Ius Comparatum – Global Studies in Comparative Law

Volume 37

As globalization proceeds, the significance of the comparative approach in legal scholarship increases. The IACL / AIDC with almost 800 members is the major universal organization promoting comparative research in law and organizing congresses with hundreds of participants in all parts of the world. The results of those congresses should be disseminated and be available for legal scholars in a single book series which would make both the Academy and its contribution to comparative law more visible. The series aims to publish the scholarship emerging from the congresses of IACL / AIDC, including: 1. of the General Congresses of Comparative Law, which take place every 4 years (Brisbane 2002; Utrecht 2006, Washington 2010, Vienna 2014, Fukuoka 2018 etc.) and which generate (a) one volume of General Reports edited by the local organizers of the Congress; (b) up to 30 volumes of selected thematic reports dealing with the topics of the single sections of the congress and containing the General Report as well as the National Reports of that section; these volumes would be edited by the General Reporters of the respective sections; 2. the volumes containing selected contributions to the smaller (2-3 days) thematic congresses which take place between the International Congresses (Mexico 2008; Taipei 2012; Montevideo 2016 etc.); these congresses have a general theme such as "Codification" or "The Enforcement of Law" and will be edited by the local organizers of the respective Congress. All publications may contain contributions in English and French, the official languages of the Academy.

More information about this series at http://www.springer.com/series/11943

Académie Internationale de Droit Comparé
International Academy of Comparative Law

Mary Keyes
Editor

Optional Choice of Court Agreements in Private International Law

Springer

Editor
Mary Keyes
Griffith Law School
Griffith University
Brisbane, Australia

ISSN 2214-6881 ISSN 2214-689X (electronic)
Ius Comparatum – Global Studies in Comparative Law
ISBN 978-3-030-23913-8 ISBN 978-3-030-23914-5 (eBook)
https://doi.org/10.1007/978-3-030-23914-5

This Springer imprint is published by the registered company Springer Nature Switzerland AG.
The registered company address is: Gewerbestrasse 11, 6330 Cham, Switzerland

Foreword

In the era of globalization, the frequent movement of people, goods, services, and capitals across borders challenges the conventional legal framework. The sovereignty of nation-states is gradually eroded by alienating its decision-making power to other bodies, entities, or non-state actors. The divide between "private" and "public" is blurring, giving priority to private ordering. This paradigm shift accords with the tendency in private international law to accentuate and extend the role of party autonomy. This is not only the case with the freedom of choice of law but also the freedom of selecting the forum.

Today, it is generally established that choice of court agreements ought to be respected, subject to limited exceptions. It is a remarkable development, considering that granting the validity and effects of choice of court agreements is a relatively recent development in quite a few countries, particularly in the USA (1972), in the Netherlands (1985), in China (1991), and in Italy (1995). This is because it required overcoming the idea of sovereignty that individuals could not confer or oust the adjudicatory jurisdiction of a court that inheres in the power of the sovereign state. It reflects a shift of the concept of international jurisdiction from "concerns of international law and interstate power" to "concerns of fairness to individual defendants," with an emphasis on the interests of private parties.[1] Designating the forum for future litigation entails notable advantages of ensuring legal certainty and predictability of the parties, allowing an effective risk calculation.

The discussions among academics and practitioners have so far concentrated on the treatment of exclusive choice of court agreements. It is presumably attributable to the growing use of exclusive forum selection clauses in practice, as well as the new legal framework established by the 2005 Hague Choice of Court Convention and the 2012 Recast of the EU Brussels I Regulation adjusting to it. These tendencies of academic and practical interests in exclusive choice of court agreements are understandable, given that the exclusivity of the available courts considerably affects the

[1]Mills, A (2018) Party Autonomy in Private International Law, Cambridge, pp. 34 ff.

interests of parties in effective dispute resolution, and requires a clear definition of the validity and effects of the agreements as well as due regard to access to justice.

Notably, unlike the ample publications on exclusive choice of court agreements, optional (or non-exclusive) choice of court agreements or asymmetric (or unilateral) choice of court agreements have attracted much less attention of academics and lawmakers so far, despite their increasing importance in practice. An optional choice of court agreement means a permissive agreement to allow parties to bring a suit to the court nominated in their contract, in addition to legally competent courts. An asymmetric choice of court agreement means a one-sided agreement on jurisdiction that is exclusive for one party and optional for the other party. These types of choice of court agreements entail a series of important questions that were largely left unresolved.

The underlying fascinating book fills these lacunae in the academia. Professor Mary Keyes, the general reporter and authority of private international law from Australia, is an expert in this area, having extensively published excellent articles and book chapters on forum selection clauses. Professor Keyes and other highly qualified national reporters from 19 jurisdictions, encompassing both civil law and common law jurisdictions, have contributed to this remarkable collection. This volume chiefly addresses the following issues on optional choice of court agreements in a comparative perspective, discerning similarities to and differences from the solutions adopted for exclusive choice of court agreements.

First, this volume deals with the threshold question of how to determine the criteria of characterizing choice of court agreement as exclusive or optional. As Professor Keyes points out, this book shows divergent solutions among various jurisdictions, including the use of the presumption of exclusivity. Conflicts rules either point to the law governing the contract, the law of the chosen court, or the law of the court seized. Second, this volume deals with the positive and negative effects of choice of court agreements. As Professor Keyes analyzes, it shows a tendency of convergence among countries as to the "positive effects" to grant jurisdiction of the selected court ("prorogation") both for exclusive and optional choice of court agreements. A certain harmony can also be observed as to the "negative effects" of exclusive choice of court agreements to deprive jurisdiction of the court ("derogation"), with the caveat of judges' discretion in common law jurisdictions. However, countries largely differ as to the negative effects of optional choice of court agreements because of its permissive character, including the applicability of *forum non conveniens,* or *lis pendens* when a nominated court has first been seized. Third, this book analyzes limitations on choice of court agreements and remedies for breach of choice of court agreements. Professor Keyes comes to the result that damages or anti-suit injunctions are generally not available to support optional choice of court agreements, on the ground that instituting proceedings elsewhere does not qualify as a breach of contract. Fourth, this volume shows that countries are divided as to the validity of an asymmetric choice of court agreement. Some countries generally take an affirmative stance, some countries rely on a case-by-case analysis, and some others answer in the negative. In conclusion, Professor Keyes indicates the role and significance of forum selection clauses in contemporary cross-border business transactions and calls for further research in view of various features and types of optional choice of court agreements.

By tackling all these crucial issues in a comparative perspective, the underlying book will highly inspire and contribute to enhance discussions among academics and practitioners, which may further influence the development of case law and law-making in different countries. Viewing its broad scope of comparative research and the highest caliber of its thorough study, the underlying collection is a fantastic achievement.

The practical relevance of optional choice of court agreements will presumably continue to rise. The Judgments Project of the Hague Conference on Private International Law was completed and adopted as a new convention on the recognition and enforcement of foreign judgments at the 22nd Diplomatic Session in June 2019. Under the Draft Convention of May 2018, Article 5 (1) (m) provides an indirect jurisdiction ground based on a choice of court agreement "other than an exclusive choice of court agreement". If this provision is included in the future convention, it will give rise to various questions on how to delineate its scope from the exclusive choice of court agreements falling under the 2005 Choice of Court Convention, how to deal with asymmetric choice of court agreements, and how to solve international parallel proceedings. This will particularly be important, now that the 2005 Choice of Court Convention has entered into force in all EU Member States including Denmark and the U.K., Montenegro, Singapore and Mexico, has been signed by the U.S., China and Ukraine, and is envisaged to be joined by Australia.

To find accurate information and effective answer to various questions surrounding optional choice of court agreements, academics and practitioners from various countries and international business communities will primarily refer to this book, which yields an invaluable insight in different legal systems, clear analyses and convincing results. This collection will provide a new perspective on the treatment of optional choice of court agreements and certainly serve as an important and useful guide for academics, attorneys and judges, and hopefully also for lawmakers in the future. I sincerely congratulate the contributors on the completion of this wonderful book, which is an enrichment for the series of *Ius Comparatum* founded by the International Academy of Comparative Law.

Kyoto University, Kyoto, Japan Yuko Nishitani

Preface

This collection comprises 19 national reports addressing the issue of the legal effects of optional choice of court agreements, by which we mean choice of court agreements that are other than purely exclusive. Whereas exclusive choice of court agreements have attracted a great deal of attention in private international law, optional choice of court agreements have been neglected by lawmakers and commentators alike, although optional choice of court agreements are quite often found in both commercial and non-commercial contracts. This collection therefore makes a significant contribution to the literature on choice of court agreements.

This project was undertaken under the auspices of the International Academy of Comparative Law, and I thank Professor Diego P. Fernández Arroyo and Professor Katharina Boele-Woelki for the invitation to me to act as General Reporter for this topic, and for the invitation to include this volume in the important Ius Comparatum series. Eleven national reporters presented their draft reports at the Congress of the International Academy of Comparative Law which was held in Fukuoka, Japan, in July 2018. Professor Yuko Nishitani graciously chaired that session of the Congress, and also agreed to write the Foreword to this volume, and I thank her for her generosity and collegiality.

I also thank Anja Trautmann and Anitha Chellamuthu at Springer for their editorial and production help with this volume. But above all I would like to record my profound thanks to the national reporters who participated in this project. They have been without exception not only brilliant in their written work but also truly delightful to work with, and I have learned a great deal from each one of them. I thank them, in particular, for their helpful comments on an earlier draft of the General Report.

Brisbane, Australia
April 2019

Mary Keyes

Contents

Part I
General Report

Optional Choice of Court Agreements in Private International Law: General Report

Mary Keyes

1 Introduction

One of the most radical recent changes in private international law internationally is the development of the law in relation to the effect of choice of court agreements. Until recently, jurisdictional litigation was less common than litigation on the issue of choice of law, and the issue of jurisdiction attracted significantly less attention than choice of law in the commentary. At the same time, it was evidently rare for the parties to include forum selection provisions in their contracts, although early cases reveal examples.[1] The substantial increase in the volume of cross-border transactions has led to far more disputes about jurisdiction. At the same time, express dispute resolution terms have become common in cross-border agreements, involving non-commercial as well as commercial parties. Both of these factors have led to a sudden development in the law about the effect of choice of court agreements, to the point that the volume of recent laws and commentary about choice of court agreements substantially eclipses that in relation to choice of law agreements.[2]

In this chapter, references to the national reports are to the names of the authors of the national reports, e.g. references to the Australian national report are to "Marshall (2019)".

[1]E.g. *Glenar v Meyer* (1796) 2 H Bl 603.

[2]The main exceptions to this are the Regulation (EC) No 593/2008 of the European Parliament and of the Council of 17 June 2008 on the law applicable to contractual obligations OJ L 177 ("Rome I Regulation"), and the Hague Principles on Choice of Law in International Commercial Contracts 2015, each of which has generated scholarly commentary: see, e.g. (2017) 22 issue 2 *Uniform Law Review*, a special issue devoted to the Hague Principles.

M. Keyes (✉)
Griffith Law School, Griffith University, Brisbane, QLD, Australia
e-mail: m.keyes@griffith.edu.au

M. Keyes (ed.), *Optional Choice of Court Agreements in Private International Law*,
Ius Comparatum – Global Studies in Comparative Law 37,
https://doi.org/10.1007/978-3-030-23914-5_1

International instruments have been influential in the development of regional and national laws. The United Nations Convention on the Recognition and Enforcement of Foreign Arbitral Awards (the "New York Convention"), concluded in 1958,[3] has influenced the development of the law relating to choice of court agreements in various ways. This influence is most clearly evident in the Hague Choice of Court Agreements Convention 2005 ("Hague Choice of Court Convention"),[4] which was inspired by and modelled on the New York Convention.[5] In turn, the Hague Choice of Court Convention influenced the 2012 revision of the Brussels I Regulation,[6] so the New York Convention has been indirectly influential in that sense. While the influence of the New York Convention is also clear in some countries' national laws,[7] where exclusive choice of court agreements are analogised to arbitration agreements,[8] in others, it evidently has had little impact.[9]

In many legal systems, there have been important recent changes to the law concerning choice of court agreements. Many countries have recently amended or introduced new legislation on civil procedure[10] and private international law, and

[3]United Nations Convention on the Recognition and Enforcement of Foreign Arbitral Awards 1958, entered into force 7 June 1959 ("New York Convention").

[4]Convention of 30 June 2005 on Choice of Court Agreements 2005, entered into force 1 October 2015.

[5]Hartley and Dogauchi (2010), p. 791, para 1; Hartley (2013), p. 19, para 1.47.

[6]The Council *Proposal for a Regulation of the European Parliament and of the Council on jurisdiction and the recognition and enforcement of judgments in civil and commercial matters (Recast)* noted that "granting priority to the chosen court to decide on its jurisdiction...would largely accord with the system established in the 2005 Hague Choice of Court Agreements Convention, thus ensuring a coherent approach within the Union and at international level were the Union to decide to conclude the 2005 Convention in the future." (Brussels, 14.12.2010 COM (2010) 748 final 2010/0383/COD, pp. 5, 9). See likewise, Council Decision of 4 December 2014 on the approval, on behalf of the European Union, of the Hague Convention of 30 June 2005 on Choice of Court Agreements (2014/887/EU, OJ L 353/5 10.12.2014), which states in recital (5) that "[w]ith the adoption of Regulation (EU) No 1215/2012 the Union paved the way for the approval of the Convention, on behalf of the Union, by ensuring coherence between the rules of the Union on the choice of court in civil and commercial matters and the rules of the Convention."

[7]Oprea (2019), Section 1.1.3.

[8]In South Africa, until recently, "South African courts treated foreign arbitration agreements in the same way as exclusive foreign choice of court agreements": Schoeman (2019), Section 4, text to note 62. The situation is similar in Taiwan: Chen (2019), Section 1.3.2. In Australia, arbitration agreements and exclusive choice of court agreements are treated as "legally cognate" (Marshall 2019, text to note 45, citing *Global Partners Fund Ltd v Babcock & Brown Ltd (in liquidation)* [2010] NSWCA 196, para 60).

[9]This includes in Greece (Panapoulos 2019, Section 1.2); Germany (Weller 2019, Section 1.2); and the People's Republic of China (Tu and Huang 2019, Section 2 (text following note 35)).

[10]For example, in Japan, amendments to the Code of Civil Procedure dealing with international jurisdiction, including choice of court agreements, came into effect in April 2012; in Switzerland, the Code of Civil Procedure was enacted in 2011. The Brussels I Recast came into effect in 2015.

regional and international instruments have had a significant effect.[11] Within Europe, the 2012 recast of the Brussels I Regulation,[12] which gave greater protection to exclusive choice of court agreements, influenced reform to national laws in some member states.[13] The European legislation also has had some influence further afield, including in Japan.[14]

The growth in importance of choice of court agreements in practice has also seen a substantial increase in the commentary devoted to the effect of these agreements. This commentary is dominated by consideration of the legal effects of exclusive choice of court agreements, which are also referred to as exclusive jurisdiction clauses,[15] exclusive or mandatory forum selection clauses, and obligatory or binding choice of court agreements.

In comparison to the amount of attention devoted to exclusive choice of court agreements, optional choice of court agreements (also referred to as non-exclusive jurisdiction clauses (sometimes abbreviated as "NEJ clauses"), non-exclusive choice of court or forum selection clauses, permissive forum selection clauses, and "imperfect" choice of court agreements) have been relatively neglected both by law makers and in the commentary.[16] While some reporters note that optional choice of court agreements are often included in contracts,[17] others remark that there are few[18] cases concerning the effect of optional agreements.

The contributions to this collection show that in some countries, the law in relation to optional choice of court agreements is undeveloped, particularly in comparison to the attention that has been given to exclusive choice of court agreements. In others, the case law is quite sophisticated. The national reports also identify a number of unresolved issues with the effect of optional choice of court agreements, and others where the law is unclear or the cases are conflicting. This collection

---

[11] Article 23 of the Brussels I Regulation "partially inspired" the Belgian Private International Law Act in relation to the effect of choice of court agreements: Van Calster and Poesen (2019), Section 2.1.

[12] Regulation (EU) No 1215/2012 of the European Parliament and of the Council of 12 December 2012, OJ l 351/1 ("Brussels I Recast").

[13] The Brussels I Recast influenced the Romanian Civil Code: Oprea (2019), Section 1.1.3. On the other hand, these instruments did not influence German law: Weller (2019), Section 1.2.

[14] This influence relates to the introduction of special rules for consumer contracts and individual employment relations. The Japanese rules in this respect are not identical to those found in the Brussels I Recast. Chen reports that the Hague Choice of Court Convention and the EU instruments "are highly valued and referred to by Taiwanese courts in some cases": (2019), Section 1.3.3.

[15] This is the term used in England and in some common law jurisdictions, including Australia and Singapore.

[16] Yeo (2005), pp. 307–308. At the time of writing this chapter in September 2018, there were no books written in English devoted solely to optional choice of court agreements. There are a number of books, in English as well as in other languages, which deal only with choice of court agreements, but these address optional choice of court agreements in passing and focus on exclusive choice of court agreements: e.g. Hartley (2013) and Joseph (2015).

[17] Van Calster and Poesen (2019), Section 5.

[18] France (Mailhé 2019, text to note 7).

contributes to the literature on choice of court agreements in calling attention to the importance of optional choice of court agreements, and the need for further research and legal development on this topic.

Much of the law and literature on choice of court agreements assumes that the agreement—whether optional or exclusive—nominates the courts of a single country. However, some choice of court agreements are more complex than this. In particular, the controversial decision of the French Cour de Cassation in the *Madame X v Société Banque Privé Edmond de Rothschild*[19] has drawn attention to asymmetric choice of court agreements. This refers to choice of court agreements containing both exclusive and optional components. This collection also considers the effect of such agreements internationally.

1.1 Scope of This Project

The national reports in this collection include a number of countries which are Member States of the European Union.[20] In those countries, there are several legal sources which determine the effect of choice of court agreements. These include the Hague Choice of Court Agreements Convention 2005, which at the time of writing applies in Mexico, Montenegro, and Singapore as well as the European Union. Singapore is represented in this collection.[21] In those countries which are Member States of the European Union, the Lugano II Convention[22] applies; as it does also in Denmark, Iceland, Norway and Switzerland. Switzerland is represented in this collection.[23] In the European Union Member States, the law on jurisdiction is dominated by the Brussels I Recast, which applies to any choice of court agreement not covered by the Hague Convention that designates the courts of a Member State. Residual national laws apply to choice of court agreements that are not covered by the Hague Convention, the Lugano II Convention, or the Brussels I Recast. In the other countries represented in this collection, the relevant laws are national laws, which are sometimes determined at the provincial level, as is the case in Canada.[24]

[19]Cass civ, 1ère, 26 September 2012. This case and a number of subsequent decisions of the French Cour de Cassation are discussed in detail by Mailhé (2019), Section 3.

[20]At the time this collection was written, in 2018, the UK was still a member state of the European Union, and the national report for the UK reflects this.

[21]Chong (2019).

[22]Convention on jurisdiction and the recognition and enforcement of judgments in civil and commercial matters, OJ L 339, 21.12.2007, entry into force 01/01/2010 ("Lugano II Convention").

[23]Haas and MacCabe (2019).

[24]The Canadian civil law and common law are both covered in this collection: Guillemard and Sabourin (2019) and Saumier (2019).

2 Attitudes to Jurisdictional Agreements

In general, the legal response to choice of court agreements has changed over time. The national reports demonstrate that, for most legal systems, much of this development has been recent, and much of it has brought about quite radical changes.

Attitudes to agreements about forum tend to cluster at opposite ends of the spectrum: at one end, they are regarded as being superior to other means of allocating jurisdiction, at least in international commercial disputes. At the other end of the spectrum, they are derided as being unacceptable as either inconsistent with, or undermining, public interests in the regulation of litigation. Historically, the latter position prevailed in many legal systems. For example, in the US and in Québec, choice of court agreements were invalid as contrary to public policy.[25] But there are some important exceptions. Mailhé notes that party autonomy was regarded by the drafters of the French Civil Code, in 1804, as "a natural exception to the rules they proposed in its articles 14 and 15".[26] In the German Code of Civil Procedure, which entered into force in 1879, "choice of court agreements could be agreed upon without any major limitations."[27] In Taiwan, the Code of Civil Procedure has allowed the parties to designate a court to exercise jurisdiction from the time of its promulgation in 1930.[28]

More recently, the former view that choice of court agreements are desirable and should be respected has become popular. For example, Saumier writes that "[t]he attitude toward choice of court agreements in Canadian common law provinces is very positive"[29]; the other reports express similar sentiments.[30] In most legal systems, the law now enables the parties to choose the forum for the resolution of disputes.

In a few countries, the laws reveal historical, ongoing, and some new, hesitations about completely accepting party autonomy. Again the German national law is an exception to the general trend; in 1974, the law relating to choice of court agreements was fundamentally reformed, and significant limitations on the parties' freedom

---

[25]Buxbaum (2019), Section 2; Guillemard and Sabourin (2019), Section 1, text to notes 30–32. See similarly, Tarman and Oba, referring to cases from the Turkish Cour de cassation, which establish that "a refusal of jurisdiction by the Turkish courts due to a jurisdiction agreement would indicate a mistrust of the adjudication of Turkish courts and would be contrary to public order": (2019), Section 3.3 (text to note 31).

[26]Mailhé (2019), Section 1.

[27]Weller (2019), Section 1.1, text to note 3, citing the Zivilprozessordnung, section 38.

[28]Chen (2019), Section 1.2.1.

[29]Saumier (2019), Section 1.

[30]Buxbaum states that "[i]n the vast majority of US states, choice of court agreements, both optional and exclusive, are viewed with approval.": (2019), Section 3.1. See similarly Belgium (Van Calster and Poesen 2019, Section 2.1); Romania (Oprea 2019, Section 1.1.3); and South Africa (Schoeman 2019, Section 3.3, text to notes 34 and 35).

were imposed,[31] which remain in force.[32] Several US states also "maintain the traditional hostility to choice of court agreements."[33] As explained below, the law in many countries now recognises that choice of court agreements involving presumptively weaker parties require different regulation to those involving commercial parties.[34]

3 The Distinction Between Exclusive and Optional Choice of Court Agreements

The distinction between exclusive and optional choice of court agreements is very well established in some legal systems. In others, particularly those in which the parties' ability to choose their forum has only recently been accepted, the distinction is less well established. For example, in China "The concept of non-exclusive choice of court agreement. . .was first formally presented in the 2005 [Supreme People's Court] Summary".[35] In the Netherlands, all choice of court agreements are "commonly referred to as 'forumkeuze' (i.e. 'choice of forum')".[36] In South Africa, there is no reference in national law to optional choice of court agreements[37]; and "no clear distinction is drawn between exclusive and optional choice of court agreements".[38] Several reporters note that their national legislation makes no reference to optional choice of court agreements, and that there is very little relevant case law.[39]

A preliminary issue is identifying the applicable law to determine whether a choice of court is exclusive or optional. There is a diversity of views on this question. In some countries, it is well settled that this is determined by the governing law of the contract as a whole,[40] or the governing law of the choice of court agreement, if that

[31] Weller (2019), Section 1.1, text to note 9, citing the Law to Change the Code of Civil Procedure of 21 March 1974, Federal Law Gazette, BGBl 1974 I 753, which came into effect on 1 April 1974.

[32] Weller (2019), Section 1.1, text to note 10.

[33] Buxbaum (2019), Section 3.1.

[34] See below, Sect. 8.

[35] Tu and Huang (2019), Section 2 (text to note 27).

[36] Rammeloo (2019), Section 1.1. Likewise, in Québec, the Civil Code does not distinguish between exclusive and optional choice of court agreements: Guillemard and Sabourin (2019), Section 2.2.1.

[37] This is the case in South Africa: Schoeman (2019), Section 3, text to note 26.

[38] Schoeman (2019), Section 6.

[39] E.g. France (Mailhé 2019, text to note 7).

[40] This is so in South Africa (Schoeman 2019, Section 3.1). The position may be different in China (Tu and Huang 2019, Section 3, text to note 42). In England, it is presumed that the applicable law for the choice of court agreement is the same as the applicable law for the contract as a whole: Merrett and Carruthers (2019), Section 2.1.1 (citing *Mauritius Commercial Bank v Hestia* [2013] EWHC 1328 (Comm)). In *Shandong Jufeng Network v MGame & Tianjin Fengyun Network*, the Supreme People's Court of China "held that the choice of law agreement and the choice of court agreement are two separate legal acts and therefore different applicable laws should be applied to

were different.[41] However, even where that is the case, the courts sometimes simply state that a choice of court agreement is exclusive or optional without justifying that conclusion.[42]

It seems to be quite common that courts do not refer to any choice of law analysis when determining whether a choice of court agreement is exclusive or optional.[43] One problem with undertaking a choice of law analysis is that it might lead to practical difficulties, given a lack of clarity under some national laws as to the distinction between exclusive and optional choice of court agreements.[44] Takahashi proposes that a clear test for distinguishing exclusive from optional choice of court agreements should be developed, and that it should be applied as an overriding mandatory rule—that is, irrespective of the otherwise applicable law.[45]

The presumption in favour of exclusivity in the Hague Choice of Court Convention might be applied either by the nominated court, to determine whether the choice of court is exclusive within the terms of the Convention, or by a non-chosen court which has been seised and which is determining whether it is obliged to suspend or dismiss those proceedings because of an exclusive choice of court agreement in favour of the courts of another contracting state.[46] When the nominated court is determining the issue, the application of the presumption should not be justified on the basis of the Hague Convention being part of the law of the exclusively chosen court, because the issue as to whether it is the exclusively chosen court has not yet been determined. That would mean that the chosen court could only be applying the presumption under the Convention on the basis that the Convention is part of the law of the forum. If the law of the forum was the governing law of the choice of court agreement, that would not be objectionable. But if the governing law of the choice of court agreement was the law of another country which was not a contracting state to the Convention, any reference to the Convention would have to be justified on the basis that the Convention was applicable as part of the law of the forum *per se*. As Chong points out in the context of the Singaporean legislation which gives effect to the Convention,[47] this might be justified on the basis that the Convention establishes

---

regulate them.": (2009) Min San Zhong Zi No 4; Model Case No 44, Notice of the Supreme People's Court on Issuing 10 Major Cases and 50 Model Cases on China's Judicial Protection of the Intellectual Property Rights in 2009 [2010] Fa No 172, promulgated on 14 April 2010, cited in Tu and Huang (2019), Section 3, text to note 46.

[41]Merrett and Carruthers (2019), Section 2.1.1, note 20 (citing Collins 2012, para 12-105 and Maher and Rodger 2010, para 17-17); Chong (2019), Section 2.2.

[42]This is so, for example, in South Africa: Schoeman (2019), Section 3.1.

[43]This is so in common law Canada (Saumier 2019, Section 2); France (Mailhé 2019, Section 1.1); Japan (Takahashi 2019, text to note 13); the Netherlands (Rammeloo 2019, Section 2.2).

[44]Takahashi (2019), text following note 22.

[45]Takahashi (2019), Section 4.

[46]Hague Choice of Court Agreements Convention, Article 6.

[47]Supreme Court of Judicature Act Cap 322, Rev Ed 2007, section 18F which relevantly provides that "if there is no express provision to the contrary" in the choice of court agreement, then "an agreement to submit to the jurisdiction of the Singapore International Commercial Court shall be

a forum mandatory rule.[48] The same reasoning might apply to the Brussels I Recast and the Lugano II Convention, although it has been suggested that the characterisation of the agreement as optional or exclusive should be governed by the law of the chosen court.[49] Of course, this presents insuperable difficulties if the choice of court agreement nominates the courts of more than one country.[50]

As just noted, another possibility is that the law of the forum should be applied to determine whether a choice of court agreement is exclusive or optional.[51] The law of Québec is applied to this question, either because the issue is one of characterisation,[52] or one of procedure.[53] In the Czech Republic, forum law applies because the "procedural character" of choice of court agreements, and because the "emphasis on the transfer of jurisdiction continues to prevail."[54]

In some countries, there are conflicting authorities as to the choice of law rule which should be applied to determine whether a choice of court agreement is optional or exclusive. For example, whereas a majority of Chinese courts take the view that this is a procedural question which should be determined according to the law of the forum,[55] a minority of Chinese courts insist that the governing law of the main contract should be applied to interpret the choice of court agreement.[56]

3.1 *Distinguishing an Exclusive from an Optional Choice of Court Agreement*

There are a number of techniques used to determine whether a particular choice of court agreement is exclusive or optional. The simplest is that used in the Hague Choice of Court Agreement Convention, which defines an exclusive choice of court agreement,[57] but also deems that a choice of court agreement is exclusive "unless the parties have agreed otherwise".[58] The solution of deeming a choice of court

considered to have agreed – (a) to submit to the exclusive jurisdiction of the Singapore International Commercial Court". This provision is discussed in Chong (2019), Section 2.2.

[48]Chong (2019), Section 2.2.

[49]Panapoulos (2019), Section 2.2.

[50]Van Calster and Poesen (2019), Section 3.3.2.

[51]Greece (Panapoulos 2019, text to note 8); Germany (Weller 2019, Section 3.2.1); Romania (Oprea 2019, Section 2.1).

[52]Under the Québec Civil Code, this is determined by the law of the court seised: art 3078. See Guillemard and Sabourin (2019), Section 2.1, text to note 74.

[53]Under the Québec Civil Code, this is determined by the law of the court seised: art 3132. See Guillemard and Sabourin (2019), Section 2.1, text to note 75.

[54]Rozehnalová et al. (2019), Section 2.2 (sentence before note 49).

[55]Tu and Huang (2019), Section 3, text to notes 42-42.

[56]Tu and Huang (2019), Section 3, text to notes 44-45.

[57]Hague Choice of Court Convention, Article 3(a). The Convention also defines "non-exclusive choice of court agreement", in Article 22(1).

[58]Hague Choice of Court Convention, Article 3(b).

agreement to be exclusive was adopted in the Brussels I Recast,[59] and in the Lugano II Convention on Jurisdiction and the Enforcement of Judgments in Civil and Commercial Matters.[60] This does not appear to have influenced the national law of most of the EU Member States, for situations falling outside the scope of the Recast, although the Romanian Civil Procedure Code provides that in the absence of contrary stipulation, the jurisdiction agreement is exclusive.[61] The same presumption is found in other countries including Greece[62] and Switzerland.[63] In the Czech Republic, it is generally assumed that choice of court agreements are exclusive, although there is no explicit presumption to that effect.[64] A suggestion made in Japan in the preparation of the reforms to the Code of Civil Procedure that foreign choice of court agreements should be deemed to be exclusive was rejected "as being contrary to international business practice", and the issue was left to interpretation of individual agreements.[65] Rather ironically, there is a tendency in Japan to characterise choice of court agreements as being exclusive.[66]

Under the national law of most countries, there is no explicit presumption of exclusivity.[67] Rather, the distinction between exclusive and optional choice of court agreements is one of interpretation of the agreement[68]; determining whether a choice of court agreement is optional or exclusive is a question of the parties' intentions.[69] In some countries, the courts tend to find that agreements are exclusive.[70] Attempting to identify the parties' intentions is often very difficult, and several reporters note that decisions are inconsistent.[71]

---

[59]Brussels I Recast Regulation, Article 25(1). The Recast does not contain a definition of non-exclusive choice of court agreements.

[60]Lugano II Convention, Article 23. This Convention does not contain a definition of non-exclusive choice of court agreements.

[61]Oprea (2019), note 42, citing the Romanian Civil Procedure Code, article 1068(1).

[62]Greek Code of Civil Procedure, Art 44.

[63]Swiss Code on Civil Procedure, Article 17(1); Swiss Private International Law Act, Article 5(1); Haas and MacCabe (2019), Section 5, text to note 53.

[64]Rozehnalová et al. (2019), Sections 2.2.1, 2.8.

[65]Takahashi (2019), Section 2.3, text to note 12.

[66]Takahashi (2019), Section 2.3.

[67]This includes Germany: Weller (2019), Section 1.2. The Scottish law is based on the Brussels Convention, and therefore does not include a presumption of exclusivity: Merrett and Carruthers (2019), Section 1.1.

[68]Netherlands (Rammeloo 2019, Section 2.3); Taiwan (Chen 2019, Section 2.2.2).

[69]Including China (Tu and Huang 2019, Section 3, text to note 48; although they also note that some courts, including the Supreme People's Court, have implicitly and explicitly adopted a presumption of exclusivity in some cases) and Taiwan (Chen 2019, Section 2.2.2).

[70]This is so in the Czech Republic (Rozehnalová et al. 2019, Section 2.1) and Japan (Takahashi 2019, Section 2.3), for example.

[71]For China, see Tu and Huang (2019), Section 3, text to and following note 51.

In common law countries, the test of whether a choice of court agreement is exclusive is whether the parties promised to commence or pursue proceedings, if at all, only in the courts of a single legal system.[72] This clearly demonstrates the contractual nature of choice of court agreements in the common law. In most countries, the courts consider a range of different factors in determining whether the choice of court agreement is exclusive. However, some reporters state that the cases have not articulated any principles of interpretation.[73]

In some jurisdictions, the courts apply a presumption against exclusivity; this is so in some US states,[74] and in Taiwan.[75]

In addition to the possibility that the courts of a single country may take different approaches and reach apparently inconsistent conclusions in different cases as to the character of choice of court agreements, the same agreement may be interpreted as being non-exclusive in one country, and as exclusive in another. For example, in *Compania Sud Americana de Vapores SA v Hin-Pro International Logistics Ltd*, the choice of court agreement in favour of the English courts was held to be non-exclusive by the Chinese courts,[76] and exclusive by the English courts.[77] In another case, a choice of court agreement which nominated Australian courts was interpreted by a US court as non-exclusive, but would have been interpreted by the Australian court as exclusive.[78] This suggests that courts may be inclined to interpret an ambiguous choice of court agreement as exclusive, if it nominates the forum court, and as optional, if it nominates a foreign court.[79]

3.2 Varieties of Choice of Court Agreements

Choice of court agreements can take many different forms, and their effect will depend in every case on what the agreement actually provides. Referring to the clause in *Sabah Shipyard (Pakistan) Ltd v Islamic Republic Of Pakistan*,[80] which the English Court of Appeal described as non-exclusive, Briggs argued that "[i]t denatures such a clause to call it non-exclusive, for it was more subtle, more complex,

[72]E.g. *BNP Paribas SA v Anchorage Capital Europe LLP* [2013] EWHC 3073 (Comm), para 87 and 88, cited by Merrett and Carruthers (2019), Section 2.2.1, text to note 47.

[73]E.g. Takahashi (2019), Section 2.3.

[74]Buxbaum (2019), Section 4.

[75]Chen (2019), Section 2.2.2.

[76]Zheijiang High People's Court (2013) Zhe Xia Zhong Zi No 42, cited by Tu and Huang (2019), Section 3, note 52.

[77][2015] EWCA 401 (Civ).

[78]*Armacel Pty Ltd v Smurfit Stone Container Corporation* [2008] FCA 592. In this case, the Australian court held that because of the US judgment, the plaintiff "was barred by an issue estoppel from contending that [the clause] was an exclusive jurisdiction clause": para 66 and 90.

[79]See likewise Tang et al. (2016), p. 65.

[80][2003] 2 Lloyd's Rep 571.

than that."[81] Briggs has argued that the distinction between exclusive and non-exclusive choice of court agreements is "unhelpful", because some choice of court agreements do not neatly fall into one or the other category.[82] In particular, while there appears to be widespread agreement about what constitutes an exclusive choice of court agreement,[83] the concept of optional choice of court agreement is often defined by reference to what it is not (i.e. purely exclusive), and many different types of choice of court agreement satisfy that criterion.[84]

The Explanatory Report to the Hague Choice of Court Convention gives some examples of non-exclusive choice of court agreements (i.e. agreements which do not come within the Convention definition of exclusive choice of court agreements). These include agreements that impose "no restrictions on the courts before which proceedings may be brought", giving as an example a clause which nominates the courts of one country but also states that "this shall not preclude the bringing of proceedings in any other court that has jurisdiction under the law of the State in which it is located."[85] This is contrasted with non-exclusive agreements "with limitation"; the example given is "an agreement that designates a court or the courts of two or more Contracting States *to the exclusion of all others*".[86] In Belgium, "scholarship distinguishes two kinds of optional choice of court agreements", namely "non-exclusive" choice of court agreements (which confer non-exclusive jurisdiction on one or more courts), and "complex" choice of court agreements (which confer jurisdiction on multiple courts, "specifying that the parties can commence proceedings in one of these courts to the exclusion of the courts which would ordinarily have jurisdiction.")[87] Oprea identifies four different types of non-exclusive choice of court agreements: simple non-exclusive choice of court agreements, hybrid choice of court agreements, multiple choice of court agreements,[88] and asymmetric choice of court agreements.[89]

---

[81]Briggs (2008), p. 118, para 4.21.

[82]Briggs (2012), p. 118, para 4.21. See, likewise, Collins (2012), para 12–102.

[83]Although it is possible that the parties can include what Merrett and Carruthers refer to as an "exclusively non-exclusive" choice of court agreement, which nominates the courts of one country as having exclusive jurisdiction if one party is claimant, and the courts of another country as having exclusive jurisdiction if the other party is claimant: (2019), Section 2.2.1, text to note 38. The choice of court agreement in *Meeth v Glacetal* Case 23/78 [1978] ECR 2133 was of this kind. See also Keyes and Marshall (2015), pp. 357–358.

[84]See also Oprea (2019), Section 2.6; *Noble Power Investments Ltd v Nissei Stomach Tokyo Co Ltd* [2008] 5 HKLRD 631, para 24.

[85]Hartley and Dogauchi (2010), p. 845, para 246.

[86]Hartley and Dogauchi (2010), p. 845, para 247 (emphasis original).

[87]Van Calster and Poesen (2019), Section 3.1.

[88]Oprea (2019), Section 1.2.

[89]Oprea (2019), Section 2.6, text to notes 36–38.

4 The Positive Effects of Choice of Court Agreements

Choice of court agreements are relevant at two different stages in a cross-border dispute. This is conventionally addressed in terms of their "positive" and "negative" effects. The first stage relates to establishing whether a chosen court is competent to hear and determine a dispute. This is referred to as prorogation, the "jurisdiction-granting" effect,[90] submission to the jurisdiction, or the positive effect of a choice of court agreement. Whether an agreement has the effect of establishing the jurisdiction of a court chosen by the parties depends on the procedural law of the forum court and whether it recognises the parties' agreement as a basis of competency. Almost all legal systems now recognise the positive effect of choice of court agreements.[91] The Brussels I Recast, for example, provides in Article 25(1) that

> If the parties, regardless of their domicile, have agreed that a court or the courts of a Member State are to have jurisdiction to settle any disputes which have arisen or which may arise in connection with a particular legal relationship, *that court or those courts shall have jurisdiction*, unless the agreement is null and void as to its substantive validity under the law of that Member State (emphasis added).

In some countries, the nominated court is obliged to accept the submission to jurisdiction.[92]

However, in a few countries, the parties' agreement is not sufficient; there must be another basis of jurisdiction.[93] At common law, a choice of court agreement in favour of the forum is not itself a separate basis of jurisdiction because jurisdictional competence depends on service.[94] This has been cured by legislation which authorises service out of the jurisdiction if the defendant submitted to the jurisdiction.[95]

Most legal systems also recognise that where the defendant participates in the proceedings in the forum without contesting jurisdiction, the forum court has jurisdiction.[96] In some legal systems, this is conceptualised as an implied or tacit choice of court agreement. In others, it is understood and described as a unilateral

[90]Hartley (2013), p. 5, para 1.08.

[91]E.g. Brussels I Recast Regulation, Article 25(1); Lugano II Convention, Article 23(1); Greece (Greek Code of Civil Procedure, Arts 42–44); Québec (Civil Code of Québec, article 3148(4)); Singapore (*Astrata (Singapore) Pte Ltd v Portcullis Escrow Pte Ltd* [2011] 3 SLR 386); Switzerland (Swiss Code on Civil Procedure, Article 17), and the UK (Merrett and Carruthers 2019, Section 1.1).

[92]Including the Czech Republic (Rozehnalová et al. 2019, Section 1.3) and Switzerland (Haas and MacCabe 2019, Section 6.1 (citing the Swiss Code on Civil Procedure, Article 17, and the Lugano II Convention, Article 23)).

[93]This is the case in South Africa (Schoeman 2019, Section 3.5) and in some US states (Buxbaum 2019, text to note 76, referring in particular to Florida).

[94]Keyes (2015), p. 225.

[95]Marshall (2019), Section 2.3.1.1.

[96]Brussels I Recast Regulation, Article 26(1); Lugano II Convention, Article 24(1); Greek Code of Civil Procedure, Art 42 § 2; Japanese Code of Civil Procedure, Article 3-8; Taiwanese Code of Civil Procedure, Article 25.

submission to the jurisdiction by the defendant, which is normally analysed in terms of a waiver of the defendant's right to object to the court's jurisdiction.

In quite a few countries, the law has only recently accepted the parties' ability to prorogate jurisdiction. For example, in the Netherlands, this was only accepted by the Dutch Hoge Raad (Supreme Court) in 1985.[97] In China, the parties' ability to contract for jurisdiction was not recognised until 1991.[98] Romanian law explicitly recognised the effectiveness of choice of court agreements for the first time in the Romanian Civil Procedure Code which came into effect in 2013.[99]

The reason that the positive effect of choice of court agreements was, historically, controversial, is that the assumption of jurisdiction in cross-border cases was justified as an aspect of sovereignty, and the parties' ability to invoke the courts' jurisdiction was inconsistent with territorial limitations on the exercise of sovereignty. This is reflected, for example, in the Dutch "traditional doctrine of sovereignty according to which jurisdiction could be attributed to courts by the law only (i.e. not by the autonomous will of the contracting parties)."[100]

Where the relevant procedural law permits prorogation, this basis of jurisdiction contrasts with the other rules establishing the courts' jurisdiction, which rely on factual connections between the forum and the parties, such as personal connections of domicile, or connections between an aspect of the dispute and the forum, such as that the contract in dispute was to be performed in the territory of the forum court. The lack of a requirement of factual connection to the chosen court was one reason for concerns about the legitimacy of prorogation as a basis of jurisdictional competency; whereas, from the perspective of parties from different legal systems, a lack of factual connection might be desirable because it would indicate that the chosen courts would be neutral as between the parties to the contract.

There is little difference between optional and exclusive choice of court agreements in terms of their positive effect.[101]

4.1 *The Problem with Prorogation*

Most courts now take a favourable attitude to choice of court agreements which nominate them. Nygh suggested that "For the prorogated forum the choice of the parties presents no challenge to State authority. Concepts of territorial sovereignty

[97]*Piscator*, HR February 1, 1985, NJ 1985, 698 (discussed by Rammeloo 2019, Sections 1.1 and 2.5).

[98]1991 Chinese Civil Procedure Law, Articles 25 and 224 (promulgated and entered into force on 9 April 1991). These provisions were replaced by Article 34 of the 2012 Chinese Civil Procedure Law (which was in turn replaced by Article 34 of the 2017 Chinese Civil Procedure Law). See Tu and Huang (2019), Section 2, text to notes 13–16.

[99]Oprea (2019), Section 1.1.3, text to notes 14–15.

[100]Rammeloo (2019), Section 1.1, text to note 1.

[101]Chen (2019), Section 2.1.

and control are not offended, but rather flattered, when foreigners submit to the jurisdiction."[102] Given the current popular view of international litigation as a product, it is hardly surprising that most legal systems welcome the parties' contractual choice of the forum. However, this fails to recognise the effect of the prorogation in potentially exacerbating, or creating, a problem of overlapping jurisdictions.

In the legal systems which allow prorogation without any requirement of connection, where the prorogation is the only basis on which a nominated court is competent, the choice of court agreement has the effect of increasing the number of competent courts in which either party could bring proceedings. If the courts of more than one legal system would have regarded themselves as competent irrespective of the agreement, prorogation exacerbates the problem of overlapping jurisdictions, by making one more court competent. If there would have only been one competent court but for the parties' choice of court agreement (admittedly an unlikely scenario, in a cross-border dispute), prorogation creates the problem of overlapping jurisdictions. If a nominated court is otherwise competent under its other rules of jurisdictional competency, the prorogation neither creates nor adds to the competency of that court, and does not exacerbate the problem of overlapping jurisdictions, which would arise in any case.

5 The Negative Effects of Choice of Court Agreements

The second stage at which a choice of court agreement is relevant relates to its effect in controlling the possibility or the reality of parallel proceedings. At this stage, a choice of court agreement might be challenged in either the chosen, or non-chosen, courts. It will not necessarily be given the same effect in the chosen and the non-chosen courts, including because the chosen court will, as Nygh observed, be flattered by the choice, whereas the non-chosen courts may be offended, especially if the factual connections to the non-chosen court are strong.[103] This may be true of optional choice of court agreements as well as of exclusive choice of court agreements.

The legal effects of choice of court agreements are regarded as a matter of procedure and for that reason subject to forum law.[104]

The following sections first address the negative effects of exclusive choice of court agreements; and then the negative effects of optional choice of court agreements.

---

[102]Nygh (1999), p. 15.

[103]Nygh (1999), pp. 15, 19.

[104]This is so in England and Scotland (Merrett and Carruthers 2019, Section 2.3); Germany (Weller 2019, Section 3.3); Japan (Takahashi 2019, Section 2.1); Singapore (Chong 2019, Section 2.2); Taiwan (Chen 2019, Section 2.3.1); the US (Buxbaum 2019, Section 6.1).

5.1 *The Negative Effect of Exclusive Choice of Court Agreements*

Much of the law and scholarship about choice of court agreements concerns the effect of exclusive agreements in non-chosen courts.[105] In this context, choice of court agreements are often said to have a negative, derogative, or "jurisdiction-depriving"[106] effect on a non-chosen court which is competent, under its own rules of jurisdiction, to hear the dispute. This only necessarily follows if the choice of court agreement is exclusive, because at least in most types of optional choice of court agreements, the parties do not by their agreement foreclose the possibility of litigating in courts other than those nominated in the choice of court agreement. An exclusive choice of court agreement only has a jurisdiction-depriving effect if the non-chosen court is obliged to enforce an exclusive choice of court agreement by staying its proceedings.[107] The Hague Choice of Court Convention,[108] the Brussels I Recast, and the national laws of some countries[109] require the non-chosen courts of the forum to stay proceedings where the parties have agreed to the exclusive jurisdiction of a foreign court.

The Brussels I Recast exemplifies this approach to the strict enforcement of exclusive choice of court agreements. Article 31(2) states

> Without prejudice to Article 26, where a court of a Member State on which an agreement as referred to in Article 25 confers exclusive jurisdiction is seised, *any court of another Member State shall stay the proceedings until such time as the court seised on the basis of the agreement declares that it has no jurisdiction* under the agreement. (emphasis added)

Article 31(3) further states that "Where the court designated in the agreement has established jurisdiction in accordance with the agreement, any court of another Member State shall decline jurisdiction in favour of that court." The introduction of article 31 is one of the most important recent developments in private international law. The Lugano II Convention has not been amended to incorporate a similar protection of exclusive choice of court agreements.

---

[105]Saumier (2019), Section 3.1.

[106]Hartley (2013), p. 5, para 1.08.

[107]Under the common law, exclusive choice of court agreements are not strictly enforceable; the courts will generally enforce them, but this is subject to the courts' discretion, and the courts may not enforce even an exclusive choice of court agreement if there are strong grounds, cause, or reasons for non-enforcement: *Donohue v Armco* [2001] UKHL 64 (UK House of Lords); *Akai Pty Ltd v The People's Insurance Co Ltd* (1996) 188 CLR 418 (Australian High Court); *ZI Pompey Industrie v ECU-Line NV* 2003 SCC 27 (Supreme Court of Canada); *Amerco Timbers Pte Ltd v Chatsworth Timber Corp Pte Ltd* [1977-78] 2 SLR 112 (Singapore Court of Appeal).

[108]Article 6.

[109]Turkey (Tarman and Oba 2019, Section 3.3, text to note 33). Note, however, that the Turkish courts sometimes establish their jurisdiction on the basis of the principle of good faith, if the respondent is domiciled in Turkey. Tarman and Oba note that this "reasoning is heavily criticized in the academic commentary": (2019), Section 3.3.2.1, text to note 43.

The common law approach is different in principle. The line of English cases commencing with *The Eleftheria*[110] have been very influential in England, and most common law countries apply the principle from that case that exclusive choice of court agreements, whether in favour of the forum or of a foreign court, should be enforced unless there are strong reasons for non-enforcement.[111] Clearly, this gives the non-chosen court a discretion whether to enforce the agreement.

Relatively speaking, the effect of an exclusive choice of court agreement which is being challenged in proceedings in the chosen court has not been the subject of much litigation or much study. Nygh's comment, mentioned above, in relation to a prorogated court being flattered by being selected is also pertinent in terms of the attitude the court will have to a litigant challenging the nominated court's jurisdiction.

In the Hague Choice of Court Convention,[112] the Brussels I Recast, and the national law of some countries,[113] the court nominated in an exclusive choice of court agreement *cannot* decline jurisdiction in favour of a foreign court. The Civil Code of Québec goes even further, stating that the

> Québec authorities *have no jurisdiction* where the parties have chosen by agreement to submit the present or future disputes between themselves relating to a specific legal relationship to a foreign authority, or to an arbitrator.[114]

In other legal systems, the court nominated in an exclusive choice of court agreement has a discretion not to exercise jurisdiction. In common law systems, although an exclusive choice of court agreement should be enforced in most cases, it may not be if the party resisting its enforcement shows "strong" reasons or cause for its non-enforcement.[115] The English House of Lords stayed proceedings in such a case, in *Donohue v Armco Inc.*[116]

As in the case of prorogation, the development of the law in relation to the negative effect of exclusive choice of court agreements is fairly recent in most countries. For example, before 1994, while the courts of Québec enforced choices

110 [1970] P 94.

111 E.g. Australia (Marshall 2019, Section 3); Singapore (Chong 2019, Section 3). This case has also been influential in South Africa (Schoeman 2019, Section 3.4).

112 Article 5(2).

113 This is so for example in China (Tu and Huang 2019, Section 3, text to note 60); and Japan, except where the foreign court is deemed to have exclusive subject matter jurisdiction (Takahashi 2019, Section 1.1, text following note 2). Australia and New Zealand have enacted reciprocal legislation regulating jurisdiction and judgments in trans-Tasman proceedings (the Trans-Tasman Proceedings Acts 2010). Inter alia, this legislation was designed to be consistent with the Hague Choice of Court Convention, and as a result, the courts nominated in an exclusive choice of court agreement cannot stay those proceedings: Trans-Tasman Proceedings Act 2010 (Cth) s 20(1)(b). See Marshall (2019), text to note 31.

114 Art 3148.

115 *Donohue v Armco Inc* [2001] UKHL 64, para 24.

116 *Donohue v Armco Inc* [2001] UKHL 64.

of court in favour of the forum, they would not give effect to choice of court agreements that nominated foreign courts.[117]

5.2 The Negative Effects of Optional Choice of Court Agreements

Whereas the law of different legal systems has shown strong signs of convergence in relation to the positive effects of both exclusive and optional choice of court agreements, and the negative effects of exclusive choice of court agreements, there are no such indications of convergence in relation to the negative effect of optional choice of court agreements.

The negative effects of optional choice of court agreements are more complicated than the negative effects of exclusive choice of court agreements, as the national reporters attest. The Hague Choice of Court Convention does not contain any direct principles in relation to the optional choice of court agreements, and the Brussels I Recast Regulation does not contain any specific principles relating to the effect of such agreements.

The Hague Choice of Court Convention does not regulate optional choice of court agreements directly, but it affects them indirectly in two ways. The first is that the Convention deems choice of court agreements to be exclusive. In some legal systems, the effect of this will be that fewer choice of court agreements will be optional, than would have otherwise been the case under national laws about the distinction between optional and exclusive choice of court agreements.[118] The second is that contracting states can opt to recognise the judgments given by a court of another contracting state, the jurisdiction of which court depends on the parties' optional choice of that court. Contracting states can make a declaration under article 22, the effect of which would be that judgments rendered by the courts of other contracting states which had also made a declaration under article 22 and the jurisdiction of which derived from a non-exclusive choice of court agreement would be recognised by the contracting state making the declaration. To date, none of the contracting states has made such a declaration.

While the Recast enables prorogation of jurisdiction, and protects exclusive choice of court agreements by requiring courts other than those nominated in an exclusive choice of court agreement to stay proceedings in favour of the jurisdiction of the nominated courts, it contains no specific provisions concerning the negative effects of an optional choice of court agreement. It therefore gives no priority to optional choice of court agreements, when it comes to the allocation of jurisdiction.

[117]Guillemard and Sabourin, Section 1 text to note 29 and following note 30.

[118]Marshall and Keyes (2017), p. 275.

Rather, "substantive jurisdiction as between Member State courts will still be determined by which court is first seised",[119] pursuant to Article 29.

It is not clear whether, if proceedings are commenced in the courts of a Member State which is nominated in an optional choice of court agreement (pursuant to the Recast, article 25), proceedings can be stayed under national procedural rules.[120] It is also unclear whether, if proceedings are commenced in the courts of a Member State pursuant to another ground of jurisdiction, those proceedings might be stayed on the basis of an optional choice of court agreement which nominated the courts of a non-Member State.[121]

Under the national law of most countries, optional choice of court agreements have a different, and much weaker, effect than exclusive choice of court agreements. However, in some countries, the forum court which is nominated in an optional choice of court agreement is obliged to exercise its jurisdiction. In China, although a version of *forum non conveniens* applies, the courts cannot decline jurisdiction in favour of a foreign court, if the parties nominated the Chinese courts in an optional choice of court agreement.[122]

The situation is similar in Japan. Article 3-9 of the Japanese Code of Civil Procedure enables a Japanese court to dismiss the proceedings

> if, taking into account the nature of the case, the burden on the defendant to answer the claim, the location of evidence and any other factors, the court finds that there are special circumstances by reason of which hearing and determining the case in Japan would impair fairness between the parties or hinder the proper and efficient conduct of proceedings,

and this clearly applies where there is an optional choice of court in favour of Japanese courts. However, Takahashi notes that "dismissal will be rare where Japanese courts are chosen by the parties because 'fairness between the parties' would usually be promoted by respecting their agreement."[123] Similarly, in Taiwan, if the parties nominated the Taiwanese courts as having jurisdiction, the court is not obliged to stay its proceedings, even if foreign proceedings were commenced first.[124]

The negative effects of optional choice of court agreements differ between different legal systems. This diversity was one of the reasons that optional choice of court agreements were excluded from the Hague Choice of Court Convention. The Explanatory Report to the Convention notes that if proceedings had been commenced first in a forum other than that nominated in an optional choice of

---

[119]Joseph (2015), p. 314, para 10.56.

[120]Merrett and Carruthers (2019), Section 2.3.4.

[121]Merrett and Carruthers (2019), Section 2.3.4.

[122]Tu and Huang (2019), Section 3, text to note 60.

[123]Takahashi (2019), Section 2.1, text to note 11, citing the Kyoto District Court, judgment on 29 January 2015 (2015WLJPCA01296002).

[124]Chen (2019), Section 2.8.1, citing the Taiwanese Code of Civil Procedure, Article 182-2 Section 1.

court agreement, "[t]his would raise issues of lis pendens and forum non conveniens that would have been difficult to resolve in an acceptable way."[125]

In those legal systems which rely on *lis pendens* to resolve problems of overlapping jurisdictions (assuming there are no issues of exclusive subject matter jurisdiction), the main issue is the sequence in which the respective courts' jurisdiction was seised.[126] In some countries, an optional choice of court agreement may be a factor to be considered but is not determinative.[127]

In those legal systems in which the courts have discretion whether to exercise jurisdiction on the basis of the appropriateness of the forum court, relative to the appropriateness of foreign countries under the doctrine of *forum non conveniens*, the parties may be precluded from asserting that a forum nominated as having non-exclusive jurisdiction is inappropriate. In a number of countries, including China, England and the United States, the effect of an optional choice of court agreement is that the defendant is taken to have waived their right to contest the court's jurisdiction.[128] In England, the parties may not challenge the appropriateness of the nominated court in an optional choice of court agreement—whether the forum or a foreign court—"on grounds foreseeable at the time of the agreement".[129] In *S & W Berisford plc v New Hampshire Insurance Co Ltd*, an influential decision in England and other common law jurisdictions, Justice Hobhouse stated that

> the fact that the parties have agreed in their contract that the English courts shall have jurisdiction (albeit a non-exclusive jurisdiction) creates a strong prima facie case that that jurisdiction is an appropriate one; it should in principle be a jurisdiction to which neither party to the contract can object as inappropriate; they have both implicitly agreed that it is appropriate.[130]

Similarly, in *Highland Crusader Offshore Partners v Deutsche Bank*, a decision of the English Court of Appeal, Lord Justice Toulson stated that

> A non-exclusive jurisdiction agreement precludes either party from later arguing that the forum identified is not an appropriate forum on grounds foreseeable at the time of the agreement, for the parties must be taken to have been aware of such matters at the time of the agreement. For that reason an application to stay on forum non conveniens grounds an action brought in England pursuant to an English non-exclusive jurisdiction clause will ordinarily fail unless the factors relied upon were unforeseeable at the time of the agreement.[131]

---

[125]Hartley and Dogauchi (2010), p. 801, para 48.

[126]E.g. Greece (Panapoulos 2019, Sections 2.4.1 and 2.4.2).

[127]E.g. Germany (Weller 2019, Section 3.5).

[128]China (Tu and Huang 2019, Section 3, text to note 61); UK (Merrett and Carruthers 2019, Section 2.3.3); US (Buxbaum 2019, Section 5.2.1.2.1).

[129]*Highland Crusader Offshore Partners LP v Deutsche Bank AG* [2009] EWCA Civ 725, para 51.

[130][1990] 2 QB 631, 646.

[131][2009] EWCA Civ 725, para 50. See likewise *British Aerospace Plc v Dee Howard Co* [1993] 1 Lloyd's Rep 368, 376; *Ace Insurance SA-NV v Zurich Insurance Co Ltd* [2001] 1 Lloyd's Rep 618, 630.

Two distinct and inconsistent lines of reasoning as to the effect of optional choice of court agreements have emerged in common law jurisdictions.[132] The first is that the existence of an optional choice of court agreement, whether in favour of the forum or of a foreign court, is relevant to the normal *forum non conveniens* enquiry. This is how most optional choice of court agreements are treated in Australia,[133] and how optional choice of courts in favour of foreign courts are treated in Singapore.[134] Most state courts in the US "apply the traditional *forum non conveniens* analysis, but place a significant burden on the defendant who seeks to dismiss from a forum to which it previously agreed."[135]

If proceedings have been commenced in the courts of two countries, then the existence of parallel proceedings will also be relevant to the *forum non conveniens* analysis. If one set of proceedings were commenced pursuant to an optional choice of court agreement, this is likely to be given significant weight. In one Canadian case, the fact that the foreign court was nominated in an optional choice of court agreement was a weighty consideration in the Canadian court's decision to stay its proceedings, even though the Canadian court was the court first seised.[136]

The second line of reasoning, which is especially evident in the English cases and has recently been adopted in Singapore, is that the party challenging the jurisdiction of the court nominated in the optional choice of court agreement is bound by their implied promise to submit to the jurisdiction of that court, unless they can show *strong* cause or reasons as to why they should be allowed to litigate in a non-chosen court.[137] This is the same test that is applied to exclusive choice of court agreements. Some English cases have used even stronger language. For example, in *Mercury Communications v Communications Telesystems International*, Justice Moore-Bick stated that

> particular weight should attach to the fact that the defendant has freely agreed as part of his bargain to submit to the jurisdiction. In principle he should be held to that bargain unless there are *overwhelming* reasons to the contrary.[138]

---

[132]*Orchard Capital I Ltd v Ravindra Kumar Jhunjhunwala* [2012] 2 SLR 519.

[133]Marshall (2019), Section 2.3.1.

[134]Chong (2019), Section 2.4. Optional choice of courts in favour of Singapore courts are dealt with quite differently: see ibid, Section 2.3.1.

[135]Buxbaum (2019), Section 5.2.1.2.1.

[136]*Silveira v FY International Auditing & Consulting Corp* 2015 ONSC 388, cited by Saumier (2019), Section 3.4.

[137]Merrett and Carruthers (2019), Section 2.3.3, text to notes 72–74; Chong (2019), Section 2.3.1. The same approach is taken in Hong Kong (*Noble Power Investments Ltd v Nissei Stomach Tokyo Co Ltd* [2008] 5 Hong Kong LRD 631).

[138][1999] 2 All England Reports (Comm) 33 (emphasis added). In another case, Justice Gloster stated that "the general rule is that the parties will be held to their contractual choice of English jurisdiction unless there are overwhelming, or at least very strong, reasons for departing from this rule": *Antec International Ltd v Biosafety USA Inc* [2006] EWHC 47 (Comm), para 7.

This line of reasoning has been criticised for blurring the distinction between exclusive and optional choice of court agreements.[139]

In some jurisdictions, there are conflicting authorities as to which of these principles should be applied to determine the effect of an optional choice of court agreement.[140] In common law Canada, the effect of an optional choice of court agreement is normally determined according to the *forum non conveniens* principle, although Canadian courts sometimes apply the test used for exclusive choice of court agreements where the choice of court agreement is apparently optional,[141] and Saumier notes that

> the weight of precedent [may have been] shifting to apply only the strong cause [test] whenever a party is seeking to avoid a choice of court agreement, whether it is the plaintiff or the defendant, whether it is exclusive or optional and whether the agreement designates the forum or a foreign court.[142]

In South Africa, while a stay could be granted in a case involving an optional choice of court agreement, it is uncertain whether this would be done by reference to *forum non conveniens*, or by reference to the principle relevant to exclusive choice of court agreements.[143]

In *Abdul Rashid bin Abdul Manaf v Hii Yii Ann*, Justice Woo of the Singapore High Court drew a distinction between an optional choice of court agreement which denoted "an" appropriate forum, and a "most appropriate jurisdiction" agreement which denoted "the" appropriate forum.[144] In the case of a "most appropriate jurisdiction" agreement, "the evidential burden shifts to a plaintiff suing in the non-contractual jurisdiction to show strong cause as to why he should be permitted to do so", in which case "this will bring the negotiated [optional choice of court agreement] very close to an [exclusive choice of court agreement]".[145] While the Singaporean courts until recently treated any optional choice of court agreement as one factor relevant to the *forum non conveniens* analysis, the Singaporean Court of Appeal recently held that "where the proper law of the contract is Singapore law and Singapore is a named forum in the optional choice of court agreement, the defendant must show 'strong cause' why he should not be bound to his contractual agreement to submit to the Singapore court's jurisdiction."[146] On the other hand, the effect of an

---

[139]Chong (2019), Section 2.3.1, text to note 36, citing *UBS AG v Telesto Investments Ltd* [2011] 4 SLR 503, para 120; Merrett and Carruthers (2019), Section 2.3.3, text to notes 75 and 76, citing *BP Plc v AON* [2005] EWHC 2554 (Comm), para 23; *Highland Crusaders Offshore Partners LP v Deutsche Bank AG* [2009] EWCA 725.

[140]Common law Canada (Saumier 2019, Section 3.3).

[141]Saumier (2019), Section 3.4.

[142]Saumier (2019), Section 3.4.

[143]Schoeman (2019), Section 5.2.

[144][2014] 4 SLR 1042, discussed in Chong (2019), Section 2.4, text to notes 58–60.

[145][2014] 4 SLR 1042, para 54, discussed in Chong (2019), Section 2.4, text to note 59.

[146]Chong (2019), Section 2.3.1, following note 38, discussing *Shanghai Turbo Enterprises Ltd v Liu Ming* [2019] SGCA 11.

optional choice of court in favour of a foreign court continues to be determined according to the *forum non conveniens* analysis.[147]

5.2.1 An Agreement That Changes Character When the Option Is Exercised

In some countries, optional choice of court agreements are regarded as changing their character when the option is exercised, at which point they become exclusive. This is so in Chinese law, but only in relation to options in favour of Chinese courts.[148] In English law, it is possible that "a non-exclusive jurisdiction clause may be one which means that a contracting party is entitled to decide later that the court chosen is to have exclusive jurisdiction, but is under no compulsion to do so."[149] Some US state courts have taken the view that "an optional choice of court agreement 'becomes mandatory' once suit is filed in the designated forum"[150]; and some Belgian scholars take a similar view.[151] In Singapore, although it is not clear whether the agreement changes character when the option is exercised, the courts will be reluctant to grant an anti-suit injunction if proceedings have not been commenced in Singapore pursuant to the optional choice of court agreement.[152]

5.2.2 Additional Provisions

Choice of court agreements sometimes include further provisions, in addition to the nomination of a particular court or courts. These additional provisions have been important in the decisions of English courts in cases involving optional choice of court agreements. They might include the nomination of an agent who is authorised to accept service of process within the nominated forum. Some choice of court agreements also include express waivers of the right to object to the jurisdiction of the nominated court. For example, part of the jurisdiction clause in *Sabah Shipyard (Pakistan) v Pakistan* stated that

> Each Party waives any objection that it may now or hereafter have to the venue of any action or proceeding brought as consented to in this Section 1.9 [the jurisdiction clause], and specifically waives any objection that any such action or proceedings was brought in any inconvenient forum and agrees not to plead or claim the same. . .[153]

---

[147]Chong (2019), Section 2.4.

[148]Tu and Huang (2019), Section 3, text to note 62.

[149]Briggs (2008), p. 115, para 4.16.

[150]Buxbaum (2019), Section 5.2.1.2.1.

[151]Van Calster and Poesen (2019), Section 3.3.3 (although they disagree with this view).

[152]Chong (2019), Section 2.3.3, text to note 103, citing *Morgan Stanley Asia (Singapore) Pte v Hong Leong Finance Ltd* [2013] 3 SLR 409, para 71.

[153][2003] 2 Lloyd's Rep 571, para 28.

Express waivers of the right to challenge jurisdiction might be unilateral.[154] For example, part of the Law and Jurisdiction clause in *Commerzbank AG v Liquimar Tankers Management Inc* provided that

> The guarantor irrevocably waives any objection which it may now or in the future have to the laying of the venue of any proceedings in any court referred to in this clause and any claim that those proceedings have been brought in an inconvenient or inappropriate court.[155]

In some cases decided by the courts in common law countries, the existence of an express waiver of the right to object to the nominated court seems to have led to the court imposing a higher standard on the party challenging the jurisdiction than is applied in other cases.[156]

Some optional choice of court agreements also include "express other jurisdiction" clauses, which "expressly contemplate the possibility of parallel proceedings".[157] For example, the clause in *Highland Crusaders Offshore Partners v Deutsche Bank* stated that "Nothing in this paragraph [containing the choice of court agreement] shall limit the right of any party to take proceedings in the courts of any other country of competent jurisdiction."[158] In cases in which there are express other jurisdiction provisions, it seems that the courts are likely to take a strict approach, although it has been suggested that the reasoning in these cases should not depend on such a provision because "in any optional jurisdiction agreement there is no promise not to sue in another jurisdiction, thus no agreement that [the nominated forum] is the sole forum, and accordingly there is an inherent risk of parallel proceedings."[159]

5.2.3 Implied Promises

In a number of English cases, the courts have held that an optional choice of court agreement might, depending on the wording of the agreement, entail implied promises that might be enforced in various ways (principally, by the grant of an anti-suit injunction).[160] These include implied obligations

- not to commence or continue parallel proceedings in a non-nominated forum;
- not to apply for a stay of proceedings in the nominated forum; or

[154] E.g. *Bambang Sutrisno v Bali International Finance Ltd* [1999] 2 SLR(R) 632.

[155] [2017] 1 WLR 3497, para 9.

[156] Chong (2019), Section 2.3, text to note 32 (citing *Transocean Offshore International Ventures Ltd v Burgundy Global Exploration Corp* [2010] 2 SLR 821) and Section 2.4, text to note 51 (citing *Bambang Sutrisno v Bali International Finance Ltd* [1999] 2 SLR(R) 632).

[157] Merrett and Carruthers (2019), Section 2.5.3, citing *Royal Bank of Canada v Cooperative Centrale* [2004] EWCA Civ 7.

[158] [2009] EWCA Civ 725.

[159] Merrett and Carruthers (2019), Section 2.5.3.

[160] Merrett and Carruthers (2019), Section 2.5.3, citing in particular *Sabah Shipyard (Pakistan) v Pakistan* [2003] 2 Lloyd's Rep 571.

- not to apply for an anti-suit injunction in a non-nominated forum, to prevent commencement or continuation of proceedings in a court nominated in an optional choice of court agreement.

5.2.4 Discrimination Between Options in Favour of Forum and Foreign Courts

Most legal systems do not openly discriminate in favour of choice of court agreements that nominate forum courts, as opposed to those that nominate foreign courts. For example, in common law systems, optional choice of court agreements whether in favour of the forum or of a foreign court are generally regarded as being relevant to the general *forum non conveniens* analysis. However, in some countries, optional choice of court agreements in favour of foreign courts are treated differently to those that nominate courts of the forum.[161] Tu and Huang note that "optional choice of court agreements in favour of Chinese courts on the one hand and those in favour of foreign courts on the other are not treated consistently."[162] Article 12 of the 2005 Supreme People's Court of China Summary states that an optional choice of court agreement nominating a foreign court does not exclude the jurisdiction of the competent courts of other countries, including China,[163] even if one party has exercised the option by commencing proceedings in the foreign court nominated in the optional choice of court agreement.[164] This contrasts with the effect of an optional choice of court agreement in favour of the Chinese courts, which is regarded as becoming exclusive when the option is exercised.[165]

In Australia, an optional choice of court agreement in favour of a foreign court will have little effect.[166] This is because of the idiosyncratic Australian version of *forum non conveniens* which requires the defendant to establish that the Australian court is clearly inappropriate, which is far more onerous on the defendant than the version of *forum non conveniens* developed in England and used in other common law jurisdictions which requires the defendant to show only that a foreign court is clearly more appropriate than the forum. In Australia, the fact that the parties have agreed to submit to the jurisdiction of a foreign court is regarded as merely one factor to take into account in deciding whether the Australian court is clearly inappropriate; Marshall notes that Australian courts have never stayed proceedings in a case in which the parties had nominated foreign courts in an optional choice of court agreement.[167]

---

[161]Including Australia (Marshall 2019, Section 2.3.1.3) and Singapore (Chong 2019, Section 2.5).

[162]Tu and Huang (2019), Section 3 (text in the sentence before note 68).

[163]Tu and Huang (2019), Section 3 (text to note 64).

[164]Tu and Huang (2019), Section 3 (text to note 67).

[165]Tu and Huang (2019), Section 3 (text to note 62).

[166]Marshall (2019), Section 2.3.1.2.

[167]Marshall (2019), Section 2.3.3.1.

6 Limitations on the Parties' Choice of Court

Most jurisdictions impose few limitations on the parties' choices of court. One of the main exceptions to this proposition relates to subject matter jurisdiction. This is not contractible, and therefore the forum's rules of exclusive subject matter jurisdiction take priority over the parties' agreements. Most legal systems explicitly nominate particular grounds of exclusive subject matter jurisdiction, which tend to be fairly similar, including disputes concerning immovable property,[168] some intellectual property rights,[169] and some matters involving companies.[170] In Chinese law, a wide range of subject matters belongs to the exclusive jurisdiction of Chinese courts. These include disputes concerning harbour operations, succession,[171] performance of contracts within Chinese territory of Chinese-foreign equity joint ventures, Chinese-foreign contractual joint ventures, and Chinese-foreign cooperative exploration and exploitation of natural resources.[172] In some legal systems, the law identifies the place of exclusive subject matter jurisdiction generally—that is, it does not only reserve the exclusive subject matter jurisdiction of the courts of the forum.

It is common to find limits on the types of relationships in which a choice of court agreement may be used; for example, many reporters state that choice of court agreements only apply to particular legal relationships,[173] and some note that the parties cannot use such agreements in family matters.[174] In Chinese law, the parties are only able to choose courts to deal with contractual disputes and disputes related to property interests.[175]

In most of the countries represented in the national reports, there is no requirement of factual connection to the foreign country the courts of which are nominated in a choice of court agreement.[176] On the other hand, there is a requirement of factual connection in Chinese law. According to Article 34 of the Chinese Civil Procedure Law,

---

[168]In South African law, the place where land is situated is regarded as having exclusive jurisdiction to deal with questions of title to that land: Schoeman (2019), Section 3.5, text to note 53.

[169]E.g. Belgium Van Calster and Poesen (2019), Section 2.2.

[170]E.g. Germany (Weller 2019, Section 2.1.1); Japan (Takahashi 2019, Section 1.2, citing the Japanese Code of Civil Procedure, Article 3-10 and 3-5); Turkey (Tarman and Oba 2019, Section 3.1.2).

[171]Chinese Civil Procedure Law, Article 33.

[172]Chinese Civil Procedure Law, Article 266.

[173]In Turkey, the dispute must arise from an "obligatory relationship": Tarman and Oba (2019), Section 3.1.3.

[174]E.g. Greece (Panapoulos 2019, text to note 2); Netherlands (Rammeloo 2019, Section 1.1); Turkey (Tarman and Oba 2019, Section 3.1.3).

[175]Tang et al. (2016), p. 69.

[176]For example, Japan (Takahashi 2019, Section 1.1).

> Parties to a dispute over a contract or any other right or interest in a property may, without violating rules concerning jurisdiction by forum level and exclusive jurisdiction, choose the court for the place where the defendant is domiciled, or where the contract is performed or signed, or where the plaintiff is domiciled, or where the subject matter is located or any other place that has actual connection with the dispute as the court having jurisdiction over their dispute by a written agreement.[177]

The requirement of factual connection has been heavily criticised by Chinese scholars.[178]

Whereas factual connection may not be a requirement for the validity of a choice of court agreement in most legal systems, the connections to the nominated court might be taken into account when a defendant challenges the choice of court agreement. For example, the Swiss Private International Law Act gives the Swiss court the discretion to decline the submission to its jurisdiction if there is no "local or factual proximity of the court designated by agreement."[179] The relevant connections are that either at least one party is domiciled, has its "main whereabouts", or its place of business in the forum; or Swiss law is the governing law.[180] Similarly, in countries which have a principle of *forum non conveniens*, factual connections may be relevant in considering whether the proceedings should be stayed or dismissed.

In the Czech Republic, prorogation of a foreign court will only be recognised if there is a "legally significant" international element present.[181] Under Greek law, a foreign court agreement in a contract that is purely internal to Greece is regarded as invalid on the basis of the theory of *fraud à la loi*.[182] In some countries, some reason for the selection of the chosen court is required.[183] In the 1985 decision of the Dutch Hoge Raad which established that the parties could prorogate the jurisdiction of Dutch courts, the parties' freedom to establish jurisdiction was stated to be subject to their having "a genuine interest".[184] This does not necessarily require a factual

---

[177] Civil Procedure Law of the PRC (as amended in June 2017), Article 34, cited by Tu and Huang (2019), Section 2, text to note 6.

[178] Tu and Huang (2019), Section 2 (note 11), citing Tang et al. (2016), p. 70; Tang (2012), p. 466; Liu and Zhou (2014), p. 50.

[179] Haas and MacCabe (2019), Section 6.1 (text to note 66), citing the Swiss Private International Law Act, Article 5(3). See likewise Van Calster and Poesen (2019), Section 3.4.2.1, citing the Belgian Private International Law Act, Article 6, paragraph 2.

[180] Haas and MacCabe (2019), Section 6.1, text to note 67, citing the Swiss Private International Law Act, Article 5(3).

[181] Rozehnalová et al. (2019), Section 1.1, text to note 10. This requirement is not defined in Czech legislation, and is therefore determined ad hoc in each case. There is similarly a requirement in Turkish law that the dispute must involve a foreign element: Tarman and Oba (2019), Section 3.1.1. As in the case of the Czech Republic, this is not defined, and the courts apply a broad interpretation.

[182] Panapoulos (2019), Section 1.1.2.

[183] Buxbaum notes that in a few US states, "courts have held that the designated forum 'must bear a reasonable relationship to the transaction'": (2019), Section 5.1, citing KC Ravens LLC v Nima Scrap, LLC 369 P 3d 341 (Ct App Kansas 2016). She suggests that these decisions are anomalous.

[184] *Piscator*, HR February 1, 1985, NJ 1985, 698, cited by Rammeloo (2019), Section 1.1 (text to note 2).

connection; the parties would have a genuine interest if the chosen court was neutral or had relevant expertise.[185]

As noted, the tendency in German law has been the converse of that observed in most other legal systems. The reason for the restrictive approach to the enforcement of choice of court agreements in the 1974 reform to the Code of Civil Procedure was that these agreements were being used in "virtually all standard terms", and their invocation in legal proceedings, particularly involving consumers, was regarded as unfair and abusive.[186] German law consequently imposes a number of limitations, which are different to those found in most other legal systems. These include that choice of court agreements are only valid if they are concluded between merchants (which generally includes corporations[187]), legal persons under public law,[188] or public trusts.[189]

In some countries, the parties' ability to choose their forum is limited by the application of the forum's internationally mandatory rules.[190] This is not the case in France, where the Cour de Cassation held in 2008 that the potential application of French *lois de police* (imperative rules) does not prevent the parties from selecting a foreign court in a choice of court agreement.[191]

Most legal systems will not enforce choice of court agreements in favour of foreign courts when that would be incompatible with fundamental public policy of the forum.[192] This is likely to affect exclusive rather than optional choice of court agreements. In Japan, the Supreme Court held that effect may be denied to a choice of court agreement if it is "extremely unreasonable and contrary to the law of public policy".[193] Similarly, a choice of court agreement would not be enforced by Singaporean courts if it was against the fundamental public policy of Singapore.[194] In

[185]Rammeloo (2019), note 4.

[186]Weller (2019), Section 1.4.

[187]Weller (2019), Section 2.1.7.

[188]Similar limitations apply in Turkey, but only in the case of the choice of Turkish courts: Tarman and Oba (2019), Section 4.1.

[189]German Code on Civil Procedure, section 38(1).

[190]E.g. Australia (Marshall 2019, text to notes 13–14); Belgium (Van Calster and Poesen 2019, Section 2.2).

[191]Mailhé (2019), text to note 5, citing Cass civ 1ére 22 October 2008, *Monster Cable*, no 07-15823, *JCP G* 2008, 10187, note L d'Avout. The same applies in Greece: Panapoulos (2019), text to note 18.

[192]E.g. Czech Republic (Rozehnalová et al. 2019, Section 1.3, text to note 36, and Section 2.8, text to note 72); Germany (Weller 2019, Section 3.11).

[193]Chisadane, Supreme Court, Judgment, November 28, 1975, 29 Minshu (1) 1554 [1975], cited in Takahashi (2019), Section 1.3. Takahashi notes that although this aspect of the judgment was not explicitly codified in the Code of Civil Procedure, it "arguably has survived the amendment of the [Code of Civil Procedure] since no statutory basis would need to be found to safeguard the fundamental legal value of Japan": (2019), Section 1.3.

[194]Chong (2019), Section 1, text to note 3, giving as an example where the parties deliberately chose a foreign court "to evade the operation of the Unfair Contract Terms Act" Cap 396, 1994 Rev Ed.

Romania, a choice of court agreement will be ineffective "if it abusively deprives one of the parties of the protection ensured by a court designated by Romanian law."[195]

7 Support of Optional Choice of Court Agreements

In most legal systems, the only protection of optional choice of court agreements is the possibility of proceedings brought in a forum other than that or those nominated in the choice of court agreement being stayed or dismissed, or the court declining jurisdiction.[196] This might be done on several bases: if the optional choice of court agreement is transformed into an exclusive choice of court agreement once the option is exercised; if the court finds itself to be *forum non conveniens*, taking into account the existence of the optional choice of court agreement; or if the court stays or refuses to stay proceedings on the basis of *lis pendens*, where the relevant court's jurisdiction is derived from the optional choice of court agreement.

Even in common law systems, there are few remedies available to support optional choice of court agreements, in comparison to the range of remedies that support exclusive choice of court agreements. It has been suggested that the "remedies to ensure the optional choice of court agreements' efficacy are not necessarily very efficient."[197]

In most countries, damages are definitely not available for breach of an optional choice of court agreement[198]; it is doubtful whether they are available in Romania.[199] Van Calster and Poesen suggest that it may be possible that "an abusive exercise of an optional choice of court agreement in favour of the Belgian courts can give rise to an award of damages to the defendant".[200] Anti-suit and anti-enforcement injunctions are not available to support an optional choice of court agreement in most countries.[201] The courts of EU Member States cannot grant anti-

[195]Oprea (2019), Section 4.4, sentence before note 81, citing the Romanian Civil Procedure Code, Article 1068.

[196]This is possible in Québec, under the Civil Code, art 3135: see Guillemard and Sabourin (2019), Section 2.2.1, text to note 90.

[197]Oprea (2019), Section 4.6.

[198]Including the Czech Republic (Rozehnalová et al. 2019, Section 2.6.2); Greece (Panapoulos 2019, Section 2.6).

[199]Oprea (2019), Section 4.6.2.

[200]Van Calster and Poesen (2019), Section 3.4.2.2.

[201]Including China (Tu and Huang 2019, Section 3 (text following note 81)), Greece (Panapoulos 2019, Section 2.6), Germany (Weller 2019, Section 3.8), Romania (Oprea 2019, Section 4.6.1), Switzerland (Haas and MacCabe 2019, Section 6.3) and Taiwan (Chen 2019, Section 2.8.3 and 2.8.4).

suit injunctions to preclude the commencement or continuation of proceedings in the courts of other Member States.[202]

In common law systems, in addition to staying or dismissing proceedings, and setting aside service of process, the main protection available for choice of court agreements is the anti-suit injunction.[203] Whereas an anti-suit injunction will readily be issued to prevent the breach of an exclusive choice of court agreement,[204] that will generally not be the basis on which an anti-suit injunction might be awarded if foreign proceedings have been commenced notwithstanding the parties' optional choice of court agreement in favour of the forum, because this is generally not regarded as a breach of contract.[205] Instead, the party applying for an anti-suit injunction will need to show that the commencement or continuation of the foreign proceedings is unconscionable, vexatious or oppressive.[206]

The English courts alone have in some cases granted anti-suit injunctions to restrain the commencement or continuation of foreign proceedings where the parties had agreed to the non-exclusive jurisdiction of English courts. Unfortunately, "the cases are inconsistent and the principles far from clear."[207] In *Sabah Shipyard (Pakistan) Ltd v Pakistan*,[208] the English Court of Appeal famously upheld the decision of the primary judge to grant an anti-suit injunction to prevent the continuation of foreign proceedings which the court held were brought to frustrate the optional choice of court agreement in favour of the English courts. This was on the basis that the foreign party's conduct was vexatious or oppressive.[209] On the other hand, the English courts have in some cases refused to grant anti-suit injunctions.[210] In other common law jurisdictions, an anti-suit injunction might be issued to prevent

[202] *Turner v Grovit* [2005] 1 AC 101.

[203] This is available, in principle, in Australia (Marshall 2019, Section 2.3.3.3), common law Canada, England and Scotland (Merrett and Carruthers 2019, Section 2.5.3), and Singapore (Chong 2019, Section 2.7, text to notes 95–103). In Scotland, this is referred to as "restraint of foreign proceedings" (Merrett and Carruthers 2019, Section 2.5.3). In common law Canada, there is no case law relating to anti-suit injunctions to protect choice of court agreements in particular: Saumier (2019), Section 4.

[204] In England, an anti-suit injunction might be granted to prevent commencement or continuation of proceedings in breach of the exclusive component of an asymmetric choice of court agreement: Merrett and Carruthers (2019), Section 3.5, citing *Bank of New York Mellon v GV Films* [2009] EWHC 2338 (Comm).

[205] *UBS AG v Telesto Investments Ltd* [2011] 4 SLR 503, para 75.

[206] Australia (Marshall (2019), Section 2.3.3.3); UK (Merrett and Carruthers 2019, Section 2.5.3).

[207] Merrett and Carruthers (2019), Section 2.5.3.

[208] [2003] 2 Lloyd's Rep 571.

[209] An injunction was also granted in *BNP Paribas SA v Anchorage Capital Europe LLP* [2015] EWHC 3077.

[210] Merrett and Carruthers (2019), Section 2.5.3, text to notes 109–116, citing *Royal Bank of Canada v Cooperative Centrale* [2004] EWCA Civ 7; *Highland Crusader Offshore Partners v Deutsche Bank AG* [2009] EWCA Civ 725; and *SwissMarine Corp Ltd v OW Supply & Trading A/S (in bankruptcy)* [2015] EWHC 1571 (Comm).

the commencement or continuation of foreign proceedings, again, if it could be shown that the foreign proceedings were vexatious or oppressive.[211]

In principle, common law courts can grant anti-enforcement injunctions, but there are no cases in which it has been argued or suggested that this remedy might be available to support an optional choice of court agreement.[212]

In principle, in at least some common law countries, damages are available for breach of exclusive choice of court agreements.[213] It has been suggested that damages should be available for breach of the exclusive component of an asymmetric choice of court agreement.[214]

In comparison, it is generally not regarded as a breach of contract for a party to commence proceedings in a court other than that nominated in an optional choice of court agreement, because such agreements are generally not regarded as imposing an obligation to refrain from litigating in courts other than that or those nominated in the optional choice of court agreement. It is highly unlikely that a court would award damages unless the choice of court agreement was more elaborate than simply nominating a court as having optional jurisdiction. In some English cases in which the courts have granted anti-suit injunctions, it has been held that an optional choice of court agreement entails implied promises, including promises not to commence or continue parallel proceedings in a forum other than that nominated; not to apply for a stay of proceedings in the forum; or not to apply for an anti-suit injunction to prevent commencement or continuation of proceedings in a court nominated in an optional choice of court agreement.[215] Merrett and Carruthers suggest that if "losses have been suffered as a result of a breach of such a promise damages may be recoverable."[216]

It is not clear whether damages for breach of a choice of court agreement might be available under the Brussels I Recast Regulation. Several reporters mention that the foreign judgment would give rise to an issue estoppel.[217] While some regard that as precluding the possibility of damages being awarded, Merrett and Carruthers suggest that

> (a) it could be argued that the procedural consequences of a jurisdiction agreement under the Regulation are different from contractual questions; and (b) furthermore, the effect of *Erich*

---

[211]Including Singapore (Chong 2019, Section 2.7).

[212]Marshall (2019), Section 2.3.3.4.

[213]See Marshall (2019), Section 2.3.3.2 (noting that while there is probably a right to damages for breach of an exclusive choice of court agreement in Australian law, there is no case in which an Australian court has awarded damages); Merrett and Carruthers (2019), Section 2.5.1 (citing *Donohue v Armco Inc* [2001] UKHL 64; *The Alexandros T* [2013] UKSC 70). In common law Canada, there is no case law on this issue in particular.

[214]Merrett and Carruthers (2019), Sections 2.5.1 and 3.4 (text to notes 98 and 195), citing *Barclays Bank plc v Ente Nazionale de Previdenza dei Medici degli Odontoiatra* [2015] EWHC 2857 (Comm) paras 127-8. Cf Marshall (2019), Section 2.3.3.2.

[215]See above, Sect. 5.2.3.

[216]Merrett and Carruthers (2019), Section 2.5.1.

[217]Merrett and Carruthers (2019), Section 2.5.1.

Gasser is now reversed by Art 31(2) which does give *competence competence* to the chosen court.[218]

They cite two English cases—*The Alexandros T*[219] and *Barclays Bank v Ente Nazionale de Presidenza*[220]—as authority for the proposition that a claim for damages for breach of a choice of court agreement does not infringe the principle of mutual trust and confidence.[221]

8 Weaker Parties

In many legal systems, the law reveals serious concerns about the use of choice of court agreements in contracts involving weaker parties, and this is one of the major limitations on the use of choice of court agreements. Some legal systems provide protection to parties who are presumed to be weaker, including consumers and employees, specifically in terms of invalidating, or limiting the effect of, choice of court agreements. This protection may take several forms: it may be implied from the exclusion of such parties from the scope of the instrument, as is done in the Hague Choice of Court Convention,[222] or it may be explicit in specific rules that apply only to choice of court agreements involving weaker parties, as in the Brussels I Recast[223] and in national laws of some countries. Countries including China,[224] the Czech Republic,[225] Germany,[226] Greece,[227] Japan,[228] Switzerland,[229] Turkey,[230] and the US[231] provide specific protection for weaker parties. Specific protective rules in favour of weaker parties generally do not distinguish between exclusive and optional

[218]Merrett and Carruthers (2019), Section 2.5.1.

[219][2013] UKSC 70, paras 39 and 131-2.

[220][2015] EWHC 2857 (Comm); approved by the Court of Appeal in [2016] EWCA Civ 1261.

[221]Compare Rozehnalová et al. (2019), Section 2.6.2.

[222]Article 2(1).

[223]Sections 3 (dealing with insurance contracts), 4 (dealing with consumer contracts) and 5 (dealing with employment contracts).

[224]Tu and Huang (2019), Section 3 (text to note 75), citing Article 31 of the Supreme People's Court of China Interpretation on Chinese Civil Procedure Law.

[225]Rozehnalová et al. (2019), Section 2.5, citing the Czech Private International Law Act, sections 86 and 88.

[226]Weller (2019), Section 3.7.

[227]Panapoulos (2019), Sections 1.1.2 and 2.5.

[228]Takahashi (2019), Section 2.2, citing the Japanese Code of Civil Procedure, article 3-7.

[229]Haas and MacCabe (2019), Section 10, citing the Swiss Code on Civil Procedure, article 35(1), Lugano Convention, articles 13, 17, 21, and the Swiss Private International Law Act, article 114(2).

[230]Tarman and Oba (2019), Section 3.2.

[231]Buxbaum (2019), Section 3.2.

choice of court agreements,[232] although some, such as those invalidating choice of court agreements that *exclude* a weaker party's right to bring proceedings in the forum, would obviously only apply to an exclusive choice of foreign courts.

In some countries, choice of court agreements involving presumptively weaker parties are completely unenforceable.[233] For example, under the Civil Code of Québec, a choice of court agreement which nominates a foreign court cannot be enforced against a consumer or employee who is domiciled in Québec.[234] It is more common that the choice of court agreement is not completely invalid; generally, it can be invoked by the weaker party, and only invoked against the weaker party in limited circumstances. For example, in the Brussels I Recast Regulation, a choice of court agreement involving insureds, consumers, and employees can be enforced if the agreement gives the weaker party a selection of courts other than those that would otherwise be available under the default rules.[235] In Taiwan, the legal protection of weaker parties only enables proceedings to be transferred from the chosen Taiwanese court to another competent Taiwanese court.[236]

The inclusion of such protective provisions is for most legal systems a new legal development.[237] Laws protecting consumers and employees are the most common, but in other legal systems they extend also to insureds. In the Swiss Code on Civil Procedure, tenants are also presumed to be weaker[238]; laws in US states protect a range of other parties presumed to be in a weaker bargaining position, including franchisees.[239]

In some countries, the primary laws make no particular provision for the protection of weaker contracting parties in the specific context of choice of court agreements.[240] It is typical of common law countries that there are no specific protections for weaker parties in the principles of jurisdiction.[241] Disputes about choice of court

---

[232]For example, in Chinese law, a choice of court agreement in a consumer contract is invalid unless the consumer receives "proper notice" of the terms: Tu and Huang (2019), Section 3 (text to note 75).

[233]This is so for most choice of court agreements involving weaker parties in German law: Weller (2019), Section 3.7. See also Panapoulos (2019), describing the unenforceability of contracts involving weaker parties under Greek law of national origin: Section 1.1.2 (referring to agreements in some employment matters, in favour of foreign courts), Section 2.5.3 (referring to consumer agreements which are "concluded or to be executed in Greece").

[234]Article 3149.

[235]Articles 15(2), 19(2), and 23(2).

[236]Chen (2019), Section 2.7, citing Taiwanese Code of Civil Procedure, Article 28 section 2.

[237]Takahashi notes that prior to the amendment of the Japanese Code of Civil Procedure which came into effect in 2012, "no special treatment was given to individual employment relations" in the context of choice of court agreements: (2019), Section 1.3.

[238]Article 35, cited in Haas and MacCabe (2019), Section 10.

[239]Buxbaum (2019), Section 3.2.

[240]This is particularly true in common law countries.

[241]This is so in Australia (Marshall 2019, Section 2.3.2); Singapore (Chong 2019, Section 2.6), the UK (Merrett and Carruthers 2019, Section 2.4); and in the US (Buxbaum 2019, Section 3.3).

agreements involving weaker parties are, in general, resolved using the same principles as those applicable in other cases.[242] A small number of cases suggest that exclusive choice of court agreements involving consumers require slightly different treatment.[243] The implications of those cases for optional choice of court agreements involving consumers are not clear, but it stands to reason that in a choice of court agreement involving a consumer, the agreement should be given less weight.[244]

9 Asymmetric Choice of Court Agreements

The decision of the French Cour de Cassation in *Madame X vs Société Banque Privé Edmond de Rothschild*[245] has attracted a great deal of attention, and stimulated controversy internationally about the effect of asymmetric choice of court agreements, sometimes called unilateral, or one-sided, choice of court agreements. While asymmetric agreements take different forms, the most common contains a combination of an exclusive choice of court agreement, which applies if one party commences proceedings, and an optional choice of court agreement, which applies if the other party commences proceedings.

While asymmetric choice of court agreements are not rare, they have not been the subject of much litigation.[246] Evidently, in most countries there are no specific statutory rules relating to their enforcement,[247] and so, to the extent that the question of their effectiveness has arisen in practice, the principles are derived from case law.

In France, choice of court agreements "in the sole interest of one party" have long been recognised: "[s]uch optional choices were discovered by interpretation: the agreement was found to allow the party the clause had been written in favour of to renounce his right and to seize an otherwise competent court."[248] In Greece, choice of court agreements "for the benefit of one of the parties, as envisaged in Art 17 §5

[242]For example, in the 2017 decision of the Canadian Supreme Court in *Douez v Facebook Inc*, involving an exclusive choice of court agreement between Facebook and Canadian users of Facebook services, the court used the same principles as those that are applied in commercial cases: 2017 SCC 33. See Saumier (2019), Section 3.2.

[243]Most importantly, in *Douez v Facebook, Inc*, 2017 SCC 33 the majority of the Supreme Court of Canada took the view that the consumer context required a "differentiated application of the "strong cause" test for refusing to enforce a choice of court agreement": Saumier (2019), Section 3.2.

[244]Marshall (2019), Section 2.3.2.

[245]Cass civ, 1ère, 26 September 2012.

[246]Chong notes that in Singapore "[t]here appear to be few reported cases dealing expressly with asymmetrical choice of court agreements and of those few, the optional portion of such agreements has not been at issue": (2019), Section 4. See similarly, in relation to Belgium, Van Calster and Poesen (2019), Section 4.2.

[247]This is so, for example, in Switzerland (Haas and MacCabe 2019, Section 11).

[248]Mailhé (2019), text to note 13.

[of the Brussels Convention], are steadily accepted as valid in the Greek legal order under provisions of national origin".[249]

The effect of asymmetric choice of court agreements under the Brussels I Recast Regulation is particularly unclear. The recent decisions of the French Cour de Cassation have in particular attracted a great deal of attention. The Cour de Cassation has now refused to enforce asymmetric choice of court agreements in four cases, including the *Rothschild* case.[250] In another two cases, *eBizcuss*[251] and *Diemme Enologia vs Etablissements Chambon & fils*[252] it held an asymmetric choice of court agreement to be enforceable. In England, on the other hand, an asymmetric choice of court agreement has been held valid under the Recast.[253] In *Commerzbank AG v Liquimar Tankers Management Inc*, Justice Cranston held that Article 31(2) of the Recast applied to the exclusive component of asymmetric choice of court agreements.[254] Joseph suggested that a choice of court agreement which benefited only one party "would simply be an example of parties making specific provision other than by way of 'exclusive jurisdiction' binding on both parties."[255] He suggested that this is because of the respect that the Recast requires for party autonomy, and that "there is therefore no reason not to uphold such a bargain."[256]

There are conflicting views as to whether asymmetric choice of court agreements come within the scope of the Hague Choice of Court Convention. One view is that the Convention does not apply to them at all. This view derives from the *Explanatory Report* on the Convention, which states that asymmetric agreements are "non-exclusive for the purpose of the Convention because they exclude the possibility of initiating proceedings in other courts for only one of the parties."[257] Some commentators base their view, that the Convention does not apply to asymmetric choice of court agreements, on this statement from the Explanatory Report.[258] The contrary view is proposed by Justice Cranston in dicta in *Commerzbank AG v Liquimar Tankers Management Inc*, where he said that "there are good arguments in my view that the words of the definition in article 3(a) of the Hague Convention cover asymmetric jurisdiction clauses."[259] Merrett and Carruthers agree, suggesting

[249] Panapoulos (2019), Section 1.3.1.3, citing the Greek Code of Civil Procedure, Art 44.

[250] The other cases are *Danne Holdings vs Crédit Suisse* Cass civ 1ère, 25 March 2015, *Crédit Suisse II* Cass. civ. 1e., 7 February 2018 and *Saint-Joseph* Cass. civ. 1e., 3 October 2018, discussed by Mailhé (2019), Section 3.

[251] *Société eBizcuss.com vs Apple* Cass. civ. 1ère, 7 October 2015, discussed by Mailhé (2019), at text to note 41.

[252] Cass. civ. 1ère, 11 May 2017, discussed by Mailhé (2019), at text to notes 42–44.

[253] *Commerzbank AG v Liquimar Tankers Management Inc* [2017] 1 WLR 3497.

[254] [2017] 1 WLR 3497, para 64.

[255] Joseph (2015), p. 98, para 3.79.

[256] Joseph (2015), p. 73, para 3.18.

[257] Hartley and Dogauchi (2010), p. 845, para 249. See also p. 811, paras 105–106.

[258] Joseph (2015), p. 73, para 3.18; Chong (2019), Section 4, text to note 108–110.

[259] [2017] 1 WLR 3497, para 74, cited by Merrett and Carruthers (2019), Section 3.3.

that if the exclusive component is in issue, it should come within the scope of the Hague Convention.[260]

In some countries the legal effects of asymmetric choice of court agreements are unknown under national laws because their effects are not explicitly provided for in legislation and have not been tested in case law.[261] Most national reporters in the remaining countries state that asymmetric agreements are regarded as valid.[262] However, in the Czech Republic, scholars continue to criticise them for "lack of clarity",[263] whereas they are enforced in some cases, at least between commercial parties; and in Turkey, there are inconsistent views about the validity of asymmetric choice of court agreements.[264] In those legal systems that have explicit protections for weaker parties, the effectiveness of an asymmetric agreement involving a weaker party is subject to those controls.[265] Concerns about asymmetric agreements are almost always due to the fact of their being used in contracts involving weaker parties.[266] Van Calster and Poesen suggest it is possible that the "Belgian courts might subject asymmetrical choice of court agreements to the requirement of good faith".[267]

It is common, in those legal systems in which asymmetric agreements have been litigated, that the different components are treated separately, depending on which aspect of the agreement is in issue.[268] Exclusive components are treated as simple exclusive choice of court agreements, and optional components are treated as simple optional choice of court agreements.[269] In China, an asymmetric choice of court agreement was held to be valid in one case; its effect was said to depend on whether the investor or the bank commenced proceedings.[270] The courts held that if the investor commenced proceedings, the nominated courts would have exclusive jurisdiction, whereas if the bank commenced proceedings, the courts would have only non-exclusive jurisdiction.

[260]Merrett and Carruthers (2019), Section 3.3.

[261]E.g. common law Canada (Saumier 2019, Section 5), Romania (Oprea 2019, Section 5.1.3, text to note 125).

[262]This is so in Germany (Weller 2019, Section 4); the Netherlands (Rammeloo 2019, Section 3.2); and the US (Buxbaum 2019, Section 3.4).

[263]Rozehnalová et al. (2019), Section 3.1.

[264]Tarman and Oba (2019), Section 5.

[265]This is so in Taiwan: Chen (2019), Section 3.1, citing the Taiwanese Code of Civil Procedure, Article 28 Section 2.

[266]Mailhé (2019), Section 2.2, text to notes 33–35.

[267]Van Calster and Poesen (2019), Section 4.3.3.

[268]Japan (Takahashi 2019, Section 3.1), Singapore (Chong 2019, Section 4), and the UK (Merrett and Carruthers 2019, Section 3).

[269]Australia (Marshall 2019, Section 4); Japan (Takahashi 2019, Section 3.2).

[270]*Lai v ABN AMRO Bank NV*, the Shanghai High People's Court (2010) Hu Gao Min Wu (Shang) Zhong Zi No 49, cited by Tu and Huang (2019), Section 4, text to notes 102-3.

In some countries, a choice of court agreement which left the choice of court entirely to the option of the plaintiff would not be enforceable.[271] In Germany, it is impermissible to leave the choice of court entirely to the plaintiff, because this would be insufficiently precise.[272] In German law, "the asymmetry raises issues of fairness and abuse",[273] and there are a range of controls to prevent this, including where one party "exploited its economic or social power" in compelling the weaker party to agree to the asymmetric agreement, and where the weaker party's access to justice is impaired, either legally or practically, "to an intolerable extent".[274] The controls are stronger where the asymmetric agreement is contained in standard terms.[275]

Common law courts, particularly the English courts, and most common law commentators[276] do not see any problem with asymmetric choice of court agreements. English courts have given effect to them under national law, the Brussels Convention, the Lugano Convention, and the Recast.[277] The English judges have stated that the fact that such agreements give an advantage to one party is not unusual in contracts generally and is not a cause for concern.[278] English commentators insist that there is nothing wrong with the parties reaching an agreement as to jurisdiction that is neither simply exclusive nor simply optional. Briggs asserted that

> there is no apparent reason why parties may not, if so advised, make an agreement for the resolution of disputes which is more complex, and better suited to their needs, than would be provided by a plain and simple "exclusive or non-exclusive" template.[279]

In those legal systems which impose general restrictions on the use of choice of court agreements involving weaker parties, those restrictions would be applied to asymmetric agreements.[280] There are other substantive provisions under the national laws of some countries which might have the effect of limiting the effect of an asymmetric choice of court agreement. For example, Takahashi suggests that a new provision of the Japanese Civil Code, due to come into force on 1 April 2020, which states that any contractual clause in a standard transaction "which purports to restrict

[271] Germany (Weller 2019, Section 2.1.1, text to note 55).

[272] Weller (2019), Section 4, text to note 163.

[273] Weller (2019), Section 4, text to note 162.

[274] Weller (2019), Section 4, text to notes 167-8.

[275] Weller (2019), Section 4, text to note 171.

[276] E.g. Briggs (2008), pp. 120–121, para 4.24.

[277] These include *Commerzbank AG v Liquimar Tankers Management Inc* [2017] 1 WLR 3497; *Barclays Bank plc v Ente Nazionale di Previdenza ed Assistenza dei Medici e Degli Odontoiatri* [2015] 2 Lloyd's Rep 527; *Mauritius Commercial Bank Ltd v Hestia Holdings Ltd* [2013] 2 All ER (Comm) 899; *Lornamead Acquisitions Ltd v Kaupthing Bank HF* [2013] 1 BCLC 73; and *Continental Bank NA v Aeakos Cia Naviera SA* [1994] 1 WLR 588.

[278] Merrett and Carruthers (2019), Section 3.1.1, text to notes 144–145 (citing *NB Three Shipping Ltd v Harebell Shipping Ltd* [2014] EWHC 2001 and *Law Debenture Trust Corporation plc v Elektrim Finance BV* [2005] EWHC 1412 (Ch), para 46.

[279] Briggs (2012), p. 376.

[280] This includes Japan: Takahashi (2019), Section 3.2, text to notes 20–21.

the rights or add to the obligations of the other party [ie the offeree] shall be deemed not to have been consented to if it is considered to harm the interests of that other party unilaterally" will apply to an asymmetric choice of court agreement contained in a commercial contract.[281]

One particularly tricky problem associated with asymmetric choice of court agreements is determining the governing law. Referring to the law of the chosen court is unhelpful because there are multiple courts chosen, which might be problematic, given that different legal systems take different views as to the validity of such agreements. Referring to the law of the forum might encourage forum shopping, given the diversity in regulation of asymmetric choice of court agreements. A possible solution would be to refer to the law governing the contract in which the choice of court agreement is contained.

10 Optional Choice of Court Agreements in Intra-national Cases

In some countries, including Canada, China and Greece, optional choice of court agreements in intra-national cases are not treated any differently to those in international cases.[282] In Germany, the same principles are applied to intra-national cases and those international cases which are subject to German national law.[283]

In other legal systems, choice of court agreements in intra-national cases are treated somewhat differently to those in international cases. In Japan, "the tendency of the courts in intra-national cases is to deem a choice of court agreement to be optional unless the contrary intent is clear".[284] This is the converse to international cases, in which the Japanese courts tend to treat choice of court agreements as exclusive. There are no special jurisdictional rules for protecting consumers and employees in the intra-national context, unlike the international context. After the amendment to the Japanese Code of Civil Procedure which inserted special provisions for protecting such weaker parties in the international context, Takahashi suggests that "if the different treatment of intra-national and international cases persists, the presence and absence of special rules for protecting weaker parties may furnish an explanation".[285]

In Australia, there is a significant difference between the effect of optional choice of court agreements in intranational, compared to international, cases.[286] While in both cases optional choice of court agreements in favour of the forum were likely to

---

[281]Takahashi (2019), Section 3.2, citing the Japanese Civil Code, new Article 548-2.

[282]Guillemard and Sabourin (2019), Section 2.3; Tu and Huang (2019), Section 3 (text to notes 89 and 90); Panapoulos (2019), Section 2.4.3.

[283]Weller (2019), Section 3.10.

[284]Takahashi (2019), Section 2.4, text to note 18.

[285]Takahashi (2019), Section 2.4, final para.

[286]Marshall (2019), Section 2.4.

be given significant weight, optional choice of court agreements in favour of other courts were much more likely to be regarded as a "strong indication" of the parties' intentions as to venue in intranational cases,[287] whereas in international cases, Australian courts have never stayed proceedings in cases involving optional choice of court agreements in favour of foreign courts.[288]

11 The Recognition of Foreign Judgments

In most countries, a judgment rendered by a foreign court nominated by the parties in an optional choice of court agreement would be recognised, assuming that other requirements of recognition are satisfied.[289] Whereas judgments rendered by foreign courts other than that which the parties nominated as having exclusive jurisdiction would not be recognised in some countries,[290] there is no such limitation on the recognition of foreign judgments rendered by courts other than those nominated in an optional choice of court agreement.[291]

As noted, the main practical difficulty with optional choice of court agreements is that they do very little to limit the prospect of parallel proceedings. Although this may be controlled in many cases by the principles of *lis pendens*, or *forum non conveniens*, there remains the prospect that, in a case involving an optional choice of court agreement, judgment is rendered by more than one court in the same matter, where one court's jurisdiction was founded on the parties' agreement. This possibility is addressed in the Hague Choice of Court Convention, which (as noted above), enables contracting states to make a declaration that they will recognise judgments of the courts of other contracting states, which were nominated by the parties as having non-exclusive jurisdiction, and which have also made a declaration under Article 22.[292] Article 22(2) anticipates the possibility of multiple proceedings, and addresses this by stipulating that the judgment will only be recognised if

> *b)* there exists neither a judgment given by any other court before which proceedings could be brought in accordance with the non-exclusive choice of court agreement, nor a proceeding pending between the same parties in any other such court on the same cause of action; and
>
> *c)* the court of origin was the court first seised.

[287] Marshall (2019), Section 2.4.

[288] Marshall (2019), Section 2.3.3.1.

[289] Japan (Takahashi 2019, Section 1.1); Taiwan (Chen 2019, Section 2.8.4).

[290] Although there is no such indirect protection of exclusive choice of court agreements in the Brussels I Recast. See Panapoulos (2019), Section 1.3.3.3, citing Greek Code of Civil Procedure, Article 323(2).

[291] Including Australia (Marshall 2019, Section 2.3.3.5); the Czech Republic (Rozehnalová et al. 2019, Section 2.6.3); Germany (Weller 2019, Section 3.9); Romania (Oprea 2019, Section 4.6.3); Singapore (Chong 2019, Section 2.7, text following note 88); Taiwan (Chen 2019, Section 2.8.5).

[292] To date, none of the contracting states has entered this reservation.

12 Justifications for Enforcing Choice of Court Agreements

While there has been a rapid increase in the volume of laws and commentary on choice of court agreements, there has been relatively limited discussion of the justifications for the enforcement of agreements on choice of court. It is generally assumed that the benefits of agreements speak for themselves, and that as much as party autonomy might be beneficial in other contexts, it can be assumed to be beneficial in the context of choices of court.

A number of arguments are made in favour of the enforcement of agreements about dispute resolution. Most of these arguments are not specific either to the context of international dispute resolution, or to the issue of jurisdiction, and therefore many of these justifications are also found in the context of the use of agreements in domestic private law and domestic civil procedure: indeed, one argument in favour of the use of agreements in the context of international litigation is that this is consistent with the domestic law of obligations. Many of these arguments are proposed at a level of generality and abstraction, and almost all assume that the choice of court agreement is exclusive. There has been very limited discussion of the justification for the enforcement of optional choice of court agreements, in particular.

The justifications include that enforcing agreements creates or enhances legal certainty and predictability.[293] This has two applications. The first relates to enabling the parties to predict how any jurisdictional dispute between them would be resolved, and the second, to establishing the legal framework for the main contract. The first aspect of certainty—enabling the parties to anticipate the resolution of a jurisdictional dispute—is particularly important in relation to the selection of forum because, so the argument goes, without a choice of court agreement, it is very likely that any dispute could be heard in the courts of a number of different countries because of the expansive circumstances in which the courts of most legal systems assert jurisdictional competence. Further exacerbating this problem, disputes about the allocation of jurisdiction in the absence of any agreement are resolved according to default principles that are regarded as being problematic. The default principle of *lis pendens* is regarded as too blunt, if not liable to incentivise the hasty commencement of proceedings, and therefore disincentivise and frustrate amicable settlement of disputes. The default principle of *forum non conveniens* on the other hand is regarded as too unpredictable, if not unfair to foreign defendants. Both types of default principle, in conjunction with broad rules of jurisdictional competence, are also criticised for their propensity to foster forum shopping. The use of choice of court agreements therefore is promoted on the basis that it minimises the scope for opportunistic, unilateral forum shopping.

[293]This is referred to by the European Court of Justice in cases such as *Benincasa v Dentalkit Srl* [1997] ECJ Case C-269/95, para 29; and *Trasporti Castelletti* [1999] ECJ Case C-159/97, para 48. See also Van Calster and Poesen (2019), Section 2.1.

It will be obvious that the foregoing argument applies best to, and indeed is usually made in the context of, exclusive choice of court agreements. In some cases, courts have commented on the value of exclusive choice of court agreements in creating certainty. For example, in *Armacel v Smurfit Stone Container Corp*, Justice Jacobson of the Federal Court of Australia said that the choice of court agreement had to be interpreted

> against the background that this was a contract made between business people negotiating at arms' length who must be presumed to have intended some certainty as to where their disputes would be litigated....It is therefore difficult to see why they would not have intended that all their disputes be resolved in New South Wales.[294]

The assumption that reasonable business people would not intend a multiplicity of proceedings is also relevant in the broad interpretation applied in some countries to the material scope of choice of court agreements.[295]

The application of arguments about certainty to optional choice of court agreements is very complicated. Optional choice of court agreements merely create an option for one party, or both, to commence proceedings in a nominated court, or several nominated courts. Because they do not necessarily affect the parties' ability to commence proceedings in courts other than that or those nominated, they do not reduce the number of potential forums, and clearly, they do not do so to the same degree that exclusive choice of court agreements do. It is therefore questionable whether they can be defended on the basis that they create legal certainty.

The second aspect of the argument that choice of court agreements create certainty is that the parties need to know the legal framework for their contract (particularly, the forum in which any disputes will be resolved) in order appropriately to draft the contract,[296] and to perform their obligations under it. This argument has a much weaker application in the context of optional choice of court agreements than in the context of exclusive choice of court agreements, unless the parties nominate only one court.

According to an economic analysis of law, the use of agreements is desirable because of consumer sovereignty: that is, the parties are better judges of what is in their interests than any third party, including a court. Economic analysts also argue that if agreements are strictly enforced, the private and public costs of dispute resolution will be reduced. Optional choice of court agreements do not lend themselves to strict enforcement in the way that exclusive choice of court agreements do. The principle of *lis pendens* is usually applied in a strict way; but it is not possible to predict which court will be first seised. The principle of *forum non conveniens* has also been criticised as making it difficult to predict whether a court

---

[294] [2008] FCA 592, para 88.

[295] Germany (Weller 2019, Section 2.1.5, text to note 77, referring to the assumption that "reasonable business parties typically . . .want to avoid several proceedings about the same facts in different courts").

[296] Hartley (2013), p. 4, para 1.01.

will decline jurisdiction. Under either principle, there is not a strong argument that the use of optional choice of court agreements will be efficient.

Enforcing agreements is also justified on the basis that the agreement generates reasonable or legitimate expectations by the parties that should be protected. This argument is circular because the expectation can only be legitimate or reasonable if it reflects the legal status of agreements.

The enforcement of agreements is usually justified primarily on the basis that it promotes respect for party autonomy.[297] For example, recital 19 of the Preamble to the Brussels I Recast Regulation states that

> The autonomy of the parties to a contract, other than an insurance, consumer or employment contract, where only limited autonomy to determine the courts having jurisdiction is allowed, should be respected subject to the exclusive grounds of jurisdiction laid down in this Regulation.

Almost all of the above referenced discussion about the justifications for enforcing choice of court agreements assumes that the choice of court agreement is exclusive. Whereas exclusive choice of court agreements are generally regarded as being highly rational (because they generate a high degree of certainty about forum), there is a perception that optional choice of court agreements are the opposite. In the influential English case *Sohio Supply Co v Gatoil (USA) Inc*, Lord Justice Staughton said that he could

> *think of no reason at all* why [the parties] should choose to go to the trouble of saying that the English courts should have non-exclusive jurisdiction. I can think of every reason why they should choose that some court, in this case the English court, should have exclusive jurisdiction. Then, both sides would know where all cases were to be tried.[298]

Guillemard and Sabourin also question the utility of optional choice of court agreements, given that the legal certainty generated by such agreements tends to be very limited.[299]

Clearly, there are reasons for using optional choice of court agreements that might be quite rational. Briggs points out that

> Agreeing in advance that a particular court or courts would, as far as the parties are concerned, be available, would reduce the risk of jurisdictional challenges if proceedings are brought before them; but for the parties to tie their hands to litigation in a court which may become unattractive in the period between the making of the contract and the dispute arising is not always sensible.[300]

[297] Schoeman (2019), Section 3.3, text to notes 34 and 35, citing *MV Spartan-Runner v Jotun-Henry Clark Ltd* 1991 (3) SA 803 (N), 806G-H and *Blanchard, Krasner & French v Evans* 2002 (4) SA 144 (T), para 11; and *Foize Africa (Pty) Ltd v Foize Beheer BV and Others* 2013 (3) SA 91 (SCA), para 28*(a)*.

[298] [1989] 1 Lloyd's Rep 588, 591-2.

[299] Guillemard and Sabourin (2019), Introduction, text following note 17.

[300] Briggs (2008), pp. 114–115, para 4.15.

That is particularly so if one party is, or its assets are, mobile, in which case, the flexibility which optional choice of court agreements offer may be attractive at least to one party.[301]

One reason that optional choice of court agreements are regarded as irrational is that they do not eliminate or substantially reduce the prospect of parallel proceedings. Not only is this prospect problematic from the perspective of public policy, but it has also been regarded as being, in general, unlikely to reflect the intentions of rational businesspeople. Guillemard and Sabourin suggest that optional choice of court agreements encourage a race to commence proceedings.[302]

13 Reform

The national reports demonstrate that there are many unresolved issues associated with the effects of optional choice of court agreements. Even in those countries where the law in relation to optional choice of court agreements is relatively well developed, there remain a number of issues that have not been determined, and incompatible decisions. These issues do not appear to have attracted the attention of lawmakers, in that none of the national reports refers to current reform projects. A few national reporters take the view that there is no obvious need for reform to the law, whereas others suggest reform is required. The latter tends to be the case in those countries in which the recognition of choice of court agreements is relatively recent. But most reporters identify aspects of the law relating to the effect of optional choice of court agreements which would benefit from greater clarity and certainty.

Aspects of the law which have been identified as being problematic and therefore requiring reform include a lack of certainty on the distinction between exclusive and optional choice of court agreements[303]; a lack of clarity on the governing law to determine whether a choice of court agreement is optional or exclusive[304]; a lack of consistency in the treatment of optional agreements[305]; a lack of consistency in the treatment of optional choice of court agreements in favour of the forum and those in favour of foreign courts[306]; and a lack of consistency in the treatment of optional choice of court agreements in international and intranational cases.[307] It has been

[301]Oprea (2019), Section 1.2, text in para above note 16.

[302]Guillemard and Sabourin (2019), Introduction.

[303]E.g. Japan (Takahashi 2019, Section 4); South Africa (Schoeman 2019, Section 6). Weller notes this issue but also suggests that "this is a minor problem because it is easy for the parties to express themselves clearly in this respect.": (2019), Section 5.

[304]Van Calster and Poesen note that the parties "can minimize the risk of litigation on this issue by explicitly subjecting the optional choice of court agreement to one particular law": (2019), Section 3.3.2 (text to note 43).

[305]Common law Canada: Saumier (2019).

[306]Australia (Marshall 2019, Sections 2.3.1.3 and 5); Singapore (Chong 2019, Section 5, para 3).

[307]Marshall (2019), Section 2.4.

suggested that the general *lis pendens* rule may not be suitable to resolve parallel proceedings where one of the courts' jurisdiction is derived from an optional choice of court agreement.[308] The national reports also disclose some quite significant differences in the definition of and treatment of optional choice of court agreements, which means that if there are parallel proceedings, the same choice of court agreement may well be given very different effects in the different legal systems. Several reporters also suggest that greater clarity is required in terms of the effect of asymmetric choice of court agreements.

Some of the national reporters include suggestions for the reform of the law. In particular, it is suggested that it would be desirable to develop statutory solutions to maximise certainty and clarity. There is a fairly high level of support for the Hague Choice of Court Convention, but those reporters who suggested that their country acceding to the convention would be an improvement do not comment on whether they also support their country making a declaration under Article 22, which indirectly addresses the treatment of optional choice of court agreements.

14 Conclusion

The national reports confirm that there have been significant changes in the law relating to the effect of choice of court agreements. They also show convergences in terms of the legal effect of choice of court agreements, particularly in terms of a widespread acknowledgment of the virtues of party autonomy. This convergence is reflected in the Brussels instruments, particularly the Recast, which has had a strong influence within the European Union Member States,[309] but also influenced the development of the law further afield.[310] The Brussels I Recast was designed to integrate with the Hague Choice of Court Convention. That Convention creates the possibility of greater international coordination in the treatment of choice of court agreements, but so far has not been widely adopted beyond the European Union. In all events, the Hague Convention only deals directly with exclusive choice of court agreements, and the Brussels I Recast only modified the treatment of exclusive choice of court agreements, leaving other choice of court agreements regulated by the default principle of *lis pendens*.

The most significant recent development in relation to optional choice of court agreements concerns the now common, although not universal, position that the parties' agreement as to forum is effective in establishing the competence of a court

[308] Oprea (2019), Section 6.

[309] See, for example, Rozehnalová et al. (2019), Section 1.3.

[310] Takahashi acknowledges the influence of the Brussels I Regulation in terms of the introduction in the 2012 amendments to the Japanese Code of Civil Procedure of the protective provisions relating to consumer and individual employment contracts: (2019), Section 1.

to hear a dispute, notwithstanding a lack of any factual connection to the chosen court.

There remain important differences between the legal treatment of optional choice of court agreements internationally. For example, the conceptualisation and treatment of optional choice of court agreements in common law jurisdictions is fairly similar, but important differences persist between the common law treatment of such agreements, and the treatment in other legal systems. This is clearly evident in the kinds of remedies available to support optional choice of court agreements. There are also significant differences in terms of the legal treatment of asymmetric agreements, and agreements involving weaker parties.

As Briggs observed,

> though the expression 'non-exclusive jurisdiction clause' may suggest it describes a class of terms which is as internally coherent as that of exclusive jurisdiction clauses, it does not. . . .unlike exclusive jurisdiction clauses, non-exclusive jurisdiction is neither straightforward nor uniform.[311]

Briggs argued strongly that, because optional choice of court agreements may have different effects, depending on exactly what the agreement provides, "it would be beneficial to lay aside the unhelpful terminology of 'non-exclusive jurisdiction agreement', and to focus instead on precisely what obligations the parties wished to create and impose on each other."[312] The focus on the obligations entailed in the choice of court agreement is consistent with the law in some, but not all, countries represented in the national reports. Disagreeing with Briggs' argument, Joseph pointed out that the distinction between exclusive and non-exclusive jurisdiction agreements "was of central importance" to the Brussels I Recast, the Lugano Convention, and the Hague Choice of Court Agreements Convention.[313] As Oprea notes, the distinction is important in practice for several reasons. First, the Hague Convention does not apply to optional agreements[314]; and second, a number of specific rules have been developed which apply only to exclusive agreements.[315]

In short, it seems clear that the category of optional choice of court agreements is here to stay. This collection suggests the need for further work at the international, regional, and national levels in order to improve the certainty, clarity, and consistency of the law relating to optional choice of court agreements, which is already important in practice and only likely to become more so.

[311]Briggs (2008), p. 116, para 4.19.

[312]Briggs (2008), p. 120, para 4.23.

[313]Joseph (2015), p. 102, para 4.03.

[314]Oprea (2019), Section 2, text to note 19.

[315]In particular, see Brussels I Recast Regulation, Article 31(2).

References

Briggs A (2008) Agreements on jurisdiction and choice of law. Oxford University Press, Oxford
Briggs A (2012) The subtle variety of jurisdiction agreements. Lloyd's Maritime Commer Law Q:364
Collins L (ed) (2012) Dicey, Morris & Collins on the conflict of laws, 15th edn. Sweet & Maxwell, London
Hartley T (2013) Choice-of-court agreements under the European and international instruments. Oxford University Press, Oxford
Hartley T, Dogauchi D (2010) Explanatory report on the Convention of 30 June 2005 on Choice of Court Agreements. In: Permanent Bureau of the Conference (ed) Proceedings of the twentieth session, Tome III. Intersentia, Antwerp
Joseph D (2015) Jurisdiction and arbitration agreements and their enforcement, 3rd edn. Sweet & Maxwell, London
Keyes M (2015) Party autonomy in dispute resolution: implied choices in the context of jurisdiction. Jpn Yearb Int Law 58:223–246
Keyes M, Marshall BA (2015) Jurisdiction agreements – exclusive, optional and asymmetrical. J Priv Int Law 11:345–378
Liu X, Zhou Q (2014) The actual connection principle and forum non conveniens in Chinese contractual jurisdiction system. Legal Sci 12:50
Maher G, Rodger B (2010) Civil jurisdiction in the Scottish Courts. W Green, Edinburgh
Marshall BA, Keyes M (2017) Australia's accession to the Hague Convention on choice of court agreements. Melb Univ Law Rev 41:246
Nygh P (1999) Autonomy in international contracts. Clarendon Press, Oxford
Tang ZS (2012) Effectiveness of exclusive jurisdiction clauses in the Chinese Courts – a pragmatic study. Int Comp Law Q 61:459
Tang ZS, Xiao Y, Huo Z (2016) Conflict of laws in the People's Republic of China. Edward Elgar, Cheltenham
Yeo TM (2005) The contractual basis of the enforcement of exclusive and non-exclusive choice of court agreements. Singapore Acad Law J 17:306

National Reports Cited in This Chapter

Buxbaum H (2019) United States: the interpretation and effect of permissive forum selection clauses, in this collection
Chen R-C (2019) Taiwan: legislation and practice on choice of court agreements in Taiwan, in this collection
Chong A (2019) Singapore: a mix of traditional and new rules, in this collection
Guillemard S, Sabourin F (2019) Canada – Civil Law (*Québec)*: Les clauses d'élection de for facultatives en droit international privé québécois, in this collection
Haas E, MacCabe K (2019) Switzerland: choice of court agreements according to the code on civil procedure, the Private International Law Act and the Lugano Convention, in this collection
Mailhé F (2019) France: a game of asymmetries, optional and asymmetrical choice of court agreements under French Case Law, in this collection
Marshall B (2019) Australia: inconsistencies in the treatment of optional choice of court agreements, in this collection
Merrett L, Carruthers J (2019) United Kingdom: giving effect to optional choice of court agreements – interpretation, operation and enforcement, in this collection
Oprea EA (2019) Romania: interpretation and effects of optional jurisdiction agreements in international disputes, in this collection

Panapoulos G (2019) Greece: a forum favorable to optional choice of court agreements, in this collection
Rammeloo S (2019) Netherlands: optional choice of court agreements in a globalizing world, in this collection
Rozehnalová N, Mahdalová S, Zavadilová L (2019) Czech Republic: the treatment of optional and exclusive choice of court agreements, in this collection
Saumier G (2019) Canada – common law: choice of court agreements in common law Canada, in this collection
Schoeman E (2019) South Africa: Time for Reform, in this collection
Takahashi K (2019) Japan: quests for equilibrium and certainty, in this collection
Tarman ZD, Oba ME (2019) Turkey: optional choice of court agreements in Turkish Law, in this collection
Tu G, Huang Z (2019) China: optional choice of court agreements in the Vibrant Age, in this collection
Van Calster G, Poesen M (2019) Belgium: optional choice of court agreements, legal uncertainty despite a modern legal framework, in this collection
Weller M (2019) Germany: optional choice of court agreements – German National Report, in this collection

Mary Keyes is a professor at Griffith Law School, at Griffith University, in Brisbane, Australia. Her teaching and research interests are in the areas of jurisdiction, particularly choice of court; and international family law and litigation.

Part II
National Reports

Australia: Inconsistencies in the Treatment of Optional Choice of Court Agreements

Brooke Marshall

As creatures of the common law, optional choice of court agreements are alive and well in Australia. This chapter describes and critiques the treatment of optional agreements, generally called "non-exclusive jurisdiction agreements",[1] under the laws of Australia. As a federal state, Australia is composed of the Commonwealth of Australia, six States and ten Territories, two of which are relevant for this chapter.[2] As among these intra-national units, the law which applies to the character and effects of optional choice of court agreements is the same. Despite this horizontal uniformity, there is no vertical uniformity among the legal regimes which the courts of these intra-national units must apply to optional choice of court agreements in different cases. Very different principles apply to the effect of optional agreements in intra-national cases as opposed to those in international cases. Even within the broad categories of "intra-national" and "international", different principles apply and even where the same principles apply, their application does not necessarily lead to consistent results.

There are, this chapter argues, a number of inconsistencies in the treatment of optional choice of court agreements under Australian law, the most notable of which is the disparity of treatment between the effect given to optional agreements nominating Australian courts (forum courts) and those nominating foreign courts. This lamentable homeward trend is the product of the uniquely Australian iteration of the

I have attempted to state the law as it stood at 8 March 2018. I thank Tilman Koops and Max Winterhalder for proof-reading and assistance with the house style.

[1]Or "non-exclusive jurisdiction clauses".

[2]See further Sect. 2.1.

B. Marshall (✉)
Faculty of Law, University of New South Wales, Sydney, NSW, Australia
e-mail: brooke.marshall@unsw.edu.au

M. Keyes (ed.), *Optional Choice of Court Agreements in Private International Law*, Ius Comparatum – Global Studies in Comparative Law 37,
https://doi.org/10.1007/978-3-030-23914-5_2

forum non conveniens doctrine. Because of this doctrine, Australian law, despite its English common law roots and the continuing influence of English appellate authority,[3] differs in several respects from the law of the other common law jurisdictions discussed in this volume.

This chapter comprises five sections. It begins by describing the treatment of choice of court agreements in general, both exclusive and optional under Australian law (Sect. 1). Section 2 explores the legal sources, choice of law rules and legal principles which dictate how optional choice of court agreements are treated in international and intra-national cases. The law relating to exclusive and optional choice of court agreements is then compared in Sect. 3. Section 4 considers what are collectively described as "asymmetric choice of court agreements", one type of which is an agreement that is exclusive, if one party initiates proceedings, and optional, if the other party initiates proceedings. The chapter closes in Sect. 5 with an evaluation of the legal treatment of optional agreements in Australia, predictions as to how parties, through drafting, may respond to the deficiencies in the law, and reflections as to law reform.

1 The Treatment of Choice of Court Agreements in General

There is a policy in Australia to enforce express[4] choice of court agreements in cross-border transactions. It is informed by at least three factors. First, a strong curial disposition to hold parties to their contractual bargain,[5] an exclusive choice of court agreement[6] being, from an Australian perspective, a contract creating rights and obligations between the parties.[7] Second, the policy favouring enforcement is informed by the role that exclusive choice of court agreements perform, at least in theory, in reducing the scope for unilateral forum shopping by the claimant, once a dispute has arisen.[8] In this second sense, exclusive choice of court agreements produce fairness between parties to civil litigation, because the forum is determined by a mutual choice pre-dispute rather than a unilateral choice post-dispute. Third, exclusive choice of court agreements promote efficiency insofar as they reduce the

[3]"Ordinarily a decision of the Court of Appeal of England and Wales on a common law question not affected by statutory interpretation or constitutional or other considerations special to Australia ought be followed unless there is some sound basis for concluding that it was erroneous": *Independent Trustee Services Ltd v Morris* (2010) 79 NSWLR 425, 430 (Bryson AJ).

[4]This chapter does not deal with implied or tacit choice of court agreements which, in some countries, refer to the situation whereby the defendant enters an unconditional appearance in proceedings commenced by the claimant.

[5]*Huddart Parker Ltd v The Ship Mill Hill* [1950] HCA 43, (1950) 81 CLR 502, 508–509; *Incitec Ltd v Alkimos Shipping Corporation* (2004) 138 FCR 496, [47]; Bell (2003), p. 277.

[6]Otherwise referred to as "exclusive jurisdiction clauses" or "agreements".

[7]*ACE Insurance v Moose Enterprise Ltd* [2009] NSWSC 724, [53].

[8]See Bell (2003), pp. 13, 122, and 128.

likelihood that each party will call upon the publically-funded civil justice systems of several countries in parallel to resolve their dispute.

Only the first of these factors—holding parties to their bargain—is relevant to optional choice of court agreements, though Australian courts often fail to appreciate or respect the actual content of the bargain. As to the second factor, optional agreements increase rather than decrease the scope for forum shopping enjoyed by the claimant by providing a further forum in which it may bring proceedings. Contrary to the third factor, the treatment of optional agreements by Australian courts promotes inefficiency by increasing the likelihood of parallel litigation: an Australian court nominated in an optional choice of court agreement is very likely to exercise jurisdiction, even if proceedings are on foot in a more suitable forum. That treatment is peculiar, because commencing proceedings in a foreign court is permitted by the parties' agreement and therefore holding parties to their contractual bargain (the first factor) does not require the Australian court to exercise jurisdiction. An Australian court seised of a dispute within the scope of an optional agreement nominating a foreign court will only stay proceedings if, by reference to numerous factors, including the agreement, it considers itself to be clearly inappropriate for the resolution of the dispute ("the clearly inappropriate forum test" or "*Voth* principle").[9] Although a decision to retain jurisdiction is compatible with the first factor (enforcing the parties' agreement—because the agreement does not require the Australian court to decline jurisdiction in favour of the nominated foreign court—[10]), that decision is incompatible with the second factor, namely efficiency. Multiple sets of proceedings on the same issues drain the public resources of several states. It would be more efficient for an Australian court to stay its proceedings if the foreign, nominated court is, on balance, more appropriate for the resolution of the dispute or if proceedings in the foreign court are well advanced and there is no possibility, according to the foreign court's rules, for the foreign court to stay its proceedings because, for example, it was the court first seised.

1.1 Limitations

There are multiple limitations under Australian law which, in effect, limit parties' freedom to contract about jurisdiction, by rendering those agreements unenforceable.[11] An agreement which purports to confer on an Australian court subject-matter jurisdiction that it does not have, for example, jurisdiction in

[9]The exception to this test is where proceedings are on foot in both the forum and the foreign nominated court involving the same parties but different issues: see below note 106 and accompanying text.

[10]Keyes (2009), p. 202.

[11]Technically, the law controls the enforcement of the agreement, rather than the parties' freedom to reach the agreement.

proceedings concerning rights *in rem* or title to and possession of foreign land,[12] could not be enforced. The contractibility of personal jurisdiction is also subject to certain limits in both commercial and non-commercial contexts. Although a court always has a discretion not to enforce a choice of court agreement, it is particularly likely to exercise that discretion where the agreement is contrary to Australian public policy or internationally mandatory rules[13] or where its enforcement will result in the non-application of Australia's internationally mandatory rules.[14] Those rules and policies are generally, though not exclusively, embodied in legislation. Legislation will require an Australian court to stay proceedings, brought pursuant to a choice of court agreement, exclusive or optional, where those proceedings concern a dispute which falls within the scope of an international arbitration agreement.[15] Legislation also restricts the enforcement of choice of court agreements nominating foreign courts involving franchisees,[16] consumer and commercial insureds,[17] Australian exporters and importers of goods by sea,[18] and, arguably, consumers and small businesses party to standard form contracts for the supply of goods or services, or financial products or services.[19] While the legislation applicable to franchisees, insureds, and exporters and importers clearly applies to exclusive and asymmetric choice of court agreements,[20] its application to optional agreements is less clear. For example, the Franchising Code prohibits clauses which *require* a party to bring

[12] *British South Africa Co v Companhia de Moçambique* [1893] AC 602 (HL).

[13] *Compagnie des Messageries Maritimes v Wilson* (1954) 94 CLR 577.

[14] *Akai Pty Ltd v The People's Insurance Company Ltd* (1996) 188 CLR 418, 445.

[15] *International Arbitration Act 1974* (Cth), s 7(2). Martin CJ recently observed, "While there is an obvious tension between an agreement to confer exclusive jurisdiction upon a court or courts and an arbitration agreement, there is no such tension between an arbitration agreement and an agreement to submit to the non-exclusive jurisdiction of the courts": *Fitzpatrick v Emerald Grain Pty Ltd* [2017] WASC 206, [77]. His Honour explained that the purpose of the optional agreement is a residual one: it is to give the nominated court jurisdiction "to supervise the performance of their arbitration agreement and enforce the terms of any award made ... and, perhaps, [to make] ... provision for the possibility that there may be disputes which do not fall within the scope of their arbitration agreement": at [78].

[16] Competition and Consumer (Industry Codes—Franchising) Regulation 2014 (Cth) sch 1, cl 21.

[17] Section 52 of the *Insurance Contracts Act 1984* (Cth) prevents parties to insurance contracts from excluding, restricting or modifying the application of the Act to the prejudice of the insured. This includes where parties do so via an exclusive choice of court agreement which obliges the insured to bring disputes before a foreign court: *Akai Pty Ltd v The People's Insurance Co Ltd* (1996) 188 CLR 418, 447–448. The Act does not protect reinsureds: *Insurance Contracts Act 1984* (Cth), s 9(1)(a).

[18] *Carriage of Goods by Sea Act 1991* (Cth) ss 11(2)(b), (c): "An agreement ... has no effect so far as it purports to ... preclude or limit the jurisdiction of a court of the Commonwealth or of a State or Territory". See Forrest (2009), p. 504; *Dampskibsselskabet Nordon A/S v Gladstone Civil Pty Ltd* [2013] FCAFC 107, [71].

[19] *Australian Securities and Investments Commission Act 2001* (Cth) s 12BF, 12BH(1)(k); *Competition and Consumer Act 2010* (Cth), sch 1, s 23(3),(4) both of which are discussed further below at text to notes 229–238.

[20] See text to notes 239–240 below.

proceedings outside the jurisdiction where the franchisee is based:[21] optional choice of court agreements do not have that effect. Similarly, the *Carriage of Goods by Sea Act 1991* (Cth) renders ineffective agreements which preclude or limit the jurisdiction of Australian courts:[22] optional choice of court agreements do not have that effect.

In family law matters, the enforceability of choice of court agreements appears to be limited. It is probable that such an agreement will have no effect for the purposes of establishing an Australian court's jurisdiction, though an agreement designating forum courts may be relevant to the court's exercise of jurisdiction.[23] In *Costigan v Costigan*, Carew J considered an *exclusive* choice of court agreement in favour of the Family Court of Australia in a financial agreement (a marital property agreement)[24] between a husband and wife to be a factor relevant to whether the court should *exercise* jurisdiction or whether proceedings should be stayed on *forum non conveniens* grounds.[25] The court did not, nor did it need to, consider whether the agreement had any relevance in establishing the court's jurisdiction, given that it had jurisdiction based on the parties' Australian citizenship.[26] The financial agreement also contained an exclusive agreement in favour of the Israeli courts whose scope concerned rights and obligations arising out of an Israeli marital property agreement, which had been incorporated into the Australian agreement. Notably, the court gave no weight to this agreement in deciding whether to exercise jurisdiction.[27]

1.2 Influence of Bilateral and Multilateral Instruments

The law in relation to choice of court agreements in Australia has been, and continues to be, influenced directly and indirectly by bilateral and multilateral instruments. In October 2013, a bilateral arrangement entered into force[28] which governs *inter alia* choice of court agreements in cases involving Australian and New Zealand courts between commercial parties.[29] The provisions of the *Trans-Tasman Proceedings Act 2010* (Cth), concerning optional choice of agreements,

[21]Competition and Consumer (Industry Codes—Franchising) Regulation 2014 (Cth) sch 1, cl 21(2)(a).

[22]*Carriage of Goods by Sea Act 1991* (Cth) ss 11(2)(b), (c).

[23]Keyes (2014), pp. 15, 18, and 23.

[24]See generally Keyes (2011).

[25][2017] FamCA 879 [39], [51]. See *Henry v Henry* (1995) 185 CLR 571.

[26]*Costigan v Costigan* [2017] FamCA 879, [43].

[27]Ibid, [52].

[28]Agreement between the Government of Australia and the Government of New Zealand on Trans-Tasman Proceedings and Regulatory Enforcement, signed 24 July 2008 [2013] ATS 32 (entered into force 11 October 2013). See generally Mortensen (2014), pp. 113, 113–114, 120, and 131–134.

[29]Contracts involving consumers and employees are excluded from the scope of the Act: *Trans-Tasman Proceedings Act 2010* (Cth) ss 20(3)(b)–(c).

were modelled on Commonwealth legislation governing intra-national disputes.[30] By contrast, the provisions of the Act governing exclusive choice of court agreements were largely[31] inspired by the Hague Choice of Court Agreements Convention 2005 (Hague Convention).

The Hague Convention is set to have a direct influence on the Australian law concerning choice of court agreements governing disputes between commercial parties[32] to some types of contract.[33] The Hague Convention seeks to ensure the uniform treatment internationally of "exclusive" choice of court agreements and of judgments rendered by courts whose jurisdiction was based on an exclusive agreement. Under the Convention, an exclusive choice of court agreement is one which designates the jurisdiction of the courts of a single country to the exclusion of all others. In November 2016, the Parliament of Australia's Joint Standing Committee on Treaties recommended that Australia take binding treaty action to accede to the Hague Convention. At the time of writing, the Commonwealth government is preparing an International Civil Law Bill which would allow for the Convention to be implemented in Australia.[34]

The Hague Convention will affect the treatment of *optional* choice of court agreements in international cases[35] by Australian courts in a limited way.[36] Some choice of court agreements which Australian courts would, applying the principles under the current law,[37] characterize as optional, will, under the Hague Convention,

[30]See *Australian Gourmet Pastes Pty Ltd v IAG New Zealand Ltd* [2017] VSCA 155, [26]; *Service and Execution of Process Act 1992* (Cth) s 20; *Trans-Tasman Proceedings Act 2010* (Cth) s 19.

[31]The *Trans-Tasman Proceedings Act 2010* (Cth) s 20 and the Hague Convention s 3 b) differ in an important respect: the Hague Convention's presumption that an agreement will be exclusive unless the parties have provided otherwise is not reflected in the Act.

[32]The Convention excludes contracts to which consumers or employees are party from its scope: art 2(1).

[33]See art 2(2) of the Hague Convention for a list of exclusions.

[34]Melissa-Jane Ford, A/g Principal Legal Officer, Private International Law and Commercial Policy Unit, Australian Government Attorney-General's Department, "Update on the Implementation of the Hague Choice of Court Convention and Negotiations on the Draft Hague Judgments Convention on the Recognition and Enforcement of Judgments in Civil and Commercial Matters" (Speech delivered at the University of Sydney Law School, "Commercial Issues in Private International Law" Conference, 16 February 2018). See further National Interest Analysis: Australia's Accession to the Convention on Choice of Court Agreements [2016] ATNIA 7, [21].

[35]cf. choice of court agreements in intra-national cases which fall outside the scope of the Convention: Hague Convention, arts 1(1), 25(2); Hartley and Dogauchi (2010), paragraphs 261–262.

[36]The Hague Convention may also impact the recognition and enforcement in Australia of foreign judgments rendered by courts whose jurisdiction was based on an optional choice of court agreement. That will be the case if Australia chooses to extend the Convention's provisions governing recognition and enforcement to judgments rendered by courts which had jurisdiction under an optional agreement by making a reciprocal declaration under art 22 of the Convention.

[37]Discussed at text to notes 66–79.

be characterized as exclusive.[38] The Hague Convention presumes an agreement which designates a court or the courts of one Contracting State to be exclusive, unless the parties have expressly provided otherwise.[39] As will be seen, Australian law contains no such presumption,[40] meaning that agreements which designate a court or the courts of one state may equally be treated as optional under the current law. But once an Australian court has, by reference to the Hague Convention, characterized an agreement as optional, the effect the court will give to that agreement will not be impacted by the Convention. An agreement's effect will continue to be governed by the principles set out below.[41]

The Hague Convention was itself inspired by the United Nations Convention on the Recognition and Enforcement of Foreign Arbitral Awards 1958 (the New York Convention),[42] which has also influenced the judicial development of legal principles applicable to choice of court agreements in Australia.[43] Although practice tells a different tale,[44] in principle, arbitration agreements and exclusive choice of court agreements are "treated as legally cognate" under Australian law.[45] While it might be thought that the parallelism between arbitration agreements optional choice of court agreements is weaker, Australian courts have not considered this to be so. For example, in *Telesto Investments Ltd v UBS AG* Sackar J applied the principle of construction that applies to determine the scope of arbitration and exclusive choice of court agreements to an optional choice of court agreement.[46] In the context of optional agreements, which contemplate the possibility of litigation in multiple courts,[47] the suitability of that principle—namely that parties "are unlikely to have intended that different disputes should be resolved before different tribunals"[48]—is less apparent.

---

[38]Mortensen (2009), p. 231; Marshall and Keyes (2017), p. 275. For examples, see Marshall (2019), pp. 97–100.

[39]Art 3(b).

[40]Text to notes 66–79.

[41]Text to notes 82–117.

[42]Keyes (2014), p. 23.

[43]Mortensen et al. (2015), p. 72.

[44]Keyes (2009), p. 181 (observing that "Australian courts are much more likely to retain jurisdiction where the parties have agreed to litigate in a foreign court, than they are to retain jurisdiction in the face of an effective agreement to arbitrate.").

[45]*Global Partners Fund Ltd v Babcock & Brown Ltd (in liq)* [2010] NSWCA 196, (2010) 79 ACSR 383, [60] (Spigelman CJ with whom Giles and Tobias JJA agreed).

[46][2013] NSWSC 503, 94 ACSR 29, [269]–[272].

[47]Compare *Deutsche Bank AG v Highland Crusader Offshore Partners LP* [2009] EWCA Civ 725; [2010] 1 WLR 1023, [105] with Mills (2018), pp. 99 and 151–152 (observing at 99 that an optional jurisdiction agreement "merely preserves a flexible choice of forum at the time commencing litigation, and is not incompatible with ensuring that only a single forum will, in the end, hear all related claims").

[48]*Francis Travel Marketing Pty Ltd v Virgin Atlantic Airways Ltd* (1996) 39 NSWLR 160, 165.

2 Optional Choice of Court Agreements

This section first sets out the various legal regimes which apply to optional choice of court agreements in international cases as compared with intra-national cases (Sect. 2.1). The content of those regimes for optional agreements in international cases (Sect. 2.3) and for optional agreements in intra-national cases (Sect. 2.4) will then be considered in turn.

2.1 Legal Regimes Applicable to Optional Choice of Court Agreements

As explained above,[49] Australia is a federal state comprising the Commonwealth of Australia, six States (New South Wales, Queensland, South Australia, Tasmania, Victoria and Western Australia) and ten Territories, the two relevant for this chapter being the Northern Territory and the Australian Capital Territory.[50] As also mentioned, horizontally, the law about *the character* and *effect* of optional choice of court agreements among the Commonwealth, Australia's States, the Northern Territory and the Australian Capital Territory is identical.

The Australian common law, which applies in all of Australia's component units, provides the choice of law rule which designates the law according to which a choice of court agreement will be *characterized* as exclusive or optional. If the law which that rule designates is Australian, the common law also provides the relevant principles according to which that characterization will be made. The common law provides the choice of law rule (and the relevant principles if Australian law is the proper law) in international cases[51] as well as in intra-national cases.[52] This rule and those principles are discussed in Sect. 2.2 below.

[49]Text to note 2.

[50]Australia's other mainland territory, Jervis Bay, and its seven external territories are not discussed here.

[51]Though it is less clear whether the common law applies residually to these questions in Trans-Tasman cases. The *Trans-Tasman Proceedings Act 2010* (Cth), s 20(3)(a) contains a definition of an exclusive choice of court agreement and an optional agreement is anything which falls outside that definition: s19(2)(d). In *Re Douglas Webber Events Pty Ltd* (2014) 291 FLR 173, Brereton J did not engage in any choice of law analysis to determine the proper law applicable to the character of a jurisdiction clause described as "non-exclusive", simply treating it as non-exclusive for the purposes of the Act: at [27], [41]. Nor did Judge Anderson engage in any choice of law analysis to determine the proper law applicable to the character of a jurisdiction clause governed by the Act and described as "exclusive" in *Australian Gourmet Pastes Pty Ltd v Endeavour Packaging Pty Ltd* [2016] VCC 455, [15]–[27]. On appeal, Tate JA, with whom Santamaria and Beach JJA agreed, did not do so either: *Australian Gourmet Pastes Pty Ltd v IAG New Zealand Ltd* [2017] VSCA 155.

[52]*Asciano Services Pty Ltd v Australian Rail Track Corp Ltd* [2008] NSWSC 652, [16]–[17].

The common law governs the *effect* of optional choice of court agreements in international cases, except for those in cases involving proceedings in Australian and New Zealand courts, which are regulated by the Commonwealth *Trans-Tasman Proceedings Act*[53] introduced above.[54] The law about the legal effect of optional choice of court agreements is governed by the same common law principle ("the clearly inappropriate forum test" or "*Voth* principle"), explained in Sect. 2.3.1 below, in all Commonwealth, State and Territory cases. The rules of court also govern the effect of optional choice of court agreements in international cases in New South Wales,[55] Victoria,[56] the Australian Capital Territory,[57] Tasmania[58] and South Australia.[59] Despite differences in the wording of those rules when compared to the common law test, (they all refer to the forum court being "*an* inappropriate forum") the High Court has assimilated that wording to the *Voth* principle.[60]

The law governing the *effect* of optional choice of court agreements in intra-national cases, before the superior courts of these component units is identical due to the cross-vesting scheme; a harmonized set of identical legislation implemented by the Commonwealth, the States and the Territories.[61] Commonwealth legislation also applies to the effect of optional choice of court agreements before inferior and intermediate courts, in intra-national cases, meaning that the law is identical among the component units.[62] Both pieces of Commonwealth legislation are discussed in Sect. 2.4 below.

---

[53] *Trans-Tasman Proceedings Act 2010* (Cth) s 19(2)(d).

[54] Text to notes 28–30. See Marshall and Keyes (2017), pp. 249–250 and 253–254.

[55] Uniform Civil Procedure Rules 2005 (NSW) r 11.6 (as amended in 2016) which provides in (1) that the forum court "may dismiss or stay the proceeding or set aside service of the originating process", on application of the person served outside Australia if (2)(b) "the court is an inappropriate forum for the trial of the proceeding".

[56] Supreme Court (General Civil Procedure) Rules 2015 (Vic) r 7.04(1)(2)(b), which is in materially identical terms to UCPR (NSW) r 11.6.

[57] Court Procedures Rules 2006 (ACT) r 6504(2)(b).

[58] Supreme Court Rules 2000 (Tas) r 147C(2)(b).

[59] Supreme Court Civil Rules 2006 (SA) r 40C(2)(b). The rules in all these jurisdictions were recently amended "to give effect to harmonized rules approved by the Council of Chief Justices": Douglas and Bath (2017), p. 160. For criticism, see Dickinson (2019), pp. 30–54.

[60] The wording in r 11.6 (2)(b) of the Uniform Civil Procedure Rules 2005 (NSW) is identical to an earlier version of the rule which the High Court of Australia assimilated to the *Voth* principle: *Renault v Zhang* (2002) 210 CLR 491, 503. For analysis of judgments in *Renault v Zhang* on this point, see Keyes (2014), pp. 28–29.

[61] See e.g. *Jurisdiction of Courts (Cross-Vesting) Act 1987* (Cth) s 5. On the cross-vesting scheme generally, see Keyes (2011), pp. 20 and 26.

[62] *Service and Execution of Process Act 1992* (Cth) s 20(3), (4)(d).

2.2 Characterization of an Agreement as Optional or Exclusive

Ascertaining whether an agreement is optional or exclusive at common law is a question of construction.[63] The choice of law rule is that construction of the choice of court agreement is governed by the proper law of the contract within which it is contained,[64] although there has historically been a tendency in Australia to apply Australian law, as the law of the forum, to this question.[65]

If Australian law is the applicable law, the test for determining whether a choice of court agreement is characterized as exclusive or optional is whether or not the agreement obliges parties to sue in the nominated jurisdiction.[66] Courts interpret the agreement by reference to objective factors which are assumed to indicate the intentions of reasonable contracting parties, there generally being no evidence of the parties' subjective intentions.[67]

Factors tending in favour of an agreement being characterized as optional are: the absence of the word "exclusive" which, although not determinative, is, as Brereton J put it in *ACE Insurance Ltd v Moose Enterprise Pty Ltd,* "not merely neutral";[68] the use of the precatory language, such as the word, "should";[69] and a lack of mutuality in the language used.[70] A further factor to consider is whether the agreement is intransitive: whether the parties have agreed to submit only themselves (rather than their disputes) to the nominated court.[71] For instance, "the parties submit to the jurisdiction of the competent courts of England (London)."[72] Parties, by submitting

---

[63] *Faxtech Pty Ltd v ITL Optronics Ltd* [2011] FCA 1320, [5]. See also *Trina Solar (US) Inc v Jasmin Solar Pty Ltd* [2017] FCAFC 6, (2017) 247 FCR 1, [37], [128] (which concerned an arbitration agreement).

[64] *Hoerter (Trading as CF Mumm) v Hanover Caoutchouc, Gutta Percha & Telegraph Works* (1893) 10 TLR 103 (CA), 104 (Lord Esher, Master of the Rolls); *Parnell Manufacturing Pty Ltd v Lonza Ltd* [2017] NSWSC 562, [21]; *Faxtech Pty Ltd v ITL Optronics Ltd* [2011] FCA 1320, [5]; *Proactive Building Solutions v MacKenzie Keck Pty Ltd* [2013] NSWSC 1500, [16]–[17].

[65] Davies et al. (2014), para 7.63. See e.g. *Re Bulong Nickel Pty Ltd* [2002] WASC 126, (2002) 42 ACSR 52, [35].

[66] *Akai Pty Ltd v The People's Insurance Co Ltd* (1996) 188 CLR 418, 425; Marshall and Keyes (2017), p. 251.

[67] *FAI General Insurance Co Ltd v Ocean Marine Mutual Protection and Indemnity Association* (1997) 41 NSWLR 117, 126; Marshall and Keyes (2017), p. 251.

[68] *ACE Insurance v Moose Enterprise Ltd* [2009] NSWSC 724, [33].

[69] As opposed to the mandatory word "shall" which has been held to "be apposite to create the language of obligation": *British Aerospace PLC v Dee Howard Co* [1993] 1 Lloyd's Rep 368, 375 (Waller J). See *ACE Insurance v Moose Enterprise Pty Ltd* [2009] NSWSC 724, [33].

[70] *FAI General Insurance Co Ltd v Ocean Marine Mutual Protection and Indemnity Association* (1997) 41 NSWLR 117, 126.

[71] *Faxtech Pty Ltd v ITL Optronics Ltd* [2011] FCA 1320, [12]–[14].

[72] *Faxtech Pty Ltd v ITL Optronics Ltd* [2011] FCA 1320, [4].

only themselves, are agreeing to *defend* in the nominated court if sued there, with the implication that they are free to *bring* proceedings (i.e. their disputes) in other courts.

A factor telling in favour of exclusivity is if the Australian court would in any event have jurisdiction,[73] for example, if the forum is the place where the obligation the subject of the suit should have been performed,[74] or if the parties expressly or impliedly chose Australian law as the applicable law.[75] By expressly agreeing to forum jurisdiction, when the forum already has jurisdiction, is said to suggest that the parties "must be seeking to add something", namely, exclusivity.[76] A second factor is whether the agreement uses the "language of obligation and not option", for example, the use of the phrase "all disputes" or "any dispute" (which is equated with "all disputes").[77] A further factor suggesting exclusivity is if the agreement is transitive, that is, if the parties have agreed to submit their disputes, not only themselves to the nominated court. Such an agreement to initiate and defend eventual proceedings in the nominated court indicates that the agreement is exclusive.[78] A final factor suggesting exclusivity is if the parties have chosen a neutral jurisdiction with which neither party had any connection.[79]

2.3 Optional Choice of Court Agreements in International Cases

As already mentioned,[80] common law principles, or rules of court assimilated to common law principles, govern optional choice of court agreements in all international cases, except in Trans-Tasman cases. Accordingly, the focus of the analysis in the following sections is on the common law.[81] The analysis begins by setting out the legal effects of optional agreements under Australian law. It then explores those effects in the context of agreements involving weaker parties. Finally, the

[73] *FAI General Insurance Co Ltd v Ocean Marine Mutual Protection and Indemnity Association* (1997) 41 NSWLR 117, 127 (though observing that "the clause may have been intended only to put beyond doubt the existing jurisdiction" (Giles CJ)); *ACE Insurance v Moose Enterprise Pty Ltd* [2009] NSWSC 724, [33].

[74] e.g. Uniform Civil Procedure Rules 2005 (NSW) sch 6 item (b)(iii).

[75] e.g. Uniform Civil Procedure Rules 2005 (NSW) sch 6 item (b)(iv).

[76] *British Aerospace PLC v Dee Howard Co* [1993] 1 Lloyd's Rep 368, 374 (Waller J). See also *Compania Sud Americana de Vapores SA v Hin-Pro International Logistics Ltd* [2016] 1 All ER (Comm) 417, 436, [64] (Christopher Clarke LJ).

[77] *Sinochem International Oil (London) Co Ltd v Mobil Sales and Supply Corp* [2000] 1 Lloyd's Rep 670, 676 (Rix J). See also *British Aerospace v Dee Howard* [1993] 1 Lloyd's Rep 368, 375.

[78] Marshall and Keyes (2017), p. 252.

[79] *Parnell Manufacturing Pty Ltd v Lonza Ltd* [2017] NSWSC 562, [25].

[80] Section 2.1.

[81] The effect of optional choice of court agreements in Trans-Tasman cases is discussed briefly below in Sect. 3.

consequences of a party bringing proceedings outside the court nominated in an optional choice of court agreement will be examined.

2.3.1 Legal Effects

The law applicable to determining the legal effect of an optional choice of court agreement is the law of the forum, irrespective of whether the agreement nominates the courts of the forum or foreign courts.[82] The effect Australian courts give to forum agreements, on the one hand, and foreign agreements, on the other, will be described in turn, followed by a comparison.

Agreement in Favour of the Courts of the Forum

An optional choice of court agreement allows a claimant, under common law principles[83] and the relevant rules of court,[84] to serve originating process on a defendant (who is physically not present in Australia) *outside* the agreed jurisdiction. It also provides a basis on which a service of process clause, providing for a method by which service is to be effected or authorizing an agent to accept service *within* the agreed jurisdiction, can be given effect. Provided service is effective, the forum court would regard itself as jurisdictionally competent. It is arguably incorrect to describe the agreement as a submission to the jurisdiction.[85] That is because the forum court cannot regard itself as jurisdictionally competent unless the defendant physically appears before the court and enters an appearance,[86] is served with the court's originating process within the court's territorial limits,[87] or is properly served outside the court's territorial limits under the relevant rules of court.[88] The fact that a choice of court agreement, without a service of process clause, will be insufficient to found the court's jurisdiction[89] also supports that view.

Regrettably, the recently developed harmonized rules of court, implemented in four Australian States and one Territory, use the language "has submitted" to

[82]See *Re Bulong Nickel Pty Ltd* [2002] WASC 126, (2002) 42 ACSR 52, [35] (where the court applied Australian law to determine the effect of an asymmetric choice of court agreement (which the court characterized as optional) designating New York courts in the anchor limb.)

[83]*Flaherty v Girgis* [1987] HCA 17, (1987) 162 CLR 574, 599 (Brennan J).

[84]e.g. Federal Court Rules 2011 (Cth) r 10.42 item 19; Uniform Civil Procedure Rules 1999 (Qld), r 124(1)(i); Supreme Court (General Civil Procedure) Rules 2015 (Vic) r 7.02(k), Court Procedures Rules 2006 (ACT) r 6502(k).

[85]Dickinson (2015), *passim*; cf. Bell (2003), p. 305.

[86]*Laurie v Carroll* (1958) CLR 310 (HCA) 323. See Dickinson (2015), pp. 14, 37, and 66.

[87]Ibid. See Keyes (2015), p. 225; Dickinson (2015), pp. 21–22 and 66.

[88]See e.g. Federal Court Rules 2011 (Cth) rules 10.42 item 19, 10.45–10.49.

[89]*Mondial Trading Pty Ltd v Interocean Marine Transport Inc* (1985) 60 ALJR 277, (1985) 65 ALR 155, [20].

encompass (one presumes)[90] the situation in which a defendant is party to an agreement to submit to the jurisdiction of the forum court, via an optional choice of court agreement.[91] That rule provides that an originating process may be served outside Australia without leave "when the person to be served has submitted to the jurisdiction of the court".[92] This language is misleading, because if the person to be served has already submitted to the jurisdiction of the court in the proceedings commenced by the originating process, there would be no need to serve that process on the person outside the court's territorial limits. The better view is that an optional choice of court agreement in favour of an Australian court is an agreement *to* submit to the jurisdiction of that court.

An optional choice of court in favour of an Australian court does not appear to be treated as a waiver of the parties' rights to contest the exercise of that jurisdiction under forum law.[93] That view is supported by the fact that an Australian court, nominated in an optional choice of court agreement can consider an application to contest the exercise of its jurisdiction,[94] even when the optional choice of court agreement is accompanied by an express waiver by the parties not to object to proceedings in the nominated court.[95] That said, any attempt to contest the exercise of jurisdiction by an Australian court with jurisdiction under an optional agreement is likely to fail.[96] That probability of failure is explicable by the uniquely Australian iteration of the *forum non conveniens* doctrine, which controls the question of whether a court that is jurisdictionally competent will exercise jurisdiction. The doctrine requires an Australian court that is jurisdictionally competent, whether by virtue of an optional choice of court agreement or on some other ground, to retain jurisdiction unless it considers itself to be a *clearly* inappropriate forum.[97] Unless the

[90]Compare with Dickinson who remarks that "New sub-para. (k) replaces old sub-para. (h), but (in excluding reference to an agreement to submit) is arguably narrower." (2019), p. 34 text in fn 136 of Dickinson's chapter.

[91]The former version of the rule, for example in the State of New South Wales, clearly encompassed optional jurisdiction agreements on its terms: sch 6 item (h) provided that originating process may be served outside Australia "if the proceedings are proceedings in respect of which the person to be served has submitted or *agreed to submit* to the jurisdiction of the court" (my emphasis).

[92]e.g. Uniform Civil Procedure Rules 2005 (NSW) sch 6 item (k).

[93]Compare with Keyes (2015), p. 238.

[94]e.g. *Centrebet Pty Ltd v Baasland* [2013] NTSC 59.

[95]See *Centrebet Pty Ltd v Baasland* [2013] NTSC 59, [158]–[163]. The court's willingness to consider the defendant's request to stay the Northern Territory proceedings on *forum non conveniens* grounds, despite the parties' contractual waiver to that course, may be explained by the fact that the Norwegian defendant had no legal representation and not entered an appearance: see [132].

[96]But see *Armacel Pty Ltd v Smurfit Stone Container Corp* [2008] FCA 592 (2008) 248 ALR 573, [122].

[97]See *Voth v Manildra Flour Mills Pty Ltd* (1990) 171 CLR 538, adopting at 564 the reasoning of Deane J in *Oceanic Sun Line Special Shipping Co Inc v Fay* (1988) 165 CLR 197, 247; affirmed in *Puttick v Tenon Ltd* [2008] HCA 54, 238 CLR 265, [28]–[30], [38]. For a discussion of the development of the test, see Thomson et al. (2015), pp. 631–632.

nominated court considers that continuance of its proceedings would be unjust, oppressive or vexatious to the defendant, it will not grant a stay.[98] Given that an optional choice of court agreement amounts to an admission by the parties as to the appropriateness of the forum,[99] an argument that the forum is *clearly* inappropriate will generally be futile.

The operation of the Australian test can be appreciated by comparison to English law. The test under English law requires an English court to retain jurisdiction, unless there is "some other forum which is clearly *more* appropriate for the trial of the action".[100] Given that an optional choice of court agreement amounts to an admission by the parties as to the appropriateness of the forum,[101] not an admission as to the forum's appropriateness relative to other fora, an argument that another jurisdiction is more appropriate can evidently be made.[102]

The effect of an optional choice of court agreement in favour of the forum does not, in principle, change once the option has been exercised by commencing proceedings in the forum. Whether proceedings in the forum are brought first or after proceedings have already been initiated in another jurisdiction between the same parties on the same issues, the forum court will apply the test described at text to notes 96–99 above. The fact that forum proceedings were commenced second will be "a highly relevant consideration" in assessing whether the forum proceedings, brought pursuant to the optional agreement, are as a whole vexatious or oppressive to the defendant and thus whether the forum is clearly inappropriate.[103] The pendency of foreign proceedings does not, however, alone render litigation in the forum inappropriate[104] and may be outweighed by the fact that the forum was nominated in the optional agreement, especially if forum law had also expressly been chosen by the parties and if the foreign proceedings are not particularly advanced.[105] If the parties in the forum proceedings and foreign proceedings are the same but the issues

[98] *Oceanic Sun Line Special Shipping Co Inc v Fay* (1988) 165 CLR 197, 248 (Deane J) applied to cases involving optional choice of court agreements in e.g. *Centrebet Pty Ltd v Baasland* [2013] NTSC 59, [158].

[99] Fawcett (2001), p. 245.

[100] *Spiliada Maritime Co v Cansulex Ltd* [1987] AC 460 (HL) 476, 477–478 (Lord Goff) (my emphasis). See generally in this volume, Merrett and Carruthers, "United Kingdom: Giving Effect to Optional Choice of Court Agreements: Interpretation, Operation and Enforcement".

[101] *Deutsche Bank AG and another v Highland Crusader Offshore Partners LP* [2009] EWCA Civ 725, [2010] 1 WLR 1023, [64].

[102] See *Deutsche Bank AG v Sebastian Holdings Inc* [2009] EWHC 3069 (Comm Ct), [21] (Burton J) ("an application for a stay can be considered in a non-exclusive jurisdiction case, where there is no FNC [*forum non conveniens*] waiver clause. The significant factor is that there is no breach of contract involved in the party seeking to persuade the chosen court to decline jurisdiction"); a conclusion untouched by the decision on appeal: *Sebastian Holdings Inc v Deutsche Bank AG* [2010] EWCA Civ 998.

[103] *Armacel Pty Ltd v Smurfit Stone Container Corp* [2008] FCA 592, (2008) 248 ALR 573, [6], [82]–[83], [95]–[97].

[104] *Henry v Henry* (1995) 185 CLR 571, 591.

[105] *Centrebet Pty Ltd v Baasland* [2013] NTSC 59; Thomson et al. (2015), p. 650.

are not, the relevant question "is not whether the Australian court is clearly inappropriate" but rather

> whether, *having regard to the controversy as a whole*, the Australian proceedings are vexatious or oppressive in the *Voth* sense of those terms, . . . namely, that they are 'productive of serious and unjustified trouble and harassment' or 'seriously and unfairly burdensome, prejudicial or damaging'.[106]

Agreement in Favour of Foreign Courts

The legal effect of an optional choice of court agreement in favour of foreign courts is a submission to the jurisdiction of the foreign courts.[107] A foreign optional agreement will be a factor in considering whether Australia is a clearly inappropriate forum for the proceedings.[108] Keyes explains that:

> This is because commencing proceedings in a forum other than the chosen court is not inconsistent with the terms of the agreement, and therefore enforcing the agreement does not mandate declining jurisdiction in favour of the chosen court.[109]

A foreign optional choice of court agreement does not indicate any "preference" for litigation in the foreign court, even when accompanied by an express choice of law clause designating the law of the foreign court.[110] Again, if the parties in the forum proceedings and foreign proceedings are the same but the issues are not, the forum court will not ask itself whether it is a clearly inappropriate forum, but rather whether its proceedings are vexatious or oppressive in light of the controversy as a whole.[111]

The legal effect of an optional choice of court agreement in favour of foreign courts does not, in principle, change after the option has been exercised by commencing proceedings in a nominated foreign court. As with optional agreements in favour of forum courts, whether proceedings in the forum are brought first or after proceedings have already been initiated in the foreign nominated court between the same parties on the same issues or even if no proceedings have been initiated in the foreign nominated court at all,[112] the forum court will assess whether it is a clearly inappropriate forum. The pendency of parallel foreign proceedings initiated first will

---

[106] *CSR Ltd v Cigna Insurance Australia Ltd* (1997) 189 CLR 345, 400–401 (my emphasis).

[107] *Akai Pty Ltd v The People's Insurance Company Ltd* (1996) 188 CLR 418, 425.

[108] *Telesto Investments Ltd v UBS AG* [2012] NSWSC 44, (2012) 262 FLR 119, [204]; *Green v Australian Industrial Investment Ltd* (1989) 25 FCR 532, (1989) 90 ALR 500, 512 cf. *Trans-Tasman Proceedings Act 2010* (Cth) s 19(2)(d).

[109] Keyes (2009), p. 202.

[110] *Bagsfirst Global Pty Ltd v Global Brands (Football) Pty Ltd* [2010] NSWSC 988, [24] (concerning a clause that was described as non-exclusive); Garnett (2013), p. 147.

[111] See above note 106 and accompanying text.

[112] e.g. *Autotrop Sdn Bhd v Powercrank Batteries Pty Ltd* [2006] VSC 401.

be very relevant,[113] but those factors will not alone render litigation in the forum clearly inappropriate. For example, in *Green v Australian Industrial Investment Ltd*, the pendency of parallel[114] proceedings initiated first in the foreign court, nominated in an optional agreement, were outweighed by the fact that the claimant was seeking relief under Commonwealth legislation, which did not form part of the law expressly chosen by the parties to govern the contract.[115]

Forum Versus Foreign Agreements: A Tale of Inconsistency

Under Australian law, optional choice of court agreements in favour of forum courts on the one hand, and in favour of foreign courts on the other, are not treated consistently. The explanation for the inconsistency is that the "clearly inappropriate forum" test, applied by Australian courts to determine whether it should exercise jurisdiction in both these situations, is evidently skewed towards a conclusion that Australian courts should exercise jurisdiction. A forum agreement is an admission by the parties that the forum is appropriate, such that an argument that the forum is *clearly* inappropriate will be extremely difficult to make.[116] Conversely, a foreign agreement is just one factor among competing factors suggesting that the forum court is clearly inappropriate. As will be shown below, in no case in which a foreign court was nominated in an optional agreement has an Australian court considered itself to be clearly inappropriate.[117]

2.3.2 Agreements Involving Presumptively Weaker Parties

Optional choice of court agreements involving presumptively weaker parties—consumers, certain insureds, franchisees and employees—are governed by the same principles as optional agreements in commercial contracts, though legislation

[113] *Henry v Henry* (1995) 185 CLR 571, 591.

[114] French J described the two sets of proceedings as "related" at 502 though they were in fact parallel: they involved the same parties and the same legal issue or controversy, namely whether Australian Industrial Investment Ltd and two of its directors made fraudulent or misleading representations: *Green v Australian Industrial Investment Ltd* (1989) 25 FCR 532, (1989) 90 ALR 500. See *Henry v Henry* (1995) 185 CLR 571, 590 where Dawson, Gaudron, McHugh and Gummow JJ drew a distinction between related and parallel proceedings.

[115] (1989) 25 FCR 532, (1989) 90 ALR 500, 503, 511–512. See further text to note 120. The High Court in *Voth v Manildra Flour Mills Pty Ltd* criticised French J in *Green v Australian Industrial Investment Ltd* for having "placed too much weight upon the notion that a proceeding regularly invoked [in Australia] provides a prima facie right to have the proceeding continue in that forum": (1990) 171 CLR 538, 566.

[116] This point was made more fully above at text to notes 99–102.

[117] Text to note 131.

may limit their effect in some cases, as has been seen.[118] An Australian court, with jurisdiction under an optional agreement, or an Australian court, with jurisdiction seised in spite of an optional agreement, will determine whether to exercise jurisdiction by asking itself whether it is a clearly inappropriate forum.[119] A particularly relevant factor in cases involving consumers and insureds, which will weigh in favour of the forum court retaining jurisdiction in spite of the foreign optional agreement, is if the Australian court forms the view that the foreign nominated court would not apply Australia's legislation protecting consumers and insureds. This view will more readily be formed where the law of the cause is a foreign law.[120] Conversely, there is authority to suggest that where staying forum proceedings in favour of a foreign optional agreement has the effect of displacing legislation protecting consumers and small businesses but the optional agreement was not inserted for that very purpose, an Australian court would grant a stay.[121]

By reference to authority concerning the effect of exclusive choice of court agreements nominating foreign courts in cases involving consumers, the weight given to an optional agreement nominating a foreign court, in determining whether the forum court is clearly inappropriate, may be reduced where the case has no "real connection" with the nominated, foreign court[122] or where the choice of court agreement was part of terms offered on a "take it or leave it" basis.[123] The principles which a court is required to consider when confronted with a stay application in light of a foreign exclusive choice of court agreement are different from those which

---

[118]Section 1.1.

[119]This applies both to international cases governed by the common law and to Trans-Tasman cases that involve consumers or employees, those categories of party being excluded from the scope of the *Trans-Tasman Proceedings Act 2010* (Cth): ss 20(3)(b)–(c).

[120]See e.g. *Green v Australian Industrial Investment Ltd* (1989) 25 FCR 532, (1989) 90 ALR 500, 503, 511–512. This is also a factor to which Australian courts have given weight in deciding whether to stay forum proceedings to enforce exclusive foreign choice of court agreements: e.g. *Vautin v BY Winddown Inc* (No 2) [2016] FCA 1235, [23], [55]; *Commonwealth Bank of Australia v White* [1999] 2 VR 681, [11], [89] (a case in which Mr White successfully alleged that the insertion of English exclusive jurisdiction and choice of law agreements in a new underwriting agreement which he was asked to execute 5 years after the original agreement, were inserted for the very purpose of avoiding Australian legislation protecting consumers from misleading and deceptive conduct).

[121]So much can be deduced from Sackar J's decision to stay permanently forum proceedings in light of a Singaporean judgment rendered by a Singaporean court with jurisdiction under an asymmetric choice of court agreement: *Telesto Investments Ltd v UBS AG* [2013] NSWSC 503, [280], [286]. Although the clause was asymmetric (see Sect. 4 below), Sackar J described the clause as an agreement by "the parties ... to submit to the non-exclusive jurisdiction of Singapore".

[122]*Knight v Adventure Associates Pty Ltd* [1991] NSWSC 861, [14], [32], [39]–[40]. But see *Benson v Rational Entertainment Enterprises Ltd* [2015] NSWSC 906 [132]. The relevance of the exclusive choice of court agreement was not reagitated on appeal: *Benson v Rational Entertainment Enterprises Ltd* [2018] NSWCA 111 [37].

[123]*Quinlan v Safe International Försäkrings AB* [2005] FCA 1362, (2006) 14 ANZ Ins Cas ¶ 61-693, [46], [49], [53]. But see *Gonzalez v Agoda Company Pte Ltd* [2017] NSWSC 1133, discussed in Keyes (2019), p. 285.

apply to optional choice of court agreements. Notwithstanding it seems reasonable to infer that *if* an Australian court will give less weight to a foreign exclusive choice of court agreement in deciding whether to exercise jurisdiction despite the agreement in a consumer/insured case, it will similarly give less weight to a foreign optional agreement in deciding whether it is a clearly inappropriate forum.

Whether legislation would directly restrict the enforcement of optional choice of court agreements in cases involving insureds and franchisees was doubted in Sect. 1.1 above. The application of legislation, designed to protect consumers and small businesses party to standard form contracts for the supply of goods or services, or financial products or services, to an optional choice of court agreement is unclear, as will be seen below.[124]

There appear to be no reported international cases involving an employee whose employment contract contained an optional choice of court agreement, though there is authority suggesting that an exclusive agreement nominating Australian courts will be readily enforced against a foreign employee.[125]

2.3.3 Limited Consequences if a Party Brings Proceedings Outside the Nominated Court

This section assesses five possible consequences of a party bringing proceedings outside the court nominated in an optional choice of court agreement, including where that court is a foreign court or a court of the forum.

Improbability of a Stay of Forum Proceedings

If a party brings proceedings in the forum, in circumstances in which the parties had nominated a foreign court in an optional choice of court agreement, *in principle*, the forum court may exercise its discretion to stay its proceedings, if it considers itself to be a clearly inappropriate forum (see the section "Agreement in Favour of Foreign Courts" above). Factors relevant to determining whether a stay will be granted encompass both "connecting factors" with the forum and "legitimate personal or juridical advantages" of proceedings in the forum available to one or the other of the parties.[126] Factors connecting the case to the forum refer to matters of convenience and expense, such as the location of witnesses, as well as other matters including the law applicable to the dispute and the location of the parties.[127] Legitimate personal

[124] See text to notes 229–238 below.

[125] *Alstom Ltd v Sirakas (No 2)* [2012] NSWSC 64, [1], [103] (obiter).

[126] *Voth v Manildra Flour Mills Pty Ltd* (1990) 171 CLR 538, 564–565 referring to *Spiliada Maritime Co v Cansulex Ltd* [1987] AC 460 (HL) 476, 477–478, 482–484 (Lord Goff).

[127] *Voth v Manildra Flour Mills Pty Ltd* (1990) 171 CLR 538, 564–565 referring to *Spiliada Maritime Co v Cansulex Ltd* [1987] AC 460 (HL) 476, 477–478, 482–484 (Lord Goff).

advantages include the ability of one or the other party to have proceedings heard in its "home" court.[128] Juridical advantages include the likelihood that the claimant in the forum proceedings would be able to obtain the relief it seeks in the foreign proceedings.[129] Given the high threshold set by the clearly inappropriate forum test,[130] Australian courts, in practice, appear never to have exercised their discretion to stay proceedings in a published decision involving a foreign optional choice of court agreement.[131] If there are proceedings pending before the foreign nominated court that were commenced first and proceedings in the forum that were commenced second, an Australian court may have regard to additional factors, not in isolation by reference to its proceedings alone, but by comparison to the foreign proceedings.[132] These include the extent to which the judgment of one court is likely to be recognized by the other, the enforceability of either court's orders in third countries, the stage each of the proceedings have reached, and the costs the parties have incurred, together with the parties' relative abilities to participate in one or other of the proceedings.[133]

No Contractual Claim to Damages

Unlike an exclusive choice of court agreement, "which imposes contractual obligations on the parties",[134] an optional agreement is not an agreement to sue only in the nominated court.[135] That being so, if one party commences proceedings in a foreign court when an Australian court is nominated in an optional choice of court agreement, the counterparty will have no contractual claim to damages for breach before the Australian court.

[128] *Bagsfirst Global Pty Ltd v Global Brands (Football) Pty Ltd* [2010] NSWSC 988, [22].

[129] *Armacel Pty Ltd v Smurfit Stone Container Corp* [2008] FCA 592, (2008) 248 ALR 573, [98].

[130] *Bagsfirst Global Pty Ltd v Global Brands (Football) Pty Ltd* [2010] NSWSC 988, [35].

[131] See *Bagsfirst Global Pty Ltd v Global Brands (Football) Pty Ltd* [2010] NSWSC 988, [35]; *Green v Australian Industrial Investment Ltd* (1989) 25 FCR 532, (1989) 90 ALR 500; *Autotrop Sdn Bhd v Powercrank Batteries Pty Ltd* [2006] VSC 401, [27]–[33]; *Parnell Manufacturing Pty Ltd v Lonza Ltd* [2017] NSWSC 562, [29] (obiter).

[132] *Henry v Henry* (1995) 185 CLR 571, 592–593. See further Mortensen et al. (2015), p. 106.

[133] *Henry v Henry* (1995) 185 CLR 571, 592–593.

[134] *ACE Insurance v Moose Enterprise Ltd* [2009] NSWSC 724, [53]. Breach of an exclusive choice of court agreement appears to give rise to a right to damages under Australian law, although an Australian court has not yet awarded them: *Commonwealth Bank v White [No 2 of 2004]* [2004] VSC 268, [5] (obiter); Garnett (2013), pp. 148–149. See also *Compagnie des Messageries Maritime v Wilson* (1954) 94 CLR 577, 587 (Fullagar J) (obiter) (a case concerning choice of court agreement nominating two courts, albeit within one country). The dicta as to the availability of damages is consistent with English law: *Starlight Shipping Co v Allianz Marine Aviation Versicherungs AG* [2014] EWCA Civ 1010. On damages and exclusive choice of court agreements, see generally Dinelli (2015).

[135] See Davies et al. (2014), para 7.61 ("A non-exclusive jurisdiction clause says nothing as to the parties' collective attitude to litigation in a forum other than that nominated.").

Anti-suit Injunction Only Where Foreign Proceedings Are Vexatious or Oppressive

An optional choice of court agreement, nominating the courts of the forum, will not give rise to an injunction except in the circumstance where commencement or continuation of foreign proceedings is vexatious or oppressive.[136] Provided that an Australian court has personal jurisdiction over the defendant in the forum proceedings,[137] it may grant an anti-suit injunction on equitable grounds.[138] Optional choice of court agreements differ from exclusive agreements for which an equitable anti-suit injunction may also be granted in aid of the legal right not to be sued in a court other than the nominated court.[139] Optional agreements contain no such right. And while it could be said that an optional choice of court agreement contains a legal right "to insist that the other party may not oppose jurisdiction in that forum",[140] that right seems to be hollow, because courts do entertain applications in which the other party opposes jurisdiction in the forum, even if they are unsuccessful.[141] In any event, it is not "a right which will by itself . . . warrant the restraint of proceedings commenced by the other party in another forum".[142]

For the forum court to grant anti-suit injunctive relief on equitable grounds, on the basis of vexation and oppression, it must engage in the two-stage process articulated in *CSR Ltd v Cigna Insurance Australia Ltd*.[143] First, the forum court must satisfy itself that the *forum* court is not clearly inappropriate,[144] as explained above.[145] Provided the forum is not clearly inappropriate, the court will then assess whether the *foreign* proceedings are vexatious or oppressive, by considering whether there is anything that can be gained in the foreign proceedings over and above what can be

---

136 See Raphael (2008), paras 9.12, 14.03–14.11; *Deutsche Bank AG and another v Highland Crusader Offshore Partners LP* [2009] EWCA Civ 725, [2010] 1 WLR 1023, [105]; Fawcett (2001), p. 256.

137 As explained in the section "Agreement in Favour of the Courts of the Forum", an optional choice of court agreement nominating the courts of the forum, coupled with service of process on the defendant, gives the court personal jurisdiction.

138 *Armacel Pty Ltd v Smurfit Stone Container Corp* [2008] FCA 592, (2008) 248 ALR 573, [123]–[126]; *CSR Ltd v Cigna Insurance Australia Ltd* (1997) 189 CLR 345, 393.

139 See *CSR Ltd v Cigna Insurance Australia Ltd* (1997) 189 CLR 345, 373. On anti-suit injunctions in aid of legal rights, see Douglas (2017), pp. 71–73.

140 Bell (2003), p. 306.

141 This argument was developed in the section "Agreement in Favour of the Courts of the Forum" above, in arguing that an optional choice of court agreement cannot properly be a waiver of the right to contest jurisdiction.

142 Bell (2003), p. 306.

143 *CSR Ltd v Cigna Insurance Australia Ltd* (1997) 189 CLR 345, 397.

144 See *Armacel Pty Ltd v Smurfit Stone Container Corp* [2008] FCA 592, (2008) 248 ALR 573, [123], [126].

145 Text to notes 97–99.

gained in the forum proceedings.[146] Unlike the first stage of the test, this second stage calls for a comparative exercise by reference to both fora. It requires an assessment of the relative injustice which each party will suffer if the claimant in the foreign court is or is not allowed to proceed.[147] Factors that are relevant to determining whether an anti-suit injunction will be granted include procedural advantages in each forum,[148] as well as the propriety of the intentions of the respective claimants in bringing the proceedings in the respective fora, and the effect of the intentions of the claimant in the foreign proceedings on the other party and the forum.[149] A further factor is comity, which will assume particular importance if the foreign proceedings are well advanced.[150] Other relevant factors include the opportunity under foreign procedural law for the claimant in the forum proceedings to seek a stay of the foreign proceedings and whether any equitable defences apply.[151] A final factor may be the availability of alternative remedies; contractual damages,[152] as has been seen,[153] will not be available.

Apart from equitable anti-suit injunctions, an Australian court nominated in an optional agreement, once proceedings have been brought before it, has an inherent jurisdiction to protect its processes, which will also found the award of an anti-suit injunction. Douglas has recently differentiated the principles applicable to equitable as opposed to inherent jurisdiction injunctions in Australia, so these will not be repeated here.[154]

Improbability of an Anti-enforcement Injunction

There appears to be no published Australian case in which a party has applied for an anti-enforcement injunction to restrain an application for the enforcement of a judgment, given by a court other than that nominated in an optional choice of court agreement, or given by a court or tribunal other than that nominated in an exclusive jurisdiction or arbitration agreement for that matter.[155] If Australian law

---

[146] *CSR Ltd v Cigna Insurance Australia Ltd* (1997) 189 CLR 345, 393.

[147] See *Sunland Waterfront (BVI) Ltd v Prudentia Investments Pty Ltd* [2013] VSCA 237, [442]; Douglas (2017), p. 75.

[148] Compare *CSR Ltd v Cigna Insurance Australia Ltd* (1997) 189 CLR 345, 395 with *Sunland Waterfront (BVI) Ltd v Prudentia Investments Pty Ltd* [2013] VSCA 237, [480]–[481].

[149] Douglas (2017), pp. 76–77.

[150] *Armacel Pty Ltd v Smurfit Stone Container Corp* [2008] FCA 592 (2008) 248 ALR 573, [125].

[151] Douglas (2017), p. 78.

[152] On equitable damages, see Douglas (2017), p. 94.

[153] Section "No Contractual Claim to Damages".

[154] Douglas (2017), pp. 79–89.

[155] This is perhaps unsurprising, given that there appears to be no English case in which "an anti-enforcement injunction has been granted simply on the basis that the proceedings sought to be restrained were commenced in breach of an exclusive jurisdiction or arbitration clause.": *Ecobank*

were eventually to follow English law on this point,[156] it would seem that something close to fraud or deceit by the respondent to the application would be needed for a court to grant an anti-enforcement injunction, and, even then, if the applicant delayed in applying for the injunction, comity and fairness would weigh heavily against the grant of the injunction.[157]

No Non-recognition of the Non-nominated Court's Judgment

A judgment rendered by a foreign court, other than a court which was nominated in an optional choice of court agreement, would be recognized and enforced by Australian courts, under common law principles or the *Foreign Judgments Act 1991* (Cth), if there were no other bars to its recognition and enforcement, provided the foreign court was exercising a recognized ground of international jurisdiction.[158] Again, optional choice of court agreements differ in this respect from exclusive choice of court agreements. A judgment rendered by a foreign court, in a matter which parties had agreed to submit exclusively to the jurisdiction of another court, if registered under the *Foreign Judgments Act 1991* (Cth), may (subject to limited exceptions) be set aside on application of the judgment debtor.[159]

2.4 Optional Choice of Court Agreements in Intra-National Cases

It was explained above[160] that in international cases an Australian court with jurisdiction under an optional choice of court agreement or an Australian court with jurisdiction seised in spite of an optional agreement, will determine whether to exercise jurisdiction by asking itself whether it is a clearly inappropriate forum for the proceedings. Although there is scope for an Australian court to apply this principle in an intra-national case so as to stay its proceedings in the exceptional circumstance where the proceedings before it amount to an abuse of its processes, in intra-national cases, the treatment of optional agreements is generally different.

Transnational Inc v Tanoh [2015] EWCA Civ 1309, [118] (Christopher Clarke LJ with whom the Chancellor, Sir Terence Etherton, and Patten LJ agreed).

[156] See the quote of Bryson AJ in *Independent Trustee Services Ltd v Morris* (2010) 79 NSWLR 425, 430 extracted above at note 3.

[157] See *Ecobank Transnational Inc v Tanoh* [2015] EWCA Civ 1309, [118], [130], [134].

[158] See *Foreign Judgments Act 1991* (Cth), s 7(1)(a)(iv); *Emanuel v Symon* [1908] 1 KB 302, 309 referred to with approval in e.g. *de Santis v Russo* [2001] QCA 457, [2002] 2 Qd R 230, [9].

[159] s 7(4)(b).

[160] Section "Forum Versus Foreign Agreements: A Tale of Inconsistency".

The question of whether a superior court will exercise jurisdiction either on the basis of, or in spite of, an optional choice of court agreement will be determined by the cross-vesting scheme.[161] This scheme applies where both sets of proceedings are pending in the Supreme Courts of two States[162] and where one set of proceedings is pending in the Federal Court and the other in a State Supreme Court.[163] There is a statutory requirement for a court to *transfer* proceedings to another Australian court under section 5 of the Cross-Vesting Acts where it appears that the other court is the "more appropriate court",[164] or the transfer is in the "interests of justice".[165] As Keyes points out, the leading cases treat these terms "as being identical",[166] which reduces the importance of assessing within which roman numeral sub-clause the case falls under the relevant paragraph in section 5 of the Acts. Again, "[i]t is not necessary that it should appear that the first court is a 'clearly inappropriate' forum."[167]

Recent decisions suggest that an optional choice of court agreement will be a material factor in the assessment of whether a transfer is in the interests of justice,[168] though, in practice, it will be a more material factor if it nominates the court of the forum[169] and a less material factor if it nominates another Australian court.[170] The weight to be accorded to an optional agreement as a factor may depend on how many of the parties' claims can be adjudicated in the nominated court as opposed to the other court,[171] and whether litigation in the nominated court would be more onerous

[161] *Plantagenet Wines Pty Ltd v Lion Nathan Wine Group Australia Ltd* [2006] FCA 247, 229 ALR 327, [39]–[44].

[162] *Schmidt v Won* [1998] 3 VR 435, 453–454, 455; *McEntee v Connor* (1994) 4 Tas R 18, 24.

[163] *Plantagenet Wines Pty Ltd v Lion Nathan Wine Group Australia Ltd* [2006] FCA 247, 229 ALR 327, [42].

[164] *BHP Billiton Ltd v Schultz* [2004] HCA 61, (2004) 221 CLR 400, [175].

[165] *BHP Billiton Ltd v Schultz* [2004] HCA 61, (2004) 221 CLR 400, [14], [175]. See Keyes (2014), p. 27.

[166] Keyes (2014), p. 27.

[167] *BHP Billiton Ltd v Schultz* [2004] HCA 61, (2004) 221 CLR 400, [14]. See also *Bankinvest AG v Seabrook* (1988) 14 NSWLR 711, 730.

[168] *Mineralogy Pty Ltd v Sino Iron Pty Ltd* [2013] NSWSC 466, [27] (optional agreement nominating another Australian court; transfer ordered).

[169] *Monash IVF Pty Ltd v Burmeister (No 2)* [2017] NSWSC 903, [19], [24]–[25] (optional agreement nominating the court of the forum; transfer refused). See also *Balescope Pty Ltd v Pegasus Leasing Ltd* (1994) 63 SASR 51, 58 (optional agreement nominating the court of the forum; appeal against the decision to refuse a transfer dismissed).

[170] *Open Universities Australia Pty Ltd v TAFE Commission* [2017] VSC 617, [6]–[7], [19], [23] (optional agreement nominating another Australian court; transfer refused); *Santos Ltd v Helix Energy Services Pty Ltd* [2009] VSC 282, (2009) 28 VR 595 (optional agreement nominating another Australian court; transfer refused). But see *Mineralogy Pty Ltd v Sino Iron Pty Ltd* [2013] NSWSC 466, [27] (optional agreement nominating another Australian court; transfer ordered).

[171] *Plantagenet Wines Pty Ltd v Lion Nathan Wine Group Australia Ltd* [2006] FCA 247, 229 ALR 327, [59] (optional agreement nominating another Australian court; transfer refused).

to one of the parties in comparison to litigation in the other court.[172] Less weight will, in principle, be given to an optional agreement than an exclusive one,[173] though in *Taurus Funds Management Pty Ltd v Aurox Resources Ltd*, Einstein J treated an optional agreement, nominating the court of the forum, as "a critical and decisive factor" in determining the Supreme Court of New South Wales to be a more appropriate forum than the Supreme Court of Western Australia.[174] Equally in several New South Wales cases, the court has found it unnecessary to decide whether the agreement was exclusive or optional, considering the agreement either way to be "a strong indication . . . of where their disputes should be tried".[175] In both those cases, the court ordered a transfer to the nominated court.

This reasoning of the New South Wales Supreme Court reveals a remarkable difference in the judicial perception of parties' intentions in concluding an optional choice of court agreement in intra-national as compared with international cases. The same court, in an international case, considered that an optional agreement did not indicate any "preference" of the parties for litigation in the chosen court.[176] Unlike optional and exclusive choice of court agreements, an asymmetric choice of court agreement (which combines both exclusive and optional aspects)[177] was given no weight in one of the leading intra-national cases in considering whether to transfer proceedings.[178]

The effect of optional agreements before inferior and intermediate courts is specifically regulated by the *Service and Execution of Process Act 1992* (Cth) (SEPA). Section 20(4) of the Act lists a number of matters to be taken into account by the court in deciding whether to *stay* (rather than transfer) its proceedings on the basis that "the court of another State is *the appropriate court* for the proceeding".[179] One of those matters is "any agreement between the parties about the court or place in which the proceeding should be instituted".[180] Although the SEPA uses the term "the appropriate court", the Victorian Court of Appeal has recently suggested that this term is to be assimilated with "the more appropriate court", which is the term

[172] *Plantagenet Wines Pty Ltd v Lion Nathan Wine Group Australia Ltd* [2006] FCA 247, 229 ALR 327, [82].

[173] *Anderson Formrite Pty Ltd v Baulderstone Hornibrook Pty Ltd* (2004) 206 ALR 614, [2004] WASC 115, [15].

[174] [2010] NSWSC 1223, [35]–[39].

[175] *Asciano Services Pty Ltd v Australian Rail Track Corp Ltd* [2008] NSWSC 652, [5], [18], [19], [22] (Palmer J). The quote is at [19]. See also *Patrick Badges Pty Ltd v Commonwealth* [2002] NSWSC 221, [14] (obiter—the court in that case ultimately did characterize the derogation agreement as exclusive) (Howie J).

[176] *Bagsfirst Global Pty Ltd v Global Brands (Football) Pty Ltd* [2010] NSWSC 988, [24] (McDougall J).

[177] See Sect. 4 below.

[178] *Bankinvest AG v Seabrook* (1988) 14 NSWLR 711, 719, 729–730.

[179] (My emphasis). See also *Service and Execution of Process Act 1992* (Cth) s 20(3).

[180] *Service and Execution of Process Act 1992* (Cth) s 20(4)(d).

employed by the equivalent provision of the *Trans-Tasman Proceedings Act*[181] that was modelled on the SEPA.[182] The Queensland Court of Appeal, in interpreting the term "the appropriate court" in the SEPA, had refrained from deciding whether that term meant "*more* appropriate court".[183] The Victorian Court of Appeal observed in obiter that "the more appropriate" court test in the *Trans-Tasman Proceedings Act* is not the same as the English test in *Spiliada Maritime Corp v Cansulex Ltd*,[184] which requires the alternative court to be "clearly and distinctly more appropriate".[185]

3 Exclusive and Optional Choice of Court Agreements Compared

An exclusive choice of court agreement in favour of an Australian court has the same effect as an optional agreement in favour of an Australian court in establishing, together with service, the nominated court's jurisdiction in an international case.[186] An Australian court nominated in an exclusive agreement will exercise jurisdiction, unless the defendant can establish strong reasons for the court to decline jurisdiction.[187] Strong reasons include where the dispute affects interests of third parties, not bound by the exclusive agreement, or involves issues outside the agreement's scope.[188] This is a different test than the "clearly inappropriate forum" test which applies to the exercise of jurisdiction in cases involving optional choice of court agreements nominating Australian courts, though both tests are likely to lead to the forum court exercising jurisdiction where it is the nominated court. Mortensen, Garnett and Keyes also note that, "in practice", courts tend to apply the "clearly inappropriate forum" test to exclusive agreements nominating Australian courts.[189]

Similarly, an Australian court seised of proceedings governed by an exclusive choice of court agreement in favour of a foreign court, and called upon to stay those proceedings, will in principle enforce the agreement by staying its proceedings.

---

[181] s 19(2)(d).

[182] *Australian Gourmet Pastes Pty Ltd v IAG New Zealand Ltd* [2017] VSCA 155, [26].

[183] *St George Bank Ltd v McTaggart* [2003] QCA 59, [2003] 2 Qd R 568, [9] (emphasis in original). See further Keyes (2014), pp. 27–28.

[184] [1987] AC 460, 477. The English test is discussed further in the section "Agreement in Favour of the Courts of the Forum" above.

[185] *Australian Gourmet Pastes Pty Ltd v IAG New Zealand Ltd* [2017] VSCA 155, [88], footnote 71 (Tate JA with whom Santamaria and Beach JJA agreed).

[186] See the section "Agreement in Favour of the Courts of the Forum" above.

[187] *Donohue v Armco Inc* [2001] UKHL 64, [2002] 1 All ER 97, 107–108, 112–114, 117, 121–122. See Marshall and Keyes (2017), pp. 254–255.

[188] *Donohue v Armco Inc* [2001] UKHL 64, [2002] 1 All ER 97, 108 considered in *Incitec Ltd v Alkimos Shipping Corporation* (2004) 138 FCR 496, [48]–[49] (a case concerning an exclusive choice of court agreement nominating a foreign court).

[189] Mortensen et al. (2015), p. 97.

Strong countervailing reasons are needed for the court not to stay its proceedings,[190] which include the circumstance where the agreement itself[191] or its effect[192] is contrary to Australian public policy or internationally mandatory rules,[193] and where the proceedings pending in the forum involve third parties or issues outside the scope of the choice of court agreement.[194] Again, this is a different test to the "clearly inappropriate forum" test which applies to optional choice of court agreements nominating foreign courts. The difference between the strong reasons test and the "clearly inappropriate forum" test means that an Australian court is far more likely to stay its proceedings in favour of foreign proceedings, brought pursuant to an exclusive choice of court agreement, than foreign proceedings brought pursuant to an optional choice of court agreement.[195]

It follows that in international cases, to which common law principles apply, Australian law is more developed in its treatment of exclusive choice of court agreements than in its treatment of optional agreements: in principle, the test for determining whether an Australian court should *exercise* jurisdiction in light of an exclusive agreement nominating the courts of the forum, or in spite of an exclusive agreement, nominating a foreign court, is the same.[196] That is not true of the test which an Australian court applies in determining whether to exercise jurisdiction in light of an optional choice of court agreement nominating the courts of the forum or in spite of an optional choice of court agreement nominating a foreign court. The lack of equality of treatment between optional agreements nominating foreign courts and those nominating forum courts is troubling.

Different principles apply to exclusive and optional choice of court agreements in Trans-Tasman and intra-national cases. Under the *Trans-Tasman Proceedings Act*, an Australian court must not stay its proceedings in favour of a more appropriate New Zealand court, if the parties had agreed to the exclusive jurisdiction of the

[190] *The "Eleftheria"* [1970] P 94, 99; *Akai Pty Ltd v The People's Insurance Company Ltd* (1996) 188 CLR 418, 428–429, 444–445; *Incitec Ltd v Alkimos Shipping Corporation* (2004) 138 FCR 496, [43]; *Global Partners Fund Ltd v Babcock & Brown Ltd (in liq)* [2010] NSWCA 196, (2010) 79 ACSR 383, [88]–[89] (Spigelman CJ with whom Giles and Tobias JJA agreed).

[191] i.e. the agreement is rendered unenforceable by legislation embodying Australia's internationally mandatory rules: *Compagnie des Messageries Maritimes v Wilson* (1954) 94 CLR 577.

[192] i.e. enforcing the agreement is likely to mean that Australia's internationally mandatory rules will be not applied by the foreign court: *Akai Pty Ltd v The People's Insurance Company Ltd* (1996) 188 CLR 418, 445.

[193] *Akai Pty Ltd v The People's Insurance Company Ltd* (1996) 188 CLR 418, 428–429 (Dawson and McHugh JJ), 445 (Toohey, Gaudron and Gummow JJ). See further Marshall and Keyes (2017), pp. 263–265.

[194] See *Incitec Ltd v Alkimos Shipping Corporation* (2004) 138 FCR 496, [47].

[195] See *Parnell Manufacturing Pty Ltd v Lonza Ltd* [2017] NSWSC 562, [29].

[196] In practice, the test differs because the public policy of the forum will be considered a strong reason not to enforce an exclusive agreement nominating *foreign* courts, whereas, the public policy of the forum/fora, from which an exclusive agreement nominating the courts of the forum derogates, will not be considered a strong reason not to enforce an exclusive agreement nominating *forum* courts.

Australian court.[197] Correlatively, an Australian court seised of proceedings governed by an exclusive agreement nominating a New Zealand court must stay its proceedings.[198] These rules are subject to limited exceptions, similar to those contained in the Hague Convention.[199] An optional choice of court agreement designating an Australian or New Zealand court, by contrast, will be one matter, among enumerated others, which an Australian court *must* take into account under the *Trans-Tasman Proceedings Act* in determining whether a New Zealand court is "the more appropriate court".[200] In an intra-national case, an exclusive choice of court agreement, like an optional agreement, will only be treated as one discretionary factor among others, which a superior court *may* take into account[201] and which an inferior or intermediate court *must* take into account,[202] even though, as pointed out above,[203] more weight will, in principle, be given to an exclusive agreement than an optional one.

It follows that in Trans-Tasman cases, the law relating to exclusive and optional choice of court agreements is equally well-developed: a clear distinction is drawn between the principles applicable to exclusive and optional choice of court agreements, and within each of these distinct categories, agreements designating Australian courts and agreements designating New Zealand courts are treated identically. In intra-national cases, by contrast, although the same principles apply irrespective of whether the agreement nominates the court of the forum or another Australian court, which is encouraging, the law is underdeveloped in its understanding of parties' intentions: in intra-national cases, exclusive and optional agreements are treated as almost equivalent, which would seem to defeat parties' intentions, and in some intra-national cases, choice of court agreements are given no weight at all.[204]

---

[197]s 20(1)(b).

[198]*Trans-Tasman Proceedings Act 2010* (Cth) s 20(1)(a).

[199]Ibid s 20(2), (2A); Hague Convention, arts 5–6. Dickinson has argued that s 20 of the Trans-Tasman Proceedings Act should be extended to all exclusive choice of court agreements nominating foreign courts: (2014a), p. 176.

[200]*Trans-Tasman Proceedings Act 2010* (Cth) s 19(1)(b), (2)(d). See *Re Douglas Webber Events Pty Ltd* (2014) 291 FLR 173, [41].

[201]See cases cited in notes 168–175.

[202]*Service and Execution of Process Act 1992* (Cth) s 20(4)(d). For criticism, see Keyes (2014), pp. 40–41; Dickinson (2014b), p. 282.

[203]Text to note 173.

[204]See e.g. *Techtronic Industries Pty Ltd v Mitre 10 Australia Ltd* [2008] NSWSC 740, [5]–[15] (relying exclusively on the factors identified in *James Hardie & Coy Pty Ltd v Barry* (2000) 50 NSWLR 357, 379 (none of which refers to a choice of court agreement) despite counsel for the party seeking to resist the transfer having pointed to the relevance of the optional derogation agreement.)

4 Asymmetric Choice of Court Agreements

A choice of court agreement that combines both exclusive and optional aspects is a variant of one broad type of agreement known as an asymmetric choice of court agreement. Given that this was the broad type of agreement in issue in the widely-discussed French Supreme Court (*Cour de cassation*) *Rothschild* case,[205] to distinguish these from other types of asymmetric agreement, I will call these Rothschild clauses. Rothschild clauses are themselves of different variants[206] and can be found in multiple Australian cases.[207] For instance, in *Telesto Investments Ltd v UBS AG* one of several choice of court agreements in related contracts provided:

> the exclusive place of jurisdiction ... shall be the jurisdiction in which the Account is booked. Notwithstanding this, the Bank shall have the right, but not the duty or obligation, to take legal action against the Client in the jurisdiction in which UBS e-banking Services is offered, in the Client's place of residence or domicile or any other jurisdiction ....[208]

The Federal Court of Australia considered the effect of a Rothschild clause in *Reinsurance Australia Corporation Ltd v HIH Casualty & General Insurance Ltd (in liq)*.[209] The clause relevantly provided:

> Each of the insurers hereby irrevocably submits itself to the jurisdiction of the United States District Court for the Southern District of New York. ... Each of the insurers agrees ... that the insured may at its option bring suit, or institute other judicial proceedings against the insurers or any of their respective assets in any State or Federal Court of the United States or of any country or place where such insurer or such assets may be found.[210]

Jacobson J reasoned that the clause required the insurer "to submit to the exclusive jurisdiction of the New York courts" but held that the insurer's statutory

---

[205] Cass civ, 1ère, 26.9.2012, *Madame X v Banque Privée Edmond de Rothschild*, No 11-26.022 discussed in e.g. Keyes and Marshall (2015), pp. 366–370; Fentiman (2013), p. 24; in this volume, Mailhé, "France: A Game of Asymmetries, Optional and Asymmetrical Choice of Court Agreements under French Case Law".

[206] Marshall (2019), pp. 101–102.

[207] *Bankinvest AG v Seabrook* (1988) 14 NSWLR 711, 719; *Telesto Investments Ltd v UBS AG* [2013] NSWSC 503, 94 ACSR 29, [5]; *Reinsurance Australia Corporation Ltd v HIH Casualty & General Insurance Ltd (in liq)* [2003] FCA 56, (2003) 254 ALR 29, [339]; *Venter v Ilona MY Ltd* [2012] NSWSC 1029, [28]; *Re Bulong Nickel Pty Ltd* [2002] WASC 126, (2002) 42 ACSR 52, [34]–[35].

[208] *Telesto Investments Ltd v UBS AG* [2013] NSWSC 503, 94 ACSR 29, [5]. It should be noted that Mr Tyne, the sole beneficial owner of Telesto Investments Ltd, was involved in his capacity as trustee of the Argot Unit Trust in related proceedings in the Federal Court: *Tyne v UBS AG (No 2)* (2017) 250 FCR 341 reversed by *Tyne v UBS AG (No 2)* [2017] FCAFC 5, (2017) 250 FCR 341 but reinstated by *UBS AG v Tyne* [2018] HCA 45, [8], [60] (Kiefel CJ, Bell and Keane JJ), [61] (Gageler J), in dissent: [83], [124] (Nettle and Edelman JJ), [135], [170] (Gordon J).

[209] [2003] FCA 56, (2003) 254 ALR 29, [339], [341], [343]–[346]; Garnett (2013), p. 137.

[210] *Reinsurance Australia Corporation Ltd v HIH Casualty & General Insurance Ltd (in liq)* [2003] FCA 56, (2003) 254 ALR 29, [339].

claim for misleading conduct was outside the clause's scope.[211] Jacobson J's reasoning as to the clause's "exclusive" effect is consistent with the approach taken by the Supreme Court of New South Wales in *Venter v Ilona MY Ltd.*[212] That case concerned a narrow variant of Rothschild clause, nominating the courts of Bochum, Germany, with an option for the ship-hoist manufacturer to bring proceedings at the ship-owners' place of commercial residence.[213] The manufacturer sought to stay the New South Wales proceedings because of the "exclusive" German choice of court agreement.[214] Rein J held that the clause "is an exclusive jurisdiction clause contractually binding upon the Owners" and stayed the proceedings.[215]

Another type of asymmetric choice of court agreement can be observed in Australian case law. A unilateral non-exclusive choice of court agreement requires one named party to submit to the jurisdiction of a foreign court. For example, "... the Client irrevocably and unconditionally submits to the non-exclusive jurisdiction of the courts of [the country in which the relevant Account is booked] ...".[216] That clause is likely to be treated as having the same effect as an optional choice of court agreement, namely as a submission to the jurisdiction of the foreign court, albeit by one party.[217]

In other Australian cases, various combinations of these types of asymmetric agreement can be observed. A unilateral non-exclusive choice of court agreement accompanied by an option allowing the bank to sue in any other court was considered by the Queensland Court of Appeal in *Marks v Australia and New Zealand Banking Group Ltd.*[218] The clause provided that "The Guarantor irrevocably submits to the non-exclusive jurisdiction of the courts of Singapore or of any other court as the Bank may elect...".[219] The clause in *Oceanic Sun Line Special Shipping Co Inc*

---

[211] *Reinsurance Australia Corporation Ltd v HIH Casualty & General Insurance Ltd (in liq)* [2003] FCA 56, (2003) 254 ALR 29, [343], [349]. (The quote is at [343].)

[212] [2012] NSWSC 1029.

[213] [2012] NSWSC 1029, [28]: "Bochum shall be the place of jurisdiction. However, MD engineering [the ship-hoist manufacturer] shall be entitled to also take legal action against the Customer [the ship-owners] in the court which is competent for their commercial residence".

[214] Rogers A-JA also described the Rothschild clause in *Bankinvest AG v Seabrook* (1988) 14 NSWLR 711 as "exclusive": at 720.

[215] *Venter v Ilona MY Ltd* [2012] NSWSC 1029, [29], [46].

[216] *Telesto Investments Ltd v UBS AG* [2013] NSWSC 503, 94 ACSR 29, [5].

[217] *Telesto Investments Ltd v UBS AG* [2013] NSWSC 503, 94 ACSR 29, [262]–[266], [272] (although the court here was concerned with the question of whether that party had "submitted" to the foreign proceedings for the purposes of establishing whether the foreign court exercised international jurisdiction, such that an Australia court would recognize and enforce the foreign judgment).

[218] [2014] QCA 102.

[219] *Marks v Australia and New Zealand Banking Group Ltd* [2014] QCA 102, [31].

v Fay[220] concerned what might be called a unilateral exclusive choice of court[221] agreement, which required only the passenger to bring proceedings exclusively in Athens, Greece. The clause said nothing about the obligations of the carrier in proceedings against the passenger. The High Court did not appear to notice the asymmetric character of the clause but, in any event, it did not enforce it on the basis that the clause did not form part of the carriage contract.[222] A unilateral exclusive choice of court agreement also appeared in the recent case of *Valve Corporation v Australian Competition and Consumer Commission*, purporting to require Australian consumers to sue in Washington.[223]

There is limited consideration by Australian courts of the effect of the optional component of an asymmetric agreement. In *Marks v Australia and New Zealand Banking Group Ltd*, the Queensland Court of Appeal stated that the effect of the clause is that:

> [t]he first limb is a submission by the Guarantor to the non-exclusive jurisdiction of the courts of Singapore and the second limb is a submission by the Guarantor to the non-exclusive jurisdiction of any other court as the ANZ Bank may elect.[224]

Gotterson JA observed in obiter that, had the bank first commenced proceedings in Queensland, pursuant to the second limb (the optional component), those proceedings would have had no impact on the optional jurisdiction of the Singaporean courts or on the jurisdiction of any other court which would have regarded itself as competent.[225] Based on that obiter, it appears that the effect of the type of asymmetric agreement, set out above,[226] with which that case was concerned does not depend on whether the option has been exercised.

---

[220](1988) 165 CLR 197, 205: "any action *against the Carrier* must be brought only before the courts of Athens Greece to the jurisdiction of which *the Passenger submits* himself formally *excluding the jurisdiction of all* and *other* court or *courts* of any other country or countries which court or courts otherwise would have been competent to deal with such action." (my emphasis).

[221]Compare with Yeo (2005), p. 316 (using this term to describe a Rothschild clause).

[222]*Oceanic Sun Line Special Shipping Co Inc v Fay* (1988) 165 CLR 197, 205, 207–208, 229, 256, 261.

[223][2017] FCAFC 224, [53]: "*You* agree that any claim asserted in any legal proceeding *by you* against Valve shall be commenced and maintained exclusively in any state or federal court located in King County, Washington, ... and *you* hereby consent to the exclusive jurisdiction of such courts." (my emphasis). See also [55]. A similar clause appears in Facebook's standard terms and conditions, which the Supreme Court of Canada recently refused to enforce. The clause provides: "*You* will resolve any claim, cause of action or dispute (claim) you have with us arising out of or relating to this Statement or Facebook exclusively in a state or federal court located in Santa Clara County ...*You* agree to submit to the personal jurisdiction of the courts located in Santa Clara County, California for purpose of litigating all such claims": *Douez v Facebook Inc* 2017 SCC 33, [8] (my emphasis). For a discussion of this case, see in this volume Saumier, "Choice of Court Agreements in Common Law Canada".

[224]*Marks v Australia and New Zealand Banking Group Ltd* [2014] QCA 102, [34] (Gotterson JA with whom Muir JA and Daubney J agreed).

[225]*Marks v Australia and New Zealand Banking Group Ltd* [2014] QCA 102, [34]–[35].

[226]Text to note 219.

The case of *Marks v Australia and New Zealand Banking Group Ltd*[227] equally suggests that the effect of an asymmetric choice of court agreement does not depend on whether the party in whose favour the option is drafted is, or is presumed to be, the stronger party to the transaction. The asymmetric choice of court agreement in that case,[228] in a contract between one of Australia's largest banks and an individual guarantor, was effective. That said, in principle, asymmetric choice of court agreements may be rendered ineffective by statutory provisions relating to unfair contract terms. For example, section 12BF of the *Australian Securities and Investments Commission Act 2001* (Cth) (ASIC Act) provides that an unfair term in a contract of adhesion for a financial product or the supply of financial services is void.[229] This applies both to consumer contracts[230] and to small business contracts,[231] although it is unclear whether the relevant provisions have internationally mandatory effect and thus whether they have any effect when the proper law of the contract is foreign. A term is unfair if:

> it would cause a significant imbalance in the parties' rights and obligations arising under the contract; and it is not reasonably necessary in order to protect the legitimate interests of the party who would be advantaged by the term; and it would cause detriment (whether financial or otherwise) to a party if it were to be applied or relied on.[232]

A "term that limits, or has the effect of limiting, one party's right to sue another party" is an example of an unfair term.[233] An asymmetric choice of court agreement which requires a consumer or small business to bring proceedings outside Australia may have the effect of limiting that party's right to sue the bank.[234] That having been said, High Court authority on section 12BF of the ASIC Act, in relation to the imposition of late payment credit card fees by a bank, casts some doubt on whether claims of unfairness in individual cases will be made out where the clause in

[227] [2014] QCA 102.

[228] The clause is set out above at text to note 219.

[229] *Australian Securities and Investments Commission Act 2001* (Cth) s 12BF(1).

[230] *Australian Securities and Investments Commission Act 2001* (Cth) s 12BF(1), (3). A consumer contract is "a contract at least one of the parties to which is an individual whose acquisition of what is supplied under the contract is wholly or predominantly an acquisition for personal, domestic or household use or consumption."

[231] *Australian Securities and Investments Commission Act 2001* (Cth) s 12BF(1), (4). Small business contracts are those to which at least one party at the time the contract is entered into employs fewer than 20 persons on a regular and systematic basis (s 12BF(4)(a), (5)) and the upfront contract price does not exceed AUD$300,000 (s 4(b)(i)) or the contract has a duration of more than 12 months and the upfront contract price does not exceed AUD$1,000,000 (s 4(b)(ii)).

[232] *Australian Securities and Investments Commission Act 2001* (Cth) s 12BG(1). See generally *ACC v CLA Trading Pty Ltd* [2016] FCA 377, (2016) ATPR 43,055, 43,057-6–43,057-13.

[233] *Australian Securities and Investments Commission Act 2001* (Cth) s 12BH(1)(k).

[234] The same argument can be made in respect of exclusive choice of court agreements: Marshall and Keyes (2017), p. 265.

question is widespread in a given market.[235] European commentators attest that asymmetric clauses are "widespread",[236] or even "ubiquitous",[237] at least in European financial markets. Identical provisions to those in the ASIC Act exist in respect of all standard form contracts involving consumers or small businesses for a supply of goods or services.[238]

The effect that other legislation would have on asymmetric choice of court agreements requiring the weaker party to sue outside Australia is clear. Clause 21 of the Franchising Code would render of no effect an asymmetric choice of court agreement in a franchising contract, which requires the franchisee to bring proceedings in a foreign court.[239] The same would apply to an asymmetric choice of court agreement which requires the insured to sue in a foreign court.[240]

5 Evaluation and Reform

The legal treatment of optional choice of court agreements in Australia is deficient in multiple respects, foreshadowed in this chapter. First, optional agreements nominating forum courts and those nominating foreign courts are treated inconsistently, because the effect that Australian courts give to them is subject to the "clearly inappropriate forum test".[241] This test is inadequate in many ways, but most relevantly to optional agreements, it yields the result that an Australian court will almost never stay its proceedings if proceedings are on foot before a foreign court nominated in an optional choice of court agreement. It follows that application of this test to optional agreements nominating foreign courts may create uncertainty for any party unfamiliar with it and will invariably duplicate the costs of litigation: it is unlikely that a foreign court, nominated in an optional agreement, that is seised of proceedings will stay those proceedings, whether because it was the court first seised or because, on application of its law, the parties' agreement is characterized as exclusive. The clearly inappropriate forum test also means that Australian courts nominated in optional agreements will almost always exercise jurisdiction, even though the parties' agreement does not require that course. Accordingly, its application to optional agreements nominating forum courts erodes much of the value

[235] See *Paciocco v ANZ Banking Group Ltd* [2016] HCA 28, (2016) 258 CLR 525, 618 (Keane J with whom French CJ and Kiefel J agreed).

[236] Bälz and Stompfe (2017), p. 158 (my translation).

[237] Fentiman (2013), p. 24.

[238] *Competition and Consumer Act 2010* (Cth), sch 1, s 23(3), (4). Although this provision is yet to be tested before an Australian court, the legislation is unambiguous.

[239] *Competition and Consumer (Industry Codes—Franchising) Regulation 2014* (Cth) sch 1, cl 21 (2).

[240] *Insurance Contracts Act 1984* (Cth), s 52; *Akai Pty Ltd v The People's Insurance Co Ltd* (1996) 188 CLR 418, 447–448.

[241] See the section "Forum Versus Foreign Agreements: A Tale of Inconsistency".

inherent in a court having discretion as to whether or not to exercise jurisdiction: the test means that an Australian court nominated in an optional agreement cannot stay its proceedings if another forum is more suitable, even when doing so would arguably be more consistent with the intentions of the parties.

The second deficiency is that there is a noticeable and unexplained difference in judicial perceptions as to the parties' intentions in concluding an optional choice of court agreement in intra-national as compared with international cases. The Supreme Court of New South Wales has considered an optional agreement nominating another Australian court to be "a strong indication [by the parties] ... of where their disputes should be tried",[242] in an intra-national case, and as not indicating *any* "preference" for litigation in the chosen, foreign court in an international case.[243] In some intra-national cases, the parties' intentions are ignored entirely, no weight being given to their choice of court agreement in deciding whether to transfer proceedings to another Australian court.[244] The divergence in judicial perceptions as to the parties' intentions in concluding an optional choice of court agreement in intra-national and international cases reveals confusion as to exactly what an optional choice of agreement is and is intended to do. Further research on this point would be welcome.

Third, the tendency to develop the law applicable to optional choice of court agreements by transposing principles applicable to arbitration agreements is insufficiently thoughtful.[245] While such an extension may be justified in respect of some issues, it is less clear that it is in respect of others. For instance, an optional agreement should, like an exclusive agreement and an arbitration agreement, be treated as separable from the contract within which it is contained for the purposes of ascertaining its validity.[246] But the extension to optional agreements of the principle of construction relevant to determining the scope of an arbitration agreement, namely that parties intended all disputes to be resolved in one forum, does not seem cogent in the context of an agreement which contemplates that possibility.

Fourth, despite horizontal uniformity among Australia's component units,[247] there is no vertical uniformity among the regimes which apply to optional choice of court agreements in intra-national, Trans-Tasman and international cases. The principles which an Australian court applies to determine whether to exercise jurisdiction in light of or in spite of an optional agreement in Trans-Tasman cases differ from the principles applicable in international cases, which themselves differ from the principles applicable in intra-national cases.[248] Even in intra-national cases,

[242] *Asciano Services Pty Ltd v Australian Rail Track Corp Ltd* [2008] NSWSC 652, [19].

[243] *Bagsfirst Global Pty Ltd v Global Brands (Football) Pty Ltd* [2010] NSWSC 988, [24].

[244] See note 204 above.

[245] See text to notes 46–48 above.

[246] *FAI General Insurance Co Ltd v Ocean Marine Mutual Protection and Indemnity Association* (1997) 41 NSWLR 559, 567 (a case concerning an exclusive choice of court agreement).

[247] Section 2.

[248] Sections 2.3–3.

the principles to be applied by superior courts differ from the principles to be applied by inferior or intermediate courts.[249] A lack of uniformity in the different regimes applicable to optional agreements under Australian law creates complexity in the law. Some academics have lamented this lack of uniformity.[250]

Of all these deficiencies, the lack of weight that Australian courts give to optional choice of court agreements nominating foreign courts in deciding whether to exercise jurisdiction or stay proceedings in international cases is especially problematic. In response, it may be that parties in the future will become more specific in their drafting. For example, in some cases it may be the parties' intentions, in using an optional agreement, that once the foreign, nominated court has been seised, no proceedings can be brought in any other court.[251] Assume the parties were to make those intentions clear in wording of their agreement by providing, for instance: "either party may bring proceedings in the courts of England and Wales. This clause does not prevent either party from bringing proceedings in other competent courts unless or until one of them seises the courts of England and Wales." It is not clear how an Australian court would treat such a clause. Would such an agreement continue to be one factor in determining whether the Australian court is a clearly inappropriate forum?[252] Or would an Australian court treat the agreement as an "activated"[253] exclusive agreement, applying the principles applicable to foreign exclusive choice of agreements to determine whether to stay its proceedings as soon the nominated foreign court has been seised?[254]

At the time of writing, there are no existing proposals to reform the law relating to the treatment of optional choice of court agreements in, or affecting, Australia. The Hague Convention, which Australia proposes to implement, only applies to jurisdiction arising out of *exclusive* agreements.[255] The most pressing reform to the law is an amendment to the common law test that Australian courts apply in deciding whether to exercise jurisdiction in light of or in spite of an optional jurisdiction agreement. The inequality in treatment between optional forum and optional foreign agreements, which the "clearly inappropriate forum" test produces, is flawed as a matter of principle. Until the High Court has a change of heart on the matter, or the test is legislatively changed,[256] parties would be well-advised to conclude exclusive choice of court agreements where there is a risk that their dispute may come before

[249] Section 2.4.

[250] Compare Keyes (2014), pp. 27 and 41 with Dickinson (2014b), p. 287 (although Dickinson does not comment on the law applicable in international cases: see p. 276).

[251] See *Deutsche Bank AG and another v Highland Crusader Offshore Partners LP* [2009] EWCA Civ 725, [2010] 1 WLR 1023, [105] (where Toulson LJ observed that such an agreement is conceivable).

[252] Section "Agreement in Favour of Foreign Courts".

[253] Fentiman (2015), para 2.67.

[254] Section 3.

[255] Art 1(1). On the limited effect the Convention will have on optional agreements, see text to notes 38–39.

[256] See Keyes (2014), p. 41.

an Australian court. As has been seen, Australian courts are more likely to stay their proceedings in light of an exclusive foreign choice of court agreement than they are in light of an optional foreign one. Notwithstanding, parties ought to be aware of the mandatory legislation[257] which may impact the effectiveness of an exclusive choice of court agreement nominating foreign courts. The extent to which the Hague Convention will alter that situation, if Australia accedes to it, remains to be seen.

There are no impediments *per se* to the reform of the law relating to the effect of optional choice of court agreements. That said, if the "clearly inappropriate forum" test were to be changed by Commonwealth legislation, because of Australia's constitutional structure, the States would have to refer relevant powers to the Commonwealth, or the Commonwealth, the states and the territories would need to enact uniform rules. Either of those courses would be necessary, because it is not clear that the Commonwealth has competence to legislate with respect to state and territory courts not exercising federal jurisdiction.[258]

References

Bälz K, Stompfe P (2017) Asymmetrische Streitbeilegungsklauseln in internationalen Wirtschaftsverträgen. SchiedsVZ 15:157–164

Bell A (2003) Forum shopping and venue in transnational litigation. Oxford University Press, Oxford

Davies M, Bell AS, Brereton PLG (2014) Nygh's conflict of laws in Australia, 9th edn. LexisNexis Butterworths, Chatswood

Dickinson A (2014a) What, if anything, can Australia learn from the EU? In: Dickinson A, Keyes M, John T (eds) Australian private international law for the 21st century: facing outwards. Hart, Oxford, pp 157–189

Dickinson A (2014b) Harmonisation of the forum conveniens tests in Australia and trans-Tasman proceedings: a discussion paper. In: Dickinson A, Keyes M, John T (eds) Australian private international law for the 21st century: facing outwards. Hart, Oxford, pp 275–293

Dickinson A (2015) Keeping up appearances: the development of adjudicatory jurisdiction in the English courts. Br Yearb Int Law 86:6–67

Dickinson A (2019) In absentia: evolution and reform of Australian rules of adjudicatory jurisdiction. In: Douglas M, Bath V, Keyes M, Dickinson A (eds) Commercial issues in private international law. Hart, Oxford, pp 13–44

Dinelli A (2015) The limits on the remedy of damages for breach of jurisdiction agreements: the law of contract meets private international law. Melbourne Univ Law Rev 38:1023–1040

Douglas M (2017) Anti-suit injunctions in Australia. Melbourne Univ Law Rev 41:66–105

Douglas M, Bath V (2017) A new approach to service outside the jurisdiction and outside Australia under the Uniform Civil Procedure Rules. Australian Bar Rev 44:160–185

Fawcett J (2001) Non-exclusive jurisdiction agreements in private international law. LMCLQ: 234–261

Fentiman R (2013) Unilateral jurisdiction agreements in Europe. Cambridge Law J: 24–27

Fentiman R (2015) International commercial litigation, 2nd edn. Oxford University Press, Oxford

[257] See Sect. 1.1.

[258] For a fuller discussion of these issues, see Marshall and Keyes (2017), pp. 272–273.

Forrest C (2009) The Hague Convention on Choice of Court Agreements: the maritime exceptions. J Private Int Law 5:491–516
Garnett R (2013) Jurisdiction clauses since Akai. Australian Law J 87:134–149
Hartley T, Dogauchi D (2010) Explanatory report on the Convention of 30 June 2005 on Choice of Court Agreements. In: Permanent Bureau of the Conference (ed) Proceedings of the twentieth session, Tome III. Intersentia, Antwerp, pp 783–862
Keyes M (2009) Jurisdiction under the Hague Choice of Courts Convention: its likely impact on Australian practice. J Private Int Law 5:181–211
Keyes M (2011) Financial agreements in international family litigation. Australian J Family Law 25:167–184
Keyes M (2014) Improving private international law. In: Dickinson A, Keyes M, John T (eds) Australian private international law for the 21st century: facing outwards. Hart, Oxford, pp 15–45
Keyes M (2015) Party autonomy in dispute resolution: implied choices and waiver. Japanese Yearb Int Law 58:223–246
Keyes M (2019) Developing Australian private international law: the Hague choice of court convention & the Hague principles of choice of law in international commercial contracts. In: Douglas M, Bath V, Keyes M, Dickinson A (eds) Commercial issues in private international law. Hart, Oxford, pp 277–309
Keyes M, Marshall BA (2015) Jurisdiction agreements: exclusive, optional and asymmetrical. J Private Int Law 11:345–378
Marshall B (2019) The 2005 Hague convention: a panacea for non-exclusive and asymmetric jurisdiction agreements too? In: Douglas M, Bath V, Keyes M, Dickinson A (eds) Commercial issues in private international law. Hart, Oxford, pp 91–127
Marshall BA, Keyes M (2017) Australia's accession to the Hague Convention on Choice of Court Agreements. Melbourne Univ Law Rev 41:246–283
Mills A (2018) Party autonomy in private international law. Cambridge University Press, Cambridge
Mortensen R (2009) The Hague and the ditch: the trans-Tasman judicial area and the Choice of Court Convention. J Private Int Law 5:213–242
Mortensen R (2014) Together alone: integrating the Tasman world. In: Dickinson A, Keyes M, John T (eds) Australian private international law for the 21st century: facing outwards. Hart, Oxford, pp 113–144
Mortensen R, Garnett R, Keyes M (2015) Private international law in Australia, 3rd edn. LexisNexis, Chatswood
Raphael T (2008) The anti-suit injunction. Oxford University Press, Oxford
Thomson J, Martin K, Warnick L (2015) Commercial contract clauses: principles and interpretation, 2nd edn. Lawbook Co., Pyrmont
Yeo TM (2005) The contractual basis of the enforcement of exclusive and non-exclusive choice of court agreements. Singapore Acad Law J 17:306–360

Brooke Marshall is a Lecturer in private international law at the Faculty of Law, University of New South Wales, Australia. Prior to moving to Sydney, she worked as a Senior Research Fellow at the Max Planck Institute for Comparative and International Private Law in Hamburg, Germany, where she wrote her doctoral thesis on the topic of asymmetric choice of court agreements. Ms Marshall was awarded, in 2016, the Diploma of The Hague Academy of International Law in Private International Law. She has published several articles in the field and is the Regional Editor for Australasia of the forthcoming book *Choice of Law in International Commercial Contracts* (Oxford University Press).

Belgium: Optional Choice of Court Agreements, Legal Uncertainty Despite a Modern Legal Framework

Geert Van Calster and Michiel Poesen

1 Introduction

This chapter covers the legal regime of optional choice of court agreements in the Belgian legal order. There are a multitude of European Union (EU) and international instruments that govern choice of court agreements. There is also relevant case law on the issue in a number of EU Member States, whether or not with reference to EU law. However, as this contribution focuses on the Belgian legal regime regarding the issue under consideration, the chapter's discussion is limited as much as practically possible to the application by the Belgian courts and interpretation by Belgian scholarship of said EU and international instruments.

An English translation of the Belgian Private International Law Act 2004 (hereafter Act 2004) can be consulted online.[1] The authentic Dutch and French version (the German version not being authentic) may be consulted on the website of the Belgian State Gazette.[2] EU regulations and international conventions can be consulted online in various languages.

With regard to terminology, we use "optional choice of court agreement" to refer to a choice of court agreement conferring jurisdiction to multiple courts. We use "asymmetrical choice of court agreement" to refer to a choice of court agreement that

[1] Available on http://bit.ly/2z0AIsR.

[2] Wet van 16 juli 2004 houdende het Wetboek van internationaal privaatrecht, *Belgian Official Gazette* 27 July 2004, 57344. Available on http://bit.ly/2z0vHQQ.

G. Van Calster (✉)
Department of International and European Law, KU Leuven, Leuven, Belgium
e-mail: gavc@kuleuven.be

M. Poesen
Institute of Private International Law, KU Leuven, Leuven, Belgium
e-mail: michiel.poesen@kuleuven.be

M. Keyes (ed.), *Optional Choice of Court Agreements in Private International Law*, Ius Comparatum – Global Studies in Comparative Law 37, https://doi.org/10.1007/978-3-030-23914-5_3

is exclusive with regard to one party and optional with regard to the other. Note that the legal terminology used in Belgian legal scholarship might differ. We will indicate this in the text below (see Sects. 3.1 and 4.1 below).

2 Choice of Court Agreements in General

2.1 The Legal Treatment of Choice of Court Agreements

Belgian private international law has traditionally been favourable to choice of court agreements, acknowledging the importance of these agreements for legal certainty and predictability of the forum.[3] The legal framework regarding choice of court agreements in Belgium has been harmonized to a very large extent at the EU level by the Brussels regime, first by Article 17 of the Brussels Convention, later by Article 23 of the Brussels I Regulation and now by Article 25 of the Brussels I Recast Regulation.[4]

Moreover, Belgium is party to a multitude of bilateral and multilateral conventions regarding private international law. The most recent and most relevant convention as regards choice of court agreements is the 2005 Hague Choice of Court Convention. As a Member State of the EU, Belgium is bound by the 2005 Hague Choice of Court Convention.[5]

Prior to the Act 2004, Belgian case law generally accepted choice of court agreements.[6] This was formally recognized in the 2004 Act. The Act codifies residual private international law, which is applicable if no EU or international instruments applies.[7] The Belgian regime of choice of court agreements is partially inspired by Article 23 of the Brussels I Regulation, and partially by the abolished Article 635 of the Belgian Code of Civil Procedure.[8]

[3]Recital 15 of the Brussels I Recast Regulation; Hartley and Dogauchi (2013), p. 31, para 1; Wautelet (2013), p. 1705; Erauw and Storme (2009), p. 121, para 55; Fallon and Rigaux (2005), p. 375, para 9.14; Erauw and Fallon (2004), p. 92; Laenens (1981), p. 160, para 544–545.

[4]1968 Brussels Convention on jurisdiction and the enforcement of judgments in civil and commercial matters, [1972] OJ L 299/32; Regulation 44/2001on jurisdiction and the recognition and enforcement of judgments in civil and commercial matters, [2001] OJ L12/1; Regulation 1215/2012 on jurisdiction and the recognition and enforcement of judgments in civil and commercial matters, [2012] OJ L351/1.

[5]Council Decision 2014/887 on the approval, on behalf of the European Union, of the Hague Convention of 30 June 2005 on Choice of Court Agreements, [2014] OJ L353/5.

[6]Cass. 2 November 2001, *RCJB* 2003, 263, case note Fallon; Wautelet (2008), pp. 135–136.

[7]Article 21 Act 2004: Kruger and Verhellen (2016), p. 36; Van Calster (2016), p. 129; Van Calster (2015), p. 17, para 31.

[8]Nuyts (2005), p. 177, para 6173; Erauw (2004–2005), p. 124.

2.2 *The Importance of Party Autonomy and the Limitations Thereto*

Parties do not have an unlimited autonomy to enter into choice of court agreement. Note that we will only briefly discuss the limitations of the Brussels I Recast Regulation, the Lugano Convention and the 2005 Hague Choice of Court Convention. Belgian national private international law (referred to below as residual private international law) will be discussed in more detail.

The Brussels I Recast Regulation[9] governs the limitations to choice of court agreements in civil and commercial matters if parties have agreed to confer jurisdiction to a court or the courts of an EU Member State.[10] The following limitations apply:

- Parties cannot derogate from the exclusive jurisdictional rules listed in Article 24 of the Brussels I Recast Regulation.[11]
- Choice of court agreements are subject to limitations in insurance contracts, consumer contracts, and individual contracts of employment. For these contracts party autonomy is limited in the sense that parties can confer jurisdiction to a limited number of courts, or after the dispute arose.[12]
- The agreement must be validly entered into. Article 25(1) of the Brussels I Recast Regulation imposes conditions only as to the *formal expression of consent* to the choice of court agreement.[13] *Material validity* is now, following the amendments made to the Brussels I Regulation, assessed in the light of the *lex fori prorogati*, including its conflict rules,[14] in other words, including *renvoi*. In Belgian law this approach entails the applicability of the Rome I Regulation, even though choice of court agreements are explicitly excluded from the Regulation's scope. The Act 2004 states in Article 98, paragraph 1 that the Rome I Regulation (which governs the law applicable to contracts) applies even to subject-matters excluded from the Regulation's scope of application. Choice of court agreements are one of these excluded matters, to which Belgian courts will consequently apply Rome I's mechanism: Belgium's lex fori prorogati is in other words the *lex contractus*, to be applied using the Rome I rules. It is yet to be seen how the Belgian courts will

---

[9]In general, these limitations also apply under the Brussels I Regulation. The reference to the *lex fori prorogati* has been added in the Brussels I Recast Regulation and did not feature in the Brussels I Regulation.

[10]Article 25 of the Brussels I Recast Regulation; Van Calster (2016), p. 129; Van Calster (2015), pp. 1453–1457.

[11]Van Calster (2016), p. 73; Senechal (2008), p. 38, para 10.

[12]Specifically for employment contracts see Gangsted and Van Calster (2017), pp. 83–141; Senechal (2008), p. 39, para 11.

[13]Van Calster (2016), pp. 119–120.

[14]Recital 20 of the Brussels I Recast Regulation. The Belgian Supreme Court in ordinary, however, applied Art 25 without following Recital 20's *renvoi* instruction: Cass. 8 February 2019, docket number C.18.0354.N.

apply this conflict rule, in that it is not sure what issues are to be regarded as being covered by the expression "material validity".[15]

- A choice of court agreement should relate to "disputes which have arisen or which may arise in connection with a particular legal relationship".[16]

The 2007 Lugano Convention applies to a choice of court agreement when parties confer jurisdiction to a court located in Iceland, Norway or Switzerland.[17] Its provisions regarding choice of court agreements largely align with the Brussels I (not: the Recast)[18] Regulation.

The 2005 Hague Convention is applicable if parties confer exclusive jurisdiction to a court located in one of the ratifying states. Only if both parties reside in an EU member state does the Recast Regulation supersede the Hague Convention.[19] The limitations and conditions of (formal and substantive) validity coincide to a large extent with those of Article 25 of the Brussels I Recast Regulation.[20]

Unlike Article 25(1), which contains one single regime governing choice of court agreements, the provisions of the Act 2004 draw a distinction between *prorogation* of jurisdiction in favour of the Belgian courts on the one hand, and *derogation* of jurisdiction of the Belgian courts in favour of foreign courts on the other. These issues are governed by Article 6 and 7 Act 2004 respectively. Both regimes impose the following limitations:

- A limited number of jurisdictional rules are exclusive, such as jurisdiction regarding matters relating to intellectual property (Article 86 Act 2004).[21]
- Choice of court agreements in consumer and employment contracts can only be made after the dispute has arisen.[22]
- The choice of court agreement should be "valid" and "admissible".[23] Under Belgian law the validity of the agreement—including the formal validity,[24] and only excluding expression of consent—as noted is governed by the *lex contractus* which is applicable to the choice of court agreement by virtue of the relevant conflict rules. This is what the Brussels regime now calls "substantive validity".[25] Admissibility on the other hand is governed by Belgian law. A choice of court agreement is in any event inadmissible if the foreign court that is nominated in the choice of court agreement will not apply Belgian mandatory law such as the law

[15] See also, along similar lines, Francq (2015), p. 97, para 30.

[16] Article 25(1) of the Brussels I Recast Regulation.

[17] Hartley (2013), p. 107, para 6.05.

[18] The Brussels I Recast Regulation refers to the *lex fori prorogati* with regard to material validity of a choice of court agreement; Kruger and Verhellen (2016), p. 98; Francq (2015), p. 96, para 28.

[19] Kruger and Verhellen (2016), p. 84; Hartley (2013), p. 122, para 6.51.

[20] Kruger and Verhellen (2016), pp. 84–85.

[21] Van Boxstael (2010), p. 192, para 94.

[22] Article 97, paragraph 3 Act 2004; De Meyer and Storme (2014), p. 499.

[23] Fallon and Rigaux (2005), p. 778, para 14.17.

[24] Pertegas Sender (2005), p. 178, para 35.

[25] Article 98, paragraph 1 Act 2004.

concerning commercial agency contracts,[26] or in matters relating to the status and legal capacity of natural persons.[27]

- A choice of court agreement must relate to a legal relationship. The wording of the Act 2004 is less strict than that of Article 25(1) of the Brussels I Regulation Recast, since the latter requires that a choice of court agreement relates to a "particular" legal relationship.[28]

3 Optional Choice of Court Agreements

3.1 Definition

Belgian scholarship distinguishes two kinds of optional choice of court agreements. The first kind is referred to as "non-exclusive" choice of court agreements (*clause attributive de juridiction non-exclusives*[29]; *niet-exclusief beding*[30]). These are agreements conferring jurisdiction to one or more courts, specifying that the choice to confer jurisdiction to said court(s) is not exclusive, implying that the parties can bring their claims before the courts that would ordinarily have jurisdiction.[31]

The second kind of optional choice of court agreements are referred to as "complex" choice of court agreements (*clause de juridiction non-exclusive complexe*[32]; *meervoudig beding*[33]). These are clauses that confer jurisdiction to multiple courts, specifying that the parties can commence proceedings in one of these courts to the exclusion of the courts which would ordinarily have jurisdiction.[34]

3.2 Relevant Sources

Taking into account their respective scope of application, the issue of optional choice of court agreements is governed by the Brussels I Recast Regulation, the Brussels I

[26] Wautelet (2008), p. 139; Fallon and Rigaux (2005), p. 780, para 14.18.
[27] Pertegas and Samyn (2006), p. 34.
[28] Pertegas Sender (2005), p. 178, para 35.
[29] Verbruggen (2013), p. 446, para 12.
[30] Van Calster (2015), p. 21, para 40; Van Calster (2015), p. 1455, para 34.
[31] Wautelet (2013), p. 1726; Marquette (2013), p. 65, para 57; Verbruggen (2013), p. 446, para 12.
[32] Marquette (2013), p. 66, para 58.
[33] Van Calster (2015), p. 1455, para 34.
[34] Van Calster (2015), p. 1455, para 34.

Regulation or the 2007 Lugano Convention.[35] It should be noted, for the sake of completeness, that the 2005 Hague Choice of Court Convention does not apply to non-exclusive choice of court agreements.[36]

As to residual private international law, Articles 6 and 7 Act 2004 do not apply to optional choice of court agreements. Scholarship explicitly reserves applicability of the aforementioned provisions to exclusive choice of court agreements.[37] Moreover, the text of Article 6 Act 2004 (regarding prorogation of jurisdiction of the Belgian courts) explicitly refers to agreements that confer "exclusive" jurisdiction. Furthermore, Article 7 Act 2004 (regarding derogation of jurisdiction of the Belgian courts) in principle requires the Belgian courts to decline jurisdiction or to grant a stay, when parties conferred jurisdiction to a foreign court/foreign courts. Consequently, this provision only seems relevant in case of an agreement conferring exclusive jurisdiction.

However, arguably, *praeter legem* optional choice of court agreements should be subject to the conditions of validity and admissibility of Articles 6 and 7 Act 2004 (see Sect. 2.2 above). There would seem to be no pertinent reason not to subject exclusive and optional choice of court agreements to the same rules, for they both essentially are parties' agreements concerning jurisdiction. Moreover, this interpretation provides legal certainty to parties who have entered into an optional choice of court agreement that is governed by residual private international law.

3.3 *Legal Effect*

3.3.1 Interpretation

The optional nature of a choice of court agreement is determined by the intention of the parties. A choice of court agreement is said to be optional, if the parties grant jurisdiction to a court or the courts of a certain state, whilst explicitly[38] clarifying that said jurisdiction is not exclusive.

Another question concerns what law is applicable to issues of interpretation of a choice of court agreement: we refer to the discussion above.[39]

[35] Hartley (2013), p. 14, para 1.32; Marquette (2013), p. 65, para 56; Verbruggen (2013), pp. 446–447, para 12.

[36] Hartley and Dogauchi (2013), p. 31, para 9; Hartley (2013), pp. 143–144, para 7.42. The 2019 HCCH Judgments Convention will complement the 2005 Hague Choice of Court Convention by providing for a base of recognition and enforcement of judgments given by a court designated in an agreement "other than an exclusive choice of court agreement" (Art 5(1)(m)).

[37] Pertegas and Samyn (2006), pp. 33 and 40; Van Houtte and Verlinden (2004), p. 14, para 46.

[38] Article 25(1) of the Brussels I Recast Regulation; van Calster (2015), p. 1455, para 34.

[39] Magnus and Mankowski (2016), pp. 655–656, para 141; Erauw and Storme (2009), p. 123 *in initio*, para 56; Francq (2015), p. 97, para 30.

3.3.2 Validity of Optional Choice of Court Agreements Under Belgian Law

There are no published judgments which cover the validity of optional choice of court agreements under Belgian law. As a preliminary note, it is crucial to underline that Belgium has an abysmal method of publishing, more appropriately hiding, case law. The very highest courts of the land, the Constitutional Court, the Supreme Court in ordinary (*Cour de Cassation/Hof van Cassatie*) and the Supreme Administrative Court (*Raad van State/Conseil d'Etat*) publish their case law on a dedicated website (all three of which have search functions that are very wanting). All other courts do not. Belgium does not seriously take part in ECLI. Further, Belgium's page on the EU's e-justice portal links to juridat.org only contains a selection of relevant case-law. The unacceptable reality in Belgium is that editorial committees of legal reviews scramble to network courts and clerks to get their hands on interesting case law. This results in a rather haphazard selection of published material of which one can be sure it does not represent a proper image of the application of EU law, indeed any other law, in the country.[40] Moreover anonymity of judgments in Belgium takes absurd lengths. Even in commercial cases, the identity of parties is limited to the use of their initials. Finally, the Supreme Court in ordinary (*Cour de Cassation/Hof van Cassatie*) applies an extreme form of judicial economy, often sufficing with an observation that the lower courts (typically a Court of Appeal) have correctly or incorrectly applied the law, without much verbatim analysis of the legal reasoning behind it. Its judgments are often extremely short with little indication of how the court suggests the future interpretation ought to be directed.

In any event, Belgian scholarship accepted the validity of *optional* choice of court agreements under the Brussels Convention and the (old) Brussels I Regulation.[41] Legal scholarship argued that the validity of such agreements was exclusively subject to Article 17 of the Convention and Article 23 of the Brussels I Regulation. The applicability of national law by virtue of any conflict rule they suggested was excluded.[42]

Determination of the substantive validity of optional choice of court agreements becomes more complicated when applying Article 25 of the Brussels I Recast Regulation. As noted Article 25 explicitly subjects the issue of substantive validity of choice of court agreements to the *lex fori prorogati*.

However, applying the *lex fori prorogati* to the substantive validity of optional choice of court agreement is quite impracticable, since optional choice of court agreements do not confer exclusive jurisdiction to one forum. Parties can minimize

---

[40] A good free source for collated case law (taken from judgments published in reviews) is the site managed by my colleague at Antwerp, prof Thalia Kruger: http://www.eurprocedure.be/?language=nl&form_type=basic.

[41] Verbruggen (2013), p. 447, para 12 *in fine*.

[42] Marquette (2013), pp. 65–66, para 57; Verbruggen (2013), p. 447, para 12.

the risk of litigation on this issue by explicitly subjecting the optional choice of court agreement to one particular law.[43]

Belgian scholarship argues that *"complex" optional* choice of court agreements are invalid. This variant, pursuant to which party have the choice to bring proceedings in a number of courts in different member states which are nominated in an optional choice of court agreement (see Sect. 3.1 above), would, it is argued, be incompatible with the main goal of the Brussels regime because such an agreement would imply that the forum is unforeseeable for the defendant.[44]

The validity of optional choice of court agreements that are subject to *residual private international law* is a topic that has not at all been entertained in Belgian scholarship. This is most likely due to the fact that commercial private international law has been (practically) completely harmonised by EU law, combined with the fact that optional choice of court agreements are mostly used in commercial contracts.[45] Validity under residual PIL seems less problematic than under EU PIL. By analogy with exclusive choice of court agreements, validity is subject to the *lex contractus* pursuant to Article 98, paragraph 1 Act 2004—as discussed above.[46]

3.3.3 No Submission to Forum

An optional choice of court agreement *in favour of the Belgian courts* does not imply a submission to the exclusive jurisdiction of the Belgian courts. This applies both to the Brussels regime as well as residual private international law. Parties can still start proceedings in other jurisdictions.

Optional choice of court agreements *in favour of a foreign court* have a similar effect. Belgian courts will not be obliged to decline jurisdiction if they have jurisdiction under statutory jurisdiction rules in the event of a "non-exclusive" choice of court agreement, since the jurisdiction of the foreign court appointed in the optional choice of court agreement is not exclusive. However, if the Belgian courts are not appointed in a "complex" choice of court agreement as one of the courts which have jurisdiction, Belgian courts in any event cannot assume jurisdiction.

However, some Belgian scholars suggest that the legal effect of an optional choice of court agreement changes once the option has been exercised by commencing proceedings in one of the courts appointed in the optional choice of court agreement. Once the option has been exercised, jurisdiction of the court seized becomes exclusive.[47] This point of view is hard to reconcile with the non-exclusive nature of optional choice of court agreement.

---

[43]Van Calster (2016), p. 129; Van Calster (2015), p. 1455, para 34.

[44]Marquette (2013), p. 66, para 58; Verbruggen (2013), pp. 448–449, para 15.

[45]Marquette (2013), p. 67, para 59; Van Calster and Verhulst (2013), p. 15, para 53.

[46]See above note 26.

[47]Verbruggen (2013), p. 449, para 16.

3.3.4 Parallel Proceedings

In EU law, in the event of parallel proceedings (*lis alibis pendens*; *aanhangigheid*; *litispendence*) before a court nominated in an optional choice of court agreement and a court which would ordinarily have jurisdiction, general *lis alibis pendens* rules apply. Article 29 of the Brussels I Recast Regulation stipulates that any court other than the court first seized shall of its own motion stay its proceedings until such time as the jurisdiction of the court first seized is established.[48]

Article 31 of the Brussels I Recast Regulation contains a rule that prioritizes the court which is nominated in an *exclusive* choice of court agreement. Hence, courts nominated in an *optional* choice of court agreement do not come under the scope of that provision.[49]

In residual private international law, the Belgian courts have the option to stay proceedings if proceedings were started in a foreign court first, on the condition that it can be presumed that a decision of the foreign court will be enforceable in Belgium. If there is no doubt regarding the enforceability of a decision of the foreign court, the Belgian courts have to decline jurisdiction (Article 14 Act 2004).[50] Assuming that jurisdiction of the Belgian courts becomes exclusive after the option in favour of the Belgian courts pursuant to the optional choice of court agreement has been exercised (see Sect. 3.3.3 above), the reason for refusal of enforcement of Article 25, paragraph 1, 7° of the Act 2004 comes into play. This reason of refusal relates to the non-respect of the exclusive jurisdiction of the Belgian courts (see Sect. 3.3.5 below).

3.3.5 Enforcement

Under Belgian residual private international law, enforcement is refused pursuant to Article 25, paragraph 1, 7° Act 2004 when a foreign court entered a judgment notwithstanding an exclusive choice of court agreement in favour of the Belgian courts.[51] When we assume that optional choice of court agreements have no exclusive nature, enforcement will not be refused when a foreign court disregarded an optional choice of court agreement in favour of the Belgian courts. However, that question is contested in Belgian scholarship (see Sect. 3.3.3 above).

More importantly, pursuant to Article 25, paragraph 1, 6° Act 2004 enforcement of a foreign judgment is refused if it was issued while parallel proceedings were still pending in a Belgian court.[52] Given the doctrinal uncertainty regarding the question

[48]Dickinson and Lein (2015), pp. 326–330, para 11.16–11.29.

[49]Dickinson and Lein (2015), p. 341, para 11.54.

[50]Erauw and Storme (2009), p. 149, nr 77; Pertegas and Samyn (2006), pp. 79–83; Wautelet (2004), p. 215, para 21.

[51]Storme (2006), p. 147; Wautelet (2004), pp. 214–215, para. 21.

[52]Storme (2006), p. 147; Wautelet (2004), p. 216, para 24.

whether jurisdiction becomes exclusive after exercise of the option pursuant to the optional choice of court agreement (see Sect. 3.3.3 above), litigants have to be aware of this reason for refusal.

3.4 Treatment of Weaker Parties

There is no published case law regarding the position of weaker parties with respect to optional choice of court agreements. However, the general principles regarding choice of court agreements can be applied by analogy. Note that we will not discuss the general rules concerning admissibility of choice of court agreements regarding consumer, employment and insurance contracts (see Sect. 4 below concerning asymmetrical choice of court agreements).

3.4.1 Unfair Market Practices

In *Happy Flights v Ryanair*, the commercial court (*rechtbank van koophandel; tribunal de commerce; Handelsgericht*) of Charleroi ruled that an exclusive choice of court agreement must not create an unreasonable situation for consumers.[53] The clause under consideration was a clause in Ryanair's general terms and conditions.[54] Said clause conferred jurisdiction on the Irish courts. A number of Belgian consumers brought a claim against Ryanair, due to their flights having been cancelled. They started proceedings in the commercial court at Charleroi, Belgium. Ryanair argued that the Charleroi court lacked jurisdiction to hear the claims, the Irish courts having exclusive jurisdiction by virtue of the choice of court clause in Ryanair's general terms and conditions.

The commercial court disregarded the choice of court clause in Ryanair's general terms and conditions. Surprisingly, the commercial court does not mention the legal basis for its decision. Hence, there is no reference to, for example, Article 25 of the Brussels I Recast Regulation. Legal commentators refer to the provisions of the Belgian Economic Law Act,[55] which transpose the Unfair Commercial Practices Directive—arguably *lex specialis* vis-à-vis the Brussels I Recast Regulation.[56] In that respect, reference is made to inter alia *Oceano Grupo*; the clause conferring jurisdiction to courts which are a long way from the consumer's domicile and in the

[53]Commercial court Henegouwen, section Charleroi 24 March 2017, docket number A/16/01963, and docket number A/16/01964, unpublished case law; Verhoeven (2017), p. 3.

[54]Contracts of carriage are excluded from the scope of the consumer section of the Brussels I Regulation and the Brussels I Recast Regulation: Magnus and Mankowski (2016), pp. 504–505, para 115.

[55]Article VI.82, 23° Code of Economic Law. See Article XIV.50, 23° Code of Economic Law.

[56]Directive 2005/29 concerning unfair business-to-consumer commercial practices in the internal market [2005] OJ L149/22.

territorial jurisdiction of Ryanair, should be regarded as unfair and contrary to good faith.[57]

Although the commercial court's judgment concerns an exclusive choice of court agreement, the same principle *a fortiori* applies to its optional variant. A clause conferring optional jurisdiction to a court which is a long way from the consumer's domicile might equally be unfair. As stated in *Oceano Grupo*, "the costs relating to the consumer's entering an appearance could be a deterrent and cause him to forgo any legal remedy or defence", making the clause unfair.[58]

3.4.2 Good Faith

Although there are no precedents in this sense, there is a case for subjecting the exercise of optional choice of court agreements in favour of the Belgian courts to the requirement of good faith. This would imply that the exercise of the option granted by an optional choice of court agreement must not be manifestly unreasonable. In Belgian procedural law, this theory is known as abuse of process (*"misbruik van procesrecht*"; *"abus de droit d'agir en justice"*).[59]

In what follows, we discuss two aspects of good faith in relation to optional choice of court agreements in favour of the Belgian courts. First, we focus on the impact of good faith on forum selection pursuant to an optional choice of court agreement. Secondly, we consider whether the abuse of an optional choice of court agreement can give rise to damages.

Forum Selection

The application of the theory of abuse of process to optional choice of court agreements would imply that the Belgian courts decline jurisdiction, if the exercise of an optional choice of court agreement is manifestly unreasonable. Such an approach could be necessary to safeguard procedural economy and fairness with respect to the defendant.[60]

However, applying this theory would lead to a result which is very similar to the theory of *forum non conveniens*, since it would essentially allow a Belgian court to decide that another forum is more appropriate to hear a case.[61] Under the Brussels I

---

[57]CJEU Joined cases C-240/98 to C-244/98 *Oceano Grupo*, ECLI:EU:C:2000:346.

[58]CJEU Joined cases C-240/98 to C-244/98 *Oceano Grupo*, ECLI:EU:C:2000:346, para. 22.

[59]Vanlergberghe (2015), pp. 117–119, para 3; p. 128, para 14.

[60]Nuyts (2003), p. 412, para 308.

[61]Rodger (2006), p. 71 defines the doctrine of *forum non conveniens* as "a plea to the effect that a court with jurisdiction should decline to exercise its jurisdiction because the just determination of the dispute requires that the action should be tried elsewhere in a more appropriate forum."

regime, *forum non conveniens* was clearly not accepted,[62] which arguably also excluded the theory of abuse of right with respect to the exercise of optional choice of court agreements. However the Brussels I Recast Regulation regime does have a *forum non conveniens*-light provision, allowing courts seized in the EU to give way to non-EU courts where this is in the interest of the "proper administration of justice" (see inter alia recital 24).

Residual private international law allows Belgian courts to decline jurisdiction on the basis of grounds akin to *forum non conveniens*, pursuant to Article 6, paragraph 2 Act 2004 (prorogation of jurisdiction in favour of the Belgian courts). Belgian courts can decline jurisdiction when it appears that the dispute has no meaningful connection with Belgium.[63] Hence by analogy with Article 6, paragraph 2 Act 2004, Belgian courts can decline jurisdiction in the event of an abusive exercise of an optional choice of court agreement, when that optional choice of court agreement is governed by residual private international law.

A similar reasoning applies under Article 7, juncto Article 11 Act 2004. If a case displays a close connection with Belgium and if requiring a claimant to start proceedings abroad would be impossible or unreasonable, Belgian courts can assert jurisdiction despite a clause that confers jurisdiction to one or more foreign courts.

Of note is also that Belgian case law might already apply the theory of abuse to disregard an exclusive choice of court in favour of foreign courts. In the aforementioned *Happy Flights v Ryanair* case, the commercial court disregarded an exclusive choice of court clause in Ryanair's general terms and conditions in favour of the Irish courts. It did so by stating that Ryanair acted unreasonably by invoking the choice of court agreement, hence contesting the jurisdiction of the Belgian courts. According to the court, Ryanair's defence exclusively aimed at stalling proceedings, whilst Ryanair expressly acknowledged that the claimant's claim was founded on the merits.[64] That approach might be transposed to optional choice of court agreements. This implies that a Belgian court could decide to exercise jurisdiction in spite of an optional choice of court agreement pointing away from Belgium.

Award of Damages

Another question is whether abusive exercise of an optional choice of court agreement in favour of the Belgian courts can give rise to an award of damages to the defendant, if the claimant opted to commence proceedings in Belgium with the sole purpose of stalling proceedings and hence causing harm to the defendant.

---

[62]Case C-281/02, *Owusu*, ECLI:EU:C:2005:120, para. 46.

[63]Wautelet (2008), pp. 142–143; Pertegas and Samyn (2006), p. 37; Carlier (2005), para 15.

[64]Commercial Court Henegouwen, section Charleroi 24 March 2017, docket number A/16/01963, p. 3, and docket number A/16/01964, p. 3, unpublished case-law.

In any event, the civil sanction of Article 780*bis* Judiciary Code can be applied. This provision allows the Belgian courts to fine a claimant who commits abuse of process. The beneficiary of that fine is the Belgian state.[65]

Under what conditions Belgian courts may condemn a claimant to pay damages to the defendant, and what law would apply, is less clear, especially within the remit of residual Belgian PIL.[66] In our view the *locus damni* for an abusive application of choice of court is clearly *not* in the place where the defendant is being sued: rather, where it ought to have been sued. This is not an easy decision to make in cases of non-exclusive choice of court involving more than one jurisdiction. *Locus delicti commissi* arguably may also be both the place where the suit went ahead (which is where the positive action occurred) and the place(s) where no proceedings were introduced (the place(s) of inaction). Races to court would therefore seem inevitable. Under EU private international law, the UK Supreme Court insisted, with reluctance, on autonomous interpretation under EU law and located the *locus delicti commissi* in the case of *incitement* (in the case at issue by legal advice) to breach choice of court, as the location of the advice.[67]

3.5 *Intranational Cases*

Belgian case law accepts the validity of optional choice of court agreements[68] in intranational cases (i.e. cases without a cross-border element).[69] Article 624 of the Belgian Code of Civil Procedure 1967 lays out their status in Belgian civil procedure.[70] Scholarship states that the optional nature of a choice of court agreement in an intranational setting should be clearly stipulated by the parties.[71] When the wording of a clause does not reflect its optional nature, the court should try to determine the mutual intention of the parties to the choice of court agreement. If that intention cannot be established, the court should opt for the interpretation that is least

[65]Vanlergberghe (2015), pp. 117–119, para 3; p. 128, para 14.

[66]Vanlergberghe (2015), p. 120, para 5; Taelman (1988), p. 101, para 13; Fallon and Rigaux (2005), p. 469, para 11.3.

[67]*AMT v Marzillier* [2017] UKSC 13. See analysis, including of the High Court and Court of Appeal judgment, by Van Calster (2017b).

[68]*"Territoriaal bevoegdheidsbeding"* (Dutch), *"Clause de compétence territorial"* (French).

[69]Regional court Brussels 29 March 2000, *AJT* 2000-01, 215.

[70]Gerechtelijk Wetboek, *Belgian Official Gazette* 10 October 1967, 11360.

[71]Laenens (1981), p. 109, para 390.

favourable for the party in whose favour the optional choice of court agreement is made.[72]

It is worth noting that older case law, exclusive intranational choice of court agreements could be deviated from by the party "for the benefit of whom" the choice of court had been made.[73] This meant that exclusive clauses were in fact "optional". This approach is reminiscent of Article 17(1) of the Brussels Convention: *"If an agreement conferring jurisdiction was concluded for the benefit of only one of the parties, that party shall retain the right to bring proceedings in any other court which has jurisdiction by virtue of this Convention."* This line of case law was strongly criticised by scholarship.[74] More recent case law accepts the binding force of a choice of court agreement, without allowing deviation by the party in whose favour the choice of court was made.[75]

3.6 Comparison of Exclusive and Optional Choice of Court Agreements

In conclusion, the legal effect in Belgium of exclusive choice of court agreements and their optional variant differ significantly:

- The conflict rule for the *lex fori prorogati* of Article 25 of the Brussels I Recast Regulation is difficult to apply to determine the validity of *optional* choice of court agreements, since these clauses do not confer jurisdiction to one forum exclusively. Parties can avoid legal uncertainty by subjecting the optional choice of court agreement to a choice of law, in which they should, in our view, exclude renvoi.
- An *optional* choice of court agreement does not equate to a submission to the jurisdiction of the courts nominated in the agreement. The parties can still seize the courts which would ordinarily have jurisdiction.
- General *lis alibis pendens* rules apply in case of parallel proceedings in the court(s) nominated in the *optional* choice of court agreement and the courts which ordinarily would have jurisdiction. This means that the court(s) nominated in the optional choice of court agreement is (are) not prioritized over other courts.

[72]Interpretation *contra proferentem* pursuant to Article 1162 of the Belgian Civil Code; Laenens (1981), pp. 107–108, para 382–395.

[73]Regional court Brussels 30 January 1967, *Pas.* 1967, II, 205. District court (*burgerlijke rechtbank; tribunal civil; Zivilgericht*) Hoei 14 November 1882, *Pas.* 1883, III, 15.

[74]Laenens (1981), p. 109, para 389–390; Voet (2007), p. 326.

[75]Commercial court Ghent 2 February 2007, *RW* 2007-08, 324, case note S Voet; Commercial court; Tongeren 19 December 2006, *P&B* 2007, 65.

4 Asymmetrical Choice of Court Agreements

4.1 Definition

Asymmetrical choice of court agreements are choice of court agreements which are exclusive with regard to one party, and optional with regard to the other.[76] In Belgium, they are sometimes referred to as unilateral choice of court agreements (*clauses attributives de juridiction optionnelles unilatérales*[77] *eenzijdige forumbedingen*[78]).

4.2 Legal Effect

Belgian case law and scholarship regarding the legal effect of asymmetrical choice of court agreements under the Brussels regime is rare.

In a judgment of 2009, the Ghent regional court (*Hof van Beroep; Cour d'Appel; Appellationshof*) ruled that an asymmetrical choice of court agreement concluded between two businesses was valid in the light of (then) Article 23 of the Brussels I Regulation.[79] The clause conferred exclusive jurisdiction to the courts of Linz (Austria), whilst providing the option for one party to start proceedings in the courts where the other party was domiciled. The court decided that Article 23 does not oblige parties to confer jurisdiction to only one court, and the asymmetrical choice of court agreement under scrutiny was sufficiently precise as to the courts to which jurisdiction was conferred.

However, Belgian scholarship argues that one specific form of asymmetrical choice of court agreements is invalid. It is suggested the variant pursuant to which one party has the choice to bring proceedings in a number of courts in different member states which are nominated in an asymmetrical choice of court agreement would be incompatible with the main goal of the Brussels regime because such an agreement would imply that the forum is unforeseeable for the defendant.[80]

As to parallel proceedings, scholarship argues that Article 31 of the Brussels I Recast Regulation does not apply to asymmetrical choice of court agreements. This provision refers to exclusive choice of court agreements as such, without leaving room for asymmetrical choice of court agreements which are unilaterally exclusive.[81] For further discussion of the effect of asymmetrical choice of court

[76]Hartley (2013), p. 141, para 7.34.

[77]Marquette (2013), pp. 66–67, para 59; Verbruggen (2013), p. 447, para 13.

[78]Van Calster (2015), p. 21, para 40.

[79]Regional court Ghent 14 January 2009, *RABG* 2011, 291.

[80]Marquette (2013), p. 66, para 58; Verbruggen (2013), pp. 448–449, para 15.

[81]Dickinson and Lein (2015), p. 341, para 11.54.

agreements on parallel proceedings, we refer to the heading on optional choice of court agreements (see Sect. 3.3.4 above).

4.3 *Treatment of Weaker Parties*

4.3.1 Protected Categories in the Brussels Regime

The Brussels I Regulation and Recast Regulation limit the possibility of concluding a choice of court agreement in consumer, insurance and employment contracts. In general, choice of court agreements in these categories which have been entered into before the dispute has arisen are only enforceable if they are optional in favour of the consumer, insured or employee.[82] They can only allow the consumer, insured or employee to bring proceedings in courts other than indicated in the consumer, insurance of employment section of the Regulations.[83] Claims against a consumer, an insured or an employee can only be brought in the Member State where they are domiciled.[84]

Hence, asymmetrical choice of court agreements in consumer, insurance and employment contracts are only valid if the option to bring proceedings in different courts is granted to these weaker parties, without derogating from the protection granted to them by the consumer, insurance and employment section of the Regulation.[85]

4.3.2 Unfair Market Practices

In B2C relations, one can imagine Belgian courts applying the doctrine of unfair commercial practices in case an asymmetrical choice of court agreement is disproportionate, to the detriment of a consumer (see Sect. 3.4.1 above).

4.3.3 Good Faith

Although there are no precedents in this sense, Belgian courts might subject asymmetrical choice of court agreements to the requirement of good faith (see Sect. 3.4.1 above).[86] According to this increasingly popular theory of Belgian private law, no

[82]Magnus and Mankowski (2016), p. 429, para 1; p. 557, para 8.

[83]Magnus and Mankowski (2016), p. 522, para. 22.

[84]Magnus and Mankowski (2016), p. 513, para. 11; p. 553, para. 1.

[85]Hartley (2013), p. 141, para 7.34, footnote 37.

[86]It is worth noting that Turkish case law takes a similar approach: Van Calster (2017a).

right can be exercised in a discretionary way. If the exercise of a right fails to meet the requirements of good faith, a court can disregard the exercise of that right.[87]

The application of this theory could imply that Belgian courts can disregard the exclusive component of an asymmetrical choice of court agreement, which confers exclusive jurisdiction to other than Belgian courts. A defendant in whose favour the asymmetrical choice of court agreement is made could act contrary to good faith when he contests the jurisdiction of the Belgian courts, with the exclusive aim of causing harm to the claimant ("*animo nocendi*"), or if he would not benefit from the case being brought in the court nominated in the asymmetrical choice of court agreement's exclusive component.[88] Note that this was the Charleroi commercial court's approach in *Happy Flights v Ryanair.*[89]

The main argument against this approach is that it is reminiscent of *forum non conveniens*, which has been dismissed by the CJEU in *Owusu.*[90] However, this point of criticism only applies to the Brussels regime. There seems to be no such objection regarding asymmetrical choice of court agreements that are subject to Belgian residual private international law. *Forum non conveniens* is an accepted theory in residual private international law (see Sect. 3.4.2 above).[91]

As to the exercise of the optional component of an asymmetrical choice of court agreement, the principles discussed in the chapter concerning optional choice of court agreements can be applied by analogy (see Sect. 3.4.2 above). The same applies to the possibility to award damages.

5 Conclusion

There is a lot of ambiguity surrounding optional and asymmetrical choice of court agreements. The first important issue concerns their substantive validity. The conflict rule of the *lex fori prorogati* in Article 25 of the Brussels I Recast Regulation is quite unpractical when the parties have not conferred exclusive jurisdiction to a particular court of the courts of a particular member state. Parties can resolve this ambiguity by subjecting the optional or asymmetrical choice of court agreement to a choice of law (preferably excluding renvoi in the process).

Moreover, Belgian case-law seems to suggest that there is still room for the application of the unfair market practices legislation in B2C relations that are not subject to the consumer section of the Brussels I Regulation and the Recast Regulation, such as transport contracts. Moreover, Belgian courts might be inclined to subject optional and asymmetrical choice of court agreements to the requirement of

[87] Vanlergberghe (2015), pp. 117–119, para 3; p. 128, para 14.

[88] Vanlergberghe (2015), pp. 125–126, para 11; Taelman (1988), pp. 94–95, para 6.

[89] See above Sect. 3.4.2.

[90] CJEU, joined cases C-240/98 to C-244/98, ECLI:EU:C:2000:346, *Oceano Grupo*, para 22.

[91] Erauw and Storme (2009), p. 149, para 77.

good faith. It is questionable whether this approach is compatible with the absence of *forum non conveniens* under the Brussels regime, to the extent that the litigation concerned is subject to that regime.

Consequently, there still is a lot of legal uncertainty with regard to the legal effect of optional and asymmetrical choice of court agreements in Belgium. The lack of litigation regarding their legal effect might imply that legal practitioners have not yet picked up on these issues—or indeed that such litigation is typically taken away from the Belgian courts by virtue of the very choice of court agreement. Given the fact that optional and asymmetrical choice of court agreements are widely used in commercial and financial practice, it is likely that Belgian case law will develop. Brexit might be a potential factor in this respect, as it is possible that an increasing amount of cross-border commercial and financial disputes will be brought in the courts of Belgium.[92]

Legislative intervention would be preferable. This would effectively prevent unnecessary litigation and legal uncertainty.

References

Bambust I (2017) Brussels international business court. Juristenkrant:16

Carlier J-Y (2005) Le Code belge de droit international privé. RCDIP:11

de Meyer J, Storme H (2014) Artikel 97 WIPR. In: Couwenberg I, Hansenbout A, Vanfraechem L (eds) Internationaal Privaatrecht. Duiding. Larcier, Brussel, pp 757–758

Dickinson A, Lein E (2015) The Brussels I regulation recast. Oxford University Press, Oxford

Erauw J (2004–2005) Het vernieuwde internationaal privaatrecht van België wordt van kracht. RW:121

Erauw J, Fallon M (2004) De nieuwe wet op het internationaal privaatrecht. Kluwer, Antwerp

Erauw J, Storme H (2009) Beginselen van het Belgisch Privaatrecht. Internationaal privaatrecht. Kluwer, Mechelen

Fallon M, Rigaux F (2005) Droit international privé. Larcier, Brussels

Francq S (2015) De Bruxelles I à Bruxelles *Ibis*. JT:89

Gangsted J, Van Calster G (2017) Protected parties in European and American conflict of laws: a comparative analysis of individual employment contracts. Eur Yearb Private Int Law 18:83–142

Hartley T (2013) Choice-of-court agreements under the European and international instruments. Oxford University Press, Oxford

Kruger T, Verhellen J (2016) Internationaal privaatrecht. De essentie. Die Keure, Bruges

Laenens J (1981) De bevoegdheidsovereenkomst naar Belgisch recht. Kluwer, Antwerp

Magnus U, Mankowski P (2016) European commentaries on private international law, vol 1. Verlag Dr Otto Schmidt, Munich

[92]The Belgian government attempted to establish the Brussels International Business Court (BIBC): Wetsontwerp houdende de oprichting van het Brussels International Business Court, *Parl. St.* Kamer 2017-2018, nr. 3072/001; Bambust (2017), p. 16. The BIBC's aim was to promote Belgium as a jurisdiction for post-Brexit cross-border commercial and financial dispute resolution. If the BIBC had achieved its goal, it would have been bound to develop extensive case law on choice of court agreements, including optional and asymmetrical ones. Unfortunately, the bill that was meant to establish the BIBC did not pass the scrutiny of the federal parliament: Van Calster (2019).

Marquette V (2013) Contracter dans un contexte international: les frontières a l'autonomie de la volonté. In: IJE/IBJ (ed) Le droit des affaires en évolution/Tendensen in het bedrijfsrecht. Bruylant, Brussels, pp 15–75

Nuyts A (2003) L'exception de forum non conveniens. Bruylant, Brussels

Nuyts A (2005) Le nouveau droit international privé belge. JT:177

Pertegas M, Samyn L (2006) Artikel 6, Uitbreiding van de internationale bevoegdheid door wilskeuze. In: Erauw J, Fallon M, Guldix E, Meeusen J, Pertegas Sender M, van Houtte H, Watté N, Wautelet P (eds) Het Wetboek Internationaal Privaatrecht becommentarieerd. Intersentia, Antwerp, pp 32–49

Pertegas Sender M (2005) Le nouveau droit international prive belge. JT:173

Rodger B (2006) Forum Non Conveniens Post-Owusu. J Private Int Law 2:71–97

Senechal J (2008) Le règlement Bruxelles I, les clauses internationales d'élection de for et d'arbitrage. In: Defossez M, Senechal J (eds) Enforcing contracts. Aspects procéduraux de l'exécution des contrats transfrontaliers en droit européen et international. Larcier, Brussels

Storme H (2006) Artikel 25, Gronden voor weigering van de erkenning of de uitvoerbaarverklaring. In: Erauw J, Fallon M, Guldix E, Meeusen J, Pertgeas Sender M, van Houtte H, Watté N, Wautelet P (eds) Het Wetboek Internationaal Privaatrecht becommentarieerd. Intersentia, Antwerp, pp 117–123

Taelman P (1988) Gebruik en misbruik van procesrecht. TPR:89

Van Boxstael JL (2010) Code DIP. Premiers commentaires. Larcier, Brussels

Van Calster G, Verhulst M (2013) "Bevoegdheid: Europese ontwikkelingen" in Themis 76 - Internationaal privaatrecht. Die Keure, Bruges

Van Calster G (2015) L'EEX nouveau (ofte Brussel Ibis) est arrivé. De hervorming van de moeder van het Europees Internationaal Privaatrecht. RW:1443

Van Calster G (2016) European private international law. Hart, Oxford

Van Calster G (2019) The Brussels international business court. A carrot sunk by caviar. In Kramer X, Sorabji J (eds) International business courts – a European and global perspective. Eleven, Den Haag, forthcoming

Van Houtte H, Verlinden J (2004) Het wetboek internationaal privaatrecht - Een inleiding. In: Van Houtte H (ed) Internationaal privaatrecht. Themis, vol 28. Intersentia, Antwerp, pp 7–16

Vanlergberghe B (2015) Rechtsmisbruik in het procesrecht. In: Van Oevelen A, Rutten S, Rozie J (eds) Rechtsmisbruik. Intersentia, Antwerp, pp 115–147

Verbruggen C (2013) La compatibilité d'une clause (unilatérale) optionnelle de juridiction avec l'article 23 du Règlement Bruxelles I. TBH:443

Verhoeven M (2017) Vliegtuigpassagiers hoeven niet naar buitenlandse rechtbank. Juristenkrant:3

Voet S (2007) Over de bindende bevoegdheidsovereenkomst. P&B, pp 67–68

Wautelet P (2004) Le nouveau régime des décisions étrangères dans le Code de droit international privé. P&B:208

Wautelet P (2008) Les litiges contractuels transfrontaliers - le domaine résiduel du droit international privé: le droit belge. In: Defossez M, Senechal J (eds) Enforcing contracts. Aspects procéduraux de l'exécution de contrats transfrontaliers en droit européen et international. Larcier, Brussels, pp 133–159

Wautelet P (2013) Forumkeuzebeding. In: Ballon G-L, De Decker H, Sagaert V, Terryn E, Tilleman B, Verbeke AL (eds) Gemeenrechtelijke clausules. Intersentia, Antwerp, pp 1697–1738

Online Sources

Hartley T, Dogauchi M (2013) Explanatory Report on the 2005 Hague Choice of Court Agreements Convention. Available on https://bit.ly/2z1QCmC. Accessed 2 Sept 2018

Van Calster G (2017a) Turkish Supreme Court rejects choice of court agreement on basis of 'good faith'. Accepts asymmetric clauses. Available on https://bit.ly/2hHNvMf. Accessed 2 Sept 2018

Van Calster G (2017b) AMT v Marzillier: UK Supreme Court sides with reluctant Court of Appeal on inducement to breach choice of court agreement. Available on http://bit.ly/2LLkOY0. Accessed 2 Sept 2018

Geert Van Calster is full professor (professor ordinarius) in the University of Leuven and Head of Leuven Law's department of European and international law. He is also an independent legal practitioner at the Brussels Bar, focusing on international litigation and private international law.

Michiel Poesen is a PhD candidate at the institute of private international law of the KU Leuven Law Faculty. Prior to joining the institute of private international law, he was a junior associate at the litigation department of a Brussels based law firm and a teaching assistant of civil procedure.

Québec : Les Clauses D'Élection De For facultatives En droit international Privé Québécois

Sylvette Guillemard and Frédérique Sabourin

Résumé Le *Code civil du Québec* ne fait pas de différence entre les clauses d'élection de for exclusives et les clauses d'élection de for facultatives, sauf de façon très alambiquée dans le cadre de la reconnaissance des décisions étrangères (art. 3165 C.c.Q.). Les clauses d'élection de for « facultatives » sont rares en droit international privé québécois. L'adhésion à la Convention de La Haye sur les accords d'élection de for, bien que ce texte comporte un certain nombre de défauts, permettrait d'aplanir plusieurs difficultés. En particulier, la loi applicable aux accords d'élection de for mériterait d'être clarifiée.

1 Introduction

Le texte qui suit répond aux questions posées par Mme Mary Keyes, professeur de droit à l'université Griffith, à Brisbane, en Australie, et rapporteure générale au XXe Congrès de l'Académie internationale de droit comparé qui s'est déroulé à Fukuoka, au Japon, du 22 au 28 juillet 2018.

Conformément aux instructions reçues pour assurer la cohérence avec les autres textes dans le présent volume, les termes « facultative » et « exclusive » seront utilisés pour qualifier l'élection de for dans le présent texte.

Trois remarques préliminaires doivent être faites.

La première est qu'au Québec les sources juridiques sont la législation, la jurisprudence et la doctrine, ces dernières interprétant la première. Or, la lettre du *Code civil du Québec* ne fait pas de différence entre les clauses d'élection de for

Les opinions exprimées dans ce texte n'engagent que l'auteure.

S. Guillemard (✉)
Faculté de droit, Université Laval, Québec, QC, Canada
e-mail: Sylvette.Guillemard@fd.ulaval.ca

F. Sabourin
Ministère de la Justice du Québec, Québec, QC, Canada
e-mail: frederique.sabourin@mri.gouv.qc.ca

M. Keyes (ed.), *Optional Choice of Court Agreements in Private International Law*,
Ius Comparatum – Global Studies in Comparative Law 37,
https://doi.org/10.1007/978-3-030-23914-5_4

exclusives et les clauses d'élection de for facultatives, sauf de façon très alambiquée dans le cadre de la reconnaissance des décisions étrangères (art. 3165 C.c.Q.[1]).

Plusieurs décisions parlent de l'effet obligatoire[2] de la clause sans même mentionner son prétendu caractère exclusif : « [L'article 3148 C.c.Q.[3]] reconnaît [. . .] une pleine valeur juridique aux clauses d'élection de for [. . .][4] » sans qu'il soit question de compétence exclusive. Quand le législateur tenait à une compétence

---

[1] Art.3165 C.c.Q.. La compétence des autorités étrangères n'est pas reconnue par les autorités québécoises dans les cas suivants:

1° Lorsque, en raison de la matière ou d'une convention entre les parties, le droit du Québec attribue à ses autorités une compétence exclusive pour connaître de l'action qui a donné lieu à la décision étrangère;

2° Lorsque le droit du Québec admet, en raison de la matière ou d'une convention entre les parties, la compétence exclusive d'une autre autorité étrangère; [. . .]

Art. 3165 C.c.Q.: *The jurisdiction of foreign authorities is not recognized by Québec authorities in the following cases:*

(1) where, by reason of the subject matter or an agreement between the parties, Québec law grants exclusive jurisdiction to its authorities to hear the action which gave rise to the foreign decision;

(2) where, by reason of the subject matter or an agreement between the parties, Québec law recognizes the exclusive jurisdiction of another foreign authority; [. . .].

[2] Voir *Eagle River International Ltd (Faillite de)*, qui n'envisage pas l'exclusivité mais plutôt l'impérativité prévue par le code, ce qui n'est pas équivalent : *Eagle River International Ltd (Faillite de)*, 1999 CanLII 11910 (CS), <http://canlii.ca/t/1krhm>, consulté le 2017-10-18; confirmé par: 2000 CanLII 9546 (CA), <http://canlii.ca/t/1f8lw>, consulté le 2017-10-18, par. 44. La Cour suprême du Canada a rejeté le pourvoi sans se prononcer explicitement sur la clause d'« attornment »: *Sam Lévy & Associés c. Azco Mining inc.*, 2001 CSC 92 à https://scc-csc.lexum.com/scc-csc/scc-csc/fr/item/1934/index.do (version anglaise à https://scc-csc.lexum.com/scc-csc/scc-csc/en/item/1934/index.do).

[3] Article 3148 du Code civil du Québec:

Dans les actions personnelles à caractère patrimonial, les autorités québécoises sont compétentes dans les cas suivants: [. . .]

4° Les parties, par convention, leur ont soumis les litiges nés ou à naître entre elles à l'occasion d'un rapport de droit déterminé;

[. . .]

Cependant, les autorités québécoises ne sont pas compétentes lorsque les parties ont choisi, par convention, de soumettre les litiges nés ou à naître entre elles, à propos d'un rapport juridique déterminé, à une autorité étrangère ou à un arbitre, à moins que le défendeur n'ait reconnu la compétence des autorités québécoises.

Art. 3148 C.C.Q.: *In personal actions of a patrimonial nature, Québec authorities have jurisdiction in the following cases: [. . .]*

(4) the parties have by agreement submitted to them the present or future disputes between themselves arising out of a specific legal relationship;

However, Québec authorities have no jurisdiction where the parties have chosen by agreement to submit the present or future disputes between themselves relating to a specific legal relationship to a foreign authority or to an arbitrator, unless the defendant submits to the jurisdiction of the Québec authorities.

[4] Voir notamment *Lamborghini (Canada) inc.* c. *Automobili Lamborghini S.P.A.*, 1996 CanLII 6047 (QC CA) <http://canlii.ca/t/1ngqt>, consulté le 2017-10-19.

exclusive, il l'a indiqué en toutes lettres (art. 3151 C.c.Q.[5]). Pourrait-on dire que selon le Code civil, toutes les clauses d'élection de for sont exclusives, sauf celles contenues dans un contrat avec un consommateur ou un travailleur dans la mesure où elles ne leur sont pas opposables, en vertu de l'article 3149 C.c.Q.[6]?

Il y a quelques années, une des coauteures de ce texte, comparant la *Convention sur les accords d'élection de for* conclue à La Haye le 30 juin 2005 et le *Code civil du Québec*, notait qu'ils « divergent sur certains points. Ainsi, la Convention établit une présomption d'exclusivité de la clause d'élection de for[7] ». Si le texte international le dit en toutes lettres[8], le *Code civil du Québec* n'est pas aussi explicite.

La seconde remarque préliminaire est qu'il règne au Québec une grande confusion terminologique de la part de la jurisprudence et de la doctrine, ce qui n'aide pas à y voir clair et complique la tâche du chercheur. Le plus souvent, lorsque confusion il y a, l'expression clause d'élection de for désigne tout accord intervenu entre les parties portant sur la compétence, aussi bien judiciaire qu'arbitrale. En effet, plusieurs tribunaux utilisent les expressions clause d'élection de for et clause compromissoire indistinctement[9]. Or, normalement, l'expression « clause compromissoire » est réservée pour désigner la volonté des parties d'avoir recours à l'arbitrage et non à des tribunaux étatiques[10].

[5]Art. 3151 C.c.Q. : Les autorités québécoises ont compétence exclusive pour connaître en première instance de toute action fondée sur la responsabilité prévue à l'article 3129.

Art. 3151 C.c.Q: *Québec authorities have exclusive jurisdiction to hear in first instance all actions based on liability under article 3129.*

[6]Art. 3149 C.c.Q. : Les autorités québécoises sont, en outre, compétentes pour connaître d'une action fondée sur un contrat de consommation ou sur un contrat de travail si le consommateur ou le travailleur a son domicile ou sa résidence au Québec; la renonciation du consommateur ou du travailleur à cette compétence ne peut lui être opposée.

Art. 3149 C.c.Q. : *Québec authorities also have jurisdiction to hear an action based on a consumer contract or a contract of employment if the consumer or worker has his domicile or residence in Québec; the waiver of such jurisdiction by the consumer or worker may not be set up against him.*

[7]Sabourin (2007), par. 60.

[8]*Convention sur les accords d'élection de for*, La Haye, le 30 juin 2005, article 3 b) : « Aux fins de la présente Convention :

[...] b) un accord d'élection de for qui désigne les tribunaux d'un Etat contractant, ou un ou plusieurs tribunaux particuliers d'un Etat contractant, est réputé exclusif sauf si les parties sont convenues expressément du contraire ; ». Aux termes de la Convention, la présomption n'a pas tout à fait le même sens qu'en droit québécois. En droit québécois, selon l'article 2847 C.c.Q., la présomption légale qui concerne des faits réputés est absolue et aucune preuve ne peut lui être opposée.

[9]Voir comme exemple de confusion: *Kom International Inc.* c. *Swiednicki*, 2018 QCCS 546 ; « clause compromissoire parfaite »: *SMC Pneumatiques (Canada) ltée* c. Ressort Deziel *inc.*, 2014 QCCA 300 (CanLII), <http://canlii.ca/t/g35q6>, consulté le 2017-10-20; *JS finance Canada inc.* c. *JS Holding SA*, 1999 CanLII 13870 (QC CA), <http://canlii.ca/t/1n8wq>, consulté le 2017-10-19.

[10]Guillemard et Édouard Onguene Onana (2007), p. 663, note 95.

Il est parfois également incorrectement question de clause d'élection de for pour désigner une clause par laquelle le choix de la loi applicable est effectué[11]. À leur décharge, les clauses des contrats sont parfois ainsi rédigées alors les juges s'y réfèrent dans leurs décisions comme elles sont nommées.

De même, alors que la jurisprudence avait qualifié de « parfaite » la clause compromissoire pouvant donner sans l'ombre d'un doute compétence à un tribunal arbitral, l'adjectif est parfois repris pour évaluer une clause d'élection de for « obligatoire », « contraignante » ou « exclusive[12] ». Plus généralement il est question de son caractère « impératif » ou « irrévocable ». Là encore ces termes empruntent à l'arbitrage, l'irrévocabilité se rattachant au caractère final de la sentence arbitrale[13]. Il arrive que la jurisprudence considère qu'une clause d'élection de for qui n'a pas ces qualités n'a tout simplement pas l'effet d'une clause d'élection de for, plutôt que de la qualifier de clause « facultative[14] ».

En fait, les clauses d'élection de for « facultatives » sont rares en droit international privé québécois[15], nous n'avons pu retracer qu'une dizaine de décisions rapportées à cet égard. Il n'y a pas de terminologie particulière pour désigner ces clauses, dispositions ou accords d'élection de for. D'ailleurs, les expressions « facultatives », « non exclusive », « attributive de compétence facultative » et « optionnelles » ne sont pas couramment utilisées. Des décisions retiennent le qualificatif « imparfaites » pour les désigner[16].

---

[11]*eBay Canada Ltd.* c. *Mofo Moko*, 2013 QCCA 1912 (CanLII), <http://canlii.ca/t/g1sx6>, consulté le 2017-10-19, par. 5: « la convention intervenue entre les parties contient une clause d'élection de for rendant le droit de la province de l'Ontario applicable aux litiges entre les parties et déclarant la Californie comme étant la juridiction compétente ». Dans le même sens, « [l]a clause d'élection de for peut déterminer tantôt la loi applicable au contrat, tantôt le lieu d'introduction d'un recours exercé en vertu du contrat, tantôt l'un et l'autre » (*United European Bank and Trust Nassau Ltd.* c. *Duchesneau*, 2006 QCCA 652 (CanLII), http://canlii.ca/t/1n773 par. 37, consulté le 2017-10-18.

[12]Voir, entre autres, *Lemieux, Nolet* c. *Marcus Evans (Amérique du Nord) ltée*, 2008 QCCQ 1235 (CanLII), <http://canlii.ca/t/1w121>, par. 33, consulté le 2017-10-19: « En conséquence, le Tribunal est d'avis que la Cour du Québec a juridiction dans le présent dossier, la clause d'élection de for étant imparfaite. »

[13]*Importations Cimel Ltée* c. *Pier Augé Produits de Beauté*, 1987 CanLII 1165 (QC CA), <http://canlii.ca/t/1stlg>, consulté le 2017-10-25. Dans cette affaire, la convention des parties prévoyait que les litiges seraient tranchés par les tribunaux français ou la Chambre de Commerce Internationale de Paris.

[14]*STMicroelectronics Inc.* c. *Matrox Graphics Inc.*, 2007 QCCA 1784, 2007 QCCA 1784 (CanLII), <http://canlii.ca/t/1v8b6>, consulté le 2017-10-18 (version anglaise à <http://canlii.ca/t/fqbbv>), par. 126. Voir également *Wheelhouse* c. *Crête*, 2017 QCCQ 4241 (CanLII), <http://canlii.ca/t/h3t2h>, consulté le 2017-10-25, qui prévoyait expressément la compétence non-exclusive des tribunaux ontariens.

[15]Hartley et Dogauchi (2005), par. 240, « les accords non exclusifs sont assez courants, notamment dans le secteur bancaire international ».

[16]*Investia Services financiers inc.* c. *Services financiers Dundee inc.*, 2012 QCCS 4411 (CanLII), <http://canlii.ca/t/fssnc>, consulté le 2017-10-20, (version anglaise à http://canlii.ca/t/fvz18); *Lemieux, Nolet* c. *Marcus Evans (Amérique du Nord) ltée*, 2008 QCCQ 1235 (CanLII), <http://

Enfin la troisième remarque est la suivante. On peut se demander quel avantage ont les parties à conclure une clause d'élection de for facultative. Après tout, les clauses d'élection de for sont là pour assurer la prévisibilité, la stabilité et la sécurité juridique[17]. Or, la sécurité obtenue par une clause d'élection de for facultative peut être bien limitée selon la forme qu'elle revêt.

Trevor Hartley et Masato Dogauchi[18] en distinguent deux. La première forme qu'ils appellent « accords non exclusifs sans restriction » est celle des clauses qui ajoutent la compétence d'un tribunal aux tribunaux par ailleurs compétents en vertu d'autres bases prévues par leur droit national. Certaines affaires québécoises l'illustrent bien. Dans *Wheelhouse* c. *Crête*[19] et dans *Investia Services financiers inc.* c. *Services financiers Dundee*[20], les clauses prévoyaient expressément la compétence non-exclusive des tribunaux ontariens, et dans *Air Nostrum Lineas Aeras Del Mediterraneo* c. *DAC Aviation Internationale Ltée*[21], celle des tribunaux anglais. Dans *Eagle River International Ltd (Faillite de)*[22], la clause se lisait ainsi: « the Company hereby expressly acknowledges and agrees [. . .] to attorn, if required, to any courts of competent jurisdiction in the Province of British Columbia in order to either administer or interpret this Debenture in accordance with the laws

canlii.ca/t/1w121>, consulté le 2017-10-19. C'est aussi le cas dans *Duchesneau* c. *Duplessis*, [2005] n° AZ-50298589, J.E. 2005-483 (C.S.) et *Huppé* c. *Duplessis*, 2005 CanLII 5985 (C.S.), <http://canlii.ca/t/1jxg9>, consulté le 2017-10-20, mais pas en appel de ces décisions, respectivement: *United European Bank and Trust Nassau Ltd.* c. *Duchesneau*, 2006 QCCA 652 (CanLII), <http://canlii.ca/t/1n773>, consulté le 2017-10-18 et *United European Bank and Trust Nassau Ltd.* c. *Huppé*, 2006 QCCA 653 (CanLII), <http://canlii.ca/t/1n774>, consulté le 2017-10-20.

[17] « On s'accorde, en général, sur la très grande utilité pratique des clauses attributives de juridiction dans l'ordre international. Grâce à elles il est, en effet, possible de diminuer sensiblement l'insécurité inhérente à l'absence d'organisation de la société internationale » (Ancel et Lequette 2001, p. 661). La clause d'élection de for est tellement utile qu'elle est devenue, d'après Catherine Kessedjian, « très courante dans les contrats internationaux à tel point que l'on ne devrait plus s'interroger, semble-t-il, sur le principe de sa validité » (1997) ; Guillemard (2006), p 19.

[18] Hartley et Dogauchi (2005), par 246–247.

[19] *Wheelhouse* c. *Crête*, 2017 QCCQ 4241 (CanLII), <http://canlii.ca/t/h3t2h>, consulté le 2017-10-25.

[20] *Investia Services financiers inc.* c. *Services financiers Dundee inc.*, 2012 QCCS 4411 (CanLII), <http://canlii.ca/t/fssnc>, consulté le 2017-10-20 (version anglaise à http://canlii.ca/t/fvz18).

[21] *Air Nostrum Lineas Aeras Del Mediterraneo* c. *DAC Aviation Internationale Ltée*, 2017 QCCS 5421, par. 4.

[22] *Eagle River International Ltd (Faillite de)*, 1999 CanLII 11910 (C.S.), <http://canlii.ca/t/1krhm>, consulté le 2017-10-18 ; confirmé par : 2000 CanLII 9546 (C.A.), <http://canlii.ca/t/1f8lw>, consulté le 2017-10-18. La Cour suprême du Canada a rejeté le pourvoi sans se prononcer explicitement sur la clause d'« attornment »: *Sam Lévy & Associés* c. *Azco Mining inc.*, 2001 CSC 92 à https://scc-csc.lexum.com/scc-csc/scc-csc/fr/item/1934/index.do (version anglaise à https://scc-csc.lexum.com/scc-csc/scc-csc/en/item/1934/index.do).

prevailing in the Province of British Columbia ». Dans *M.F.I. Export Finance Inc.* c. *Rother International S.A. de C.V. Inc.*[23], telle était la clause:

> This Agreement shall be governed and construed in accordance with the laws of the Province of Ontario and the Government of Canada and ROTHER and MFI hereby attorn to the jurisdiction and courts thereof. Any collection action or legal enforcement relating to the collection of Cuban accounts receivable from customers of ROTHER located in Cuba, may at the option of MFI be governed and construed in accordance with the laws of the Republic of Cuba and, for these purposes only, ROTHER hereby attorns to the Cuban jurisdiction and the courts thereof.

Dans *STMicroelectronics Inc.* c. *Matrox Graphics Inc.*[24], la clause se lisait comme suit: « Buyer agrees that it will submit to the personal jurisdiction of the competent courts of the State of Texas and of the United States sitting in Dallas County, Texas, in any controversy or claim arising out of the sale contract, [...] ». Dans *Intergaz inc.* c. *Atlas Copco Canada inc.*[25], elle prévoyait que: « it is agreed that the parties shall be entitled to an injunction or injunctions to prevent breaches of this Agreement and to enforce specifically the terms and provisions hereof in any court of the United States or any state having jurisdiction, this being in addition to any other remedy to which they are entitled at law or in equity ».

La seconde forme qu'ils appellent « accords non exclusifs avec restriction » est celle des clauses qui limitent la compétence des tribunaux pour les parties, ou pour une seule d'entre elle. Ainsi, dans *Corporate Cars Quebec*[26], les parties avaient prévu: « no actions shall be brought against Corporate Cars to construe or enforce this Lease or otherwise with respect to this Lease except in the courts of Ontario » et dans *Axara* c. *4021487 Canada inc.*[27], que « [t]out différend entre les parties relatif à la conclusion, à la validité, à l'interprétation, à l'exécution du contrat, ou plus généralement qui résulterait du présent contrat, sera de la compétence de la juridiction dont dépend territorialement la partie contre laquelle l'action est engagée ».

Il nous semble que les clauses d'élection de for facultatives encouragent une course contre la montre où la première partie qui saisira un tribunal s'assurera de sa saisine. Pour le professeur Talpis[28], une clause asymétrique permettrait aux parties de résoudre à l'amiable leur litige. Nous pensons au contraire que ces clauses

---

[23] *M.F.I. Export Finance Inc.* c. *Rother International S.A. de C.V. Inc.*, 2004 CanLII 16200 (C.S.), (en anglais) à <http://canlii.ca/t/1gv7b> consulté le 2017-10-18.

[24] *STMicroelectronics Inc.* c. *Matrox Graphics Inc.*, 2007 QCCA 1784, 2007 QCCA 1784 (CanLII), <http://canlii.ca/t/1v8b6>, consulté le 2017-10-18 (version anglaise à <http://canlii.ca/t/fqbbv>), par. 126.

[25] *Intergaz inc.* c. *Atlas Copco Canada inc.*, 1997 CanLII 9248 (C.S.), http://canlii.ca/t/1kn44, par. 8, consulté le 2017-10-18.

[26] *Corporate Cars Quebec, l.p.* c. *9098-0038 Quebec inc.*, 2007 QCCQ 1690 (CanLII), <http://canlii.ca/t/1qt46>, consulté le 2017-10-25.

[27] *Axara* c. *4021487 Canada inc.*, 2017 QCCS 5588.

[28] Talpis (1993), pp. 183 et 225.

favorisent la partie la plus forte à imposer ses choix. Ce qui peut également se produire avec une clause exclusive.

Le texte qui suit fera état du traitement des clauses d'élection de for en général avant d'aborder celui des clauses d'élection de for facultatives dont une variété particulière, ces clauses dites asymétriques.

2 Le traitement des clauses d'élection de for en general

Avant 1994, la jurisprudence appliquait les articles du *Code de procédure civile* relatifs à la compétence territoriale interne des tribunaux québécois aux situations internationales. Elle admettait que les parties puissent choisir les tribunaux québécois, dans la mesure où ils avaient par ailleurs compétence sur la matière[29]. Elle admettait également que les parties puissent écarter la compétence des tribunaux québécois au profit d'un arbitre[30] mais refusait de reconnaître la validité d'une clause de juridiction par laquelle les parties écartaient la compétence des tribunaux québécois au profit d'un tribunal judiciaire étranger. Ce refus était justifié par les dispositions de l'article 68 C.p.c., qui envisageaient la compétence des tribunaux québécois « nonobstant convention contraire[31] ». Comme l'indique la Cour d'appel :

> Le dernier paragraphe de cet article [3148 C.c.Q. écarte] [...] la jurisprudence jusqu'alors suivie. Jusqu'à l'entrée en vigueur du Code civil du Québec, existait, en effet, un courant jurisprudentiel selon lequel les tribunaux québécois refusaient de se dessaisir en présence d'une telle clause qu'ils considéraient comme contraire à l'ordre public.
>
> [...] la jurisprudence québécoise [...] refusait d'accorder à la clause d'élection de for visant les tribunaux judiciaires l'exclusivité habituellement recherchée par ses termes[32] ».

La situation allait changer avec l'entrée en vigueur du *Code civil du Québec*, en 1994, dont les articles 3148 et 3168 C.c.Q. permettent expressément les clauses d'élection de for. Par conséquent, pour la Cour d'appel, « L'article 3148 écarte la jurisprudence antérieure sur les clauses d'élection de for, en les reconnaissant

---

[29]*Alimport (Empresa Cubana Importadora de Alimentos)* c. *Victoria Transport Ltd.*, [1977] 2 R.C.S. 858 à https://scc-csc.lexum.com/scc-csc/scc-csc/fr/item/5882/index.do (version anglaise à https://scc-csc.lexum.com/scc-csc/scc-csc/en/item/5882/index.do).

[30]*Zodiac International* v. *Polish People's Republic*, [1983] 1 R.C.S. 529 à https://scc-csc.lexum.com/scc-csc/scc-csc/fr/item/2471/index.do (version anglaise à https://scc-csc.lexum.com/scc-csc/scc-csc/fr/item/2471/index.do).

[31]Voir *GreCon Dimter inc.* c. *J.R. Normand inc.*, 2005 CSC 46 à https://scc-csc.lexum.com/scc-csc/scc-csc/fr/item/2279/index.do (en anglais à https://scc-csc.lexum.com/scc-csc/scc-csc/en/item/2279/index.do), par. 35.

[32]*Lamborghini (Canada) inc. c. Automobili Lamborghini S.P.A.*, [1997] R.J.Q. 58, p 63 (C.A.), 1996 CanLII 6047 (QC CA), <http://canlii.ca/t/1ngqt>, consulté le 2017-10-19.

explicitement comme valides[33] ». Bien accueillies par la doctrine[34], ces innovations n'ont pas été sans conséquence. La jurisprudence exhorte régulièrement les parties et les praticiens à apporter le soin nécessaire à la rédaction de ces clauses et à porter attention à leurs effets[35].

Selon la Cour suprême du Canada[36], l'article 3148 C.c.Q. participe du mouvement d'harmonisation internationale des règles de conflits de lois et de juridiction. Ce dernier se réalise, notamment, par voie d'accords internationaux que parrainent des organisations internationales comme la Conférence de La Haye de droit international privé et la Commission des Nations Unies pour le droit commercial international (« CNUDCI »). La Cour se réfère à la *Convention pour la reconnaissance et l'exécution des sentences arbitrales étrangères*[37], qui s'applique au Québec, par suite de l'adhésion tardive du Canada à cette convention entrée en vigueur au pays le 10 août 1986[38]. En outre, selon les commentaires du ministre sur le Code civil, l'article s'inspire de la *Convention sur la reconnaissance et l'exécution des jugements étrangers en matière civile et commerciale* et de la *Convention sur les accords d'élection de for* conclues à La Haye respectivement le 1er février 1971 et le 25 novembre 1965[39] auxquelles le Canada n'est pas partie. Les instruments européens ne semblent pas avoir eu d'influence sur le droit international privé québécois.

Depuis 1994, le droit international privé québécois est favorable à la faculté pour les parties de choisir de confier leurs litiges présents ou futurs, découlant d'un rapport juridique déterminé, à un tribunal québécois ou étranger[40]. Il existe une reconnaissance explicite des clauses d'élection de for. En effet, l'article 3148 du *Code civil du Québec* prévoit que :

---

[33] *Lamborghini (Canada) inc. c. Automobili Lamborghini S.P.A.*, [1997] R.J.Q. 58, p 63 (C.A.), 1996 CanLII 6047 (QC CA), <http://canlii.ca/t/1ngqt>, consulté le 2017-10-19. Voir aussi: *Sony Music Canada Inc.* c. *Kardiak Productions Inc*, 1997 CanLII 10719 (C.A.) à <http://canlii.ca/t/1nffl>, consulté le 2017-10-18; *Boutique Tania enr.* c. *Chase Paymentech Solutions*, 2007 QCCS 67 (CanLII), <http://canlii.ca/t/1qcgx>, consulté le 2017-10-30.

[34] Emanuelli (2011), par 119; Glenn (1993), pp. 752–756; Goldstein et Groffier (2003), pp. 359–363; Groffier (1993), p. 142; Talpis (1993), p. 183; Talpis et Castel (1993), p. 908, par 450.

[35] *Boutique Tania enr.* c. *Chase Paymentech Solutions*, 2007 QCCS 67 (CanLII), <http://canlii.ca/t/1qcgx>, consulté le 2017-10-19; *Robertson Building Systems Ltd.* c. *Constructions de la Source inc.*, 2006 QCCA 461 (CanLII), <http://canlii.ca/t/1n001>, consulté le 2017-10-19.

[36] *GreCon Dimter inc.* c. *J.R. Normand inc.*, 2005 CSC 46, par. 27 à https://scc-csc.lexum.com/scc-csc/scc-csc/fr/item/2279/index.do, (en anglais à https://scc-csc.lexum.com/scc-csc/scc-csc/en/item/2279/index.do).

[37] 330 R.T.N.U. 3 (« *Convention de New York* »), du 10 juin 1958.

[38] *Gazette du Canada*, partie II, vol. 120, n° 17, TR/86-154 et 155.

[39] Québec (1993), p. 2009. Le Canada n'est pas davantage partie à la *Convention de La Haye du 30 juin 2005 sur les accords d'élection de for.*

[40] Voir *GreCon Dimter inc.* c. *J.R. Normand inc.*, 2005 CSC 46 à https://scc-csc.lexum.com/scc-csc/scc-csc/fr/item/2279/index.do (en anglais à https://scc-csc.lexum.com/scc-csc/scc-csc/en/item/2279/index.do), par 19–22.

> Dans les actions personnelles à caractère patrimonial, les autorités québécoises sont compétentes dans les cas suivants: [. . .]
>
> 4° Les parties, par convention, leur ont soumis les litiges nés ou à naître entre elles à l'occasion d'un rapport de droit déterminé;
>
> [. . .]
>
> Cependant, les autorités québécoises ne sont pas compétentes lorsque les parties ont choisi, par convention, de soumettre les litiges nés ou à naître entre elles, à propos d'un rapport juridique déterminé, à une autorité étrangère ou à un arbitre, à moins que le défendeur n'ait reconnu la compétence des autorités québécoises[41].

Selon la Cour suprême, « [d]avantage qu'un simple alinéa à portée limitée, l'art. 3148, al. 2 C.c.Q. constitue, en matière de conflits de juridiction, la pierre angulaire d'une politique législative de respect de l'autonomie de la volonté des parties[42] ».

De plus, pour ce qui est de la reconnaissance et de l'exécution des décisions étrangères, les articles 3165 et 3168 C.c.Q. prévoient respectivement que :

> 3165. La compétence des autorités étrangères n'est pas reconnue par les autorités québécoises dans les cas suivants:
>
> 1° Lorsque, en raison de la matière ou d'une convention entre les parties, le droit du Québec attribue à ses autorités une compétence exclusive pour connaître de l'action qui a donné lieu à la décision étrangère;
>
> 2° Lorsque le droit du Québec admet, en raison de la matière ou d'une convention entre les parties, la compétence exclusive d'une autre autorité étrangère; [. . .][43]
>
> 3168. Dans les actions personnelles à caractère patrimonial, la compétence des autorités étrangères n'est reconnue que dans les cas suivants: [. . .]
>
> 5° Les parties leur ont soumis les litiges nés ou à naître entre elles à l'occasion d'un rapport de droit déterminé; cependant, la renonciation du consommateur ou du travailleur à la compétence de l'autorité de son domicile ne peut lui être opposée [. . .][44].

---

[41]Voir pour la version anglaise la note 3.

[42]Voir *GreCon Dimter inc.* c. *J.R. Normand inc.*, 2005 CSC 46 à https://scc-csc.lexum.com/scc-csc/scc-csc/fr/item/2279/index.do (en anglais à https://scc-csc.lexum.com/scc-csc/scc-csc/en/item/2279/index.do), par 35.

[43]Voir pour la version anglaise la note 1.

[44]Art. 3168 C.c.Q.: *In personal actions of a patrimonial nature, the jurisdiction of foreign authorities is recognized only in the following cases:*[. . .]

(5) the parties have submitted to the foreign authorities the present or future disputes between themselves arising out of a specific legal relationship; however, renunciation by a consumer or a worker of the jurisdiction of the authority of his place of domicile may not be set up against him; [. . .].

Voir *Dent Wizard International Corp.* c. *Mariano*, 2004 CanLII 11422 (QC CS), <http://canlii.ca/t/1h770>, consulté le 2017-10-20.

Il doit s'agir d'une action personnelle à caractère patrimonial. Les élections de for ne sont pas admises en matière d'actions personnelles à caractère extrapatrimonial[45], ni réelles[46], ni mixtes[47] même lorsque la clause serait par ailleurs valide[48].

En outre, il ne doit pas s'agir d'une action fondée sur la responsabilité civile pour tout préjudice subi au Québec ou hors du Québec et résultant soit de l'exposition à une matière première provenant du Québec, soit de son utilisation, que cette matière première ait été traitée ou non. En effet, dans cette matière, les tribunaux québécois ont une compétence exclusive (art. 3151[49] et 3129 C.c.Q.[50]). En vertu de l'article 3165 (1°) C.c.Q.[51], le jugement étranger ne serait pas reconnu.

Par ailleurs, les clauses d'élection de for contenues aux contrats ne seraient pas opposables au syndic qui représente et agit pour le bénéfice de la masse des créanciers[52].

---

[45]Droit de la famille – 152222, 2015 QCCA 1412, http://canlii.ca/t/gl0hl, par. 19, consulté le 2017-10-19.

[46]*Behaviour Communications inc.* c. *Virtual Image Productions*, 1999 CanLII 10658 (QC CQ), <http://canlii.ca/t/1kkrz>, consulté le 2017-10-19; Emanuelli (2011), n°206 cité par *Groupe Anderson inc.* c. *CGAO*, 2017 QCCA 923, <http://canlii.ca/t/h47c8>, par. 12, consulté le 2017-10-19; appel d'un jugement de la Cour supérieure ayant rejeté un moyen déclinatoire accueilli (*Groupe Anderson inc.* c. *CGAO*, 2017 QCCS 990 (CanLII), <http://canlii.ca/t/h2mqb>, consulté le 2017-10-19).

[47]*Groupe Anderson inc.* c. *CGAO*, 2017 QCCA 923, <http://canlii.ca/t/h47c8>, par. 11, consulté le 2017-10-19; appel d'un jugement de la Cour supérieure ayant rejeté un moyen déclinatoire accueilli (*Groupe Anderson inc.* c. *CGAO*, 2017 QCCS 990 (CanLII), <http://canlii.ca/t/h2mqb>, consulté le 2017-10-19).

[48]L'élection de for obéit aux règles générales en matière de contrat: absence de formalisme sous réserve des difficultés de preuve, capacité des parties, consentement libre et éclairé qui ne soit pas vicié par l'erreur, la crainte ou la lésion (mineurs et majeurs protégés), cause et objet qui ne soient pas prohibés par la loi ou contraire à l'ordre public (art. 1385-1415 C.c.Q.). Il doit y avoir rencontre des volontés de part et d'autre à défaut de quoi la clause est invalide: voir *Linn Products Ltd.* c. *Classé Audio inc.*, 2006 QCCA 426 (CanLII), version anglaise à <http://canlii.ca/t/1mwtq>, consulté le 2017-10-19 *Boutique Tania enr.* c. *Chase Paymentech Solutions*, 2007 QCCS 67 (CanLII), <http://canlii.ca/t/1qcgx>, consulté le 2017-10-19; *Dobexco Foods International inc.* c. *Van Barneveld Gouda Bv.*, 1997 CanLII 9210 (QC CS), <http://canlii.ca/t/1kn2v>, par. 28-29, consulté le 2017-10-19.

[49]Précité note 5.

[50]Art. 3129 C.c.Q. : Les règles du présent code s'appliquent de façon impérative à la responsabilité civile pour tout préjudice subi au Québec ou hors du Québec et résultant soit de l'exposition à une matière première provenant du Québec, soit de son utilisation, que cette matière première ait été traitée ou non.

Art. 3129 C.c.Q. : *The application of the rules of this Code is mandatory with respect to civil liability for any injury suffered in or outside Québec as a result of exposure to or the use of raw materials, whether processed or not, originating in Québec.*

[51]*Worthington Corp.* c. *Atlas Turner inc.*, 2004 CanLII 21370 (C.A.), <http://canlii.ca/t/1hqkr>, consulté le 2017-10-19, requête pour autorisation de pourvoi à la Cour suprême rejetée (C.S. Can., 30581, 2005-03-17), 30581; Glenn (1991), pp. 41–60.

[52]*Eagle River International Ltd (Faillite de)*, 1999 CanLII 11910 (CS), <http://canlii.ca/t/1krhm>, consulté le 2017-10-18; confirmé par: 2000 CanLII 9546 (CA), <http://canlii.ca/t/1f8lw>, par. 44, consulté le 2017-10-18. La Cour suprême du Canada a rejeté le pourvoi sans se prononcer

De plus, le consommateur ou le travailleur qui a son domicile ou sa résidence au Québec ne peut se voir opposer sa renonciation à la compétence des autorités québécoises (art. 3149 C.c.Q.)[53]. En vertu de l'article 3168 (5°) C.c.Q., le jugement étranger ne serait pas reconnu à l'encontre d'un consommateur ou d'un travailleur domicilié au Québec s'il a été rendu sur le fondement juridictionnel d'une élection de for en faveur d'un tribunal étranger.

C'est pour prévenir les abus qui menacent une partie « faible[54] » et protéger cette partie[55] que le législateur québécois par diverses interventions législatives tente de rétablir le déséquilibre des forces en présence dans certains contrats.

La question de savoir s'il est nécessaire, pour que soit donné effet à une clause d'élection de for étranger, que le contrat présente un quelconque élément d'extranéité a fait l'objet de quelques débats[56]. Certains ont souligné que, contrairement à l'article 3111 C.c.Q.[57] (relatif à la loi applicable), l'article 3148 C.c.Q. ne prévoit pas expressément que l'acte juridique qui ne présente aucun élément d'extranéité peut contenir une clause d'élection de for[58]. L'une des co-auteures de ce texte estime que la seule désignation d'un for étranger peut constituer l'élément d'extranéité nécessaire pour rendre le litige international[59].

---

explicitement sur la clause d'« attornment »: *Sam Lévy & Associés c. Azco Mining inc.*, 2001 CSC 92 à https://scc-csc.lexum.com/scc-csc/scc-csc/fr/item/1934/index.do (version anglaise à https://scc-csc.lexum.com/scc-csc/scc-csc/en/item/1934/index.do).

[53]Précité note 6. Voir, par exemple, *Demers* c. *Yahoo! inc.*, 2017 QCCS 4154 et *Hamamouche et Entreprise publique économique Air Algérie*, Montréal, Québec, 2018 QCTA 248.

[54]Guillemard (2004), p. 29.

[55]Ministère de la Justice (1993), p. 2011.

Ainsi, dans l'affaire qui a opposé un individu à Yahoo!, le contrat liant le premier au second a été qualifié de contrat de consommation et par conséquent, la clause d'élection de for qui y était incluse, en faveur des tribunaux ontariens, n'était pas opposable à l'utilisateur du moteur de recherche.

[56]*Dell Computer Corp.* c. *Union des consommateurs*, 2007 CSC 34 à https://scc-csc.lexum.com/scc-csc/scc-csc/fr/item/2374/index.do (version anglaise à https://scc-csc.lexum.com/scc-csc/scc-csc/en/item/2374/index.do), par. 196. À noter, dans cette affaire, il était question d'une clause d'arbitrage.

[57]Art. 3111 C.c.Q. : L'acte juridique, qu'il présente ou non un élément d'extranéité, est régi par la loi désignée expressément dans l'acte ou dont la désignation résulte d'une façon certaine des dispositions de cet acte.

Néanmoins, s'il ne présente aucun élément d'extranéité, il demeure soumis aux dispositions impératives de la loi de l'État qui s'appliquerait en l'absence de désignation.

On peut désigner expressément la loi applicable à la totalité ou à une partie seulement d'un acte juridique.

Art. 3111 C.c.Q. : *A juridical act, whether or not it contains any foreign element, is governed by the law expressly designated in the act or whose designation may be inferred with certainty from the terms of the act.*

Where a juridical act contains no foreign element, it remains nevertheless subject to the mandatory provisions of the law of the State which would apply in the absence of a designation.

The law may be expressly designated as applicable to the whole or to only part of a juridical act.

[58]Rochette (2006).

[59]Guillemard (2004), pp. 25–26, 50.

Par ailleurs, il n'est pas nécessaire que les parties ou le litige aient un lien avec l'État du tribunal choisi[60].

Finalement, selon la Cour suprême, un dernier type d'exceptions à l'autonomie de la volonté des parties tient au libellé des clauses d'élection de for[61].

Il est possible que d'autres instances aient des compétences exclusives au Québec, par exemple en matière de logement[62], qui pourraient faire échec à une clause d'élection de for, mais à notre connaissance, il n'y a pas de jurisprudence sur cette question.

3 Clauses D'élection De For Facultatives

Selon la Cour suprême, « La dérogation à la compétence des autorités québécoises dans un cas précis sera décidée en fonction de la rédaction de la clause de juridiction adoptée par les parties. [. . .] La clause doit avoir un caractère impératif et conférer une compétence exclusive de manière claire et précise à l'autorité étrangère[63] ». Elle ajoute : « Dans la mesure où la volonté des parties de soumettre leurs litiges éventuels à une autorité étrangère s'affirme de façon claire et exclusive, les tribunaux devraient respecter les clauses d'élection de for[64] ».

Dans l'affaire *M.F.I.*[65], la Cour supérieure passe en revue la jurisprudence jusqu'alors rendue et conclut :

[60]Guillemard (2004), pp. 9, 25–26, 19 et seq, 26, p 28, p 51. L'auteure souligne la possibilité d'invoquer le *forum non conveniens* prévu à l'article 3135 C.c.Q. Voir *infra*, 2.2.1 et 5.

[61]*GreCon Dimter inc.* c. *J.R. Normand inc.*, 2005 CSC 46, par. 27 à https://scc-csc.lexum.com/scc-csc/scc-csc/fr/item/2279/index.do (en anglais à https://scc-csc.lexum.com/scc-csc/scc-csc/en/item/2279/index.do), par. 27 se référant à Glenn (1993), p 756. Voir en outre *Pivotal Payments Direct Corp.* c. *6858449 Canada inc.*, 2013 QCCS 5212 (CanLII), version anglaise à <http://canlii.ca/t/g1mt1>, consulté le 2017-10-19, par. 9, où la clause d'élection de for en faveur des tribunaux québécois n'a pas trouvé application parce qu'elle ne visait pas le recours institué et qu'elle n'avait pas survécu à la résiliation de la convention entre les parties.

[62]Goldstein et Groffier (2003), pp. 729–730, par. 435 estiment qu'il pourrait s'agir de règles d'application nécessaire (art. 3076 C.c.Q. : Les règles du présent livre s'appliquent sous réserve des règles de droit en vigueur au Québec dont l'application s'impose en raison de leur but particulier. En anglais: *The rules contained in this Book apply subject to those rules of law in force in Québec which are applicable by reason of their particular object.*).

[63]*GreCon Dimter inc.* c. *J.R. Normand inc.*, 2005 CSC 46, par. 27 à https://scc-csc.lexum.com/scc-csc/scc-csc/fr/item/2279/index.do (en anglais à https://scc-csc.lexum.com/scc-csc/scc-csc/en/item/2279/index.do).

[64]*GreCon Dimter inc.* c. *J.R. Normand inc.*, 2005 CSC 46, par. 27 à https://scc-csc.lexum.com/scc-csc/scc-csc/fr/item/2279/index.do (en anglais à https://scc-csc.lexum.com/scc-csc/scc-csc/en/item/2279/index.do).

[65]*M.F.I. Export Finance Inc.* c. *Rother International S.A. de C.V. Inc.*, 2004 CanLII 16200 (C.S.), (en anglais) à <http://canlii.ca/t/1gv7b> consulté le 2017-10-18.

> [62] Not only did the parties to the Loan Agreement fail to stipulate that *only* the Ontario Courts *had jurisdiction*, or that their jurisdiction was *exclusive*, they also did not provide that their attornment to the Ontario Courts was *irrevocable*, or that the Agreement could *only be enforced* before the Ontario Courts. Nor did they state that *any or all actions had to be taken* before the Ontario Courts.
>
> [63] Finally, the absence of exclusive Ontario jurisdiction was confirmed when the parties attorned to Cuban jurisdiction for the purposes set out in sec. 18, and also to the jurisdiction of the courts of Canada.
>
> [65] In the Court's opinion, for the foregoing reasons, the parties did not express their intention "to submit all existing or future disputes" relating to the Loan Agreement to the Ontario Courts, as required by the last paragraph of art. 3148. [. . .]. (nos soulignements)

À notre connaissance, le seul cas erroné de qualification de clause facultative par un tribunal québécois est celui du dossier *Kardiak*. La clause en question se lisait ainsi :

> This Agreement has been entered into in the Province of Ontario, and the validity, interpretation and legal effect of this Agreement shall be governed by the laws of the Province of Ontario applicable to contracts entered into and performed entirely within the Province of Ontario. The Ontario courts (provincial and federal), only, will have jurisdiction of any controversies regarding this Agreement; any action or other proceeding which involves such a controversy will be brought in those courts, in the Province of Ontario, and not elsewhere[66].

Les termes souffrent peu d'interprétation et confèrent à la disposition un caractère obligatoire. Et pourtant, comme le constate la Cour d'appel, « le premier juge a décidé que la clause 19.08 constituait une simple clause d'élection de for qui "permet l'alternative additionnelle des recours devant les tribunaux québécois" ».

Face à une clause d'élection de for, les instruments de mesure que les tribunaux utilisent sont les termes et la volonté ou l'intention des parties : « En d'autres termes, le formalisme qui à une certaine époque a animé la jurisprudence sur les clauses de choix de for n'est plus de mise : il faut rechercher l'intention réelle des parties sans s'arrêter à des considérations d'ordre uniquement terminologique[67] ». Aucun élément objectif n'intervient (comme la disponibilité du tribunal étranger, etc.). Comme le souligne la Cour d'appel dans *STMicroelectronics Inc.*[68], il n'y a pas de formule sacramentelle ni d'obligation d'utiliser des mots-clés.

En recherchant l'intention des parties, les tribunaux appliquent les articles 1425 à 1432 C.c.Q.[69].

---

[66] *Sony Music Canada Inc.* c. *Kardiak Productions Inc*, 1997 CanLII 10719 (QC CA).

[67] *PIRS, s.a.* c. *Compagnie d'arrimage de Québec ltée*, 2013 QCCA 31 par.9.

[68] *STMicroelectronics Inc.* c. *Matrox Graphics Inc.*, 2007 QCCA 1784, 2007 QCCA 1784 (CanLII), <http://canlii.ca/t/1v8b6>, par. 85, consulté le 2017-10-18 (version anglaise à <http://canlii.ca/t/fqbbv>).

[69] Ces articles prévoient :

1425. Dans l'interprétation du contrat, on doit rechercher quelle a été la commune intention des parties plutôt que de s'arrêter au sens littéral des termes utilisés.

Dans la présente partie, nous traiterons successivement de la loi applicable à l'élection de for, de l'effet d'une clause d'élection de for facultative, du traitement de la clause d'élection de for en droit international privé québécois et canadien ainsi qu'en droit interne, et finalement des clauses d'élection de for asymétriques.

3.1 *Quelle loi s'applique?*

Un auteur a fait remarquer : « La détermination de la loi applicable aux accords d'élection de for soulève des questions théoriques d'une grande complexité. Il s'agit, selon la doctrine la plus autorisée, de " l'un de ces irritants problèmes de droit international privé [. . .]"[70] ». Comme nous allons le voir, cette difficulté se présente peu devant les tribunaux québécois.

1426. On tient compte, dans l'interprétation du contrat, de sa nature, des circonstances dans lesquelles il a été conclu, de l'interprétation que les parties lui ont déjà donnée ou qu'il peut avoir reçue, ainsi que des usages.

1427. Les clauses s'interprètent les unes par les autres, en donnant à chacune le sens qui résulte de l'ensemble du contrat.

1428. Une clause s'entend dans le sens qui lui confère quelque effet plutôt que dans celui qui n'en produit aucun.

1429. Les termes susceptibles de deux sens doivent être pris dans le sens qui convient le plus à la matière du contrat.

1430. La clause destinée à écarter tout doute sur l'application du contrat à un cas particulier ne restreint pas la portée du contrat par ailleurs conçu en termes généraux.

1431. Les clauses d'un contrat, même si elles sont énoncées en termes généraux, comprennent seulement ce sur quoi il paraît que les parties se sont proposé de contracter.

1432. Dans le doute, le contrat s'interprète en faveur de celui qui a contracté l'obligation et contre celui qui l'a stipulée. Dans tous les cas, il s'interprète en faveur de l'adhérent ou du consommateur.

En anglais :

1425. *The common intention of the parties rather than adherence to the literal meaning of the words shall be sought in interpreting a contract.*

1426. *In interpreting a contract, the nature of the contract, the circumstances in which it was formed, the interpretation which has already been given to it by the parties or which it may have received, and usage, are all taken into account.*

1427. *Each clause of a contract is interpreted in light of the others so that each is given the meaning derived from the contract as a whole.*

1428. *A clause is given a meaning that gives it some effect rather than one that gives it no effect.*

1429. *Words susceptible of two meanings shall be given the meaning that best conforms to the subject matter of the contract.*

1430. *A clause intended to eliminate doubt as to the application of the contract to a specific situation does not restrict the scope of a contract otherwise expressed in general terms.*

1431. *The clauses of a contract cover only what it appears that the parties intended to include, however general the terms used.*

1432. *In case of doubt, a contract is interpreted in favour of the person who contracted the obligation and against the person who stipulated it. In all cases, it is interpreted in favour of the adhering party or the consumer.*

[70] Guez (2000), par 309; Gaudemet-Tallon (1981), p. 440.

Dans *Investia Services financiers inc.* c. *Services financiers Dundee*[71], la clause d'élection de for contenue au contrat prévoyait que le contrat serait administré et interprété en vertu des lois en vigueur en Ontario et que les parties se soumettaient irrévocablement à la compétence non-exclusive des tribunaux ontariens. La Cour supérieure indique :

> [48] Dans un premier temps, nous sommes d'opinion que nous n'avons pas à nous référer au droit ontarien pour interpréter la clause d'élection de for.
>
> [49] Que les parties aient choisi à l'article 14.16 de soumettre le contrat au droit ontarien et aux lois fédérales, c'est une chose; mais ceci ne signifie pas que l'interprétation de la clause d'élection de for lorsqu'un tribunal québécois doit statuer sur sa compétence ratione materiae doive se faire en vertu du droit ontarien [15].
>
> [51] Dans cet arrêt [Spar Aerospace] ainsi que dans GreCon et STM, la Cour suprême et la Cour d'appel ont statué sur la compétence du tribunal québécois en fonction de l'article 3148 C.c.Q.
>
> [52] À nulle part dans ces arrêts, l'on ne voit que nos tribunaux se sont inspirés du droit du Texas, de la Californie ou de l'Allemagne pour statuer sur la compétence *ratione materiae* de nos tribunaux.

Il n'y a pas, à notre connaissance, d'autre cause de jurisprudence ni de doctrine sur cette question précise. Il semble qu'il s'agisse principalement d'une question d'interprétation de la clause de juridiction adoptée par les parties. Généralement, les tribunaux en viennent à appliquer le droit québécois[72]. Il en est ainsi que les tribunaux québécois soient désignés ou non par la clause d'élection de for[73].

À quel titre le font-ils?

Il peut s'agir d'une question de qualification, laquelle est demandée, selon l'article 3078 C.c.Q.: « au système juridique du tribunal saisi[74] ».

On peut aussi penser qu'il s'agit d'une question de procédure, laquelle est également régie, selon l'article 3132 C.c.Q.: « par la loi du tribunal saisi[75] ».

De l'avis de l'une des co-auteures de ce texte exprimé dans un article écrit avec Édouard Onguene Onana, « la clause d'élection de for est incontestablement conventionnelle, mais – ou même si – son objet est purement procédural[76] ». S'il s'agit d'une question de fond, celle-ci est régie par la loi désignée expressément dans

---

[71] *Investia Services financiers inc.* c. *Services financiers Dundee inc.*, 2012 QCCS 4411 (CanLII), <http://canlii.ca/t/fssnc>, consulté le 2017-10-20, (version anglaise à http://canlii.ca/t/fvz18).

[72] *STMicroelectronics Inc.* c. *Matrox Graphics Inc.*, 2007 QCCA 1784, 2007 QCCA 1784 (CanLII), <http://canlii.ca/t/1v8b6>, consulté le 2017-10-18 (version anglaise à <http://canlii.ca/t/fqbbv>).

[73] Dans *eBay Canada Ltd.* c. *Mofo Moko*, 2013 QCCA 1912 (CanLII), <http://canlii.ca/t/g1sx6>, consulté le 2017-10-19, il s'agissait d'un contrat de consommation et la convention intervenue entre les parties contenait une clause d'élection de for rendant le droit de la province de l'Ontario applicable aux litiges entre les parties et déclarant la Californie comme étant la juridiction compétente.

[74] En anglais: art. 3078 C.c.Q.: « *Characterization is made according to the legal system of the court seized of the matter* [. . .].».

[75] En anglais: art. 3132 C.c.Q.: « *Procedure is governed by the law of the court seized of the matter* ».

[76] Guillemard et Édouard Onguene Onana (2007), pp. 676–677.

l'acte ou dont la désignation résulte d'une façon certaine des dispositions de cet acte (art. 3111, 1er al. C.c.Q.)[77]. En l'absence de désignation de la loi dans l'acte ou si la loi désignée rend l'acte juridique invalide, les tribunaux québécois appliquent la loi de l'État qui, compte tenu de la nature de l'acte et des circonstances qui l'entourent, présente les liens les plus étroits avec cet acte (art. 3112 C.c.Q.)[78]. Les liens les plus étroits sont présumés exister avec la loi de l'État dans lequel la partie qui doit fournir la prestation caractéristique de l'acte a sa résidence ou, si celui-ci est conclu dans le cours des activités d'une entreprise, son établissement (art. 3113 C.c.Q.)[79]. Le Code prévoit des règles spécifiques de rattachement pour les contrats les plus usuels (art. 3114 et s. C.c.Q.). Cependant, bien qu'il y ait des règles spécifiques pour la convention d'arbitrage qui désignent la loi applicable au contrat principal, ou, si cette loi a pour effet d'invalider la convention d'arbitrage, la loi de l'État où l'arbitrage se déroule (art. 3121 C.c.Q.)[80], il n'y en a pas pour l'élection de for.

Or, pour appliquer un droit étranger que ces règles pourraient désigner, encore faudrait-il qu'il soit allégué voire éventuellement prouvé. À défaut de quoi, le droit québécois une fois de plus s'appliquerait (art. 2809 C.c.Q.)[81].

Par analogie, il faut souligner une certaine controverse dans la jurisprudence et la doctrine au sujet de la règle de conflit applicable à la validité des clauses d'élection de for dans les contrats d'adhésion[82]. En effet, pour les uns, le droit québécois

---

[77] Précité, note 49.

[78] En anglais: art. 3112 C.c.Q.: *If no law is designated in the act or if the law designated invalidates the juridical act, the courts apply the law of the State with which the act is most closely connected in view of its nature and the attendant circumstances.*

[79] En anglais: art. 3113 C.c.Q.: *A juridical act is presumed to be most closely connected with the law of the State where the party who is to perform the prestation which is characteristic of the act has his residence or, if the act is concluded in the ordinary course of business of an enterprise, has his establishment.*

[80] En anglais: art. 3121 C.c.Q.: *In the absence of a designation by the parties, an arbitration agreement is governed by the law applicable to the principal contract or, where that law invalidates the agreement, by the law of the State where arbitration takes place.*

[81] Art. 2809 C.c.Q : Le tribunal peut prendre connaissance d'office du droit des autres provinces ou territoires du Canada et du droit d'un État étranger, pourvu qu'il ait été allégué. Il peut aussi demander que la preuve en soit faite, laquelle peut l'être, entre autres, par le témoignage d'un expert ou par la production d'un certificat établi par un jurisconsulte.

Lorsque ce droit n'a pas été allégué ou que sa teneur n'a pas été établie, il applique le droit en vigueur au Québec.

En anglais: art. 2809 C.c.Q.: *Judicial notice may be taken of the law of other provinces or territories of Canada and of that of a foreign state, provided it has been pleaded. The court may also require that proof be made of such law; this may be done, among other means, by expert testimony or by the production of a certificate drawn up by a jurisconsult.*

Where such law has not been pleaded or its content has not been established, the court applies the law in force in Québec.

[82] Un contrat d'adhésion est défini à l'article 1379 C.c.Q. Une clause d'un contrat d'adhésion peut être annulée si elle est externe au contrat et n'a pas été expressément portée à la connaissance de l'adhérent, à moins que l'autre partie ne prouve que l'adhérent en avait par ailleurs connaissance (art. 1435 C.c.Q.), si elle est illisible ou incompréhensible (en application de l'article 1436 C.c.Q.)

s'applique pour déterminer si une clause d'élection de for en faveur de tribunaux étrangers peut être annulée[83]. Dans quelques décisions, il est indiqué que cette question relève du tribunal qui a juridiction pour instruire l'affaire[84]. La clause d'élection de for doit en outre recevoir application même à l'égard d'une action demandant l'annulation de la convention dans laquelle cette clause est stipulée[85]. Pour sa part, la Cour d'appel a, en *obiter*, indiqué que cette question relève de la loi applicable au litige[86].

Pour l'une des des co-auteures de ce texte dans un article écrit avec Édouard Onguene Onana[87], c'est à tort que la Cour d'appel n'a pas voulu considérer que l'article 1437 C.c.Q. est, selon les termes de l'article 3076 C.c.Q., une règle de droit dont « l'application s'impose en raison de [son] but particulier ». Ainsi, quiconque serait adhérent et soumis à une clause de rattachement juridictionnel abusive serait

---

ou abusive (en application de l'article 1437 C.c.Q.). Il en est de même dans un contrat de consommation.

[83]Dans *HSBC Bank Canada* c. *Nytschyk*, 2002 CanLII 39572 (C.S.), <http://canlii.ca/t/1djk5>, consulté le 2017-10-18, la Banque poursuivait un résident ontarien devant les tribunaux québécois conformément à une clause d'élection de for qui se lisait comme suit : « This Guarantee shall be construed in accordance with the laws of the Province of ONTARIO and shall be deemed to have been made in such Province and to be performed there, and the Courts of such Province shall have jurisdiction over all disputes which may arise under this Guarantee [...] provided that nothing herein contained shall prevent the bank from proceeding at its election against the undersigned in the courts of any other province or country ».Il est possible d'arguer qu'en l'espèce en fait le droit québécois s'est appliqué pour déterminer si une clause d'élection de for en faveur des tribunaux québécois peut être annulée, ce qui est une question différente.

Cette décision est citée avec approbation par Goldstein et Groffier (2003), par 377, pp. 545–547. Ces derniers avancent que le droit québécois s'applique parce qu'il s'agit de déterminer le domaine ou les conditions d'application d'une règle de compétence juridictionnelle québécoise en tant que question préalable qui doit être régie par la loi applicable à la question principale (la procédure). Quoi qu'il en soit, l'ordre public permettrait à leur avis d'écarter toute loi étrangère qui donnerait effet à une clause abusive.

[84]*9163-2802 Québec inc.* c. *Pioneer Steel Pre-Fabricated Buildings Ltd.*, 2009 QCCS 1010 (CanLII), <http://canlii.ca/t/22sjh>, consulté le 2017-10-18; *Québec inc. (Pizzeria Stratos Nicolet)* c. *Société de prêt First Data Canada inc.*, 2006 QCCS 6480 (CanLII), <http://canlii.ca/t/1qk0w>, consulté le 2017-10-18; *2617-3138 Québec Inc.* c. *Rogers Cantel Inc.*, 1998 CanLII 11373 (C.S.), <http://canlii.ca/t/1kpd2>, consulté le 2017-10-18; *2736349 Canada Inc.* c. *Rogers Cantel Inc.*, 1998 CanLII 9527 (C.S.), <http://canlii.ca/t/1kdc2>, consulté le 2017-10-18. Voir, en matière de contrat de consommation et d'arbitrage: *Dell Computer Corp.* c. *Union des consommateurs*, 2007 CSC 34 à https://scc-csc.lexum.com/scc-csc/scc-csc/fr/item/2374/index.do (version anglaise à https://scc-csc.lexum.com/scc-csc/scc-csc/en/item/2374/index.do).

[85]*General Motors du Canada Ltée* c. *178018 Canada inc. (Laurier Pontiac Buick GMC Cadillac Hummer Ltée)*, 2011 QCCA 1461 (CanLII), <http://canlii.ca/t/fml2j>, consulté le 2017-10-18; *TCA Global Credit Master Fund* v. *8894132 Canada inc.*, 2017 QCCS 4146.

[86]*United European Bank and Trust Nassau Ltd.* c. *Duchesneau*, 2006 QCCA 652 (CanLII), <http://canlii.ca/t/1n773>, consulté le 2017-10-18; *Industries Caron (meubles) inc.* c. *Rich-Wood Kitchens Ltd.*, 2007 QCCS 5101 (CanLII), <http://canlii.ca/t/1tp9k>, consulté le 2017-10-18; *DSD International inc.* c. *DMG Canada Inc.*, 2006 QCCS 2388, 2006 QCCS 2388 (CanLII), <http://canlii.ca/t/1n6jv>, consulté le 2017-10-18.

[87]Guillemard et Édouard Onguene Onana (2007), p. 680.

assuré de l'ineffcacité de la clause. Ils estiment avec Me Stéphane Rochette que cette solution serait préférable[88].

3.2 *L'effet d'une clause d'élection de for facultative*

De façon générale, on peut observer que la jurisprudence est moins souvent saisie de litiges contestant une clause d'élection de for en faveur des tribunaux québécois, que de clauses en faveur de tribunaux étrangers qu'ils soient canadiens, américains, européens ou autres. À cet égard, en vertu de l'article 3077 C.c.Q., une province canadienne constitue une autorité étrangère[89].

Il y a lieu de croire que, comme son nom l'indique, la clause facultative peut être utilisée ou non.

3.2.1 En présence d'une clause d'élection de for facultative en faveur des tribunaux québécois

Si le demandeur saisit le tribunal québécois compétent sur la base d'une clause d'élection de for facultative en sa faveur, ce dernier respectera généralement le choix du demandeur. Il n'y a pas règle écrite mais cela fait partie des règles de « courtoisie » implicites envers le demandeur. D'ailleurs, on voit mal ce qui inciterait le tribunal québécois à ne pas exercer sa compétence puisque la clause la lui attribue.

La solution pour le défendeur afin de tenter d'échapper dans ce cas à la saisine du tribunal québécois est d'invoquer le *forum non conveniens*. En effet, un tribunal québécois peut exceptionnellement se dessaisir à la demande d'une partie s'il estime que les autorités d'un autre État sont mieux à même de trancher le litige (art. 3135 C. c.Q.)[90].

---

[88]Guillemard et Édouard Onguene Onana (2007), p. 678; Rochette (2006).

[89]En anglais: art. 3077 C.c.Q. « *Where a State comprises several territorial units having different legislative jurisdictions, each territorial unit is regarded as a State.* [...] ».

[90]Art. 3135 C.c.Q : Bien qu'elle soit compétente pour connaître d'un litige, une autorité du Québec peut, exceptionnellement et à la demande d'une partie, décliner cette compétence si elle estime que les autorités d'un autre État sont mieux à même de trancher le litige.

Art. 3135 C.c.Q.: *Even though a Québec authority has jurisdiction to hear a dispute, it may, exceptionally and on an application by a party, decline jurisdiction if it considers that the authorities of another State are in a better position to decide the dispute.*

Voir pour des affaires où le *forum non conveniens* a été accueilli en présence d'une clause d'élection de for : *Sony Music Canada Inc.* c. *Kardiak Productions Inc*, 1997 CanLII 10719 (C.A.) à <http://canlii.ca/t/1nffl>, consulté le 2017-10-18; *Birdsall inc.* c. *In Any Events Inc.*, 1999 CanLII 13874 (C.A.). À noter que dans cette dernière affaire, le *forum non conveniens* est accueilli, dans un contexte particulier, non pas à l'égard de l'action principale, pour laquelle une clause d'élection de for attribue compétence aux tribunaux québécois, mais bien à l'égard d'un recours en garantie incident. Pour des affaires où le *forum non conveniens* a été rejeté : *Meubles D & F ltée* c. *Baby*

Cependant, à notre avis, il n'aura que peu de chances succès. En effet, le droit québécois, au moins le *Code civil du Québec*, ne connaît pas vraiment les clauses facultatives. D'ailleurs, pour ne citer que lui, l'article 3148 *in fine* C.c.Q. retire compétence aux tribunaux québécois lorsque les parties ont attribué conventionnellement compétence à un tribunal étranger. Nous voyons mal comment la question de deux clauses, facultatives, l'une en faveur du tribunal québécois, l'autre en faveur d'un tribunal étranger, pourrait être résolue par le *Code civil du Québec*.

Le fait que des parties choisissent de donner compétence au tribunal québécois puis qu'une fois ce dernier saisi, l'une d'entre elles fasse en quelque sorte machine arrière heurte la logique. Pourtant, le cas s'est présenté, de façon plus ou moins limpide, en raison de la présence de plusieurs contrats, indiscutablement liés, comportant chacun une clause d'élection de for en faveur de fors différents, dans le dossier *Kardiak*.

Ainsi, Kardiak Productions inc. avait signé avec Kathleen Sergerie (une artiste connue au Québec sous le nom de Kathleen) un contrat de gérance. Ce contrat prévoyait dans ses dispositions générales une clause d'élection de for en faveur des tribunaux ontariens et, dans une disposition particulière modifiant une autre clause, (peut-être s'agissait-il d'une erreur de référence) une clause d'élection de for en faveur des tribunaux québécois. Selon la Cour d'appel, le contrat laissait transparaître l'intention des parties de confier aux tribunaux québécois les litiges relatifs à l'interprétation et à l'application de ce contrat. Un contrat d'enregistrement avait ensuite été conclu entre Kardiak et Sony Music Canada inc. engageant les services de Kathleen. Ce contrat contenait une clause d'élection de for accordant compétence aux tribunaux ontariens pour régler tout litige découlant du contrat. Poursuivie au Québec en dommages-intérêts par Kardiak, Kathleen a obtenu le renvoi de l'action devant les tribunaux ontariens mieux à même de trancher le litige en vertu de l'article 3135 C.c.Q.[91].

L'effet juridique d'une clause d'élection de for facultative en faveur du for ne change pas une fois que le choix a été exercé par le déclenchement de la procédure devant ce tribunal, mais en pratique, il est possible que la saisine du tribunal permette de soulever la litispendance (art. 3137 C.c.Q.)[92].

Furniture Warehouse Store Inc., 2006 QCCS 5438 (CanLII), <http://canlii.ca/t/1qcct>, consulté le 2017-10-19; *Les Entreprises Exulon Inc.* c. *1220103 Ontario Limited*, [1998] n° AZ-98036269, B.E. 98 BE-627 (C.Q.).

[91]Sabourin (2007).

[92]Art. 3137 C.c.Q.: L'autorité québécoise, à la demande d'une partie, peut, quand une action est introduite devant elle, surseoir à statuer si une autre action entre les mêmes parties, fondée sur les mêmes faits et ayant le même objet, est déjà pendante devant une autorité étrangère, pourvu qu'elle puisse donner lieu à une décision pouvant être reconnue au Québec, ou si une telle décision a déjà été rendue par une autorité étrangère.

Art. 3137 C.c.Q : *On the application of a party, a Québec authority may stay its ruling on an action brought before it if another action, between the same parties, based on the same facts and having the same subject is pending before a foreign authority, provided that the latter action can*

3.2.2 Le demandeur saisit le tribunal québécois non désigné dans la clause d'élection de for facultative

La clause facultative en faveur des tribunaux du for, d'une part, et en faveur des tribunaux étrangers, de l'autre, est traitée de manière cohérente, mais il n'en a pas toujours été ainsi.

En droit québécois, une clause d'élection de for en faveur d'un tribunal étranger entraîne une dénégation de compétence du tribunal québécois. Cela signifie que la clause d'élection de for fait perdre sa compétence au tribunal québécois, comme l'exprime l'article 3148 C.c.Q. *in fine* :

> Dans les actions à caractères patrimoniales [. . .], les autorités québécoises ne sont pas compétentes lorsque les parties ont choisi, par convention, de soumettre les litiges nés ou à naître entre elles, à propos d'un rapport juridique déterminé, à une autorité étrangère [. . .].

Il y a lieu d'estimer que si le demandeur saisit le tribunal québécois non désigné dans la clause d'élection de for même facultative, en raison de l'article 3148 C.c.Q. *in fine*, le tribunal québécois devrait rejeter l'action pour cause d'incompétence. Raisonner autrement anéantirait l'efficacité des clauses d'élection de for. Or il est indéniable que l'ordre juridique québécois admet l'attribution de compétence reposant sur la volonté des parties si la clause est, selon la terminologie de Trevor Hartley et Masato Dogauchi « avec restriction ». Cependant, dans certaines situations, le défendeur, malgré une élection de for en faveur d'autorités étrangères, reconnaît par ses actes la compétence des autorités québécoises. Celles-ci seront alors valablement saisies du litige (art. 3148 *in fine* C.c.Q.)[93].

Malgré tout, en présence d'une clause d'élection de for facultative en faveur des tribunaux étrangers, les tribunaux québécois ont conservé leur compétence puisque seule une élection de for exclusive en faveur d'un for étranger les oblige à se dessaisir[94].

---

result in a decision which may be recognized in Québec, or if such a decision has already been rendered by a foreign authority.

[93]Voir à ce sujet : *M.F.I. Export Finance Inc.* c. *Rother International S.A. de C.V. Inc.*, 2004 CanLII 16200 (C.S.), par. 82 (en anglais) à <http://canlii.ca/t/1gv7b> consulté le 2017-10-18 où la demande pour prolongation du délai d'inscription, l'échéancier convenu entre les parties — dans lequel les défendeurs indiquent expressément leur intention de contester au fond l'action de la demanderesse — et la demande de transfert du dossier dans un autre district — dans laquelle les défendeurs allèguent que le seul tribunal compétent est la Cour supérieure de ce district — constituent, parce qu'ils ont été produits avant l'exception déclinatoire, une soumission claire des défendeurs à la compétence des tribunaux québécois. La Cour souligne de plus que cinq mois se sont écoulés entre la saisie avant jugement pratiquée par les demandeurs, laquelle fut contestée par les défendeurs, et l'exception déclinatoire.

Voir également : *JS finance Canada inc.* c. *JS Holding SA*, 1999 CanLII 13870 (QC CA), <http://canlii.ca/t/1n8wq>, consulté le 2017-10-19 et *Osmos Canada inc.* c. *Grgas Associates Ltd*, 2013 QCCQ 10945 (CanLII), <http://canlii.ca/t/g0pkc>, consulté le 2017-10-20.

[94]Voir à ce sujet *: Eagle River International Ltd (Faillite de)*, 1999 CanLII 11910 (CS), <http://canlii.ca/t/1krhm>, consulté le 2017-10-18; confirmé par: 2000 CanLII 9546 (CA), <http://canlii.ca/t/1f8lw>, consulté le 2017-10-18. La Cour suprême du Canada a rejeté le pourvoi sans se

Dans *Investia Services financiers inc.* c. *Services financiers Dundee*[95], la Cour supérieure indique :

> [66] Poser la question, c'est y répondre : la compétence du tribunal ontarien n'est pas exclusive.
>
> [67] D'ailleurs, l'avocat des défenderesses reconnaît qu'au 29 juin 2011, les demanderesses pouvaient s'adresser à la Cour supérieure du Québec; toutefois, l'argument des défenderesses veut que du moment où les entités Dundee ont saisi le tribunal ontarien du litige, même postérieurement, le tribunal québécois perd sa compétence.
>
> [68] La Cour supérieure est compétente ou ne l'est pas du tout; si elle l'était au 29 juin, il est illogique qu'elle ne le soit plus deux mois plus tard suite au dépôt de la requête pour jugement déclaratoire en Ontario.
>
> [69] Le tribunal partage l'affirmation de l'avocat des demanderesses : la compétence d'un tribunal québécois ne peut être soumise à une condition résolutoire du seul fait du dépôt d'une procédure de façon subséquente par l'autre partie au contrat.

De façon unanime, les tribunaux estiment que pour donner compétence, autrement dit pour avoir une valeur contraignante, la clause doit être incontournable, impérative et. . .exclusive.

Et, alors que le *Code civil du Québec* ne prévoit aucun « attribut » à la clause d'élection de for, la jurisprudence en ajoute. Ainsi, la Cour suprême du Canada impose que les clauses d'élection de for, comme les clauses d'arbitrage, aient « [...] un caractère impératif et [confèrent] [. . .] une compétence exclusive de manière claire et précise [...][96] ».

---

prononcer explicitement sur la clause d'« attornment »: *Sam Lévy & Associés c. Azco Mining inc.*, 2001 CSC 92 à https://scc-csc.lexum.com/scc-csc/scc-csc/fr/item/1934/index.do (version anglaise à https://scc-csc.lexum.com/scc-csc/scc-csc/en/item/1934/index.do). Voir également: *Groupe Germain inc.* c. *Moneris Solutions Corp.* (C.S., 2014-07-24), 2014 QCCS 4058, SOQUIJ AZ-51102978, 2014EXP-2845, J.E. 2014-1623, requêtes pour permission d'appeler et pour suspendre l'exécution du jugement accueillies (C.A., 2014-10-16), 200-09-008698-141, 2014 QCCA 1901, SOQUIJ AZ-51115616. Désistement d'appel (C.A., 2014-04-10), 500-10-005587-140; *STMicroelectronics Inc.* c. *Matrox Graphics Inc.*, 2007 QCCA 1784, 2007 QCCA 1784 (CanLII), <http://canlii.ca/t/1v8b6>, consulté le 2017-10-18 (version anglaise à <http://canlii.ca/t/fqbbv>); *M.F.I. Export Finance Inc.* c. *Rother International S.A. de C.V. Inc.*, 2004 CanLII 16200 (C.S.), (en anglais) à <http://canlii.ca/t/1gv7b> consulté le 2017-10-18; *Intergaz inc.* c. *Atlas Copco Canada inc.*, 1997 CanLII 9248 (C.S.), <http://canlii.ca/t/1kn44>, consulté le 2017-10-18; *Lemieux, Nolet* c. *Marcus Evans (Amérique du Nord) ltée*, 2008 QCCQ 1235 (CanLII), <http://canlii.ca/t/1w121>, consulté le 2017-10-19. En l'espèce, la clause d'élection de for était ainsi libellée: « [. . .] *the parties submit to the exclusive jurisdiction of the Cook County Courts in Illinois. However Marcus Evans only is entitled to waive this right and submit to the jurisdiction of the courts in which the Client's office is located*». Les deux parties avaient des établissements au Québec et l'action était intentée par Marcus Evans.

[95] *Investia Services financiers inc.* c. *Services financiers Dundee inc.*, 2012 QCCS 4411 (CanLII), <http://canlii.ca/t/fssnc>, consulté le 2017-10-20, (version anglaise à http://canlii.ca/t/fvz18).

[96] *GreCon Dimter inc.* c. *J.R. Normand inc.*, 2005 CSC 46, par. 27 à https://scc-csc.lexum.com/scc-csc/scc-csc/fr/item/2279/index.do, (en anglais à https://scc-csc.lexum.com/scc-csc/scc-csc/en/item/2279/index.do).

Si une exception déclinatoire est soulevée devant le tribunal québécois en raison d'une clause d'élection de for en faveur d'un tribunal étranger, de deux choses l'une : ou bien le tribunal québécois ne donnera pas effet à la clause d'élection de for pour cause d'invalidité, par exemple, et l'exception déclinatoire sera rejetée, le tribunal québécois restant alors saisi du dossier ; ou bien le tribunal québécois reconnaîtra la clause d'élection de for et se déclarera incompétent. Il rejettera alors l'action (art. 3148 al. 2 C.c.Q.).

Aucune possibilité de *suspension* dans de tels cas.

Si le tribunal étranger avait été saisi avant le tribunal québécois, il faut croire que ce dernier peut surseoir à statuer pour cause de litispendance (art. 3137 C.c.Q.). Les tribunaux québécois ne suspendent des procédures que dans peu de cas. Sur les questions de compétence, en dehors de la litispendance qui permet au tribunal de surseoir à statuer, soit les tribunaux rejettent le moyen déclinatoire, et l'instance se poursuit, soit ils acceptent le moyen. Dans ce cas, ils rejettent l'action pour cause de leur propre incompétence.

On peut imaginer qu'une clause d'élection de for facultative en faveur d'un tribunal étranger soit l'un des éléments que le tribunal québécois, compétent sur un autre chef, examine pour se déclarer *forum non conveniens*. L'article 3135 C.c.Q. lui permet en effet de décliner sa compétence au profit d'un autre tribunal, également compétent (ici, en vertu de la clause d'élection de for facultative) s'il considère que ce tribunal est mieux placé que lui pour connaître du litige. Dans cette évaluation, le juge tiendra compte de divers éléments, toujours repris par la jurisprudence à l'identique : « le lieu de résidence des parties et de leurs témoins ; la situation des éléments de preuve ; le lieu de formation et d'exécution du contrat ; la situation des biens du défendeur; la loi applicable au litige ; l'avantage dont jouit le demandeur dans la juridiction choisie ; l'intérêt des deux parties ; la nécessité d'une procédure d'exemplification à l'étranger ; et l'intérêt de la justice[97] ». Permettons-nous d'insister, l'article 3135 C.c.Q., donc le *forum non conveniens*, ne pourra être appliqué que si le tribunal québécois est compétent, quel que soit le fondement de la compétence.

Ajoutons que si la clause d'élection de for n'est pas facultative mais obligatoire, celui qui la viole engage théoriquement sa responsabilité contractuelle. L'exécution en nature semble incongrue ici. L'exécution par équivalent n'est pas plus adaptée car comment évaluer les dommages ? Et surtout sont-ils assez importants pour saisir la justice (*de minimis non curat praetor*) ? On peut en douter.

La question se pose à peine dans la mesure où la clause est facultative. L'adjectif implique que la clause ne peut avoir un effet contraignant et que, par conséquent, saisir le tribunal désigné est une possibilité comme est alors possible d'en saisir un autre, sans conséquence négative à cet égard.

Une injonction anti-poursuite ne peut être accordée pour empêcher le déclenchement ou la poursuite d'une procédure devant un tribunal étranger si les parties ont désigné le tribunal du for dans une clause d'élection de for facultative

[97] *Province du Nouveau-Brunswick* c. *Les Produits métalliques AT inc.*, 2017 QCCA 453, par. 16.

(art. 513 C.p.c.)[98]. Une injonction anti-exécution ne peut pas non plus être accordée pour restreindre une demande d'exécution d'un jugement rendu par un tribunal autre que celui désigné dans une clause d'élection de for facultative. Il nous semble, ici aussi, que ce n'est pas la bonne voie procédurale. Pour exécuter au Québec un jugement rendu « à l'étranger », il faut passer par les articles 3155 C.c.Q. et suivants. La partie qui estime que le tribunal qui a rendu la décision dont on demande l'exécution (au Québec) n'était pas compétent en raison d'une clause d'élection de for en faveur d'une autre juridiction doit invoquer l'article 3155 par 1 C.c.Q. puis démontrer que la clause d'élection de for ne désignait pas le dit tribunal (art. 3168 par 5 C.c.Q.) et que le défendeur – en l'occurrence elle, il faut croire – n'a pas reconnu sa compétence (art. 3168 par 6 C.c.Q.).

3.2.3 La reconnaissance et de l'exécution d'une décision étrangère rendue en contravention d'une clause d'élection de for facultative

Au stade de la procédure de la reconnaissance et de l'exécution d'une décision étrangère, en vertu des règles de droit international privé québécois, l'un des éléments que doit vérifier le tribunal québécois requis est la compétence du tribunal étranger. Or, en vertu de l'article 3168 par 5 C.c.Q., si l'action a été intentée devant un tribunal désigné dans une clause d'élection de for, la décision du tribunal saisi pourra être reconnue par un tribunal québécois.

Une fois de plus, les termes du code ne font aucune distinction entre clause d'élection de for obligatoire et clause d'élection de for facultative, en particulier à l'article 3168 C.c.Q.

Qu'en est-il si l'action a été intentée devant un tribunal autre que celui désigné dans une clause d'élection de for. Il faut supposer que le défendeur à l'étranger avait contesté la compétence du tribunal sur la base de la clause d'élection de for, et qu'il avait perdu. Il peut également n'avoir pas contesté la compétence du tribunal devant lequel il a été attrait malgré la clause d'élection de for, que le jugement ait été rendu par défaut et que le défendeur étranger invoque cette incompétence au stade de la reconnaissance. Pour que le jugement soit reconnu, il faudrait qu'un autre chef de compétence prévu à l'article 3168 C.c.Q. soit présent.

[98]Art. 513 C.p.c. : « Une injonction ne peut en aucun cas être prononcée pour empêcher des procédures judiciaires, [. . .] ».

En anglais : art. 513 C.c.p. « An injunction cannot be granted to restrain judicial proceedings ». Pour ce qui est des injonctions anti-poursuite, Prujiner et Piché (2018).

3.3 Traitement de la clause d'élection de for en droit international privé canadien ainsi qu'en droit interne

Le Québec est l'une des dix provinces du Canada. Comme l'a rappelé récemment la Cour suprême du Canada, « [l]es règles de droit international privé varient d'une province à l'autre[99] ». Le droit international privé relatif aux clauses d'élection de for n'est pas identique dans les provinces de common law et au Québec, seule province de droit civil.

Pour l'une des co-auteures de ce texte,

> Les tribunaux de common law accordent peu, voire très peu, d'importance à la clause d'élection de for, du moins à celle qui a pour effet de retirer sa compétence au tribunal canadien.
>
> [. . .]
>
> Dans les juridictions de common law, la clause d'élection de for est donc nettement moins efficace qu'au Québec, par exemple. Ici, se fondant sur le Code civil du Québec, les magistrats commencent par se demander s'ils ont compétence : si la clause la leur attribue, la réponse est affirmative et exceptionnellement, ils pourront s'en dessaisir. Si la clause ne proroge pas compétence en leur faveur, ils se déclareront non compétents, quitte à appliquer la règle du forum de nécessité, prévue par l'article 3136 C.c.Q. Au Canada anglais, le raisonnement est moins systématique et la clause d'élection de for n'est que l'un des éléments, parmi d'autres, que le juge évaluera pour déterminer s'il a compétence. Le seul exercice par les parties de leur volonté n'est pas suffisant en soi pour lier le tribunal[100].

Rappelons qu'en vertu de l'article 3077 C.c.Q., une autre province canadienne constitue une entité étrangère, au même titre qu'un État étranger *stricto sensu*. Une clause d'élection de for envers un tribunal d'une autre province canadienne a le même traitement de la part des tribunaux qu'une clause d'élection de for envers un tribunal non canadien.

Pour traiter d'une question proche, mentionnons que dorénavant les parties peuvent convenir d'une clause d'élection de for dans les relations purement internes (intra québécoises).

L'article 41 C.p.c. constitue une nouveauté au Québec, introduite par le *Code de procédure civile* entré en vigueur le 1er janvier 2016. Son dernier alinéa permet en effet aux parties, dans une relation purement québécoise, de désigner conventionnellement le tribunal compétent.

Deux conditions à cela :

> - l'ordre public doit le permettre. L'article 41 C.p.c. dans son ensemble traite de la compétence territoriale en première instance, sans se limiter à une sphère particulière du droit. Il couvre donc toutes les situations, familiales, personnelles, à caractère patrimonial ou non. Pour le moment, aucune cause de jurisprudence ne porte sur une clause d'élection de for

---

[99] *Lapointe Rosenstein March and Melançon S.E.N.C.R.L.* c. *Cassels Brock & Blackwell* LLP, [2016] 1 RCS 851, par.33.

[100] Guillemard (2004), p. 34. Voir en outre dans le présent volume Saumier, « Choice of Court Agreements in Common Law Canada ».

interne, ce qui laisse penser que ce n'est pas pratique courante, peut-être en raison de son utilité discutable.

On voit mal des raisons d'ordre public s'opposant à la désignation d'un tribunal autre que celui du domicile car en l'occurrence, les parties ne risquent pas d'échapper ainsi à l'application de la loi québécoise ; il n'y a pas non plus d'éventuelles difficultés – recherchées par une partie – de reconnaissance ou d'exécution, etc…

- la clause d'élection de for ne doit pas être contenue dans un contrat d'adhésion. Il n'y a aucun doute sur cette question, étant donné les termes du Code. Cela différencie la question du traitement du même sujet en présence d'un élément d'extranéité.

Donc, on note une opposition sur cette question en matière interne et en matière internationale puisque, dans ce cas-ci, « le législateur n'a pas voulu, dans les règles de droit international privé, rendre inopposable aux parties une pareille clause d'élection de for parce qu'elle est d'adhésion[101] ».

En matière interne, peu importe le caractère abusif ou non de la clause, le seul fait qu'elle soit incluse dans un contrat d'adhésion suffit à l'invalider.

3.4 Clauses D'élection De For Asymétriques

En général, on désigne comme asymétrique une clause qui ne confère pas les mêmes droits à chaque partie. Il pourrait en être ainsi d'une clause d'élection de for qui combine les aspects exclusifs et facultatifs.

En droit québécois, l'expression clause d'élection de for asymétrique désigne plutôt une clause qui désigne des tribunaux différents selon que l'une ou l'autre des parties est demanderesse. Par exemple, rappelons le dossier *Alimport*[102]. Un contrat de vente de pommes de terre de semence contenait une clause stipulant qu'en cas de différend, si la défenderesse était le vendeur, les parties s'en remettaient aux tribunaux de Montréal. Dans le cas contraire, si la défenderesse était l'acheteur, les parties s'engageaient à soumettre le différend aux tribunaux de la ville de La Havane. En présence d'une telle clause d'élection de for facultative en faveur des tribunaux québécois, ceux-ci se sont estimés compétents. Dans cette affaire, l'acheteur, dont le siège social était à La Havane, à Cuba, avait intenté une action en Cour supérieure à Montréal contre le vendeur, dont le siège social était à Grand Falls, Nouveau-Brunswick, pour mauvaise exécution du contrat.

---

[101] *United European Bank and Trust Nassau Ltd.* c. *Duchesneau*, 2006 QCCA 652 (CanLII), <http://canlii.ca/t/1n773>, consulté le 2017-10-18, par. 49.

[102] *Alimport (Empresa Cubana Importadora de Alimentos)* c. *Victoria Transport Ltd.*, [1977] 2 R.C.S. 858 à https://scc-csc.lexum.com/scc-csc/scc-csc/fr/item/5882/index.do (version anglaise à https://scc-csc.lexum.com/scc-csc/scc-csc/en/item/5882/index.do).

Dans *Federal Corporation* c. *Triangle Tires Inc.*[103], la convention prévoyait une élection de for à Taïwan, si Triangle ou Kebek était la partie demanderesse et au Québec, si Federal était la partie demanderesse. Puisque Federal était poursuivi par Triangle, les tribunaux québécois ont estimé qu'ils n'étaient pas compétents.

Un autre exemple d'asymétrie juridictionnelle est fourni par *Duchesneau*[104]. Dans ce cas, la clause réserve à une banque le choix unilatéral de prendre action devant le tribunal de son choix partout dans le monde, alors qu'elle ne permet à son client canadien que de poursuivre aux Bahamas. En l'espèce, si l'on peut qualifier la clause d'asymétrique, elle ne présente pas, à notre avis, de caractère facultatif pour le client de la banque. Celui-ci poursuit cette dernière en dommages-intérêts devant la Cour supérieure du Québec. La banque rétorque en plaidant l'incompétence du tribunal québécois en raison de la clause d'élection de for. La question qui se posait était de savoir si la clause est abusive, non pas parce qu'elle est « asymétrique » mais bien parce qu'elle oblige le demandeur Duchesneau, le client de la banque, à poursuivre aux Bahamas et non au Québec. Le juge de première instance donne tort à la banque, « au motif que les clauses d'élection de for en cause, parties d'un contrat d'adhésion, sont abusives et exorbitantes[105] ».

Selon la Cour d'appel, cette clause asymétrique n'est pas abusive et elle n'est par conséquent pas invalidée par la Cour d'appel. Au contraire dans *HSBC Bank Canada c. Mike Nytschyk*[106], la Cour supérieure a accueilli l'exception déclinatoire de la caution domiciliée en Ontario et rejeté l'action intentée par l'institution financière, en considérant que la dernière partie de la clause d'élection de for en cause dans cette affaire était inapplicable, parce qu'elle a été abusive et exorbitante. Par cette clause, la banque s'était réservé le choix unilatéral de poursuivre la caution devant les tribunaux de la province ou du pays de son choix.

Il ne semble y avoir aucune différence entre une clause asymétrique et une clause qui serait uniquement facultative.

L'effet d'une telle clause ne dépend pas de ce que le choix a été exercé ou non. La seule incidence pourrait être la litispendance, codifiée à l'article 3137 C.c.Q. En vertu de cet article, si une clause asymétrique donnait compétence à un tribunal québécois ou à un tribunal étranger et que ce dernier ait été saisi en premier, le tribunal québécois saisi en second pourrait surseoir à statuer. À noter que le vocabulaire utilisé dans cet article laisse un pouvoir discrétionnaire au tribunal québécois saisi en second. Par conséquent, le tribunal ne sera pas obligé de surseoir et pourra préférer statuer.

---

[103] *Federal Corporation* c. *Triangle Tires Inc.*, 2012 QCCA 434 (CanLII), <http://canlii.ca/t/fqgl0>, consulté le 2017-10-25, par.17.

[104] *United European Bank and Trust Nassau Ltd.* c. *Duchesneau*, 2006 QCCA 652 (CanLII), <http://canlii.ca/t/1n773>, consulté le 2017-10-18.

[105] *United European Bank and Trust Nassau Ltd.* c. *Duchesneau*, 2006 QCCA 652 (CanLII), <http://canlii.ca/t/1n773>, consulté le 2017-10-18, par. 20.

[106] *HSBC Bank Canada* c. *Nytschyk*, [2002] J.Q. n° 23 (QL) (C.S.).

L'effet d'une clause d'élection de for asymétrique ne dépend pas de ce que la partie en faveur de laquelle l'accord a été rédigé est, ou est présumée, la partie plus forte à la transaction. Comme toute clause contractuelle, si la clause pose un problème d'interprétation, les tribunaux rechercheront en premier la volonté des parties à cet égard. Au besoin, si aucune interprétation claire ne se dégage, la clause sera lue *contra proferentem* (art. 1432 C.c.Q.). Donc, la clause sera interprétée en faveur de la partie qui ne l'a pas rédigée. Si le contrat est un contrat d'adhésion ou de consommation, à plus forte raison, la règle est identique.

La question de l'interprétation a été au cœur du différend opposant Le Groupe Germain et Moneris Solution[107]. Le Groupe Germain a été amené à signer des contrats « ayant des objets similaires, l'un portant sur les cartes de crédit et l'autre sur les cartes de débit et accès aux terminaux Moneris » mais dont la « formulation n'est pas identique » en termes de compétence des tribunaux. Celui relatif aux cartes de crédit comportait, contrairement à l'autre, « une phrase supplémentaire [faisant] référence à une compétence non-exclusive des tribunaux de la province de l'Ontario ». L'autre contrat ne comportait pas l'adjectif « non-exclusive », au contraire. Il faut noter que les deux contrats étaient des contrats d'adhésion, imposés au Groupe Germain.

La Cour supérieure explique : « Un des principes de base lorsqu'il y a lieu d'analyser la teneur d'une clause d'élection de for est la présence ou non d'une ambigüité dans sa formulation » (para 21). Elle poursuit :

> Le droit est bien établi en ce qui concerne un contrat d'adhésion dont une clause est ambiguë. Ainsi, l'article 1432 du Code civil du Québec énonce que :
>
> Dans le doute, le contrat s'interprète en faveur de celui qui a contracté l'obligation et contre celui qui l'a stipulée. Dans tous les cas, il s'interprète en faveur de l'adhérent ou du consommateur. (par. 25).

4 Conclusion

L'une des co-auteures de ce texte écrivait avec Édouard Onguene Onana :

> Nous avons pu constater que les raisonnements proposés par les juges ne sont pas toujours satisfaisants ni efficaces. C'est pour cette raison que nous proposons, au moins au législateur québécois, quelques solutions. L'adhésion à la Convention de La Haye sur les accords d'élection de for, bien que ce texte comporte un certain nombre de défauts, permettrait certainement d'aplanir plusieurs des difficultés que nous avons relevées. À défaut d'adhérer au texte international, le législateur québécois pourrait s'en inspirer pour ajouter quelques dispositions au livre X du Code civil, la première étant, à notre avis, de reconnaître expressément au juge saisi le pouvoir de statuer sur la validité de la clause d'élection de for. À cela pourrait s'ajouter un article portant sur la loi applicable à ladite clause, de préférence celle du for. En attendant, nous avons trouvé dans le droit québécois une autre

[107] *Groupe Germain inc.* c. *Moneris Solutions Corporation*, 2014 QCCS 4058 (CanLII), <http://canlii.ca/t/g8r5p>, consulté le 2017-10-25.

piste, déjà existante, mais que la Cour d'appel n'a pas voulu exploiter : considérer que l'article 1437 C.c.Q. est, selon les termes de l'article 3076 C.c.Q., une règle de droit dont « l'application s'impose en raison de [son] but particulier ». Ainsi, quiconque serait adhérent et soumis à une clause de rattachement juridictionnel abusive serait assuré de l'inefficacité de la clause[108].

Ces auteurs recommandaient au législateur québécois de préciser que « l'autorité saisie, qu'il s'agisse de l'autorité désignée ou non, est compétente pour se prononcer sur la clause de rattachement juridictionnel[109] ». Une autre option, qu'ils privilégiaient « en raison de sa simplicité, serait de prévoir que la clause d'élection de for est régie par le droit (interne) du tribunal saisi[110] ».

Références

Ancel B, Lequette Y (2001) Grands arrêts de la jurisprudence française de droit international privé, 4e éd. Dalloz, Paris

Emanuelli C (2011) Droit international privé québécois, 3e éd. éd. Wilson & Lafleur, Montréal

Gaudemet-Tallon H (1981) Compte rendu de l'ouvrage de Kaufmann-Kohler, G, La clause d'élection de for dans les contrats internationaux. JDI : 439–440

Glenn HP (1991) La guerre de l'amiante, R.c.d.i.p 80:41–60

Glenn HP (1993) Droit international privé. Dans : Textes réunis par le Barreau du Québec et la Chambre des notaires du Québec, La réforme du Code civil, Priorités et hypothèques, preuve et prescription, publicité des droits, droit international privé, dispositions transitoires, tome 3. Éd. Presses de l'Université Laval, Sainte-Foy, Qué., pp 669–800

Goldstein G, Groffier E (2003) Droit international privé, Règles spécifiques, tome 2. Éditions Yvon Blais, Cowansville

Groffier E (1993) La réforme du droit international privé québécois : supplément au Précis de droit international privé québécois. Éditions Yvon Blais, Cowansville

Guez P (2000) L'élection de for en droit international privé, Thèse de doctorat, Université Paris X, 18 janvier 2000, en ligne à http://www.glose.org/th004-htm.htm#_ftn946. Consulté le 27 octobre 2017

Guillemard S (2004) Liberté contractuelle et rattachement juridictionnel : le droit québécois face aux droits français et européen. E.J.C.L. 8.2 : 1-63, en ligne à https://www.ejcl.org//82/abs82-1.html. Consulté le 19 octobre 2017

Guillemard S (2006) Le droit international privé face au contrat de vente cyberspatial. Éditions Yvon Blais, Cowansville

Guillemard S, Édouard Onguene Onana D (2007) Le contrat d'adhésion : actualités et droit international privé, Les Cahiers de droit 48:635–680, à https://retro.erudit.org/revue/cd/2007/v48/n4/043948ar.pdf

Hartley T, Dogauchi M (2005) Rapport explicatif de la Convention sur les accords d'élection de for conclue à La Haye le 30 juin 2005

Kessedjian C (1997) Conférence de La Haye de droit international privé, Compétence juridictionnelle internationale et effets des jugements étrangers en matière civile et commerciale,

[108]Guillemard et Édouard Onguene Onana (2007), p. 680.

[109]Guillemard et Édouard Onguene Onana (2007), p. 676.

[110]Guillemard et Édouard Onguene Onana (2007), p. 676.

Document préliminaire no 7, avril 1997, en ligne à. https://assets.hcch.net/docs/a41b52c3-20f0-4478-9532-14240382d145.pdf. Consulté le 28 novembre 2018

Ministère de la Justice (1993) Commentaires du ministre de la Justice, Le Code civil du Québec : Un mouvement de société, tome II, Publications du Québec, Québec

Prujiner A, Piché C (2018) L'injonction anti-poursuite dans la procédure d'arbitrage et juridictionnelle au XXe Congrès de l'Académie internationale de droit comparé, Fukuoka, Japon, 22 au 28 juillet 2018, à paraître

Rochette S (2006) Commentaire sur la décision United European Bank and Trust Nassau Ltd. c. Duchesneau — Le tribunal québécois doit il examiner le caractère abusif d'une clause d'élection de for incluse dans un contrat d'adhésion?. Dans Repères, EYB 2006REP504, septembre 2006

Sabourin F (2007) Convention sur les accords d'élection de for de La Haye et le droit du Québec 2007, Conférence pour l'harmonisation des lois au Canada, en ligne à. http://www.ulcc.ca/fr/reunions-annuelles/217-2007-charlottetown-pe-reunions-annuelles/documents-de-la-section-civile-2007/569-convention-sur-les-accords-delection-de-for-de-la-haye-et-le-droit-du-quebec-2007. Consulté le 25 octobre 2017

Talpis JA (1993) Choice of law and forum selection clauses under the New Civil Code of Quebec. Revue du Notariat 96:183–227

Talpis JA, Castel J-G (1993) Le Code Civil du Québec : Interprétation des règles du droit international privé. Dans : Textes réunis par le Barreau du Québec et la Chambre des notaires du Québec, La réforme du Code civil, Priorités et hypothèques, preuve et prescription, publicité des droits, droit international privé, dispositions transitoires, tome 3. Éd. Presses de l'Université Laval, Sainte-Foy, Qué., pp 801–933

Sylvette Guillemard est professeur de droit à l'Université Laval à Québec. Elle enseigne et mène des recherches en droit international privé, règlement des différends et droit comparé. Elle est membre titulaire de l'Académie internationale de droit comparé.

Frédérique Sabourin, Ad. E., (LL.D.) est avocate au ministère de la Justice du Québec depuis 1985. Elle est membre de délégations représentant le Canada à la Conférence de La Haye de droit international privé. Elle est membre associée de l'Académie internationale de droit comparé.

Choice of Court Agreements in Common Law Canada

Geneviève Saumier

1 Introduction

The attitude toward choice of court agreements in Canadian common law provinces[1] is very positive. Exclusive choice of court agreements are routinely enforced by courts called upon to do so, even though they do not consider that the parties have the capacity to "oust" the jurisdiction of the court. While the principles governing choice of court agreements are reiterated by trial courts or motion judges, the case law does not reflect a coherent and consistent approach to such agreements, particularly in terms of distinguishing optional and exclusive agreements, or in terms of applying the appropriate test with its accompanying burden of proof. Looking at decisions over the past 5 years, it appears that the weight of precedent has been

[1]Canada is comprised of ten provinces and three federal territories. Of the ten provinces, nine are usually referred to as "common law provinces" while one, Québec, is referred to as a "civil law" jurisdiction. This classification is apposite mainly for private law, whereas public law, as well as judicial and procedural law, essentially follows the common law tradition in all provinces. However, given that procedural law is within provincial legislative competence, there is not necessarily uniformity across provinces in these fields. Most notably, the jurisdictional aspects of private international law, many of which directly implicate choice of court agreements, are subject to three different approaches across the country: Québec has a comprehensive, and distinct, codification of these rules (see in this volume, Sabourin and Guillemard, "Les Clauses d'élection de For Facultatives en Droit International Privé Québécois"), British Columbia, Saskatchewan and Nova Scotia have adopted legislation on international jurisdiction, and the other provinces, including Ontario, continue to rely on court decisions in the absence of statutory sources. As a result, even as between the Canadian common law provinces, there is potential for differential treatment of choice of court agreements, although in fact there is significant uniformity, for reasons explained further in the text.

G. Saumier (✉)
Faculty of Law, McGill University, Montreal, QC, Canada
e-mail: genevieve.saumier@mcgill.ca

M. Keyes (ed.), *Optional Choice of Court Agreements in Private International Law*, Ius Comparatum – Global Studies in Comparative Law 37,
https://doi.org/10.1007/978-3-030-23914-5_5

shifting to apply the "strong cause" test whenever a party is seeking to avoid a choice of court agreement, whether it is the plaintiff or the defendant, whether it is exclusive or optional and whether the agreement designates the forum or a foreign court. While this may not have a determinative impact on the result in most cases, it still makes for a confusing and unsatisfactory body of judicial decisions, particularly for foreign litigants or researchers seeking to understand the law in the Canadian common law provinces.

This contribution will canvass the way in which courts in Canadian common law provinces have treated choice of court agreements.[2] It will begin by looking at the sources for the principles and rules governing the issue, including the question of the applicable law. The next section will examine the distinction between optional and exclusive agreements and how this is dealt with by courts, including whether damages or anti-suit injunctions are available for their breach and the treatment of asymmetrical agreements. A final section will provide an overall evaluation and indicate avenues for needed reforms.

2 Legal Sources Governing the Treatment of Choice of Court Agreements

The rules governing the treatment of choice of court agreements in Canadian common law provinces are largely found in the decided cases, including a recent decision from the Supreme Court of Canada,[3] as opposed to legislation. In three provinces that have adopted a statutory regime to deal with international jurisdiction, it is specifically provided that jurisdiction can be granted by agreement, but the legislation only speaks of agreements designating the forum and does not distinguish between optional and exclusive agreements.[4] The federal *Marine Liability Act* limits the effect of a choice of court agreement in narrow circumstances involving carriage

[2]For a detailed examination of choice of court agreements across Canada, see Saumier and Bagg (2013).

[3]*Douez v Facebook Inc.*, 2017 SCC 33. The other relevant Supreme Court of Canada case is *Z.I. Pompey Industrie v ECU-Line N.V.*, 2003 SCC 27. All cases and legislation mentioned in this report are available online, free of charge, at www.canlii.org.

[4]The *Court Jurisdiction and Proceedings Transfer Act*, developed as uniform legislation by the Uniform Law Conference of Canada, is in force in British Columbia (SBC 2003, c 28), Saskatchewan (SS 1997, c C-41.1) and Nova Scotia (SNS 2003 (2d Sess), c 2). The relevant section dealing with choice of court agreements (s. 3 in BC and s. 4 in NS and Sask) states: A court has territorial competence in a proceeding that is brought against a person only if (a) that person is the plaintiff in another proceeding in the court to which the proceeding in question is a counterclaim, (b) during the course of the proceeding that person submits to the court's jurisdiction, (c) *there is an agreement between the plaintiff and that person to the effect that the court has jurisdiction in the proceeding,* (d) that person is ordinarily resident in [the Province] at the time of the commencement of the proceeding, or (e) there is a real and substantial connection between [the Province] and the facts on which the proceeding against that person is based.

of goods.[5] Finally, the *Ontario Consumer Protection Act* implicitly guarantees access to Ontario courts for consumers making claims under the *Act*,[6] thereby restricting the impact of a choice of court agreement in such cases. This is unlike the case in Québec where the Civil Code deals with all aspects of choice of court agreements and also expressly provides that consumers and employees are not bound by choice of court agreements.[7]

As a result of this paucity of legislation in the common law provinces, court decisions supply most of the law governing the treatment of choice of court agreements. Even for the three provinces that have legislated on international jurisdiction, the Supreme Court has recently indicated that these statutes do not govern the treatment of choice of court agreements, which therefore remain subject to common law. That case involved an agreement designating a *foreign* court and, in that sense, it was accurate to state that the legislation does not address the issue. However, given that the legislation does expressly deal with choice of court agreements designating the forum, the Supreme Court's holding is not wholly satisfactory.[8] Nevertheless, the fact that choice of court agreements are said to be governed

[5] *Marine Liability Act*, Statutes of Canada 2001, chapter 6, Part 5 on Liability for Carriage of Goods by Water, s. 46 (1) If a contract for the carriage of goods by water to which the Hamburg Rules do not apply provides for the adjudication or arbitration of claims arising under the contract in a place other than Canada, a claimant may institute judicial or arbitral proceedings in a court or arbitral tribunal in Canada that would be competent to determine the claim if the contract had referred the claim to Canada, where (a) the actual port of loading or discharge, or the intended port of loading or discharge under the contract, is in Canada; (b) the person against whom the claim is made resides or has a place of business, branch or agency in Canada; or (c) the contract was made in Canada. (2) Notwithstanding subsection (1), the parties to a contract referred to in that subsection may, after a claim arises under the contract, designate by agreement the place where the claimant may institute judicial or arbitral proceedings. While this provision preserves the jurisdiction of Canadian courts despite an otherwise valid forum selection clause, this does not exclude a motion to stay based on *forum non conveniens*. See *Magic Sportswear Corp. v. Mathilde Maersk (The)*, 2006 FCA 284 (stay granted), *Mazda Canada Inc. v. Cougar Ace (The)*, 2008 FCA 219 (stay granted).

[6] Statutes of Ontario 2002, chapter 30, Schedule A, sections 7-8, of which the relevant portions are as follows: 7(1)The substantive and procedural rights given under this Act apply despite any agreement or waiver to the contrary. (2) Without limiting the generality of subsection (1), any term or acknowledgment in a consumer agreement or a related agreement that requires or has the effect of requiring that disputes arising out of the consumer agreement be submitted to arbitration is invalid insofar as it prevents a consumer from exercising a right to commence an action in the Superior Court of Justice given under this Act. 8(1) A consumer may commence a proceeding on behalf of members of a class under the Class Proceedings Act, 1992 or may become a member of a class in such a proceeding in respect of a dispute arising out of a consumer agreement despite any term or acknowledgment in the consumer agreement or a related agreement that purports to prevent or has the effect of preventing the consumer from commencing or becoming a member of a class proceeding.

[7] See articles 3148 and 3149 Civil Code of Québec and article 11.1 of the Québec *Consumer Protection Act*, CQLR c. P-40.1 For more details, see in this volume, Sabourin and Guillemard, "Les Clauses d'élection de For Facultatives en Droit International Privé Québécois".

[8] For a discussion of the decision on this point, see Saumier (2018), pp. 153–155.

by the common law provides for greater uniformity across the common law provinces.

This result also follows from the fact that Canadian common law courts assess choice of court agreements as if they raise no choice of law issue, even where the contract containing them also includes a choice of law clause.[9] Courts move directly to an interpretation of the clause, referring to previous case law from their own province or from other Canadian provinces. As such, it appears that choice of court agreements are implicitly assumed to be governed by the *lex fori*. While this may be justified on the basis that the issue is procedural in nature, the lack of any consideration of the question is not satisfactory from a methodological perspective, particularly given the contractual nature of choice of court agreements that may legitimately subject them to the law governing the contract. Moreover, when interpreting choice of court agreements, courts turn to rules on contract interpretation, not procedural law, thereby undermining the argument supporting a procedural characterization warranting recourse to the *lex fori*.

In so interpreting choice of court agreements, general principles of contract interpretation are relied upon, particularly the textual approach and the attempt to ascertain the intention of the parties.[10] Unlike in the Hague Choice of Court Convention,[11] which Canada has not ratified, there is no presumption that an agreement is exclusive unless it is expressly stated to be non-exclusive. This does not, however, indicate that the word "exclusive" must be contained in the agreement in order for a court to consider it to be exclusive.[12] For example, the B.C. Court of Appeal interpreted "irrevocably and unconditionally submits" as exclusive, rejecting a purely textual interpretation and emphasizing instead the intention of the parties.[13] With respect to terminology, courts and parties in common law provinces do not use the expression "optional choice of court agreement"; they refer instead to "non-exclusive forum selection clauses" or speak of "attornment". Where the clause designates one forum to the exclusion of all others, the term used is generally

[9]See Oppong and Gibbs (2017), pp. 400–402 and, for example, *2249659 Ontario Ltd. v. Sparkasse Siegen*, 2013 ONCA 354.

[10]See Hall (2012), pp. 237–238; Oppong and Gibbs (2017), pp. 403–406. For a thorough review of the case law in different Canadian common law provinces, see *3289444 Nova Scotia Ltd. v. RW Armstrong & Associates Inc.*, 2016 NSSC 330 at paragraphs 42–66. While that portion of the reasons is instructive, the overall judgment is weakened by the description of an arbitration clause as a forum selection clause; this conflation is surprisingly also evident in *Novatrax International Inc. v. Hägele Landtechnik GmbH*, 2016 ONCA 771.

[11]*Hague Convention of 30 June 2005 on Choice of Court Agreements*, 30 June 2005, Hague Conference on Private International Law (entered into force 1 October 2015), online: www.hcch.net/en/instruments/conventions/full-text/?cid=98.

[12]For example, in *Preymann v. Ayus Technology Corporation*, 2012 BCCA 30, the parties disagreed on the appropriate translation of the clause from German to English, in particular on whether the word "exclusive" was correct in the English version. The Court held that regardless of which English version was preferable, it considered that the agreement was exclusive.

[13]*BC Rail Partnership v. TrentonWorks Ltd.*, 2003 BCCA 597 at paragraphs 5 and 18–20.

"exclusive forum selection clause", though occasionally the expression "exclusive choice of court agreement" is used.

3 Treatment of Choice of Court Agreements in Canadian Common Law Provinces

As indicated in the introduction, choice of court agreements are considered to be valid and legitimate in Canadian common law provinces and are routinely enforced by courts. This is the case whether the law governing these agreements is covered by statute or is subject to the common law, and whether the agreement is optional or exclusive. Notwithstanding this generally cohesive approach, the decided cases do not present a coherent methodology with respect to the assessment and effect of the diverse varieties of choice of court agreements. This should be a cause for concern for parties who rely on choice of court agreements to reduce jurisdictional uncertainty relating to future litigation of disputes.

3.1 Exclusive Choice of Court Agreements

The bulk of decided cases relates to situations where the plaintiff has seized a court in contradiction to a clause designating a *foreign* court. Such a situation obviously presupposes that the court seized has jurisdiction. Because Canadian courts consider that parties cannot oust the jurisdiction of courts even by agreement, it is always possible for a court to refuse to enforce such an agreement, even if it is otherwise valid in a contractual sense.

In principle, exclusive choice of court agreements will be enforced by courts unless there is legislation specifically prohibiting choice of court agreements in particular contracts or limiting their effect. The Supreme Court has recently reiterated the approach to be taken with respect to exclusive choice of court agreements (in that case, designating a foreign court) in its 2017 decision in the *Douez v Facebook* case.[14] It is a two-step process, the first step involving a demonstration that the clause is valid and applies to the claim. Unusually, this step puts the onus on the party seeking to enforce the clause. The other party can raise any relevant contractual defense relating to consent, duress, fraud, etc. If the clause is valid and applies to the claim, then the party seeking to avoid the clause carries the burden of showing there is a "strong cause" for non-enforcement. Following on the approach in the well-known English case *The Eleftheria*, the Supreme Court of Canada held, in its first decision from 2003 on this issue, *Z.I. Pompey Industrie v. ECU-Line N.V.*, that exclusive choice of court agreements should be enforced unless there were

[14] *Douez v Facebook* 2017 SCC 33, para 28.

serious grounds not to.[15] In that case the Court held that this was a distinct test from the *forum non conveniens* test, a point reiterated most recently in the *Douez* case.[16] Despite stating that the test is different, the Court in *Pompey* took the criteria for the evaluation of "strong cause" from *The Eleftheria*, which are essentially the same as the criteria for *forum non conveniens*:

> (a) In what country the evidence on the issues of fact is situated, or more readily available, and the effect of that on the relative convenience and expense of trial as between the English and foreign Courts. (b) Whether the law of the foreign Court applies and, if so, whether it differs from English law in any material respects. (c) With what country either party is connected, and how closely. (d) Whether the defendants genuinely desire trial in the foreign country, or are only seeking procedural advantages. (e) Whether the plaintiffs would be prejudiced by having to sue in the foreign Court because they would (i) be deprived of security for that claim; (ii) be unable to enforce any judgment obtained; (iii) be faced with a time-bar not applicable in England; or (iv) for political, racial, religious or other reasons be unlikely to get a fair trial.[17]

It may well be that the strong cause test is distinct from *forum non conveniens* only in the sense that in the latter, the criteria are assessed to arrive at an overall conclusion regarding the appropriateness of the preferred foreign forum. Where an exclusive choice of court agreement designating a foreign court is present, that element carries significant weight in favour of a stay, giving the other criteria significantly less weight. Still, the fact that questions such as convenience and prejudice are considered in assessing whether to grant a stay does weaken the contractual justification for enforcing exclusive choice of court agreements in the first place. This point was made explicit in the Ontario Court of Appeal's 2010 judgment in *Expedition Helicopters*:

> Thus, even though the literal wording of the test in The 'Eleftheria' may imply a conventional *forum non conveniens* analysis, *Pompey* makes clear that such an analysis is not to be used. Rather, the forum selection clause pervades the analysis and must be given full weight in the consideration of other factors. It is not enough for the plaintiff to establish a 'strong' case that Ontario is the more convenient forum. The plaintiff must show 'strong cause' that the case is exceptional and the forum selection clause should not be enforced.
>
> [...]
>
> A forum selection clause in a commercial contract should be given effect. The factors that may justify departure from that general principle are few. The few factors that might be considered include the plaintiff was induced to agree to the clause by fraud or improper inducement or the contract is otherwise unenforceable, the court in the selected forum does not accept jurisdiction or otherwise is unable to deal with the claim, the claim or the circumstances that have arisen are outside of what was reasonably contemplated by the parties when they agreed to the clause, the plaintiff can no longer expect a fair trial in the selected forum due to subsequent events that could not have been reasonably anticipated, or

[15] *Z.I. Pompey Industrie v ECU-Line N.V.*, 2003 SCC 27.

[16] *Douez v Facebook* 2017 SCC 33, para 18.

[17] *Z.I. Pompey Industrie*, 2003 SCC 27, para 19 quoting from *The "Eleftheria"* [1969] 1 Lloyd's Rep. 237 at p. 242.

> enforcing the clause in the particular case would frustrate some clear public policy. Apart from circumstances such as these, a forum selection clause in a commercial contract should be enforced.[18]

Despite its reference to *Pompey*, this list of criteria for "strong cause" is much narrower and excludes many of the items in the list from *The Eleftheria*. Applying it would likely reduce the number of cases where an agreement would not be enforced. Although the Supreme Court in *Douez v Facebook* did refer to *Expedition Helicopters*, no account of the striking difference in approach in that case was noted.[19] It would thus appear that this attempt by the Ontario Court of Appeal to support the enforcement of exclusive choice of court agreements more vigorously has not made inroads.

3.2 Choice of Court Agreements and the Protection of Weaker Parties

In *Douez v Facebook*, the Supreme Court refused to enforce an exclusive agreement designating Californian courts in Facebook's terms and conditions in a class action claim brought under British Columbia's *Privacy Act*. There were no express statutory limitations on the enforceability of such a clause under BC law and so the question had to be addressed according to general jurisdictional rules. While the court was unanimous on the two-step approach to the question, the court was very divided on the result of its application. One judge held that the clause was invalid while three held that it was valid, but that there was strong cause not to enforce it. The remaining three judges dissented, holding that the clause was both valid and should be enforced. The decision is significant for two main reasons. First, as indicated in the previous part, the Supreme Court held, unanimously on this point, that the British Columbia statute on jurisdiction (the *CJPTA*) was not applicable to the case, leaving it to be decided according to common law rules. Second, three judges posited that the consumer context gave rise to a differentiated application of the "strong cause" test for refusing to enforce a choice of court agreement.[20] This suggests a potentially distinct approach for weaker parties that had been rejected in the Supreme Court's previous decision from 2003.[21] Because of the lack of a

[18] *Expedition Helicopters Inc. v. Honeywell Inc.*, 2010 ONCA 351, para 11 and 24.

[19] *Douez v Facebook* 2017 SCC 33, para 34. See also *Momentous.ca Corp. v. Canadian American Association of Professional Baseball Ltd.*, 2012 SCC 9, where the Supreme Court referred only to *Pompey* whereas the Ontario Court of Appeal had based its reasons (2010 ONCA 722) on the revised criteria in *Expedition Helicopters*.

[20] The lack of a plurality on this point should restrict its precedential value although recent trial decisions appear to be treating it as authoritative. See for example, *Cain v Pfizer*, 2018 ONSC 297, *Nowak*, 2018 BCSC 785, *Heller v Huber*, 2018 ONSC 718.

[21] In *ZI Pompey*, the court appeared to support an undifferentiated approach to clauses in contracts of adhesion, which would include consumer contracts, by referring with approval to the notorious US

plurality holding on this issue, *Douez v Facebook* has created uncertainty regarding the treatment of exclusive choice of court agreements in consumer cases although the importance accorded to the nature of the rights invoked (privacy rights, described as quasi-constitutional) may limit the impact of the case in more traditional contractual claims.[22] Absent legislative intervention, the enforceability of choice of court agreements in consumer cases will continue to be addressed on a case-by-case basis. As noted in Sect. 3.1, only Ontario provides protective jurisdictional treatment for consumers under the *Consumer Protection Act* by guaranteeing access to an Ontario court for claims brought under the Act, notwithstanding anything contrary in the contract.

With respect to employment contracts, there are no express or implied legislative protections against choice of court agreements in the common law provinces, unlike the situation in Québec. Despite this, in 2010, the Ontario Court of Appeal did refuse to enforce an exclusive choice of court agreement in an employment context, referring explicitly to the uneven bargaining power between the parties.[23] Interestingly, since *Douez v Facebook*, three decisions involving employment claims indicated the relevance of a discussion of relative bargaining power in deciding whether or not to enforce a choice of court agreement.[24]

Because *Z.I. Pompey Industrie v. ECU-Line N.V.* and *Douez v Facebook* involved exclusive agreements designating a foreign court, they need not have any necessary implications for agreements designating the forum court or for optional clauses. However, the rules governing those situations are not well defined and it is already apparent, only 1 year following *Douez v Facebook*, that this situation is not improving.[25]

Supreme Court decision in *Carnival Cruise Lines Inc v Shute* 499 US 585 (1991) that enforced such a clause (para 28).

[22]For a case that considered *Douez* but still enforced a choice of court agreement in a consumer case, *see Northcott v Cornerstone United Inc.*, 2017 ABPC 201 (Alberta Provincial Court). For a case discussing *Douez* in relation to an employment contract, see *Nowak v Biocomposites Inc.*, 2018 BCSC 785.

[23]See *Stubbs v. ATS Applied Tech Systems Inc.*, 2010 ONCA 879.

[24]See *Cain v Pfizer*, 2018 ONSC 297, *Nowak*, 2018 BCSC 785, *Heller v Huber*, 2018 ONSC 718.

[25]See for example *Forbes Energy Group Inc. v. Parsian Energy Rad Gas*, 2018 ONSC 5103, where the court assesses the clause designating a foreign court first under the strong cause test and then, subsequently, having found the absence of strong cause, under the *forum non conveniens* test, before granting a stay. In *Corrosion Service Company Limited v. Hydrosphere Construction Inc.*, 2018 ONSC 4434, with respect to an agreement designating the forum, the court held first that there was no strong cause not to enforce but then sent the parties to Québec, on the basis that it was the more appropriate forum under a *forum non conveniens* analysis. In *3289444 Nova Scotia Limited v R.W. Armstrong & Associates Inc.*, the trial court, deciding prior to *Douez v Facebook*, gave a rather clear judgment distinguishing between exclusive and optional clauses and applying the *forum non conveniens* analysis to the latter under the CJPTA (2016 NSSC 330); on appeal, after *Douez v Facebook*, though upholding the lower court's stay order, the decision proceeds on a much more confusing appraisal of the applicable rules (2018 NSCA 26).

3.3 Choice of Court Agreements Designating the Forum, Whether Exclusive or Optional

In the three provinces where international jurisdiction is governed by statute, the legislation specifically provides for the jurisdiction of the court if it has been designated in an agreement between the parties.[26] It is worth noting that the statute does not distinguish between optional and exclusive designations. In the other provinces, the agreement of the parties will also be considered to confer jurisdiction on the forum court.[27] In all cases the parties are considered to have submitted, or "attorned" to the jurisdiction of the forum, whether the agreement is optional or exclusive, even absent any other connection between the parties, the litigation and the forum. This will prevent the defendant from contesting jurisdiction *per se* but this does not address the other possibility, that the defendant will nevertheless request that the court decline to exercise its jurisdiction. This might be expected to occur on the basis of the *forum non conveniens* doctrine, which is well established throughout the country.[28] Under Canadian law, this analysis requires demonstrating that the foreign court is clearly more appropriate than the forum court.

In those provinces that have adopted the CJPTA, nothing in the provision on granting stays precludes its application to forum jurisdiction established on the basis of an agreement between the parties.[29] However, following *Douez v Facebook*, courts in CJPTA provinces will have to contend with the holding that the statute does not apply to choice of court agreements. The incompatibility between that

---

[26]The legislation is presented in footnote 4. There are very few decided cases on this point. In *MicroCoal Inc. v. Livneh*, 2014 BCSC 787, the court confirmed that the provision provided for an irrebuttable ground of jurisdiction that did not depend on any other connection being established with the designated forum, although on the facts it found that the clause did not apply.

[27]See for example, *Loat v. Horwath*, 2011 ONCA 509 at para 27–28.

[28]It is provided either expressly by statute (in CJPTA provinces and in Québec) or at common law, as confirmed by the Supreme Court of Canada in its seminal decision *Amchem Products Incorporated v. British Columbia (Workers' Compensation Board)*, [1993] 1 SCR 897.

[29]This is despite the fact that in *Douez v Facebook*, the Supreme Court suggested that the CJPTA does not deal with choice of court agreements, leaving these to be assessed under the common law rules. For a discussion, see Saumier (2018). The section dealing with stays in the CJPTA (s. 11 in BC, s. 12 in NS and s. 10 in Sask) states: Court may decline territorial competence (1) After considering the interests of the parties to a proceeding and the ends of justice, a court may decline to exercise its territorial competence in the proceeding on the ground that a court of another state is a more appropriate forum in which to hear the proceeding. (2) A court, in deciding the question of whether it or a court outside [the Province] is the more appropriate forum in which to hear a proceeding, must consider the circumstances relevant to the proceeding, including (a) the comparative convenience and expense for the parties to the proceeding and for their witnesses, in litigating in the court or in any alternative forum, (b) the law to be applied to issues in the proceeding, (c) the desirability of avoiding multiplicity of legal proceedings, (d) the desirability of avoiding conflicting decisions in different courts, (e) the enforcement of an eventual judgment, and (f) the fair and efficient working of the Canadian legal system as a whole. The Supreme Court held that this provision was a complete codification of the *forum non conveniens* doctrine (*Teck Cominco Metals Ltd. v. Lloyd's Underwriters*, 2009 SCC 11).

holding and the express language of the statute is problematic, although it might arguably be avoided where the agreement designating the forum is merely optional, since the Supreme Court jurisprudence has only dealt with *exclusive* agreements.[30] This leaves open the possibility that the enforcement of *optional* agreements designating the forum can continue to be assessed using the traditional *forum non conveniens* approach provided under the statute. Where the agreement designating the forum is exclusive, however, the "strong cause" test would be applicable.

In non-CJPTA jurisdictions, there is also uncertainty regarding the availability of *forum non conveniens* to avoid the jurisdiction of the optionally-designated forum court. In one case from Alberta, the court applied the "strong cause" test when considering whether to stay jurisdiction that it acquired based on an optional choice of court agreement. In so doing, it did not even refer to the optional nature of the agreement.[31] In a more recent decision from Ontario, the court assessed the agreement, which it did not even describe as optional, after having determined its jurisdiction on other grounds, within a *forum non conveniens* analysis, but using the "strong cause" test.[32] Two other Ontario cases noted the optional nature of the clause in favour of Ontario courts, referred to precedent distinguishing optional from exclusive agreements but then went on to follow cases dealing with exclusive agreements, using the "strong cause" test.[33] While stays were not granted in these cases, the reasoning certainly suggests that it is open to a defendant to seek such a stay although the actual test applicable (*forum non conveniens* or strong cause) is unclear.

3.4 *Optional Agreements Designating Foreign Courts*

Courts in Canadian common law provinces have stated, at least prior to *Douez v Facebook*, that optional choice of court agreements designating foreign courts should be considered as a factor, but not a determinative factor, within a *forum non conveniens* analysis if the defendant is seeking a stay.[34] Where parallel proceedings have been instituted in the foreign court, this fact may assist the party seeking a stay. This is particularly evident where the parallel proceedings risk giving rise to contradictory judgments. For example, in a case involving an alleged breach of a service contract, a first claim was instituted in the non-designated court and a month later, the defendant in that claim commenced proceedings in the designated

[30]This was the approach taken in *Romanchuk v Jemi Fibre Corp*, 2018 SKQB 46 at para 14.

[31]*1400467 Alberta Ltd v Adderley*, 2014 ABQB 339.

[32]*TFS RT Inc. v Kenneth Dyck*, 2017 ONSC 2780.

[33]*Mackie Research Capital Corporation v. Mackie*, 2012 ONSC 3890 and *Terracap Investments Inc. v Credit Capital Immobilliari, S.A.*, 2016 ONSC 4618.

[34]See *Sugar v. Megawheels Technologies Inc.*, 2006 CanLII 37880 at para 28; *Silveira v. FY International Auditing & Consulting Corp.*, 2015 ONSC 338.

forum. The claim was essentially in the nature of a counter-claim to the initial action. In granting a stay in the first action, the non-designated court gave significant weight to the fact that the designated court was also seized (even if not first) of a largely similar action.[35] In another case, the fact that the parallel proceedings were distinct enough to be dealt with in a separate action, though also capable of being asserted as a counterclaim, was considered by the court in deciding whether to grant a stay.[36]

Despite this potentially important distinct treatment of optional agreements, courts do not always clearly identify or consider whether an agreement is optional or exclusive, and in such cases, they often apply the test governing the treatment of exclusive agreements even where, arguably, the clause could be understood to be optional.[37] This is not insignificant, as the burden of proof on the plaintiff seeking to avoid an exclusive agreement in favour of a foreign court is greater than the burden of defending against a request for a stay under *forum non conveniens*. It is not clear why plaintiffs are not more alive to the advantage of arguing that the agreement is optional rather than exclusive and thereby insisting that their ability to remain in their preferred forum is to be analyzed under the *forum non conveniens* paradigm. It may be, however, that the weight of precedent has been shifting to apply only the strong cause test whenever a party is seeking to avoid a choice of court agreement, whether it is the plaintiff or the defendant, whether it is exclusive or optional and whether the agreement designates the forum or a foreign court.

4 Remedies for Breach of a Choice of Court Agreement: Anti-suit Injunction, Damages, Non-enforcement of Foreign Judgment

There are no cases from Canadian common law provinces establishing the availability of a remedy, other than a stay, where a party has not respected a choice of court agreement. While anti-suit injunctions can be issued by courts, there are no reported cases involving such injunctions in relation to choice of court agreements. Neither is there any evidence of damages being awarded for breach of a choice of court agreement. Both of these issues are the subject of doctrinal writing but have yet to be tested in court.[38]

If a judgment was rendered in a foreign court that was seized contrary to a choice of court agreement, this might be a bar to recognition and enforcement by courts in Canadian common law provinces. The jurisdictional requirement in the recognition

[35] *Silveira v. FY International Auditing & Consulting Corp.*, 2015 ONSC 338.

[36] See *Mackie Research Capital Corporation v. Mackie*, 2012 ONSC 3890, though that case involved an optional agreement designating the forum.

[37] See for example, *Meta4Hand Inc v Research In Motion*, 2017 ABQB 23; *2Source Manufacturing Inc. v. United Technologies Corporation*, 2017 ONSC 4409.

[38] See for example Oppong and Gibbs (2017).

and enforcement context is merely that the foreign court had a "real and substantial connection" with the parties or the litigation. Where that is established, the fact that a party sought but failed to obtain a stay based on a choice of court agreement would not appear to provide a valid jurisdictional defense to enforcement unless the agreement provided for exclusive jurisdiction, and possibly only if the designated court was the one where recognition and enforcement is sought. The British Columbia Court of Appeal decision in *Old North State Brewing Co. v Newlands Services*, from 1998, supports the view that an exclusive jurisdiction clause can stand in the way of recognition and enforcement, although this was not operative there since the clause in that case, designating B.C. courts, was held to be merely optional.[39]

5 Asymmetrical Choice of Court Agreements

There are no reported cases dealing with asymmetrical choice of court agreements in Canadian common law provinces. There is thus no basis upon which to make any statement regarding how a Canadian court would treat such agreements.

6 Conclusion

Parties who include a choice of court agreement in their contract can largely rely on its enforcement by courts in Canadian common law provinces. This is particularly true where the clause is exclusive, as has been repeated very recently by the Supreme Court of Canada in the *Douez v Facebook* case in 2017. Still, there remains some uncertainty given that a "strong cause" not to enforce even an exclusive clause can be invoked by a party seeking to avoid its enforcement. Moreover, uncertainty also remains regarding the treatment of optional clauses. While these should typically establish the jurisdiction of the designated Canadian court, they do not guarantee that the designated court will not decline to exercise its jurisdiction on *forum non conveniens* grounds. Where an optional clause points rather to a foreign court, this should also be relevant, though not determinative, in assessing whether the court seized should decline jurisdiction. While this summary of the treatment of the different types of choice of court agreements in Canadian common law provinces suggests a coherent approach, the decided cases paint a different picture. Indeed, courts do not systematically distinguish between optional and exclusive agreements, and in many cases subject all of them to the single "strong cause" test, despite its different emphasis and more exigent burden of proof. Nor is there predictability concerning the treatment of weaker parties, such as consumers and employees. The

[39] *Old North State Brewing Co. Inc. v. Newlands Services Inc.*, 1998 CanLII 6512 (BC CA); see especially para 32.

recent Supreme Court decision in *Douez v Facebook* appears to have opened the door to differentiated treatment although the precedential force of the case is unpredictable.

Does this suggest a need for reform? Certainly in those provinces that have adopted a statutory regime for international jurisdiction, it would be useful to make amendments to provide for comprehensive treatment of choice of court agreements. This would assist in filling gaps left by the Supreme Court's interpretation of that legislation in the *Douez v Facebook* decision. If such amendments were made, they could and should draw distinctions between optional and exclusive agreements and provide specific tests for each. They might also deal expressly with weaker parties, such as consumers and employees, which would provide greater national uniformity and equal treatment of these parties throughout the Canadian employment and consumer markets. Should other provinces be considering the adoption of legislation to deal with international jurisdiction, they should also consider including specific provisions to deal with choice of court agreements.

Finally, if there is any movement on the ratification of the Hague Choice of Court Convention by Canada, this will bring with it necessary modifications to the law of the common law provinces since it currently is not aligned with the approach in the Convention.[40]

References

Hall GR (2012) Canadian contractual interpretation law, 2nd edn. LexisNexis, Markham

Oppong RF, Gibbs S (2017) Damages for breach and interpretation of jurisdiction agreements in common law Canada. Canadian Bar Rev 95:393–412

Saumier G (2018) Has the CJPTA readied Canada for the Hague choice of court convention? Osgoode Hall Law J 55:141–162

Saumier G, Bagg J (2013) Forum selection clauses before Canadian Courts - a tale of two (or three?) solitudes. UBC Law Rev 46:439–487

Geneviève Saumier is the Peter M. Laing Chair and Professor of Law at the Faculty of Law of McGill University. She is also co-rapporteur for the 2019 Hague Convention on the Recognition and Enforcement of Foreign Judgments in Civil or Commercial Matters.

[40]For a discussion, see Saumier (2018).

People's Republic of China (PRC): Optional Choice of Court Agreements in the Vibrant Age

Guangjian Tu and Zeyu Huang

1 Introduction

Due to the late development of Chinese laws in general and Chinese Private International Law (PIL) in particular, Chinese treatment of choice of court agreements is relatively under-developed, compared with some other advanced jurisdictions.[1] This Report attempts to give the most detailed information possible with respect to optional choice of court agreements in the PRC. Before looking into the legal treatment of choice of court agreements in the PRC, it is, however, necessary to identify the legal sources where one can find relevant information. Since the PRC is a country of the civil law tradition, the statutes enacted by the legislature i.e. the National People's Congress (NPC) are the primary sources of law. Furthermore, owing to the special political status of power division between the legislature and the judiciary within China, the Judicial Interpretations and other similar documents issued by the Supreme People's Court (SPC) can also act as sources of law to guide Chinese lower courts to decide cases.[2] Although the doctrine of *stare decisis* is not recognized in Chinese law, Chinese courts at all levels in deciding similar cases shall pay due respect to the guiding cases publicized by the SPC, especially those publicized in its Gazette.[3] Lower courts shall quote the guiding cases as a part of the

[1]See Chen (2004), pp. 10–15; Tu (2016), p. 3.

[2]All Chinese legal instruments and cases cited in this report can be found at www.chinalawinfo.com unless otherwise indicated, this website will not be cited again in the following discussion. See Tu (2016), p. 9; Tang et al. (2016), pp. 24–27.

[3]See art. 6 of Notice of the Supreme People's Court on Issuing the Provisions on Case Guidance [2010] Fa Fa No. 51, which entered into force on 26 November 2010; Tu (2016), pp. 6–7.

G. Tu (✉) · Z. Huang
School of Law, University of Macau, Macau, PR China
e-mail: gjtu@umac.mo; gjtu@um.edu.mo; yb67213@connect.umac.mo

M. Keyes (ed.), *Optional Choice of Court Agreements in Private International Law*, Ius Comparatum – Global Studies in Comparative Law 37,
https://doi.org/10.1007/978-3-030-23914-5_6

reasoning for their judgment or ruling although they do not need to take them as the legal basis.[4] In addition, the reported cases by Chinese lower courts, for instance High Courts at the provincial level and Intermediate Courts at the prefecture (middle-city) level, cannot be totally ignored because they might have *de facto* persuasive effects in practice.[5] Therefore, in the following discussion of choice of court agreements in the PRC, all these sources are duly taken into account.

2 The Treatment of Choice of Court Agreements in General

Currently, Chinese law expressly recognizes the parties' freedom to contractual jurisdiction albeit subject to some limitations. Article 34 of the Chinese Civil Procedure Law (CCPL) provides:

> Parties to a dispute over a contract or any other right or interest in a property may, without violating rules concerning jurisdiction by forum level and exclusive jurisdiction, choose the court for the place where the defendant is domiciled, or where the contract is performed or signed, or where the plaintiff is domiciled, or where the subject matter is located or any other place that has actual connection with the dispute as the court having jurisdiction over their dispute by a written agreement.[6]

It can be inferred from this Article that Chinese law obviously adopts an explicit policy in favour of enforcing parties' agreements on jurisdiction. However, the parties' freedom to choose courts is generally limited to disputes relating to contracts or other property interests. In the areas of non-contractual disputes, such as personal injury or some other non-contractual or non-proprietary cases, the parties are generally not allowed to reach a choice of court agreement.[7] Furthermore, the parties' freedom is also compromised by the fact that in some areas Chinese courts will claim exclusive jurisdiction and the parties are not allowed to choose the adjudicatory courts at their will. According to Articles 33 and 266 of CCPL, Chinese courts shall have exclusive jurisdiction over disputes arising out of immovable property, harbour operations, successions, performance of contracts for Chinese-foreign equity joint ventures, Chinese-foreign contractual joint ventures and Chinese-foreign cooperation and development of natural resources.[8]

---

[4]See art. 10 of Detailed Rules for the Implementation of the Provisions of the Supreme People's Court on Case Guidance [2015] Fa No. 130, which entered into force on 13 May 2015.

[5]However, whether academic doctrines (writings) can be legal sources is still controversial in the PRC. According to Tu's observation, academic opinions have not yet become legal sources; but Tang et al. advocated that the opinions of Chinese academics should also be potential legal sources. See Tu (2016), p. 9; Tang et al. (2016), p. 28.

[6]See art. 34 of the Civil Procedure Law of the PRC, as amended in June 2017.

[7]See Tang et al. (2016), p. 69.

[8]See art. 33 of CCPL, which says: "The following cases shall be subject to exclusive jurisdiction of the courts specified in this Article: (1) Where a dispute is about an immovable property, the court for the place where the immovable property is located shall have jurisdiction; (2) Where a dispute is

Apart from these stipulations in statutory law, it is suggested by Chinese commentators that Chinese courts have taken *de facto* exclusive jurisdiction in disputes concerning incorporation, legal capacity and dissolution of companies, and specific intellectual property disputes in judicial practice.[9] In these certain areas, the parties are thus prevented from reaching choice of court agreements to derogate from the exclusive jurisdiction of Chinese courts.

Last but not least, the most controversial limitation on the parties' freedom in concluding their choice of court agreements stems from the "actual connection" principle.[10] This principle stipulates that the parties to such agreements can only choose the limited courts of the places having actual connection with the dispute as enumerated in the law.[11]

The legal treatment of choice of court agreements in China has changed several times along with the several amendments of the CCPL. The 1982 CCPL for Trial Implementation enacted at the initial stage of Mr. Deng Xiaoping's "reform and opening-up policy" did not uphold the parties' autonomy to choose a forum at all.[12] It was not until 1991 when Chinese law began to recognize the parties' freedom to contract about jurisdiction for the first time.[13] This change was largely brought about

arising out of harbour operation, the court for the place where the harbour is located shall have jurisdiction; (3) Where a dispute is about succession, the court for the place of the deceased's domicile upon death or where the main property to be inherited shall have jurisdiction"; art. 266 of CCPL, which says: "Actions instituted for disputes arising out of performance within the territory of the People's Republic of China of contracts for Chinese-foreign equity joint ventures, Chinese-foreign contractual joint ventures or Chinese-foreign cooperative exploration and exploitation of natural resources shall be under the exclusive jurisdiction of the people's courts of the People's Republic of China".

[9]E.g., see Tang et al. (2016), p. 60.

[10]See art. 34 of CCPL; art. 531 of the Interpretation of the Supreme People's Court on the Application of the Civil Procedure Law of the People's Republic of China [2015] Fa Shi No. 5 promulgated on 30 January 2015, which entered into force on 4 February 2015 (2015 SPC Interpretation on CCPL); Tu (2007), pp. 359, 361; Tang (2012), pp. 466, 467.

[11]See art. 34 of CCPL. Chinese scholars have heavily criticized the "actual connection" principle. E.g., Tang et al. (2016), p. 70 (suggesting that a strict interpretation of the "actual connection" principle technically invalidates choice of court agreements choosing neutral fora, and thus the best approach is to remove the principle from Chinese law completely); Tang (2012), p. 466 (saying that the "actual connection principle" is inconsistent with international practice and incompatible with commercial convenience); Liu and Zhou (2014), p. 50 (arguing that the actual connection between the chosen court and the dispute should not be considered as one of the prerequisites for the validity of choice of court agreements).

[12]See Chap. 2 Jurisdiction of the CCPL (For Trial Implementation) promulgated on 8 March 1982, which entered into force on 1 October 1982.

[13]See arts. 25 and 244 of the 1991 CCPL, which was promulgated and entered into force on 9 April 1991. Art. 25 says: "Parties to a contract may, without violating rules concerning jurisdiction by forum level and exclusive jurisdiction, choose the court for the place where the defendant is domiciled, or where the contract is performed or signed, or where the plaintiff is domiciled, or where the subject matter is located as the court having jurisdiction over the dispute by a written agreement". Art. 244 says: "Parties to a foreign-related dispute over a contract or any other right or interest in a property may choose a court for the place that has actual connection with the dispute as

by great concerns with local protectionism of Chinese courts and the need for developing the "socialist commodity economy".[14] In the 1991 CCPL, the two relevant provisions i.e. Articles 25 and 244 apply to choice of court agreements for purely domestic disputes and foreign-related disputes respectively. In the 2007 Amendment of the CCPL, these provisions were maintained without any change being made.[15] However, in the 2012 Amendment of CCPL, the provision concerning choice of court agreements specifically devised for foreign-related disputes was deleted.[16] The current Article 34 of the CCPL with respect to choice of court agreements initially devised for domestic disputes only has now been reserved for both domestic and foreign-related disputes in both the 2012 CCPL[17] and the 2017 CCPL.[18] In this more streamlined way, the treatment of choice of court agreements has been transformed from "dual track" to "single track".[19] There might be two possible explanations for the deletion of the specific provision concerning choice of court agreements for foreign-related cases: first, the legislators intend to use one set of rules to govern all choice of court agreements irrespective of domestic or foreign-related elements, being pressed by commentators' criticisms[20]; secondly, it is said that the deletion is to pave the way for implementing the 2005 Hague Choice of Court Convention[21] in the PRC in future, given the backdrop of globally increasing judicial cooperation regarding choice of court agreements.[22] However, it must be noted that the 2015 SPC Interpretation on CCPL seemingly

---

the court having jurisdiction over the dispute by a written agreement. Rules concerning jurisdiction by forum level and exclusive jurisdiction shall not be violated if a people's court of the People's Republic of China is chosen as the court having jurisdiction".

[14]See Wang Hanbin (1991) Preamble and Section 2, The Explanation on the Civil Procedure Law of the People's Republic of China (For Trial Implementation) (Amended Draft). Paper presented at the 4th Meeting of the Seventh National People's Congress on 2 April 1991, which can be found at http://www.npc.gov.cn/wxzl/gongbao/2000-12/28/content_5002547.htm (last visited on 28 August 2018).

[15]See art. 25 and 242 of the 2007 CCPL promulgated on 28 October 2007, which entered into force on 1 April 2008.

[16]See Paragraph 58 of the Decision of the Standing Committee of the National People's Congress on Amending the Civil Procedure Law of the People's Republic of China (2012) promulgated on 31 August 2012, which entered into force on 1 January 2013.

[17]See art. 34 of the 2012 CCPL promulgated on 31 August 2012, which entered into force on 1 January 2013.

[18]See art. 34 of the CCPL; Tang et al. (2016), p. 64.

[19]See Tu and Li (2013), pp. 644, 645.

[20]See Tang et al. (2016), p. 63.

[21]This refers to the Hague Convention of 30 June 2005 on Choice of Court Agreements concluded in the Twentieth Diplomatic Session of the Hague Conference on 30 June 2005, which entered into force on 1 October 2015, following the deposit of the instrument of approval by the President of the Council of the European Union on 11 June 2015. The PRC has now signed the Convention. See the webpage at https://www.hcch.net/en/news-archive/details/?varevent=569 (last visited on 28 August 2018).

[22]See Tang et al. (2016), pp. 63–64.

purports to revive the provision concerning choice of court agreements regarding foreign-related disputes.[23] Thus, it is not totally clear whether Chinese law would maintain the "single track" or not in the future.

Another noticeable change of the legal treatment of choice of court agreements is that Chinese law recognizes the choice of more than one court and the choice referring to the domicile of one party in the 2015 SPC Interpretation on CCPL.[24] In contrast with previous practice that invalidated the choice of court agreements choosing more than one court,[25] Article 30, paragraph 2 of the 2015 SPC Interpretation on CCPL now expressly permits the parties to choose more than one court in their choice of court agreements.[26]

Chinese law used not to make a clear distinction between exclusive and non-exclusive choice of court agreements (optional choice of court agreements). The concept of non-exclusive choice of court agreement (optional choice of court agreement) was first formally presented in the 2005 SPC Summary[27] and later on

[23]See art. 531 of the 2015 SPC Interpretation on CCPL says: "Parties to a dispute over a foreign-related contract or any other right or interest in a property may choose the foreign court for the place where the defendant is domiciled, or where the contract is performed or signed, or where the plaintiff is domiciled, or where the subject matter is located or any other place that has actual connection with the dispute as the court having jurisdiction over their dispute by a written agreement. For the cases over which a court of the People's Republic of China has exclusive jurisdiction under art. 33 and 266 of the Civil Procedure Law, the parties shall not choose a foreign court to have jurisdiction over their dispute by an agreement unless they agree to choose arbitration to settle the case".

[24]See art. 30, para. 2 of the 2015 SPC Interpretation on CCPL, which says: "Where a jurisdiction agreement provides that two or more people's courts for the places having actual connection with a dispute shall have jurisdiction over the dispute, the plaintiff may institute the action in one of the people's courts therein"; art. 32 of the 2015 SPC Interpretation on CCPL, which says: "Where a jurisdiction agreement provides that the people's court for the place where one party is domiciled has jurisdiction over the dispute, but the place where the party is domiciled changes after the agreement is concluded, the people's court for the place where the party is domiciled when the agreement is concluded shall have jurisdiction over the dispute, unless the parties agree otherwise". Also see Tang et al. (2016), p. 66.

[25]See art. 24 of the Opinion of the Supreme People's Court on Some Issues Concerning the Application of the Civil Procedure Law of the People's Republic of China [1992] Fa Fa No. 22 promulgated on 14 July 1992, which says: "If the jurisdiction agreement concluded by both parties to a contract is ambiguous or has chosen two or more people's courts specified in art. 25 of the Civil Procedural Law to have jurisdiction over the dispute, such a jurisdiction agreement shall be invalid, and the jurisdiction shall be determined according to art. 24 of the Civil Procedure Law".

[26]See note 24; Tang et al. (2016), p. 67.

[27]See art. 12 of the Supreme People's Court's Notice on Summary of the Second National Working Conference on the Trial of Foreign-Related Commercial and Maritime Cases [2005] Fa Fa No. 26, which was promulgated and entered into force on 26 December 2005 (2005 SPC Summary). This Article says: "If the parties in a case concerning foreign-related disputes agree that foreign courts have non-exclusive jurisdiction over their disputes, it can be deemed that such an agreement does not exclude the jurisdiction of the courts in the other countries which may assert jurisdiction. If one party institutes an action in a Chinese court, the Chinese court may accept the

further confirmed in a Reply of the SPC to lower courts.[28] Surely, it is a noticeable improvement for Chinese law to make such a distinction. Chinese scholars also have addressed the exclusive-optional dichotomy of choice of court agreements.[29] Some even touched upon the exclusive-optional-asymmetrical trichotomy.[30] The terms "exclusive jurisdiction clauses/agreements" and "non-exclusive jurisdiction clauses/ agreements" are often used in their discussions[31] while other scholars prefer the terms exclusive and non-exclusive "choice of court agreements".[32]

PRC acceded to the New York Convention[33] on recognition and enforcement of foreign arbitral awards in 1987.[34] Nowadays, Chinese law expressly and consistently recognises and enforces valid arbitration agreements in both intra-national and international cases.[35] Although China is a loyal party to the New York Convention,

---

case if the court has jurisdiction over the case pursuant to the relevant provisions of the Civil Procedure Law of the People's Republic of China".

[28]See Reply Letter of the Supreme People's Court on Request for Instructions as to the Validity of the Arbitration Clause in the Contract Dispute between *Yanzhou Haoke Weibo Mining Engineering Co., Ltd. v. A Weber S.A. and Sofirol S.A.*, the Supreme People's Court (2009) Min Si Ta Zi No. 19.

[29]E.g. see Jiao (2011), pp. 163–173; Tang (2012), pp. 459–484; Zhang (2014), pp. 122–132.

[30]See Guo and Wen (2014), pp. 48–56; Zhang (2016), pp. 125–133.

[31]See Tang et al. (2016), p. 65; Tang (2012), p. 459; Zhang (2014), p. 122.

[32]See Jiao (2011).

[33]See United Nations Convention on the Recognition and Enforcement of Foreign Arbitral Awards, New York, 10 June 1958, 330 U.N.T.S. 38 (the New York Convention).

[34]See Notice of the Supreme People's Court on Implementing the Convention on the Recognition and Enforcement of Foreign Arbitral Awards Acceded to by China (1987) Fa (Jing) Fa No. 5, which was promulgated and entered into force on 10 April 1987.

[35]See art. 124 (2) and 271 of the CCPL; art. 5 of the Arbitration Law of the People's Republic of China, which entered into force on 1 September 1995 and was amended on 27 August 2009. Art. 124 (2) of the CCPL says: "A people's court shall handle the following actions instituted in different circumstances: (2) Notifying the plaintiff to apply to an arbitral institution for arbitration where both parties have reached a written arbitration agreement, in accordance with the law, to apply for arbitration which prevents the parties from instituting an action in a people's court"; art. 271 of the CCPL says: "In the cases concerning disputes arising out of foreign-related economic and trade matters, carriage and maritime activities where the parties have concluded an arbitration clause in contracts or a written arbitration agreement after a dispute arises to submit the dispute to foreign-related arbitral institutions or any other arbitral institution for arbitration, the parties shall not institute an action in a people's court. If the parties have not concluded arbitration clauses in contracts or have failed to reach a written arbitration agreement after a dispute arises, the parties may institute an action in a people's court"; art. 5 of the Chinese Arbitration Law says: "If the parties have concluded an arbitration agreement and one party institutes an action in a people's court, the people's court shall not accept the case unless the arbitration agreement is invalid". For recognition and enforcement of arbitration agreements in intra-national (inter-regional) cases, please see Arrangements of the Supreme People's Court on Mutual Enforcement of Arbitral Awards between the Mainland and the Hong Kong SAR promulgated on 24 January 2000, which entered into force on 1 February 2000; Arrangement of the Supreme People's Court on Mutual Recognition and Enforcement of Arbitral Awards between the Mainland and the Macau SAR promulgated on 12 December 2007, which entered into force on 1January 2008; Arrangement Concerning Reciprocal Recognition and Enforcement of Arbitral Awards between the Hong Kong SAR and the Macau SAR signed on 7 January 2013.

it is hard to identify any influence Chinese experience under the Convention has had on its treatment of choice of court agreements.

As said, the 2005 Hague Choice of Court Convention probably has had some influence on Chinese law respecting choice of court agreements.[36] However, it is difficult to see any other influence resulting from a bilateral, multilateral or regional instrument although PRC has signed and ratified more than 30 bilateral treaties in this area, let alone the Brussels regime to which PRC is an outsider.[37]

3 Optional Choice of Court Agreements

As already illustrated, statutory laws, judicial interpretations of the SPC and other legal documents issued by the SPC are the primary legal sources.[38] Moreover, the cases adjudicated and/or publicized by the SPC and cases of lower Chinese courts also can act as potential sources to provide answers to questions for judicial practices.[39] As far as determining the effect of optional choice of court agreements is concerned, the relevant provisions of the CCPL, the 2015 SPC Interpretation on CCPL and any other Judicial Interpretation or guidance such as the 2005 SPC Summary and Reply Letters of the SPC, and the reported cases of the SPC and other lower Chinese courts are the legal sources that should be taken into consideration.[40] They will be discussed in detail in the following.

It is crucial to determine whether a choice of court agreement is exclusive or optional because the legal effects of the two categories of agreements are quite different.[41] To decide this question, the applicable law governing this issue should be ascertained at first. Regrettably, Chinese law does not explicitly provide the choice of law rule for such an issue. As a consequence, Chinese courts have adopted inconsistent approaches of characterizing choice of court agreements in judicial practices. The predominant one is to apply the *lex fori* to interpret and determine the nature of a choice of court agreement in dispute.[42] The justification for this approach is the presumption held by most Chinese courts that "the exclusivity and

[36]See notes 21–22 and accompanying text. For further detailed discussion, see Tu (2007).

[37]For a list of the bilateral treaties to which PRC is a Contracting Party, see the website of the SPC available at http://www.court.gov.cn/shenpan-gengduo-73.html (last visited on 28 August 2018).

[38]See Section 1 of this Report.

[39]See notes 3–5 and accompanying text.

[40]Legally speaking, the relevant sources are only those that are currently applicable. However, academically, they could cover those that do not have legal effects any longer.

[41]See Fawcett (2001), pp. 234–235; Briggs (2012), p. 376.

[42]E.g. see *Shandong Jufeng Network v. MGame & Tianjin Fengyun Network,* the Supreme People's Court (2009) Min San Zhong Zi No. 4; Model Case No. 44, Notice of the Supreme People's Court on Issuing 10 Major Cases and 50 Model Cases on China's Judicial Protection of the Intellectual Property Rights in 2009 [2010] Fa No. 172, promulgated on 14 April 2010.

the legal effects of choice of court agreements" are more related to procedure, which should be exclusively governed by the *lex fori*, namely pursuant to Chinese law.[43] Another approach was indicated in *Sumitomo Bank Ltd. v. Xinhua Estate*, where the Chinese court applied the *lex causae* of the concerned contract to interpret the choice of court agreement and decide its legal effect therein.[44] If the parties have chosen the applicable law governing the contract, the applicable law agreed by the parties shall also be applied to interpret the choice of court agreement and determine its legal effect.[45] This approach was criticized by the SPC in *Shandong Jufeng Network v. MGame*, where the Court held that the choice of law agreement and the choice of court agreement are two separate legal acts and therefore different applicable laws should be applied to regulate them.[46] Furthermore, the SPC confirmed that the *lex fori* shall be the applicable law governing the interpretation and validity of the choice of court agreement.[47]

As clarified above, Chinese law is often applied by Chinese courts to determine whether a choice of court agreement is exclusive or optional. In general, the first step to determine the issue of "exclusivity" is to interpret the choice of court agreement under Chinese law, aiming at finding out the parties' true intention.[48] If the parties' intention to conclude an exclusive or an optional choice of court agreements can be ascertained, the parties' real will shall be respected. For instance, the Chinese court in the case of *Zhong An Housing v. Merchants Bank* upheld the validity of an optional choice of court agreement designating Hong Kong courts because the

[43]E.g. see *Shandong Jufeng Network v. MGame (2009)*, Ibid.; *China Point Finance Ltd. v. Zhuhai City Commercial Bank*, the Guangdong High People's Court (2004) Yue Gao Fa Min Si Zhong Zi No. 263; *Yacheng Automobile Fittings v, HSBC Holdings*, the Jiangsu Wuxi Intermediate People's Court (2006) Xi Min San Chu Zi No. 23; *Zhiming Xu v. Yihua Zhang*, the Supreme People's Court (2015) Min Shen Zi No. 471.

[44]See *Sumitomo Bank Ltd. v. Xinhua Estate*, the Supreme People's Court (1999) Jing Zhong Zi No. 194.

[45]Ibid; art. 41 of the Law of the People's Republic of China on Choice of Law for Foreign-Related Civil Relationships promulgated on 28 October 2010, which says: "The parties, by agreement, can choose the governing law for their contract; if the parties did not make a choice, the applicable law shall be the law of the place where the party who is to effect the characteristic obligation for the contract has his habitual residence or the law of another place which has the closest connection with the contract".

[46]See *Shandong Jufeng Network v. MGame (2009)*, note 42.

[47]See *Shandong Jufeng Network v. MGame (2009)*, note 42.

[48]Once, there was a retrial case where the Supreme People's Procuratorate protested that Hong Kong law, including its case law, as chosen by the parties as *lex causae* of the concerned contract, should be applied to interpret the choice of court clause and determine whether it was exclusive. However, the SPC did not support this argument, holding that it was an error in the application of law to refer to Hong Kong case law to interpret the choice of court clause. See *Bank of China (Hong Kong) Ltd. v. Sichuan Province Foreign Economic and Trade Corporation*, the Sichuan High People's Court (2005) Chuan Min Zai Zhong Zi No. 70.

parties expressly indicated that their agreement was non-exclusive.[49] This approach has also been followed by Chinese lower courts in other cases recently.[50]

Chinese law, however, does not expressly and exactly say how to distinguish the two categories of choice of court agreements if the parties' intention cannot be ascertained through interpretation. There is no general presumption or uniform standard that has been formed to help Chinese courts to make such a decision.[51] Thus, this would unfortunately lead to inconsistent judgments in cases where the parties did not make their intentions clear. In the case of *Compania Sud Americana v. Hin-Pro International,* the Chinese court held that the choice of court clause in the bill of lading was non-exclusive because it did not expressly exclude the jurisdiction of the courts of other countries.[52] This might indicate that in some Chinese courts, a choice of court agreement is presumed to be optional if the parties have failed to clearly grant "exclusivity" to the court chosen in the agreement. It, however, has been suggested that this practice reflects the "homeward trend" and local protectionism of some Chinese courts because this approach may be readily adopted by some Chinese courts to compete for jurisdiction where the parties' intention is not so clear.[53] In contrast, in another case decided by the SPC, a choice of court agreement in favour of a foreign court was held as exclusive although the parties failed to use the word "exclusive", only saying that the claimant may bring any dispute to the court of Mongolia.[54] This case might reflect another approach by some Chinese courts that a choice of court agreement is presumed to be exclusive unless the parties clearly agreed otherwise. This approach was also adopted in an earlier case decided

[49]See *Zhong An Housing Ltd. v. Merchants Bank,* the Supreme People's Court (2001) Min Si Zhong Zi No. 1. See another similar case of the SPC, *China International Iron & Steel Investment Corp. v. Guangzhou Branch of the Deutsche Bank,* the Supreme People's Court (2000) Jing Zhong Zi No. 173.

[50]See *The Industrial and Commercial Bank of China (Asia) Ltd. v. Guangdong Shengtong Financial Leasing Ltd.*, the Guangdong Guangzhou Intermediate People's Court (2016) Yue 01 Min Chu No. 310; *Toyota Tsusho Corp. v. Zhaoqing Dawang Qichang Industry Ltd.*, the Guangdong Zhaoqing Intermediate People's Court (2017) Yue 12 Min Chu No.5.

[51]There are general presumptions to help courts in other jurisdictions. For example, under art. 25 (1) of the Brussels I Recast Regulation, a choice of court agreement is presumed to be exclusive unless the parties have agreed otherwise. At common law, the courts do not strictly presume exclusivity, but they have a tendency to conclude that choice of court agreements are exclusive which is compatible with the intention of rational commercial parties, see Tang et al. (2016), p. 64; Keyes and Marshall (2015), pp. 351, 352.

[52]See *Compania Sud Americana de Vapores SA v. Hin-Pro International Logistics Ltd.*, the Zhejiang High People's Court (2013) Zhe Xia Zhong Zi No. 142. In contrast, the same choice of court clause in this case was interpreted by the English court as exclusive and therefore an anti-suit injunction was granted to stop the proceedings in the Chinese court: *Compania Sud Americana de Vapores SA v. Hin-Pro International Logistics Ltd.* [2015] EWCA Civ 401.

[53]See Tang et al. (2016), p. 65. See another similar case where a Chinese court adopted the same approach: *CMACGMS v. Shaoxing Haoyi*, the Shanghai High People's Court (2016) Hu Min Xia Zhong No. 291.

[54]See *Zhiming Xu v. Yihua Zhang (2015)*, note 43.

by a Chinese lower court.[55] In a very recent case adjudicated by the SPC, the presumption in favour of "exclusivity" was adopted.[56] It is a pity that Chinese law lacks a unified general presumption for the nature of a choice of court agreement where there is ambiguity regarding the parties' intention, which aggravates uncertainty in practice for sure.

Under Chinese law, it is believed that the chosen court is granted with jurisdiction if the parties have chosen the forum in a valid choice of court agreement irrespective of whether it is exclusive or optional.[57] In other words, a Chinese court can take jurisdiction if the parties have chosen it in a valid optional choice of court agreement, by which the parties are supposed to have submitted themselves to the Chinese court.[58] This is called the prorogation effect of a choice of court agreement in favour of the chosen court.[59] Moreover, Chinese courts are forbidden from declining jurisdiction in favour of foreign courts on the ground of *forum non conveniens* if the parties have chosen Chinese courts by either exclusive or optional choice of court agreements.[60] Therefore, the parties to an optional choice of court agreement in favour of Chinese courts should be regarded as having actually waived their rights to contest jurisdiction of the chosen Chinese courts.[61] Once the option has been exercised by commencing proceedings in the chosen forum, the optional choice of court agreement would be treated as an exclusive one if a Chinese court is designated.[62] Generally speaking, an optional choice of court agreement does not have the same derogation effect as an exclusive choice of court agreement to exclude the potential jurisdictions of all other fora before the option is exercised. Nonetheless, Chinese law grants an optional choice of court agreement in favour of a Chinese court strong effects after the option is exercised.[63]

Under Chinese law, the legal effect of an optional choice of court agreement in favour of foreign courts is less certain than the effect of an optional choice of court in

[55]See *Yacheng Automobile Fittings v, HSBC Holdings (2006)*, note 43.

[56]See *Dignity International Development Ltd. v. Rich Profit Creation Ltd.*, the Supreme People's Court (2016) Zui Gao Fa Min Shen No. 2783.

[57]See Tang (2012), p. 470.

[58]Ibid.

[59]See Tang (2012), pp. 470–472.

[60]See art. 532 (2) of the 2015 SPC Interpretation on CCPL, which says: "In dealing with a foreign-related case, under the following circumstances, a people's court may render a ruling to dismiss the case, and inform the plaintiff to institute an action in a more convenient foreign court: (1) . . . (2) the parties do not have an agreement conferring jurisdiction on the courts of the People's Republic of China. . ." Also see art. 11 (3) of the 2005 SPC Summary, which says: "In dealing with a foreign-related commercial case, if a Chinese court finds it is not convenient to exercise jurisdiction, that court can dismiss the case by the doctrine of *forum non conveniens.* To apply the doctrine, the following conditions must be met: (1) . . . (2) . . . (3) the parties do not have an agreement conferring jurisdiction on Chinese courts. . .".

[61]See Reply Letter of the SPC on *Yanzhou Haoke Weibo Mining Engineering Co., Ltd. v. A WEBER S.A. and SOFIROL S.A. (2009)*, note 28.

[62]See Tang et al. (2016), p. 72.

[63]See Tang (2012), p. 472.

favour of Chinese courts. It is provided in Article 12 of the 2005 SPC Summary that the optional choice of court agreement in favour of foreign courts in cross-border commercial disputes does not have the derogation effect to exclude the jurisdictions of other countries' competent courts including Chinese courts.[64] That is to say, a Chinese court which has statutory jurisdiction under the CCPL can still take jurisdiction over the case if one of the parties brings the dispute to the Chinese court in face of an optional choice of court agreement favouring foreign courts.[65] This general rule was expressly recognized and adopted by Chinese courts in judicial practice.[66] As a result, Chinese courts could compete to exercise jurisdiction even if the parties have made an optional choice of court agreement in favour of foreign courts but bring their dispute to the jurisdictionally competent Chinese court under the CCPL. Pursuant to Article 533 of the 2015 SPC Interpretation on CCPL, Chinese courts still could take jurisdiction at its discretion even if one of the parties has exercised the option by commencing proceedings in the nominated foreign court, which means that the legal effect of an optional choice of court agreement in favour of foreign courts would not change even if the option is exercised.[67]

It is not difficult to infer from the previous two paragraphs that under Chinese law, optional choice of court agreements in favour of Chinese courts on the one hand and those in favour of foreign courts on the other are not treated consistently. First, a Chinese court is not allowed to apply *forum non conveniens* to decline jurisdiction if it is chosen in an optional choice of court agreement[68] while a Chinese court is permitted to compete to exercise jurisdiction despite the existence of an optional choice of court agreement in favour of foreign courts, presuming that the designated foreign court might still decline to hear the case.[69] Secondly, after the option has been exercised by any party to the optional choice of court agreement, the

[64]See art. 12 of the 2005 SPC Summary, note 27.

[65]Ibid.

[66]See *Zhong An Housing Ltd. v. Merchants Bank (2001)*, note 49; *Compania Sud Americana v. Hin-Pro International (2013)*, note 52.

[67]See art. 533 of the 2015 SPC Interpretation on CCPL, which says: "When both a Chinese court and a foreign court have jurisdiction over the same case, if one party is launching the litigation in the foreign court and the other party in the Chinese court, the Chinese court can exercise jurisdiction and accept the case…"; art. 10 of the 2005 SPC Summary, which says: "in a case where both a Chinese court and a foreign court have jurisdiction, if one party is suing in the foreign court and sues again for the same case in the Chinese court or the other party sues again for the same case in the Chinese court, the jurisdiction of the Chinese court shall not be influenced whether or not the foreign court has already accepted or made a judgment on the same case. The Chinese court, however, has some discretion to decide whether to exercise its own jurisdiction according to the circumstances of the case…".

[68]See art. 532 (2) of the 2015 SPC Interpretation on CCPL and art. 11 (3) of the 2005 SPC Summary, note 60.

[69]See e.g., *Sumitomo Bank Ltd. v. Xinhua Estate (1999)*, note 44. For a comprehensive discussion on the development of *forum non conveniens* in Chinese courts and how it interacts with optional choice of court agreements, see Tu (2012), pp. 341–365.

jurisdiction of the Chinese court nominated in the agreement is treated as exclusive[70] whereas the jurisdiction of the foreign court chosen in the agreement is still treated as non-exclusive in the sense that it cannot exclude Chinese courts with statutory jurisdiction from exercising jurisdiction.[71] There are three possible explanations for this inconsistent treatment: first, the difference in treatment is due to the "home-ward trend" and the tendency of Chinese courts to favour local jurisdiction[72]; secondly, Chinese law over-emphasizes the concept of performing judicial sovereignty in exercising international jurisdiction, which takes priority over international comity, judicial justice and efficiency[73]; thirdly, Chinese courts sometimes compete to exercise jurisdiction for enforcement purposes because of the difficulties in recognizing and enforcing foreign judgments under the current Chinese law.[74]

Compared with optional choice of court agreements in commercial contracts, Chinese law has provided more protection for presumptively weaker parties, especially consumers who have agreed to optional choice of court agreements. The greater protection is stipulated in Article 31 of the 2015 SPC Interpretation on CCPL, which states that if a business entity enters into a choice of court agreement with consumers by using standard clauses without giving "proper notice" to the consumers, the choice of court agreement shall be held invalid by the people's court.[75] The special protection given to consumers is based on the rationale of the necessity to regulate the asymmetric information in the bargaining process.[76] Only by ensuring the consumers are aware of the standard choice of court clause can the genuine intention of the consumer to conclude such an agreement be established.[77] Article 31 of the 2015 SPC Interpretation on CCPL should be applied in combination

[70]See note 62 and accompanying text.

[71]E.g., see *China International Iron & Steel Investment Corp. v. Guangzhou Branch of the Deutsche Bank (2000)*, note 49; *The Industrial and Commercial Bank of China (Asia) Ltd. v. Guangdong Shengtong Financial Leasing Ltd. (2016)*, note 49.

[72]See Tang et al. (2016), pp. 65, 72.

[73]Tang et al. (2016), p. 89; Tu (2012), note 69, p. 364.

[74]E.g., see *NKK (Japan) v. Beijing Zhuangsheng Ltd.*, the Beijing High People's Court (2008) Gao Min Zhong Zi No. 919. The Chinese courts in this case asserted their jurisdiction even though there existed an exclusive choice of court agreement choosing Hong Kong courts for the reason that the Hong Kong judgment could not be recognized and enforced in the Mainland China. For another earlier case, see *Kwok & Yih Law Firm v. Xiamen Huayang Color Printing Company*, publicized in the Gazette of the Supreme People's Court in 2004, Issue 7 and adjudicated by the Fujian Xiamen Intermediate People's Court, where a similar optional choice of court agreement in favor of the Hong Kong Court was involved and the Chinese court asserted jurisdiction for enforcement purposes.

[75]See art. 31 of the 2015 SPC Interpretation on CCPL, which says: "Where a business entity enters into a choice of court agreement with a consumer by using standard clauses without reminding the consumer in a proper way to pay attention to such clauses, the people's court shall support the consumer's claim that the choice of court agreement is invalid".

[76]See Tang et al. (2016), p. 67.

[77]Ibid.

with the provisions of Chinese Contract Law regarding standard clauses to determine the validity of choice of court agreements involving consumers.[78]

In accordance with Article 12 of the 2005 SPC Summary, an optional choice of court agreement nominating the courts of a foreign country cannot exclude the jurisdiction of courts in other countries which may be able to assert jurisdiction.[79] This provision implies that if a party commences proceedings in a court other than that nominated in the optional choice of court agreement, for example, a Chinese court, the Chinese court seized of the case does not have to stay proceedings if it considers itself jurisdictionally competent. Moreover, this stance is formally entrenched by Article 533 of the 2015 SPC Interpretation on CCPL which empowers a competent Chinese court to assert jurisdiction even though one party has commenced proceedings in a foreign court having jurisdiction over the same case including jurisdiction based on an optional choice of court agreement.[80] On the contrary, in cases where an optional choice of court agreement nominating a Chinese court is breached by one party via commencing proceedings in a foreign court, the nominated Chinese court is unlikely to stay proceedings even if the foreign court seized of the same case is considered as a more convenient court.[81] However, Chinese law does not award any damages arising out of breach of an optional choice of court agreement and does not have the machineries of anti-suit injunction and anti-enforcement injunction that can enhance the parties' choice of Chinese courts.

Traditionally, China has a very "conservative" attitude towards recognition and enforcement of foreign courts' judgments. Generally, it will not recognize and enforce a foreign judgment unless there is a treaty applicable or reciprocity in practice.[82] Chinese law does not make a distinction between foreign judgments based on the parties' choice of court agreements and those on other jurisdictional grounds.

Under the policy of "One Country, Two Systems", with the handovers of Hong Kong and Macau respectively in 1997 and 1999, the PRC is now a unitary sovereign country comprising sub-national units and multiple legal systems.[83] According to the Hong Kong and Macau Basic Laws, the Hong Kong Special Administrative Region (SAR) and the Macau SAR enjoy a high-level of autonomy and can maintain their own legal systems including private laws after the handover.[84] Due to historic

[78]More elaboration on "proper notice" and the application of this specific requirement can be found in *CMACGMS v. Zhejiang Haoyi Trade Ltd.*, the Shanghai High People's Court (2016) Hu Min Xia Zhong No. 291.

[79]See art. 12 of the 2005 SPC Summary, note 27.

[80]See art. 533 of the 2015 SPC Interpretation on CCPL, note 67.

[81]See art. 532 (2) of the 2015 SPC Interpretation on CCPL and art. 11 (3) of the 2005 SPC Summary, note 60.

[82]See art. 281–282 of CCPL; Tu (2016), pp. 169–176.

[83]See Tu (2016), p. 10.

[84]See art. 2, 8 of the Basic Law of the Hong Kong Special Administrative Region of the People's Republic of China (Hong Kong Basic Law) and the Basic Law of the Macau Special Administrative Region of the People's Republic of China (Macau Basic Law).

reasons, the laws maintained in the two SARs are largely inherited from English law and the laws of Portugal respectively, which are quite different from those in the Mainland China.[85] Accordingly, the laws of the two SARs and the Mainland China regarding optional choice of court agreements are different from one another as well. The differences create the need for inter-regional judicial cooperation in terms of choice of court agreements and recognition and enforcement of judgments resulting from them.[86] To coordinate the disparities among the three legal systems regarding choice of court agreements, special mutual arrangements have been achieved on a piece-meal approach.[87] For detailed discussion of the differences and the reasons which account for the differences, some scholars' commentaries might be helpful.[88]

In Mainland China, optional choice of court agreements in intra-national cases are treated almost in the same way as in international cases since cases related to Hong Kong and Macau are generally treated almost in the same way as foreign-related cases.[89] It is clearly stipulated in the Judicial Interpretations of the SPC and followed by lower Chinese courts that the provisions of Chinese law regarding international procedural issues and choice of law issues for foreign-related cases can be applied by analogy to cases involving Hong Kong and Macau.[90] Therefore, the legal treatment of optional choice of court agreements in intra-national and international cases is basically no different under Chinese law.

The legal effect of an exclusive choice of court agreement favouring foreign courts is expressly provided for in Article 8 of the 2005 SPC Summary, which requires Chinese courts to decline jurisdiction if the parties have reached such an

[85]See Tu (2016), p. 10.

[86]Ibid.

[87]E.g., see the Arrangement of the Supreme People's Court between the Mainland and the Hong Kong SAR on Mutual Recognition and Enforcement of the Judgments in Civil and Commercial Cases under Prorogation Jurisdiction, Fa Shi [2008] No. 9 promulgated on 3 July 2008, which entered into force on 1 August 2008); Arrangement of the Supreme People's Court between the Mainland and the Macau SAR on Mutual Recognition and Enforcement of Civil and Commercial Judgments, Fa Shi [2006] No. 2 promulgated on 21 March 2006, which entered into force on 1 April 2006.

[88]E.g., see Johnston and Harris (2017), Tu (2013), pp. 349–375; Lee (2015), pp. 331–350.

[89]See e.g. *Yacheng Automobile Fittings v, HSBC Holdings (2006)*, note 43 (where a Hong Kong court was granted with non-exclusive jurisdiction); *Zhiming Xu v. Yihua Zhang (2015)*, note 43 (where a Mongolian Court was granted with jurisdiction); Tu (2016), p, 16.

[90]E.g., see art. 19 of the Interpretation of the Supreme People's Court on the Law of the People's Republic of China on Choice of Law for Foreign-Related Civil Relationships (I) promulgated on 28 December 2012, Fa Shi [2012] No. 24 and having entered into force on 7 January 2013, which says: "Issues concerning the applicable law in relation to civil relationships involving the Hong Kong SAR and the Macau SAR are subject to the provisions of this Interpretation by analogy"; art. 3, para. 1 of the Answers of the Supreme People's Court regarding the Trials on Commercial Disputes involving Hong Kong and Macau that entered into force on 19 October 1987 but repealed on 18 January 2013, which says: "When dealing with procedural issues, the provisions of Book Five of the Civil Procedural Law (For Trial Implementation) on foreign-related civil procedures shall be applied to commercial cases involving Hong Kong and Macau".

agreement.[91] This is the so-called derogation effect of the exclusive choice of court agreement, which is the main difference from an optional choice of court agreement.[92] In judicial practice, the derogation effect of an exclusive choice of court agreement excluding jurisdiction of any court other than that nominated in the agreement has been consistently recognized by Chinese courts, regardless of whether a Chinese court or a foreign court is designated by the agreement.[93] In contrast, under Chinese law an optional choice of court agreement only has the prorogation effect and does not have the same derogation effect as an exclusive choice of court agreement of excluding the jurisdiction Chinese courts may have according to domestic Chinese jurisdictional rules.[94]

In China, the treatment of exclusive and optional choice of court agreements are both under-developed since no clear distinction has been made in either legislation or judicial interpretations.[95] The provisions about the legal treatment of exclusive and optional choice of court agreements appear sporadically in a few judicial interpretations issued by the SPC. There are no systematic dispositive provisions regarding the characterization, interpretation, validity and effects of these two basic categories of choice of court agreements, and judicial practices as to these basic issues are also diverse. It is not currently possible to tell which one is more developed than the other. The only point that could be made here is probably that the legal effect which an exclusive choice of court agreement may have under Chinese law is more certain than that of an optional choice of court agreement.

4 Asymmetrical Choice of Court Agreements

Scholars often use the exclusive-optional dichotomy to classify choice of court agreements while some do use the exclusive-optional-asymmetrical trichotomy by paying due attention to asymmetrical choice of court agreements.[96] The asymmetrical agreement comprises both exclusive and non-exclusive elements and applies to the parties differently.[97] Such agreements are commonplace in international financial contracts and are adopted to favour the financial institutions as a risk-management

[91]See art. 8 of the 2005 SPC Summary, which says: "... if the parties have made an arbitration agreement or an exclusive choice of court agreement nominating a foreign court, Chinese court shall not exercise jurisdiction". Also see Tu (2012), p. 361.

[92]See Tang (2012), p. 472.

[93]See, e.g., *Yacheng Automobile Fittings v, HSBC Holdings (2006)*, note 43; *Zhiming Xu v. Yihua Zhang (2015)*, note 43.

[94]See text to notes 51–67 above.

[95]See text to notes 12–32.

[96]See text to notes 27–32; Keyes and Marshall (2015), pp. 345–378.

[97]See Keyes and Marshall (2015), p. 364.

strategy.[98] The most well-known example was examined in the controversial decision of the French *Cour de cassation* in *Madame X v. Rothschild,*[99] where the asymmetrical clause provided that Madame X could only bring a dispute to the exclusive jurisdiction of the courts of Luxembourg while the Bank reserved the right to sue in any competent court with jurisdiction.[100] The validity of such an asymmetrical agreement is divergent in different laws. For instance, these agreements are rejected in France but well accepted by England.[101]

As regards the legal effects of such an agreement under Chinese law, lessons might be learned from the judicial practice of some Chinese courts. In *Lai v. ABN AMRO Bank*, the choice of court clause provided that the parties should irrevocably submit any potential dispute to Hong Kong courts, but this provision could not prevent the Bank from filing the lawsuit in the courts of other jurisdictions.[102] Both the Shanghai Intermediate People's Court and the Shanghai High People's Court upheld the validity of this choice of court agreement and concluded that if the investor commenced the proceedings Hong Kong courts would have exclusive jurisdiction whereas if the Bank filed the lawsuit the jurisdiction clause would be non-exclusive.[103] Therefore, it could be inferred from this case that to some Chinese courts, the legal effect of such an asymmetrical agreement depends on which party to the agreement has exercised the option. If the weaker party, normally a consumer, has exercised the option, the asymmetrical agreement would be treated as exclusive; if the stronger party, normally a bank or other financial institution, has exercised the option, the asymmetrical agreement has the legal effect of an optional choice of court agreement. As said above, Chinese law, however, also grants relatively higher protection to weaker parties such as consumers to the asymmetrical choice of court agreement. If the asymmetrical choice of court agreement is drafted by the stronger party to the agreement such as the bank as a standard clause without giving consumers proper notice in advance, the agreement shall be considered invalid by Chinese courts.[104]

---

[98]Ibid.

[99]*Cass civ, 1ère, 26.09.2012, Madame X v Banque Privée Edmond de Rothschild*, No 11-26.022 (Rothschild).

[100]Ibid.

[101]For a detailed examination of different approaches adopted by the courts of France and England to determine the effect of an asymmetrical choice of court agreement, see Keyes and Marshall (2015), pp. 363–377; Mailhé, "France: A Game of Asymmetries, Optional and Asymmetrical Choice of Court Agreements under French Case Law", in this collection, Sect. 3; Merrett and Carruthers, "United Kingdom: Giving Effect to Optional Choice of Court Agreements – Interpretation, Operation and Enforcement", in this collection, Sect. 3.

[102]See *Lai v. ABN AMRO Bank N.V.*, the Shanghai High People's Court (2010) Hu Gao Min Wu (Shang) Zhong Zi No. 49.

[103]Ibid.

[104]See art. 31 of the 2015 SPC Interpretation on CCPL, note 75.

5 Evaluation and Reform

Given the current situation that Chinese law lacks systematic and developed legal rules on choice of court agreements, it is hard to say whether the legal treatment of optional choice of court agreements in the PRC is effective and well-justified. From the perspective of history, this is partially due to the late development of Chinese laws. Although Chinese law including Chinese PIL has achieved a great leapfrog development against the backdrop of globalization and a free market economy, there are still many problems in the legal treatment of optional choice of court agreements. First, at the legislative level, Chinese law does not draw a clear-cut dividing line between exclusive and optional choice of court agreements. Instead, they are dealt with only in one provision, i.e. Article 34 of the CCPL. In order to guide Chinese courts to tackle specific issues regarding choice of court agreements, such as choice of law rules, characterization, legal effects etc., merely sporadic judicial interpretations have been issued by the SPC. As a consequence, the judicial practices as regards the exclusivity issue, choice of law, and the legal effects of optional choice of court agreements are inconsistent. Secondly, the legal treatment of optional choice of court agreements in Chinese law is attached to some sort of local protectionism and "homeward trend". In cases where choice of court agreements choosing foreign courts, Chinese courts are prone to consider them as optional so that sometimes they can exercise exorbitant jurisdiction, especially when a Chinese party or state interest is involved. Thirdly, Chinese law is not prepared to tackle newly-emerging types of choice of court agreements such as asymmetrical choice of court agreements as discussed in this Report earlier. Neither have most Chinese judges nor practitioners acquired the necessary knowledge and expertise to decide issues and resolve problems arising out of cases involving this latest type of choice of court agreements. This would create more uncertainty for the parties and make it more difficult for the parties to be convinced by the judgments of Chinese courts. This problem has been vividly revealed in *Lai v. ABN AMRO Bank,* where the losing party was not convinced by the poor interpretation of the two levels of Chinese courts on the asymmetrical choice of court agreement in dispute and finally applied to the SPC for a retrial.

It is beyond doubt that the under-developed legal treatment of choice of court agreements in Chinese law shows the need for reforms to reduce the uncertainty and costs for the parties and the concerned courts. However, to the knowledge of the current authors, there are no existing proposals to reform the current Chinese law relating to the treatment of optional choice of court agreements. Maybe, the fact that China has signed the 2005 Hague Choice of Court Convention will help to draw the attention of Chinese legislators and scholars to this significant issue.

References

Briggs A (2012) The subtle variety of jurisdiction agreements. Lloyd's Maritime Commer Law Q 364–381

Chen AHY (2004) An introduction to the legal system of the People's Republic of China, 3rd edn. LexisNexis, Hong Kong

Fawcett JJ (2001) Non-exclusive jurisdiction agreements in private international law. Lloyd's Maritime Commer Law Q 234–260

Guo Y, Wen S (2014) A brief analysis of the legal effect on one-sided jurisdiction clause. Chinese Rev Int Law 4:48

Jiao Y (2011) The legal system and the legal nature of choice of court agreements. Jurist 6:163

Johnston G, Harris P (2017) Conflict of laws in Hong Kong, 3rd edn. Sweet & Maxwell, Hong Kong

Keyes M, Marshall BA (2015) Jurisdictional agreements: exclusive, optional and asymmetrical. J Priv Int Law 3:345–378

Lee E (2015) Legal pluralism, institutionalism and judicial recognition of Hong Kong – China cross-border insolvency judgments. Hong Kong Law J 45:331–350

Liu X, Zhou Q (2014) The actual connection principle and *Forum Non Conveniens* in Chinese contractual jurisdiction system. Legal Sci 12:50

Tang ZS (2012) Effectiveness of exclusive jurisdiction clauses in the Chinese courts – a pragmatic study. Int Comp Law Q 61:459–484

Tang ZS, Xiao Y, Huo Z (2016) Conflict of laws in the People's Republic of China. Edward Elgar, England

Tu G (2007) The Hague choice of court convention—a Chinese perspective. Am J Comp Law 54:347–365

Tu G (2012) Forum non conveniens in the People's Republic of China. Chinese J Int Law 11:341–365

Tu G (2013) Arrangement on mutual recognition and enforcement of judgments in civil and commercial matters between China and Macau: inherent problems, six years' experience and the way forward. Hong Kong Law J 43:349–376

Tu G (2016) Private international law in China. Springer, Singapore

Tu G, Li X (2013) The second amendment to the PRC civil procedure law: an international litigation perspective. Hong Kong Law J 43:633–658

Wang H (1991) Preamble and Section 2, The explanation on the Civil Procedure Law of the People's Republic of China (For trial implementation)

Zhang L (2014) An exploration on non-exclusive jurisdiction agreements. Tribune Polit Sci Law 32:122

Zhang L (2016) An analysis of the legitimacy of asymmetrical jurisdiction agreements. Legal Sci 1:125

Guangjian Tu is a Full Professor of Law at the University of Macau; PhD, LLM (UK); BSC., Dip of Law; Qualifications of Lawyer and Judge (PRC).

Zeyu Huang is a PhD student in the Law Faculty of University of Macau; Renmin U (PRC); LLM (Macau).

Czech Republic: The Treatment of Optional and Exclusive Choice of Court Agreements

Naděžda Rozehnalová, Silvie Mahdalová, and Lucie Zavadilová

1 The Treatment of Choice of Court Agreements in General

1.1 Introduction

Agreements on jurisdiction are and have been regulated in the Czech Republic by a number of legal norms of domestic, European and international origin. Despite the existence of a favourable legal environment (and professional legal literature recommendations), parties' agreements on jurisdiction do not constitute the preferred manner of establishing court jurisdiction, either at the national or international level.

This is due to several reasons, some of which are historically conditioned and the outcome of a certain force of habit. With respect to the national level, it is important to note that until 1991 all disputes between companies were processed within the framework of a special economic arbitration, i.e. not before the courts. An adjustment of the Civil Procedure Code implemented in 1991[1] transferred the settlement of disputes between entrepreneurs to the courts and the establishment of court jurisdiction by an agreement of the parties was explicitly determined. This agreement is limited to disputes between entrepreneurs in business-related matters. The agreement cannot be concluded in consumer and non-business-related matters. Its use in the

The authors have published a short summary of this paper under the title "Czech National Report on Optional Choice of Court Agreements" in The Lawyer Quarterly (2018), pp. 332–347.

[1]Act No. 519/1991 Coll., amending the Civil Procedure Code. The term "*commercial relations*" was later replaced with the term "*relations between entrepreneurs within the framework of their business activities*".

N. Rozehnalová (✉) · S. Mahdalová · L. Zavadilová
Faculty of Law, Masaryk University, Brno, Czech Republic
e-mail: rozehn@law.muni.cz

M. Keyes (ed.), *Optional Choice of Court Agreements in Private International Law*,
Ius Comparatum – Global Studies in Comparative Law 37,
https://doi.org/10.1007/978-3-030-23914-5_7

domestic framework is rather marginal and agreements establishing the jurisdiction of courts other than those stipulated by legal rules are scarce.

At the international level, where the possibility of the prorogation of domestic and foreign courts has been regulated since 1950,[2] proceedings initiated before courts competed with proceedings before arbitrators. Compulsory arbitration was applicable to all disputes between entrepreneurs in Comecon countries since 1975.[3] In accordance with the so-called Moscow Convention[4] all disputes between entrepreneurs from member states were resolved before designated arbitration tribunals. In 1991, the Czech Republic withdrew from agreements linked to Comecon, eliminating its obligation to resolve disputes within the compulsory arbitration framework. As a result, it opened up to the possibility of resolving disputes before courts as well as to the possibility of resolving disputes by facultative arbitration. With respect to business partners from other countries, facultative arbitration was preferred (and recommended) due to both doctrinal and legal reasons. In particular, the complexity of the recognition and enforcement of court decisions on the international level and, on the other hand, the relatively favourable conditions associated with arbitration awards, played a crucial role.[5] The adoption of the New York Convention on the Recognition and Enforcement of Foreign Arbitral Awards[6] undoubtedly boosted the usage of arbitration proceedings. Although the law as well as some bilateral treaties on judicial cooperation did facilitate the possibility of concluding prorogation agreements, their usage by contracting parties, i.e. entrepreneurs, was limited. On the international level, the resolution of disputes was dominated by arbitration proceedings.

Changes took place especially after 1990.[7] Mandatory arbitration was abolished at both the national and international levels and disputes were thus open to resolution before the courts or within the optional arbitration framework. The prorogation agreement in favour of Czech courts is explicitly determined by law.[8] With respect to the derogation of Czech courts and the establishment of the jurisdiction of a

[2]Section 623 of the Act No. 142/1950 Coll., the Civil Procedure Code, as subsequently amended.

[3]Kučera (1980), pp. 371–374.

[4]Convention on the Settlement by Arbitration of Civil Disputes Arising out of Economic, Scientific and Technical Cooperation Relationships (Moscow, 26 May 1972). The Convention was revoked in 1995 in Moscow. See: Sedláček and Steiner (1975), p. 157; Sedláček (1982), p. 181.

[5]Růžička (2003), pp. 11–55.

[6]United Nations Convention on the Recognition and Enforcement of Foreign Arbitral Awards (New York, 1958). This Convention has been effective for the former Czechoslovakia since 10th October 1959.

[7]I.e. after the so-called Velvet Revolution when not only political changes but also significant changes of legal order occurred.

[8]Section 37, paragraphs 2, 3 of the Act No. 97/1963 Coll., on Private International Law and Rules of International Procedure, as subsequently amended (hereinafter referred to as Private International Law Act 1963). See also: Bělohlávek (2004), p. 679; Rozehnalová (2013d), pp. 53–100.

foreign court, such a procedure is only allowed in the case of legal persons.[9] Additional changes subsequently took place once the Czech Republic joined the EU, both in terms of law and with respect to the behaviour of contracting parties.

The following conclusions may thus be drawn: parties are not precluded from utilizing agreements on jurisdiction due to primarily legal (national or international) reasons, quite the contrary. Rather favourable legal conditions at both the national and international levels have existed in the past and continue to exist today. The unfavourable view of the prorogation of courts is thus the result of the above mentioned historical experience. Stereotypes also persist regarding the utilization of options other than active court choice in the form of an agreement on jurisdiction. Instead, changes take place in the area of international relations, often under the influence of a partner's dispute settlement requirements before the courts of a particular country. Reasons for the fact that prorogation agreements are infrequently used in favour of Czech courts also include a range of general problems associated with courts and the management of international proceedings. First of all, these include the duration of proceedings, and, in international disputes, also the determination of foreign law. Outside of the European Union, or where international treaties have not been concluded, the recognition and enforcement of a foreign decision is also a factor. This is guaranteed by the New York Convention on the Recognition and Enforcement of Foreign Arbitral Awards to which the Czech Republic is party.

The issue of the parties' legal limits when concluding an agreement on jurisdiction may be assessed from two points of view:

- The prorogation of a foreign court is only possible in case an international element is present. Czech doctrine specifically emphasizes the need for the existence of a legally significant international element.[10] However, as this is not defined by the Act No. 91/2012 Coll., on Private International Law, as subsequently amended,[11] its qualification is a matter of discretion in each particular case (ad hoc).
- Prorogation (or derogation) applies only to territorial jurisdiction, i.e. not to matters of material or functional jurisdiction. This is applicable to both national[12] and international[13] prorogation agreements.
- While only entrepreneurs may enter into prorogation agreements at the national level, no such limitation exists at the international level. Limitations at the

[9]Kučera and Tichý (1989), pp. 224–225; Rozehnalová (1997), pp. 93, 104–105; Bříza (2012), p. 180.

[10]More to the determination of a legally significant international element and discussions with regard to this issue see: Kučera and Tichý (1989), pp. 24–25; Pauknerová and Pfeiffer (2013), p. 5; Kučera and Pauknerová (2015), pp. 23–25; Rozehnalová (2016), pp. 202–206.

[11]Act No. 91/2012 Coll., on Private International Law, as subsequently amended (hereinafter referred to as the Private International Law Act).

[12]Jirsa (2016), p. 69.

[13]Kučera and Tichý (1989), p. 224; Rozehnalová (2013a), p. 578; Bříza and Břicháček (2014a), p. 502.

international level are associated with the scope of the subject matter: an agreement on jurisdiction may only be concluded with respect to issues associated with obligation law and property law and in matters linked to employment.[14] Restrictions associated with the so-called weaker parties will be addressed later on.
- Form also imposes some limitations: in accordance with Czech law, in both national[15] and international[16] cases an agreement on jurisdiction must be concluded exclusively in writing. No other forms are allowed.

Regional as well as international instruments binding for the Czech Republic also impose their own jurisdiction limitations or delineations. As described further on, a central role in the legal regulation of prorogation agreements is played by the Regulation (EU) No 1215/2012 of the European Parliament and of the Council of 12 December 2012 on jurisdiction and the recognition and enforcement of judgments in civil and commercial matters (recast).[17]

1.2 Recent Developments

The overview provided below in this chapter lists the many sources of legal regulation of parties' agreements on jurisdiction. Leaving changes at the European and international levels aside, let us concentrate purely on the level of Czech law. In 2012, the Private International Law Act was adopted. It was first implemented on 1 January 2014.[18] In comparison with previous national regulations, the regulation of the parties' agreements on the jurisdiction of courts underwent certain changes, in part thanks to the significant influence of the Council Regulation (EC) No 44/2001 of 22 December 2000 on jurisdiction and the recognition and enforcement of judgments in civil and commercial matters[19] and the Brussels I Recast Regulation. The new regulation may be described as follows:

- The general regulation applicable to the jurisdiction of Czech courts by parties' agreement is stipulated in section 85 of the Private International Law Act.[20]

[14]Kučera and Tichý (1989), pp. 221–222; Rozehnalová (2013a), pp. 572–573; Bříza and Břicháček (2014a), p. 499.

[15]Javůrková (2009), p. 414; Novotný (2009), pp. 580–581.

[16]Rozehnalová (2013a), pp. 576–577; Bříza and Břicháček (2014b), pp. 501–502.

[17]Regulation (EU) No 1215/2012 of the European Parliament and of the Council of 12 December 2012 on jurisdiction and the recognition and enforcement of judgments in civil and commercial matters (recast) (hereinafter referred to as Brussels I Recast Regulation).

[18]Section 125 of the Private International Law Act.

[19]Council Regulation (EC) No 44/2001 of 22 December 2000 on jurisdiction and the recognition and enforcement of judgments in civil and commercial matters (hereinafter referred to as Brussels I Regulation).

[20]This states that "Jurisdiction of the Czech courts in matters of the law of obligations and of other property rights may be established also by means of a written agreement of the parties. Nevertheless

A written agreement is explicitly required. Jurisdiction may be established in this manner for matters of obligation law and property law.[21] No distinction is made between business and consumer disputes. Labour disputes are subject to special regulations. Following the implementation of the Brussels I Recast Regulation and in view of the existence of international conventions,[22] this provision has become practically obsolete.[23]

- The provisions of section 86 of the Private International Law Act[24] specifically permit the establishment of the jurisdiction of a foreign court in matters of obligation law and property law. These provisions specifically regulate the derogation of Czech courts, including conditions under which, on the contrary, regardless of the existence of an agreement on the jurisdiction of a foreign court, a submitted case is processed by a Czech court. In consumer and insurance matters an agreement on the establishment of the jurisdiction of a foreign court may be negotiated only after a dispute has arisen. Alternatively, this also applies to cases where a policyholder, an insured person, another beneficiary, an injured party or a consumer is entitled to launch proceedings before the court of another country (i.e. a so-called asymmetrical agreement[25]).[26] In comparison with previously valid regulations, new restrictions were adopted specifically in accordance with the Brussels I Recast Regulation.[27]

---

the substantive (subject-matter) jurisdiction of the Czech courts shall not be altered by such an agreement."

[21]Rozehnalová (2013a), pp. 566–580; Bříza and Břicháček (2014a), pp. 499–504.

[22]Convention on Choice of Court Agreements (Hague, 30 June 2005) (hereinafter referred to as Hague Choice of Court Convention of 2005); Convention on Jurisdiction and the Recognition and Enforcement of Judgments in Civil and Commercial Matters (hereinafter referred to as Lugano II Convention); Treaty between the Czechoslovak Socialist Republic and Mongolia on the Provision of Legal Assistance and Legal Relations in Civil, Family and Criminal Matters (Ulan Bator, 15 October 1976) (hereinafter referred to as bilateral treaty with Mongolia).

[23]Rozehnalová (2013a), pp. 571–576; Bříza and Břicháček (2014a), pp. 498, 500, 504.

[24]This provides that "(1) Jurisdiction of a foreign court in matters of the law of obligations and of other property rights may be determined by means of a written agreement of the parties. In matters of insurance and consumer contracts such an agreement shall be admissible only after a dispute has arisen, or, provided it enables only the policyholder, the insured, another beneficiary, the injured or the consumer to initiate proceedings in the courts of another state.

(2) If jurisdiction of a foreign court is determined pursuant to the paragraph 1, jurisdiction of the Czech courts shall thereby be excluded; a Czech court shall nevertheless hear the case provided:

(a) the parties unanimously declare their intent not to insist on the agreement,
(b) a judgment given abroad would not be recognized in the Czech Republic,
(c) a foreign court declined to hear the case, or
(d) a jurisdiction agreement is contrary to the public policy."

[25]Bříza (2012), p. 180.

[26]Rozehnalová (2013b), pp. 580–594; Bříza (2014), pp. 512–519.

[27]Rozehnalová (2013b), p. 585.

- The jurisdiction of Czech courts in labour matters[28] may also be based on an agreement between parties. Again, limitations in line with the Brussels I Recast Regulation apply: the agreement may be negotiated only after a dispute has arisen or in case the arrangement allows employees to independently initiate proceedings before the court of a foreign country. The agreement must be conducted in writing.[29]

Following the implementation of the Brussels I Recast Regulation and in view of the existence of international conventions,[30] the above described provisions are seldom utilized. This is especially true of the provisions of sections 85 and 88 of the Private International Law Act which became practically obsolete after 10 January 2015. Any application outside of the EU (and the Lugano II Convention and the Hague Choice of Court Convention of 2005) thus only remains open to the provision of section 86 of the Private International Law Act.

1.3 The Influences of Multilateral, Regional, and Bilateral Instruments

The impact of multilateral and regional instruments is crucial. As an EU member state, the Czech Republic is bound by EU legislation (in our area of interest specifically by the directly applicable Brussels I Recast Regulation) and by international conventions concluded by the European Union (e.g. the Lugano II Convention, the Hague Choice of Court Convention of 2005 and the EU–Denmark Agreement). EU legislation and specifically its Brussels I Regulation and Brussels I Recast Regulation were of fundamental importance with respect to implemented changes in the provisions of the Private International Law Act. Other international conventions concluded by the Czech Republic which include the option to establish agreements on court jurisdiction did not have extensive influence on Czech legislation.

[28]See section 88 of the Private International Law Act: "(1) Jurisdiction of the Czech courts in labour matters may be established also by means of a written agreement of the parties. Nevertheless, the substantive (subject-matter) jurisdiction of the Czech courts shall not be altered by such an agreement.

(2) If the Czech courts shall otherwise have jurisdiction, jurisdiction of foreign courts may be agreed upon in writing only after a dispute has arisen, or, provided the agreement enables only an employee to initiate proceedings in the courts of another state. The provision of section 86, paragraph 2 shall apply mutatis mutandis."

[29]Rozehnalová (2013c), pp. 609–615; Bříza (2014), pp. 544–546.

[30]The Hague Choice of Court Convention of 2005; the Lugano II Convention; the bilateral treaty with Mongolia; Agreement between the European Community and the Kingdom of Denmark on jurisdiction and the recognition and enforcement of judgments in civil and commercial matters of 19 October 2005 (hereinafter referred to as EU–Denmark Agreement).

The new Czech regulations on jurisdiction agreements, as set out in the Private International Law Act, were fundamentally influenced by the Brussels I Recast Regulation (and, of course, by previous modifications) with respect to the issue of the position of the weaker party and, in certain cases, the utilization of asymmetrical agreements.[31] This differs from the previous national regulations (Private International Law Act 1963), which did not include any provisions regarding the special position of consumers, workers or insured persons.[32]

Finally, it is necessary to provide a comment on terminology as well as a comment on the concept of jurisdiction agreements from the point of view of Czech law. Neither the term "optional" (or an equivalent) nor the term "exclusive" (or an equivalent) were ever in use in Czech doctrine and legislation.[33] This explanation is significant for an understanding of the handling of some issues described in Sect. 2, explicitly focusing on optional choice of court agreements. The above listed terms only began to appear once the Czech Republic joined the European Union, i.e. with the application of the Brussels I Regulation and subsequently the Brussels I Recast Regulation and Lugano II Convention. Within the framework of Czech law (i.e. from the point of view of the Private International Law Act) only the simple term of "parties' agreement on the jurisdiction of courts" has been and is being used in reference to prorogation or derogation agreements.

However, the assessment of the concept of an agreement from the point of view of Czech law is rather more complex. It must be said that this question was not discussed in connection with the adoption of the Czech Private International Law Act and that no explanation was provided in the Explanatory Report to this Act. If we compare the features and effects of exclusive or optional agreements with the Czech regulation, it may be said that the Czech regulation, i.e. as stipulated in the Private International Law Act, constitutes a regulation of exclusive agreements, or, rather, that we proceed from the presumption that the regulation focuses on exclusive agreements.[34] The Czech regulation presupposes a choice of a court belonging to a single jurisdiction (either a specific court or a jurisdiction as a whole). In the case of the prorogation of Czech courts (section 85 of the Private International Law Act), a Czech court cannot reject jurisdiction established by a validly concluded agreement. The situation is similar in the case of derogation in favour of Czech courts and prorogation of a foreign court's jurisdiction. The explicit exclusion of the jurisdiction of Czech courts where the jurisdiction of a foreign court has been negotiated (section 86, paragraph 2 of the Private International Law Act) constitutes evidence of the concept of exclusivity.[35] Exceptions to this rule are limited and explicitly stated in the Act (section 86, paragraph 2 of the Private International Law Act). The first exception refers to the utilization of an agreement whereby the parties withdraw

[31]Rozehnalová (2013b), pp. 585–586.

[32]Kučera and Tichý (1989), pp. 215–227.

[33]Rozehnalová (2013a), p. 570.

[34]Bříza and Břicháček (2014a), p. 504.

[35]Rozehnalová (2013b), p. 587.

from a negotiated agreement. Additional reasons include: situations where a decision issued abroad could not be recognized in the Czech Republic; situations where a foreign court refused to deal with a matter; and situations where an arrangement on the jurisdiction of a foreign court would be contrary to public policy.[36] With respect to Czech courts, the prorogation agreement thus has binding positive and as well as binding negative effects.

2 Optional Choice of Court Agreements

2.1 *Legal Sources Relevant to the Determination of the Effect of Optional Choice of Court Agreements*

In the Czech Republic court selection agreements are generally regulated by regional, i.e. European, sources and by international and domestic sources. With respect to optional choice of court agreements, relevant sources include European sources (Brussels I Regulation, Brussels I Recast Regulation) and international sources associated with these European regulations (the Lugano II Convention, the EU–Denmark Agreement, the Hague Choice of Court Convention of 2005). These include an explicit assumption of the exclusivity of such agreements, i.e. the agreement may be qualified as optional only in case the parties agree to do so.[37] In the case of other sources, in particular domestic regulations included in the Private International Law Act, agreement type—as previously mentioned—is not specifically identified. However, doctrine does tend to qualify these agreements as exclusive agreements, i.e. to support the argument in favour of exclusivity.

In summary, legal regulations relevant to the choice of court agreements applicable to the Czech Republic include the following:

- The Brussels I Recast Regulation along with its predecessor, the Brussels I Regulation (the Czech Republic was not bound by the Convention of 27 September 1968 on jurisdiction and the enforcement of judgments in civil and commercial matters[38]). As the Brussels I Recast Regulation extends the scope of this regulation in terms of affected persons (article 6), its temporal scope is of interest both in relation to the preceding Brussels I Regulation and the Czech regulation stipulated in the Private International Law Act. The use of this Act has become rather limited following the application of the Brussels I Recast Regulation and, in the case of prorogation according to section 85 of the Private

[36] Rozehnalová (2013b), pp. 587–588; Bříza (2014), pp. 517–519.

[37] Keyes and Marshall (2015), p. 350.

[38] Convention of 27 September 1968 on Jurisdiction and the Enforcement of Judgments in Civil and Commercial Matters (hereinafter referred to as Brussels Convention).

International Law Act, in fact entirely obsolete.[39] With respect to agreements on jurisdiction, two fundamental moments appear to be decisive for any consideration of the application of the new regulation: the conclusion of the agreement and the initiation of proceedings.[40] The Brussels I Recast Regulation is applicable, in accordance with article 66 thereof, to proceedings instituted on or after 10 January 2015.[41] The possible validity of agreements included under section 85 of the Private International Law Act and their invalidity under the Brussels I Recast Regulation was discussed in Czech literature also with respect to the solution in Sanicentral GmbH v René Collin (Case 25/79). The author holds a position in favour of respecting the principle of autonomous will and the principle of legal certainty.[42] On the other hand, it must be said that such a solution was never required throughout the duration of the applicability of the Private International Law Act (1 year) and that the Brussels I Recast Regulation is significantly more benevolent than the Czech regulation.

- The Lugano II Convention, binding for EU member states, Denmark, Switzerland, Iceland and Norway.
- The EU–Denmark Agreement.
- The Hague Choice of Court Convention of 2005. The Czech Republic, as an EU member state, is bound to non-EU contracting parties within the framework of this international convention.
- Other multilateral international conventions no longer directly linked to the EU also include provisions allowing or restricting prorogation agreements. The Czech Republic is bound by the Montreal Convention,[43] Warsaw Convention[44] and the CMR Convention.[45]
- Bilateral treaties—in some cases agreements on judicial cooperation concluded by the Czech Republic prior to joining the European Union—also include adjustments to prorogation agreements. A currently valid convention (with the regulation of prorogation agreement) has also been concluded with Mongolia.
- Act No. 91/2012 Coll., on Private International Law, as subsequently amended, a key standard governing the area of private and procedural international law, includes relevant regulations in sections 85, 86 and 88. As previously mentioned this arrangement is somewhat residual and applies only where no European (EU) or international standards apply.

---

[39] Bříza and Břicháček (2014a), pp. 498, 500, 504.

[40] On this debate see: Magnus and Mankowski (2016), pp. 1014–1016.

[41] See also the solution given by European Court of Justice in Sanicentral GmbH v René Collin (Case 25/79 of 13 November 1979).

[42] Rozehnalová (2013a), p. 574. On this question see also: Bříza (2012), pp. 130–131.

[43] Convention for the Unification of Certain Rules for International Carriage by Air (Montreal, 28 May 1999), exhaustively listed fora in article 33.

[44] Convention for the Unification of Certain Rules to International Carriage by Air (Warsaw, 12 October 1929), article 28.

[45] Convention on the Contract for the International Carriage of Goods by Road (CMR) (Geneva, 19 May 1956), article 31.1.

2.2 *The Applicable Law to Characterise a Choice of Court Agreement as Optional or Exclusive*

Before we address the issue of applicable law with respect to qualifying whether prorogation agreements are optional or exclusive, it is necessary to inspect the nature of such agreements as viewed by Czech doctrine. The answer to this question also determines what law is applicable to the qualification of a prorogation agreement.

Under Czech doctrine, prorogation agreements are classified as agreements with procedural effects or as procedural agreements. The primary consequence of this designation is the dominance of the forum law.[46] The same applies to derogation agreements (or derogation effects) in favour of foreign courts.[47]

Although this view has been and continues to be dominant, views reflecting not only the procedural aspects of such agreements (shifts in jurisdiction) but also the private law aspects of prorogation agreements establishing the rights and obligations of the parties to such agreements have gradually emerged. As a result of this view, prorogation agreements should also "bear" a material law aspect. In accordance with the principle of the autonomous will of the parties, the parties should be able to choose the governing law applicable to the material validity of a prorogation agreement (especially with respect to issues of party will and consensus). However, the admissibility of prorogation agreements is always governed by the forum law.[48] The application of choice of law rules would only be relevant with respect to the contractual elements of prorogation agreements.

While some progress in doctrine with respect to prorogation agreements is visible, their procedural character and emphasis on the transfer of jurisdiction continue to prevail. Their nature thus also allows us to unequivocally infer the dominance of forum law with regard to the issue of qualification.[49]

Given the fact that the prorogation agreement is classified as a procedural agreement in Czech doctrine, no other approach than the application of forum law is discussed—with the exception of the above-mentioned scope of the choice of law rule.

2.2.1 The Principles Applicable to Determine Whether a Choice of Court Agreement Is Characterized as Optional, or Exclusive

The general legal principle governing private law is the autonomous will of the parties. The range and scope of this principle is determined by law. As a result, the common will of the parties is only capable of influencing a limited range of issues.

[46]Bělohlávek (2012), pp. 971 et seq; Rozehnalová (1997), p. 91; Kučera and Tichý (1989), p. 223; Bříza (2012), pp. 169, 179; Rozehnalová (2013a), p. 568.

[47]Kučera and Tichý (1989), p. 224.

[48]Bříza (2012), p. 179; Bříza and Břicháček (2014a), p. 503.

[49]Rozehnalová (2013a), p. 568.

The key issue is whether or not the parties decide to conclude a prorogation agreement. The will of the parties does not come into play in any other areas. It cannot alter e.g. the form of the prorogation agreement, which is instead stipulated by law. The parties cannot directly influence whether the prorogation agreement is negotiated as exclusive or optional. This option is not legally provided for. They only have disposal of the territorial jurisdiction of the agreement, i.e. any agreement made between them cannot alter either material or functional jurisdiction. This is in accordance with Czech domestic law. While Czech legislation does not comment on the exclusivity or non-exclusivity of prorogation agreements, the presumption of exclusivity is prevalent in its doctrine. The situation is different where the Brussels I Recast Regulation or international instruments are applied.

2.3 *The Applicable Law to Determine the Legal Effect of an Optional Choice of Court Agreement*

As explained above, Czech legislation does not expressly mention agreement type. In view of the character of agreements regulated by the Private International Law Act, it is, however, possible to assume a tendency towards their exclusive nature. Nevertheless, it is impossible to say how Czech law might react to a hypothetical situation where parties concluding an agreement explicitly classified it as optional.

In the case of the prorogation of a Czech court in such a manner, previously mentioned regional or international instruments would be applied. This would be outside of the scope of the Private International Law Act.

In the event that a Czech court should be asked to assess the derogation effects of an agreement on the jurisdiction of a court whereby the parties explicitly "non-exclusively" opt for the jurisdiction of a foreign court (i.e. outside the scope of European or international instruments), the issue of the effects of such an agreement would be settled in accordance with Czech law. This point of view, if considered further, allows us to model the following situations:

1. The jurisdiction of a Czech court may apply despite the existence of a prorogation agreement in case the parties affirm, in accordance with section 86, paragraph 2 of the Private International Law Act, that they do not insist on the prorogation of jurisdiction of a foreign court. This constitutes the application of a legally explicitly stipulated exemption from the statutory derogation of jurisdiction of Czech courts. It also comprises an exception to the written form of the agreement—an affirmative statement of the parties, included in the protocol, is sufficient. Submission by itself is not sufficient.
2. Despite the existence of an agreement explicitly described as optional, proceedings will be initiated before a Czech court. The court is under an obligation to investigate ex officio the conditions of such proceedings, i.e. including its jurisdiction. The outcome in this case is entirely uncertain, with all variants being conceivable. An outcome in favour of maintaining the validity of such an

agreement may be based either on the principle of the autonomous will of the parties or the severability of invalid provisions. The court may also reject jurisdiction, in which case the issue of exclusivity or non-exclusivity would not be processed. Alternatively, the court may declare such an agreement invalid.

Regarding situations described in point 2, no such question has yet been addressed by the courts.

From the point of view of Czech law this is not a choice of law issue but rather a question of procedural law dominated by the forum law. Procedural standards relevant to jurisdiction are used, as applicable.

2.4 The Legal Effect of an Optional Choice of Court Agreement

2.4.1 Optional Choice of Court Agreement in Favour of the Courts of the Forum

Legal regulation relevant to the prorogation of Czech courts in accordance with section 85 of the Private International Law Act is obsolete. In this case, we are proceeding in accordance with the Brussels I Recast Regulation (or according to international instruments, if applicable to a given situation), specifically in accordance with article 25 thereof. This is not a matter of submission to jurisdiction, but one of establishing jurisdiction on the basis of an agreement between parties. This situation is thus different from submission regulated by the provision of article 26 of the Brussels I Recast Regulation.

2.4.2 Optional Choice of Court Agreement in Favour of a Foreign Court

From a domestic regulations perspective it may be said that the Private International Law Act operates with the concept of the exclusive nature of agreements on jurisdiction. We may however ask what the effects of an optional choice agreement (an agreement expressly determining the jurisdiction of a foreign court) would be, i.e. whether they would be identical to the effects of an agreement not based on this concept. Or, on the contrary, whether the absence of this aspect of the prorogation agreement might result in a derogation effect with respect to the Czech courts.

2.4.3 The Effect of Exercising the Option by Commencing Proceedings in a Nominated Foreign Court

Providing an answer to this question is rather difficult. In general, in case a valid agreement on the jurisdiction of a foreign court is concluded, the jurisdiction of the

Czech courts is thereby derogated. This modification of the resulting effects is explicitly stipulated in section 86 of the Private International Law Act. Whether these effects are also triggered by the optional choice of court agreement remains uncertain, as stated above on several occasions. Naturally, the situation is quite different under the Brussels I Recast Regulation, which resolves this situation in accordance with general *lis pendens* rules.

2.4.4 Consistency in the Treatment of Optional Choice of Court Agreements in Favour of Forum and Foreign Courts

The question, whether optional choice of court agreements in favour of forum and foreign courts are treated consistently, cannot be answered from the point of view of domestic legislation as set out in the Private International Law Act. The Private International Law Act is based on the presumption of exclusive prorogation. However, this question is relevant in connection with the application of article 25 of the Brussels I Recast Regulation, which allows parties to negotiate an optional prorogation agreement. Nevertheless, not even the provisions of the Brussels I Recast Regulation distinguish between prorogation in favour of forum courts or, on the other hand, in favour of the courts of other member states. Given the principle of mutual trust between member states, it may be assumed that member states will not distinguish between the prorogation in favour of forum courts or in favour of those of other member states.

2.5 Optional Choice of Court Agreements Involving Presumptively Weaker Parties

Following the example of regional regulations, Czech national legislation sets out provisions for the protection of weaker parties. The adoption of protection for weaker parties was led in particular by efforts designed to balance the economic, legal and factual inequalities in society.[50] Simultaneously, Czech legislation also enables weaker parties to litigate in their home jurisdiction, to facilitate access to the courts.[51]

The nature of the parties is not decisive in the case of prorogation of Czech courts in accordance with section 85 of the Private International Law Act. However, weaker parties are protected when negotiating agreements on the jurisdiction of foreign courts in accordance with sections 86 and 88 of the Private International Law Act.[52] In the case of insurance and consumer agreements, the jurisdiction of a foreign court

[50]Rozehnalová (2013a), p. 569; Rozehnalová (2013b), pp. 585–586.

[51]Rozehnalová (2013b), p. 586.

[52]Bříza and Břicháček (2014b), pp. 513–514.

in accordance with section 86 of the Private International Law Act may only be established after a dispute has arisen, or in case it allows a weaker party (policy-holder, insured, another beneficiary, injured party or consumer) to initiate proceedings before the court of another country. Likewise, in accordance with section 88, paragraph 2 of the Private International Law Act, the jurisdiction of a foreign court may be established in labour matters only after a dispute has arisen or in case it allows the employee to initiate proceedings before the court of another country.[53]

The provision of section 86, paragraph 2 of the Private International Law Act (as well as section 88, paragraph 2 thereof, which refers to it) expressly provides for a derogation of jurisdiction of Czech courts.[54]

Although we generally proceed from the concept of exclusivity, the Private International Law Act does apply the concept of optional prorogation in connection with asymmetrical agreements in favour of weaker parties.[55] In cases where the provisions of the Brussels I Recast Regulation are prioritized, special provisions for the protection of weaker parties established in articles 15, 19 and 23 of this Regulation must be respected. These provisions do not include a presumption of exclusivity, as is the case with article 25 of the Brussels I Recast Regulation.

2.6 *The Consequences if a Party Brings Proceedings in a Court Other than that Nominated in an Optional Choice of Court Agreement*

2.6.1 Lis Pendens

A general *lis pendens* rule is included in section 8, paragraph 2 of the Private International Law Act. According to this provision, if proceedings before a Czech court are initiated later than related proceedings before a foreign court, the Czech court may suspend proceedings in a justified case. Such an interruption may only be carried out by the court in case the decision of the foreign court is deemed recognizable in the Czech Republic.[56]

Nevertheless, the provision of section 86, paragraph 2 of the Private International Law Act specifically stipulates the derogation of the jurisdiction of Czech courts in the case of the prorogation of jurisdiction of a foreign court. Due to a lack of jurisdiction, the Czech court should stop any proceedings and the *lis pendens* rule would thus not be applied. This solution is fully in line with the concept of exclusivity utilized in the Czech rule of law. However, whether the autonomous will of the parties would outweigh an explicitly established derogation of jurisdiction

[53] Rozehnalová (2013c), pp. 612–613; Bříza (2014), p. 546.

[54] Rozehnalová (2013b), p. 587.

[55] Rozehnalová (2013b), p. 586.

[56] Belloňová (2013), pp. 74–75; Břicháček (2014a), pp. 68–69.

of a Czech court in the event of a negotiated optional prorogation agreement is unclear. Although the issue has not yet been addressed by Czech courts in practice, we believe that it would be up to the court to consider whether it would prefer a restrictive interpretation of the law or whether it would be willing to stand by the autonomous will of the parties.

With regard to the presumption of exclusivity as established by the Private International Law Act, the issue is of greater relevance in connection with the application of the Brussels I Recast Regulation, which presupposes optional prorogation. Exclusive prorogation requires the application of a special *lis pendens* rule as set out in article 31, paragraph 2 of the Brussels I Recast Regulation. In case proceedings were initiated before a court seised in accordance with an exclusive choice of court agreement, the courts of other member states are under an obligation to suspend proceedings. The jurisdiction of a prorogated court prevails even if proceedings were initiated before another court at an earlier date. In relation to optional prorogation, the general *lis pendens* rule stipulated in article 29 of the Brussels I Recast Regulation is applied. In such a situation, proceedings must be interrupted by the court which initiated proceedings at a later date.

2.6.2 Damages for Breach of an Optional Choice of Court Agreement Are Not Available

The possibility of awarding damages for breach of contract if one party commences proceedings in a court other than that nominated in an optional choice of court agreement may be considered problematic within the EU as it violates the principle of mutual trust between EU courts. Furthermore, in the Czech legal environment, the prorogation agreement is considered to constitute a procedural agreement or an agreement with a procedural effect. An opinion expressed in literature (and shared by the authors of this chapter) states that claims for damages resulting from the breach of an agreement on court jurisdiction cannot be enforced. One of the basic prerequisites for claiming damages is absent in this case: by concluding a prorogation agreement, no subjective substantive law—the breach of which would give rise to damages—was created in the first place.[57]

2.6.3 Enforceability of a Foreign Judgment

Apart from legally stipulated exceptions, a court may not review the jurisdiction of a court whose decision should be recognized and enforced. In accordance with section 15, paragraph 1, letter a) of the Private International Law Act, a Czech court may refuse to recognize a judgement rendered by a foreign court in case a given matter

[57] Bříza (2012), pp. 168–169, 171.

falls under the exclusive jurisdiction of the Czech courts (i.e. jurisdiction established in accordance with Czech legislation).[58]

In accordance with article 45, paragraph 1, letter e) of the Brussels I Recast Regulation, a court shall refuse a motion to recognize and enforce a judgement rendered by a foreign court in case doing so would constitute a violation of the rules of exclusive jurisdiction and selected special provisions associated with the protection of weaker parties.

In accordance with the Private International Law Act as well as with the Brussels I Recast Regulation (or other international instruments), the establishment of jurisdiction at odds with the parties' prorogation agreement does not constitute grounds for the denial of recognition and enforcement of a judgement rendered by a foreign court.

2.7 Intranational Vs. International Cases

In intranational cases, prorogation is governed by a separate regulation, the Act No. 99/1963, the Civil Procedure Code, as subsequently amended.[59] The provision of section 89a of the Civil Procedure Code[60] allows entrepreneurs to have disposal of the territorial jurisdiction of a court of first instance. An agreement cannot be concluded in cases where the law establishes exclusive territorial jurisdiction.[61] In accordance with legally stipulated provision, the agreement must be concluded in writing.[62] Prorogation is accepted in matters associated with business-to-business relations. Prorogation is entirely excluded in consumer matters. An agreement concluded in consumer matters would be considered invalid by the court ex officio.[63]

A prorogation agreement may be concluded for the purpose of deciding both a particular dispute and, in general, all future disputes arising in connection with a particular legal relationship. The prorogation agreement may also be concluded ex post for the purpose of deciding a dispute which has already arisen.[64]

Practices espoused by Czech courts infer that even in the case of an existing applicable prorogation agreement concluded in accordance with section 89a of the

---

[58] Jirmanová (2013), pp. 109–110; Břicháček (2014b), pp. 101–105.

[59] Act No. 99/1963, the Civil Procedure Code, as subsequently amended (hereinafter referred to as Civil Procedure Code).

[60] This provides that "Parties in matters concerning relations between entrepreneurs within the framework of their business activities may agree in writing to the local jurisdiction of another court of first instance, unless the law provides for exclusive local jurisdiction."

[61] Jirsa (2016), pp. 68–69.

[62] Novotný (2009), pp. 580–581; Přidal (2013), p. 315; Javůrková (2009), p. 414.

[63] Novotný (2009), pp. 580–581; Přidal (2013), pp. 315–316; Jirsa (2016), pp. 68–69.

[64] Jirsa (2016), pp. 69–70.

Civil Procedure Code, it is up to the plaintiff to choose a court with territorial jurisdiction. Unless the parties agree otherwise, the jurisdiction according to section 89a of the Civil Procedure Code shall be optional.[65] The territorial jurisdiction of a prorogated court may only be invoked by the plaintiff.[66]

In comparison to prorogation regulations containing an international element, prorogation in domestic relations is available to a narrower definition of entities: an agreement may only be concluded by entrepreneurs within the framework of their business activities.[67] From a formal requirements point of view, this arrangement is identical to the provisions of the Private International Law Act.

For the purposes of prorogation in domestic relations, the designation of a particular court with territorial jurisdiction is required. On the other hand, a prorogation agreement in matters with an international element need not include the designation of a court with territorial jurisdiction in a designated country. In case a court with territorial jurisdiction cannot be designated in accordance with the parties' agreement or the general rules for determining the territorial jurisdiction of a court, a court which shall hear and decide the case shall be designated by the Supreme Court.[68]

2.8 *The Effect of an Exclusive Choice of Court Agreement*

The term "exclusive prorogation agreement" does not exist and is thus not used in Czech law. Where this aspect is considered in literature, it is based on the presumption or concept of exclusivity. In accordance with this approach, prorogation is associated with two effects, namely prorogation and derogation. The choice of jurisdiction of a court of another country in accordance with section 86 of the Private International Law Act constitutes the establishment of jurisdiction of such a foreign court and, at the same time, the derogation of the jurisdiction of Czech courts.[69] Maintaining the jurisdiction of Czech courts would be contrary to the purpose of the regulation of international relations.[70]

The derogation of the jurisdiction of Czech courts as a result of the establishment of a foreign court's jurisdiction is stipulated in section 86, paragraph 2 of the Private International Law Act. The effect of this provision indicates a preference for the

[65]Javůrková (2009), pp. 414–415.

[66]Judgment of the Municipal Court in Prague of 11 July 2005, No. 16 Co 144/2005. See: Jirsa (2016), p. 69.

[67]Jirsa (2016), p. 68.

[68]Judgment of the Supreme Court of 29 August 2002, No. 29 Odo 524/2002. See: Rozehnalová (1997), pp. 105–106; Bříza and Břicháček (2014a), p. 502.

[69]Rozehnalová (2013a), p. 570.

[70]Kučera and Tichý (1989), p. 225.

concept of exclusivity.[71] This thus eliminates uncertainty as to whether it is still possible to initiate proceedings before the Czech courts in the event of the existence of a prorogation agreement in favour of a foreign court. The jurisdiction of Czech courts to hear and adjudicate in a given matter will be established only in legally enumerated cases. Exceptions to the derogation of Czech courts constitute these situations: where participants unanimously declare that they do not insist on the prorogation of jurisdiction of a foreign court; in case a decision issued in a foreign country cannot be recognized in the Czech Republic; in case a foreign court refuses to hear the case; and in case the prorogation of a foreign court would be contrary to public policy (ordre public) of the forum.[72]

Although the law mentions the prorogation of a "foreign court", the derogation of jurisdiction of Czech courts may also be waived as a result of the selection of several courts of a foreign country.[73] An opposing interpretation would thus be unjustifiably formalistic. In the case of a prorogation agreement in favour of a foreign court, Czech courts are not authorized to investigate whether such an agreement may establish the jurisdiction of a foreign court in a valid manner. This agreement may only be reviewed by the prorogated foreign court.[74]

2.8.1 Differences in the Effect of Optional and Exclusive Choice of Court Agreements

Differences between the effects of exclusive and optional prorogation agreements are identifiable. However, it is impossible to say how the effects of optional agreements might be perceived by Czech courts. Differences lie mainly in the derogation and *lis pendens* effects of prorogation agreements. Their form depends on the application of specific legal regulations.

Regulations relevant to prorogation in favour of Czech courts in accordance with section 85 of the Private International Law Act are obsolete. In case the parties prorogate the jurisdiction of Czech courts, the provisions of the Brussels I Recast Regulation (or the provisions of international instruments) have precedence.

In case the parties prorogate the jurisdiction of a foreign court, the situation differs with respect to whether the court in question is a court of EU member state or a court in a third state. In the case of the prorogation of a court of another member state, the provisions of the Brussels I Recast Regulation have precedence. The provision of section 86 of the Private International Law Act only applies to situations where parties agree on the jurisdiction of a court in a third state, i.e. a non-EU member state court, in matters not regulated by international instruments. The effects of

[71] Rozehnalová (2013b), p. 587.

[72] Rozehnalová (2013b), pp. 587–588; Bříza (2014), pp. 517–519.

[73] Bříza (2014), p. 517.

[74] Kučera and Tichý (1989), p. 225; Rozehnalová (2013b), pp. 581–582; Bříza (2014), p. 517; Kučera and Pfeiffer (2015), p. 315.

prorogation in favour of foreign courts in accordance with section 86 of the Private International Law Act were analysed above. At this point, it may be summarized that the law associates prorogation agreement with prorogation and specifically also with derogation effects.

The Brussels I Recast Regulation is based on an explicit presumption of exclusivity. A prorogation agreement according to this regulation is associated with both prorogation and derogation effects. In case parties specifically agree on optional prorogation, the agreement only carries a prorogation effect. The difference, therefore, is that by utilizing optional prorogation, the parties do not derogate the jurisdiction of courts in accordance with generally valid international jurisdiction rules.[75] The situation is similar in the case of international instruments binding for the Czech Republic.

Another distinction between exclusive and optional prorogation agreements may be identified in connection with *lis pendens*.

2.8.2 Comparing the Treatment of Exclusive and Optional Choice of Court Agreements

In the Czech legal environment, the basic point of departure is the presumption of the exclusivity of prorogation agreements, despite the fact that no such presumption is stipulated explicitly. The concept of the exclusivity of prorogation agreements is specifically regulated by regional and international instruments. The same concept has been discussed in professional legal literature.[76]

Czech domestic regulations do not take into account an optional prorogation agreement. However, we may address the issue of whether such an agreement may in fact be validly concluded and whether it would thus carry a derogation effect with respect to the jurisdiction of the Czech courts. We have already mentioned the possibilities which may arise, specifically noting the legal uncertainty arising as a result of the conclusion of an explicitly optional agreement on jurisdiction.

The following may be concluded on this issue: Czech legislation, as has been mentioned more than once, does not explicitly address the question of exclusivity and non-exclusivity. Our analysis shows that such a distinction would be beneficial; both in view of article 25 of the Brussels I Recast Regulation, which includes admissibility, and in order to avoid previously mentioned uncertainties. It may be said that from this point of view the existing legal regulation is rather inadequate and that an explicitly formulated regulation of admissibility would contribute to legal certainty.

[75]Keyes and Marshall (2015), pp. 353–355.

[76]Kučera and Tichý (1989), p. 224; Rozehnalová (2013a), p. 570; Bříza and Břicháček (2014a), p. 504.

3 Asymmetrical Choice of Court Agreements

3.1 The Legal Effect of a Choice of Court Agreement that Combines Both Exclusive and Optional Aspects ("Asymmetrical Choice of Court Agreement")

The regulation of asymmetrical agreements in accordance with sections 86 and 88 of the Private International Law Act raises questions about the range of options it covers. The Private International Law Act does not include legislation addressing the issue of asymmetrical agreements in general, i.e. legislation which would regulate their conclusion and effects for all purposes. The same applies to the previous regulation (Private International Law Act 1963, valid until 2014). Furthermore, these agreements did not appear in practice. Instead, we previously encountered asymmetrical clauses regulating the selection among entrepreneurs between litigation and arbitration, with the right to select limited to one party. While these clauses were criticized for lack of clarity in literature, they were being accepted and enforced in practice.

Most likely in connection with the Brussels I Regulation and the Brussels I Recast Regulation, new regulations incorporated into the Private International Law Act include asymmetrical choice of court agreements applicable to cases involving so-called weaker parties. This option, specifically stipulated by section 86, paragraph 1, sentence two, of the Private International Law Act (and similarly also by section 88 with respect to employment agreements[77]) is linked to the derogation of the jurisdiction of Czech courts and the choice of a foreign court. The application of the provision of section 86 of the Private International Law Act is possible in cases where the jurisdiction of the court of a third country would be prorogated.[78] The option thus granted to the weaker party is formulated as an explicit exception to the general rule. It may be asked whether or not the wording of section 86, paragraph 1 of the Private International Law Act in fact allows for considerations regarding the possibility of the conclusion of an asymmetrical agreement in additional cases, i.e. where parties have equal standing. Regulating the conclusion of asymmetrical agreements in favour of so-called weaker parties as an explicitly amended exception to the general rule on the possible prorogation of foreign courts does not contradict this view. Furthermore, the wording of paragraph 1 allows us to deduce that in the case of parties of equal standing, this option may be available to any contracting party, i.e. with the exception of insurance situations and consumer issues where such

[77]However, application of this provision, similarly to section 85 of the Private International Law Act, is limited with regard to the scope of application of the Brussels I Recast Regulation. In addition, formulation of the second paragraph of this section does not raise those questions, which are mentioned in relation to section 86.

[78]I. e. a situation which does not fall within the scope of the Brussels I Recast Regulation, the Lugano II Convention, the Hague Choice of Court Convention of 2005, and the EU–Denmark Agreement.

treatment would be limited to designated persons. This view has not been discussed in any literature, nor has it been verified in a decision-making process. It is clearly possible to find both arguments for its utilization (the principle of the autonomous will of the parties) as well as arguments against (the unequal standing of the parties; and unpredictability and uncertainty with respect to the determination of the forum, in effect destroying all of the benefits of prorogation agreements). The Explanatory Report to the Act which provides guidance in a range of other cases provides no solutions in this specific case. Neither do existing commentaries. The assessment of this solution is thus uncertain. In the future, given the circumstances outlined above, it may be expected that, possibly also thanks to the influence of the Brussels I Recast Regulation, the provision may be interpreted in favour of asymmetrical agreements of parties of equal standing, i.e. with the exception of cases specifically stipulated by law.

3.1.1 The Effect of the Optional Component of an Asymmetric Agreement

An answer to the question seeking to establish the effects of an optional component of such an agreement is determined by two facts with respect to the analysed Private International Law Act: (a) we are analysing a national regulation, i.e. a regulation which defines the jurisdiction of domestic courts and specifies cases respecting the jurisdiction of foreign courts; (b) the Czech regulation is based on the presumption of the exclusive nature of agreements regulated by this Act. It should also be borne in mind that the provision of section 86 of the Private International Law Act is limited to cases of derogation of Czech courts and the choice of courts of third countries (i.e. non-EU countries with restrictions where international conventions would apply). The party in whose favour the option is drafted may initiate proceedings both before Czech courts whose jurisdiction is established by law as well as before a court designated in accordance with the option. In the latter case, when the option is exercised, the jurisdiction of the Czech courts is derogated as a result. This effect is explicitly regulated by law. In case proceedings are initiated by the other party, only the jurisdiction of Czech courts is established (determined by law). The derogation of Czech courts does not take place only under conditions specifically set out in the same regulation (agreement of parties, public order dispute, the future decision of a third country court will not be enforced and the foreign court will refuse to handle it). In such a case, the dispute will be processed by a Czech court. Situations outside of the above are regulated by the Brussels I Recast Regulation or by international instruments.

3.1.2 Does the Effect of Such an Agreement Depend on Whether the Option Has Been Exercised?

An agreement on the choice of courts includes the possibility of one party—the option holder—to sue in a court other than the Czech court with established jurisdiction. This is an agreement between parties. The option is consumed once proceedings are initiated. The situation is clear where proceedings have been initiated before a foreign court in whose favour the option is drafted. The jurisdiction of Czech courts is derogated, with the exception of specifically mentioned cases. If, on the other hand, the proceedings were initiated before a Czech court, the situation would be uncertain. This situation would entail party A which would initiate proceedings before a Czech court and party B, favoured by the option, which would initiate proceedings before a foreign court. In such a case, the general *lis pendens* rule set out in section 8 of the Private International Law Act would apply. At the level of Czech law, this situation does not influence cases where either the Brussels I Recast Regulation or other international instrument applies.

3.2 *The Effect of an Asymmetrical Choice of Court Agreement and the Position of the Party in Whose Favour the Option Is Drafted*

As stated above, the Czech regulation expressly allows for the conclusion of an asymmetrical agreement in the case of specifically enumerated parties. These are considered to be the weaker parties (policyholder, insured, another beneficiaries, injured or consumer[79]). This scenario is thus explicitly regulated and explicitly admitted. The choice is specifically in their favour and at their disposal. In case an agreement is concluded in favour of the other party, i.e. the contractual partner in any of the enumerated matters, the agreement is invalid. As a result, the negative effects of the agreement do not occur and the jurisdiction of the Czech courts is not derogated. This case is thus clear and distinct. It is, however, limited to a group of enumerated cases, i.e. insurance and consumer matters.

In the case mentioned at the beginning of this section, i.e. in the event of an asymmetrical agreement on jurisdiction in cases where the parties are of equal standing, the standing itself would not be factually investigated. A possible exception could be the case of the so-called adhesion contracts and the potential invalidity of an arrangement concluded in accordance with section 1801 of the Act No. 89/2012 Coll., the Civil Code, as subsequently amended (a clause outside the

[79]The Explanatory Report to the Act does not expressly mention weaker parties. However, commentaries associate the text with position of a weaker party. Some doubts were expressed with regard to insurance issues.

text of the agreement proposed by the other party grossly contradicts business practices and the principle of fair business practices).

4 Evaluation and Reform

4.1 Effectiveness of the Legal Treatment of Optional Choice of Court Agreements in the Czech Republic

The conclusion of optional choice of court agreements is explicitly regulated by regional and international sources which are binding for the Czech Republic and which take precedence. The discussion outlined in article 25 of the Brussels I Recast Regulation (or article 17 of the Lugano II Convention) is relevant for the Czech legal environment, as is the initiation of a debate on cross-border financial services in connection with prorogation agreements.

A different position, however, is enshrined in the Czech Private International Law Act. As previously mentioned, the regulation has been limited by the impact of aforementioned regional and international sources only to the issue of the derogation of jurisdiction of Czech courts and the prorogation of the courts of non-EU countries or international treaties (the Lugano II Convention, the Hague Choice of Court Convention of 2005). Czech domestic legislation is based on the presumption of exclusive choice of court agreement; however, neither doctrine nor the text of the Private International Law Act labels agreements as such, i.e. this qualification may only be inferred from the features of the regulation. Clarifying the position—either at the level of legal regulations or at the level of decision-making practices and doctrine—would undoubtedly help increase legal certainty. This concerns in particular cases where asymmetrical agreements are allowed, such as in the case of situations outlined in article 25 of the Brussels I Recast Regulation.

4.2 Issues and Problems Arising in the Legal Treatment of Optional Choice of Court Agreements and Their Consequences

With respect to Czech domestic legislation, the conclusion of asymmetrical choice of court agreements in so-called general situations requires further clarification, i.e. in situations where no exceptions to such agreements are made for the benefit of specifically enumerated parties associated with insurance and consumer matters and, at the same time, where the courts of non-EU countries and the courts of countries not covered by international treaties are concerned. We consider this uncertainty to be the most serious current issue. Furthermore, due to the prevailing impact of regional and international instruments, it may also be worthwhile to resolve the issue of the exclusivity and non-exclusivity of agreements on the jurisdiction of courts in an explicit manner. Indeed, this has already been carried out in Slovakia.

As regards the consequences of these issues and problems, disputes over jurisdiction may occur due to the unclear or uncertain interpretation of the provision of section 86, paragraph 1 of the Private International Law Act. Doubts regarding the validity of the derogation of Czech courts may lead to parallel proceedings—conducted at a foreign and at a Czech court.

If, at the domestic level of the regulation, we were to follow the *lis pendens* rule, proceedings would be regulated by section 8 of the Private International Law Act. However, in cases where a valid agreement was present, proceedings would adhere directly to the provision of section 86, paragraph 1 of the Private International Law Act—the jurisdiction of Czech courts would be waived and they would be obliged to stop the proceedings. The situation would differ in case of any doubt about the validity of the agreement. In this case the provision of section 8 of the Private International Law Act would apply. In such a case, the court would be under no obligation to respect the jurisdiction of a foreign court. It would be up to the court to decide whether or not to do so.

Nevertheless, no reform regarding the law relating to the treatment of optional choice of court agreements is being proposed at the national level. It is also necessary to note the limited scope of the provision in question. On the other hand, the situation at the EU level is quite different, with a substantial number of calls for the clarification of the position in asymmetrical agreements found in the field of financial services falling under article 25 of the Brussels I Recast Regulation and the Lugano II Convention[80]; proposals for reform range from potential legislative changes to clarifications before the CJEU.

5 Conclusion

Modifications (at the level of the Private International Law Act) would seem to be appropriate in two areas. Firstly, a clarification of the possibility of concluding asymmetrical agreements not only in cases of insurance, employment and consumer matters, but also generally between parties of equal standing is required. The provision of section 86 of the Private International Law Act is not clear in this respect. Secondly, an explicit regulation with respect to the nature of agreements on jurisdiction enshrined in the Czech Private International Law Act would be desirable. The current concept, with all considerations based on an assumption of exclusivity, does not seem satisfactory, in particular, if, under the influence of dominant regulations enshrined in the Brussels I Recast Regulation, the usage of optional agreements becomes more widespread in practice.

[80]Ahmed (2017), pp. 403–425.

References

Ahmed M (2017) The legal regulation and enforcement of asymmetric jurisdiction agreements in the European Union. Eur Bus Law Rev 28:403–425

Belloňová P (2013) § 8 Základní ustanovení. In: Pauknerová M, Rozehnalová N, Zavadilová M et al. Zákon o mezinárodním právu soukromém: komentář. Wolters Kluwer ČR, Prague, pp 73–76

Bělohlávek AJ (2004) Zákon o rozhodčím řízení a o výkonu rozhodčích nálezů: komentář. C. H. Beck, Prague

Bělohlávek AJ (2012) Procesní smlouvy a kvalifikace rozhodčích a prorogačních smluv. Aplikace hmotněprávní úpravy na smlouvy s procesním účinkem pro futuro. Právník, pp 971–1101

Břicháček T (2014a) § 8 Základní ustanovení. In: Bříza P, Břicháček P, Fišerová Z et al. Zákon o mezinárodním právu soukromém: komentář. C. H. Beck, Pilsen, pp 66–71

Břicháček T (2014b) § 15 (Důvody pro odepření uznání cizího rozhodnutí). In: Bříza P, Břicháček P, Fišerová Z et al. Zákon o mezinárodním právu soukromém: komentář. C. H. Beck, Pilsen, pp 100–108

Bříza P (2012) Volba práva a volba soudu v mezinárodním obchodě. C. H. Beck, Prague

Bříza P (2014) § 88 Pravomoc. In: Bříza P, Břicháček P, Fišerová Z et al. Zákon o mezinárodním právu soukromém: komentář. C. H. Beck, Pilsen, pp 544–547

Bříza P, Břicháček T (2014a) § 85 Pravomoc. In: Bříza P, Břicháček P, Fišerová Z et al. Zákon o mezinárodním právu soukromém: komentář. C. H. Beck, Pilsen, pp 498–511

Bříza P, Břicháček T (2014b) § 86 Sjednání příslušnosti zahraničního soudu. In: Bříza P, Břicháček P, Fišerová Z et al. Zákon o mezinárodním právu soukromém: komentář. C. H. Beck, Pilsen, pp 512–525

Javůrková N (2009) § 89a (Dohoda sporných stran o příslušnosti soudu) In: David L, Ištvánek F, Javůrková N et al. Občanský soudní řád: komentář: I. díl (§ 1 až 200za). Wolters Kluwer ČR, Prague, pp 414–416

Jirmanová M (2013) § 15 (Odepření uznání cizího rozhodnutí). In: Pauknerová M, Rozehnalová N, Zavadilová M et al. Zákon o mezinárodním právu soukromém: komentář. Wolters Kluwer ČR, Prague, pp 107–115

Jirsa J (2016) Komentář k § 89a. In: Jirsa J, Doležal M, Vančurová K et al. Občanské soudní řízení: soudcovský komentář. Wolters Kluwer ČR, Prague, pp 68–70

Keyes M, Marshall BA (2015) Jurisdiction agreements: exclusive, optional and asymmetrical. J Priv Int Law 11:345–378

Kučera Z (1980) Mezinárodní právo soukromé. Panorama, Prague

Kučera Z, Pauknerová M (2015) Pojem a předmět mezinárodního práva soukromého. In: Kučera Pauknerová, Růžička et al. Mezinárodní právo soukromé. Aleš Čeněk, Pilsen–Brno, pp 23–31

Kučera Z, Pfeiffer M (2015) Závazkové právo. In: Kučera Z, Pauknerová M, Růžička K et al. Mezinárodní právo soukromé. Aleš Čeněk–Doplněk, Pilsen–Brno, pp 283–317

Kučera Z, Tichý L (1989) Zákon o mezinárodním právu soukromém a procesním: komentář. Panorama, Prague

Magnus U, Mankowski P (2016) European Commentaries on Private International Law: Commentary: Brussels Ibis Regulation. Otto Schmidt: Köln

Novotný Z (2009) § 89a (Prorogace). In: Drápal L, Bureš J et al. Občanský soudní řád I: komentář: § 1 až 200 za. C. H. Beck, Prague, pp 580–582

Pauknerová M, Pfeiffer M (2013) § 1 Předmět úpravy. In: Pauknerová, Rozehnalová, Zavadilová et al. Zákon o mezinárodním právu soukromém: komentář. Wolters Kluwer ČR, Prague, pp 1–15

Přidal O (2013) § 89a (Prorogace). In: Svoboda K, Smolík P, Levý J et al. Občanský soudní řád: komentář. C. H. Beck, Prague, pp 315–316

Rozehnalová N (1997) Smlouva o příslušnosti soudu z pohledu Úmluvy o soudní pravomoci a příslušnosti a výkonu rozhodnutí v občanských a obchodních věcech z roku 1968. In: Ročenka evropského práva. Masarykova univerzita, Brno, pp 85–107

Rozehnalová N (2013a) § 85 Pravomoc. In: Pauknerová M, Rozehnalová N, Zavadilová M et al. Zákon o mezinárodním právu soukromém: komentář. Wolters Kluwer ČR, Prague, pp 566–580
Rozehnalová N (2013b) § 86 Sjednání příslušnosti zahraničního soudu. In: Pauknerová M, Rozehnalová N, Zavadilová M et al. Zákon o mezinárodním právu soukromém: komentář. Wolters Kluwer ČR, Prague, pp 580–594
Rozehnalová N (2013c) § 88 Pravomoc. In: Pauknerová M, Rozehnalová N, Zavadilová M et al. Zákon o mezinárodním právu soukromém: komentář. Wolters Kluwer ČR, Prague, pp 609–615
Rozehnalová N (2013d) Rozhodčí řízení v mezinárodním a vnitrostátním obchodním styku. Wolters Kluwer ČR, Prague
Rozehnalová N (2016) Instituty českého mezinárodního práva soukromého. Wolters Kluwer ČR, Prague
Růžička K (2003) Rozhodčí řízení před Rozhodčím soudem při Hospodářské komoře České republiky a Agrární komoře České republiky. Aleš Čeněk, Pilsen
Sedláček V (1982) Rozhodčí řízení v československém zahraničním obchodě. ČSOPK, Prague
Sedláček V, Steiner V (1975) Mezinárodní obchodní arbitráž (se zřetelem k právní úpravě v ČSSR). ČSOPK, Prague

Legal Documents

Act No. 142/1950 Coll., the Civil Procedure Code, as subsequently amended
Act No. 97/1963 Coll., on Private International Law and Rules of International Procedure, as subsequently amended
Act No. 99/1963, the Civil Procedure Code, as subsequently amended
Act No. 519/1991 Coll., amending the Civil Procedure Code
Act No. 89/2012 Coll., the Civil Code, as subsequently amended
Act No. 91/2012 Coll., on Private International Law, as subsequently amended
Agreement between the European Community and the Kingdom of Denmark on jurisdiction and the recognition and enforcement of judgments in civil and commercial matters of 19 October 2005
Convention for the Unification of Certain Rules for International Carriage by Air (Montreal, 28 May 1999)
Convention for the Unification of Certain Rules to International Carriage by Air (Warsaw, 12 October 1929)
Convention of 27 September 1968 on Jurisdiction and the Enforcement of Judgments in Civil and Commercial Matters
Convention on Choice of Court Agreements (Hague, 30 June 2005)
Convention on Jurisdiction and the Recognition and Enforcement of Judgments in Civil and Commercial Matters (Lugano II Convention)
Convention on the Contract for the International Carriage of Goods by Road (CMR) (Geneva, 19 May 1956)
Convention on the Recognition and Enforcement of Foreign Arbitral Awards (New York, 1958)
Convention on the Settlement by Arbitration of Civil Disputes Arising out of Economic, Scientific and Technical Cooperation Relationships (Moscow, 26 May 1972)
Council Regulation (EC) No 44/2001 of 22 December 2000 on jurisdiction and the recognition and enforcement of judgments in civil and commercial matters
Regulation (EU) No 1215/2012 of the European Parliament and of the Council of 12 December 2012 on jurisdiction and the recognition and enforcement of judgments in civil and commercial matters (recast)
The Explanatory Report to the Act No. 91/2012 Coll., on Private International Law

Treaty between the Czechoslovak Socialist Republic and Mongolia on the Provision of Legal Assistance and Legal Relations in Civil, Family and Criminal Matters (Ulan Bator, 15 October 1976)

Case Law

Judgment of the European Court of Justice of 13 November 1979, case No. 25/79
Judgment of the Supreme Court of 29 August 2002, No. 29 Odo 524/2002
Judgment of the Municipal Court in Prague of 11 July 2005, No. 16 Co 144/2005

Naděžda Rozehnalová is a Professor at the Faculty of Law, Masaryk University, Czech Republic. She focuses in her research on Private International Law, International Procedural Law and Arbitration Law.

Silvie Mahdalová is a PhD student at the Faculty of Law, Masaryk University, Czech Republic. She studies Private International Law. She is primarily interested in the European Insolvency Law.

Lucie Zavadilová is a PhD student at the Faculty of Law, Masaryk University, Czech Republic. In her research, she focuses on Private International Law, especially matrimonial property regimes having cross-border implications.

France: A Game of Asymmetries, Optional and Asymmetrical Choice of Court Agreements Under French Case Law

François Mailhé

1 Introduction

France has always been very favourable to choice of court agreements. Acceptance of such agreements in commercial matters was even understood as such an important principle that the drafters of the *Code civil*, in 1804, considered it a natural exception to the rules they proposed in its articles 14 and 15 (competence of French courts for French nationals) together with the competence of French courts for disputes about immovables located in France.[1] The rule was notoriously confirmed by the *Mardelé* and *Dambricourt* cases in 1930 and 1931[2] and, though it was never expressly proclaimed in the same way as it has been for arbitration, the favour derives clearly from the policy followed both by French governments[3] and, above all, by case law.

The extent of French liberalism towards choice of court agreements may best be assessed by mentioning the issue of the applicability of "*loi de police*" or overriding

The author would like to thank Marie Goré for the exceptional opportunity and Mary Keyes for such an efficient and kind editorship.

[1]Locré (1805), p. 321.

[2]Cass. civ. 19 feb. 1930 and 27 jan. 1931, *Rev. crit. DIP* 1931, p. 514; *S.* 1933, 1, 41, comm. by Niboyet. If those decisions were mainly addressing the validity of arbitration clauses, the Cour de cassation also annulled the court of appeal decision for overlooking choice of court clauses.

[3]See recently, a semi-public authority report on the development of International business chambers in the Paris Tribunal de commerce ("*Préconisations sur la mise en place à Paris de chambres spécialisées pour le traitement du contentieux international des affaires*", available at http://hcjp.fr), and the creation of the International Commercial Chamber of the Paris Court of Appeal in March 2018.

F. Mailhé (✉)
Picardy-Jules Verne University, Amiens, France

M. Keyes (ed.), *Optional Choice of Court Agreements in Private International Law*, Ius Comparatum – Global Studies in Comparative Law 37,
https://doi.org/10.1007/978-3-030-23914-5_8

mandatory provisions. Those are the rules "*regarded as crucial by a country for safeguarding its public interests, such as its political, social or economic organisation, to such an extent that they are applicable to any situation falling within their scope, irrespective of the law otherwise applicable to the contract under this Regulation*", as Article 9 Rome I Regulation defines them. Still, according to consistent case law, the fact that the litigation requires the application of a French *loi de police* does not allow a French court to disregard a clause designating a foreign court.[4] Despite some criticism, arguing that allowing parties to "take off" meant allowing them to avoid such rules,[5] the *Cour de cassation* has not changed its solution.[6]

But if French law has long known and supported choice of court agreements, its case law dealing with dozens of cases every year, *optional* choice of court agreements could not be based on the same volume of precedents.

Indeed, if the exact translation of "optional" would be "*facultative*", the phrase "*clause attributive de juridiction facultative*" (or its equivalent, "*clause d'élection de for facultative*" or "*convention de juridiction facultative*") finds no match in case law.[7] The literal translation of the phrase ("*clause attributive de juridiction optionnelle*" or "*clause d'élection de for optionnelle*") is quite rare in French doctrine and almost absent from French case law. Non-exclusive clauses ("*clause non exclusive*") were observed, but not really studied.[8] The "right of option" ("*droit d'option*") is more frequent but used to describe the situations where the claimant is offered a choice among different courts by the legislation itself.[9] To add to the

[4]Cass. civ. 1ere 22 oct. 2008, *Monster Cable*, n° 07-15823, *JCP G* 2008, 10187, note L. d'Avout; *D.* 2009, p. 200, note F. Jault-Seseke; *D.* 2009, p. 684, chron. A. Huet; *D.* 2009, p. 2384, obs. L. d'Avout et S. Bollée; *Gaz. Pal.* 21 févr. 2009, n° 52, p. 27 note P. Guez; *JDI* 2009, p. 599, note M.-N. Jobard-Bachellier et F.-X. Train; *Rev. crit. DIP* 2009, p. 1, chron. D. Bureau et H. Muir Watt; *RDC* 2009, p. 691, obs. E. Treppoz; *Procédures* 2008, comm. 311, obs. C. Nourissat; *Procédures* 2009, étude 2, M. Attal.

[5]See especially the commentary by Bureau and Muir Watt (2009), referring to Wai (2002).

[6]Cass. civ. 1ere, 24 nov. 2015, *Lauterbach*, n° 14-14924, *JDI* 2016, p. 939, note L. Usunier; *D.* 2015. 2509, et 2016. 1045, obs. F. Jault-Seseke; *RTD civ.* 2016. 98, obs. H. Barbier; *JCP* 2016. 241, obs. C. Nourrissat.

[7]Research has been mainly conducted on the very rich, public and free access website Legifrance. gouv.fr. This website keeps record of every *Cour de cassation* decision (the higher court in the private law judiciary in France) since 1987, all published ones since 1960, and the most important older ones. Courts of appeal decisions are numerous but not exhaustive, and first instance tribunal ones quite scarce, so that research cannot be deemed complete on the lower levels of judicial practice (and few of them actually proved useful for the research).

[8]Two cases could be found. The first one, Cass. civ. 1e, 23 jan. 2008, n° 06-21011, discussed the effect of such a clause on art. 14 and 15 code civil, see below at note 27. A more recent case, Com. 12 may 2015, n° 13-28504 and 14-11028, rejected the argument based on the interpretation of the clause on a procedural ground (the argument was targeting a contract which was not the object of the litigation).

[9]Cass. civ. 1e, 7 dec. 2011, *West Caribbean Airways*, *JDI* 2012, p. 1384, note S. Clavel; *RCDIP* 2012, p. 138, Rapp. A. Maitrepierre; *D.* 2012, p. 254, obs. X. Delpech et note P. Delebecque et p. 1237, obs. F. Jault-Seseke et 1439, note H. Kenfack; *JCP G* 2012, p. 414, note 264 L. d'Avout;

confusion, "*clauses optionnelles*" is now employed to describe agreements opening a choice between a court and an arbitral tribunal (sometimes, pathologically, with mediation and conciliation).[10]

The absence of a specific word, though, does not entail absence of the object. Optional choice of court agreements are not ignored by French courts, at least when the option is opened to only one of the parties. An old series of cases first discussed them as clauses "in the sole interest of one party", or "for the sole benefit of one party" ("*dans le seul intérêt/seul bénéfice d'une partie*").[11] Such optional choices were discovered by interpretation: the agreement was found to allow the party the clause had been written in favour of to renounce his right and to seize an otherwise competent court.[12] One can infer from this case law a general neutrality towards optional clauses, allowing for lower judges to interpret the clauses this way.

But a recent development has turned this question into a battlefield in French case law. Since the *Rothschild* case, in 2012,[13] six cases have been studied by the *Cour de cassation*, the French supreme court for private law cases, where several optional clauses, expressly asymmetric, have been mostly set aside as an inefficient means of defence for the party who benefited from the option. Litigation on those clauses has become so problematic than no less than two decisions were rendered by the *Cour* since this report was first drafted in 2017, and another 2 months after the report was presented in Fukuoka in July 2018.

For the sake of clarity, these two quite opposite tendencies among French case law are not exactly based on the same sets of rules. On one hand, the interpretation of clauses as being in the sole interest or benefit of one party comes from French domestic law on jurisdiction clauses, both domestic and international.[14] The

---

RTD civ. 2012, p. 367, note P. Théry; *RDC* 2012, p. 957, note A. Lapart. Interestingly, this decision was part of a struggle with some US courts to convince them to consider that such a right could not be undermined by the use of *forum non conveniens* in *In re West Caribbean Airways*, 619 F. Supp. 2d 1299; *Pierre-Louis v. Newvac Corp.*, 584 F.3d 1052, 2009, In vain.

[10]See the absence of distinction in Barbet and Rosher (2010).

[11]The oldest available cases are Trib. civ. Doullens, 5 nov. 1948, *Gaz. Pal.* 1948. 2. 272; Paris, 4 juil. 1963, *D.* 1964, p. 151; *Gaz. Pal.* 1964, I, 39.

[12]See last Cass. com., 14 juin 2016, n° 15-11.338.

[13]Cass. civ. 1ère, 26 sept. 2012, *Rothschild*, n° 11-26.022, Keyes and Marshall (2015); *Rev. crit. DIP* 2013, p. 256, note D. Bureau; *Banque et droit* 2013, n°148, p. 3 note M.-E. Ancel, L. Marion et L. Wynaendts (available in English at SSRN: https://ssrn.com/abstract=2258419); *D.* 2012, p. 2876, note D. Martel et 2013, p. 2293, obs. L. d'Avout, p. 1503, obs. F. Jault-Seseke; *Rev. dr. com. belge* 2013, p. 443, note C. Verbruggen; *Gaz. Pal.* 12 avril 2013, p. 37, obs. J. Morel-Maroger and 7 déc. 2012, obs. M. Nioche; *Cah. Arb.* 2013, p. 443, note J. Barbet; *RTD Com.* 2013, p. 383, obs. Ph. Delebecque; *RDC* 2013, p. 661, note J.-B. Racine; *RDC* 2013, p. 265, note J. Klein; *Décid. jurid. et fi.* 2013, n°147, p. 24, note D. Mondoloni; *JCP E* 2013, 1134, obs. C. Nourissat et 1003, note Ph. Grignon; *JCP G* 2013, 105, note L. Degos and D. Akchoti; *RGDA* 2013, p. 220, note R. Schulz; *Option finance* 2012, n° 1198, p. 31 obs. G. Benteux and A. Chazot; *LPA* 14 nov. 2012, p. 7, note J.-G. Mahinga; *RJC* 2012, n° 6 p. 21 note P. Berlioz; *JCP G* 2012, 1065, obs. E. Cornut. See also Ancel (2015).

[14]See for example Cass. civ. 2e, 1 june 2017, 16-18739; Cass. com. 23 sept. 2014, n° 13-19.108 and 13-21.934.

Rothschild line of cases, on the other hand, was exclusively determined under article 23 Brussels I Regulation, i.e. rules of private international law enacted by the European Union.

As for the rest of the European Union countries, choice of court agreements are now indeed mainly governed by European Union rules when controlled by French courts. International agreements designating French or other EU State courts are governed by Brussels I (Recast) Regulation or, for some, by the Lugano Convention, its twin convention for relations with some other European countries (Iceland, Lichtenstein, Norway and Switzerland). Then, as the EU has ratified the Hague Convention on Choice of Court Agreements 2005 ("Hague Convention"), this convention applies to clauses designating either a court of a non-EU State party to the Convention, or a court of a member State of the EU when one of the parties reside in such a third State (as at the date of writing, in November 2018, Montenegro, Mexico and Singapore). Last, France is party to a certain number of international conventions in specific fields, for example, in matters of international transportation contracts, the Geneva, Montreal, Brussels, Rhine and COTIF conventions.

In practice, considering that international activities of French nationals and French companies are mainly turned towards other EU States, it is therefore no surprise that relatively few cases are now governed by rules stemming from French sources and most are by the Brussels I (Recast) Regulation. As a Report for the European Commission puts it, national law only deals with "residual jurisdiction".[15] French case law on such residual competence issues therefore mainly concerns choice of courts when the designated courts are those of one of the states of the USA (Russia, with African and Middle Eastern countries, are also represented).

Developing a report on French law would have therefore been ambiguous, since introducing only purely French sources would first have mostly excluded recent case law, and second forgotten a specifically French case law interpreting the Brussels I Regulation. It will also be argued that the diverging approaches in French case law does not stem from any divergence in those sources.

The choice has therefore been made to stick as much as possible to the discussion of French law as was the purpose of the report, but to develop also on this specific case law on asymmetric jurisdiction clauses which, though developed on cases where Brussels I Regulation was applicable, could certainly be extended to French law on jurisdiction clauses.

Considering this ambiguity of French case law on the effect of optional clauses, between openness in general and antagonism to asymmetrical clauses, I will leave the traditional French path of the two parts and two subparts. The discussion indeed needs a more German (Hegelian) approach with a Thesis (Sect. 2), Antithesis (Sect. 3) and (proposed) Synthesis (Sect. 4) to the description of French law regarding optional jurisdiction clauses.

[15] Nuyts (2007).

2 Thesis: Optional Choice of Court Agreements Under French Law

France is no exception: optional choice of court agreements were seldom met in case law, the primary source of French law on choice of court agreements. So it is necessary to introduce briefly choice of court agreements under French law (that is to say, mainly exclusive choice of court agreements) before turning to optional ones.

2.1 Choice of Court Agreements, in General

To understand the effect of jurisdiction clauses in general and optional ones in particular, one has first to address the way French law, like most continental European systems, deals with competence. Indeed, contrary to some other systems where it is first understood as an issue of power of the court, French law now generally deals with international competence the same as with domestic competence, i.e. as a problem of allocation of cases between courts decided over by the legislator (either French, European or international). International competence is therefore treated much the same as venue rules, with some exceptions only, and judges have no power to alter legislative solutions. The effect of choice of court clauses is identical, since, unless those clauses don't comply with mostly formal rules of validity and some scarce rules on exclusive competence, French courts have no power but to either accept their designation or the exclusion of their intervention for a foreign one. This is, as a side note, a reason why the term "competence" is not perfectly adapted to French law. The latter carries too much weight and an irrelevant idea of power and freedom of the judge.[16]

Like most French private international law before the rising of EU sources, choice of court agreements were, as was said, governed by case law. From the cases *Mardelé* and *Dambricourt* in 1930 and 1931 until it was reaffirmed in the case *Sorelec* in 1985,[17] after the reform of the French code of civil procedure, the *Cour de cassation* slowly developed a regime for those clauses. As with many case law developed regimes, that of choice of court agreements is partially uncertain. One thing is clear at least: French case law does not expressly enter into this issue under a conflict of law analysis.[18] The interpretation, validity and effects of the clause were

[16]As to the divergence between the two terms "jurisdiction" and "competence", see already Smit (1961). The role and nature of "competence" of courts was the topic of my PhD research: Mailhé (2016). Some of its findings were discussed in Mailhé (2015).

[17]Cass. civ. 1e, 17 dec. 1985, n° 84-16.338, *Rev. crit. DIP* 1986, p. 537 comm. By H. Gaudemet-Tallon; *D.* 1986, IR, p. 265, obs. By B. Audit; B. Ancel et Y. Lequette, *Grands Arrêts de droit international privé,* Dalloz 2006, 5e ed., n° 72.

[18]One exception: Cass. civ. 1ere, 3 dec. 1991, n° 90-10.078, *Rev. crit. DIP* 1992, p. 340, note H. Gaudemet-Tallon.

dealt with according to French rules close to—but more liberal than—those applied for domestic choice of court clauses.

Freeing such international clauses from the domestic limitations imposed by the *Nouveau code de procedure civile* enacted in the 1970s, *Sorelec* presumes the validity of the clause. Two elements may be brought as a means of defence against it: the existence of an imperative competence of French courts,[19] and evidence that the clause was not known and accepted by the other party, which goes through mainly practical arguments about access and acceptance of standard documents.[20]

As regards the protection of choice of court agreements, French law protects them with mere procedural effects. First, anti-suit injunctions are not available under French law.[21] It is assumed to be incompatible with the paradigm French law entertains as to the sovereignty of other State courts in deciding over their own competence. Paradoxically, French courts have not been reluctant to enforce anti-suit injunctions in France, even when a procedure had already started before a French judge.[22] Second, and maybe for the same reason, no money damages have ever been allocated for such a violation. Instead, choice of court agreements, in their exclusive effects, are sanctioned by specific *lis pendens* and enforcement of foreign judgment effects.

As for *lis pendens*, for a dismissal (or a stay, in case of related actions) to be granted under French law, both courts must have competence. If a foreign court outside the scope of the exclusive designation is seized, the dismissal (nor the stay)

---

[19]Such a situation is rare. If courts refuse to protect their competence when a *loi de police* is at stake, it is not to take it back on the basis of any random factor connecting the case to France. In practice, such exclusivity has seldom been observed, and it is usually considered that exclusivity is limited to issues on rights in rem in immovable property (art. 44 code of civil procedure), on the validity of registrations on public registries (including those of industrial property rights), on recourse to force such as for the enforcement of judgment and other usual exclusive competence situations. A specific difficulty stems from employment and consumer contracts. Where it now seems ascertained that clauses in employment contracts need to be limited to additional options offered to employees, consumer contracts have quite recently been protected by the Paris court of appeal through consumer law and unfair terms regulation (Paris 12 feb. 2016, n° 15/08624, *D.* 2016. 422, 1045, obs. F. Jault-Seseke, 2141, obs. J. Larrieu, and 2017. 539, obs. N. Sauphanor-Brouillaud; *Dalloz IP/IT* 2016. 214, obs. S. André et C. Lallemand; *RTD civ.* 2016. 310, obs. L. Usunier; *CCE* 2016 comm. 33, obs. G. Loiseau, and étude 12, note F. Mailhé). Both are now governed by Brussels I Recast anyway, at least as long as the consumer is domiciled in the EU and the employee working in the same area (art. 18 and 21).

[20]See, as examples, Cass. com. 23 sept. 2014, n° 13-19.108 13-21.934; Cass. com. 28 feb. 2012, n° 11-16.156.

[21]One exception: Cass. civ. 1e, 19 nov. 2002, n° 00-22334; D. 2003, jurispr. p. 797, note G. Khairallah; *JCP G* 2002, II, 10 201, concl. J. Sainte-Rose, note S. Chaillé de Néré; *JCP E* 2003, p. 1675, note M. Menjucq; *Gaz. Pal.* 26 june 2003, p. 29 note M.-L. Niboyet; *RTD com.* 2003, p. 169, obs. J.-L. Vallens; *JDI* 2003, p. 132, note Ph. Roussel-Galle; *Rev. crit. DIP* 2003, 631, note H. Muir Watt.

[22]Cass. civ. 1e, 14 oct. 2009, *D.* 2010, p. 177, note S. Bollée, *RCDIP* 2010, p. 158, note H. Muir Watt, *Gaz. Pal.* 2009, p. 332 note M.-L. Niboyet.

may therefore not be granted, as the violation of the clause makes that court incompetent.

The same goes for recognition of the decision of a court not designated by the exclusive choice of court agreement. It has recently been confirmed by the *Cour de cassation* that the violation of a clause designating French courts entails refusal of enforcement[23] and another case, though isolated and older than the actual principle, did the same for a clause designating a Luxemburg tribunal.[24]

2.2 *Optional Choice of Court Clauses, in Particular*

Exclusive choice of court agreements are understood as having two effects under French law: exclusion of other courts, and prorogation of competence for the chosen one.[25] Non-exclusive choice of court agreements only aim at benefiting from the latter effect,[26] allowing for the alternative competence of other courts, and opening the possibility of *lis pendens* situations to be solved in favour of a non-designated court as well as the recognition and enforcement of its judgment. A particular effect was also applicable for a while: when article 14 and 15 of the French civil code were considered specific privileges, it could be claimed that they were always available unless waived by the French national.[27] The waiver seems to be now interpreted

[23]Cass. civ. 1e, 15 may 2018, n° 17-17546, *JCP G* 2018, 919, note F. Mailhé, *JCP E* 2018, 196, obs. C. Nourrissat. See also Lyon, 3 july 1912, *Gaz. Pal.* 1912, 2, p. 655; CA Paris, 20 june 1961, *JDI* 1962, p. 718 and *Rev. crit. DIP* 1962, p. 63, note Y. Loussouarn; TGI Seine, 10 jan. 1962, *Rev. crit. DIP* 1963, p. 607, note J. Déprez.

[24]Cass. civ. 1e, 3 may 1977: *Rev. crit. DIP* 1978, p. 367, note D. A. The case is older than the *Simitch* decision which set the standard for refusal of enforcement on the ground of a problem of competence of the foreign court (Cass. civ. 1e, 18 feb. 1985). This case sets forth a double condition: there should be no violation of an exclusive competence of French courts (which is the reason for the May 15, 2018 case), and there should be a "characterized connection" between the case and the State of the foreign court. This double standard does not seem to allow to take into consideration the exclusive competence of a third State, but it has been argued that a choice of court agreement designating courts in such a State would prevent any "characterized connection" with another State.

[25]See for a detailed discussion and a comparison with English law, Keyes and Marshall (2015).

[26]This statement only considers the option as concerning the use of the clause itself, and not the various courts designated. If the choice offered by the clause is construed as exclusive of other options, the effect of the clause should be identical to the ones previously considered for exclusive agreements. Additionally, This rather simple presentation derives from the understanding of the clause as having a purely procedural effect, securing a forum while rejecting others. In the absence of additional contractual obligations (of damages in case of breach, for example), French law does not need to detail other consequences which derive from the law of competence itself. Comp., under English law, Merrett (2018), p. 40ff.

[27]Now abandonned by both Cass civ. 1e, 23 may 2006, *Prieur*, *D.* 2006, p. 1846, chr. B. Audit and pan. 1751, obs. P. Courbe; *JCP* 2006, 10134, note Callé; *RCDIP* 2006, p. 870, note H. Gaudemet-Tallon; *JDI* 2006, p. 1377, note C. Chalas; *PA* 22 sept. 2006, p. 10, obs. P. Courbe; *Grands Arrêts*

even more liberally.[28] This was an interesting decision as the non-exclusive character of the clause should have meant the non-exclusion of objective competence rules such as those ones. But the contractual interpretation of the clause here superseded its procedural aspects.

Apart from this decision, though, case law on optional clauses is restricted to a specific trend born in 1966 in the *Cour de cassation*, France's highest court for private law, about clauses "in the sole interest of one party".[29] This phrase has been used several times in case law to describe a certain interpretation of what looked like a classical exclusive jurisdiction clause. To allow for the "violation" of the choice in favour of otherwise competent French courts, some accepted an interpretation of such clauses as being optional for one of the parties, for whom the clause was "in the sole interest" or "the sole benefit".[30]

Such options were therefore found through factual analysis and interpretation of the clause and the contract. As had already been the case in the early *Mardelé* and *Dambricourt* cases, the *Cour de cassation* then merely mentioned article 1134 of the French *Code civil* (now article 1103) as a reference to the limited power of the courts over contractual matters and the even more limited controlling power of the *Cour* over the interpretation of documents by lower courts: the *Cour de cassation* can only reverse their decisions in cases where it appears they have blatantly betrayed the clear meaning of such documents. Lower courts are therefore free to characterize agreements as optional, though it does not seem they have often done so. The regime of optional clauses is therefore mostly derived and adapted from that of exclusive ones, both for their effect and their violation.

A first consequence of the procedural context of such case law, the interpretation of clauses as "in the sole interest of one party" has only been found in cases where that allowed French courts to affirm their competence in spite of an agreement designating a foreign court. But the reciprocal situation, where such an agreement designating French courts would have so been waived by its beneficiary before a foreign court, has never been found in case law. It would indeed require a party opposing the enforcement of such a decision to raise that defence. Since the violation of a choice of court agreement is already, in itself, a very rare argument in enforcement proceedings, statistics do not allow any conclusion as to a potential bias of

---

n° 87 and Cass. civ. 1e, 22 may 2007, *Fercométal*, *D.* 2007, AJ p. 1586 and chron. B. Audit, p. 2548; *JCP* 2007, actu. 258 obs. C. Chabert; *RCDIP* 2007, p. 610, note H. Gaudemet-Tallon; *JDI* 2007, p. 956, note B. Ancel and H. Muir Watt; *Gaz. Pal.* 21–22 march 2008, p. 28, obs. M.-L. Niboyet.

[28] In a case decided after the change of interpretation of the article 14 and 15 *code civil* as privileges (the Cour de cassation decided to uphold a decision where the court of appeal had enforced a choice of court clause against article 14 code civil, even though the clause was construed as non-exclusive, see Cass. civ. 1e, 23 jan. 2008, n° 06-21011, *JDI* 2009, comm. 14 note A. Sinay-Cytermann.

[29] Cass. civ. 2e, 15 june 1966, *D.* 1967, p. 84; *Gaz. Pal.* 1966, 2, p. 184. Some cases before the Paris tribunal and some courts of appeal had already dealt with such clauses in the same way even prior to that.

[30] As examples reaching the higher court: Cass. com., 14 feb.1989, n° 86-17.140; Cass. Civ. 1ere, 29 june 2011, n° 10-22.933; Cass. com., 14 june 2016, n° 15-11.338.

French courts in favour of their competence. But two court of appeal decisions at least show that the argument did not always convince the French judges to set the clause aside to keep the litigation in France,[31] and this interpretation is not limited to international choice of court clauses.[32]

A second consequence is that it has never been entertained that the beneficiary could decline the competence of the chosen court when this one is seized. Once the option had been exercised, defences were only relying on the validity of the clause and not its asymmetrical character.

Other effects flow from the same line of reasoning. If raised before a French court, an optional choice of court agreement for a foreign court would get the same effect as for exclusive clauses: it would be verified whether or not the dispute falls under the exclusive competence of French courts. If not, it would remain to be verified whether the claimant was a beneficiary of the option. If that was so, the right enclosed in the agreement would be considered waived. If it wasn't, only provided for the benefit of the other party, that party could then refuse French jurisdiction.

A specific kind of optional clauses has been legally ascertained though. As they have been in Brussels I (and Recast) Regulation, choice of court clauses in employment contracts are efficient only if they open an additional forum for the sole benefit of the employee.[33] In matters of consumer and insurance relations, it seems to stem from the latest decisions on clauses covered by French common law that the protection for weaker parties rather runs through the exclusion of any choice of court agreement,[34] thus differing from the option offered by EU law.[35]

Those two elements taken into consideration, and reminding the reader of the "venue" character of international competence in French law, where the judge has no power but to accept the allocated case, a negative effect of the optional choice of court simply does not seem possible.

3 Antithesis: Asymmetrical Choice of Court Agreements

Unfortunately and paradoxically, this stand is opposite to the previous one: asymmetrical choice of court agreements are inefficient. In French doctrine (case law did not name it), the phrase "asymmetrical choice of court agreement" is used in a specific way. It points at clauses which not only answer to the description of balancing exclusive and optional aspects, but which also do so by attributing each of those elements to only one of the parties, the exclusivity binding a "weak" party

[31]Versailles, 16 feb. 2006, n° ct0141; Versailles 30 nov. 2000, RG n° 1997-5188.

[32]See e.g., Civ. 2e, 13 july 1999, n° 97-22489.

[33]See e.g. Cass. soc. 29 may 2013, n° 12-15966.

[34]See e.g. CA Paris, 12 feb. 2016, n° 15/08624, already quoted footnote 19.

[35]Articles 15 and 19 Brussels I Recast.

while optionality is opened for the stronger one, the drafter of the contract in all published available cases.

For some time, expressly asymmetrical clauses had met an ambiguous treatment by French courts. Court of appeals mostly enforced them, while some denied them efficiency.[36] To the great surprise of the whole doctrine, the *Cour de cassation*, when first asked to consider this specific character, decided in favour of this last tendency. In 2012, a *Banque de Rothschild* case opposed a French citizen to a Luxemburg bank, the investment contract she had signed compelling her to sue in Luxemburg while the bank was also allowed to sue "before any other competent court" according to the choice of court clause. The first civil chamber of the *Cour de cassation* met the clause with hostility, considering it "*potestative*" which was a way to say it was at the discretion of one party. The word was overshooting the objective since the discretion it is meant to stigmatize is not that of using a clause, but more radically of allowing one to exist.[37] The existence of the clause was not at stake in this case, so that the *Cour* later abandoned it. But it maintained its hostility towards the clause.

In *Danne Holding vs Crédit Suisse*,[38] a company created for the management of a farm in the Loire valley had taken a loan with a Swiss company. The borrower later challenged the validity of the whole financial operation that involved the Swiss bank together with a French bank and an English company, but the Swiss bank claimed the loan was covered by a choice of court clause compelling the borrower "to recognize the exclusive competence of the Zurich courts", where the bank "was allowed to sue the borrower before any otherwise competent court".[39] The court of appeal had upheld the clause, severing the action towards the Swiss bank from the French litigation. The *Cour de cassation* quashed the decision, finding that the court of appeal should have inquired whether "the unbalance in the clause was not contrary to the objective of predictability and legal certainty that article 23 of the Brussels I Regulation was aiming at, since the clause was allowing the bank to sue before any competent tribunal and did not specify according to which objective

[36]CA Paris, 30 nov. 1988 and 14 dec. 1988, *JDI* 1990, p. 153; CA Rouen, 8 dec. 1994, *DMF* 1995, p. 554. See also cases cited *in DMF* 1993, p. 525, obs. P. Bonassies. Others were favourable: CA Rouen, 21 oct. 1992, *DMF* 1993, p. 529, obs. Y. Tassel; CA Aix, 17 july 2014, *DMF* 2014, p. 764, note Ph. Delebecque.

[37]"*Potestativité*" is, under French law, a reason for setting aside the obligation that it impairs. A contractual obligation is "*potestative*" when its very existence depends upon the discretionary will of one of the parties only, in contradiction with its contractual character.

[38]Cass. civ. 1ère, 25 march 2015, *Danne Holding*, n° 13-27.264, Marshall (2016); L. d'Avout, *JCP G* 2015, 600; S. Bollée, *D.* 2015, p. 2031; L. Usunier, *RTD Civ.* 2015, p. 844; M.-E. Ancel, *Banque et droit* 2015, n° 163, p. 4; J. Morel-Maroger, *Gaz. Pal.* 31 july 2015, p. 29; J.-P. Mattout et A. Prüm, *Dr. et pat.* 2015, n°250, p. 90; J. Mestre et A.-S. Mestre-Chami, *RLDA* 2016, n° 115, p. 43.

[39]« *l'emprunteur reconnaît que le for exclusif pour toute procédure est Zurich ou au lieu de la succursale de la banque où la relation est établie, [...] la banque est toutefois en droit d'ouvrir action contre l'emprunteur devant tout autre tribunal compétent* ».

elements this competence was based".[40] Switching its basis from "potestativity" to "predictability" was a more solid ground, but still did not convince most of the doctrine and lower courts.

Eight months later, in *eBizcuss vs. Apple*,[41] still the same chamber of the *Cour* had to deal with a clause stating that "*(t)his Agreement and the corresponding relationship between the parties shall be governed by and construed in accordance with the laws of the Republic of Ireland and the parties shall submit to the jurisdiction of the courts of the Republic of Ireland. Apple reserves the right to institute proceedings against Reseller in the courts having jurisdiction in the place where Reseller has its seat or in any jurisdiction where a harm to Apple is occurring*". The Agreement was an exclusive distributorship contract between a French company and Apple that Apple had terminated when it had opened its new flagship store in Paris. The French distributor had consequently sued Apple for abrupt termination of the contract, which may give rise to damages under French law. There again, the *Cour* enhanced the predictability imperative those clauses had to ensure. But the fact that the clause offered "objective elements" to determine where Apple could sue ("*where a harm to Apple is occurring*") satisfied the *Cour*. This last decision was interpreted by some scholars as demonstrating that the *Cour de cassation* was progressively abandoning its *Rothschild* stance.

It actually seemed abandoned when the commercial chamber of the *Cour de cassation* decided over the *Diemme Enologia vs Etablissements Chambon & fils case*, in May 2017, where the latter company, exclusive distributor of Diemme Enologia wine production machines, sued the former company, registered in Italy, for abrupt termination of the contract.[42] The clause here at stake provided for the exclusive competence of the courts of Ravenna, Italy, but added that Diemme could also "refer to other competent courts, according to the legal procedural rules".[43] The

[40]*« si le déséquilibre dénoncé, en ce que la clause litigieuse réservait à la banque le droit d'agir contre l'emprunteur devant « tout autre tribunal compétent » et ne précisait pas sur quels éléments objectifs cette compétence alternative était fondée, n'était pas contraire à l'objectif de prévisibilité et de sécurité juridique poursuivi par le texte susvisé »*.

[41]Cass. civ. 1ère, 7 oct. 2015, *eBizcuss*, n° 14-16.898, *RDC* 2016, p. 282 note E. Treppoz; *D.* 2015, p. 2620, obs F. Jault-Seseke; *Dr. et pat.* 2016, n° 256, p. 102, obs. J.-P. Mattout et A. Prüm; *Gaz. Pal.* 11 nov. 2015, p. 19, C. Dupoirier et V. Bouvard; *Procédures* 2015, n° 12, p. 80, obs. C. Nourissat; *Rev. dr. banc. et fi.* 2016, n° 1, p. 25, note A. Vrignaud; *JCP E* 2016, 1087, note M.-E. Ancel and L. Marion; *RCA* 2016, Etud. 5, note N. Ciron; *Banque et droit* 2016, n° 166, p. 68, note G. Affaki; *JCP G* 2015, 1123, obs. F. Mailhé.

[42]Cass. civ. 1ère, 11 mai 2017, n° 15-18758, *D.* 2017, p. 2054, obs. L. d'Avout; *JDI* 2017, p. 1338, note M.-E. Ancel et L. Marion; *Rev. crit. DIP* 2017, p. 483, note D. Bureau.

[43]*« Toute réclamation ou litige relative à l'exécution ou à l'interprétation du présent contrat, à son application, interprétation, annulation ou résiliation, sera soumise exclusivement à la seule et unique juridiction de la cour d'appel de Ravenne (Italie). La société DIEMME aura toutefois le droit de se référer à d'autres cours compétentes, conformément aux règles de procédure légale »*.

court of appeal had set the clause aside based on the *Banque Rothschild* formula ("potestativity" of the clause). The commercial chamber of the *Cour* quashed the decision, noting the court of appeal had evidenced an agreement on a choice of court, "regardless of the fact that the clause only [bound] one party".[44]

While most were then convinced this regrettable case law was forgotten, including the author of this report,[45] the first chamber of the *Cour de cassation* later issued two more decisions, in *Crédit Suisse II* (in February 2018)[46] and *Saint-Joseph* (in October 2018),[47] where it reaffirmed its opposition to those clauses. *Crédit Suisse II* is a return of the first of its name (*Danne Holding vs Crédit Suisse*) before the higher court, while *Saint-Joseph* opposed a French company to a Luxembourg bank. Once again, the Cour de cassation chose to quash the decisions that had refused to set the clause aside (*Saint-Joseph*) and confirmed that which had accepted to do it (*Crédit Suisse II*). The decisions are both justified at length, but the most interesting is the last one in time. Referring to the "high degree of predictability" that such clauses should ensure and to the ECJ *Coreck Maritime* decision about the necessity of "objective elements" to allow for the determinability of the designated courts,[48] the higher court decides that the fact that the clause "did not correspond to the objective of predictability" because it "did not hold any reference to a rule of competence applicable in a Member-State (of the European Union) nor any objective element precise enough to allow for the identification of the courts which could be seized".[49]

At this moment in time, unless such clauses therefore refine the option offered to one of the parties to limit it to a specific connecting factor (even as vague as "the place of the harm" from the *eBizcuss* case) or to specific rules of competence (article 7.1 Brussels I on contractual matters, as may be supposed, for example), they may be set aside.

[44]« *avait constaté la volonté des parties de convenir d'une prorogation de compétence dans les termes du contrat, peu important que cette clause attributive ne s'impose qu'à l'une des parties* ».

[45]See Mailhé (2017).

[46]Cass. civ. 1e., 7 feb. 2018, n° 16-24.497, *D.* 2018, p. 1934, S. Bollée; *JDI* 2018, comm. 16, note M.-E. Ancel et L. Marion.

[47]Cass. civ. 1e., 3 oct. 2018, n° 17-21.309, *JDI* 2018, comm. 16, note M.-E. Ancel et L. Marion, *JCP G* 2018, note F. Mailhé, to be published.

[48]CJCE, 9 nov. 2000, case C-387/98, *JDI* 2001, p. 701, note J.-M. Bischoff; *Rev. crit. DIP* 2001, p. 359, note F. Bernard-Fertier.

[49]The clause stated that « *ne contenait aucun renvoi à une règle de compétence en vigueur dans un Etat membre ni aucun élément objectif suffisamment précis pour identifier la juridiction qui pourrait être saisie, de sorte qu'elle ne répondait pas à l'objectif de prévisibilité* ».

4 Synthesis: Voluntary or Compulsory Reform

France is in dire need of reconciliation between those two case law trends. Its system is sound enough, though, to allow for the expectation of a new, authoritative, decision soon. But it would certainly not erase the reasons for this case law, which calls for a deeper reform.

4.1 In Need of an Authoritative Decision

How to reconcile both trends of that case law? Of course, it could be said that the latest trend has just reversed the oldest one.[50] It may not be so simple, though, as some recent decisions by the *Cour de cassation* have still enforced the latter as lately as 2016.[51]

Another way to look at it is that those clauses are different in the way they are drafted. Clauses "in the sole interest (or benefit) of" a party always seem to be written in a symmetric way. It is only through the interpretation of the courts that those clauses get their asymmetry. On the contrary, the whole ambition of the *Cour de cassation* since *Danne Holding* at least has been to compel clause writers to make their designations predictable enough, so that it has set aside clauses which were asymmetrical but also "unclear". Such an argument, though, fails to convince. It would be quite hypocritical to sanction contract writers where they were keen enough to explain the asymmetry (stopping just short of explaining the option offered), and to uphold clauses where they simply weren't.

It may be noticed, though, that all those openly asymmetrical clauses were either in favour of a bank or of a very powerful party (Apple), where to the contrary the *Diemme* case does not seem to have dealt with such a powerful party. The idea then quickly comes that this case law was simply dealing with the imbalance between the parties. It has been our opinion since *Danne Holding*[52]: *Rothschild*, with its "potestativity" argument, and above all *Danne Holding*, which strangely connected the balance between the parties to predictability,[53] tend to show that it was this

---

[50]That was the interpretation followed once by a court of appeal: Versailles, 21 oct. 2014, RG n° 14/03184.

[51]Cass. com. 14 june 2016, 15-11338.

[52]Mailhé (2018), published in the new *Assas International Law Review*. We take the liberty to signal this journal to the reader: launched this year, the *RDIA/AILR* contains articles both in French and English with an annual chronicle of French decisions on international law in English.

[53]« *Qu'en se déterminant ainsi, sans rechercher si le déséquilibre dénoncé, en ce que la clause litigieuse réservait à la banque le droit d'agir contre l'emprunteur devant « tout autre tribunal compétent » et ne précisait pas sur quels éléments objectifs cette compétence alternative était fondée, n'était pas contraire à l'objectif de prévisibilité et de sécurité juridique poursuivi par le texte susvisé* ». The underlined part translates as: "in so deciding, without any verification that this unbalance [...] wasn't contrary to the objective of predictability and legal certainty...".

aspect of the relation that struck the *Cour de cassation*. It must be connected to the extension of the "significant imbalance" test in French law, that entered the civil code in 2016 after appearing in the consumer code and developing in the business code.[54] Such an explanation, though, may not be of great help, since the Cour de cassation did not decide to connect the cause to the effect. Indeed, there is no condition of imbalance for this case law to apply. In the words of the *Cour*, the sole asymmetry is a reason to check the optional part of the clause with a predictability test.

A last way to look at it, which is not very comforting, is that two of the six chambers of the *Cour de cassation* are diverging. Indeed, the last time the first civil chamber (in charge of international issues) upheld a decision on a clause "in the sole interest of" a party dates back to 2011, hence a year before *Rothschild.*[55] To the contrary, the commercial chamber last upheld this case law in 2016.[56] If the issue is that of a divergence between the chambers, which France knows occasionally,[57] the solution might come with the reunion of a "Joint chamber" (*chambre mixte*) or, if the matter is considered important enough, a Plenary assembly (*Assemblée plénière*), the highest formation of the *Cour de cassation*. If that was the case, it must be noted that, in similar but domestic cases, the second civil chamber (in charge of most procedural matters) accepts the interpretation of clauses "in the sole interest of" a party,[58] so that if strength is to be found in numbers, this last trend may have an advantage.

Without trying to sum up all the arguments ranged against the *Rothschild – Danne Holding* case law, it should be stressed that those cases were all based on European law, which also allows for an intervention of the European Court of Justice. France has recently been sanctioned by the Court for the refusal by its other Supreme Court, the *Conseil d'Etat*, to submit a prejudicial question on a point of ambiguity of European law,[59] so that the *Cour de cassation* may acknowledge the necessity of a referral to the ECJ as soon as a new case is brought in. And, even if the *Cour* referred in *Saint-Joseph* to both a "whereas" of the Brussels I Regulation and one of the famous cases of the ECJ (*Coreck Maritime*),[60] neither may convince the ECJ: "whereas" has no independent normative value, and *Coreck Maritime* did not deal with an optional or asymmetrical clause, but with a symmetrical exclusive one. If the determinability of a court is necessary for the effectiveness such a clause, none is required where the sole point is to allow a party to be free to seize another one...

[54]New article 1171 civil code: "*Any term of a standard form contract which creates a significant imbalance in the rights and obligations of the parties to the contract is deemed not written*", translated by Cartwright et al. (2016).

[55]Civ. 1^e^, 29 june 2011, n° 10-22933.

[56]Cass. com. 14 june 2016, n° 15-11338.

[57]See e.g. Deumier (2013).

[58]Civ. 2^e^, 1 june 2017, n° 16-18739.

[59]ECJ, 4 Oct. 2018, case C-416/97.

[60]CJCE, 9 nov. 2000, quoted above at note 43.

4.2 *In Need of a Modernization of Choice of Court Agreement Regimes*

It has not yet been brought to the attention of the *Cour de cassation* that its opposition to asymmetrical clauses is quite contradictory with its interpretation of clauses "to the sole benefit of" one of the parties. It may be hoped that some future papers may give it food for thought. At any rate, it seems probable that a new decision by the *Cour*—or even by a judgmental ECJ—will put French law back on track. But it may not suffice to solve all related problems.

As regards optional choice of court agreements, French law will face the same problems as most other systems in dealing with optional choice of court agreements. Interpretation of the agreement gets more difficult when conditions, alternatives, connecting factors are multiplied.[61] The treatment of competing procedures (*lis pendens*, related cases) is also more complicated to deal with. More importantly, and more specifically to French law as to other EU systems, articulating the several applicable regimes (Hague Convention 2005, Brussels I Regulation, ordinary rules) becomes tricky when a clause may point at several jurisdictions, within or outside the EU and the Hague Convention domain, since the chosen court is often a standard of applicability.[62] Indeed, even though some of those regimes (Brussels I Recast, the Hague Convention for example) are quite close to each other, there are still important differences between them, which could grow further through their local interpretation. All those issues concern clauses which specify the option offered between several courts, and they are especially serious for asymmetrical clauses, but French law has apparently rarely encountered other kinds of clauses, which may be a hint as to their frequency relatively to French-related international business.

There is an impediment anyway, inherent to such relations. Choice of court agreements are indeed procedural agreements, dealing with a public organisation, that of competence. As such, it is necessary to consider the courts chosen, at least the States of the chosen courts. At the same time, it is a private agreement, drafted as the parties see fit, and therefore as diverse as their imagination and interests may find them. There will therefore always be problems, interferences, between those two elements. A radical solution would be to prohibit such clauses, but the resulting restriction to parties' autonomy does not seem either desirable or respectful of many legal traditions. A wiser solution would be to try to deal with the most common examples, allowing for the courts to solve the other models, and the experience of French case law would reassuringly tend to say that such clauses are not so numerous; but on that matter, French law is far from applying for a seat at the elder counsel.

Still, one has to remember what started the whole *Banque de Rothschild* case law: imbalance. French law has a long tradition of moralizing contractual relations, up to

[61]It may have been an additional reason for the temptation of some courts to limit them to "predictable" ones.

[62]On this issue of rules of applicability, see Audit and Berman (2005).

its important 2016 reform of contract law.[63] This trend is in line with growing sensitivity to the need of protecting traditionally unprotected categories, such as small and medium enterprises, non-profit organizations or unprotected consumers. The asymmetry between the treatment of asymmetrical clauses and clauses "to the sole benefit of" may therefore be the consequence of another, more serious asymmetry, an asymmetry which grows together with the democratization of globalization. This last asymmetry, this conflicting movement, is that opposing the half century of liberalism supporting international transactions to a renewed need to protect weaker parties. The same as contract law needed the development of a consumer law, that commercial law needed the development of a law of regulation, the time seems ripe for private international law to develop a more comprehensive set of protective rules and go beyond those developed more than 40 years ago, for an economy where consumers were mainly buying local and international business was only for multinational companies.

References

Ancel M-E (2015) A French introspection. In: Affaki G, Naon HG (eds) Jurisdiction choices in times of trouble. ICC, Paris, pp 64–70

Audit B, Berman G (2005) The application of private international norms to "third countries": the jurisdiction and judgments example. In: Nuyts A, Watté N (eds) International civil litigation in Europe and relations with third states. Bruylant, Bruxelles, p 55

Barbet J, Rosher P (2010) Les clauses de résolution de litiges optionnelles. Rev arb, 45

Cartwright J, Fauvarque-Cosson B, Whittaker S (2016) The law of contract, the general regime of obligations, and proof of obligations. http://www.textes.justice.gouv.fr/art_pix/THE-LAW-OF-CONTRACT-2-5-16.pdf

Deumier P (2013) Les divergences de jurisprudence: nécessité de leur existence, nécessité de leur résorption. RTD Civ. p 557

Keyes M, Marshall B (2015) Jurisdiction agreements: exclusive, optional and asymmetrical. J Priv Int Law 11:345–378

Locré JG (1805) Esprit du Code Napoléon tiré de la discussion. Impr. Impériale, Paris

Mailhé F (2015) International competence as a cooperation tool: jurisdiction, sovereignty and justice within the European Union. In: Cadiet L, Hess B, Requejo Isidro M (eds) Procedural science at the crossroads of different generations. Nomos, Baden-Baden, pp 341–370

Mailhé F (2016) L'organisation de la compétence internationale des juridictions. Economica, Paris

Mailhé F (2017) National Report: French Law. Draft prepared for the General Congress of the International Academy of Comparative Law: on file with editor

Mailhé F (2018) Les clauses attributives de compétence asymétriques dans les relations d'affaires. RDIA/Assas Int Law Rev 1:422. Available at https://www.u-paris2.fr/fr/revue-de-droit-international-dassas-rdia

Marshall BA (2016) Imbalanced jurisdiction clauses under the Lugano Convention. Zeitschrift für Europäisches Privatrecht, 515–527

Merrett L (2018) The future enforcement of asymmetric jurisdiction agreements. Int Comp Law Q, 37–61

---

[63] *Ordonnance n° 2016-131 du 10 février 2016 portant réforme du droit des contrats, du régime général et de la preuve des obligations*. For a translation, see Cartwright et al. (2016).

Nuyts A (2007) Study on "residual jurisdiction", General Report. 3 September 2007. http://ec.europa.eu/civiljustice/news/docs/study_residual_jurisdiction_en.pdf
Smit H (1961) The terms jurisdiction and competence in comparative law. Am J Comp Law 10:164–169
Wai R (2002) Transnational lift-off and juridical touchdown: the regulatory function of private international law in a global age. Columbia J Transnational Law 40(2):209–274

François Mailhé is Professor of law and Vice-Dean for the Faculty of law and political science of the University of Picardy-Jules Verne. After defending his PhD on international jurisdiction, its function and regime (awarded the national Robert Dennery Award by the Chancelry of Universities and published under the title "*L'organisation de la concurrence internationale des juridictions – La compétence internationale face à la mondialisation économique*", Economica, Paris 2016), in Paris II Panthéon-Assas University in 2013, he was appointed Assistant Lecturer in this University before accessing to the full professorship in 2017. Aside from Paris II and Picardy-Jules Verne, he has regularly delivered lectures in both French (Toulouse, Montpellier, Paris XII) and foreign (Normal university of Beijing, Doshisha university of Kyoto, University of Urbino) universities. He is also scientific director for the Lynxlex (www.lynxlex.com) project, a free and open access database of the text and case-law on European private international law. He is a member of the International Law Association, Trans-Europe Expert and the Comité français de droit international privé.

Optional Choice of Court Agreements: German National Report

Matthias Weller

1 The Treatment of Choice of Court Agreements in General

1.1 Historical Development in Germany: From Liberty to Protectionism

The treatment of choice of court agreements in Germany used to be quite liberal: When the German Code of Civil Procedure, the *Zivilprozessordnung,*[1] hereinafter "ZPO", entered into force, as "CPO", in 1879,[2] choice of court agreements could be agreed upon without any major limitations.[3] There were not even formal requirements.[4]

> Section 38 CPO of 1879 (in translation): An otherwise incompetent court of first instance receives jurisdiction by express or implied agreement by the parties.[5]

Special thanks go to Stephan Walter, Research Fellow at the Institute, for excellent research work in preparation of this text.

[1]Zivilprozessordnung as published on 5 December 2005 (Federal Law Gazette [Bundesgesetzblatt], BGBl. I 3202; 2006 I 431; 2007 I 1781), amended most recently by Article 1 of the Law of 31 January 2019 (BGBl. I 54).

[2]Civilprozeßordnung ("CPO") of 30 January 1877, Imperial Law Gazette (Reichgesetzblatt) 1877, 83.

[3]Section 38 CPO.

[4]Party autonomy was limited only by section 40 CPO.

[5]Section 38 CPO reads in German: "Ein an sich unzuständiges Gericht erster Instanz wird durch ausdrückliche oder stillschweigende Vereinbarung der Parteien zuständig".

M. Weller (✉)
Institute for German and International Civil Procedure Law, University of Bonn, Bonn, Germany
e-mail: weller@jura.uni-bonn.de

M. Keyes (ed.), *Optional Choice of Court Agreements in Private International Law*, Ius Comparatum – Global Studies in Comparative Law 37,
https://doi.org/10.1007/978-3-030-23914-5_9

> Section 40 CPO of 1879: (1) The agreement is ineffective if it does not relate to a specific legal relationship and the legal dispute arising from it. (2) The agreement is inadmissible if the legal dispute is about non-monetary claims or of there is an exclusive ground of jurisdiction.[6]

The parties' choice was (and is today) fully binding on the court.[7] Thus, the regime of choice of court agreements at the time when the nineteenth century was drawing to its close, may be taken as an expression of a generally liberal approach in civil law and civil procedure in Germany.[8] Meanwhile, the regulatory approach has become much more restrictive, both on the level of substantive and procedural law. In 1974, the German legislator reformed the law on the choice of court fundamentally and introduced far-reaching limitations on the freedom of the parties.[9] These limitations remain in place within the autonomous German law on choice of court agreements.[10]

1.2 *Impact of International Instruments: Only Residual Relevance of German Law*

Even though Germany is a Member State of the EU and as such bound by both the Brussels regime on jurisdiction[11] and the Hague Convention on Choice of Court

[6]Section 40 CPO reads in German: "(1) Die Vereinbarung hat keine rechtliche Wirkung, wenn sie nicht auf ein bestimmtes Rechtsverhältniß und die aus demselben entspringenden Rechtsstreitigkeiten sich bezieht. (2) Die Vereinbarung ist unzulässig, wenn der Rechtsstreit andere als vermögensrechtliche Ansprüche betrifft, oder wenn für die Klage ein ausschließlicher Gerichtsstand begründet ist".

[7]Hüßtege (2017b), § 38 para 31; Bendtsen (2017), § 38 para 30.

[8]Hahn (1881), p. 160: "Im Einklangmit der Tendenz der neueren deutschen Prozeßgesetze (. . .) und Entwürfe (. . .) gewähren die Vorschriften des dritten Teils der prorogation fori einen weiten Spielraum". In translation: "In accordance with the tendency of the recent German legislation on procedure. . .and drafts. . .the provisions of the third part of the prorogatio fori leave a large margin".

[9]Law to Change the Code of Civil Procedure ("Gesetz zur Änderung der Zivilprozessordnung") of 21 March 1974, Federal Law Gazette (Bundesgesetzblatt), BGBl. 1974 I 753, taking effect on 1 April 1974.

[10]A detailed analysis will follow below Sect. 2.

[11]Regulation (EU) No 1215/2012 of the European Parliament and of the Council of 12 December 2012 on jurisdiction and the recognition and enforcement of judgments in civil and commercial matters (recast), OJ L 351 of 20 December 2012, 1; 1968 Brussels Convention on jurisdiction and the enforcement of judgments in civil and commercial matters, OJ L 299 of 31 December 1972, 32. The latter instrument was a purely intergovernmental measure envisaged by Article 220 EEC but was ratified by all founding EEC Member States soon after the EEC came into being and was acceded to by all States later joining the EU.

Agreements,[12,13] and even though Germany is a Contracting State to the Lugano Convention[14] and the New York Convention on the Recognition and Enforcement of Foreign Arbitral Awards,[15] these international instruments did not influence the state of the autonomous German law on choice of court agreements.[16] For example, as opposed to both Article 25 Brussels Ibis and Article 3 lit. b Hague Convention,[17] there is no presumption for an exclusive effect of a choice of court agreement.[18] However, the residual scope of application of the autonomous German law has become quite limited after the aforementioned international instruments were put in place. Basically, German autonomous law on choice of court agreements only applies (to the derogation) when the parties agree upon the courts in a state that is neither an EU Member State, nor a Lugano State, nor a Contracting State to the Hague Convention.[19] Thus, current German case law and academic debate mainly revolve around the international instruments rather than the residual rules on autonomous choice of court agreements.[20]

---

[12]Convention of 30 June 2005 on Choice of Court Agreements. On 5 October 2006, the Council of the European Union (EU) adopted the decision on the accession of the (then) European Community to the Hague Conference on Private International Law and the European Community became a formal member of the Hague Conference on Private International Law on 3 April 2007. On 1 April 2009, the Hague Convention on Choice of Court Agreements was signed by the European Community and ratified by the European Union on 11 June 2015 with effect to all EU Member States except Denmark. However, Denmark ratified the Convention in 2018. On the EU's way into the Hague Conference see e.g. Weller (2016a), p. 53 et seq., paras 40 et seq.

[13]See on these two instruments from a comparative viewpoint e.g. Weller (2017), p. 91. See also e.g. Weller (2016b), p. 393.

[14]Convention on jurisdiction and the recognition and enforcement of judgments in civil and commercial matters, OJ L 339 of 21 December 2007, 3.

[15]United Nations Convention on the Recognition and Enforcement of Foreign Arbitral Awards, New York 1958. The Convention applies to Germany since 30 June 1961.

[16]One exception are the formal requirements for choice of court agreements under section 38 (2) ZPO that were autonomously harmonized with Article 17 Brussels Convention, see Bey (2017a), § 38 para 12; Toussaint (2017), § 38 para 34. Arguably, the new formal requirements under Article 23 Brussels I Regulation/Article 25 Brussels Ibis Regulation should be transplanted, by way of interpretation, to section 38 (2) ZPO as well, see e.g. Vollkommer (2016), § 38 para 28.

[17]On this presumption in the Hague Convention see Weller (2015), Haager Prorogationsübereinkommen para 9; see also Schulz (2006), p. 253 et seq.: "the presumption under common law is normally the opposite".

[18]See e.g. Federal Court of Justice (Bundesgerichtshof) Neue Juristische Wochenschrift 2015, 1118; Federal Court of Justice (Bundesgerichtshof) Monatsschrift für Deutsches Recht 1968, 474; Imperial Court (Reichsgericht) Juristische Wochenschrift 1911, 49; Hüßtege (2017b), § 38 para 32.

[19]See e.g. Weller (2014), p. 257. Aditionally, the autonomous jurisdictional law applies as a standard of control according to section 328 (1) no 1 ZPO when it comes to the recognition of a judgment from such a third state.

[20]But Weller (2005), p. 302 et seq. on the central point in autonomous German jurisdictional law whether the derogation of German courts (governed by autonmous German jurisdictional law exclusively, on this aspect see below at note 93 and accompanying text in more detail) must be

1.3 "Double Function": (Expressly) Venue and (Implicitly) Jurisdiction

These rules (like all autonomous rules on jurisdiction), although they deal with venue only, are generally understood as encompassing international choice of court agreements (and generally international jurisdiction) likewise by way of analogy.[21] German courts characterize the agreement concluded prior to the institution of proceedings as a contract by which the parties dispose of a procedural right of access to the otherwise competent court,[22] but a growing number of commentators understand the agreement as an entirely "procedural" agreement solely governed by procedural law even if concluded prior to the institution of proceedings[23] (but since there are no rules in the ZPO on e.g. formation of contracts etc., analogies must be drawn from the rules on contracts in substantive law).

1.4 Abuse Under the Old Liberal Approach

The former liberal approach to the choice of forum brought about a widely unfair practice to include choice of court agreements in virtually all standard terms, in particular in contracts with consumers. These choice of court agreements would typically grant optional or even exclusive jurisdiction to the business party at that party's domicile or another forum convenient to that party,[24] and many claims by the party using such standard terms resulted in default judgments against the other (weaker) party. Default judgments in Germany are solely based on the plaintiff's submissions.[25] Therefore, defences to be raised by the defendant would not be taken into account and facts submitted by the plaintiff would be supposed to be accepted

---

deemed null and void in order to protect fundamental values and notions of justice of the German legal order.

[21] "Double functionality" (Doppelfunktionalität) of the venue rules of sections 12 et seq. ZPO; see Federal Court of Justice (Bundesgerichtshof) NJW-Rechtsprechung-Report Zivilrecht 2010, 1554 para 10; Federal Court of Justice (Bundesgerichtshof) Neue Juristische Wochenschrift 1965, 1665.

[22] Federal Court of Justice (Bundesgerichtshof) Neue Juristische Wochenschrift 1968, 1233; Federal Court of Justice (Bundesgerichtshof) Neue Juristische Wochenschrift 1972, 1622; Higher Regional Court (Oberlandesgericht) München Praxis des Internationalen Privat- und Verfahrensrechts 1991, 46, 48.

[23] Bork (2014), § 38 ZPO para 50; Hüßtege (2017b), Vorb § 38 para 2; Vollkommer (2016), § 38 para 4.

[24] Vollkommer (2016), Vor § 38 para 4; Patzina (2016), § 38 para 1.

[25] See section 331 (1) ZPO: "Beantragt der Kläger gegen den im Termin zur mündlichen Verhandlung nicht erschienenen Beklagten das Versäumnisurteil, so ist das tatsächliche mündliche Vorbringen des Klägers als zugestanden anzunehmen". In translation: "If the plaintiff applies for a default judgment after the defendant has not appeared in the hearing, the factual submissions of the plaintiff are deemed to be accepted by the defendant".

by the defendant (*zugestanden*). Thus, many judgments emerged that presumably did not reflect the actual legal situation to the detriment of the defendant.[26] This is why courts started invalidating such agreements in standard terms.[27]

1.5 Protectionist Reform in 1974

Therefore, in 1974,[28] the legislator reformed the law on choice of court agreements, sections 38 et seq. ZPO, fundamentally by introducing a general prohibition of choice of court agreements.[29] The old sections 38 et seq. CPO were removed and replaced by certain exceptions from the new general prohibition laid down in an entirely newly designed text for section 38 ZPO, and section 40 ZPO adds further conditions (some of which existed already before under the old version of that provision).[30] Section 39 ZPO deals with jurisdiction by submission through appearance (and is not part of the further analysis here). These provisions still expressly deal with venue only but are, as was mentioned before,[31] understood as encompassing international jurisdiction likewise by analogy.

1.6 Relevant Autonomous German Legislation Today: Sections 38 and 40 ZPO

Sections 38 and 40 ZPO of 1974 are still in effect and read as follows[32]:

> Section 38: Admissible agreement as to the choice of venue.
>
> (1) A court of first instance that as such is not competent will become the forum by express or tacit agreement of the parties should the parties to the agreement be merchants, legal persons under public law, or special assets (Sondervermögen) under public law.

---

[26]Patzina (2016), § 38 para 1; Vollkommer (2016), Vor § 38 para 4. See also the Reasoning in the Legislative Proposal to the 1974 Reform Act, BT-Drucks. 7/268, 1: "Wirtschaftlich schwache und geschäftlich unerfahrene Personen gehen beim Abschluß von Verträgen oft Erfüllungsorts- oder Gerichtsstandsvereinbarungen ein, ohne deren Bedeutung zu erkennen. Im Streifalle führt dies oft zum Versäumnisurteil am weit entfernten, aber als zuständig vereinbarten Gericht, obwohl die Sache materiell-rechtlich für die beklagte Partei nicht aussichtlos war".

[27]See e.g. Higher Regional Court (Oberlandesgericht) München Neue Juristische Wochenschrift 1973, 1885; Higher Regional Court (Oberlandesgericht) Frankfurt Neue Juristische Wochenschrift 1974, 194.

[28]See above note 9.

[29]Federal Court of Justice (Bundesgerichtshof) Neue Juristische Wochenschrift 1983, 162; Bork (2014), § 38 ZPO para 4; Heinrich (2017), § 38 para 1.

[30]Vollkommer (2016), Vor § 38 para 5.

[31]See above at note 21 and accompanying text.

[32]Translation provided by the German Federal Ministry of Justice, https://www.gesetze-im-internet.de/englisch_zpo/englisch_zpo.html.

(2) The competence of a court of first instance may be agreed, furthermore, wherever at least one of the parties to the agreement has no general venue in Germany. Such agreement must be concluded in writing or, should it have been concluded orally, must be confirmed in writing. If one of the parties has its general venue in Germany, a court may be selected in Germany only if that party has its general venue in that court's jurisdiction, or if a specific jurisdiction is given.
(3) In all other regards, a choice-of-court agreement shall be admissible only where it was concluded, expressly and in writing:

1. After the dispute has arisen, or
2. For the event that, following the conclusion of the agreement, the party to whom claim is to be laid relocated his place of residence or habitual place of abode to a location outside the territorial scope of this Code, or for the event that the party's place of residence or habitual place of abode is not known at the time the proceedings are brought in the courts.

Section 40: Invalid and inadmissible choice of court agreement

(1) The choice-of-court agreement shall have no legal effect if it does not refer to a certain legal relationship and to the legal disputes arising therefrom.
(2) A choice-of-court agreement shall be inadmissible where:

1. The legal dispute concerns non-pecuniary claims that are assigned to the local courts (Amtsgerichte, AG) without consideration of the value of the subject matter being litigated, or
2. An exclusive jurisdiction has been established for the complaint.

In these cases, the competence of a court will not be established by a party making an appearance in oral argument on the merits of the case without asserting the court's lack of jurisdiction.

It has been contested that after the reform of 1974 there would still be a principle of party autonomy in place.[33] Others criticized the paternalistic touch of the new legislation.[34] At any rate, the new sections 38 and 40 ZPO must be understood as expressing mandatory notions of procedural justice and equity (*Billigkeit*),[35] which is part of a general understanding today in Germany that norms of procedural law are no longer to be taken as being just of a technical nature but rather as implementing, just like substantive law, justice and fairness.[36] As a consequence, the essential notions of procedural justice and fairness are protected against an unlimited and uncontrolled exercise of party autonomy,[37] in particular in relation to typically weaker parties.[38] From a different viewpoint, one might also consider the reform as strengthening party autonomy by better steering the powers of control of choice of

[33]Vollkommer (2016), Vor § 38 para 5; Gottwald (1985), p. 95 et seq.

[34]Jauernig (2002), p. 41: "autoritäre Sozialpolitik".

[35]Federal Court of Justice (Bundesgerichtshof) Neue Juristische Wochenschrift 1983, 1320, 1322.

[36]Bey (2017a), § 38 para 1; Vollkommer (2016), Vor § 38 para 5.

[37]Bey (2017a), § 38 para 1.

[38]Vollkommer (2016), Vor § 38 para 5.

court agreements by the courts under general clauses and abstract prohibitions of abuse of rights (*Rechtsmissbrauch*).[39]

In case of a violation of sections 38 et seq. ZPO, i.e. when the agreement in question turns out not to be covered by one of the exceptions, most commentators assume that the agreement is entirely invalid (for both sides),[40] whereas other commentators conclude from the protective *ratio* of the prohibitions that the protected party is still allowed to institute proceedings at the *forum prorogatum* and the other party gaining advantages from the agreement is barred from arguing invalidity as a matter of abuse of rights (*Rechtsmissbrauch*).[41]

1.7 No Doctrine of Forum Non Conveniens, But Residual Control of Abuse and Fairness

There is no doctrine of *forum non conveniens*. But there is a residual control of fairness of an agreement in standard terms even if the agreement satisfies the conditions for validity set up in sections 38 and 40 ZPO.[42] This residual control of standard terms for fairness will play a central role when it comes to asymmetrical choice of court agreements.[43]

2 Sections 38 and 40 ZPO in Detail

Turning now to sections 38 and 40 ZPO in detail, first of all it has to be noted that section 38 ZPO describes the range of "admissible choice of court agreements" (*zugelassene Gerichtsstandsvereinbarungen*) whereas section 40 ZPO contains certain special cases of "invalid and inadmissible choice of court agreements" (*unwirksame und unzulässige Gerichtsstandsvereinbarungen*) which would otherwise be amongst the range of admissible choice of court agreements under section 38 ZPO. The following analysis starts with the basic range of admissible choice of court agreements under section 38 ZPO and then turns to the special grounds of invalidity and inadmissibility under section 40 ZPO. In a third step, other grounds of invalidity outside section 40 ZPO will be discussed.

[39]Hartmann (2017), § 38 para 2.

[40]Bork (2014), § 38 ZPO para 4.

[41]Hüßtege (2017b), Vorb § 38 ZPO para 11.

[42]Federal Court of Justice (Bundesgerichtshof) Neue Juristische Wochenschrift 1983, 1322; Higher Regional Court (Oberlandesgericht) Hamburg Monatsschrift für Deutsches Recht 2000, 170; Patzina (2016), § 38 para 22.

[43]See below Sect. 4.

2.1 Section 38 ZPO: General Prohibition of Prorogations and Certain Exceptions

Section 38 ZPO sets up certain general conditions for the validity of choice of court agreements.

2.1.1 Remaining Options for the Parties in General

(Only) subject to these conditions, choice of court agreements may deal with venue, subject-matter jurisdiction and/or international jurisdiction in respect to any proceedings governed by the ZPO (including e.g. interim relief),[44] but not with functional jurisdiction within a certain court (*funktionale Zuständigkeit*),[45] i.e. a choice of the family, insolvency, or commercial bench within a given civil court. The parties may agree to withdraw the agreement[46] or submit its validity to conditions.[47] Theoretically, the parties may also just derogate a certain court without prorogating any other court (even though the statutory provisions address the admissibility of prorogations only),[48] but this is very rare in practice. And the parties may, by agreement, turn an optional agreement into an exclusive one and vice versa,[49] even though again this case is not directly addressed by sections 38 et seq. ZPO. Further, the parties may exclude the jurisdiction of all courts. Such an agreement may be interpreted either as an arbitration agreement (if the agreement contains the necessary elements for such an agreement)[50] or an agreement to exclude access to courts entirely (*Ausschluss der Klagbarkeit*), at least for a certain period of time,[51] a type of agreement that is sometimes used to guarantee the chance for a mediation.[52] The agreement must be sufficiently specific but it suffices if the chosen court can be determined at the moment in which that court is seized with the matter.[53] Parties may

[44] Hüßtege (2017b), Vorb § 38 para 3; Bendtsen (2017), § 38 para 1.

[45] Hüßtege (2017b), Vorb § 38 para 4; Bey (2017a), § 38 para 4; but compare Schilken (2004), p. 450.

[46] Bork (2014), § 38 ZPO para 64.

[47] Bork (2014), § 38 ZPO para 64; see Toussaint (2017), § 38 para 6.

[48] Bork (2014), § 38 ZPO para 71; Smid and Hartmann (2015), § 38 ZPO para 70.

[49] Bork (2014), § 38 ZPO para 71.

[50] Bork (2014), § 38 ZPO para 71.

[51] Smid and Hartmann (2015), § 38 ZPO para 70; Bork (2014), § 38 ZPO para 71.

[52] Conceptually, such an agreement is no longer conceived as a choice of court agreement but rather as an agreement that bars proceedings as such (Prozesshindernis), see e.g. Bacher (2017), § 253 ZPO, para 18.2.

[53] Federal Court of Justice (Bundesgerichtshof) Neue Juristische Wochenschrift 1996, 3013, 3014; Higher Regional Court (Oberlandesgericht) Brandenburg Neue Juristische Wochenschrift 2006, 3444, 3446; Hüßtege (2017b), § 38 para 28. See also, in respect to international agreements, Bork (2014), § 38 ZPO para 69. Under section 38 (3) ZPO, however, a certain specific court must be chosen (Ausdrücklichkeitserfordernis), see Smid and Hartmann (2015), § 38 ZPO para 58.

also agree upon the jurisdiction of several courts.[54] According to section 35 ZPO, the plaintiff may then choose amongst these (and other competent) courts. However, it would not be possible to leave all choices entirely to the respective plaintiff.[55] But the parties may agree on alternatively exclusive jurisdictions depending on who will be the plaintiff.[56] If the main contract turns out to be invalid, this has no effects on the respective choice of court agreement because the parties are deemed to have concluded the agreement to cover also disputes about the validity of the main contract.[57] Sometimes, however, the reason for invalidity of the main contract may become relevant as self-standing reason for invalidity of the choice of court agreement, such as a lack of capacity of one party to conclude contracts.[58]

2.1.2 Legal Capacity, Agency, Effects for Successors in Law (e.g. Assignees)

The agreement must be concluded by those who intend to be bound by it,[59] and these persons must act with general legal capacity (*Geschäftsfähigkeit*), not necessarily the capacity to institute and conduct the proceedings (*Prozessfähigkeit*).[60] However, if the choice of court agreement is concluded within pending proceedings, the parties must have procedural capacity.[61] Of course, agency (*Stellvertretung*) is possible.[62] The agreement is effective for successsors in law, i.e. for the assignee of a claim subject to a choice of court agreement, unless the original choice of court agreement must be interpreted that such effect be excluded as a matter of exception.[63] Choice of court agreements in the articles of a company or association (*Satzung*) are admissible and generally effective for new corporate members.[64]

---

[54] Federal Court of Justice (Bundesgerichtshof) Neue Juristische Wochenschrift 1983, 996; Higher Regional Court (Oberlandesgericht) Brandenburg Neue Juristische Wochenschrift 2006, 3444, 3446; Bey (2017a), § 38 para 2.

[55] Higher Regional Court (Oberlandesgericht) Karlsruhe Entscheidungen der Oberlandesgerichte in Zivilsachen 1973, 479; Vollkommer (2016), § 38 para 13; Patzina (2016), § 38 para 41.

[56] Federal Court of Justice (Bundesgerichtshof) NJW-Rechtsprechung-Report Zivilrecht 1986, 1311; Vollkommer (2016), § 38 para 13.

[57] Federal Court of Justice (Bundesgerichtshof) Zeitschrift für Zivilprozess 73 (1960), 255; Higher Regional Court (Kammergericht) Berlin Betriebs-Berater 1983, 213; Bork (2014), § 38 ZPO para 64 with further references.

[58] Bork (2014), § 38 ZPO para 64.

[59] Bork (2014), § 38 ZPO para 52.

[60] Bork (2014), § 38 ZPO para 56; Toussaint (2017), § 38 para 5; for a different view see Häsemeyer (2005), p. 299.

[61] Hüßtege (2017b), Vorb § 38 para 2; Bendtsen (2017), § 38 para 3.

[62] Bork (2014), § 38 ZPO para 52; Vollkommer (2016), § 38 para 6.

[63] Bork (2014), § 38 ZPO para 53.

[64] Bork (2014), § 38 ZPO para 60; Vollkommer (2016), § 38 para 9a. See also section 1066 ZPO for arbitration agreements. The *ratio* of this provision applies to choice of court agreements as well.

2.1.3 Time of Conclusion of the Agreement and Perpetuatio Fori

As to the time of concluding the agreement, principally an agreement is still possible after instituting the proceedings.[65] However, the principle of *perpetuatio fori*[66] bars the parties from agreements to the effect that the court where the proceedings were instituted loses its jurisdiction.[67] Conversely, where there is doubt about jurisdiction of the court originally seized with the matter, the parties may well agree upon the jurisdiction of that court still within the proceedings (but of course such cases will generally be dealt with under the notion of jurisdiction by appearance).[68] The situation is different if an (admissible) change of the claim results in the loss of the jurisdiction of the court originally seized with the matter. Then the parties are allowed to choose other courts as well.[69]

2.1.4 (No) Formal Requirements (in General)

There is no general requirement for a specific form of the agreement. Nor does the agreement have to meet the form requirements of the main contract.[70] However, in certain special situations regulated by sections 38 (2) and (3), written form or at least confirmation in writing is required additionally to other measures of protection.[71]

2.1.5 Interpretation

There is no general rule or presumption for a wide or narrow interpretation, nor is there, as has already been mentioned above,[72] such approach in respect to the

[65]Bork (2014), § 38 ZPO para 65.

[66]See section 261 (3) no. 2 ZPO.

[67]Federal Court of Justice (Bundesgerichtshof) NJW-Rechtsprechung-Report Zivilrecht 2010, 891; Federal Court of Justice (Bundesgerichtshof) NJW-Rechtsprechung-Report Zivilrecht 1995, 513; Higher Regional Court (Oberlandesgericht) München, decision of 23 May 2016—docket no. 34 AR 65/16, para 11; Bork (2014), § 38 ZPO para 65 n. 160 with further references.

[68]Federal Court of Justice (Bundesgerichtshof) Neue Juristische Wochenschrift 1976, 626; Federal Court of Justice (Bundesgerichtshof) Neue Juristische Wochenschrift 1963, 585, 586; Higher Regional Court (Oberlandesgericht) NJW-Rechtsprechung-Report Zivilrecht 1989, 716.

[69]Bork (2014), § 38 ZPO para 65.

[70]Federal Court of Justice (Bundesgerichtshof) Entscheidungen des Bundesgerichtshofes in Zivilsachen 69, 265 et seq.; Vollkommer (2016), § 38 para 8.

[71]See below Sects. 2.1.8 and 2.1.9 for more detail.

[72]See above Sect. 1.2.

question whether the agreement is to be understood as exclusive or non-exclusive.[73] Consequently, it is a matter of interpretation in the particular case at hand whether for example the agreement only covers contractual claims or additionally delictual claims arising from the same facts or even delictual claims arising only in connection with the respective main contract.[74] For example, there has recently been a large debate on the interpretation of choice of court agreements between cartellists and their damaged customers as to whether such agreements should be interpreted as encompassing the delictual claims or not.[75] However, since the agreements in the case at hand fell within the scope of the Brussels I Regulation, the debate did not touch much upon autonomous German law.[76] In general, German courts tend to a wide and inclusive interpretation on the grounds that reasonable business parties typically want to subject the entire legal relationship in question under a choice of court agreement and want to avoid several proceedings about the same facts in different courts.[77] If the agreement is agreed upon in standard terms, there is a more restrictive approach (typically, only contractual claims are deemed to be covered).[78]

2.1.6 Ex Officio Examination; Judicial Review

Choice of court agreements are to be considered *ex officio*.[79] However, the decision of the court of first instance on venue cannot be reviewed whereas the decision on international jurisdiction will be subject to judicial review (*Berufung*) and even second appeal (*Revision*).[80]

---

[73]Federal Court of Justice (Bundesgerichtshof) Neue Juristische Wochenschrift 2015, 1118; Federal Court of Justice (Bundesgerichtshof) NJW-Rechtsprechung-Report Zivilrecht 1999, 137, 138; Bork (2014), § 38 ZPO para 4.

[74]Federal Court of Justice (Bundesgerichtshof) Neue Juristische Wochenschrift 1965, 300; Higher Regional Court (Oberlandesgericht) Hamm, decision of 5 February 2016—docket no. 32 Sa 79/15, para 18; Higher Regional Court (Oberlandesgericht) Stuttgart Neue Juristische Online-Zeitschrift 2008, 2290, 2292 et seq.

[75]Wurmnest (2013), p. 75.

[76]But see e.g. Pfeiffer (2012), p. 2057.

[77]Higher Regional Court (Oberlandesgericht) Stuttgart Neue Juristische Online-Zeitschrift 2008, 2290, 2293; Vollkommer (2016), § 40 para 4; Bork (2014), § 40 ZPO para 1 with further references.

[78]Higher Regional Court (Oberlandesgericht) Hamburg Versicherungsrecht 1982, 341; Bendtsen (2017), § 38 para 31; but compare Higher Regional Court (Oberlandesgericht) Stuttgart Neue Juristische Online-Zeitschrift 2008, 2290, 2293.

[79]Bey (2017b), § 40 para 2; Vollkommer (2016), § 40 para 2.

[80]Federal Court of Justice (Bundesgerichtshof) Entscheidungen des Bundesgerichtshofes in Zivilsachen 157, 224, 227 et seq.; Federal Court of Justice (Bundesgerichtshof) Entscheidungen des Bundesgerichtshofes in Zivilsachen 153, 82, 84; Krüger (2016), § 545 para 17; for a different view see e.g. Hartmann (2017), Übers § 38 para 10.

2.1.7 Section 38 (1) ZPO: Agreement on Venue (by Certain Categories of Parties Only)

According to section 38 (1) ZPO, choice of court agreements are only valid if concluded (on both sides,[81] even if the prorogation would be favorable to the other party not being eligible under section 38 (1) ZPO[82]) by merchants (*Kaufleute*), legal persons under public law (*juristische Personen des öffentlichen Rechts*) or public trusts (*öffentlich-rechtliches Sondervermögen*), as understood according to the *lex fori*[83] at the time of the conclusion of the agreement.[84] Legal persons under private law, i.e. mainly corporations, are generally deemed merchants in the sense of the German Commercial Code (*Handelsgesetzbuch*). Thus, legal persons under private law are, of course, in most cases able to agree on a choice of court,[85] whereas non-merchants are fully excluded from agreements on venue.[86] There is no general formal requirement under section 38 (1) ZPO, thus the parties may agree on the choice of court implicitly and by standard terms (then subject of course to the general control of standard terms on its valid inclusion and fairness[87]). Commercial customs

---

[81] Hüßtege (2017b), § 38 para 7; Smid and Hartmann (2015), § 38 ZPO para 84.

[82] Hüßtege (2017b), § 38 para 7.

[83] Bork (2014), § 38 ZPO para 10; Bey (2017a), § 38 para 6.

[84] Bork (2014), § 38 ZPO para 17; Hüßtege (2017b), § 38 para 9. It is of no relevance whether the status ceases to exist after the conclusion of the agreement, Bendtsen (2017), § 38 para 12. Conversely, it does not cure the invalidity if the necessary status is acquired after the conclusion of the agreement. However, the parties are of course free to enter into a new agreement. Successors in law such as an assignee of the claim subject to the agreement remain bound even if they do not themselves have the necessary status to conclude a choice of court agreement, see Vollkommer (2016), § 38 para 10; for a different view see Regional Court (Landgericht) Trier Neue Juristische Wochenschrift 1982, 286.

[85] There are, however, legal persons under private law without the status of a merchant, i.e. small, but registered non-profit associations (Idealverein), section 21 German Civil Code.

[86] It has to be noted, that the group of "non-merchants" is not congruent with the group of "consumers" as merchants acting in their capacity as consumers, i.e. transacting for private purposes, are still capable of concluding choice of court agreements under section 38 (1) ZPO and do not fall under the stricter provision for non-merchants under section 38 (2) ZPO. This does not appear to be convincing but rather illustrates the outdated state of sections 38 and 40 ZPO as opposed to modern notions of consumer protection law to which these provisions from 1974 have not yet been adjusted to.

[87] See sections 305 et seq. German Civil Code. According to the standards laid down there, choice of court agreements in standard terms will not be considered as surprising terms and thus not included but if none of the parties has its domicile at the place of the chosen court and if there is no other substantial connection to the chosen court, there will be an issue, see Bork (2014), § 38 ZPO para 20. Furthermore, a choice of court as such will not be considered as unfair. However, there will be an issue if the agreement unilaterally favors the party using the standard terms, see Higher Regional Court (Oberlandesgericht) Hamburg Monatsschrift für Deutsches Recht 2000, 170, 171; Bey (2017a), § 38 para 8. If there is a valid and an invalid component of the agreement, a "blue pencil test" applies, Higher Regional Court (Oberlandesgericht) Karlsruhe, judgment of 10 March 2015—docket no. 8 U 208/13; Bey (2017a), § 38 para 8.

will be considered,[88] but acceptance of an invoice without opposition will usually not be considered sufficient to introduce a choice of court agreement.[89] In sum, section 38 (1) ZPO provides for nearly unlimited freedom of the parties covered by this provision to agree on choice of court agreements. The *ratio* obviously is that the status of the persons covered by the provisions will usually have sufficient business experience and will usually be able to effectively pursue their rights in a remote venue[90] or even foreign jurisdiction.[91]

2.1.8 Section 38 (2) ZPO: Agreements on International Jurisdiction

In addition, according to section 38 (2) ZPO, choice of court agreements are admissible if at least one party is not subject to the general jurisdiction of German courts based on a domestic domicile according to sections 12 et seq. ZPO (specific jurisdiction such as that based on the place of tort according to section 32 ZPO does not suffice[92]). Under section 38 (2) ZPO, as opposed to subsection (1), the agreement must be in writing or at least confirmed in writing (which can be effectuated in the context of the document for the main contract[93]). If at least one party does have a domestic domicile, the parties may only choose either that domicile or the jurisdiction of the courts at one of the special grounds of jurisdiction laid down by legislation but not entirely freely (within Germany) wherever they like.[94]

This restriction does not apply for the choice of foreign courts.[95] For, section 38 (2) ZPO does not deal expressly with derogations, but only with conditions for prorogation. Thus, even consumers may validly derogate the jurisdiction of German courts under section 38 (2) ZPO if the other party has a foreign domicile.[96] There

[88]Bork (2014), § 38 ZPO para 19; Hüßtege (2017b), § 38 para 25.

[89]This is disputed, see Hüßtege (2017b), § 38 para 25 with further references.

[90]Patzina (2016), § 38 para 5; Bendtsen (2017), § 38 para 9.

[91]According to most commentators and courts, section 38 (1) ZPO extends to international choice of court agreements of the persons covered by this provision, see Federal Court of Justice (Bundesgerichtshof) Neue Juristische Wochenschrift 2016, 2328, 2329 et seq.; Federal Court of Justice (Bundesgerichtshof) Zeitschrift für Wirtschafts- und Bankrecht 1985, 1507, 1509; Higher Regional Court (Oberlandesgericht) Saarbrücken Neue Juristische Wochenschrift 2000, 670, 671; Heinrich (2017), § 38 para 13; others want to apply both section 38 (1) and (2) ZPO, see Local Court (Amtsgericht) Berlin-Charlottenburg Neue Juristische Wochenschrift 1975, 502 or only section 38 (2) ZPO, see Higher Regional Court (Oberlandesgericht) Nürnberg Neue Juristische Wochenschrift 1985, 1296 et seq.; Vollkommer (2016), § 38 para 25.

[92]Federal Court of Justice (Bundesgerichtshof), judgment of 9 June 2016—docket no. IX ZR 314/14, para 38; Bork (2014), § 38 ZPO para 25; for a different view see Hartmann (2017), § 38 para 21.

[93]Bork (2014), § 38 ZPO para 29.

[94]See section 38 (2) Sentence 3 ZPO.

[95]Bork (2014), § 38 ZPO para 32; Bendtsen (2017), § 38 para 19.

[96]Federal Court of Justice (Bundesgerichtshof) Neue Juristische Wochenschrift 1971, 325; Hüßtege (2017b), Vorb § 38 para 5.

might be other limitations on the derogation in such cases such as standard terms control or specific protections in other areas of the law such as under labour law[97] etc., but even then the generally liberal approach in international cases for non-merchant parties is obviously in contradiction to the extremely restrictive approach for venue for such parties under section 38 (1) ZPO. Conversely, two foreign parties may agree upon any court within Germany, and there is no need of any link to Germany other than the parties' choice (subject to a residual control of abusiveness[98]).[99] However, this constellation is now dealt with by Article 25 Brussels Ibis Regulation.[100]

On a general level, it has to be added to these reflections on the German autonomous law on international choice of court agreements in section 38 (2) ZPO, that, as was mentioned before, special and certain further implicit rules and principles apply to the choice of a foreign court. First of all, the Brussels Ibis Regulation (and the Lugano Convention) is understood as not generally regulating the derogation of fora within the European Union.[101] Thus, if the parties choose a court in a state outside the EU (or outside the territorial scope of the Lugano Convention), the autonomous law of the respective EU Member (or Lugano Contracting) State applies to the effects of the derogation. The parties may choose a specific foreign court or generally the courts of a foreign state and leave the determination of the venue to the foreign law.[102] The parties may agree on the choice of a foreign court implicitly, and the choice of foreign law is a factor that contributes to establishing an implicit choice of court but generally is not in itself

[97]Federal Labour Court (Bundesarbeitsgericht) Neue Juristische Wochenschrift 1973, 963: No derogation by an employee in international cases if such derogation would impair the legitimate interests of the employee. See also section 48 (2) German Labour Court Law (Arbeitsgerichtsgesetz) in relation to choice of court agreements in collective labour agreements (Tarifverträgen).

[98]Bork (2014), § 38 ZPO para 32; Bendtsen (2017), § 38 para 19.

[99]Geimer (2016), IZPR para 77 et seq.; Nagel and Gottwald (2013), § 3 para 462; also see Higher Regional Court (Oberlandesgericht) München Praxis des Internationalen Privat- und Verfahrensrechts 1984, 318; Higher Regional Court (Oberlandesgericht) Hamburg Versicherungsrecht 1983, 1149; for a different view see Wagner (1998), p. 358 et seq.

[100]In the Recast of the Brussels I Regulation, the requirement in Article 23 Brussels I Regulation that one party must have its domicile within an EU Member State was removed to the effect that now Article 25 Brussels Ibis Regulation applies to any international agreement in favor of a court located in an EU Member State.

[101]Schlosser (1979), 71, 124 para 176: "In cases where parties agree to bring their disputes before the courts of a State which is not a party to the 1968 Convention there is obviously nothing in the 1968 Convention to prevent such courts from declaring themselves competent, if their law recognizes the validity of such an agreement. (. . .) There is nothing in the 1968 Convention to support the conclusion that such agreements must be inadmissible in principle. However, the 1968 Convention does not contain any rules as to their validity either".

[102]Bork (2014), § 38 ZPO para 33 and 69.

sufficient.[103] The validity of the derogation of the German courts does not generally depend on whether the foreign judgment will be recognizable and enforceable in Germany.[104]

However, the derogation of the German courts (not regulated in section 38 (2) ZPO) is deemed invalid if the chosen court will not accept the choice and no other grounds of jurisdiction in the chosen state are available because a valid derogation would result in a denial of justice typically unwanted by the parties in the moment of concluding the agreement.[105] Furthermore, the derogation is deemed invalid if, as a matter of a prognosis, in the foreign court chosen by the parties the fundamental values of fair proceedings as understood in Germany will not be respected.[106] Likewise, the derogation will be invalidated if, as a matter of prognosis, the foreign judgment expected to emerge from the foreign proceedings will not be recognizable in Germany because of a violation of public policy, be it on substantive, be it on procedural grounds.[107] Of course, these kinds of a residual and/or public policy control of the derogation are always a matter of last resort and must be handled with care but it still is valid case law, even in respect to the protection of fundamental values of substantive law (albeit contested by some academic commentators[108]) although cases become more and more infrequent.

2.1.9 Section 38 (3) ZPO: Some Additional Cases

In all other cases, as is made clear by section 38 (3) ZPO, an agreement is only allowed if concluded expressly (including standard terms, but generally using the

[103]Higher Regional Court (Oberlandesgericht) München Praxis des Internationalen Privat- und Verfahrensrechts 1984, 319; Higher Regional Court (Oberlandesgericht) Hamburg Monatsschrift für Deutsches Recht 1973, 1025; Bork (2014), § 38 ZPO para 33.

[104]Federal Court of Justice (Bundesgerichtshof) Versicherungsrecht 1974, 471; Federal Court of Justice (Bundesgerichtshof) Neue Juristische Wochenschrift 1971, 325; Patzina (2016), § 38 para 43; Bork (2014), § 38 ZPO para 34 with further references; for a different view (no exclusive choice of court agreement possible) see Higher Regional Court (Oberlandesgericht) München Monatsschrift für Deutsches Recht 1957, 45; Vollkommer (2016), § 38 para 14.

[105]Federal Court of Justice (Bundesgerichtshof) Versicherungsrecht 1974, 470; Heinrich (2017), § 38 para 20; Bey (2017a), § 38 para 4.

[106]See Weller (2005), p. 302 et seq.; also see Federal Court of Justice (Bundesgerichtshof) Zeitschrift für Zivilprozess 78 (1975), 318; Geimer (2016), IZPR para 83. See also, in respect to internationally mandatory norms that would otherwise not be enforced, Federal Court of Justice (Bundesgerichtshof) Internationales Handelsrecht 2013, 35; Federal Court of Justice (Bundesgerichtshof) Neue Juristische Wochenschrift 1984, 2037; Higher Regional Court (Oberlandesgericht) Stuttgart Internationales Handelsrecht 2012, 163; Bey (2017b), § 40 para 6; for a different view see Geimer (2016), para 65.

[107]Weller (2005), p. 302 et seq. with further references.

[108]E.g. Schack (2017), p. 201, para 516.

terms "court" and "jurisdiction"[109]) and after a controversy has arisen[110] or for dealing in advance with the special cases that either the defendant, after the conclusion of a contract, relocates to a foreign country or if the defendant's domicile is unknown at the moment of instituting the proceedings. It is a matter of debate whether section 38 (2) ZPO preempts subsection (3), thereby limiting the choice of venue of the parties when one party is foreign even in cases that would be covered by subsection (3),[111] or whether subsection (3) prevails once its conditions are fulfilled.[112]

2.2 Section 40 ZPO: Certain Cases of "General" Invalidity and Inadmissibility

Section 40 ZPO provides for certain "general" cases of invalidity and inadmissibility amongst those agreements that are, in principle, admissible under section 38 ZPO. In addition to these general cases, there are a number of special provisions prohibiting choice of court agreements in certain sectors of the law.[113]

According to section 40 (1) ZPO, the agreement must relate to a specific legal relation and to a dispute arising from this legal relation.[114] Thus, an agreement between two parties covering "all controversies" between them would be invalid.[115] Agreements on future legal relations are possible.[116] Agreements on (already existing) delictual claims are possible as well.[117] In relation to delictual claims

[109]Bendtsen (2017), § 38 para 23; Bey (2017a), § 38 para 17.

[110]Different views by the parties on a certain legal relationship that were mutually communicated suffice to open the door for this exception, see Bork (2014), § 38 ZPO para 37; Hüßtege (2017b), § 38 para 17a. Other commentators require that a court proceeding is imminent, Vollkommer (2016), § 38 para 33 with further references. Some commentators let suffice any kind of legal doubts communicated to the other party, Hartmann (2017), § 38 para 34. Once a party has instituted proceedings, however, it is too late to ground an agreement on this option, Federal Court of Justice (Bundesgerichtshof) NJW-Rechtsprechung-Report Zivilrecht 2010, 891, para 9; Federal Court of Justice (Bundesgerichtshof) Neue Juristische Wochenschrift 1953, 1140; Bey (2017a), § 38 para 16; for a different view see Regional Court (Landgericht) Flensburg Schleswig-Holsteinische Anzeigen 79, 39; Regional Court (Landgericht) Waldshut-Tiengen, Monatsschrift für Deutsches Recht 1985, 941.

[111]Bey (2017a), § 38 para 15; Vollkommer (2016), § 38 para 35a.

[112]Bork (2014), § 38 ZPO para 40.

[113]On these see below Sect. 2.3.

[114]Hüßtege (2017b), § 40 para 4.

[115]Bork (2014), § 40 ZPO para 1.

[116]Bork (2014), § 40 ZPO para 1; Hüßtege (2017b), § 40 para 4.

[117]Toussaint (2017), § 40 para 2; Smid and Hartmann (2015), § 40 ZPO para 4.

potentially arising in the future, there are restrictions (the scope of which is controversial[118]).

According to section 40 (2) no 1 ZPO, an agreement is inadmissible if the controvery relates to non-pecuniary claims attributed to the subject-matter jurisdiction of local courts (*Amtsgericht*) irrespective of their value. This restriction related to marriage and parental custody and other family matters, but has become obsolete by parallel legislation on the reorganization of the judiciary for non-contentious proceedings (*freiwillige Gerichtsbarkeit*).[119]

Section 40 (2) ZPO states the obvious by "providing" that an agreement will be inadmissible if there is a conflicting exclusive ground of jurisdiction that applies to the case such as section 29a ZPO. According to this latter provision the courts of the place of the immovable property have exclusive jurisdictions for landlord and tenant matters as well as lease matters. Exclusive grounds of jurisdiction under foreign law are of no effect unless there is an equivalent ground of exclusive jurisdiction under German law.[120] But again, this constellation of a prorogation of a German court (controlled by a kind of jurisdictional "mirror principle" or "theorie reflexive") is now covered by Article 25 Brussels Ibis Regulation.

2.3 *Special Rules*

Additionally, there are a number of statutory special rules with regard to certain contract types, which take precedence over the general rule of section 38 ZPO. They can be subdivided into two categories: The first category deals with the admissibility of choice of court agreements, for example sections 29c (3) ZPO, section 26 (2) Distance Learning Protection Act (*Fernunterrichtsschutzgesetz*) and section 215 Insurance Contract Act (*Versicherungsvertragsgesetz*). These rules mirror—with minor deviations—the requirements of section 38 (3) ZPO. The second category of rules precludes a derogation of the jurisdiction of certain courts. A prorogation of additional courts is, however, possible. This applies e.g. to section 53 (3) Banking Act (*Kreditwesengesetz*) and section 319 (2) Capital Investment Code (*Kapitalanlagegesetzbuch*).

[118]Some require a parallel contractual claim based on the same facts, Federal Court of Justice (Bundesgerichtshof) Neue Juristische Wochenschrift 1970, 2180; Federal Court of Justice (Bundesgerichtshof) Neue Juristische Wochenschrift 1965, 300; Bork (2014), § 40 ZPO para 1; others exclude derogations but allow prorogations, Geimer (2016), IZPR, para 70; Geimer (2014), p. 731 with further references.

[119]See sections 111, 121, 151 Act on Proceedings in Family Matters and in Matters of Non-contentious Jurisdiction (FamFG), also see sections 23a (1) no. 1, 23b (1) Courts Constitution Act (GVG), and section 122 FamFG.

[120]Bork (2014), § 40 ZPO para 11 with further references; for a different view see Rosenberg et al. (2010), § 31 para 49 et seq.

3 Specific Questions on Optional Choice of Court Agreements

3.1 Relevant Legal Sources

The relevant legal sources to determine the effect of optional choice of court agreements are sections 38 and 40 ZPO,[121] certain special provisions invalidating choice of court agreements[122] and sections 133, 157 of the German Civil Code on contractual interpretation when it comes to the interpretation of the agreement.

3.2 The Applicable Law to Determine Whether a Choice of Court Agreement Is Characterized as Optional or Exclusive

3.2.1 Choice of Law

The question whether a choice of court agreement is optional or exclusive is understood as a question of interpretation of the agreement. However, as opposed to other questions of interpretation such as the material scope of the agreement,[123] this issue is exclusively governed by the *lex fori processualis*.[124]

---

[121]See above Sect. 2.1.

[122]See above Sect. 2.3.

[123]These general matters of interpretation are goverend by the law applicable to the agreement in general, the *lex prorogationis* ("Prorogationsstatut"). There is a debate on whether such a distinct *lex prorogationis* or *lex causae* exists at all, see e.g. Antomo (2012), pp. 183, 193; von Hoffmann and Thorn (2007), p. 87 et seq. para 79; Wagner (1998), p. 369 et seq. At any rate, there is consensus that the parties remain free to choose the applicable law for the agreement even though this will occur only rarely in practice. A follow-up question then is, how such a *lex prorogationis* is to be determined. Most commentators hold that the parties may freely choose the *lex prorogationis* in analogy to the choice of law rules of the Rome I Regulation. In practice and thus in the absence of any express will of the parties in regard to the *lex prorogationis*, the law of the main contract, the *lex contractus*, is deemed to also govern the choice of court agreement, see e.g. Hüßtege (2017b), Vorb § 38 para 6; Martiny (2015), Vor Art. 1 Rom I-VO para 61; but compare Thorn (2017), Art. 1 Rom I-VO para 11: Article 4 (4) Rome I Regulation should apply by analogy but would lead to the German *lex fori processualis*.

[124]Federal Court of Justice (Bundesgerichtshof) NJW-Rechtsprechung-Report Zivilrecht 2005, 929, 930 et seq.; Federal Court of Justice (Bundesgerichtshof) Neue Juristische Wochenschrift 1997, 2885, 2886; Heinrich (2017), § 38 para 3.

3.2.2 Determining Whether a Choice of Court Agreement Is Characterized as Optional or Exclusive

The question whether a choice of court agreement is characterized as optional or exclusive is a matter of interpretation in light of the circumstances of the particular case at hand, and the general rules on interpretation of contracts in sections 133 and 157 of the German Civil Code apply by way of analogy.[125] As was mentioned before, there is no general interpretative rule such as a presumption in favor of or against exclusivity.[126] For example, it has been decided that an agreement should be interpreted as being exclusive if the chosen German court would have to apply its own law as the *lex causae*.[127] Further, it has been decided that the prospects of recognition or non-recognition of the future judgment should be taken into account.[128] If, for example, the domestic party does not have assets abroad, this would be a factor against exclusive jurisdiction of the domestic court (at least for claims by the foreign party against the domestic party).[129] If the parties prorogate one court and then, in a distinct paragraph of the agreement, derogate all other courts, the agreement is deemed to be exclusive.[130] The prorogation of the court at the plaintiff's domicile is not as such interpreted as excluding the courts at the domicile of the defendant.[131] It is also a matter of interpretation whether the agreement is mutually or only unilaterally exclusive.[132] For example, an agreement on the

[125]Federal Court of Justice (Bundesgerichtshof) Neue Juristische Wochenschrift 2015, 1118 para 22; Hüßtege (2017b), § 38 para 32.

[126]This is almost uncontested today, see Federal Court of Justice (Bundesgerichtshof) Neue Juristische Wochenschrift 2015, 1118; Federal Court of Justice (Bundesgerichtshof) Neue Juristische Wochenschrift 1973, 422; Imperial Court (Reichsgericht) Juristische Wochenschrift 1911, 49; Vollkommer (2016), § 38 para 14; for different views see Kohler (1886), p. 484 (presumption against exclusivity) and Higher Regional Court (Kammergericht) Berlin Die Rechtsprechung der Oberlandesgerichte 2 (1901), 106; Westerburg (1877), p. 591; Hüßtege (2017b), Vorb § 38 para 8 (presumption in favor of exclusivity).

[127]Higher Regional Court (Oberlandesgericht) Düsseldorf Recht der internationalen Wirtschaft 1990, 220; Nagel and Gottwald (2013), § 3 para 481.

[128]Federal Court of Justice (Bundesgerichtshof) Neue Juristische Wochenschrift 1971, 325; Federal Court of Justice (Bundesgerichtshof) Neue Juristische Wochenschrift 1968, 356; Hüßtege (2017b), Vorb § 38 para 8.

[129]Bork (2014), § 38 ZPO para 34 with further references; this view is rejected by other commentators, see Schütze (1984), p. 247; Smid and Hartmann (2015), § 38 ZPO para 125.

[130]Vollkommer (2016), § 38 para 2.

[131]Higher Regional Court (Oberlandesgericht) Frankfurt OLG-Report 1996, 95; Higher Regional Court (Oberlandesgericht) Bamberg NJW-Rechtsprechung-Report Zivilrecht 1989, 371; Vollkommer (2016), § 38 para 14; but compare Higher Regional Court (Oberlandesgericht) Koblenz Zeitschrift für Miet- und Raumrecht 1997, 187; Higher Regional Court (Oberlandesgericht) Frankfurt Recht der internationalen Wirtschaft 1985, 71.

[132]Higher Regional Court (Oberlandesgericht) Frankfurt Praxis des Internationalen Privat- und Verfahrensrechts 1998, 35, 36; Higher Regional Court (Oberlandesgericht) Hamburg Neue Juristische Wochenschrift 1952, 1020; Bork (2014), § 38 ZPO para 70.

jurisdiction of a foreign court might be interpreted as exclusive (only) for claims against the foreign party, but not for claims against the domestic party.[133] It has also been decided that the fact that one party is a state enterprise might be an indication that the agreement is exclusive for claims against that state party.[134] Likewise, if the parties agree on the jurisdiction of a court at the domicile of one party for all controversies out of or in connection with a certain legal relationship, then such an agreement should be interpreted as being exclusive for claims against that party.[135] Further, if a party uses standard terms and provides for jurisdiction of the courts at its own domicile, such an agreement may be interpreted as exclusive for claims against that party, but as optional otherwise.[136] An agreement which states that "the courts of the respective claimant have jurisdiction" creates an option.[137]

3.3 *The Legal Effect of an Optional Choice of Court Agreement*

The applicable law to determine the legal effect of an optional choice of court agreement is the *lex fori processualis*, i.e. the procedural law of the court, hence German procedural law.[138] It is that law in particular that decides upon the effect of a derogation of the German courts, but also on the validity of the prorogation of a foreign court if this is relevant for the proceedings in Germany.[139]

[133]Bork (2014), § 38 ZPO para 33.

[134]Federal Court of Justice (Bundesgerichtshof) Neue Juristische Wochenschrift 1968, 356, 357.

[135]Federal Court of Justice (Bundesgerichtshof) Neue Juristische Wochenschrift 2015, 1118; Federal Court of Justice (Bundesgerichtshof) Neue Juristische Wochenschrift 1997, 2885, 2886; Federal Court of Justice (Bundesgerichtshof) Neue Juristische Wochenschrift 1973, 422; Bey (2017a), § 38 para 2.

[136]Higher Regional Court (Oberlandesgericht) Hamm, judgment of 13 December 2013—docket no. 32 SA 84/13; Higher Regional Court (Oberlandesgericht) Schleswig Neue Juristische Wochenschrift 2006, 3360, 3361; Regional Court (Landgericht) Karlsruhe, decision of 26 September 2017—docket no. 6 O 102/17; Bork (2014), § 38 ZPO para 70. It is unclear how this case law relates to the contra proferentem rule under the law on the control of standard terms, but it seems to be the approach of the courts that in many cases the interpretation is so clear that there is no room for that rule.

[137]Jayme and Haack (1985), p. 323.

[138]Bork (2014), § 38 ZPO para 23; Hüßtege (2017b), Vorb § 38 para 7.

[139]Federal Court of Justice (Bundesgerichtshof) Neue Juristische Wochenschrift 1986, 1438; Hüßtege (2017b), Vorb § 38 para 7.

3.4 *The Effect of an Optional Choice of Court Agreement in Favor of the Courts of the Forum*

The effect of an optional choice of court agreement in favor of the courts of the forum, i.e. of the German courts, is governed by the Brussels Ibis Regulation. The effect of an optional choice of court agreement under this instrument is that, irrespective of otherwise potentially available grounds of jurisdiction, the court assumes jurisdiction based on the parties' consent, unless there has already been a valid submission to the jurisdiction of the court by appearance. The court has to examine its jurisdiction *ex officio*, including cases of default.[140] The defendant remains free to contest the validity of the agreement on its own account and the court must hear the defendant on that point and take a decision. Not only the law, but also all facts relating to that point must be assessed *ex officio*.[141] The burden of proof for jurisdiction lies with the party who seeks to rely on that jurisdiction.[142] The legal effect of an optional choice of court agreement in favor of the forum does not change once the option has been exercised by commencing proceedings in the forum.

3.5 *The Legal Effect of an Optional Choice of Court Agreement in Favor of Foreign Courts*

Since the agreement only constitutes an additional option for the parties, there is no direct effect. In particular, the non-exclusive choice of a foreign court does not bar a counterclaim against the foreign party in domestic proceedings.[143] If there is a weaker party protected by mandatory provisions guaranteeing this party domestic jurisdiction, even the optional prorogation in favor of a foreign court would be considered invalid for the other party. If a party makes use of the option and institutes proceedings at the foreign court, then a German court seized by the defendant of the foreign proceedings in the same matter will have to check whether the *lis alibi pendens* is to be taken account of to the effect that parallel domestic

[140]Hüßtege (2017a), Art. 25 EuGVVO para 24; Gottwald (2017), Art. 28 VO (EU) 1215/2012 para 1.

[141]See Mankowski (2015), Art. 25 Brüssel-Ia-VO para 3; also see Court of Justice of the European Union, judgment of 16 June 2016 – C-12/15 (Universal Music International Holding/Schilling et al), para 45 et seq.

[142]Federal Court of Justice (Bundesgerichtshof) NJW-Rechtsprechung-Report Zivilrecht 2004, 935; Higher Regional Court (Oberlandesgericht) Frankfurt Monatsschrift für Deutsches Recht 1975, 232; Stadler (2017), Art. 25 EuGVVO para 2.

[143]Federal Court of Justice (Bundesgerichtshof) Entscheidungen des Bundesgerichtshofes in Zivilsachen 59, 113.

proceedings are barred.[144] This will not be the case if, on the basis of a prognosis, the judgment emerging from the foreign proceedings will not be recognized in Germany. In order to be recognized in Germany under autonomous recognition rules, the foreign court must have had jurisdiction according to the German rules on jurisdiction as if they had been applicable to the foreign court ("mirror principle", section 328 (1) no. 1 ZPO). Thus, the German court will have to check the validity of the prorogation under German standards (or resort to other heads of jurisdiction). The legal effect of an optional choice of court agreement in favor of foreign courts does not change after the option has been exercised by commencing proceedings in a nominated foreign court, but the foreign proceedings may produce *lis pendens* effects in Germany.

3.6 Consistency in the Treatment of Optional Choice of Court Agreements

In Germany, optional choice of court agreements in favor of forum courts on the one hand, and in favor of foreign courts on the other, are not treated consistently because the latter fall partly under international regimes,[145] partly not,[146] whereas the former are always covered by Article 25 Brussels Ibis Regulation.

3.7 Presumptively Weaker Parties

Optional choice of court agreements involving presumptively weaker parties (such as employees, consumers, and insured parties) are not principally treated differently compared to optional choice of court agreements in commercial contracts. Rather, protective prohibitions of agreements in favor of weaker parties usually invalidate the entire agreement irrespective of whether it is exclusively or optionally extending the other party's position. However, in some cases of protective legislation, the weaker party is allowed to agree upon optional choice of court agreements in his own favor.[147] If it comes to the question whether the agreement is to be interpreted as

[144] See Section 261 (3) no 1 ZPO (by way of analogous application, see Federal Court of Justice (Bundesgerichtshof) Neue Juristische Wochenschrift 2001, 524, 525; Federal Court of Justice (Bundesgerichtshof) Neue Juristische Wochenschrift 1986, 2195) and Article 29 (1) Brussels Ibis Regulation.

[145] The Brussels Ibis Regulation, the Lugano Convention and the Hague Choice of Court Convention, see Sect. 1.

[146] In case of third states not participating in any of the aforementioned international instruments.

[147] See e.g. section 29 lit. c (1) sentence 1 ZPO (optional jurisdiction in favor the consumer at the consumer's domicile in doorstep selling cases) as opposed to sentence 2 (exclusive jurisdiction for claims against the consumer).

optional or exclusive, the status of one of the parties as a weaker one may be of influence.[148]

3.8 *Proceedings Brought in a Court Other Than That Nominated in an Optional Choice of Court Agreement*

If a party brings proceedings in a court other than that nominated in an optional choice of court agreement, there will be no stay since there is merely an optional choice of court agreement without a derogation, and, as has been mentioned before, there is no doctrine of *forum non conveniens* that would grant the court discretion in light of the optional agreement. Nor will there be damages awarded.[149] As a matter of principle, anti-suit injunctions are not available under the German *lex fori.* Only in the case where proceedings have already been instituted in the *forum prorogatum* and then parallel proceedings are to be instituted in Germany, the general question for coordinating internationally parallel proceedings (outside the international instruments) arises as to whether the foreign *lis alibi pendens* should be taken account of. As has been outlined above,[150] this will be the case if the judgment to be expected from the foreign proceedings will be presumably recognizable in Germany. Then the German court as second seized with the matter will stay the German proceedings.[151]

3.9 *Recognition of Foreign Judgments*

A judgment rendered by a foreign court, other than a court which was nominated in an optional choice of court agreement, would be recognized and enforced by German courts (if there were no other bars to its recognition and enforcement). Under Article 45 (3) Brussels Ibis Regulation, there is anyway no second review of jurisdiction by the court asked to recognize the judgment from the courts of another Member State, subject to very limited exceptions (such as in case of the protection of

[148]See generally Federal Court of Justice (Bundesgerichtshof) Neue Juristische Wochenschrift 2015, 1118, 1119; Hüßtege (2017b), § 38 para 32.

[149]It is even controversial in Germany whether the violation of an exclusive choice of court agreement may bring about damages since procedural law attributing the winning party a claim for the recovery of all costs may well be considered to be sufficient (at least in general), see e.g. Antomo (2017), passim; Schlosser (1979), p. 111; Wagner (1998), p. 556 et seq.; Sandrock (2004), p. 809.

[150]See above Sect. 3.5.

[151]See Section 261 (3) no 1 ZPO (by way of analogous application, see Federal Court of Justice (Bundesgerichtshof) Neue Juristische Wochenschrift 2001, 524, 525; Federal Court of Justice (Bundesgerichtshof) Neue Juristische Wochenschrift 1986, 2195) and Article 29 (1) Brussels Ibis Regulation; see also Schack (2017), p. 310 et seq., paras 830 et seq.

exclusive heads of jurisdiction or weaker parties) which do not apply.[152] The same applies *ceteris paribus* in relation to cases falling within the scope of the Lugano Convention.[153] Under autonomous German recognition law, the aforementioned "mirror principle" applies, section 328 (1) no 1 ZPO, which means that the German jurisdictional law is projected on the foreign court as if it were a German court and as if the German jurisdictional law had to be applied by that court. And since there is no derogation in case of an optional choice of court agreement, there is only the issue whether the foreign court would have had jurisdiction under German jurisdictional law.

3.10 Intra-National Cases

Even though the Federal Republic of Germany is composed of sub-national units, the *Bundesländer*, the entire law of civil procedure is federal law and as such the same for all sub-national units.

Optional choice of court agreements are not treated differently in intranational cases, to their treatment in international cases, as long as the case falls within the autonomous German law. Once the case falls under international instruments, there is a different treatment by virtue of these instruments only covering international cases.

3.11 Exclusive Choice of Court Agreements

As opposed to optional choice of court agreements, the main effect of an exclusive choice of court agreement is of course that it includes a derogation.[154] The derogation excludes all other competent courts, including an annex jurisdiction of the chosen court for counterclaims that would otherwise be available.[155] Further, an exclusive choice of court agreement in favor of a foreign court is usually taken as a prohibition of set-off against claims covered by the agreement with claims for which German courts would be competent.[156]

The derogational effect of an exclusive choice of court agreement raises the issue of a public policy control of the agreement in order to protect fundamental values

---

[152]See Article 45 (1) lit. e Brussels Ibis Regulation.

[153]See Articles 35 (1) and (3) Lugano Convention.

[154]Bork (2014), § 38 ZPO para 70.

[155]Federal Court of Justice (Bundesgerichtshof) Entscheidungen des Bundesgerichtshofes in Zivilsachen 59, 118; Federal Court of Justice (Bundesgerichtshof) Entscheidungen des Bundesgerichtshofes in Zivilsachen 52, 36; Bork (2014), § 38 ZPO para 19.

[156]Bork (2014), § 38 ZPO para 33 with further references.

and policies of the legal order of the derogated forum. Even though such a public policy control is well established both in many states as well as under the Hague Convention,[157] it finds itself again and again under critique in Germany.[158] In addition, it is only indirectly regulated in German law.[159] Of course such a control must be a measure of last resort, but as such it is indispensable.[160]

German law on optional choice of court agreements is not generally underdeveloped compared to the law on exclusive choice of court agreements. Rather, the same principles and rules apply. But since the effects of the exclusive agreement are much more drastic, there are much more judgments and academic comments on these effects and its limits.

4 Asymmetrical Choice of Court Agreements

A choice of court agreement that combines both exclusive and optional aspects (referred to as an asymmetrical choice of court agreement) is admissible in principle.[161] There is no special effect of the optional component within the asymmetrical agreement as such, but the asymmetry raises issues of fairness and abuse.[162] The legal effects do not depend on whether the option has been exercised or not. Whereas asymmetrical agreements are admissible in principle, it would not be possible for the parties to go even further and leave the determination of the court entirely to the respective claimant (which would be a perfectly symmetrical, but otherwise inadmissible agreement, namely for lack of precision of the choice)[163] or to one side. Yet, the parties may agree upon several courts and leave the choice amongst them to one side.[164] In case that the option is granted to the plaintiff, German doctrine speaks of "unilaterally favorable choice of court agreements" (*einseitig begünstigende Gerichtsstandsvereinbarung*).[165] In case of an option for the defendant in the particular case at hand, the plaintiff is required to request the defendant to make

[157] For a comparative account see Weller (2017), p. 91, 102 et seq. See also Basedow (2014), p. 344 et seq.

[158] See e.g. Schack (2017), p. 200, para 515, with further references.

[159] For an in-depth analysis and a justification of the public policy control as a necessary and inevitable element of the law on exclusive choice of court agreements Weller (2005), passim.

[160] Weller (2005), p. 302 et seq. with further references.

[161] Bälz and Stompfe (2017), p. 157; also see Smid and Hartmann (2015), § 38 ZPO para 126.

[162] See in more detail below text to notes 169–175.

[163] Higher Regional Court (Oberlandesgericht) Karlsruhe Entscheidungen der Oberlandesgerichte in Zivilsachen 1973, 479; Bork (2014), § 38 ZPO para 69.

[164] Higher Regional Court (Oberlandesgericht) Karlsruhe Entscheidungen der Oberlandesgerichte in Zivilsachen 1973, 479; Vollkommer (2016), § 38 para 13.

[165] Vollkommer (2016), § 38 para 13.

use of his right to choose prior to instituting proceedings. The defendant must do so within reasonable time.[166]

The main issue in respect to asymmetrical agreements is the court's control of abuse and fairness. There are several levels of this control. Outside standard terms the general control of abuse under contract law according to section 138 German Civil Code applies given that German law applies to the agreement as such. Under a foreign *lex prorogationis* the matter of abuse would reappear as a public policy control of the applicable foreign law (with slightly more generous standards of control due to the internationality of the case). An agreement would be held to be *contra bonos mores* under section 138 German Civil Code and thus null and void if one party has exploited its economic or social power to push the other party into the asymmetrical agreement[167] or if the superior party curtails the other party's access to justice, legally or practically (e.g. in international cases), to an intolerable extent,[168] in particular in comparison to the options for access to justice for the superior party.[169] "Compensatory" clauses, i.e. advantages for the inferior party on another level of the contract, may make up for the disadvantages on the level of jurisdiction.[170] If the asymmetrical choice of court agreement is included in standard terms, the standards of control are much stricter.[171] In that case, the agreement will be held null and void if it appears to be unfair to the disadvantaged party, for example if the user of standard terms inserts an option for himself to sue at home but keeps the option to sue elsewhere whereas the other party is to be restricted to the forum at the domicile of the first party[172] or if the clause aims at making it deliberately difficult for the other party to have access to justice.[173] Finally, under the law on the control of standard terms, the terms must generally be transparent,[174] and this has been an issue in the past when it came to complex options and asymmetrical advantages within choice of court clauses.[175]

[166]Federal Court of Justice (Bundesgerichtshof) Neue Juristische Wochenschrift 1983, 996; Vollkommer (2016), § 38 para 13.

[167]See Federal Court of Justice (Bundesgerichtshof) Zeitschrift für Zivilprozess 88 (1975), 318; Nagel and Gottwald (2013), § 3 para 474; also see Bälz and Stompfe (2017), pp. 157, 159 and 160.

[168]Federal Court of Justice (Bundesgerichtshof) Neue Juristische Wochenschrift 1989, 1477.

[169]Bälz and Stompfe (2017), p. 160 et seq.

[170]Bälz and Stompfe (2017), p. 161.

[171]Nagel and Gottwald (2013), § 3 para 475; Bälz and Stompfe (2017), p. 160; also see Wais (2017), p. 848 et seq.

[172]Pfeiffer (1998), pp. 17, 25; also see Smid and Hartmann (2015), § 38 ZPO para 95.

[173]Bälz and Stompfe (2017), p. 163.

[174]Section 307 (1) s. 2 German Civil Code.

[175]See Federal Court of Justice (Bundesgerichtshof) Neue Juristische Wochenschrift 1999, 282; Bälz and Stompfe (2017), p. 163.

5 Evaluation and Reform

In sum, the legal treatment of optional choice of court agreements in Germany is effective and justified. However, some points of the 1974 reform may be seen today as an overreaction to previous tendencies towards abuse, for example the extremely restrictive approach to agreements on venue by non-merchant parties, other points may be seen as no longer in line with today's policies such as the rather liberal approach for non-merchant parties in respect to international choice of court agreements, but this liberty has been curtailed to a large extent in the meantime by the law on the control of standard terms and by enactment of the Brussels Ibis Regulation/ Brussels I Regulation that protects consumers effectively. One remaining issue in practice is the interpretation of an agreement as optional or exclusive, since there is no presumption on this point in German autonomous law. But this is a minor problem because it is easy for the parties to express themselves clearly in this respect. On the other hand, the dominance of the international instruments, in particular of the Brussels Ibis Regulation, but increasingly also of the Hague Convention, and their respective rules of presumption might lead to the impression that a rule of presumption is standard. Thus, one might consider adjusting the autonomous law for the sake of clarity and party expectation. Yet, no proposals for a reform of the autonomous German law are on the table, nor are there any discussed in the academic community. The most important issue in the context of choice of court agreements certainly is the public policy control of international choice of court agreements, as this control, albeit standard in many states as well as under the Hague Convention,[176] finds itself again and again under critique and is only indirectly regulated in German law,[177] but of course this issue only relates to the derogation of German courts, the central point to which autonomous German law on choice of court agreements is still applicable, hence only to exclusive choice of court agreements, and these are not at issue here.

References

Antomo J (2012) Das auf internationale Gerichtsstandsvereinbarungen nach § 38 ZPO anwendbare Recht. Zeitschrift für Zivilprozess International 17:183–205

Antomo J (2017) Schadensersatz wegen der Verletzung einer internationalen Gerichtsstandsvereinbarung? Mohr Siebeck, Tübingen

Bälz K, Stompfe P (2017) Asymmetrische Streitbeilegungsklauseln in internationalen Wirtschaftsverträgen: Zulässigkeit, Grenzen, Gestaltungsmöglichkeiten. Zeitschrift für Schiedsverfahren 4:157–164

[176] For a comparative account see Weller (2017), p. 102 et seq.

[177] For an in-depth analysis and a justification of the public policy control as a necessary and inevitable element of the law on exclusive choice of court agreements Weller (2005), passim.

Basedow J (2014) Zuständigkeitsderogation, Eingriffsnormen und ordre public. In: Mankowski P, Wurmnest W (eds) Festschrift für Ulrich Magnus zum 70. Geburtstag. Sellier, Munich, pp 255–272
Bendtsen R (2017) 38 ZPO. In: Saenger I (ed) Zivilprozessordnung, 7th edn. Nomos, Baden-Baden
Bey R (2017a) § 38 ZPO. In: Prütting H, Gehrlein M (eds) Zivilprozessordnung, 9th edn. Luchterhand, Munich
Bey R (2017b) § 40 ZPO. In: Prütting H, Gehrlein M (eds) Zivilprozessordnung, 9th edn. Luchterhand, Munich
Bork R (2014) § 38 ZPO. In: Stein F, Jonas M (founders) Zivilprozessordnung, vol 1, 23rd edn. Mohr Siebeck, Tübingen
Geimer G (2016) Internationales Zivilprozessrecht. In: Zöller R (founder) Zöller Zivilprozessordnung, 31st edn. Otto Schmidt, Cologne, pp 40–60
Geimer R (2014) Forum actoris für Kapitalanlegerklagen. In: Witzleb N et al (eds) Festschrift für Dieter Martiny zum 70. Geburtstag. Mohr Siebeck, Tübingen, pp 711–734
Gottwald P (1985) Grenzen internationaler Gerichtsstandsvereinbarungen. In: Henrich D (ed) Festschrift für Karl Firsching zum 70. Geburtstag. CH Beck, Munich, pp 89–110
Gottwald P (2017) Art. 28 VO (EU) 1215/2012. In: Krüger W, Rauscher T (eds) Münchener Kommentar zur Zivilprozessordnung, vol 3, 5th edn. CH Beck, Munich
Hahn C (1881) Die gesamten Materialien zu den Reichs-Justizgesetzen: Materialien zur Zivilprozeßordnung, vol 2, part 1. R.v. decker, Berlin
Hartmann P (2017) § 38 ZPO. In: Baumbach A et al (eds) Zivilprozessordnung, 75th edn. C.H. Beck, Munich
Häsemeyer L (2005) Beteiligtenverhalten im Zivilprozess. Zeitschrift für Zivilprozess 118(3):265–312
Heinrich C (2017) § 38 ZPO. In: Musielak H-J, Voit W (eds) Zivilprozessordnung, 14th edn. Franz Vahlen, Munich
Hüßtege R (2017a) Art. 25 EuGVVO. In: Thomas H, Putzo H (founders) Zivilprozessordnung, 38th edn. CH Beck, Munich
Hüßtege R (2017b) § 38 ZPO. In: Thomas H, Putzo H (founders) Zivilprozessordnung, 38th edn. CH Beck, Munich
Jauernig O (2002) Zivilprozessrecht, 27th edn. CH Beck, Munich
Jayme E, Haack H (1985) Reziproke Gerichtsstandsklauseln – EuGVÜ und Drittstaaten. Praxis des Internationalen Privat- und Verfahrensrechts, p 323
Kohler J (1886) Prorogation, Kombinationsgerichtsstand, Prinzipalintervention. Beiträge zur Erläuterung des deutschen Rechts 30:481–499
Krüger W (2016) § 545 ZPO. In: Krüger W, Rauscher T (eds) Münchener Kommentar zur Zivilprozessordnung, vol 2, 5th edn. CH Beck, Munich, pp 620–626
Mankowski P (2015) Art. 25 Brüssel-Ia-VO. In: Rauscher T (ed) Europäisches Zivilprozess- und Kollisionsrecht, vol 1, 4th edn. Otto Schmidt, Cologne
Martiny D (2015) Art. 1 Rom I-VO. In: von Hein J (ed) Münchener Kommentar zum Bürgerlichen Gesetzbuch: Internationales Privatrecht I, Europäisches Kollisionsrecht, Einführungsgesetz zum Bürgerlichen Gesetzbuche (Art. 1-24), vol 10, 6th edn. CH Beck, Munich
Nagel H, Gottwald P (2013) Internationales Zivilprozessrecht, 7th edn. Otto Schmidt, Cologne
Patzina R (2016) § 38 ZPO. In: Krüger W, Rauscher T (eds) Münchener Kommentar zur Zivilprozessordnung, vol 1, 5th edn. CH Beck, Munich
Pfeiffer T (1998) Halbseitig fakultative Gerichtsstandsvereinbarungen in stillschweigend vereinbarten AGB?. Praxis des Internationalen Privat- und Verfahrensrechts, pp 17–25
Pfeiffer T (2012) German jurisdiction clauses in anti-cartel cases before English Courts. In: Hestermeyer HP et al (eds) Coexistence, cooperation and solidarity. Liber Amicorum Rüdiger Wolfrum, vol 2. Martinus Nijhoff, Leiden, pp 2057–2069
Rosenberg L et al (2010) Zivilprozessrecht, 17th edn. CH Beck, Munich
Sandrock O (2004) Prorogierter Gerichtsstand in Deutschland, Kosten in den USA: Erstattungsfähigkeit in Deutschland? Recht der internationalen Wirtschaft 10:809–815

Schack H (2017) Internationales Zivilverfahrensrecht mit internationalem Insolvenz- und Schiedsverfahrensrecht: ein Studienbuch, 7th edn. CH Beck, Munich

Schilken E (2004) Zur Zulässigkeit von Zuständigkeitsvereinbarungen bei Beteiligung von Nichtkaufleuten (§§ 38 Abs. 3, 40 ZPO). In: Heinrich C (ed) Festschrift für Hans-Joachim Musielak zum 70. Geburtstag. CH Beck, Munich, pp 435–455

Schlosser P (1979) Report on the Convention of 9 October 1978 on the Association of the Kingdom of Denmark, Ireland and the United Kingdom of Great Britain and Northern Ireland to the Convention on jurisdiction and the enforcement of judgments in civil and commercial matters and to the Protocol on its interpretation by the Court of Justice, OJ C 59 of 5 March 1979

Schulz A (2006) The Hague Convention of 30 June 2005 on choice of court agreements. J Priv Int Law 2:243–286

Schütze R (1984) Bedeutung der im Forum Prorogatum ergehenden Entscheidung für die Wirksamkeit einer ausschließlichen internationalen Gerichtsstandsvereinbarung. Praxis des Internationalen Privat- und Verfahrensrechts, pp 246–249

Smid S, Hartmann P (2015) § 38 ZPO. In: Wieczorek B, Schütze RA (eds) Zivilprozessordnung, vol 1/2, 4th edn. de Gruyter, Berlin

Stadler A (2017) Art. 25 EuGVVO. In: Musielak H-J, Voit W (eds) Zivilprozessordnung, 14th edn. Franz Vahlen, Munich

Thorn K (2017) Art. 1 Rom I-VO. In: Palandt O (founder) Bürgerliches Gesetzbuch, 76th edn. CH Beck, Munich

Toussaint G (2017) § 38 ZPO. In: Vorwerk V, Wolf C (eds) BeckOK ZPO, 25th edn. CH Beck, Munich

Vollkommer M (2016) § 38 ZPO. In: Zöller R (founder) Zöller Zivilprozessordnung, 31st edn. Otto Schmidt, Cologne

von Hoffmann B, Thorn K (2007) Internationales Privatrecht, 9th edn. CH Beck, Munich

Wagner G (1998) Prozeßverträge: Privatautonomie im Verfahrensrecht. Mohr Siebeck, Tübingen

Wais H (2017) Einseitige Gerichtsstandsvereinbarungen und die Schranken der Parteiautonomie. Rabels Zeitschrift für ausländisches und internationales Privatrecht 81(4):815–857

Weller M (2005) Ordre-public-Kontrolle internationaler Gerichtsstandsvereinbarugen im autonomen Zusständigkeitsrecht. Mohr Siebeck, Tübingen

Weller M (2014) Die "verbesserte Wirksamkeit" der europäischen Gerichtsstandsvereinbarung nach der Reform der Brüssel I-VO. Zeitschrift für Zivilprozess International 19:251–279

Weller M (2015) Haager Prorogationsübereinkommen. In: Rauscher T (ed) Europäisches Zivilprozess- und Kollisionsrecht, vol 2, 4th edn. Otto Schmidt, Cologne, pp 705–751

Weller M (2016a) Allgemeine Lehren. In: Weller M (ed) Europäisches Kollisionsrecht. Nomos, Baden-Baden, pp 19–125

Weller M (2016b) Validity and interpretation of international choice of court agreements: validity and interpretation of international choice of court agreements: the case for an extended use of transnational non- state contract law. In: UNIDROIT (ed) Eppur si muove: The Age of Uniform Law, Essays in Honour of Michael Joachim Bonell to celebrate his 70th birthday, vol 1. UNIDROIT, Rome, pp 393–406

Weller M (2017) Choice of court agreements under Brussels Ia and under the Hague convention: coherences and clashes. J Priv Int Law 13:91–129

Westerburg A (1877) Glossen zur Civilprozeßordnung für das Deutsche Reich. Beiträge zur Erläuterung des deutschen Rechts (Gruchot) 21:551–601

Wurmnest W (2013) Gerichtsstandsvereinbarungen im grenzüberschreitenden Kartellprozesss. In: Nietsch M, Weller M (eds) Private Enforcement: Brennpunkte kartellprivatrechtlicher Schadensersatzklagen, Workshop des EBS Law School Research Center for Transnational Commercial Dispute Resolution. Nomos, Baden-Baden, pp 75–102

Matthias Weller Mag.rer.publ., studied law in Heidelberg and Cambridge. In 1998/99 he was a Joseph Story Research Fellow in Private International Law at Harvard Law School. He received his PhD from the University of Heidelberg in 2004. Afterwards, he was a research assistant at the Institute for Foreign and International Private and Business Law at the University of Heidelberg and worked as a research assistant with Prof. Dr. Achim Krämer, one of the few attorneys admitted at the Federal Court of Justice (BGH). He habilitated in 2011 and was the Vice Dean of the EBS Law School (Wiesbaden) where he held the Chair for Civil Law, Civil Procedure Law and Private International Law. Since 2018, he has been Director of the Institute for German and International Civil Procedure Law at the University of Bonn, Germany, and the holder of an Alfried Krupp von Bohlen und Halbach Professorship for Provenance Research, Art and Cultural Property Law. Prof. Matthias Weller regularly speaks in international conferences and is the author of many publications in international and European civil procedure, as well as cultural property and private international law.

Greece: A Forum Favorable to Optional Choice of Court Agreements

Georgios Panopoulos

1 Choice of Court Agreements in General

1.1 Law of National Origin

1.1.1 Principle and Procedural Limitations

Greece is a Member State of the European Union, and, in consequence, European Regulations on jurisdiction apply directly in the Greek legal order within their scope of application. Nevertheless, it is not useless for a presentation of the treatment of choice of court agreements in Greece to begin with an examination of the sources of national origin regarding the matter.

The legal sources of national origin are to be found in the jurisdiction rules of the Greek Code of Civil Procedure (GCCP) and provisions and principles of substantive law, mainly in the Greek Civil Code (GCC). By virtue of Art. 3 § 1 GCCP, Greek courts have jurisdiction over any dispute falling under the territorial competence of any Greek court in accordance with the relevant rules of Art. 22 et seq., notwithstanding nationality of the parties. Among these rules, Art. 42–44 provide that territorial competence of a Greek court may be instituted by virtue of an agreement of the parties. In principle thus, jurisdiction of Greek courts may be established, pursuant to Art. 42–44 and 3 § 1, on an agreement of the parties.[1]

This principle enshrines a clear policy in favor of parties' agreements on jurisdiction, which is nevertheless confined by certain limitations, deriving both from

[1]See e.g. Athens Court of Appeal (CA) 6177/1975, *Armenopoulos* [Thessaloniki Bar Law Review] (*Arm.*) 1976, 406.

G. Panopoulos (✉)
Lambadarios Law Firm, Athens, Greece
e-mail: g.panopoulos@lambalaw.gr

M. Keyes (ed.), *Optional Choice of Court Agreements in Private International Law*, Ius Comparatum – Global Studies in Comparative Law 37,
https://doi.org/10.1007/978-3-030-23914-5_10

Art. 42–44 GCCP themselves and from other provisions and general principles of law. In particular, first, the principle does not apply to disputes with non-economic objects (Art. 42 § 1 (1), e.g. marital and family disputes of Art. 592 et seq.[2]) and to non-contentious proceedings (*juridiction gracieuse, freiwillige Gerichtsbarkeit*) (Art. 740 § 2). Second, there is no requirement with regard to formal validity of the choice of court agreement, which can even be tacit (Art. 42 § 1 (1)), and there is a tacit agreement when the defendant enters an appearance without (timely) contesting jurisdiction (Art. 42 § 2); provided however that the agreement concerns existing disputes for which no other court has exclusive territorial competence (e.g. disputes regarding rights *in rem* on immovable property, Art. 29; succession disputes, Art. 30) (Art. 42 § 1 (2)). In the latter case, the choice of court agreement must be express (Art. 42 § 1 (2)); with regard to future disputes, the agreement must be in writing and cover disputes which may arise in connection with a particular legal relationship (Art. 43),[3] including, when with regard to a contract, claims in tort related to the contractual nexus.[4] Finally, the agreement establishes exclusive jurisdiction of the prorogated court, unless otherwise agreed by the parties (Art. 44); however, such exclusivity does not lead to derogation from the jurisdiction of a court to order any kind of injunctive relief if competent pursuant to Art. 638 § 3. In addition to the limitations deriving from the territorial rules of Art. 42–44, jurisdiction of Greek courts may not be based on prorogation regarding disputes over rights *in rem* on immovable property abroad (Art. 4 (1)).

The choice of court agreement of Art. 42–44 GCCP not only establishes territorial competence of the chosen Greek court but also (in principle, Art. 44) excludes territorial competence of all other Greek courts. Coupled with Art. 3 § 1, application of Art. 42–44 excludes the jurisdiction of all foreign courts. However, since a choice of court agreement has a function of exclusion of the territorial competence of all Greek courts if in favor of a Greek court, it also excludes jurisdiction of the Greek courts when in favor of a foreign court; it must be noted that derogation from the jurisdiction of Greek courts is not valid if it can lead to denial of justice, i.e. when it is not fairly predictable that a foreign court has jurisdiction to hear the dispute at hand, either on the basis of prorogation of its jurisdiction or by virtue of jurisdiction rules, and can exercise such jurisdiction. A Greek court may thus not hear a dispute in the face of an agreement instituting the jurisdiction of a foreign court, provided that such agreement validly excludes jurisdiction of Greek courts, i.e. provided that it be valid in accordance with Greek law.

Mirroring the exclusion, in Art. 4 (1) GCCP, of the jurisdiction of Greek courts over disputes regarding rights *in rem* on immovable property abroad, disputes regarding such rights on immovable property in Greek territory may not, pursuant

---

[2]See Athens CA 5744/1976, *Nomiko Vima* [Athens Bar Law Review] (*NoV*) 1977, 397.

[3]Areopage [the Greek Supreme Court for civil and criminal matters] 196/1974, *NoV* 1974, 1063.

[4]Areopage 755/1993, *Ephimeris Ellinon Nomikon* [Journal of Greek Lawyers] (*EEN*) 1994, 529; also e.g. Athens CA 4609/2012 & 5973/2013, *NoV* 2014, 581, note P Giannopoulos.

to Art. 3 § 2, be removed from the jurisdiction of Greek courts.[5] The reasons that underpin this solution, i.e. the exclusivity of the sovereign power over the state territory, also justify the exclusive jurisdiction of Greek courts with regard to measures for the enforcement of judgments and disputes relating thereto[6]; but agreements on territorial competence of one or the other Greek court, in case of enforcement in Greece, are permitted.[7]

These rules regulate jurisdiction of Greek courts (directly for prorogation, by extension with regard to derogation); they also serve, applied indirectly to jurisdiction of foreign courts, in order to verify one of the conditions for recognition of foreign judgments. In particular, by virtue of Art. 323 (2) GCCP, a foreign judgment is recognised in Greece provided that, *inter alia*, the foreign court of origin had jurisdiction over the relevant dispute in accordance with the provisions of Greek law, i.e., Art. 3 § 1 and 22 et seq., including Art. 42–44.

In all cases, the validity of the choice of court agreement is governed by Greek law *qua lex fori* on the basis that the agreement has jurisdictional effects and that such effects are *ipso facto* governed by the *lex fori*.[8]

1.1.2 Substantive Limitations

A choice of court agreement is autonomous vis-à-vis the main contract, to which the former refers or of which it forms part as a clause.[9] Parties' agreements on jurisdiction must nevertheless also respect substantive limitations, deriving from provisions other than those of the Greek Code of Civil Procedure and from rules and principles of substantive law.[10] It is clear that, for instance, the formality requirement of Art. 43 GCCP caters for the protection of the weaker party's right to access to justice, in particular in cross-border pre-formulated standard contracts: pursuant to Art. 160 GCC, in order that an agreement, required by law (here Art. 43 GCCP) to be in writing, is validly concluded, the signatures of both parties must be set on the same document or, in case of more than one original, each party's signature must be set on the original held by the other party; thus, in order, for instance, for a foreign provider to contest jurisdiction of Greek courts, she must hold an original document bearing the signature of the Greek consumer and covering the jurisdiction clause

[5]Areopage 12/1986, *NoV* 1986, 1239.

[6]Brinias (1983), p. 22.

[7]Athens CA 2556/1980, *NoV* 1980, 1547; 10683/1986, *Elliniki Dikaiossini* [Law Review of the Association of Judges] (*EllDni*) 1987, 890.

[8]See all judgments referred to herein with regard to Greek law of national origin and more generally (and with critique) Chr. Tsouka (1990), pp. 13–35.

[9]See also Sect. 1.3.3.2 below.

[10]See in general Doris (1988).

contained in the agreement.[11] In addition, a choice of court agreement is not valid if written in a language unknown to one of the parties.[12] The concern for the protection of the weaker party also forms the basis for the refusal by Greek courts, until recently, to uphold the substantial validity of agreements in favor not of one (or more) specifically determined foreign court, but of the courts of a country as a whole, leaving the determination of the territorial competence to the foreign country's procedural rules.[13]

In any case, a choice of court agreement is, like any other agreement, always subject, as to its *per se* validity and to the validity of the exercise of the rights deriving therefrom, to the benchmarks set by the principle of good faith, expressly enshrined in Art. 116 GCCP, a provision whose content is informed by the rich case-law on Art. 281 GCC (prohibition of abuse of right). Good faith has served Greek courts to treat, on a strictly case-by-case basis, as invalid an agreement in favor of foreign courts.[14] In addition, general provisions on fraud, error, as well as on formation of contracts apply also to choice of court agreements.[15] Finally, it is considered that it is invalid (also on the basis of the theory of *fraude à la loi*) to exclude jurisdiction of Greek courts in the framework of a contract that is otherwise purely internal vis-à-vis the Greek legal order. On the other hand, it has been submitted as early as in 1990[16] and recently confirmed,[17] that the fact that a dispute falls under the scope of a Greek *loi de police* or *d'application immédiate*, does not affect the substantive validity of an agreement in favor of a foreign court.[18]

The protection afforded to the weaker party through case law on the relevant provisions of the Greek Code of Civil Procedure and of the Greek Civil Code has been considered to be inadequate. In view of the then imminent entry into force of the Brussels Convention (1968), to which Greece had acceded in 1982, the Greek Parliament enacted Law 1429/1984 on the protection of Greek citizens working in countries of Asia or Africa, stipulating, *inter alia*, that jurisdiction of Greek courts may not be excluded by any clause contained in an employment contract between a

[11]See Athens multimember Court of First Instance (CFI(m)) 2919/1982, *EllDni* 1983, 122; also Thessaloniki CA 9/1998, *Episkopissi Emporikou Dikaiou* [Commercial Law Review] (*EpiskED*) 1999, 130: insurance policy.

[12]*In casu* the employee, Piraeus single-member Court of First Instance (CFI(s)) 1079/1979, *Epitheorissi Naftiliakou Dikaiou* [Maritime Law Review] (*END*) 1979, 562.

[13]Areopage 339/1986, *NoV* 1987, 33, where the choice of court clause was contained in an individual contract of employment of a Greek worker in Saudi Arabia; and the *revirement jurisprudentiel* by the Full Court of Areopage 4/1992, *NoV* 1992, 707.

[14]See e.g. Athens CA 2466/1985, *EllDni* 1985, 725.

[15]See e.g. Athens CA 4262/1990, *EllDni* 1991, 576.

[16]Chr. Tsouka (1990), p. 50.

[17]*Cf.* Areopage 1542/2014, *NoV* 2015, 276; also 313/2009, *Dikaio Epikhirisseon & Etairion* [Business and Company Law Review] (*DEE*) 2009, 828; 1697/2013, *Chronika Idiotikou Dikaiou* [Private Law Review] (*ChrID*) 2014, 371.

[18]*Cf.* also ECJ 16.3.1999, *Castelletti*, C-159/97, *ECR* I 1597.

Greek citizen and a company having its seat or "center of interests" in Greece.[19] In consequence, a choice of court agreement under these circumstances in favor of a foreign court is always considered *de iure* as optional.

The protection was going to be widened in the framework of the Brussels Convention, eventually ratified by Law 1814/1988 and having entered into force on 1 April 1989, and of the subsequent Brussels I Regulations.

1.2 Foreign Influences

Treatment of choice of court agreements under Greek law of national origin does not seem to have been influenced by treatment of arbitration agreements, either under the UN New York Convention (1958), ratified by legislative decree 4220/1961 and in force since 1.10.1962, or in the framework of the UNCITRAL Model Law on International Commercial Arbitration, incorporated in the Greek legal order through International Commercial Arbitration Law 2735/1999, or otherwise, notably in the relevant Art. 867 et seq. GCCP. For instance, the fact that, pursuant to Art. 34 § 2 (a) (aa) of the International Commercial Arbitration Law and Art. V § 1 (a) of the New York Convention, the arbitration agreement is governed by the law "to which the parties have subjected it", has never affected the constant case law according to which choice of court agreements are governed by Greek law *qua lex fori* irrespective of the chosen court. In addition, while disputes arising out of individual contracts of employment have always been held as not arbitrable under Art. 867 in conjunction with Art. 614 (3) GCCP (see also Art. 1 § 4 (1) of the International Commercial Arbitration Law), choice of court agreements for disputes arising from the same kind of contracts have always been held valid in principle; and much of the case law on the limitations on the freedom to choose a court has been produced in disputes from such contracts.[20] In sum, while there are notable similarities between the two regimes (e.g. the requirement for an agreement in writing applies also for arbitration agreements regarding future disputes, Art. 868 GCCP, Art. 7 International Commercial Arbitration Law), it is difficult to discern any force of attraction between them with regard to their differences.

1.3 Recent Changes

The influence exercised on Greek law relating to choice of court agreements by the membership of Greece in the European Union has been twofold: on the one hand, there is the obvious influence of European Regulations on jurisdiction that, within

[19] See Papassiopi-Passia (1990), pp. 641 et seq.

[20] See Sect. 1.1.2 above.

their respective scope of application, have replaced the provisions of national origin; on the other, and sometimes less discernibly, the law relating to choice of court agreements has suffered significant changes through substantive provisions of acts passed in transposition of European Directives. Greece is also bound by the Hague Choice of Court Agreements Convention (2005) as a result of its approval by the European Union, with effect from 1.10.2015, however, due to the Union having taken into consideration the Convention upon drafting of the Brussels I Recast Regulation, the Convention is not expected to exercise by itself any considerable influence over the overall treatment of choice of court agreements in the Greek legal order.

The scope of application of the Brussels Convention and its successor Regulations with regard to choice of court agreements has been gradually extended, eventually covering all and any international choice of court agreement. It is thus useful to look to the changes that the European instruments have brought to the Greek legal order on a step-by-step basis, taking also into account provisions passed in transposition of European Directives. Reference is not made to Regulations relating to jurisdiction over disputes regarding to matrimonial (or equivalent) property relations, maintenance obligations, wills and succession, that have provided for a limited freedom of the parties to choose the court bound to hear their disputes.

The state of Greek law prior to the entry into force of the Brussels Convention has been already presented.[21] The focus shall be directed to the European instruments.

1.3.1 The Brussels Convention

By virtue of Law 1814/1988, the Brussels Convention entered into force in Greece on 1 April 1989.

Tacit Prorogation

Through Art. 18, the Convention immediately regulated tacit prorogation through appearance without (timely) contest of jurisdiction[22]; application of Art. 42 § 2 GCCP has since been limited to purely internal disputes, as, according to legal literature (there is no decisive case law on the matter), application of Art. 18 is not conditional upon the defendant being domiciled in a Contracting State (as per Art. 2 Conv.).[23]

---

[21] See Sect. 1.1 above.

[22] See e.g. Piraeus CA 854/2006, *END* 2007, 107; Piraeus CFI(m) 4635/2008, *Efarmoges Astikou Dikaiou* [Civil Law Review] (*EfAD*) 2009, 446, comm. A. Gova.

[23] See Kerameus et al. (1989) art. 18 n° 11; *arg.* ECJ 13.7.2000, *Josi*, C-412/98, *ECR* I 5925.

Scope

Art. 17 Conv. applies where (1) the agreement is in favor of the courts of a Contracting State and (2) at least one of the parties is domiciled in a Contracting State. In consequence

(a) if the agreement is in favor of the courts of a non-contracting State, as well as if it is in favor of the Greek courts and none of the parties is domiciled in a Contracting State, then Art. 42–44 GCCP shall apply[24];
(b) if the agreement is in favor of the courts of a Contracting State and none of the parties is domiciled in a Contracting State, Art. 17 § 2 Conv. applies, and Greek courts, if seised, shall stay proceedings until the court chosen decides on its jurisdiction and, if the agreement is deemed to be invalid by the court chosen, only then may the Greek courts examine their jurisdiction on other bases.

Differences

Art. 17 Conv. differs from the provisions of Art. 42–44 GCCP in some respects, and certain observations are in order:

(a) Whereas, pursuant to Art. 42 § 1 (1) GCCP, derogation from the exclusive territorial competence of a court is possible, provided that the choice of court agreement be express, under Art. 17 Conv. derogation (both express and tacit) from the exclusive jurisdiction of the courts of a member State as per Art. 16 Conv. is forbidden, marking the close connection of the exclusive jurisdictional bases with sovereignty of the member States.
(b) Whereas Art. 17 Conv. requires that the choice of court agreement be in writing or evidenced in writing not only for future (as Art. 43 GCCP) but also for existent disputes (where Greek law of national origin has no such requirement), it must be noted that there is no recorded case where a Greek court has based its jurisdiction on an oral agreement. In addition, Art. 17 allows for a form "which accords with practices" established by the parties themselves[25] or, in international trade or commerce, with a widely known "usage of which the parties are or ought to have been aware".
(c) The strictness of Greek law of national origin (Art. 160 CC)[26] has been loosened, since under the Convention it has been admitted that it is not obligatory that the document containing the choice of court agreement be signed by both parties or that both parties have signed the same original.
(d) Choice of court agreements for the benefit of one of the parties, as envisaged in Art. 17 § 5 Conv., are steadily accepted as valid in the Greek legal order under

[24]See Areopage 1542/2014, *ChrID* 2015, 25.
[25]See Areopage 8/2015, *EfAD* 2015, 914.
[26]See Sect. 1.1.2 above.

provisions of national origin, through Art. 44 GCCP; whereas there is no such express provision in favor of optional agreements in Art. 17, it is accepted (*arg.* also from § 5), that such agreements are allowed also under this provision.

Applicable Law

In the absence of any indication, in Art. 17 Conv., as to the law applicable to the choice of court agreement, Greek courts continued to apply Greek law *qua lex fori.*[27,28]

1.3.2 Interim Developments

By virtue of Law 2004/1992, Greece ratified the Donostia—San Sebastian Convention which modified the Brussels Convention, with effect in Greece from 1 July 1992, with respect to the jurisdictional protection of employees.[29]

In the meantime, jurisdictional protection of consumers (including policy holders) vis-à-vis choice of court agreements has been granted in relation to consumer contracts not covered by the Convention, in a manner not fully consistent with the latter.[30]

1.3.3 The Brussels I Regulation and Recast

The entry into force, on 1 March 2002, of the Brussels I Regulation, which replaced the Brussels Convention, did not bring any significant change with respect to choice of court agreements. On the one hand, paragraph 5 of Art. 17 Conv. has not found an explicit counterpart in Art. 23 Reg., however § 1 expressly now allows for optional (non-exclusive) agreements, which, drafted appropriately, can also benefit only one of the parties (in any case, the European instruments themselves allow such agreements in cases of insurance, consumer, and employment contracts). On the other hand, the new provision inserted in Art. 23 § 2 Reg. has merely aligned the text of the instrument to technological advancements that had been already taken into consideration in case law.

---

[27] See e.g. Athens CA 6359/2003, *EllDni* 2004, 1466; 676/2009, *EllDni* 2009, 559; 4467/2010, *DEE* 2011, 218.

[28] On the jurisdictional protection of weaker parties see Sect. 2.5 below; on recognition and enforcement of foreign judgments rendered in violation of a choice-of-court agreement see Sect. 2.6 below.

[29] See Sect. 2.5.2 below.

[30] See Sect. 2.5.3 below.

The Brussels I Recast Regulation, that entered into force on 10 January 2015, has been a breakthrough with regard to prorogation of jurisdiction, in more than one respect:

Scope

Art. 25 Recast applies regardless of the domicile of the parties, provided only that the agreement is in favor of a court of an EU Member State and that the dispute has an international character. It follows that Greek law of national origin only applies with regard to purely internal disputes and where the court chosen belongs to a non-EU Member State.[31]

Principle of Autonomy

Art. 25 § 5 Recast explicitly enshrines the (already established[32]) principle of the autonomy of the choice of court agreement vis-à-vis the main contract, to which the former refers and of which it usually forms part as a clause.

Applicable Law

Whenever the agreement is in favor of an EU Member State court, it is governed, as to its substantive validity, by the law (including the choice of law provisions, recital (20) Recast, same under the Hague Convention) of that Member State. It follows that application of Greek law *qua lex fori* in this case is not possible any more.

.

Lis pendens

In the framework of the Brussels I system, where proceedings involving the same cause of action between the same parties are brought in the courts of different Member States, any court other than the one first seised shall of its own motion stay its proceedings until such time as the jurisdiction of the court first seised is established and, in the affirmative, decline jurisdiction (see e.g. Art. 29 Recast). This rule applied, pursuant to the ECJ ruling in the case *Gasser*,[33] even in the case that the court second seised was the one chosen by the parties by virtue of an exclusive

[31]On the modifications regarding the specific jurisdictional protections for consumers and employees see Sect. 2.5.4 below.

[32]See under the Brussels Convention ECJ 3.7.1997, *Benincasa*, C-269/95, *ECR* I 3767, and under the Greek Code of Civil Procedure Athens CA 4340/1988, *EllDni* 1990, 377.

[33]ECJ 9.12.2003, C-116/02, *ECR* I 14693.

choice of court agreement: in this case, this court should have to stay its proceedings until the court first seised upholds (or not) the validity of the choice of court agreement.

Under Greek law of national origin, the question does not arise in similar terms: if the court second seised is a Greek court having jurisdiction by virtue of an exclusive choice of court agreement, then no foreign court has jurisdiction to hear the case in accordance with Greek procedural law and no foreign judgment would be capable of recognition in accordance with Art. 323 (2) GCCP; this condition not being met, the fact that proceedings are brought before the foreign court does not constitute a *lis pendens* that would otherwise oblige the Greek court to stay its proceedings pursuant to Art. 222 § 1.

The Brussels I Recast Regulation overruled, in Art. 31 §§ 2–4, the *Gasser* ruling and brought a more reasonable solution, similar to that of Greek law of national origin: the EU Member State court seised on the basis of an *exclusive* choice of court agreement shall not stay its proceedings, even if a court of another Member State is seised first; it is the latter court that must stay its proceedings (until the chosen court declares that it has no jurisdiction under the agreement) or decline jurisdiction if the chosen court establishes its own in accordance with the agreement.

2 Optional Choice of Court Agreements

2.1 Legal Sources

The duality of the legal regime applicable to exclusive choice of court agreements also holds in relation to optional ones. In particular, where the agreement is in favor of an EU Member State court, the Brussels I Recast Regulation applies; where the agreement is in favor of a non-EU Member State court or in favor of a Greek court in a purely internal case, Greek provisions of national origin apply. It should be noted that the Hague Convention on choice of court agreement applies solely to exclusive agreements. Said duality influences practically all the following developments.

2.2 Applicable Law

Under the Brussels I system as it stood before the Recast Regulation and under Greek law of national origin (still applicable when the agreement is in favor of the courts of a non-EU Member State), a choice of court agreement is governed, including as to its interpretation and, in consequence, as to whether it is optional or exclusive, by Greek law *qua lex fori*.

Pursuant to Art. 25 and recital (20) of the Brussels I Recast Regulation, the choice of court agreement is governed by the law designated by the choice of law rules of the EU Member State of the court chosen; this law is also applicable to the determination of the character of the agreement as exclusive or optional.

2.3 Greek Law

Both under Art. 25 Brussels Recast and under 44 GCCP, a choice of court agreement is in principle exclusive, unless the parties have agreed otherwise. In case the parties' intention is not clear, Art. 200 GCC on interpretation of contracts applies, in accordance to which agreements are interpreted as required by good faith and taking into account the relevant business usages. It must be noted that good faith may only serve the interpretation of an unclear agreement and not invalidate a clear agreement granting a jurisdictional option to one of the parties; cases of manifest imbalance between the parties would have already been treated through the special regimes protecting insureds, consumers and employees. If, following the interpretative process, a doubt as to the meaning of the agreement persists, its character shall be deemed to be exclusive.

2.4 Effect of Agreement

2.4.1 In Favor of Domestic Courts

The effect of any valid choice of court agreement (both optional and exclusive) in favor of Greek courts is to establish their jurisdiction to hear the case regardless of whether such jurisdiction exists otherwise (i.e. pursuant to other jurisdiction rules). The choice has thus a positive function and not a negative one, in the sense of a waiver of the right to contest jurisdiction, though the result seems to be the same.

The commencement of proceedings before a Greek court by virtue of an optional choice of court agreement does not alter the character and legal effect of the agreement, as it can be shown in the example of multiple proceedings: On the one hand, in the case of an *exclusive* choice, Art. 31 §§ 2–4 of the Recast Regulation empowers the chosen court to disregard any proceedings initiated before the courts of another EU Member State court; and Greek law of national origin has equivalent effect. On the other hand, the new rules of the Recast Regulation on *lis pendens* do not, by their own terms, apply to *optional* choice of court agreements, and multiple proceedings in this case are treated on the basis of the rule of the "court first seised"; the same holds under Greek law of national origin: the Greek court seised by virtue of an optional agreement must stay its proceedings pursuant to Art. 222 § 1 GCCP, if a foreign (non-EU Member State) court has already been seised and is competent in accordance with Greek jurisdiction rules pursuant to Art. 323 (2).

2.4.2 In Favor of Foreign Courts

The commencement of proceedings before a foreign court by virtue of an optional choice of court agreement does not alter the character and legal effect of the agreement, as it can be shown in the example of multiple proceedings: on the one hand, in the case of an *exclusive* choice in favor of a court of an EU Member State other than Greece, Art. 31 §§ 2–4 of the Recast Regulation obliges the Greek court to stay its proceedings, even if it has been first seised; and Greek law of national origin has equivalent effect. On the other hand, the new rules of the Recast Regulation on *lis pendens* do not, by their own terms, apply to *optional* choice of court agreements, and multiple proceedings in this case are treated on the basis of the rule of the "court first seised". The same holds under Greek law of national origin: the Greek court must stay its proceedings pursuant to Art. 222 § 1 GCCP, if a foreign (non-EU Member State) court has already been seised by virtue of an optional choice of court agreement and is thus competent in accordance with Greek jurisdiction rules pursuant to Art. 323 (2); on the contrary, if the Greek court is first seised, it has no obligation to stay proceedings. It must be noted that Greek law of national origin has a limited scope of application since the enactment, in the Recast Regulation, of the provisions of Art. 33 on *international lis pendens*, where proceedings have been initiated by virtue of an optional choice of court agreement before a court of a non-EU Member State. Nevertheless, the two sets of provisions lead to equivalent results.

2.4.3 Consistency

As already shown, treatment of optional choice of court agreements in favor of forum courts and foreign courts is fairly symmetrical and thus consistent.

2.5 *Presumptively Weaker Parties*

2.5.1 Insurance and Consumer Contracts

By virtue of Art. 12 and 15 Conv., there has been granted specific jurisdictional protection with regard to choice of court agreements for policy-holders, insured persons and beneficiaries, on the one hand, and consumers, on the other, where they are, or their counterparty is, domiciled in a Contracting State. In a nutshell, such an agreement is considered to be valid only if entered into after the dispute has arisen or in favor of the weaker party (choice both optional and asymmetrical). In comparison to the state of Greek law prior to the entry into force of the Brussels Convention, this has been a considerable step towards protection of weaker contract parties.

2.5.2 Individual Contracts of Employment

Pursuant to Art. 17 § 6 Conv., as added by the Donostia—Sebastian Convention, choice of court clauses in individual contracts of employment are valid only if entered into after the dispute has arisen or invoked by the employee (choice both optional and asymmetrical).[34] In the Brussels I Regulation, the jurisdictional protection of employees has been removed from the provision on prorogation and inserted in the new section 5 on individual contracts of employment, in Art. 21.

However, the Brussels I system was only applicable if the defendant was domiciled in a Member State (Art. 2 Conv.). In all other cases, Greek law of national origin, including Law 1429/1984 on the protection of Greek citizens working in countries of Asia or Africa, applies.

2.5.3 Consumer Protection Laws

In the meantime, jurisdictional protection of consumers (including policy-holders) vis-à-vis choice of court agreements has been granted in relation to consumer contracts not covered by the Convention, in a manner not fully consistent with the latter. By virtue of Art. 25 § 3 (xxvi) Law 1961/1991 on Consumer Protection, all choice of court agreements either in favor of Greek or foreign courts (as well as arbitration agreements) are held to be invalid as *ipso facto* abusive, if forming part of pre-formulated general terms of a contract concluded or to be executed in Greece (*arg.* Art. 22 § 3), and irrespective of the law normally applicable to the consumer contract. Law 2251/1994, which replaced Law 1961, has not considerably modified the protection granted, as, within the same territorial scope (Art. 2 § 9) it permitted agreements in favor of only Greek courts other than those normally territorially competent (Art. 2 § 7 (xxxi)).[35] The protection thus granted is far-reaching, taking also into consideration that (a) first, under both Laws, not only natural persons but also legal entities qualify as a consumer, and that, (b) contrary to the initial definition of Art. 2 (1) Law 1961, in order for a person to be a consumer, he needs just be the end user of the product or the service bought, irrespective whether the purpose of the contract can be regarded as being outside his trade or profession (Art. 1 § 4 (a) Law 2251). Delicate problems thus arise with regard to the delimitation of the respective scopes of the Brussels Convention and the Consumer Protection Law. These problems should be resolved by virtue of Art. 100 § 5 Law 4512/2018, which has recently replaced Art. 1 § 4 Law 2251 with a new Art. 1a, containing a narrower definition of consumer, limiting this concept only to natural persons acting for purposes outside their trade or profession.

---

[34]Applying this provision see e.g. Piraeus CA 501/2001, *END* 2001, 437.

[35]On the rationale of this change see Areopage 1219/2001, *EllDni* 2001, 1609.

2.5.4 Brussels I Recast

The scope of the above provisions is now considerably limited, since under the Brussels I Recast Regulation the specific jurisdictional protections for consumers and employees apply irrespective of the domicile of the defendant, provided, respectively, that the consumer is domiciled in an EU Member State (Art. 18 § 1 and 19) and that the employee carries out his work in an EU Member State (Art. 21 § 2 and 23).

2.5.5 Tacit Prorogation

It must be borne in mind that in all cases, both under the Brussels texts and Greek law of national origin, the special regimes do not protect the weak party from a tacit prorogation,[36] provided that this party has been given some kind of information by the judge with respect to his non-contest of the jurisdiction of the court seised.

2.6 Violation of Optional Choice of Court Agreement

The new rules of the Recast Regulation on *lis pendens* do not, by their own terms, apply to optional choice of court agreements, and multiple proceedings in this case are treated on the basis of the rule of the "court first seised", both under the rules of European and of Greek origin.[37] Further, Greek law, both of national origin and in the Brussels I system, and both in relation to optional and exclusive choice of court agreements, does not provide for damages or for anti-suit or—enforcement injunctions in case of breach of such an agreement.

In addition to the changes concerning the choice of court agreements themselves, the Brussels regime innovated, in comparison to the past, in one more respect: under Greek law of national origin (Art. 323 (2) GCCP), a foreign judgment issued in violation of an *exclusive* choice of court agreement by a court other than that chosen is not (in the absence of a tacit prorogation of the jurisdiction of the court of origin) capable of recognition in Greece. On the contrary, under Art. 27 Conv., such a violation does not constitute a ground of non-recognition of judgments originating from other EU Member States. With regard to judgments rendered in the face of an *optional* choice of court agreement by a foreign court other than the chosen one, there is no impediment, for that reason, to their recognition and enforcement in Greece under either (European or of national origin) recognition and enforcement regime.

[36] See ECJ, 20.5.2010, *Bilas*, C-111/09, *ECR* I 4545.

[37] See Sect. 1.3.3.3 above.

2.7 *Exclusive and Optional Choice: A Succinct Comparison*

As exclusive choice of court agreements are more common than optional ones, case law is more developed with regard to the treatment of the former than of the latter, and this holds also true in purely internal disputes, i.e. in relation to territorial competence of Greek courts. This is also mirrored in the state of the law, where, first, the *Gasser* jurisprudence, though overruled as to *exclusive* choice of court agreements, still applies with regard to optional ones; and, second, where the new Recast Regulation provisions on international *lis pendens* apply where the court of the non-EU Member State has been seised on the basis of an optional choice but not where an EU Member State court is seised on the same basis, this latter case having been left to EU Member State laws of national origin and to the differentiations in treatment that may derive therefrom.

3 Asymmetrical Choice of Court Agreements

Commonly, optional choice of court agreements are asymmetrical, without this characteristic having any influence on the more general developments already made regarding purely optional agreements.

Under Greek law of national origin, an asymmetrical choice of court agreement in favor of the stronger party would be found to be invalid in view of the substantive limitations on the parties' freedom of contract, which apply also in relation to choice of court agreements[38]; more significantly, under Greek law originating from the consumer protection directives, such an agreement would be *per se* invalid.[39] On the other hand, under the Brussels I system, in order for a choice of court clause inserted in an insurance policy, consumer contract or individual contract of employment to be valid, it must be asymmetrical in favor of the weaker party.[40]

References

Brinias I (1983) Enforcement of judgments I. Ant N Sakkoulas, Athens-Komotini

Doris P (1988) Limitations to freedom of contracts in exclusive jurisdiction clauses. Ant N Sakkoulas, Athens-Komotini

[38]See Sect. 1.1.2 above.

[39]See Sect. 2.5.3 above.

[40]See Sects. 2.5.1, 2.5.2, 2.5.4 above.

Kerameus K, Kremlis G, Tagaras H (1989) The Brussels Convention. Ant N Sakkoulas, Athens-Komotini

Papassiopi-Passia Z (1990) in Mélanges Vavouskos III. Sakkoulas, Thessaloniki

Tsouka C (1990) Choice of court clauses: private international law questions. Ant N Sakkoulas, Athens-Komotini

Dr Georgios Panopoulos was born in 1978 in Tripolis, Arcadia, Greece. He studied law at the University of Athens (LL.B., 2000; LL.M. in Civil Law, 2001) and at the University of Paris I (Panthéon-Sorbonne) (DEA droit international privé et droit du commerce international, 2002), where he obtained a Ph.D. in 2007. Following that he became involved in practice as an attorney-at-law. Since 2014 he has been a partner at "Lambadarios Law Firm". He is a scientific fellow of the Hellenic Institute for International and Foreign Law; he is also a scientific fellow at the University of Piraeus and the Faculty of Law of the University of Athens. His publications focus mainly on private international law and European economic law.

Japan: Quests for Equilibrium and Certainty

Koji Takahashi

1 The Treatment of Choice of Court Agreements in General

1.1 General Attitude to Choice of Court Agreements

Japanese law is generally in favour of enforcing the parties' agreements about jurisdiction. That policy is enshrined in paragraphs 1 through 4 of Article 3-7 of the Code of Civil Procedure (hereinafter, "CCP"). It reads[1]:

(1) The parties may decide by agreement the country in which they may file an action.
(2) The agreement provided in the preceding paragraph shall have no effect unless it is in writing and is concerned with an action arising from specific legal relationships.
(3) For the purpose of the preceding paragraph, an agreement is deemed to be in writing if it is recorded in an electromagnetic record (viz. a record made in an electronic form, a magnetic form, or any other form unrecognizable to human perception, which is used for information processing by computers).
(4) An agreement to file an action exclusively with the courts of a particular foreign country may not be invoked if those courts are legally or factually unable to exercise jurisdiction.

It should be noted that the lack of connection between the facts of the case and the place of the chosen court would not be a valid ground for denying effect to the choice of court agreement. Thus, a choice of court agreement choosing a neutral forum can be enforced.

The heads of jurisdiction set out in the CCP are those for direct jurisdiction. But indirect jurisdiction, which is one of the prerequisites for the recognition and

[1]There is no official English translation of Japanese law. All the translation of Japanese legislation in this article is the work of the present author.

K. Takahashi (✉)
Doshisha University Law School, Kyoto, Japan
e-mail: ktakahas@mail.doshisha.ac.jp

M. Keyes (ed.), *Optional Choice of Court Agreements in Private International Law*, Ius Comparatum – Global Studies in Comparative Law 37,
https://doi.org/10.1007/978-3-030-23914-5_11

enforcement of foreign judgments laid down in Article 118 of the CCP, is interpreted in general as a mirror image of direct jurisdiction. It follows that a foreign judgment rendered on the basis of a choice of court agreement which satisfies the requirements of paragraphs 2 and 3 of Article 3-7 of the CCP is recognised and can be enforced in Japan, provided that the other prerequisites are also satisfied.

Almost all heads of jurisdiction of the CCP are subject to Article 3-9 of the CCP, which provides for dismissal of proceedings when there are special circumstances.[2] It reads:

> Even where the Japanese courts have jurisdiction over an action (except where the action has been brought on the basis of an exclusive choice of court agreement in favour of the Japanese courts), the court may dismiss the whole or part of the proceedings if, taking into account the nature of the case, the burden on the defendant to answer the claim, the location of evidence and any other factors, the court finds that there are special circumstances by reason of which hearing and determining the case in Japan would impair fairness between the parties or hinder the proper and efficient conduct of hearings.

It should be noted that an exclusive choice of court agreement constitutes the only exception to the application of this provision. It also demonstrates the strong policy in favour of the enforcement of such a choice of court agreement.

1.2 Limitations to the Parties' Choice

There are two sets of limitations to the enforcement of choice of court agreements. The first set concerns consumer contracts and individual employment relations. Consumers and employees are categorically deemed to be the weaker parties. A choice of court agreement having as its object a dispute which may arise in connection with such a contract or relation has effect only in the limited circumstances set forth in paragraphs 5 and 6 of Article 3-7 of the CCP. Those provisions read:

> (5) The agreement provided in Paragraph (1) having as its object disputes which may arise in connection with a consumer contract shall have effect only in the circumstances set forth below:
>
> (i) where it is an agreement which allows an action to be filed in the country where the consumer was domiciled at the time of the conclusion of the contract (If the agreement purports to allow an action to be filed exclusively in that country, it shall be without prejudice to the right to file in other countries except in the cases provided in the following sub-paragraph.); or
>
> (ii) where the consumer filed an action in the country specified by the agreement or where the consumer invoked the agreement in response to an action brought by the trader in Japan or in a foreign country.

[2]For details, see Takahashi (2015a), pp. 104–110.

(6) The agreement provided in Paragraph (1) having as its object civil disputes which may arise over individual employment relations shall have effect only in the circumstances set forth below:

(i) where it is an agreement which was concluded when the employment contract was terminated and stipulates that an action may be brought in the country in which the labor was being supplied at the time of the conclusion of the agreement (If the agreement purports to allow an action to be filed exclusively in that country, it shall be without prejudice to the right to file in other countries except in the cases provided in the following sub-paragraph.); or

(ii) where the employee filed an action in the country specified by the agreement or where the employee invoked the agreement in response to an action brought by the employer in Japan or in a foreign country.

Another set of limitations to the enforcement of choice of court agreements exists where the case falls within what Japanese law regards as the realm of exclusive jurisdiction. Though poorly drafted, Article 3-10 provides:

The provisions contained in Article 3-2 to Article 3-4 and those contained in Article 3-6 to the preceding Article shall have no application where, with respect to the action in question, the exclusive jurisdiction of the Japanese courts is prescribed by legislation.

It follows that the Japanese courts have no jurisdiction under Article 3-7(1) in cases where legislation concerning exclusive jurisdiction (which in the Act corresponds to the provisions in Article 3-5) points to the courts of a foreign country. Article 3-5 provides for exclusive jurisdiction with respect to certain actions related to companies, actions with respect to registration, and actions with respect to the existence and effect of the intellectual property rights which come into existence by registration. Thus, for example, a choice of court agreement in favour of Japanese courts is not enforced where the action relates to the registration of immovable property situated in a foreign country.

1.3 Background to the Present Law

The CPP was amended with effect from 1 April 2012 to codify the rules of international jurisdiction for the first time in its history.[3] Among the provisions inserted by the amendment, Article 3-7 largely reflects the pre-existing case law. The leading case is Chisadane,[4] the only case in which the Supreme Court has had an opportunity to consider international choice of court agreements. In that case, the Supreme Court set forth the following principles (hereinafter, "the Chisadane principles"): (i) regarding the formal validity of an international choice of court agreement, it is not necessary for both offer and acceptance to be delivered by means of a

[3] For details, see e.g. Takahashi (2011), p. 146.

[4] Supreme Court, Judgment, November 28, 1975, 29 Minshu (10) 1554 [1975]. An English translation of the judgment is available in the Japanese Annual of International Law, No. 20 (1976) p. 106.

signed document but it is sufficient if the chosen courts are expressly specified in a document made by either or both of the parties and the existence and content of the agreement are clear; (ii) under the civil procedure law of Japan, effect will in principle be given to a foreign choice of court agreement excluding the jurisdiction of the Japanese courts, if the case does not belong to the realm of exclusive jurisdiction of the Japanese courts, and if the chosen foreign courts would have jurisdiction in the case; and (iii) effect may, however, be denied to a choice of court agreement if it is "extremely unreasonable and contrary to the law of public policy" (hereinafter, "the public policy test").

With respect to formal validity, Article 3-7(2) has confirmed the writing requirement. The component of the Chisadane principles which is concerned with formal validity has arguably survived the amendment of the CCP as furnishing the precise meaning of the writing requirement.

The prerequisites for giving effect to exclusive foreign choice of court agreements as enunciated in the Chisadane principles have been enshrined in Article 3-7(4) as well as Article 3-10 of the CCP which provides that Article 3-7, among other provisions, has no application where, with respect to the action in question, the exclusive jurisdiction of the Japanese courts is prescribed by legislation.

The public policy test contained in the Chisadane principles was not given statutory footing but arguably has survived the amendment of the CCP since no statutory basis would need to be found to safeguard the fundamental legal value of Japan. Thus, the public policy test may be necessary to deny effect to an exclusive choice of court agreement, if it specifies a country whose judiciary is corrupt or biased, or if it is concluded to oust the application of Japanese rules of mandatory nature. The need to rely on it, however, has been greatly curtailed by the enactment of paragraphs 5 and 6 of Article 3-7. While the courts have been reluctant to find a violation of public policy until several years ago,[5] there have been several more recent cases in which the courts found violations.[6] These were cases involving consumer contracts or individual employment relations.[7] They fell outside the temporal scope of application of Article 3-7[8] but they would today be decided

[5]In the corresponding period, there was only one known case (Tokyo District Court, Judgment, September 13, 1999, *Kaijiho Kenkyukaishi* [Maritime Law Research Journal] Vol. 154 (2000) p. 89) in which public policy was found to be violated.

[6]Tokyo High Court, Judgment, June 28, 2012, LEX/DB 25504140; Tokyo District Court, Judgment, November 14, 2012, LEX/DB 25483568; Osaka High Court, Judgment, February 20, 2014, H.J. (2225) 77 [2014]; and the Tokyo High Court, Judgment, November 17, 2014, H.T. (1409) 200 [2015].

[7]Among the cases mentioned in the preceding footnote, the cases of the Tokyo High Court and the Osaka High Court involved consumer contracts. The Tokyo District Court case concerned individual employment relations.

[8]This provision has application to choice-of-court agreements concluded on or after April 1, 2012.

under paragraphs 5 and 6 of that article. It is not hard to believe that the findings of violation in those decisions were influenced by the Act for the amendment of the CCP whose promulgation preceded those decisions.

Article 3-9, the relevance of which to the present discussion has been explained above, also reflects the pre-existing case law. In a clear departure from the case-law based principle, however, it makes an exception for an exclusive choice of court agreement in favour of Japanese courts. The effect of such an agreement has, to that extent, been strengthened.

Another departure from the pre-existing case law concerns the limitations with respect to consumer contracts and individual employment relations. As detailed above, those limitations are contained in paragraphs 5 and 6 of Article 3-7 which were inserted at the time of the amendment to the CCP. Prior to the amendment, no special treatment was given to individual employment relations. Thus, in a case involving an exclusive choice of court agreement between United Airlines and its employee which specified the Illinois courts, the Tokyo District Court observed that such an agreement would allow the airline to efficiently manage disputes with its employees of various nationalities. But the Court did not find that the agreement failed the public policy test and decided to give effect to it.[9] The courts deciding on the same facts today under Article 3-7(6) would have no choice but to deny effect to the agreement.

1.4 Influence of International Instruments

Japan has neither signed nor acceded to the Hague Convention on Choice of Court Agreements 2005. The General Assembly of the Legislative Council of the Ministry of Justice stated in its decision on 6 September 2005 that it would seem appropriate for Japan to start considering whether to ratify this Convention when major countries had moved towards ratification and it had become certain that this Convention would play the role of a globally uniform agreement concerning choice of court agreements.[10]

It may be said generally that the European Union instruments such as the Brussels I Regulation have influenced the recent Japanese legislation on international litigation as much as it has introduced special rules for the protection of consumers and employees as the weaker parties.

[9]Tokyo High Court, Judgment, November 28, 2000 (United Airlines case) H.J. (1743) 137 [2001].

[10]http://www.moj.go.jp/shingi1/shingi2_050906-1-1.html (in Japanese).

2 Optional Choice of Court Agreements

2.1 Effect of Optional Choice of Court Agreements

The effect of a choice of court agreement is a procedural matter and, in accordance with the maxim *forum regit processum*, is subject to the law of the forum. Where the issue is brought before a Japanese court, the following rules of Japanese law will be applied.

Article 3-7 of the CCP, outlined above, is applicable to optional choice of court agreements except for the following provisions: paragraph (4), the second half of (ii) of paragraph (5) and the second half of (ii) of paragraph (6). Articles 3-9 and 3-10, too, are applicable.

Whereas an exclusive choice of court agreement purports to give jurisdiction to the courts chosen and oust the jurisdiction of the other courts, an optional choice of court agreement only purports to confer jurisdiction on the courts chosen. Thus, the Japanese courts have jurisdiction by virtue of an optional choice of court agreement in their favour. An optional choice of court agreement in favour of foreign courts, on the other hand, does not deprive the Japanese courts of the jurisdiction which they have under the provisions of the CCP. It remains so even if the option of suing in a nominated foreign court is actually exercised. The existence of such an agreement may, however, be given some weight in favour of the foreign proceedings when the Japanese court decides whether to dismiss the parallel proceedings of Japan under Article 3-9 of the CCP or under other theories for international *lis pendens*. It goes without saying that commencing proceedings in a court other than that nominated in an optional choice of court agreement does not constitute a breach of the agreement. So a judgment rendered by a foreign court is not denied recognition or enforcement in Japan solely on the ground that the court is other than that nominated in an optional choice of court agreement.

Article 3-9 does not make an exception for an optional choice of court agreement. Nevertheless, dismissal under that provision will be rare where Japanese courts are chosen by the parties because "fairness between the parties" would usually be promoted by respecting their agreement.[11]

2.2 Optional Choice of Court Agreements Involving Presumptively Weaker Parties

The CCP contains special rules (paragraphs (5) and (6) of Article 3-7) which are meant to protect consumers and employees as the presumptively weaker parties.

[11] e.g. The Kyoto District Court in its judgment on 29 January 2015 (2015WLJPCA01296002) refused to dismiss proceedings under Article 3-9 where there was a non-exclusive choice-of-court agreement in favour of the Japanese courts.

A choice of court agreement having as its object disputes which may arise in connection with a consumer contract is given effect in limited circumstances and, in most of such circumstances, only as an optional choice of court agreement. Thus, such an agreement may be relied upon by the consumer to file an action (the first half of paragraph (5)(ii)). It may also be relied on by the trader but only where it is an agreement which allows an action to be filed in the country where the consumer was domiciled at the time of the conclusion of the contract (paragraph (5)(i)). The traders cannot, however, rely on such an agreement to contest jurisdiction even if it purports to be an exclusive choice of court agreement (See the bracket of paragraph (5)(i)). Thus, where a Japanese trader and a consumer domiciled in State X have concluded an exclusive choice of court agreement in favour of the courts of X, if the consumer files an action in Japan, the trader cannot rely on it to contest the jurisdiction of the Japanese courts.

Again, a choice of court agreement having as its object civil disputes which may arise over individual employment relations is given effect in limited circumstances and, in most of such circumstances, only as an optional choice of court agreement. Thus, such an agreement may be relied upon by the employee to file an action (the first half of (ii) of paragraph (6)). Such an agreement may also be relied on by the employer but only where it is an agreement which was concluded when the employment contract was terminated and stipulates that an action may be brought in the country in which the labor was being supplied at that time (paragraph (6)(i)). The employers cannot, however, rely on such an agreement to contest jurisdiction even if it purports to be an exclusive choice of court agreement (See the bracket of paragraph (6)(i)). Thus, suppose that a Japanese employer and an employee supplying labour in State Y concluded an exclusive choice of court agreement in favour of the courts of Y at the time of terminating the employment contract. If the employee files an action in Japan to seek the payment of a severance allowance, the employer cannot rely on the agreement to contest the jurisdiction of the Japanese courts.

These special rules are operationally neutral in terms of the nationality and domicile of the parties. Consequently, it can happen that they work against the interest of traders and employers based in Japan. Thus, for example, where a Japanese souvenir shop files an action in Japan against its former customer from a foreign country, seeking payment of the price for the souvenir it has sold to the customer, the Japanese courts have no jurisdiction to hear the claim even if the shop relies on a choice of court agreement choosing the Japanese courts.

2.3 Distinguishing Optional from Exclusive Choice of Court Agreements

Japanese law has no statutory provision laying out a test for distinguishing optional choice of court agreements from exclusive choice of court agreements. In the run up to the amendment of the CCP, the law makers considered the idea of deeming a foreign choice of court agreement to be an agreement to oust the jurisdiction of the Japanese courts unless there is a contrary agreement but rejected it as being contrary to international business practice. They instead decided to leave the matter to the interpretation of agreements.[12]

The case law has produced no clear principles. The Japanese courts have the tendency of relying on factual appreciation and their own sense of reasonableness, rather than engaging in choice-of-law analysis, in interpreting choice of court agreements to see whether they are exclusive or optional.[13] Thus, the Chisadane case featured a choice of court agreement contained in a bill of lading which stipulated[14]: "All actions under this contract of carriage shall be brought before the court in Amsterdam and no other court shall have jurisdiction with regard to any other action unless the carrier brings such an action before a court of other jurisdiction or voluntarily accepts the jurisdiction of such court." The Supreme Court found that this agreement was an exclusive choice of court agreement on the reasoning that it clearly purported to leave intact the option of suing in one of the fora having jurisdiction in the case, namely Amsterdam, and exclude other fora. However, the Court did not formulate rules for distinguishing exclusive from optional choice of court agreements in general terms. Nor did the Court enunciate any canon of interpretation which should be applied to interpret choice of court agreements.

The tendency of the Japanese courts is to characterise a choice of court agreement as exclusive unless otherwise indicated. Thus, in a case featuring an agreement giving one of the parties the right to decide where to sue from a list of fora, the Tokyo District Court held it to be an exclusive choice of court agreement in accordance with what it perceived to be the obvious purport of the agreement as gleaned from the right of choice.[15] But the opposite characterization can be taken. Thus, in a case involving an agreement stating "... any dispute between the parties shall be submitted to the Commercial Court in Paris, France," the Tokyo District Court found it to be an optional choice of court agreement, noting that it did not purport to exclude the jurisdiction of other courts. The Court acknowledged that the Commercial Court in Paris would have jurisdiction over the dispute even without the agreement but held that it would not be inconsistent with interpreting the agreement as conferring jurisdiction on that court.[16] The Tokyo District Court adopted the contrary reasoning

[12]Ministry of Justice (2009) p. 30 (in Japanese).

[13]e.g. Supreme Court, Judgment on the Chisadane case, *supra* note 4; Tokyo District Court, Judgment, April 11, 2008, H.T. (1276) 332; Tokyo District Court, Judgment, September 24, 2008, 2008WLJPCA09248005; Tokyo District Court, Judgment, March 26, 2014, 2014WLJPCA03269011.

[14]The original text of the choice-of-court agreement was in English. But the judgment, written in Japanese, only contains some English words from the agreement. The translation is a reconstruction by the present author using those English words.

[15]Tokyo District Court, Judgment, September 24, 2008, *supra* note 13. Other decisions adopting the same characterisation include the Tokyo District Court, Judgment, February 28, 1994, H.T. (876) 268.

[16]Tokyo District Court, Judgment, March 26, 2014, *supra* note 13.

in another case which involved an agreement choosing the Arbitration Court of Primorsk Region of the Russian Federation. The Court noted that the Russian court would have jurisdiction over the dispute even without the agreement and held that it would be reasonable to interpret the agreement as purporting to exclude the jurisdiction of other courts.[17]

2.4 *In Intra-national Cases*

Optional choice of court agreements are not treated differently in intra-national cases to the way they are treated in international cases. However, the tendency of the courts in intra-national cases is to deem a choice of court agreement to be optional unless the contrary intent is clear as in the cases where the agreement specifies one of the courts which would have jurisdiction even without the agreement.[18] It is opposite to the tendency in international cases (See Sect. 2.3 above). This is curious because, in the intra-national context, the courts have discretion to transfer the case to another otherwise competent court even if they are seised on the basis of an exclusive choice of court agreement (Article 17 of the CCP). Moreover, because of various procedural differences and the long distance involved, the consequence of ousting jurisdiction is arguably greater in the international context than in the intra-national context. In the latter context, the courts characterised a choice of court agreement as optional rather than exclusive on the reasoning that it was contained in a standard form of contract and/or that weaker parties ought to be protected. There are in fact no such special rules for protecting consumers and employees in the intra-national context as paragraphs (5) and (6) of Article 3-7 which are only applicable in the international context. After the amendment to the CCP which inserted those provisions, if the different treatment of intra-national and international cases persists, the presence and absence of special rules for protecting weaker parties may furnish an explanation.

3 Asymmetrical Choice of Court Agreements

3.1 *Effect of an Asymmetrical Choice of Court Agreement*

An asymmetrical choice of court agreement refers to a choice of court agreement that combines both exclusive and optional aspects. Where an asymmetrical choice of court agreement is validly formed, each aspect of such an agreement is given effect

[17]Tokyo District Court, Judgment, March 27, 2015, H.T. (1421) 238.

[18]E.g. Osaka High Court, February 21, 1990 H.T. (732) 270; Kobe District Court Amagasaki Branch, Judgment, October 14, 2011, H.J. (2133) 96. The latter even overrode the word "exclusive" used in the choice-of-court agreement.

according to its purport. Thus, an exclusive aspect is given effect as if it were an exclusive choice of court agreement and an optional aspect is given effect as if it were an optional choice of court agreement.

3.2 *Formation and Validity of an Asymmetrical Choice of Court Agreement*

A question which seems more important is whether such an agreement is validly formed in spite of the lack of equilibrium between the parties. The choice of court agreement featured in the Chisadane case was in fact asymmetrical.[19] But the Supreme Court only looked at the exclusive aspect of this agreement when finding that it did not fall foul of the public policy test.

Where Japanese law governs the validity of a choice of court agreement in a consumer contract, the Consumer Contract Act would be applicable. It reads in Article 10:

> Any clause in a consumer contract which purports to restrict the rights or add to the obligations of the consumer as provided, through the application of the provisions unrelated to the public order, in the Civil Code, the Commercial Code or other statutes or statutory instruments shall be null and void if it unilaterally harms the interests of the consumer in contravention of the fundamental principle enshrined in Article 1(2) of the Civil Code.[20]

In no case has a choice of court agreement been found null and void under this provision. Such a likelihood would be slimmer now with the introduction of Article 3-7(5). Under the latter, the trader cannot rely on an exclusive choice of court agreement to contest the consumer's choice of forum. Besides, the trader can only rely on an optional choice of court agreement under the limited situation prescribed. The lack of equilibrium stemming from the text of an asymmetrical choice of court agreement would thus be drastically redressed. Consequently, it would hardly be possible to say that such an agreement would "unilaterally harm the interests of the consumer."

Where Japanese law governs the formation of a choice of court agreement in a standard form contract (whether or not it is a consumer contract falling within the scope of the Consumer Contract Act), it will become subject to the new Article 548-2 which is to be inserted in the Civil Code with effect from 1 April 2020. It provides:

> (1) Those who have made an agreement to engage in a standard transaction (a transaction engaged in by a specific party with an opposite party drawn from the rank of many and unspecified persons, for both of whom the standardization of the whole or part of its content is reasonable) shall be deemed to have agreed to individual clauses contained in

[19] See the text accompanying supra note 14.

[20] Article 1(2) of the Civil Code provides:
The exercise of rights and the performance of obligations shall be done in good faith.

the standard form (the entirety of the clauses prepared by the specific party as the content of the contract in a standard transaction) if:

(i) they have agreed to make the standard form the content of their contract; or
(ii) the party who has prepared the standard form has indicated beforehand to the opposite party that it shall become the content of the contract.

(2) Notwithstanding the provision of the preceding paragraph, any clause falling within the description of the preceding paragraph which purports to restrict the rights or add to the obligations of the other party shall be deemed not to have been consented to if it is considered to harm the interests of that other party unilaterally in contravention of the fundamental principle enshrined in Article 1(2), having regard to the manners and actual circumstances of the standard transaction as well as the social norms relevant to the transaction.

This provision is applicable to, for example, a choice of court agreement in a standard form loan contract which purports to confer jurisdiction on the chosen courts and, only where the borrower acts as the plaintiff, oust the jurisdiction of the other courts. Where the contract is B2B, Article 3-7(5) of the CCP would not help redress the lack of equilibrium. Consequently, such an agreement will be considered to harm the interests of the borrower unilaterally. It remains to be seen whether the courts will consider that the fundamental principle enshrined in Article 1(2), *i.e.* the principle of good faith which permeates the Civil Code, is accordingly contravened.

4 Need for Reform

In the area of optional choice of court agreements,[21] Japanese law should be reformed to provide for a clear test for distinguishing optional from exclusive choice of court agreements. As seen in Sect. 2.3 above, there is no statutory provision laying out a test for distinguishing these two types of agreements. Neither has the case law produced any clear test. The uncertainty as to whether any specific choice of court agreement is optional or exclusive would result in time and expenses being wasted at the jurisdictional stage of the litigation.

It may be thought that the cause of uncertainty lies in the courts' tendency to treat this issue as a factual question. But treating it as a legal question would not promote certainty if a choice-of-law analysis were applied to ascertain the applicable law because there is uncertainty over what should be the choice-of-law rules for interpreting choice of court agreements.[22] Moreover, legal systems often fail to

[21]For a suggestion of law reform on choice-of-court agreements in general, see Takahashi (2015b), p. 395.

[22]The present author believes that where a choice-of-court agreement is contained in a contract, it should, like other terms in the same contract, be submitted to the choice-of-law analysis for that contract, with the result that it becomes subject to the law governing the contract except in what will be a rare situation where the parties have chosen a different law specifically for the choice-of-court agreement. Other authors prefer severing a choice-of-court agreement from the remainder of the contract and applying a separate choice-of-law analysis to it from the remainder of the contract.

provide an unequivocal answer to the question how to distinguish between optional and exclusive choice of court agreements. Consequently, even if the court has managed to ascertain the applicable law through a choice-of-law analysis, it will often face the difficulty of actually applying that law.

The present author believes that a solution to this problem lies in establishing a clear test which is applicable regardless of the law governing the interpretation of choice of court agreements. It can, for example, be a rebuttable presumption in favor of exclusiveness as stipulated by Article 3(b) of the Hague Choice of Court Convention. Such a rule may be categorised as an overriding mandatory rule because it is a rule applicable irrespective of the law governing the interpretation of choice of court agreements. The promotion of certainty and predictability with respect to the interpretation of choice of court agreements merits being pursued by enacting overriding mandatory rules since such agreements are invariably concluded with the aim of avoiding the uncertainty which would otherwise result from the application and interpretation of jurisdictional rules in general.

References

Ministry of Justice (2009) Kokusai Saiban Kankatsu Hôsei ni kansuru Chûkan Shian no Hosoku Setsumei [Explanatory Notes on Interim Proposal concerning Legislation on International Jurisdiction] p 30 (in Japanese)

Takahashi K (2011) Japan's newly enacted rules on international jurisdiction: with a reflection on some issues of interpretation. Jpn Yearb Priv Int Law 13:146–170

Takahashi K (2015a) The jurisdiction of Japanese courts in a comparative context. J Priv Int Law 11:103–127

Takahashi K (2015b) Law applicable to choice of court agreements. Jpn Yearb Int Law 58:384–396

Koji Takahashi is a professor at the Doshisha University Law School in Kyoto, Japan. After completing his LLB and LLM in Kyoto and LLM and PhD in London, he started his full-time career in England. First as a researcher at the Institute of Maritime Law of Southampton University and then as a lecturer at the Birmingham University, he taught and researched in various areas of English law. After returning to his native country, Japan, his focus shifted to Japanese law and comparative law. He has been on the editorial board of the Journal of Private International Law since 2005. He was on the advisory board for the Foreign Direct Investment International Moot Competition from 2011 to 2015. Since 2012, he is an adjunct Professor at the Michigan State University in the United States, teaching international litigation and arbitration. He has written extensively in English and Japanese on diverse issues of private international law, international trade law and international arbitration. In the past several years, he is also productive in his research on the legal aspects of blockchain and cryptocurrencies.

The Netherlands: Optional Choice of Court Agreements in a Globalizing World

Stephan F. G. Rammeloo

1 The Treatment of Choice of Court Agreements in General

1.1 Attitude to the Parties' Agreements About Jurisdiction in General. Party Autonomy

As a preliminary observation, this Report concentrates on choice of court agreements under *national* Private International Law of the Netherlands (i.e. not on uniform and/or harmonized international and/or EU law).

In the year 1985 the Dutch Supreme Court (*Hoge Raad*) broke with the traditional doctrine of sovereignty according to which jurisdiction could be attributed to courts by the law only (i.e. not by the autonomous will of the contracting parties).[1] In its *Piscator* judgment[2] the Supreme Court, while taking into consideration international law developments and the needs of international legal practice, endowed contracting parties with the power to establish jurisdiction (*forumkeuzevrijheid*: discretion to agree on choice of court) with a view to adjudicating conflicts that in a cross-border context are at their disposal[3] provided that the contracting parties have a genuine interest.[4]

[1]For detailed treatment of (optional) choice of court agreements, cf Kuijpers (2008).

[2]HR February 1, 1985, NJ 1985, 698 (*Piscator*).

[3]For example family law matters being excluded therefrom.

[4]More specifically, the parties may have a genuine interest because of the neutrality or expertise in view of the conflict or of the *lex fori*, diminishing forum shopping options. Cf, with further details, Strikwerda (2015a), p. 46, with references to case law, and p. 85.

S. F. G. Rammeloo (✉)
Law Faculty, Maastricht University, Private Law Department, Maastricht, Netherlands
e-mail: S.Rammeloo@maastrichtuniversity.nl

M. Keyes (ed.), *Optional Choice of Court Agreements in Private International Law*, Ius Comparatum – Global Studies in Comparative Law 37,
https://doi.org/10.1007/978-3-030-23914-5_12

The foregoing principles were codified (after the 2002 law reform on civil procedural law) in article 8 of the Code of Civil Procedure Law of the Netherlands (*Wetboek van Burgerlijke Rechtsvordering*), this provision being compliant with article 25 of EU Regulation 1215/2012 on Jurisdiction and Recognition and Enforcement of Judgments in Civil and Commercial Matters.[5] Netherlands courts are thus willing to enforce choice of court agreements, even more in the awareness that the Recast comes into play even when (cf the first line of article 25 of the Recast) neither of the contracting parties is established within the European Union.

As regards the terminology used in Dutch Private International Law, it must be underscored that Netherlands law sources tend to speak of "*exclusive jurisdiction*" mainly in respect of disputes falling within the reign of article 24 of Brussels I *bis*. Consequently and in contrast with many Common Law oriented systems of law, the term "exclusive jurisdiction" does not encompass non-optional choice of court arrangements. One can say that any choice of court agreement is commonly referred to as "*forumkeuze*" (i.e. "choice of forum") and that only contextual reading unveils the nature of choice of court agreements (i.e. optional or not, symmetrical or asymmetrical).

1.2 Status of Choice of Court Agreements. Influence of Multilateral, Regional, and Bilateral Instruments on the Law Relating to Choice of Court Agreements

Pursuant to case law of the Dutch Supreme Court as described under Sect. 1.1 above, legal treatment of choice of court underwent a major change in 1985. October 1, 2015 led to another major change as the Hague Convention on Choice of Court Agreements entered in force for, inter alia, all EU Member States (Denmark being excluded), i.e. also for the Netherlands.[6] Due to the widened formal (geographical) scope of article 25 of Brussels I *bis* as described above, positive jurisdiction clashes may occur between both Private International Law instruments ruling choice of court agreements.[7] So far, however, there is no Dutch case law on this international conflict of law source.

As an EU Member State, the Netherlands are *de iure* bound by both "Brussels I *bis*" and, as the European Union as a REIO[8] signed and ratified it, the Hague Conference Convention on Choice of Court Agreements. These instruments did not fundamentally influence the law in the Netherlands, as since the 2002 law reform article 8 of the Dutch Code on Civil Procedural Law purportedly more or less

[5]In the following to be referred to as "Brussels I *bis*".

[6]For an overview on the actual status of ratifications, signatures, etc. of this Convention, cf https://www.hcch.net/en/instruments/conventions/specialised-sections/choice-of-court.

[7]This may become even more relevant pursuant to Brexit.

[8]Regional Economic International Organisation.

enshrined the "regime" of, currently, article 25 Brussels I *bis* on choice of court agreements.

2 Optional Choice of Court Agreements

2.1 Legal Sources Relevant in Determining the Effect of Optional Choice of Court Agreements

As to legal sources determining the legal effect of optional choice of court agreements, distinctions must be drawn between various issues. Formal requirements[9] are governed by the regime of article 25 Brussels I *bis* jo. article 8 of the aforementioned Dutch Code on Civil Procedural Law, the latter provision as mentioned clearly seeking parallels with the Recast regime. In view of the "substantive" validity of the choice of court agreement, the question whether the choice of court is allowed for, as well as matters relating to procedural law aspects, both aspects are governed by the *lex fori* of the court chosen for the prorogation effects, and of the court excluded for the derogation effects.[10] Another question is whether there is real consent between the parties in respect of the choice of court agreement. This question in particular tends to be answered with the help of Private International Law of the forum seized, that is for the Netherlands EU Regulation 593/2008 on the Law Applicable to Contractual Obligations.[11] It must be underscored though that article 6 of the Hague Convention on Choice of Court Agreements seems to submit this question to the competence of the court which is exclusively chosen by the parties. Despite the fact that article 8 of the Dutch Civil Code on procedural law does not require that the choice of court is in writing (subsection 5), the writing may be considered as evidence.[12]

[9]A choice of court agreement is required to be "(a) in writing or evidenced in writing, (b) in a form which accords with practices which the parties have established between themselves; or (c) in international trade or commerce, in a form which accords with a usage of which the parties are or ought to have been aware and which in such trade or commerce is widely known to, and regularly observed by, parties to contracts of the type involved in the particular trade or commerce concerned."

[10]Cf Strikwerda (2015a), p. 86, with further reference.

[11]Idem, with referral to the Explanatory Memorandum to article 8 of the Dutch Civil Procedural Law Code, and p. 110. In the same sense the Preamble to article 25 of the Recast, Observ. 20. Although choice of court agreements are explicitly excluded from the scope of Regulation 593/2008 (art.1(2)(e)), Netherlands private international law tends to apply the Regulation to this issue by way of analogy.

[12]The legislator thus sought parallels with arbitration on one hand and the Recast regime on the other, cf Strikwerda (2015a), p. 86.

2.2 *Law Applicable to the Nature of a Choice of Court Agreement (Optional or Exclusive)*

Whether or not the choice of court agreement must be considered as optional or exclusive appears to be a matter of "interpretation" (*uitleg*) of the parties' common intentions to be taken from the wording of the choice of forum clause and the circumstances of each case to be examined. This approach follows from case law of the highest court based on the Explanatory Memorandum on article 8 of the Netherlands Civil Procedural Code.[13]

As follows from the preceding lines the answer to this question is not first submitted to any conflict rule but has to be taken directly from substantive law notions on the interpretation of the contract, in particular the parties' intentions derived from the wording of the contract and the circumstances to be examined on a case by case analysis.[14]

2.3 *Characterization of Choice of Court Agreement Under the* lex fori

Not surprisingly, the starting point is whether the wording of the choice of court agreement is unequivocally clear or not.[15] However, fact constellations that are of an in between nature result in a twilight zone.

An attempt to classify[16] the wording of ambiguous clauses leads to some guidelines: (1) even when the wording of the agreement does not speak of "exclusive", or "only", one cannot conclude there is no exclusive choice of court agreement; (2) a choice of court clause is often already considered to be of an exclusive nature if it reads, for example, "Parties submit to the jurisdiction of the court of. . .", or "Seller agrees to the jurisdiction of the province Alberta, Canada"; (3) An indication of a non-imperative choice of court agreement is, for example: "may be submitted", "are authorized to solve disputes"; (4) On the contrary other words may suggest the exclusive nature of the choice of court agreement, cf "the court (. . .) shall be", or "parties are waiving the jurisdiction of any other court"; (5) A clause obliging each of the contracting parties to initiate court proceedings in the domicile of the defendant is considered as conclusive by its own nature, as in the absence of such a clause

[13]HR November 9, 2012, NJ 2012, 638.

[14]Cf Kuijpers (2008), p. 252 et seq. Recent case law, cf District Court Amsterdam July 20, 2016, NiPR 2016, 443 (engagement letter: no exclusive agreement court of choice in the Netherlands).

[15]Cf the opinion of Advocate-General Vranken preceding HR December 17, 1993, NJ 1994, 350 (*Esmil/PGSP*), underscoring that the word 'exclusive' can be decisive. In line with this approach any choice of court which is 'not exclusive' does not derogate from another court's jurisdiction, cf District Court Dordrecht August 20, 1993, KG 1993, 327.

[16]Cf Kuijpers (2008), par. 10.3.4, with further reference to case law.

other courts would remain competent under e.g. article 7.1 of the Recast (*forum contractus*); (6) Finally, it is self-evident that the words "for all future conflicts…" only widens the scope of choice of court clauses, yet without touching upon the question whether any such choice is of an exclusive nature or not.

In case the wording is ambiguous some circumstances may be taken into account: (1) adjustments of wording during negotiation; (2) the choice of court is combined with a choice for the *lex fori* as the governing law of the contract; (3) the possibility to concentrate (potentially related) actions in the same court (avoidance of irreconcilable court judgments); (4) the fact that the court of a "third" country has been designated (neutral court) may increase exclusivity of the agreement; (5) any choice of a court of which a court order would not be enforceable may be an indicator of its non-exclusive nature.

2.4 Law Applicable to the Legal Effect of an Optional Choice of Court Agreement

There is no choice of law rule governing and designating the applicable law with a view to determining the legal effect of an optional choice of court agreement. Answers to this question are to be taken from the regime of article 8 of the Dutch Civil Procedural Law Code as described above and from case law.

As described article 8 does not itself presume that any choice of court agreement is exclusive in the sense of, currently, article 25 Recast. At the end of the day, whether an optional choice in favour of the courts of the forum must be treated as a waiver of the parties' right to contest jurisdiction under forum law depends on the parties' intentions, assessed on a case by case analysis.[17]

Usually the issue of appearance in court of the defendant in line with an optional jurisdiction clause and without contesting the court's jurisdiction leads to an absorption of the issue of jurisdiction. No case law can be traced.

In terms of the legal effect of an optional choice of court agreement in favour of foreign courts: pursuant to article 8 subsection 2 of the Dutch Code on Civil Procedural Law notably an exclusive choice for a foreign court excludes the jurisdiction of a Dutch court. If, however, any such choice is of a non-exclusive nature the Dutch court remains competent (article 8 subsection 2 of the same Code).[18] As regards the recognition and enforceability of any foreign judgment emanating from a choice of court by the parties, it is well-established under Netherlands Private International Law that if a foreign court has assumed jurisdiction "legally" (here: as a consequence of free submission by the contracting parties)

[17]HR March 13, 1981, NJ 1981, 635 (*Haviltex*).

[18]Cf Strikwerda (2015a), p. 85; Kuijpers (2008), p. 252, both with further reference.

Article 431 of the Dutch Civil Procedural Code allows for recognition and enforcement of such a foreign court judgment.[19]

2.5 Optional Choice of Court Agreements in Favour of Forum and in Favour of Foreign Courts: Consistent Treatment

To a large extent prorogation and derogation are treated consistently, as follows from the mirroring nature of Dutch Supreme Court jurisprudence, the "Piscator" judgment having regard to prorogation in favour of a Dutch court, and the "Harvest Trader" judgment concerning the derogative "power" of any choice in favour of a foreign court.[20] The complementary concept of both these cases was more or less "codified" under article 8 of the Dutch Civil Procedural Law Code.

Meanwhile, one may not ignore that under Private International Law of the Netherlands courts are bound by, depending on their substantive and formal scopes, the legal regimes of "Europe" (the Recast), international law (the Hague 2005 Convention on Choice of Court Agreements) and national Private International Procedural Law (article 8 of the Dutch Civil Procedural Law Code), each being built on different legal premises.[21] This may result in slight material divergences having been observed above already.[22] In particular, the presumptive exclusive nature of a choice of court agreement under the regime of article 25 Recast differs from the approach under article 8 of the Dutch Civil Procedural Law Code.[23]

2.6 Optional Choice of Court Agreements Involving Presumptively Weaker Parties

In line with the Recast article 15 (insurance of individuals), article 19 (consumer relationships), and article 23 (employment relationships) article 8 subsection 3 *littera*

[19]Cf Strikwerda (2015b), p. 292, with further reference.

[20]Cf what has been observed above already.

[21]It must be recalled here that Netherlands legislator yet seeks to establish harmony between Communautary, international and national law relevant with regard to the contractual choice of court.

[22]To be recalled briefly: there are some differences as regards the "writing" aspect (formal validity) but also of the additional requirement set by the Supreme Court in its "Piscator" judgment, namely that parties agreeing on choice of court in the Netherlands are presupposed to have a genuine interest of a Netherlands Court adjudicating their conflict, this element not being a prerequisite under the Recast or the 2005 Hague Convention on choice of courts.

[23]Cf what has been said on the parties' intentions being decisive for the conclusion whether or not the choice of court agreement must be held exclusive or non-exclusive.

c to be read in conjunction with article 6 of the Dutch Civil Procedural Law Code establishes the principle that employees and consumers (not: insured individuals) are not bound by any choice of court agreement unless it is entered into after the dispute has arisen; or allowing the consumer or employee to bring proceedings in courts other than those nominated in the choice of court agreement. This principle boils down to the nature of asymmetrical choice of court clauses.

2.7 Proceedings Commenced in a Court Other Than That Nominated in an Optional Choice of Court Agreement. Damages for Breach of Contract on Choice of Court

Pursuant to article 8 subsection 2 Dutch courts do not have jurisdiction any longer when parties with a view to conflicts that are deemed to be at their free disposition (cf earlier observations) agreed on an exclusive choice of forum.[24] This proviso however has to be read in in conjunction with article 11 of the Dutch Code on Civil Procedural Law, and therefore the court has wide discretion to accept or deny jurisdiction.

As (at least a potential) a consequence of jurisdiction and applicable law not running parallel, complications may arise. In case proceedings are started in a court other than that designated by the parties, it is assumed that it is for the court which was chosen by the parties from the beginning to adjudicate this matter, including compensation of (not procedural law related[25]) substantive damages, the amount of compensation to be governed by the *lex causae* (i.e. *lex contractus*).[26]

2.8 Legal Status of Judgments of Foreign Court Other Than Those Nominated in an Optional Choice of Court Agreement

In case a choice of court is of a non-exclusive nature this means that parties are allowed to start proceedings in another court, provided this court would have jurisdiction on a basis other than prorogation. This legal basis for jurisdiction of the foreign court then has to follow from either EU Regulation 1215/2012, or from any other court as a consequence of bilateral treaties, of, ultimately, on the basis of

[24]Under the exception of contracts relating to employment relationships (article 8 subsection 3).

[25]For *procedural* law related damages, understandably the assumption is that the *lex fori* applies, Kuijpers (2008), p. 264.

[26]Kuijpers (2008), p. 264. In a Dutch court the proper law of the contract would follow from applying EU Regulation 593/2008 ("Rome I").

the first title of the Dutch Code of Civil Procedural Law. When affirmed, such a foreign court judgment would be enforceable.

2.9 *Choice of Court: Interregional Law*

For the "Caribbean" territories of the Kingdom of the Netherlands it remained unclear for a long time which civil procedural laws applied.[27] As concerns choice of court agreements, a Kingdom Act (*Rijkswet Gemeenschappelijk Hof van Justitie*) in conjunction with article 103 of the Caribbean Civil Procedural Law Act apply. This boils down to courts of the "European" territory of the Netherlands applying article 8 of the Dutch Civil Procedural Law Act analogously in cases involving "Caribbean-Dutch" choice of court cases, and courts in the Caribbean territory of the Netherlands applying article 14 subsection 1 and 2 concerning international and interregional choice of forum agreements as enshrined in the Kingdom Act (*Rijkswet Gemeenschappelijk Hof van Justitie*). Case law is hardly available. As described with regard to the preceding questions Private Interregional law of the Netherlands is of a rather lacunous nature. A certain paralleled approach (concordance principle) seems to be adhered to though, also in view of case law.[28]

2.10 *Legal Effect of an Exclusive Choice of Court Agreement*

Under the complementary functioning of article 6 of the Hague Convention on the choice of courts and the—widely formulated—proviso of article 25 Recast I ("regardless of the domicile" of either of the litigating parties) there is hardly any room left for national Private International Law rules. The primacy lies with the court chosen, other courts being obliged to stay proceedings. When it comes to establishing whether any such choice of forum must be deemed to be of an exclusive nature or not, this ultimately depends on a case by case analysis of the Dutch court.[29] It is relatively complicated to distinguish, as the "range" from optional to exclusive choice of court agreements is based on a sliding scale. Correspondingly, courts try to establish the (genuine) intention of the parties as described above.

---

[27]Lewin (2016), par. 3.6.2 and 3.6.3. Cf with a view to jurisdiction in Netherlands Interregional Private Law general Dutch Supreme Court May 2, 2014, (ECLI:NL:HR:2014:1063. Cf further Lock (2011), p. 31).

[28]Lewin quotes case law, p. 94. GEA Curacao January 15, 2009, concerning a case in which the court held itself not competent to adjudicate a conflict on the basis of a choice of court designating the Curacao court, the conflict between an employer and his employee, as the latter was residing and carrying out employment in the European territory in the Netherlands.

[29]Cf Sects. 2.1 and 2.2 above.

3 Asymmetrical Choice of Court Agreements

3.1 Legal Effect of a Choice of Court Agreement Combining Both Exclusive and Optional Aspects ('Asymmetrical' Choice of Court Agreement)

In view of choice of court agreements favouring only one of the parties in the sense that this party may (as well) turn to another court, EU Regulation 1215/2012 ("Brussels I *bis*") article 25 subsection 1 in fine reading establishes that a choice of court "shall be exclusive unless the parties have agreed otherwise".[30] This provision obviously gained importance due to its extremely wide formal scope: any Dutch court will apply the regime of this provision, "regardless of where (litigating) parties are domiciled". Although article 8 of the Dutch Civil Procedural Law Code does not explicitly allow for asymmetrical choice of court agreements, article 8 still justifies, or at least allows for, this option.[31]

3.2 Legal Effect of the Optional Component of Choice of Court Agreement

Asymmetrical choices of forum are allowed for: there is no proviso or case law in Dutch law demanding that parties mutually (*over en weer*) are bound to the "same" conditions. One of the parties may stipulate a choice of court for himself, unilaterally. This approach has further ramifications for situations involving multi-party relationships containing choice of court agreements.[32]

4 Evaluation and Reform

Doctrine in the Netherlands does not classify meticulously the categories of what exactly constitutes an optional or exclusive choice of court agreement. The emphasis in case law seems to lie more on the question whether "at the end of the day" there is

---

[30]Cf in particular ECJ jurisprudence, notably its judgment from June 24, 1986 C-22/85 (*Anterist/ Crédit Lyonnais*), Rec 1986, 1951.

[31]Kuijpers (2008), p. 354, speaks of "*zeer grote contracteervrijheid*" (contracting parties are endowed with far reaching party autonomy), this freedom inter alia allowing for (i) designating the courts of more than just one legal order; (ii) dépeçage (i.e. splitting the choice of court, depending on e.g. the dispute or part of the legal relationship involved); (iii) choice of court leaving that choice to one of the parties only.

[32]Cf Kuijpers (2008), p. 18, with referral to choice of forum clauses contained in the articles of association of companies or trusts.

a valid choice of court clause than on the distinction between optional or exclusive agreements. To some extent this is explained by the methodology used, namely the direct (substantive law natured) search for the parties' intent, to be deduced from the wording and the circumstances as described above. Inasmuch as problems may arise, they will have to be solved under the reign of the Recast as a consequence of the widened formal scope (as article 25 applies irrespective of where the parties are domiciled). Interpretation of many matters are left to the CJEU, substantive elements like parties' consent however being submitted to conflict of laws of the forum seized, ultimately to be solved under the proper law of the contract.

It is comprehensible that any lack of legal certainty entails the risk of higher "transaction costs". These costs, however, tend to be hard to calculate: as legal costs in itself cannot provide for any jurisdiction rule or choice of court agreement these legal costs usually remain below the surface. A scan of Private International Law sources (PhD research, monographs, etc.) demonstrates that often costs are hard to unravel and attribute to courts. Versatile cost "categories" may even urge the plaintiff to initiate proceedings in different courts (forum chosen, or *forum derogatum*),[33] a concentration of dispute adjudication not always being possible A scan of "law & economics" related materials however does not provide for cost-related "data". Currently there are no legislative initiatives (pending). One may well ask to which extent this issue is still left to national law (of the Netherlands), given the widened, if not even potentially speaking unlimited formal scope of article 25 Recast (which applies irrespective of where the parties are domiciled) in conjunction with the Hague Convention on choice of courts. This ongoing process of internationalization is reflected by the Netherlands legislator's policy to regulate national civil procedural law in accordance with EU law and international conventions to the extent possible.

References

Kuijpers PHL (2008) Forumkeuze in het Nederlandse Internationaal Privaatrecht. Dissertation, Leiden University

Lewin GCC (2016) Interregionaal privaatrecht. MAKLU, Antwerp

[33]Kuijpers does refer to costs in Section 10.5.3 extensively, and further, on the occasion, in respect of e.g. court fees, p. 51; travelling and stay expenses of lawyers, p. 59; the weighing of (additional) costs in relation to the claim, p. 60; showing as defendant without contesting the court's competence, p. 223; procedural costs to be distinguished from civil claims resulting from a breach of choice of court agreement, pp. 242 and 243; the procedural costs in a strict sense (article 237 of the Dutch Civil Code on procedural law), to be paid according to certain standards (*barema's*), p. 265, and to be distinguished from other expenses ("*buitengerechtelijke kosten*", article 6:96 subsection 2 of the Dutch Civil Code) to be lodged in the court chosen, p. 263 and, as a consequence of its contractual nature, to be paid in full, p. 264; claims for breaking a choice of court agreement however to be lodged in in the *forum derogatum*, p. 263.

Lock FPJ (2011) Burgerlijk procesrecht in de Nederlandse Antillen en Aruba. Tijdschrift voor Civiele Rechtspleging 1:31–40
Strikwerda L (2015a) De overeenkomst in het IPR, 4th edn. MAKLU, Antwerp
Strikwerda L (2015b) Inleiding tot het Nederlandse Internationaal privaatrecht. Wolters-Kluwer, Deventer

Stephan F. G. Rammeloo is Associate Professor of Private International Law, Comparative Company Law, International Commercial Arbitration and Litigation at Maastricht University. Prior to his promotion to Associate Professor, he was Lecturer in Law at Maastricht University from 1992 to 2001. From 1986 to 1989, he was Assistant Professor at the University of Groningen, during which time he conducted research at the Max Planck Institut für ausländisches und internationales Privat- und Wirtschaftsrecht, in Hamburg. He worked as research assistant at the TMC Asser-Institute of International and European law (1989–1990) and the University of Groningen (1990–1991). From 2005 to 2010, he was the Managing Director of a one year postgraduate course in European and International Law Magister Iuris Commune (MIC), and from 2008 to 2012, he was a member of the Grotius Lawyers Consortium Academy, in the Netherlands. From 2008 onwards he lectured as flying staff professor at CESL/CUPL Beijing, China.

Romania: Interpretation and Effects of Optional Jurisdiction Agreements in International Disputes

Elena-Alina Oprea

1 Introductory Aspects

The parties' freedom to select the competent court is a clear expression of the party autonomy principle in international contracts. Widely recognised by and beyond the European Union (EU) Member States, it presents incontestable advantages: the designation of the competent court(s) for actual or future disputes ensures a welcomed predictability in the field and satisfies objectives of convenience or particular professionalism, sought by the parties.

In the European Union's Member States, the utilisation of jurisdiction agreements for international business disputes was encouraged by the adoption of the Brussels Convention on Jurisdiction and the Enforcement of Judgments in Civil and Commercial Matters (1968),[1] transformed into the Regulation (EC) no 44/2001 (Brussels I),[2] which was later reformed and replaced by the Regulation (EU) no 1215/2012 (Brussels I bis).[3] Within these instruments, Article 17 of the Convention, which became Article 23 and subsequently Article 25 in the Regulations, has acknowledged in very flexible conditions the enforceability of these agreements for cross-

[1] *Convention on Jurisdiction and the Enforcement of Judgments in Civil and Commercial Matters of 27 September 1968* [1998] OJ C27/01 (Brussels Convention).

[2] *Regulation (EC) no 44/2001 of 22 December 2000 on Jurisdiction and the Recognition and Enforcement of Judgments in Civil and Commercial Matters* [2001] OJ L12/1 (Brussels I Regulation).

[3] *Regulation (EU) no 1215/2012 of the European Parliament and of the Council of 12 December 2012 on Jurisdiction and the Recognition and Enforcement of Judgments in Civil and Commercial Matters* [2012] OJ L351/1 (Brussels I bis Regulation); it applies to proceedings instituted in the European Union Member States from 10th January 2015.

E.-A. Oprea (✉)
Babeş-Bolyai University, Faculty of Law, Private Law Department, Cluj-Napoca, Romania

M. Keyes (ed.), *Optional Choice of Court Agreements in Private International Law*, Ius Comparatum – Global Studies in Comparative Law 37,
https://doi.org/10.1007/978-3-030-23914-5_13

border commercial operations, when they select the jurisdiction of Member States' courts.[4] The autonomy recognized for the parties was at least as wide as that accepted in the field of arbitration, no connection being required between the dispute and the State of the elected forum.

1.1 Recent Changes and Influences

In Romania, the last decade has brought a series of important changes regarding the legal sources and, consequently, the legal treatment of choice of court agreements in international disputes.

1.1.1 The Regulations

In 2007, Romania became a Member State of the European Union; thereby the regime of choice of court agreements for disputes in civil and commercial matters started to be dictated by the Regulation no 44/2001. As from 10th January 2015 this was replaced by the Regulation no 1215/2012. Its provisions regulate the international jurisdiction of Member States' courts, including Romanian courts. In relations with Iceland, Norway and Switzerland, the provisions of the Lugano II Convention will apply.[5] The Regulation Brussels I bis establishes minimal provisions for the validity of jurisdiction agreements (in general). First, the European legislator has imposed a rule of a substantial nature, requiring the parties' consent as to the courts' competence to hear the disputes arising from a particular legal relationship.[6] For the formal validity of those agreements, it imposed strict requirements, the regime of which was carefully detailed and developed in the ECJ case-law.[7] The parties' freedom to contract about jurisdiction is limited in two ways: first, by the consecration of imperative criteria of exclusive jurisdiction (designed to protect important

[4]On these instruments, see Gaudemet-Tallon (2015), pp. 169 et seq., paras 153 et seq.; Magnus (2016), pp. 593 et seq.; Garcimartín (2015), pp. 277 et seq. See also Briggs (2008).

[5]*Lugano Convention on jurisdiction and the recognition and enforcement of judgments in civil and commercial matters*, JOUE 21.12.2007, L 339.

[6]In the case-law, see for example ECJ, Case C-543/10 *Refcomp SpA v Axa Corporate Solutions Assurance SA* [2013].

[7]The exhaustive character of the formal requirements stipulated in the Regulation results clearly from the ECJ's jurisprudence: often, the Court has stated that Member States do not enjoy the freedom to dictate formal validity requirements supplementary to those provided in Article 25 of the Brussels I bis Regulation (ex Art. 17 Brussels Convention, Art. 23 Brussels I Regulation). See for example, ECJ, Case 150/80 *Elefanten Schuh v Jacqmain* [1981] paras 25–27; see also ECJ, Case 159/97 *Trasporti Castelletti Spedizioni Internazionali SpA v Hugo Trumpy SpA* [1999] para 38. Oprea (2017).

State interests)[8] and secondly, by the consecration of special jurisdictional rules designed to protect weaker parties (employees, consumers, insured persons) in international disputes.[9]

The EU Member States are not free to supplement or modify through internal norms the solutions provided by the Regulation as regards the existence of the agreement or the formal validity requirements. Notwithstanding, because the Regulation cannot solve every problem related to the validity of jurisdiction agreements, the intervention of national law is not entirely forbidden. Under the Brussels I Regulation's empire, a question has arisen on how to proceed in case of substantial aspects of validity (like lack of capacity or vitiated consent), for which the judicial text did not provide a solution.[10] Completing the existing blank in the Brussels Convention and in the Brussels I Regulation, Article 25 of the Brussels I bis Regulation nowadays provides that the substantial validity of choice of court agreements has to be established according to the law of the Member State whose courts were chosen (including its conflict of laws rules).[11]

1.1.2 The Hague Convention

In 2009, the European Union—covering all Member States except Denmark—signed The Hague Convention on Choice of Court Agreements, which came into effect in October 2015.[12] As an EU Member State, Romania became bound by this instrument. In business-to-business disputes regarding the contracting members of the Convention (but not in those regarding the Member States of the European Union), its provisions on exclusive choice of court agreements shall prevail.[13] The Convention is not applicable, notably, to jurisdiction agreements concerning consumer and employment contracts, liability for marine pollution, emergency towage and salvage, liability for nuclear damage, anti-trust (competition) matters, infringement of intellectual property rights, claims for personal injury brought by or on behalf of natural persons, and tort or delict claims for damage to tangible property that do not arise from a contractual relationship (art. 2).

[8]See Article 24 of the Brussels I bis Regulation.

[9]See Sections III, IV and V in the Brussels I bis Regulation.

[10]See Briggs (2008), paras 7.12 and 7.25. Also, Merrett (2009), p. 545.

[11]On this rule and the corresponding Recital 20 from the Preamble of Brussels I bis Regulation, see Herranz Ballesteros (2014), pp. 291 et seq.; Forner Delaygua (2015), pp. 394 et seq.

[12]*Hague Convention of 30 June 2005 on Choice of Court Agreements*, available on the site www.hcch.net. On 4 and 5 December 2014, the Council of the EU adopted the decision on the ratification, on behalf of the European Union, of The Hague Convention; on 1st October 2015, the Convention entered into force, being applicable now in all EU Member States, as well as in Mexico, Singapore and Montenegro. Denmark and United Kingdom also separately ratified the Convention.

[13]See Art. 1(1), Art. 2 (1) and (2), Art. 26(6)(a) of The Hague Convention.

1.1.3 The Civil Procedure Code

For the (rare) jurisdiction agreements excluded from the scope of these supranational instruments, the applicable norms can be found in the new Romanian Civil Procedure Code (CPC), article 1067 and the following.[14] The provisions of the Code are in line with the principles comprised in the New York Convention (to which Romania has been a contracting state since 1961), in the Brussels I bis Regulation, in the Hague Convention, and the Lugano Convention. In the previous Private International Law Act no 105/1992 (now repealed) the jurisdiction of the Romanian courts was not regulated solely through imperative and exclusive jurisdiction rules; nevertheless, texts regarding jurisdiction agreements were totally missing and, because of this, the parties faced great uncertainty.

In the Code, the Romanian legislator has opted for a liberal solution, expressly recognising the effectiveness of choice-of-court agreements in international disputes. The limitations imposed on the parties' autonomy regard the subject-matter of the dispute, which must concern patrimonial rights of which the parties can freely decide. The Code has set up provisions regarding only the admissibility conditions and the formal validity requirements of choice-of-court agreements; it is silent as to the substantive validity aspects and this allows controversies in the field.[15]

1.2 Forms of Jurisdiction Agreements

As an expression of the parties' freedom to contract, choice of court agreements can be drafted in extremely various ways. The classical and simplest version is the exclusive jurisdiction agreement: the parties designate a single court, exclusively competent to decide on all disputes regarding the validity, the interpretation, the performance and the termination of their contract.

---

[14]The Code entered into force on the 15th February 2013. On the new text, see Popovici (2013), pp. 81–98; Păncescu (2013), pp. 679 et seq.; Leş (2013), pp. 1351 et seq.

[15]Normally, the substantive validity requirements should be established according to the law designated by the Romanian private international law norms. Choice of court agreements are conventions generating obligations but, because they are expressly excluded from the scope of the Rome I Regulation (see Art. 1(2)(e), Heinze 2011, p. 586), the correlative private international law norms would be those established in the Civil Code for juridical acts (Art. 2637–2638). Nevertheless, a different position can also be sustained. Given the procedural effects of these agreements, they could be governed by the *lex fori* (normally applicable for procedural aspects); this solution is difficult to accept, since the *lex fori* will be applied not only to those procedural aspects, but specially to substantive aspects (like the existence of a real free and informed consent). The doctrine did not give a solution to this. In our opinion, a distinction must be made: for the strict procedural aspects, the *lex fori* should be applied and for purely substantive aspects, *lex obligations*. For the parties' legal capacity, *lex personalis* must apply.

Under the Anglo-American influence, more nuanced and complex jurisdiction agreements have emerged: the parties designate not one, but more courts as having jurisdiction for their possible disputes regarding a contract. Also known as multiple/optional forum selection clauses, these are frequently used in international contracts, for which the normal connections with multiple jurisdictions may harden an agreement on the exclusive competence of a single court. Their practical advantages (as compared with exclusive choice of court agreements) cannot be neglected. Depending on the object of the dispute and on the specific circumstances of the case, the parties may seise one court or another, whose jurisdiction was agreed in advance. Hence, such flexible clauses facilitate the judicial resolution of disputes, preventing possible tactical manoeuvres by one of the parties (like the movement of assets to a forum which was not designated) and avoiding some of the difficulties generated by the international circulation of judgments (the parties can seise directly the courts of the State where the assets on which the judgment will be enforced are located).

The legal provisions especially devoted to these optional choice of court agreements are not very consistent. In Romania, the legal sources to be taken into consideration for the establishment of optional choice of court agreements' effects are the European instruments and, eventually, the Code of Civil Procedure.[16] Since The Hague Convention on Choice of Court Agreements only applies to exclusive jurisdiction agreements,[17] it is not relevant to this discussion.

The following provides an overview of some essential issues regarding the admissibility and the obligatory and jurisdictional effects of non-exclusive jurisdiction agreements in international disputes in front of the Romanian courts, clarifying their regime and emphasizing the difficulties, the inconveniences and the uncertainties raised by the existing applicable norms. The preliminary observations on the characterisation of these agreements (Sect. 2) will be followed by an analysis of the requirements for their admissibility and validity (Sect. 3). Then, we will address the effects of such agreements—which is the most obscure aspect in practice and doctrine (Sect. 4), before turning to asymmetric jurisdiction agreements, a current theme of discussion in comparative law (Sect. 5).

[16] Since Romania is a Member State of the European Union, the direct applicability of Regulation 1215/2012 by the Romanian judges is uncontested (see also Art. 288 TFEU). Considering the principle of supremacy, the European law has priority of application for the disputes within its scope; more precisely, in the context analysed, the European law will be applied as regards the admissibility of a choice of court agreements (see ECJ, Case C-269/95 *Benincasa v Dentalkit Srl* [1997] para 25). The national law can be applied only as far as the Regulation is not materially and geographically applicable or when the European text expressly provides for its application.

[17] Art. 1(1) of The Hague Convention: "This Convention shall apply in international cases to exclusive choice of court agreements concluded in civil or commercial matters". Beaumont (2009), p. 134; Hartley and Dogauchi (2007), para 106. Optional and unilateral jurisdiction agreements are not within the scope of The Hague Convention.

2 Characterization of Jurisdiction Agreements

The classification of jurisdiction agreements as exclusive or optional is very important in practice. On the one hand, it may entail the application of different legal instruments[18]: for example, the 2005 Hague Convention only concerns exclusive choice of court agreements, while the Brussels I bis Regulation does not include such a delimitation. On the other hand, the legal treatment reserved by the governing instrument may differ for each type of agreement. For example, the Regulation—applicable both for exclusive and non-exclusive jurisdiction agreements—imposes in its Article 31(1) an exception to the regular *lis pendens* rule that only concerns jurisdiction based on exclusive jurisdiction agreements.[19] Finally, the implications of these agreements for the courts' competence (prorogation or derogation effect), respectively on the parties' rights and duties, are distinct. In case of exclusive choice of court agreements, the parties are bound to start proceedings before the single chosen court; any non-elected court must declare itself as not having jurisdiction. On the contrary, in case of optional choice of court agreements, the parties have (or sometimes only one of them has) the possibility to choose between more than one court[20]; the derogatory effect is much attenuated or even non-existent.

2.1 *Lex fori* Characterization

Normally, under Romanian law the characterization must be done according to *lex fori*; this comprises not only the national law, but also the principles and rules included in the international instruments to which Romania is party.

In international disputes, the point of departure in the determination of the nature of a choice of court agreement (as exclusive or not) is thus represented by the texts of the international instruments in force in Romania, that may offer helpful clarifications. Supplementary to this, the pertinent case-law and the general principles of contractual interpretation may also be consulted.

2.2 *Hague Convention*

The 2005 Hague Convention, applicable only to exclusive choice of court agreements, delineates its scope, offering a definition of exclusive choice of court agreements in Article 3(1)(a):

[18]Keyes and Marshall (2015), p. 349.

[19]See Keyes and Marshall (2015), p. 350; Ahmed (2017), p. 4.

[20]Keyes and Marshall (2015), pp. 350 et seq.

> "exclusive choice of court agreement" means an agreement concluded by two or more parties that meets the requirements of paragraph c) and designates, for the purpose of deciding disputes which have arisen or may arise in connection with a particular legal relationship, the courts of one Contracting State or one or more specific courts of one Contracting State to the exclusion of the jurisdiction of any other courts.[21]

Article 3(1)(b) provides further clarification, stating that "a choice of court agreement which designates the courts of one Contracting State or one or more specific courts of one Contracting State shall be deemed to be exclusive unless the parties have expressly provided otherwise".[22]

2.3 European Regulations

Article 25(1) of the Brussels I bis Regulation also stipulates that the jurisdiction of a court nominated by the parties "shall be exclusive unless the parties have agreed otherwise."

2.4 Rules of Interpretation

Although normally the law governing the agreement should be taken into consideration for its interpretation,[23] the courts consider this to be a factual question and follow the *lex fori* solutions (which governs the power of interpretation of the *forum* State courts). The European Court of Justice seems to indirectly validate this approach. For example, in *Powell Duffryn plc. v Wolfgang Petereit*,[24] the court affirms that "The question whether in the present case the clause conferring jurisdiction is to be regarded as having such an effect is a question of interpretation which is a matter for the national court to resolve"; it does not specify that the *lex contractus* should be considered in this respect.

---

[21]The other texts in the Convention were drafted taking into account this exclusive character of jurisdiction agreements. Article 5 stipulates that the court or courts of a contracting State designated in the exclusive choice of court agreement shall have jurisdiction and cannot decline to hear the case on the ground that the dispute should be solved by another (foreign) court. Also, according to Article 6, any non-chosen court shall suspend or dismiss proceedings to which an exclusive choice of court agreement applies. These later rules could not be applied in case of non-exclusive jurisdiction agreements.

[22]For details, see Hartley and Dogauchi (2007), paras 40, 47–48, and 104–105. Any agreement which does not exclude the jurisdiction of courts from all other states (excepting for the unique chosen court/courts of a contracting State) is regarded as non-exclusive, notwithstanding that the parties may have characterised their agreement as being exclusive or may have drafted their agreement as exclusive, but only for one party.

[23]See Magnus (2016), pp. 656–657, para 143.

[24]ECJ, Case 214/89 *Powell Duffryn plc v Wolfgang Petereit* [1992] para 33.

More importantly, the European Court has also tried to offer some indications, designed to reduce the inconveniences related to the existence of different principles of interpretation in the Member States[25] and starting to give shape to an autonomous interpretation method at the EU level. For example, in a case from 1978, the court stated that national courts should take into consideration "the letter and spirit of the clause conferring jurisdiction".[26] This autonomous method, which supports a uniform application of the Regulation in all Member States, should be favoured as much as possible.[27]

2.5 *Case-Law Precisions on the Definition of the Exclusive Choice of Court Agreements*

During its activity, the Court of Justice has indirectly provided guidance on the characterisation of exclusive choice of court agreements. According to the *Meeth v Glacetal* judgment,[28] the agreement will have an exclusive character if the jurisdiction of a court is established with the exclusion, in the relations between the parties, of the jurisdiction of all other (possible) competent courts. In its subsequent case-law, the ECJ has further refined this definition, insisting on the derogatory effect of this kind of agreement.[29]

In practice, the simplest situation is where the parties expressly provided for the "exclusive" jurisdiction of the designated court, whatever the wording used might be (for example, "in case of litigation, (1) the chosen court is the only one having jurisdiction, (2) the chosen court has exclusive jurisdiction, (3) it is possible to seise only the designated court").[30] Normally, the agreement must be respected and any departure from its terms (by approaching another court) represents an infringement that can be sanctioned.

However, the terms used by the parties are not always relevant. An agreement in which the parties mentioned some courts as having exclusive jurisdiction, but allowing variations depending on the subject matter of the dispute or depending on the procedural position of one of the parties is difficult to interpret as designating

[25]See for example ECJ, Case 387/98 *Coreck Maritime* [2000], on the precision required as to the identification of the chosen court.

[26]ECJ, Case 23/78 *Meeth v Glacetal Sarl* [1978] para 8.

[27]Magnus (2016), p. 656, para 143.

[28]ECJ, Case 23/78 *Meeth v Glacetal Sarl* [1978] para 5 final.

[29]ECJ, Case 24/76 *Estasis Salotti* [1976] para 7; ECJ, Case 25/76 *Segoura v Bonakdarian* [1976] para 6: "the effect of the conferment of jurisdiction by consent . . . is to exclude both the jurisdiction determined by the general principle laid down in Article 2 and the special jurisdictions provided for in Articles 5 and 6 of the Convention".

[30]Briggs (2008), pp. 110–111, para 4.09: "an agreement for the exclusive jurisdiction of a court is an agreement that the nominated court, and only the nominated court, will be seised with jurisdiction by whichever party takes the role of claimant".

exclusively a (single) court; the agreement itself leaves open the possibility of some parallel and strongly connected proceedings, brought before the courts of different States.[31] Nevertheless, this position is controversial[32] and, thus, the risk of legal uncertainty is present.

Some complications may also arise when the parties choose a court, but the wording of the agreement does not clearly indicate that this court has exclusive jurisdiction. The solution of "exclusivity", which can be supported by textual arguments, should be favoured. Article 25(1) Brussels I bis Regulation states that when the parties agreed on the jurisdiction of a court, "this jurisdiction is exclusive, unless the parties have agreed otherwise". In our opinion, this formulation is a simple presumption in favour of the exclusive character of the chosen court's jurisdiction[33] and the party who claims that this was not exclusive, must effectively prove the corresponding parties' (different) intention.

2.6 *The Optional Jurisdiction Agreement: Definition*

The category of optional choice of court agreements is larger. It could be delimitated in a negative way, as including all agreements by which the parties do not designate the exclusive jurisdiction of a single court for any disputes which have arisen or which may arise between them in connection with a particular legal relationship.[34] A positive definition could also be given, referring to all agreements by which the parties are designating more than one court as having jurisdiction to settle the disputes between them; at least one of the parties will have the possibility to seise a different court than the one expressly designated or one of the various designated courts.

---

[31] A similar interpretation is counseled as regards the 2005 Hague Convention: according to the Hartley and Dogauchi Report, "in order to be covered by the Convention, the agreement must be exclusive irrespective of the party bringing the proceedings" (para 106).

[32] See the position of ECJ in the *Meeth v Glacetal* judgment, in which the Court interpreted a reciprocal choice of court agreement, depending on which party was claimant, as being exclusive. See also Keyes and Marshall (2015), pp. 355–356, analysing the incertitude that exists about the possible qualification of non-unique jurisdiction agreements as exclusive.

[33] See Magnus (2016), p. 657, para 144. Contra: Briggs (2008), p. 115, para 4.16: "attempts to short-circuit the analysis of what the parties actually agreed with presumptions about what they must rationally have wanted, or must have understood about the nuances of meaning, are insecure and unreliable [...] The answer is that the court must ascertain the meaning of words used, assuming commercial sense on the part of contracting parties, and without undue assistance or presumption in favour of one or another conclusion: did they agree that the proceedings in question could or would not be brought?".

[34] The doctrine refers to the clauses that do not fit into the "fully, bilaterally and immediately exclusive type"—see Briggs (2008), p. 116, para 4.19.

The forms that these optional choice of courts agreements can take are not unitary.[35] The practice revealed the existence of *simple non-exclusive choice of court agreements* (through which the parties mention a single court that can be seised, but which will not enjoy exclusive jurisdiction[36]), *hybrid choice of court agreements* (which combine jurisdiction of State courts with the intervention of arbitrators or experts[37]), *multiple choice of court agreements* (in which the parties designate not one but more (alternative) competent courts, each of them being mentioned, or not, in the clause) or, finally, *asymmetric choice of court agreements*[38] (which stipulate in favour of one of the contracting parties—usually the one who drafted the contract or who is in a superior economical position—a wider freedom regarding the courts before which the proceedings can be brought).

3 Admissibility and Validity of the Optional Jurisdiction Agreements

3.1 Applicable Norms: lex fori

Taking into consideration their procedural effects, (optional) choice of court agreements are usually governed by the *lex fori* provisions, which include not only the national norms, but also the international instruments in force in the forum State. *Lex fori* establishes the conditions for the conventional extensions and limitations of the jurisdiction of the forum State's courts, the conditions for allowing (or not) the jurisdictional effects of the agreements and the extent of those effects (for example, the derogatory effect, the consequences over the derived jurisdiction).

In the EU Member States, Brussels I bis Regulation will prevail over Member States' corresponding rules for international disputes in civil and commercial matters,[39] even if those were of public order.[40] The European legislator's point of view on optional choice of court agreements is liberal: Article 25 of the Brussels I bis Regulation (as well as Article 23 of the Regulation 44/2001) states that the jurisdiction of the chosen court is exclusive "unless the parties have agreed otherwise". The legal text itself recognizes the parties' right to conclude optional choice of court

[35]Keyes and Marshall (2015), pp. 345–378; Draguiev (2014), p. 37.

[36]According to Briggs (2008), p. 111, para 4.09: "an agreement for non-exclusive jurisdiction of a court is an agreement that the nominated court may be seised with jurisdiction by which party is the claimant, but does not necessarily involve an immediate promise that no other court will be asked to exercise jurisdiction."

[37]For the resolution of the possible conflicts, see Garnett (2013), pp. 361 et seq.

[38]Asymmetrical jurisdiction agreements are frequent in banking contracts (but are not limited to this category)—Fentiman (2013), p. 24; Draguiev (2014), p. 23.

[39]The expression "civil and commercial matters" is to be interpreted according to the provisions of the Brussels I bis Regulation and to the ECJ's corresponding case-law.

[40]Magnus (2016), p. 597, para 14.

agreements for disputes that might arise between them.[41] A similar position is found in the Romanian Civil Procedure Code.[42]

The condition of the sufficient certainty as to the court or the courts agreed by the parties is fully applicable. On this point, the ECJ did not pretend, while applying the Brussels Convention or the Regulations, a precise identification of the chosen court (s) in the text of the agreement, being satisfied by objective elements that allow, based on the circumstances of the case, its determination (at the time of the dispute).[43]

The efficacy of optional choice of court agreements in the European area also militates in favour of ensuring legal certainty[44] and respecting the party autonomy principle, to which the European legislator is undoubtedly devoted[45] and which was carefully valued by the European Court of Justice.[46] In its case-law, relying precisely

---

[41]Magnus (2016), p. 657, para 144; Forner Delaygua (2015), p. 396.

[42]According to article 1068(1) CPC, in the absence of contrary stipulation, the jurisdiction agreement is exclusive. Hence, indirectly, the Code recognizes the efficacy of optional choice-of-court agreements. Parties are free to conclude a contract in which they stipulate through a jurisdiction agreement the competence of one or more courts in case of dispute, or the possibility of one party to sue in more than one country, while the other is bound by the jurisdiction of a single court.

[43]See the *Coreck* judgment (ECJ, C-387/98 [2000] para 15): "It follows that the words have agreed in the first sentence of the first paragraph of Article 17 of the Convention cannot be interpreted as meaning that it is necessary for a jurisdiction clause to be formulated in such a way that the competent court can be determined on its wording alone. It is sufficient that the clause states the objective factors on the basis of which the parties have agreed to choose a court or the courts to which they wish to submit disputes which have arisen or which may arise between them. Those factors, which must be sufficiently precise to enable the court seised to ascertain whether it has jurisdiction, may, where appropriate, be determined by the particular circumstances of the case". See also ECJ, C-222/15 *Hoszig* [2016] para 43: "As regards the precision of the content of a jurisdiction clause, in relation to determining a court or courts of a Member State to settle any disputes which have arisen or which may arise between the parties, the Court has held, with regard to Article 17 of the Brussels Convention, that the terms of that provision cannot be interpreted as meaning that it is necessary for such a clause to be formulated in such a way that the competent court can be determined on its wording alone. It is sufficient that the clause states the objective factors on the basis of which the parties have agreed to choose a court or the courts to which they wish to submit disputes which have arisen or which may arise between them. Those factors, which must be sufficiently precise to enable the court seised to ascertain whether it has jurisdiction, may, where appropriate, be determined by the particular circumstances of the case".

[44]ECJ, Case C-269/95 *Benincasa v Dentalkit Srl* [1997] para 29; ECJ, Case C-159/97 *Trasporti Castelletti* [1999] para 48.

[45]See, for example, the Recital 19 of the Preamble (having an identical correspondent in the Recital 14 of the Preamble of the Regulation 44/2001) stating that: "The autonomy of the parties to a contract, other than an insurance, consumer or employment contract, where only limited autonomy to determine the courts having jurisdiction is allowed, should be respected subject to the exclusive grounds of jurisdiction laid down in this Regulation".

[46]ECJ, Case 23/78 *Meeth v Glacetal Sarl* [1978] para 8; ECJ, Case 387/98 *Coreck Maritime* [2000] para 14: "if the purpose of Article 17 of the Convention is to protect the wishes of the parties concerned, it must be construed in a manner consistent with those wishes where they are established. Article 17 is based on a recognition of the independent will of the parties to a contract

on party autonomy, the ECJ validated for instance the reciprocal clauses—through which each party is obliged to seise only the courts of the Member State of its counter-party.[47] The text of the Brussels Convention (applicable in that case) spoke about the designation, by the parties, of the "court or the courts from *the Member State*" (in the singular, which formula was unchanged in the Regulations) and was somehow ambiguous. Very firm on its position, the Court eliminated possible doubts:

> the interpretation of that provision gives rise to difficulty because of the fact that Article 17, as it is worded, refers to the choice by the parties to the contract of a single court or the courts of a single State. That wording, which is based on the most widespread business practice, cannot, however, be interpreted as intending to exclude the right of the parties to agree on two or more courts for the purpose of settling any disputes which may arise. This interpretation is justified on the ground that Article 17 is based on a recognition of the independent will of the parties to a contract in deciding which courts are to have jurisdiction to settle disputes falling within the scope of the convention, other than those which are expressly excluded pursuant to the second paragraph of Article 17.[48]

3.2 *Possible Interference of the National Choice-of-Law Rules*

Despite this seemingly clear frame, an aspect which has to be discussed in this context concerns the possible intervention of the rule contained in Article 25(1) of the Brussels I bis Regulation, which states that the choice of court agreement's substantive validity is determined by the rules of the chosen court's State (including its conflict of law rules[49]). Although the problem of optional choice of court agreements does not concern at least at first sight the substantive validity of the agreement (its valid formation), but mainly its jurisdictional effect (the impact on the jurisdiction or lack of jurisdiction of a court), however, once with the French

---

in deciding which courts are to have jurisdiction to settle disputes falling within the scope of the Convention, other than those which are expressly excluded pursuant to the fourth paragraph of Article 17"; ECJ, Case 322/14 *El Majdoub* [2015] para 26: "the provisions of Article 23(1) of the Brussels I Regulation clearly indicate that its scope is limited to cases in which the parties have 'agreed' on a court. As appears from Recital 11 in the Preamble to that Regulation, it is that consensus between the parties which justifies the primacy granted, in the name of the principle of the freedom of choice, to the choice of a court other than that which may have had jurisdiction under that Regulation".

[47]ECJ, Case 23/78 *Meeth v Glacetal Sarl* [1978].

[48]ECJ, Case 23/78 *Meeth v Glacetal Sarl* [1978] para 5.

[49]See Recital 20 from the Preamble: "Where a question arises as to whether a choice-of-court agreement in favour of a court or the courts of a Member State is null and void as to its substantive validity, that question should be decided in accordance with the law of the Member State of the court or courts designated in the agreement, including the conflict-of-laws rules of that Member State". On this rule, see Forner Delaygua (2015), pp. 396 et seq.

Supreme Court's judgment in the *Rothschild* case[50]—invalidating a multiple asymmetrical choice of court agreement as being purely potestative—the discussions did not hesitate to appear.[51]

The arguments in favour of such a solution—applicability of the rules of the chosen court's State—are not missing. *Pure potestativity* concerns precisely the agreement's substantive validity (because *pure potestativity* equates with the absence of any commitment from the debtor); thus, the application of the national law could appear to be justified.

Nevertheless, in our opinion, this interference of national law might be actually avoided. Generally, committed to an application as uniform as possible of the European instruments, the European Court of Justice has tried in its case-law to limit this interference, promoting autonomous solutions and interpretations, based on the legal text, its purposes and system.[52] With the 1997 *Benincasa* judgment (raising issues of substantive validity), the Court of Justice has opened the way to an autonomous regulation of the choice of court agreements. In particular, the Court stated that the agreement was "validly concluded under the rules of the Convention" and that it was "governed by the provisions of the Convention"; the references to the national statutory provisions were rejected. The position has been confirmed later, for example in the *Casteletti* judgment: "the choice of court in a jurisdiction clause may be assessed only in the light of considerations connected with the requirements laid down in art. 17 of the Convention".[53]

Given the broad jurisprudential application of the Regulation to substantive aspects—like the parties' consent or the choice of court agreement's effect on third parties[54]—and the fact that the need for its uniform application in the European Area imposes a restrictive interpretation of the provisions referring to the national law, we believe that the problem of the admissibility of the potestative choice of court agreements should be governed exclusively by the provisions of the Regulation.[55] The ECJ case-law on the "agreement" and on the "effective consent" could be used with no difficulties to invalidate purely potestative agreements

---

[50]Cass. 1 Civ., 26th September 2012, *Ms X v Banque Privée Edmond de Rothschild*, No 11-26.022.

[51]See Scherer and Lange (2013), p. 1, evoking the solution of the applicability of the conflict of laws rules from the State of the designated court. See also Ancel et al. (2013), para 8; Ancel and Cuniberti (2013), p. 8; Forner Delaygua (2015), p. 395, who argues that the issue of unilateral/asymmetrical jurisdiction agreements should normally be placed into the "substantive validity" category; nevertheless, the author recognizes that, given the problems generated by this solution, a broader interpretation and a more extended application of the category "admissibility" are recommended, to cover also this type of clause (as for the admissibility of optional choice of court agreements).

[52]ECJ, Case C-269/95 *Benincasa v Dentalkit Srl* [1997]. See more recently ECJ, Case C-543/10 *Refcomp* [2013].

[53]ECJ, Case C-159/97 *Trasporti Casteletti* [1999] paras 49–52.

[54]On this, see Oprea (2016), pp. 33–46.

[55]Ancel et al. (2013), p. 5, para 8. These authors introduce a distinction: as long as the subject-matter of the dispute falls within the scope of the European Regulation and the parties choose through the clause courts from two or more Member States, this text should be taken into consideration. However, when the choice of court agreement does not concern the Member States'

(in which the real obligations/promises are missing).[56] The occidental doctrine is favourable to this interpretation. As professor U. Magnus mentions, after the *Rothschild* judgment, "a growing number of supporters favours the view that the Regulation contains an inherent competence to deny the validity of a jurisdiction agreement if the agreement constitutes a clear misuse by one party of the freedom granted by Article 25".[57]

Of course, in the absence of a clarifying intervention of the European Court of Justice on this point, the solution can still be discussed. It is not entirely clear if the implications of the eventual potestativity of jurisdiction agreements must be solved by using national law solutions or by taking into consideration the Regulation's provisions (on the basis of which a possible autonomous, unitary position could be formed). Thus, there is a significant risk that the different Member States' courts decide in a different way and sometimes invalidate the choice of court agreement, contradicting the parties' will. Also, the uncertainty as to the solution to be followed has a dissuasive effect on the professionals interested in the use of such agreements. Subsequently it may cause an increase in the price of credit, because of the risk that the agreement may be held invalid.

4 Effects of Optional Jurisdiction Agreements

More issues and uncertainties arise as regard the effects of optional jurisdiction agreements, which are insufficiently regulated in comparison with exclusive jurisdiction agreements.

---

courts, the application of the national law (the solutions from the Civil Procedure Code and the local case-law) could be taken into consideration.

[56]This is actually what the French Supreme Court tried to do in the *Rothschild* judgment: it justified its position not by applying directly the French national law, but by taking into consideration the objectives of the Regulation—see Ancel and Cuniberti (2013), p. 8.

[57]See Magnus (2016), p. 623, para 73. In another context, the same author argued that "a jurisdiction agreement lacks the necessary precision if the choice of the competent court is entirely left at the claimant option"— see Magnus (2016), p. 622, para 71 and the extra references cited by this author. See also Herranz Ballesteros (2014), pp. 302 et seq.: according to this author, the previous case-law of the CJEU retains its validity. In some cases, there are opinions of the CJEU touching not only the purely formal aspects, but also the substantive aspects (the existence of the agreement); so far as the procedural rules contained in the Regulation cover also the problem of the conclusion of the agreement (existence of a contract), there is no longer any need to apply national law. Hence, the problem of the potestativity of the agreement should not be considered to be covered by the reference to national law. Previously, the French doctrine sustained also a restrictive interpretation: a clause which would state in favour of a party an unlimited option/the possibility to seise any court could not be validated in the light of the Regulation—see Gaudemet-Tallon (2010), para 132: "Il faut quand même que la clause désigne directement ou permette indirectement de désigner le ou les tribunaux compétents: ainsi, une clause abandonnant à une partie le choix de n'importe quelle juridiction ne relève pas de l'Article 17 (C) ou 23 (R)".

4.1 Effects of Exclusive Jurisdiction Agreements

Regarding the courts' jurisdiction, exclusive choice of court agreements have a double effect (prorogation and derogation).

The chosen court will be competent to hear any disputes which have arisen or which could arise from the legal relationship in relation to which the choice of court agreement has been established. For this, the choice of court agreement must be validly stipulated and, particularly, must not contravene the Articles 15, 19, 23 (stipulating a set of special protective jurisdiction rules for disputes involving weaker parties) or 24 of the Regulation (which consecrates a set of mandatory rules of exclusive jurisdiction).[58] The Regulation confers a high level of protection on exclusive choice of court agreements in favour of Member States' courts. When the chosen court is approached by one of the parties, the court must accept jurisdiction (Article 25),[59] even in the event of a *lis pendens* situation (Article 31) and even if it would have lacked jurisdiction in the absence of the parties' agreement.[60]

Correlative to the effect of prorogation, exclusive choice of court agreements have also a derogatory effect: they exclude the jurisdiction of all courts other than the one designated by the parties. If contested, any court other than the designated one has to declare its lack of jurisdiction.[61] This negative (derogatory) effect is strongly protected also in the case of parallel proceedings. Although with the *Gasser* judgment,[62] the European Court of Justice undermined the efficacy of choice of court agreements, the European legislator instituted a new (special) rule in the Regulation 1215/2012 and the new Article 31(2) excepts exclusive choice of court agreements from the application of the general *lis pendens* rule. Consequently, the chosen court shall have priority to determine the validity of the jurisdiction agreement and, correlatively, to hear the case. Also, according to Article 31(3): "Where the court designated in the agreement has established jurisdiction in accordance with the agreement, any court of another Member State shall decline jurisdiction in favour of that court".

58See Art. 25(4) of the Regulation.

59In The Hague Convention, see Art. 5(2): "A court that has jurisdiction under paragraph 1 shall not decline to exercise jurisdiction on the ground that the dispute should be decided in a court of another State".

60Magnus (2016), p. 658, para 146; Garcimartín (2015), p. 301, para 9.84.

61On this, see Garcimartín (2015), p. 301, para 9.84. In The Hague Convention, Article 6 clearly states that: "A court of a Contracting State other than that of the chosen court shall suspend or dismiss proceedings to which an exclusive choice of court agreement applies unless…". The Brussels I bis Regulation is vaguer as regards this derogative effect, nuanced only as regards parallel proceedings: in fact, taking into account Article 31(2), a non-designated court must first stay proceedings (if requested and if the chosen court has been seised); it has to decline jurisdiction only when the designated court has accepted its jurisdiction.

62ECJ, Case C-116/02 *Gasser v MISAT* [2003].

4.2 *Effects of Optional Jurisdiction Agreements*

By comparison, the effects of optional choice of court agreements are not sufficiently clearly stipulated in the Brussels I bis Regulation, even if the Recital 19 of its Preamble provides, in a general way, that the parties' autonomy must be respected.

The Regulation does not provide a textual solution regarding expressly the effects of optional choice of court agreements. When delimitating such effects, some distinctions are to be made in practice, taking into consideration the effective drafting of the clauses. The law of obligations clearly influences the procedural solutions.

A. In a first hypothesis, the choice of court agreement may establish in a simple and reciprocal way, the non-exclusive jurisdiction of courts from a certain country ("for any disputes arising from the present contract, the parties can (also) seise the Romanian courts"[63]). Although there is no national case-law on the matter, we consider that the solution should be a nuanced one. The optional jurisdiction agreement implies that the precise determination of the (sole) court having jurisdiction to settle the dispute will be postponed until the moment when a party decides to seise a court.

4.2.1 Disputes Brought Before the Designated Court

Under the agreement, any party will have the freedom to seise the facultative designated court which will retain the case (if the agreement was validly drafted and is applicable to the merits of the dispute). The adequate valorisation of the parties' will and economic rationality requires that, from the time of the initiation of the proceedings, the designated and seised court remains the only one having jurisdiction. The agreement does not impose an obligation to the parties to address the designated courts, but just a possibility. When this possibility has in fact materialised (at the claimant's initiative), the defendant is bound to litigate in front of this court (otherwise being in breach of its own commitment). The parties' agreement in favour of the "chosen" court is conditional on the effective seisure of that court by the claimant; once the condition is fulfilled, the agreement becomes enforceable.

If one of the parties later seises a different court, not designated in the optional jurisdiction agreement, but whose competence could be based on the objective jurisdictional rules in force in the forum State, this court shall take into account not only its *lis pendens* norms when deciding eventually whether to decline

[63]The Hartley and Dogauchi Report (2007) offers two examples of such clauses: "The courts of State X shall have non-exclusive jurisdiction to hear proceedings under this contract"; "Proceedings under this contract may be brought before the courts of State X, but this shall not preclude proceedings before the courts of any other State having jurisdiction under its law" (para 109).

jurisdiction, but also the valid stipulation of the jurisdiction agreement and its proper utilisation in the court first seised.

4.2.2 Disputes Brought Before a Non-designated Court

By definition, optional choice of court agreements allow parties to bring action in front of court(s) other than the one designated; indirectly, the parties agree on the right to seise any other competent courts. If one of the parties (first) starts proceedings before a non-designated court, but having jurisdiction according to the objective jurisdiction norms, the optional forum selection agreement could not be validly invoked in order to oblige this non-designated court to decline jurisdiction, nor to sustain the priority of the designated court's competence. This interpretation is a consequence of the optional character of the chosen court's competence. In such a case, the parties' agreement is not breached. In fact, it just allows the parties to seise the designated court, without imposing an obligation (the jurisdiction agreement has only a prorogative, but not also a derogatory, effect). The plaintiff has the possibility to choose to start proceedings before the designated court or any other court having jurisdiction under the normal international civil procedure norms. The defendant could not object, nor is his renewed consent necessary for this.

B. A second hypothesis concerns jurisdiction agreements providing for the parties' freedom to seise two or more courts, which will be alternatively competent ("In case of litigation, the courts of Cluj-Napoca, Budapest or Prague shall have jurisdiction").[64] Regarding the effects of such agreements, the solutions are similar, but not identical to those presented above.

The parties (or the beneficiary of the option, in case of an optional unilateral agreement) have the freedom to bring proceedings in front of any of the designated courts, respecting, of course, the eventual limitations conventionally provided depending on the subject-matter of the dispute. To establish the beneficiary or beneficiaries of this freedom, the parties' will should be taken into consideration. If the jurisdiction agreement does not expressly provide that only one of the parties enjoys it, the benefit of the option shall belong to the claimant.

If the claimant seises one of the courts designated by the jurisdiction agreement, this will be fully operative and the seised court will retain the case (the prorogative effect is recognised). The claimant does nothing but profits from the agreement's provisions. The defendant will not be allowed to contest that court's competence, he must respect the claimant's option. The respondent's consent as to the jurisdiction of the seised court results from the choice of court agreement itself and his eventual opposition at the time of the litigation is irrelevant.

[64]For another example, see Hartley and Dogauchi Report (2007), para 109: "Proceedings under this contract may be brought before court A in State X or court B in State Y, to the exclusion of all other courts".

"The option" will operate for all possible aspects of the dispute. The claimant is not entitled to impose on the respondent a division of the litigation between several courts. The exercise of the option is definitive for the litigation in progress and once one of the designated courts has been seised, the plaintiff cannot reconsider his decision, which is treated as a renunciation of the other available options.[65] Once the option has been exercised, the jurisdiction of the court changes from optional to exclusive[66] and starting proceedings before another (designated) court will represent a breach of the commitment. Of course, in their contract, the parties could provide expressly that seising a court does not deprive them (or just one of them) of the right to seise a different court. In these cases, subject to the *lis pendens* provisions, the parties' will should be respected.

Normally, the parties to an optional jurisdiction agreement have not only rights, but some obligations also bind them. If the agreement is a closed one (as in the hypothetical clause under discussion), the claimant is obliged to start proceedings in one of the designated courts. Seising other courts, on which the parties did not agree, should be without effect. The optional jurisdiction agreement will have a derogatory effect, which the seised court will respect (if it is asked to).[67] If the jurisdiction agreement is opened, in a combination of the hypotheses A and B presented above, it will not have also a derogatory effect and thus the claimant enjoys the freedom to choose among one of the designated courts and any other competent court (according to the objective international jurisdiction rules).

4.3 *Optional Choice of Court Agreements Involving Presumptively Weaker Parties*

Inspired by the desire to prevent the detrimental effects that unfair choice of court agreements may have on presumptively weaker parties,[68] the European legislator has established derogatory rules in the field.

[65]This solution can be deduced from the interpretation of the legal provision of the Civil Code devoted to the alternative obligations—see Vasilescu (2017), p. 14; Pop et al. (2015), p. 457, para 408.

[66]See Draguiev (2014), p. 24: "The options 'crystallize' at this point and the sole, mandatory exclusive place for settlement of the dispute is reduced to the one where the claim has been brought".

[67]If the respondent appears before the court and pleads the case on its merits, he tacitly accepts a prorogation of the jurisdiction of the seised court (see Art. 26 of the Brussels I bis Regulation and the corresponding case-law of the ECJ).

[68]See ECJ, C-240/98 *Océano Grupo* [2004].

4.3.1 Non-exclusive Jurisdiction Agreements

In consumer contracts, jurisdiction agreements are only allowed in three particular situations,[69] one of which explicitly addresses the optional (and asymmetrical) choice of court agreement's situation. According to Article 19(2) of the Brussels I bis Regulation, derogations from the (otherwise mandatory) rules of jurisdiction are permitted only by conventions which allow "the consumer to bring proceedings in courts other than those indicated in this section". The "optional" nature of the jurisdiction conferred by the clause is obvious. The weaker party will enjoy the (possibly) additional options, without having limited the possibilities to bring proceedings in front of the courts already having jurisdiction (the courts of the State of their own domicile or the domicile of the professional, according to Article 18(1) of the Regulation).[70] If the clause confers "exclusive" jurisdiction on the courts of a particular Member State and deprives, in a correlative way, the weaker party of the jurisdictional options reserved by the legal texts, it will not be effective.

Similar provisions are also found for choice of court agreements in insurance[71] and employment[72] disputes. It is about establishing additional jurisdictional alternatives; if the jurisdiction agreement also seeks to limit the options of the vulnerable party (excluding the jurisdiction of some of the courts that could be seised), it will not be effective.[73]

---

[69]See Article 19(1) of the Regulation: The choice of court agreement is valid if (1) it is entered into after the dispute has arisen; 2) it gives the consumer additional options of courts having jurisdictions or 3) it designates as having jurisdiction the courts of the Member State in which both the consumer and the professional are habitually resident at the time of the conclusion of the agreement.

[70]Although national law may be applied to substantive issues, the intervention of some restrictive solutions (such as the one from French law), which would censor these optional clauses stipulated for the benefit of the consumer, would contradict the letter and spirit of the legal text (the admission of autonomy of will in a sense of favour, to facilitate the consumer's access to justice) and we do not believe that it can be accepted. However, the issue at stake is not of high importance here, because in practice this kind of clause will rarely be found in contracts (probably standardized and written by a professional, thus best suited to his own interests).

[71]Article 15(2) of the Brussels I bis Regulation validates choice of court agreements (prior to the occurrence of the dispute) when they "enable the policyholder, the insured or a beneficiary to bring proceedings in courts other than those indicated" by the protective rules of jurisdiction from Section 3.

[72]Article 23(2) of the Brussels I bis Regulation provides that the mandatory rules of jurisdiction established by the legislator may only be derogated from by agreements which allow "the employee to bring proceedings in courts other than those indicated in Section V of the Regulation".

[73]See indirectly the Jenard Report (1979), p. 33. See Heiss (2016), p. 429, para 1; Mankowski and Nielsen (2016), p. 522, paras 22–23; Esplugues Motta and Palao Moreno (2016), p. 557, para 8.

4.3.2 Exclusive Jurisdiction Agreements

Besides post-dispute jurisdiction agreements, to which the limitations described above do not apply, the European legislator provided, for consumer and insurance contracts, a number of special provisions which also permit pre-dispute *exclusive* choice of court agreements. Article 19(3) of the Brussels I bis Regulation recognizes the admissibility of choice of court agreements entered into between a consumer and a professional, both domiciled or habitually resident in the same Member State at the time of conclusion of the contract, and which confer jurisdiction on the courts of that Member State (provided that such an agreement is not contrary to the law of that Member State).[74] The rule is particularly advantageous for the professional, "protected" in the event of a change of domicile or residence of the consumer.[75] With this exclusive and symmetrical jurisdiction agreement, the professional can limit the options which the consumer normally enjoys in international disputes. Similarly, with respect to insurance disputes, Article 15(3) of the Brussels I bis Regulation admits jurisdiction agreements concluded before the dispute arose, between a policyholder and an insurer, both of whom are at the time of conclusion of the contract domiciled or habitually resident in the same Member State, and which have the effect of conferring jurisdiction on the courts of that Member State even if the harmful event were to occur abroad, provided that such an agreement is not contrary to the law of that Member State. This provision clearly benefits the insurer, who may limit the policyholder's legal options of jurisdiction.[76] Although in a conditional and restricted way, the EU legislator validates some exclusive jurisdiction agreements in the field.

4.4 Jurisdiction Agreements in Favour of Third States' Courts: Uncertainties

When analysing the effects of choice of courts agreements, a further, complex, factor should also be considered. If the efficacy of choice of court agreements (optional or not) in favour of the European Union's Member States' courts is governed by the rules of the Brussels I bis Regulation, the situation of optional choice of court agreements in favour of third-countries' courts is less clear and this may undermine their efficacy.

The European Union does not have the authority to regulate matters concerning the jurisdiction of courts located outside its borders, thus Article 25 of the Brussels I bis Regulation does not contain provisions regarding choice of court agreements in

[74] On this rule, see Mankowski and Nielsen (2016), pp. 524–528, paras 30–42.

[75] See Report Schlosser (1979), p. 119, para 161; Mankowski and Nielsen (2016), p. 527, para 37.

[76] Given the *Peloux v AXA* judgment (ECJ, Case C-112/03 [2005]), a jurisdiction agreement cannot have a detrimental effect against a third-party beneficiary.

favour of third countries' courts. However, because this kind of choice of court agreement (optional or not) may derogate from the jurisdiction of the Member States' courts, taking the European provisions into consideration, at least so far as the agreement's derogatory effect is concerned, seems perfectly justified.[77] In fact, in its 2012 *Mahamdia* judgment,[78] the European Court of Justice has declared ineffective a choice of court agreement in favour of a third State court, concluded in violation of Article 21 of Regulation 44/2001 (now Article 23 of Regulation 1215/2012). Thus, for the question of whether it is possible to derogate from the jurisdiction of some Member States' courts, the mandatory rules laid down by the Regulation as regards the exclusive jurisdiction criteria (Article 24) and the protection of vulnerable parties (Sections 3, 4 and 5 of the Regulation) should be clearly respected. A Member State court noting a violation of such rules should invalidate the jurisdiction agreement.

More complicated is the situation of choice of court agreements which do not violate those mandatory rules of jurisdiction. The difficulties are related to determining the exact role that the European law and Member States' laws should have in such situations.

In 2000, in its *Coreck* judgment,[79] the Court of Justice stated that Article 17 of the Brussels Convention (recognizing the parties' freedom to choose the competent court) applies only under a double condition—first, one party is domiciled in the territory of a Member State, second, the clause designates a court or courts of the Member States as having jurisdiction. When either of these is not fulfilled (in particular, when the clause designates the courts of a third State), the Member States' courts must assess the effectiveness of such a clause by applying their national rules of international civil procedure. A similar solution was indicated in the *Schlosser Report*: no provision of the Brussels Convention prevents Member States' courts from declaring their lack of jurisdiction in favour of the third states' courts chosen by the parties, the validity of the choice of court agreements being assessed on the basis of the national rules of international civil procedure.[80]

This position means, in particular, that the Romanian courts would be allowed to take into consideration Article 1068 CPC which permits the parties, in patrimonial matters, to conventionally designate the competent court to hear their disputes. This

[77]Taking into account the rules of international civil procedure of the Member State of the seised court would allow parties more easily to elude the mandatory rules of the Regulation, provided that the laws of the Member States (beyond the divergences between them) do not guarantee the same standards of protection. See Magnus (2016), p. 609, para 37.

[78]ECJ, Case C-154/11 *Mahamdia v Algeria* [2012]. Committed to the objective of ensuring proper access to justice for the weaker party, the Court decided that a jurisdiction agreement in favour of non-EU Member States' courts is admissible only when it complies with the requirements of the Regulation: it was stipulated for the benefit of the employee, it created additional jurisdictional alternatives for the employee and did not exclude the jurisdiction of the otherwise competent Member States' courts.

[79]ECJ, Case C-387/98 *Coreck* [2000], para 19.

[80]Schlosser (1979), para 176.

text is extremely permissive. The choice will lack effect only "if it abusively deprives of one of the parties of the protection ensured by a court designated by Romanian law", respectively when "the chosen court belongs to foreign country, while the Romanian courts enjoy exclusive jurisdiction". As a result, if the Romanian seised court is not (expressly or indirectly) designated and one of the parties objects to its jurisdiction,[81] the court will declare itself non-competent, since the choice of court agreement is licit.[82]

This solution, respecting the principles of international cooperation, was inspired by the desire to respect the parties' autonomy—the conventional designation of one or more (foreign) courts implies the parties' will to derogate from the jurisdiction of the unassigned courts. In our opinion, it should prevail in practice. In the same sense, arguing that there is no reason to accept the parties' autonomy only when they have agreed on the jurisdiction of Member States' courts, authors like Garcimartín[83] and Gaudemet-Tallon[84] clearly affirm that the derogatory effect of choice of court agreements in favour of third States' courts should be established in accordance with each Member State's rules of civil procedure.

This application of the Member States' international civil procedure laws is, nevertheless, controversial. For example, referring to the European Court of Justice's position in the *Mahamdia* judgment, Magnus considers that even though the parties have previously concluded a jurisdiction agreement in favour of a non-member State court, it is the Regulation (and not the national civil procedure rules) that should be generally considered to asses the efficacy of that agreement, when a Member State's court is seised.[85] In addition to the arguments of practicability and uniformity in the application of the Regulation, referred to by the reputed author, this last solution could be supported by some ECJ recent judgments.

In 2005, in the *Owusu* case,[86] the European Court of Justice stated, in very general terms, that the *forum actoris* rule (Article 2 Brussels Convention/Article 4 Brussels I bis Regulation) is mandatory in nature and there can be no derogation from the principle it lays down except in the cases expressly provided by the European instruments (para 37). Given the fact that Article 25 of the Brussels I bis Regulation governs (and declares admissible) only agreements that prorogate the jurisdiction of the Member States' courts, it may be concluded that choice of court agreements in favour of third States courts have no effect. A similar position could

---

[81]Not contesting the jurisdiction of the seised court is interpreted as a tacit acceptance of jurisdiction; the prorogation results from the procedural behaviour of the defendant—see Article 26 of the Regulation.

[82]See Fentiman (2010), p. 465; Dickinson (2010), p. 47.

[83]Garcimartín (2015), p. 280, para 9.13.

[84]Gaudemet-Tallon (2015), pp. 144–145, para 131.

[85]See Magnus (2016), p. 610, para 37a.

[86]ECJ, Case C-281/02 *Owusu* [2005] para 37.

be found, with direct focus on choice of court agreements, in the *Opinion 1/03*,[87] where the ECJ was consulted on the competence of the European authorities to negotiate and conclude a new Lugano (bis) Convention on jurisdiction and the recognition and enforcement of judgments in civil and commercial matters.[88] In the Court's opinion, a jurisdiction agreement in favour of a non-member State's court does not affect the jurisdiction of the Member State's courts in whose territory the defendant is domiciled (the situation would be different in case of a supranational instrument prevailing over the Regulation and expressly accepting a different solution). This position implies an extension of the role of the European law, detrimental to the national laws of civil procedure. If it should be followed, Article 1068 CPC, admitting the effectiveness of jurisdiction agreements, could no longer be applied by the Romanian courts when the defendant is domiciled in a Member State.

The existence of two different doctrinal positions illustrates the uncertainty existing in the matter (at least until the European Court of Justice expressly decides in favour of one of them). Because the parties' autonomy itself could be affected, it is regrettable that the European legislator did not clarify the situation, although the opportunities to do so were present in the context of the discussions on the reform of Regulation no 44/2001.[89]

4.5 *International lis pendens and Jurisdiction Agreements*

An analysis of the efficacy of jurisdiction agreements—exclusive or optional—requires also consideration of the provisions devoted to international *lis pendens*.

The European legislator consecrates a series of differences, not negligible, nuancing the effects of jurisdiction agreements as the parties have designated (and eventually seised) courts of the EU Member States or courts from third States.

These differences stem from the specificity of the European law-making power. Given the particular legal bases in the European treaties—now, Article 67(4) and Article 81(2)(a), (c) and (e) TFEU—and the corresponding transfer of sovereignty from the Member States to the Union, the European legislator set up strict rules managing parallel proceedings pending before different Member States' courts, designed to prevent the pronouncement of irreconcilable judgments (which could not freely circulate in the EU). On the contrary, although it has the prerogative to

[87]Opinion of the Court (Full Court) of 7 February 2006, *Competence of the Community to conclude the new Lugano Convention on jurisdiction and the recognition and enforcement of judgments in civil and commercial matters* (Opinion 1/03) (ECLI:EU:C:2006:81).

[88]See Para 153 final of the Opinion: "Thus, where the new Lugano Convention contains articles identical to Articles 22 and 23 of Regulation No 44/2001 and leads on that basis to selection as the appropriate forum of a court of a non-member country which is a party to that Convention, where the defendant is domiciled in a Member State, in the absence of the Convention, that latter State would be the appropriate forum, whereas under the Convention it is the non-member country".

[89]See Garcimartín (2015), p. 281, para 9.14.

establish rules of international civil procedure also for litigation not entirely linked with the European Union,[90] the European legislator cannot regulate directly the jurisdiction of non-EU States' courts and, as it will be seen, this affects directly the solutions for *lis pendens* cases and the treatment of (optional) choice of court agreements in *lis pendens* cases.

The provisions found in Article 29 and seq. of the Regulation require some short clarifications.

4.5.1 Parallel Proceedings Brought in Front of EU Member States' Courts and Exclusive Jurisdiction Agreements

If the *lis pendens* situation concerns disputes brought before courts of EU Member States (intra-European *lis pendens*), the Regulation retains as a matter of principle the *prior tempore* rule (the priority of the first seised court—Article 29). An identical solution was previously stated by the Regulation Brussels I, and in the *Gasser* case,[91] the ECJ decided that it should be respected even when the court second seised was designated in a choice of court agreement. Given the inconveniences caused by this solution—facilitation of procedural manoeuvres, undermining the overall effectiveness of choice of court agreements—the European legislator reconsidered it in 2012.

Nowadays, Article 31(2) of the Regulation Brussels I bis establishes a derogatory solution to the general rule, reinforcing the efficacy of exclusive choice of court agreements. The chosen court shall have priority in assessing the validity and effectiveness of the choice of court agreement; the court not designated (but first seised) will have to stay proceedings.

4.5.2 Parallel Proceedings Brought in Front of EU Member States' Courts and Optional Jurisdiction Agreements

Given the restrictive terms used by the legislator in the Article 31(2), it is clear that this text cannot be utilised if at least one of the courts simultaneously seised can declare its jurisdiction on the basis of a non-exclusive *bilateral* choice of court agreement.[92] When, under the provisions of an optional choice of court agreement, one of the parties has seised a Romanian court and the other seised a court of another Member State, the two parallel proceedings will be managed by applying Article

[90]See Opinion 1/03 from 7 February 2006 in which the ECJ recognized the exclusive competence of the EU for the conclusion of international agreements with third States in the field of jurisdiction, recognition and enforcement of judgments in civil and commercial matters.

[91]ECJ, Case C-116/02 *Gasser v MISAT* [2003].

[92]See Ratković and Zgrabljić Rotar (2013), pp. 261–263. Fentiman (2016), p. 716, para 10: although it does not expressly refer to procedures initiated under optional choice of court agreements, the rule contained in Article 29 of the Regulation is fully operational in their case.

29 of the Regulation.[93] The court second seised, even "designated" by the parties, is obliged to stay proceedings until the court first seised (designated or not in the choice of court agreement) rules on its own jurisdiction and, obviously, also on the effectiveness of the agreement. It will also be obliged to decline its jurisdiction in favour of the court first seised, who has established her jurisdiction (accepting the validity of the choice of court agreement by which it was designated or deciding that the choice of court agreement designating other courts is not valid or operative).[94] Considering the divergences of solutions existing nowadays in the Member States' legal systems as regards the effectiveness of optional jurisdiction agreements, this encourages the party willing to obtain a procedural advantage to approach its preferred court.[95] Also, with the priority given to the court first seised (and non-designated) to analyse the jurisdiction agreement and to determine its validity, party autonomy appears insufficiently protected in those cases.

Where the optional choice of court agreement is *unilateral*, providing, for litigation initiated by one of the parties, exclusive jurisdiction of a particular court, and for disputes initiated by the other party the optional jurisdiction of several courts, a controversy may arise as to the application of Article 29 or of Article 31(2) of the Regulation. Well known European authors consider that the rule established by Article 31(2) should be applied to protect the "exclusive" component of the agreement: if the party who has to expressly approach a certain court does not respect its commitment, the rule of the priority of the first seised court could be invoked by the beneficiary of the exclusivity.[96] This interpretation is able to limit the risk that the party who has accepted the "exclusivity" reconsiders its promise, by initiating proceedings in front of another court (torpedo claim). This interpretation, preferable in our opinion, remains to be confirmed by the European Court of Justice. Until an eventual clarifying decision, uncertainty persists along with all its related negative consequences, in particular dissuading the parties from entering these agreements and the facilitation of procedural manoeuvres.

4.5.3 Parallel Proceedings in Front of EU Member States' Courts and Third States' Courts

When parallel proceedings between the same parties, having the same cause and object, were initiated in a Member State and also in a third State, the EU Member States' (including Romanian) courts will apply the provisions of Article 33 of the

[93]On this rule, see Fentiman (2016), pp. 713 et seq.

[94]Magnus (2016), p. 665, para 163a.

[95]See Ahmed (2017), p. 19.

[96]Fentiman (2016), pp. 752–753, para 17. Contra Garcimartín (2015), p. 341, para 11.54.

Regulation,[97] which establishes only the possibility (and not the obligation) to stay the proceedings.

The conditions for staying the proceedings are strict and limitative. First, the EU Member State's court has to be able to establish its jurisdiction on the basis of Article 4 of the Regulation (the forum of the defendant's domicile) or of Articles 7, 8 or 9 of the Regulation (special jurisdiction criteria). On the contrary, if jurisdiction can be founded on the rules in Sections 3, 4 or 5 of the Regulation (jurisdiction in litigation involving vulnerable parties), on Article 24 (exclusive jurisdiction) or on the basis of Article 25 (choice of court agreement, exclusive or not), the EU Member States' courts are not allowed to stay the proceedings. A second condition must also be satisfied. The possibility of staying proceedings is admitted only if the proceedings in the third State were already started at the time of the seisure of the European State courts; if the EU Member State courts were seised first, Article 33 could not be used, and the proceedings must be continued.

If the foreign court has been seised on the basis of a choice of court agreement (exclusive or optional), the Member State's courts having jurisdiction under Article 4, 7, 8 or 9 of the Regulation, seised second, have the possibility to stay the proceedings.[98] The decision is influenced by the probability of recognition/enforcement of the foreign judgment in the forum State (a condition absent for intra-European *lis pendens* cases), respectively by the need of sound administration of justice.[99] In this context, Article 33 is truly useful, offering appropriate support and respect for the party autonomy principle.

If both the foreign court and the EU court were designated and seised on the basis of an optional choice of court agreement, Article 33 is not applicable (the jurisdiction of the EU court being based on the provisions of Article 25 of the Regulation) and an eventual stay of proceeding is not permitted. This solution seems contrary to the economic interests of the parties, as well as to the objective pursued by the Regulation—the prevention of contradictory judgments—and it should be rethought.

---

[97]The solution is a new one in Regulation 1215/2012. Before the entry into force of this text, Member States' courts took into consideration their own rules of international civil procedure [in Romania, Article 1075 CPC, on which see Păncescu 2013, pp. 696–697; Leş 2013, pp. 1359–1361; Deleanu et al. 2013, pp. 758–760, para 287].

[98]If the foreign (non-EU) judgment was pronounced and is likely to be recognized and enforced in the forum state, the EU seised court shall dismiss the proceedings—Art. 33(3) of the Regulation.

[99]See Article 33(1)(a), (b). See also Recital 24: "When taking into account the proper administration of justice, the court of the Member State concerned should assess all the circumstances of the case before it. Such circumstances may include connections between the facts of the case and the parties and the third State concerned, the stage to which the proceedings in the third State have progressed by the time proceedings are initiated in the court of the Member State and whether or not the court of the third State can be expected to give a judgment within a reasonable time. That assessment may also include consideration of the question whether the court of the third State has exclusive jurisdiction in the particular case in circumstances where a court of a Member State would have exclusive jurisdiction".

4.6 *Deficiency of Other Remedies Sustaining the Optional Choice of Court Agreements' Efficacy*

Beyond these limited rules, the (other) remedies that might ensure the optional choice of court agreements' efficacy—anti-suit injunctions or anti-enforcement injunctions, awards of damages or refusal of the circulation of judgments—are not necessarily very efficient.

4.6.1 No Availability of Anti-suit Injunctions or of Anti-enforcement Injunctions

The anti-suit injunction institution—an order addressed by a court to a person not to start or not to continue litigation in front of another forum—is not consecrated by the Romanian law. Thus, this kind of procedural instrument cannot be used to block the commencement or the continuation of proceedings abroad (in violation of a choice of court agreement). Moreover, particularly in the intra-European space, the European Court of Justice prohibits the practice of anti-suit injunctions, considered contrary to the principle of mutual trust between the Member States as regards their legal systems and judicial institutions, which inspires the European instruments.[100] The *Turner* judgment[101] did not expressly address the possibility of using an anti-suit injunction to sustain the efficacy of choice of court agreements, but the terms and arguments of the ECJ were sufficiently wide as to be able to limit the use of this instrument each time the dispute falls within the scope of the Regulation. Anti-enforcement injunctions—orders by which the court (or the arbitral tribunal) restrains a party to a choice of court agreement (or to an arbitration convention) from seeking recognition or enforcement in the forum State of a foreign judgment or arbitral award obtained in violation of this choice of court agreement/arbitration convention—cannot either be granted under Romanian law.

4.6.2 Award of Damages

The occidental doctrine (specially that belonging to *common law*) advanced the possibility of awarding damages to compensate the violation of the optional

[100]See ECJ, C-159/02 *Turner v Grovit* [2004]: "The Brussels Convention . . . is to be interpreted as precluding the grant of an injunction whereby a court of a Contracting State prohibits a party to proceedings pending before it from commencing or continuing legal proceedings before a court of another Contracting State, even where that party is acting in bad faith with a view to frustrating the existing proceedings". The *Turner* judgment was confirmed by the *West Tankers* judgment (ECJ, Case C-185/07 [2009]): the anti-suit injunction cannot be used in the European area to sustain the efficacy of an arbitration agreement.

[101]ECJ, Case C-159/02 *Turner v Grovit* [2004].

jurisdiction agreements by one of the parties.[102] The opportunity of this remedy has also been discussed by the Green Paper on the review of the Brussels I Regulation.[103] In Romania, the doctrine did not take a position on this issue, and there are no clarifying judgments to justify an eventual affirmative answer in the matter. Taking into consideration the fact that the choice of court agreement is an agreement concerning the procedural relationships between the parties and its effects regard basically the courts' jurisdiction or lack of jurisdiction (procedural effects), obtaining damages in case of breach should not be possible.[104]

More generally, in the light of the ECJ's arguments in the *Turner* case,[105] the award of damages by a Member State's court when, in breach of a choice of court agreement, one of the parties has brought proceedings in front of a Member State's court (which invalidated or considered as inoperative that choice of court agreement), would be inadmissible in the EU judicial area. It implies an indirect evaluation of the way in which the seised court established its jurisdiction and, thus, it contradicts directly the mutual trust principle.[106] According to the doctrine, derogation can nevertheless be envisaged. If (1) the award of damages was conventionally stipulated by the parties and (2) the seised court declared its lack of jurisdiction (validating the jurisdiction agreement), then another court could take into account these aspects—without impeding the right of the court initially seised to decide on its competence, which is forbidden by the ECJ—and the injured party could obtain compensation.[107]

4.6.3 Liberal Rules on the Circulation of Judgments and Limited Protection for Optional Jurisdiction Agreements

At the European Union level, the Brussels I bis Regulation establishes nowadays extremely liberal rules regarding the circulation of judgments of Member States' courts, in disputes in civil and commercial matters. The grounds for refusal of recognition and enforcement are provided in an extremely limitative manner.[108] The control of the competence of the court of origin is admissible only in exceptional circumstances and the eventual breach of a choice of court agreement does not appear among these. Even if the court of origin incorrectly evaluated the validity or

[102] See Magnus (2016), p. 666, para 166.

[103] *Green Paper on the review of Council Regulation (EC) no 44/2001 on jurisdiction and the recognition and enforcement of judgments in civil and commercial matters* (COM/2009/0175 final) para 3.

[104] Moreover, in case of optional choice of court agreements, the parties only establish the right for one or both parties to seise certain courts (and not also an obligation, whose violation could be sanctioned).

[105] ECJ, Case C-159/02 *Turner v Grovit* [2004].

[106] Cuniberti and Requejo (2010), pp. 15 et seq.

[107] See Cuniberti and Requejo (2010), p. 18.

[108] See Article 45 of the Brussel I bis Regulation.

the effects of an optional choice of court agreement which, consequently, was not respected, the judgment is entitled to freely circulate in the European space.[109] Special (and more protective) rules are devoted to judgments in disputes involving weaker parties.

If the judgment originates from a non-EU Member State and, consequently, does not benefit from the provisions of the Regulation no 1215/2012, the national rules of international civil procedure will be followed for its recognition and enforcement (in Romania, Article 1096 *et seq.* CPC[110]).

Among the recognition conditions, the legislator mentioned the competence of the court of origin, evaluated according to the law of the State of origin, and the absence of a (legal) exclusive jurisdiction of the Romanian courts.[111] The corresponding texts are interpreted restrictively. Thus, even if we could not identify any pertinent case law, the refusal of recognition or enforcement of a foreign judgment for the sole ground that the foreign court evaluated a choice of court agreement differently to how it would have been evaluated according to Romanian law is highly unlikely.

Additionally, it could be discussed if the international public policy exception (Article 1097(1)(a) CPC) might be utilized to block the circulation of a foreign judgment given in breach of an (optional) choice of court agreement. Once more, considering the extremely restrictive interpretation and application of this exception in practice—essentially, only to sanction the violation of principles of loyalty and justice, characteristic to the fundamental right to a fair trial—it is submitted that this mechanism cannot be used in this context. Moreover, Article 1098 CPC prohibits the examination on the merits of the foreign judgment; verifying the foreign court's treatment of an (optional) choice of court agreement would amount to such an appreciation on the merits and, thus, is inadmissible.

Given this general and liberal frame, a foreign judgment will freely circulate in Romania, despite the fact the foreign court of origin decided to ignore a jurisdiction agreement that Romanian courts would have recognised as valid or operative. The only effective tool to block this circulation is represented by Article 1097(1)(c) CPC, which states that the recognition of the foreign (non-European) judgment can be refused when "...the dispute has been decided between the same parties through a

[109]See Magnus (2016), p. 665, para 165. See also the *Gothaer* judgment (ECJ, Case C-456/11 [2012]), in which the Court of Justice of the European Union ruled that "Articles 32 and 33 of Regulation No 44/2001 must be interpreted as meaning that the court before which recognition is sought of a judgment by which a court of another Member State has declined jurisdiction on the basis of a jurisdiction clause is bound by the finding – made in the grounds of a judgment, which has since become final, declaring the action inadmissible – regarding the validity of that clause" (para 43).

[110]Given the fact that the 2005 Hague Convention only applies to the circulation of the judgments given by courts (of a Contracting State) designated in an exclusive choice of court agreement, it will not be applicable in the discussed situation.

[111]On these rules, see Păncescu (2013), pp. 734–741; Leş (2013), pp. 1378–1380; Deleanu et al. (2013), pp. 783–787, para 302.

judgment, even a non-definitive one, ruled by the Romanian courts, or the proceedings were already started in front of the Romanian courts at the time the foreign court has been seised". If this text might save the effects of an optional jurisdiction agreement, it may equally work against them, when the dispute was brought and continued in front of the Romanian courts in violation of that agreement.

5 Asymmetrical Jurisdiction Agreements

If bilateral jurisdiction agreements are more commonly utilized in practice, unilateral or asymmetrical jurisdiction agreements are not rare, either. These are characterised by the fact that one party enjoys a greater freedom than the other as regards the court/courts which can be seised; usually, one of the parties has the obligation to approach exclusively a certain court, while the other has several available alternatives.[112]

Asymmetrical jurisdiction agreements create greater flexibility and are likely to prevent the risks of a multiplication of litigation (on the merits and, subsequently, on the recognition of foreign judgments), in the case of an important displacement of the assets susceptible of an eventual forced execution or in the case of change of domicile/headquarters of the partner after the conclusion of the contract. These agreements are frequent in the finance domain; the standard clauses of the Loan Market Association recommend such a unilateral jurisdiction agreement, stipulating that the bank (the lender) reserves the right to approach any competent court with a claim to recover the borrowed money, while the client (the borrower) is entitled to approach exclusively the courts of the state from the bank's headquarters.

5.1 Asymmetric Jurisdiction Agreements in Contracts Between Professionals

5.1.1 Elusive Regulations

The European rules in the matter are elusive. EU Regulation no 1215/2012 does not directly address the effectiveness of asymmetric choice of court agreements in contracts between professionals, and their validity is difficult to substantiate from the terms of the legal text.

The 1968 Brussels Convention contained an Article 17(5), considered to be at the origin of unilateral/asymmetrical choice of court agreements. Normally, under Article 17(1) of Brussels Convention the choice-of-court agreement had to be "exclusive". However, Article 17(5) provided that when a choice of court agreement was concluded for the benefit of one of the parties, that party had the right to

[112] D'Avout (2015), p. 995.

approach any of the courts having jurisdiction by virtue of the Convention. Given this text, the admissibility of asymmetrical jurisdiction agreements was not seriously disputed.

In the Brussels I and Brussels I bis Regulations, this provision is not found anymore and the arguments for its deletion are not necessarily very apparent. Some authors explain the solution by the fact that the Regulations consecrated, as a general rule, the possibility of optional choice of court agreements (of which the asymmetrical choice of court agreements are a subcategory)[113] and thus, the stipulation of the older provision would have been redundant. A supplementary justification may reside in the fact that, although the European Court of Justice offered indications regarding the qualification of a choice of court agreement as being stipulated for the benefit of a single party,[114] Article 17(5) of the Convention was likely to generate incertitude and unpredictability (unwanted results, affecting the objectives followed by the European legislator).[115]

5.1.2 Disparities in Comparative Law

In the absence of clear provisions, the question whether unilateral/asymmetrical choice of court agreements are effective has not received a uniform solution in comparative law.[116]

English law is favourable to the full effect of these clauses.[117] The unilateral choice of court agreement which confers an advantage on one of the parties must be treated in the same way as any other contractual clause. It is not contradictory that, for a particular aspect of the contract (like the courts which can be seised in case of dispute), one of the parties enjoys a better position. On the contrary, these

---

[113]See Droz and Gaudemet-Tallon (2001), para 51.

[114]See ECJ, Case C-22/85 *Rudolf Anterist v Crédit Lyonnais* [1986] paras 14–15: "Since Article 17 of the convention embodies the principle of the parties' autonomy to determine the court or courts with jurisdiction, the third paragraph of that provision must be interpreted in such a way as to respect the parties' common intention when the contract was concluded. The common intention to confer an advantage on one of the parties must therefore be clear from the terms of the jurisdiction clause or from all the evidence to be found therein or from the circumstances in which the contract was concluded. . . . Clauses which expressly state the name of the party for whose benefit they were agreed and those which, whilst specifying the courts in which either party may sue the other, give one of them a wider choice of courts must be regarded as clauses whose wording shows that they were agreed for the exclusive benefit of one of the parties".

[115]See Magnus (2016), p. 659, para 148.

[116]See Keyes and Marshall (2015), pp. 366 et seq.; Draguiev (2014), p. 37.

[117]See, for example, judgments *NB Three Shipping Ltd v Harebell Shipping Ltd* [2005] 1 Lloyds Rep 509; *Law Debenture Trust Corp. PLC v. Elektrim Finance BV, Elektrim SA, Concord Trust* [2005] EWHC 1412 (Ch), *Mauritius Commercial Bank Ltd v Hestia Holdings Ltd & Sujana Universal Industries Ltd* [2013] EWHC 1328, cited by Keyes and Marshall (2015), pp. 373–377; Draguiev (2014), p. 26.

asymmetrical jurisdiction agreements serve economic purposes and, as a result of the autonomy of will, they can produce effects. A similar solution is found in Italy.[118]

On the contrary, the French case-law is more severe. In 2012, in the *Rothschild* judgment,[119] the French Court of Cassation refused the efficacy of a clause reserving the right for the bank to bring an action before the Courts of the client's domicile or before any other court of competent jurisdiction. The argument invoked by the Court was the potestative character of the clause, considered contrary to Article 23 of Regulation no 44/2001.[120] The solution was confirmed in a judgment from 2015, *ICH c. Credit Suisse*,[121] but this time, indirectly, the Court accepted that an asymmetrical choice of court agreement might be declared valid if it mentions some objective elements that could ensure the predictability as regards the courts that might be approached by its beneficiary in case of dispute. In 2015, the French Court of Cassation pronounced a new decision, *Apple Sales international*,[122] validating an asymmetrical jurisdiction agreement. The indirect holding of the *Crédit Suisse* judgment was confirmed and a slight change of perspective was brought: asymmetrical choice of court agreements are not automatically invalidated given their asymmetry. Nevertheless, because in the particular case, the agreement was carefully drafted and limited in its scope, it is not obvious that the *Apple Sales* solution can be

[118]See Perrella and Massutti (2013), who evoke two recent decisions of the Court of Cassation (judgment 5705, 11th April 2012, Grinka in liquidazione v Intesa San Paolo, Simest, HSBC), respectively of the Court of Appeal of Milano (22nd of September 2010, Sportal Italia v Microsoft Corporation). See also Lupoi, in this collection.

[119]Cass 1 Civ, 26th September 2012, *Ms X v Banque Privée Edmond de Rothschild*, No 11-26.022.

[120]The relationship between the national law and the European law is not clear in the judgment. The Court refers to the object and the finalities of Article 23, but the solution is strongly influenced by the (domestic) French conception of potestativity. Despite the limitation contained (the bank could seise "any court having jurisdiction", and not any court in general), the clause in the litigation was widely interpreted and treated with high severity.

[121]Cass 1 Civ, 25th March 2015, *ICH v Crédit Suisse*, No 13-27264. In this decision, the Court of Cassation censored a decision of the Court of Appeal of Angers, which allowed the validity of a choice of court agreement stipulating the right of the bank to approach "any others courts having jurisdiction"; the invoked argument was that the Court of Appeal declared the clause as being valid without verifying if the imbalance invoked by ICH, caused by the fact that the agreement simply conferred on the bank the right to seise any court having jurisdiction, without any particular specification on the way to determine it, contravenes the objectives of predictability and legal certainty which inspire the Lugano Convention (applicable in the case). Although expressly invoked by the appellant, the argument of the potestative character of the jurisdiction clause, essential in the Rothschild judgment and which raised strong criticism, was deliberately avoided this time by the Court; it insisted on the lack of objective elements to determine the court having jurisdiction and on the fact that the imbalance which the asymmetrical jurisdiction agreement establishes is contrary to the objectives of the Lugano Convention.

[122]Cass 1 Civ, 7th October 2015, No 14-16.898. The asymmetrical jurisdiction agreement declaring that one of the parties enjoys "the right to institute proceedings against Reseller in the courts having jurisdiction in the place where Reseller has its seat or in any jurisdiction where a harm to A. is occurring" was validated. The argument was that this agreement made possible the identification of the courts that could be seised for eventual disputes between the parties regarding the performance or the interpretation of their contract and, thus, met the necessary requirement of predictability.

applied in future for any asymmetrical choice of court agreements (and specially those frequently used in the finance sector, providing the liberty for one of the parties to seise any competent court).

Despite these new clarifications, juridical incertitude is still present. The French judgments can be invoked as persuasive arguments also in disputes outside France and the efficacy of asymmetrical jurisdiction agreements becomes indirectly undermined throughout the European Union.[123] Also, the possibility of the invalidation in France of such agreements encourages the parties wishing to avoid their application to bring proceedings in this State. Correlatively, the risk of invalidation—and thus the risk for the "beneficiary" of pleading the case in front of other courts than those designated—will inform its business decisions, implying probably an increase in the price of credit.[124]

5.1.3 Romania

The Romanian case-law does not offer examples of cases discussing the efficacy of asymmetrical choice of court agreements in disputes between professionals and the doctrine also is silent on the matter.[125] Despite the fact that French case-law is frequently used as a guide by the doctrine and case-law of Romania, we do not believe that it should be followed in this specific aspect.

In fact, although the Brussels I bis Regulation does not contain provisions regarding asymmetrical choice of court agreements in contracts between professionals, neither does it provide (anywhere) that the parties to the jurisdiction agreement must enjoy the same rights and obligations. Since the disparity of rights and obligations has been freely agreed (sometimes probably in exchange for concessions regarding other contractual clauses), it should not be taken into account as a serious obstacle to the admission of the effectiveness of asymmetrical choice of court agreements.[126] Also, although the principle of nullity of the obligations assumed under a purely potestative condition is consecrated by the Romanian Law (Article 1043 of the Civil Code), it is very unlikely to be applied to jurisdiction agreements

[123]See for example Supreme Court of Bulgaria, judgment 71 from 2nd September 2011, Case 1193/2010, in which, with arguments similar to those in the *Rothschild* judgment, the court invalidated a mixed arbitration and jurisdiction agreement stipulated for the benefit of one of the contracting parties—case reported by Cuniberti (2012).

[124]Fentiman (2013), p. 27.

[125]For purely internal disputes, the situation is different, the admissibility of the asymmetrical jurisdiction agreements has been indirectly consecrated: see for example the High Court of Justice, decision no 4613 from 27th May 2011 reported in (2011) Dreptul 6: 221: "if the choice of court agreement was stipulated for the benefit of the claimant, it has the freedom to bring proceedings in front of the conventionally designated court or in front of any other legally competent court". In the doctrine, see Leş (2013), p. 211; Deleanu (2013), p. 677. There is no reason to believe that this position will not be followed in international cases.

[126]In general, arguing that asymmetrical jurisdiction agreements are compatible with the Brussels I bis Regulation's provisions, see Ahmed (2017), p. 16.

allowing one of the parties to choose between more (competent) courts. When the Civil Code sanctions the obligations assumed under a purely potestative condition, it does not impose, *per a contrario*, equal rights and obligations of the parties, but only aims to eliminate the arbitrary and discretionary power of one of them as regards its obligations and their performance.

Or, when one of the parties reserves its right to seise "any other competent court", it is more than questionable whether it enjoys effectively a discretionary power in the matter. In fact, determining the competent court will depend on the forum State's rules—in the European Union, the Regulation no 1215/2012, and in a non-EU State, its particular rules of international civil procedure. Even if the range of options may seem extremely wide, this is not really true. The claimant will not be able to seise any court in the world, but only the courts which, in the absence of any jurisdiction agreement, could have been seised anyway, on the basis of the objective jurisdictional rules.[127] In this interpretation, the claimant's commitment and the possibility of having the dispute settled by certain courts is not exclusively reliant on its own will. When the jurisdiction agreement allows one of the parties to seise some limited and precisely determined or determinable courts, the problem of potestativity can be avoided even more easily. The parties have expressly agreed the possibility of approaching those courts and the beneficiary has to act within the limits of that option (mixed condition): the right of the beneficiary of the option to seise a certain court does not depend on its discretionary will, but is objectively limited by the common will of the parties, previously expressed in the jurisdiction agreement and subject to the control of courts. This interpretation proposed by us remains nevertheless to be confirmed in practice.

5.2 Asymmetrical Jurisdiction Agreements in Disputes Involving Weak Parties

The Brussels I bis Regulation expressly addresses asymmetrical choice of court agreements included in contracts with vulnerable parties. These are validated, but only in particular circumstances, aiming to ensure that the weak parties' access to justice is not affected.[128]

Choice of court agreements concluded before the dispute arises are admissible only if they offer supplementary options of jurisdiction to the vulnerable party (supra

[127] Arguing that at the European Union level, an asymmetrical jurisdiction agreement stipulating one party's right to seise "any other court having jurisdiction" is not discretionary, because it permits with reasonable certainty and clarity an anticipative determination of the courts in front of which the proceedings may be brought, see Ahmed (2017), p. 13.

[128] See for example the Recital 18 of the Preamble of the Brussels I bis Regulation; see also the Jenard-Moller Report, para 60 (OJ 1990 C-189/77) and the Cruz-Real-Jenard Report, para 27 (OJ 1990 C-1 89/47).

Sect. 4.3).[129] These agreements are, of course, asymmetrical: they can be established only for the benefit of the consumer/employee/insured, only the weak party will be able to choose between the available courts—those provided by the Regulation or, in a supplementary way, by the jurisdiction agreement. On the contrary, the European legislator strictly limits the professional/employer/insurer's options. These parties are obliged to seise exclusively the Member State's courts of the vulnerable party's domicile[130] and a choice of court agreement providing something else would be ineffective (except when it was concluded after the occurrence of the dispute, or relates to the requirements of Articles 15(3) or 19(3) of the Regulation). An optional choice of court agreement opening jurisdictional alternatives for both the vulnerable party and the professional cannot be validly stipulated and invoked by the professional in order to derogate from the protective rules contained in Sections 3, 4 and 5 of the Brussels I bis Regulation.[131] For employment contracts, the European Court of Justice has expressly confirmed in its case-law that jurisdiction agreements are valid only if they stipulate additional options for the employee, without excluding the jurisdiction of the courts otherwise competent according to the objective jurisdictional rules.[132]

The asymmetry of jurisdiction agreements in contracts concluded with weaker parties is also consolidated by the *lis pendens* rules in the Regulation. Normally, as explained above, in case of the conventional prorogation of jurisdiction, the designated court has priority in deciding the validity of the jurisdiction agreement and the extent to which this applies in the case of the pending litigation before it, although another court from another Member State has been seised (Article 31(2) of the Regulation). In case of litigation involving vulnerable parties, the situation is

[129]See Article 15(2) for insurance contracts, Article 19(2) for consumer contracts, Article 23(2) for employment contracts.

[130]See Article 14 for insurance contracts, Article 18(2) for consumer contracts, Article 22(2) for employment contracts.

[131]See Bariatti (2015), p. 208, para 5.57 (insurance contracts); indirectly, Bonomi (2015), p. 236, para 6.85 (consumer contracts); Esplugues Motta and Palao Moreno (2016), p. 557, paras 6–8 (employment contracts); Mankowski and Nielsen (2016), pp. 516 and 522, paras 5 and 23; Lazic (2014), p. 111.

[132]See for example the ECJ, Case C-154/11 *Ahmed Mahamdia v Algeria* [2012]. In this judgment, in the light of the objective inspiring Section V, Chapter II of the Regulation—the protection of weaker parties—the Court considered, like the Advocate General, that the rule contained in Article 21(2) of the Regulation 44/2001 (Article 23(2) of the Brussels I bis Regulation) must "...be understood as meaning that such an agreement, concluded before the dispute arose, must confer jurisdiction over the action brought by the employee on courts additional to those provided for in Articles 18 and 19 of Regulation No 44/2001. The effect of the agreement is thus not to exclude the jurisdiction of the latter courts but to extend the employee's possibility of choosing between several courts with jurisdiction" (para 62). The Court took into consideration also the terms of the legal text, which validates only choice of court agreements allowing the employee to seise courts other than those provided by Section 5 of the Regulation and deduced that the related disposition "cannot be interpreted as meaning that a choice of court agreement may be applied exclusively and could therefore prohibit to the employee to seise the courts which have jurisdiction under the mentioned Articles 18 and 19" (para 63).

partially different. According to Article 31(4) of the Regulation, the (exceptional) rule of priority will not be followed when the claimant is the vulnerable party and the professional (defendant) tries to rely against it on a choice of court agreement stipulated in their contract (eventually in violation of the Regulation's mandatory provisions).[133] The *lis pendens* rule from Article 29—first come, first served—becomes fully operational and "reverse" torpedo actions detrimental to the weaker party are prevented. On the contrary, given the restrictive words of Article 31(4) of the Regulation, when the choice of court agreement is invoked by the vulnerable party, the non-chosen court, seised by the professional, has to stay proceedings and wait for the chosen court's decision on jurisdiction.

Finally, the asymmetrical effect of jurisdiction agreements in contracts concluded with weaker parties appears indirectly reinforced by the rules regarding the recognition and enforcement of judgments originating from other Member States. Article 45(3) of the Brussels I bis Regulation provides that the jurisdiction of the court of origin may be reviewed only in exceptional circumstances and Article 45(1)(e) precisely mentions among these the disputes in which weaker parties are defendant(s).[134] A judgment originating from a Member State's court, violating one of Articles 15(2), 19(2) or 23(2) of the Regulation, is not entitled to free circulation in the European Area. As was mentioned *supra* (Sect. 4.6.3), this is not the case for judgments in disputes between professionals and regarding asymmetrical jurisdiction agreements.

6 Final Remarks

While the occurrence of optional choice of court agreements is more and more frequent in practice, the related applicable norms are extremely summary. The freedom recognised to the parties in the field of jurisdiction is not accompanied by mechanisms able to ensure in an adequate manner the binding force of these agreements, whose admissibility and practical efficacy are subject to controversy.

The delimitation between exclusive and optional jurisdiction agreements is sometimes problematic, and this impacts negatively on the effective respect of the parties' will.

The optional jurisdiction agreements' effects are also insufficiently regulated. The existing rules in the European space for *lis pendens* situations are a solution, but not a panacea for the management of parallel proceedings. They do not guarantee the full respect of the parties' will, as expressed in the jurisdiction agreement, nor the elimination of parallel proceedings (with the inconveniences caused by these in

[133] Fentiman (2016), p. 750, para 7; Ratković and Zgrabljić Rotar (2013), p. 265.

[134] On this, see Mankowski (2016), pp. 932 et seq., paras 91 et seq.; Fitchen (2015), pp. 474 et seq., paras 13.372 et seq.

terms of additional costs for the parties and possible irreconcilable judgments), and encourage litigation.

Sometimes, the interpretation of the parties' agreement allows punctual solutions to the problems, but the fact that this is done in the context or with a direct application of the national law (substantial or procedural) impedes real uniformity in the EU Member States. Moreover, these solutions are not always unequivocal, which increases the risk that a court designated through an optional jurisdiction agreement (valid according to the standards of that court) to be deprived of the possibility to settle the dispute when the court first seised invalidated the agreement. This indicates not only an insufficient protection of the parties' will, but also support and encouragement for procedural strategies and manoeuvres. The legal incertitude is high and, correlatively, the cost of credit may rise.

At the EU level, an intervention of the European Court of Justice for the interpretation of Articles 25, 31 or 33 of the Brussels I bis Regulation might bring answers and partially clarify some of the existing difficulties. However, although the (supreme) courts from various European Member States have had the occasion to address preliminary questions on controversial aspects, in fact they did not consider necessary to proceed this way, so the state of incertitude and disparate solutions are perpetuated.

Of course, the best alternative would be the consecration of uniform norms (at European or supranational level) on the matter, but the correction of problems is taking time to materialize.[135] These uniform norms would simplify the reasoning and would bring the necessary certainty for the parties, would properly protect the autonomy of will and support procedural economy. In the European Union, the improvement might come with (1) clearer rules on the definition and effects of optional jurisdiction agreements, with (2) a more precise solution regarding the possibility to derogate the Brussels I bis Regulation's provisions by choice of court agreements in favour of non-Member States' courts, with (3) adapted and reconfigured provisions for extra-European *lis pendens* cases.

References

Ahmed M (2017) The legal regulation and enforcement of asymmetric jurisdiction agreements in the European Union. Eur Bus Law Rev 28(3):403–425

Ancel P, Cuniberti G (2013) One sided jurisdiction clauses – a Casenote on Rothschild. Journal des Tribunaux Luxemburg 1:7–12

Ancel ME, Marion L, Wynaendts L (2013) Reflections on one-sided jurisdiction clauses in international litigation (about the Rothschild decision, French Cour de cassation, 26 September 2012). Banque & Droit 2(148):3–9

[135] The recast of the Regulation no 44/2001 and the adoption of The Hague Convention were some missed opportunities to adopt such rules. Particularly, as regards the last instrument, Switzerland's proposal to include the unilateral choice of court agreements within the scope of the Convention was rejected during the diplomatic proceedings.

Bariatti S (2015) Jurisdiction in matters relating to insurance. In: Dickinson A, Lein E (eds) The Brussels I Regulation Recast. Oxford University Press, Oxford, pp 197–211
Beaumont P (2009) Hague Choice of Court Agreements Convention 2005: background, negotiations, analysis and current status. J Private Int Law 5(1):125–159
Bonomi A (2015) Jurisdiction over consumer contracts. In: Dickinson A, Lein E (eds) The Brussels I Regulation Recast. Oxford University Press, Oxford, pp 213–237
Briggs A (2008) Agreements on jurisdiction and choice of law. Oxford University Press, Oxford
Cuniberti G (2012) Bulgarian Court strikes down one-way jurisdiction clause, 13th November 2012. http://conflictoflaws.net. Accessed 10 Sept 2018
Cuniberti G, Requejo M (2010) La sanction des clauses d'élection de for par l'octroi de dommages et intérêts. ERA Forum 11:7–18
D'Avout L (2015) Pour une réhabilitation des clauses attributives de juridiction dissymétriques. JCP G 21:995–999
Deleanu I (2013) Tratat de procedură civilă, vol I. UJ, Bucuresti
Deleanu I, Mitea V, Deleanu S (2013) Tratat de procedură civilă, vol III. UJ, Bucuresti
Dickinson A (2010) Surveying the proposed Brussels I bis regulation-solid foundations but renovation needed. Yearb Private Int Law 12:247–309
Draguiev D (2014) Unilateral jurisdiction clauses: the case for invalidity, severability or enforceability. J Int Arbitration 31(1):19–46
Droz GAL, Gaudemet-Tallon H (2001) La transformation de la Convention de Bruxelles du 27 septembre 1968 en règlement du Conseil concernant la compétence judiciaire, la reconnaissance et exécution des décisions en matière civile et commerciale. Rev Crit DIP 90(4):601–652
Esplugues Motta C, Palao Moreno G (2016) Jurisdiction over individual contracts of employment. In: Magnus U, Mankowski P (eds) European commentaries on private international law, vol 1: Brussels I bis regulation. Otto Schmidt, Köln, pp 534–558
Fentiman R (2010) International Commercial Litigation. Oxford University Press, Oxford
Fentiman R (2013) Unilateral jurisdiction agreements in Europe. Cambridge Law J 72(1):24–27
Fentiman R (2016) Section 9: Lis pendens – related actions. In: Magnus U, Mankowski P (eds) European commentaries on private international law, vol 1: Brussels I bis regulation. Otto Schmidt, Köln, pp 712–778
Fitchen J (2015) The refusal of recognition and enforcement. In: Dickinson A, Lein E (eds) The Brussels I Regulation Recast. Oxford University Press, Oxford, pp 432–496
Forner Delaygua Q (2015) Changes to jurisdiction based on exclusive jurisdiction agreements under the Brussels I Regulation Recast. J Private Int Law 11(3):379–405
Garcimartín F (2015) Prorogation of jurisdiction. In: Dickinson A, Lein E (eds) The Brussels I Regulation Recast. Oxford University Press, Oxford, pp 277–306
Garnett R (2013) Coexisting and conflicting jurisdiction and arbitration clauses. J Private Int Law 9 (3):361–386
Gaudemet-Tallon H (2010) Compétence et exécution des judgements en Europe, 4th edn. LGDJ, Paris
Gaudemet-Tallon H (2015) Compétence et exécution des judgements en Europe, Matières civile et commerciale, 5th edn. LGDJ, Paris
Hartley T, Dogauchi M (2007) Explanatory report on the 2005 Hague Choice of Court Agreements Convention. HCCH Publications
Heinze C (2011) Choice of courts agreements, coordination of proceedings and provisional measures in the reform of the Brussels I Regulation. RabelsZ 75(3):581–618
Heiss H (2016) Jurisdiction in matters relating to insurance. In: Magnus U, Mankowski P (eds) European commentaries on private international law, vol 1: Brussels I bis Regulation. Otto Schmidt, Köln, pp 407–436
Herranz Ballesteros H (2014) The regime of party autonomy in the Brussels I Recast: the solutions adopted for agreements on jurisdiction. J Private Int Law 10(2):291–308

Jenard P (1979) Report on the Convention on jurisdiction and the enforcement of judgments in civil and commercial matters (Signed at Brussels, 27 September 1968). OJ C 59/1

Keyes M, Marshall BA (2015) Jurisdiction agreements: exclusive, optional and asymmetrical. J Private Int Law 11(3):345–378

Lazic V (2014) Procedural justice for 'Weaker Parties' in cross-border litigation under the EU Regulatory Scheme. Utrecht Law Rev 10(4):100–117

Leş I (2013) Noul cod de procedură civilă. Comentariu pe articole. CH Beck, Bucuresti

Magnus U (2016) Prorogation of jurisdiction. In: Magnus U, Mankowski P (eds) European commentaries on private international law, vol 1: Brussels Ibis Regulation – Commentary. Otto Schmidt, Köln, pp 583–669

Mankowski P (2016) Principle of non-review of jurisdiction of the court of origin. In: Magnus U, Mankowski P (eds) European commentaries on private international law, vol 1: Brussels I bis Regulation. Otto Schmidt, Köln, pp 928–953

Mankowski P, Nielsen P (2016) Jurisdiction over consumer contracts. In: Magnus U, Mankowski P (eds) European commentaries on private international law, vol 1: Brussels I bis Regulation. Otto Schmidt, Köln, pp 437–534

Merrett L (2009) Article 23 of the Brussels I Regulation: a comprehensive code for jurisdiction agreements. Int Comp Law Q 58:545–564

Oprea A (2016) Regards sur opposabilité à l'égard des tiers des conventions attributives de juridiction dans les litiges internationaux. Perspect Bus Law J 5(1):33–46

Oprea A (2017) Repères jurisprudentiels européens sur l'efficacité des conventions attributives de juridiction incluses dans les conditions générales d'affaires. Revue juridique Thémis de l'Université de Montreal 51:161–198

Păncescu FG (2013) Competenta internationala a instantelor romane. In: Boroi G (ed) Noul cod de procedură civilă. Comentariu pe articole, vol 2. Hamangiu, Bucuresti, pp 679–700

Perrella C, Massutti A (2013) Supreme Court considers unilateral jurisdiction clauses, International Law Office. http://www.internationallawoffice.com/Newsletters/Litigation/Italy/LS-Lexjus-Sinacta/Supreme-Court-considers-unilateral-jurisdiction-clauses. Accessed 10 Sept 2018

Pop L, Popa IF, Vidu SI (2015) Curs de drept civil. Obligațiile. UJ, Bucuresti

Popovici S (2013) Procesul civil international in reglementarea noului Cod de procedura civila. Partea I: Competenta internationala a instantelor romane (art. 1064–1069). Revista Romana de Drept al Afacerilor 5:81–98

Ratković T, Zgrabljić Rotar D (2013) Choice-of-court agreements under the Brussels I Regulation (Recast). J Private Int Law 9(2):245–268

Scherer M, Lange S (2013) The French Rothschild Case: a threat for unilateral dispute resolution clauses? 18th July 2013. http://kluwerarbitrationblog.com/2013/07/18/the-french-rothschild-case-a-threat-for-unilateral-dispute-resolution-clauses/. Accessed 10 Sept 2018

Schlosser P (1979) Report on the Convention on the Association of the Kingdom of Denmark, Ireland and the United Kingdom of Great Britain and Northern Ireland to the Convention on jurisdiction and the enforcement of judgments in civil and commercial matters and to the Protocol on its interpretation by the Court of Justice (Signed at Luxembourg, 9 October 1978). OJ C59/71

Vasilescu P (2017) Drept civil, Obligații. Hamangiu, Bucuresti

Elena-Alina Oprea is senior lecturer at Babeș-Bolyai University, Cluj-Napoca (Faculty of Law), where she teaches International Business Law, Internal and International Business Contracts, Private International Law. She graduated UBB Faculty of Law in 2003 and pursued her studies at Panthéon Assas University, obtaining a Master's degree in Private International Law and International Commercial Law (2004). She prepared her doctoral thesis—*European Union Law and Internationally Mandatory Rules*—under the supervision of emeritus professor Bernard Audit and since March 2011 she holds a PhD from Panthéon Assas University. She has authored a series of studies in the field of International Business Law and Private International Law, different manuals on Business Law and International Business Law and the monograph *Droit de l'Union européenne et lois de police* (L'Harmattan, 2015).

Singapore: A Mix of Traditional and New Rules

Adeline Chong

1 The Treatment of Choice of Court Agreements in General

Singapore law evinces a strong respect for choice of court agreements. The policy in favour of enforcing choice of court agreements as far as possible can be discerned when considering how Singapore courts deal with choice of court agreements in the jurisdictional context, both in terms of establishing the existence of jurisdiction and on the exercise of jurisdiction. This policy extends not just to exclusive choice of court agreements, but also optional choice of court agreements.[1] Further, legislative support for enforcing choice of court agreements is illustrated by the fact that Singapore signed up to the Hague Convention on Choice of Court Agreements 2005 ("HCCCA") on 25th March 2015. The HCCCA is implemented into Singapore law by the Choice of Court Agreements Act 2016 ("CCAA"),[2] which entered into force on 1st October 2016.

Choice of court agreements are normally categorised as being exclusive or non-exclusive in nature. Use of the terminology of "optional choice of court agreement" as a label for the latter type of agreement is uncommon in Singapore. In general terms, parties are free to contract for any jurisdiction of their choice. However, enforcement of the choice of court agreement must not be against the fundamental public policy of Singapore. For example, it is possible that a foreign

[1] "Jurisdiction agreements, though they may be [optional] in nature, should be respected and, when possible, upheld": *PT Jaya Putra Kundur Indah v Guthrie Overseas Investments Pte Ltd* [1996] SGHC 285, [64].

[2] Act No 14 of 2016.

A. Chong (✉)
Singapore Management University, School of Law, Singapore, Singapore
e-mail: adelinechong@smu.edu.sg

M. Keyes (ed.), *Optional Choice of Court Agreements in Private International Law*, Ius Comparatum – Global Studies in Comparative Law 37,
https://doi.org/10.1007/978-3-030-23914-5_14

choice of court agreement will be ignored if parties deliberately chose the foreign forum to evade the operation of the Unfair Contract Terms Act.[3]

Two recent developments have had an impact on the legal treatment of choice of court agreements. The first is the enactment of the HCCCA into Singapore law. The HCCCA has as its aim making exclusive choice of court agreements legally effective from the jurisdictional and recognition and enforcement of foreign judgments aspects. The second is the establishment of the Singapore International Commercial Court ("SICC") on 5th January 2015. The SICC is a division of the Singapore High Court[4] which specialises in actions which are international and commercial in nature. As will be seen below, traditional private international law rules are modified when there is a choice of court agreement, whether exclusive or optional in nature, in favour of the SICC.

While the Singapore courts do refer to decisions and developments in other countries, these tend to be English and Commonwealth authorities. The rules contained in the Brussels regime have not influenced Singapore law in any significant manner in this area of the law.[5]

2 Optional Choice of Court Agreements

2.1 *Legal Sources*

Statute and the common law are both relevant when one is trying to determine the effect of optional choice of court agreements. The relevant statutory provisions are mainly those which deal with the issue of the jurisdiction of the Singapore courts. Depending on how the optional choice of court agreement is construed, the Reciprocal Enforcement of Foreign Judgments Act[6] may also be relevant. It should be noted that Singapore did not avail itself of the option of extending the HCCCA to optional choice of court agreements.[7]

[3]Cap 396, 1994 Rev Ed. This Act offers protection against certain types of exclusion and limitation clauses.

[4]Unless the context provides otherwise, references to the "Singapore High Court" in this chapter should be taken as references to the Singapore High Court excluding the SICC.

[5]Although, similarly to procedural rules which implement the Brussels regime in the UK (Civil Procedure Rule 6.33(2)), no leave is required to serve a writ on a defendant abroad for a case commenced before the Singapore International Commercial Court (SICC) regime. It is unclear if the UK CPR provided the inspiration for this.

[6]Cap 265, 2001 Rev Ed. Specifically, section 5(3)(b) thereof. See below, text n 109 et seq.

[7]HCCCA, Article 22.

2.2 Applicable Law

At common law, the issue of whether a choice of court agreement is optional or exclusive in nature is one of construction of the agreement which is to be determined by the proper law of the contract.[8] In principle, the parties may choose one law to govern the choice of court agreement, and another law to govern the rest of the contract, but in practice this would be unusual. However, if this were to be the case, the proper law of the choice of court agreement would apply to determine whether the choice of court agreement is optional or exclusive in nature. The rest of the report proceeds on the assumption that the parties have not split the proper law in this manner.

Under Singapore law, there are three stages in determining what law governs a contract.[9] First, the court will determine if the parties have made an express choice of law. If there is no express choice, the court will see if any intention of the parties as to the governing law can be discerned by considering the circumstances of the case.[10] If no implied intention can be found, the court will lastly determine what is the law of closest connection to the contract.[11]

Where an express choice of law has been made, "it is virtually conclusive of the proper law governing the contract."[12] However, party autonomy is not unfettered: any choice cannot be contrary to public policy and must be *bona fide* and legal.[13] A choice is not *bona fide* when the parties have chosen a law solely to evade the provisions of another law.[14] Further, it should be noted that floating choice of law clauses are not valid as a matter of Singapore law.[15]

Singapore law could be the proper law of the contract on the basis of one of the three stages above and therefore applicable to the issue of construction of the choice

---

[8] *PT Jaya Putra Kundur Indah v Guthrie Overseas Investments Pte Ltd* [1996] SGHC 285, [62].

[9] *Pacific Recreation Pte Ltd v S Y Technology Inc* [2008] 2 SLR(R) 491.

[10] The list of factors was summarised in *Las Vegas Hilton Corp v Khoo Teng Hock Sunny* [1996] 2 SLR(R) 589, [39] as including: the language and terminology used, the form of documents involved in the transaction, whether there is any connection with a prior transaction, the currency of the contract or the currency for payment, the places of residence or business of the parties and the commercial purpose of the transaction.

[11] The factors that are considered at this third stage are the same as those considered in the search for an implied choice of law; however, while the weight attributed to specific factors may differ according to the context, equal weight is to be placed on all factors at the third stage. See *Pacific Recreation Pte Ltd v S Y Technology Inc* [2008] 2 SLR(R) 491, [48].

[12] *Peh Teck Quee v Bayerische Landesbank Girozentrale* [1999] 3 SLR(R) 842, [17].

[13] *Peh Teck Quee v Bayerische Landesbank Girozentrale* [1999] 3 SLR(R) 842, [12].

[14] *Peh Teck Quee v Bayerische Landesbank Girozentrale* [1999] 3 SLR(R) 842, [17].

[15] *Shanghai Turbo Enterprises Ltd v Liu Ming* [2018] SGHC 172, [31]; overruled on another point [2019] 1 SLR 779. It is ambiguous whether this is a statement of general principle applicable irrespective of the proper law's position on floating choice of law agreements, or confined to situations where Singapore law is the proper law of the contract: compare *Shanghai Turbo Enterprises Ltd v Liu Ming* [2018] SGHC 172, [31] and [52]. The former is more persuasive.

of court agreement. Alternatively, Singapore law could be the applicable law because no proof of the foreign proper law of the contract has been tendered by the parties.[16] If Singapore law were to be the applicable law, use of the word "exclusive" or "optional", as the case may be, is not necessarily determinative.[17] The Singapore courts' approach towards contractual construction in general is that while the text is of first importance, both the text and the context of the contract must be ascertained to determine the objective intentions of the parties.[18]

Special considerations arise if the choice of court agreement is in favour of the SICC, or if the choice of court agreement is one which falls within the scope of the CCAA. The approach taken under the SICC's rules and under the CCAA represent a departure from the common law approach, as both regimes rely on a presumption of exclusivity.

Section 18F of the Supreme Court of Judicature Act[19] provides:

(1) Subject to subsection (2), the parties to an agreement to submit to the jurisdiction of the Singapore International Commercial Court shall be considered to have agreed-

   (a) to submit to the exclusive jurisdiction of the Singapore International Commercial Court;
   (b) to carry out any judgment or order of the Singapore International Commercial Court without undue delay; and
   (c) to waive any recourse to any court or tribunal outside Singapore against any judgment or order of the Singapore International Commercial Court, and against the enforcement of such judgment or order, insofar as such recourse can be validly waived.

(2) Subsection (1)(*a*), (*b*) and (*c*) applies only if there is no express provision to the contrary in the agreement.

It is unclear whether the various presumptions set out in section 18F apply if the proper law of the contract is not Singapore law. In other words, is section 18F a forum mandatory rule? There are good grounds for arguing that the usual presumption against extraterritorial legislation is rebutted as the SICC deals with

[16]E.g., as in *Orchard Capital I Ltd v Ravindra Kumar Jhunjhunwala* [2012] 2 SLR 519. This is on the basis of the common law presumption of similarity between the *lex fori* and the applicable foreign law if the content of the latter law is not proven.

[17]In *PT Jaya Putra Kundur Indah v Guthrie Overseas Investments Pte Ltd* [1996] SGHC 285, the clause read: "Each of the parties to this Agreement hereby irrevocably and unconditionally submits to the exclusive jurisdiction of the District Courts of Central Jakarta but without prejudice to the right of any thereof to commence action or bring suit against each and every other party in any Court having Jurisdiction but for this Section.... In relation to any proceedings in Singapore, ...". The proper law of the agreement was Indonesian law but without helpful evidence on Indonesian law on construction of the agreement, the court proceeded on the basis that Indonesian law on construction of the agreement was the same as Singapore law. The High Court held that on normal Singapore principles of construction, the clause was an optional choice of court agreement. See [1996] SGHC 285, [61]–[63].

[18]*YES F&B Group Pte Ltd v Soup Restaurant Singapore Pte Ltd* [2015] 5 SLR 1187; *Yap Son On v Ding Pei Zhen* [2017] 1 SLR 219.

[19]Cap 322, Rev Ed 2007.

international cases.[20] Furthermore, this ties in with the situation when there is an overlap between the SICC and the CCAA. If the choice of court agreement falls within the scope of the CCAA, section 3(2) of the CCAA provides that the agreement is deemed to be exclusive unless the parties to the agreement expressly provide otherwise. Section 3(2) of the CCAA implements Article 3*b*) of the HCCCA which Singapore, by signing up to the HCCCA, is obliged to carry into effect. There is little doubt that the deeming provision of Article 3*b*) is intended to override the usual canons of construction. Section 3(2) of the CCAA is thus a forum mandatory rule. Hence, if the parties' choice of the SICC as the forum for dispute resolution falls within the scope of the CCAA, the presumption of exclusivity prevails regardless of the proper law of the contract.

Three points could be made which collectively set out a persuasive case that section 18F of the Supreme Court of Judicature Act ought to be construed as a forum mandatory rule: first, the presumption against extraterritorial application is rebutted as the SICC is set up to hear cases with international elements; secondly, Article 3*b*) of the HCCCA, which has been transposed into section 3(2) of the CCAA, provided the inspiration for section 18F(1)(*a*) of the Supreme Court of Judicature Act[21] and, as argued above, is itself a forum mandatory rule; and thirdly, this makes for consistency of approach between SICC/non-CCAA choice of court agreements and SICC/CCAA choice of court agreements. All of these agreements will be presumed to be exclusive regardless of the proper law of the contract.

However, the presumption of exclusivity will be rebutted under both the SICC and the CCAA regimes if the parties have expressly provided to the contrary. It has been argued that if the parties have expressly chosen another law to govern their contract, this would qualify as an express provision against the presumption of exclusivity of the forum.[22] The effect of the argument is that section 18F would remain applicable (on the assumption that it is a forum mandatory rule) if the parties have not expressly chosen a law to govern the contract and the proper law in the absence of an express choice, either on the basis that it is the parties' implied choice of law or the applicable law of the contract in the absence of choice, is the law of a foreign country. This is because proper laws derived in this manner could not be said to serve as "express provision(s) to the contrary" within the meaning of section 18F (2) of the Supreme Court of Judicature Act. The overall effect, that whether section 18F applies in a contract governed by a foreign law depends on whether the parties have expressly chosen that foreign proper law or not, is arguably rather mercurial. It cannot be justified as being in line with the SICC's ethos of championing party autonomy as the parties' implied choice of a foreign law, which is also an exercise in party autonomy, would not prevent section 18F from being superimposed onto the contract. It is submitted that the preferable view is that a clearer expression of dissent, rather than merely expressly choosing a foreign proper law, should be required to rebut the presumption.

[20] Yeo (2015), para 22.

[21] Yeo (2015), para 36.

[22] Yeo (2015), para 22.

Once it is determined that a choice of court agreement is optional in nature, its legal effect, in the sense of determining what the parties have agreed to, is determined by the proper law of the contract. However, the effect of an optional choice of court agreement on Singapore proceedings, whether Singapore is the named forum or not, is purely a procedural matter to be governed by the *lex fori*.[23]

2.3 *Optional Choice of Court Agreement for Singapore*

2.3.1 Singapore High Court (Not Including the Singapore International Commercial Court)

Non-SICC situations will first be considered as different rules apply when the choice of court agreement is for the SICC.

If there is an optional choice of court agreement in favour of Singapore, the courts have held that the parties are taken to have submitted to the jurisdiction of the Singapore courts.[24] This contractual submission, coupled with proper service of the Singapore writ, would found jurisdiction in the Singapore courts. If the choice of court agreement stipulates a method of service within Singapore, service in accordance with the contractual terms will confer jurisdiction on the Singapore courts.[25] If the choice of court agreement is silent on how service is to be effected or provides for a method of service outside of Singapore, leave will have to be obtained from the court to serve the writ on a defendant who is abroad.[26] The plaintiff will have to show[27]:

(a) a good arguable case[28] that his or her claim falls within one of the heads of Order 11 of the Rules of Court;
(b) a serious issue to be tried on the merits; and
(c) Singapore is *forum conveniens*.

[23] *Abdul Rashid bin Abdul Manaf v Hii Yii Ann* [2014] 4 SLR 1042, [12].

[24] *Astrata (Singapore) Pte Ltd v Portcullis Escrow Pte Ltd* [2011] 3 SLR 386.

[25] Rules of Court, Order 10, rule 3.

[26] Of course, service can be effected within Singapore if the defendant is present in Singapore, but the basis of service within jurisdiction in this instance will be the presence of the defendant and not the optional choice of court agreement.

[27] *Bradley Lomas Elektrolok Ltd v Colt Ventilation East Asia Pte Ltd* [1999] 3 SLR(R) 1156. The specific procedural rules are set out in the Rules of Court, Order 11, rule 2.

[28] This requires the applicant to have "the better of the argument": *Shanghai Turbo Enterprises Ltd v Liu Ming* [2019] 1 SLR 779, [49].

Order 11 rule 1(r)[29] and, specifically for contractual claims, rule (1)(d)(iv),[30] are the heads of Order 11 that can be relied upon by the plaintiff. The *forum conveniens* (and *forum non conveniens*) test which applies in Singapore is that set out in *Spiliada Maritime Corporation v Cansulex Ltd* ("*Spiliada*").[31]

The court retains a discretion to stay proceedings or to set aside service of a writ abroad even if it had assumed jurisdiction on the basis of an optional choice of court agreement in its favour. Until recently, the impact of an express or implied waiver of objection to the jurisdiction of the Singapore court in the choice of court agreement was unclear. *A fortiori* whether a waiver was to be presumed into the optional choice of court agreement. For example, in *Transocean Offshore International Ventures Ltd v Burgundy Global Exploration Corp*,[32] an optional choice of court agreement for Singapore which included an express waiver of objection[33] was held to be akin to an exclusive jurisdiction clause such that the defendant seeking a stay of the Singapore proceedings had to establish exceptional circumstances amounting to "strong cause" why he should be allowed to breach the agreement.[34] This is a higher threshold than the *Spiliada* test. However, the Singapore High Court in *UBS AG v Telesto Investments Ltd*[35] applied the *Spiliada* test to a similarly constituted agreement for Singapore which included an express waiver of objection to Singaporean proceedings. The court cautioned that the line between exclusive and optional choice of court agreements should not be blurred.[36] The balance of authority supported the *UBS AG* position, where the optional choice of court agreement is a factor to be weighed in determination of which is the "clearly and distinctly more appropriate forum."[37]

[29] "the claim is in respect of matters in which the defendant has submitted or agreed to submit to the jurisdiction of the Court".

[30] "the claim is brought to enforce, rescind, dissolve, annul or otherwise affect a contract, or to recover damages or obtain other relief in respect of the breach of a contract, being (in either case) a contract which . . . contains a term to the effect that that Court shall have jurisdiction to hear and determine any action in respect of the contract."

[31] [1987] AC 460. This test is elaborated below, see text to n 88 et seq. See also *JIO Minerals FZC v Mineral Enterprises Ltd* [2011] 1 SLR 391, [45]–[52], where the Court of Appeal rejected the Australian "clearly inappropriate forum" test.

[32] [2010] 2 SLR 821.

[33] The relevant sub-clause provided: "Each of the parties *irrevocably waives any objection* it may now or in the future have to the venue of any action or proceedings, and any claim it may now or in the future have that the action or proceeding has been brought in an inconvenient forum." See [2010] 2 SLR 821, [12] (emphasis in judgment).

[34] This test is elaborated below, see text to n 53–62. See also *Societe Generale v Tai Kee Sing @ Tai Hean Sing* [2003] SGHC 139 ("strong cause" test applied even though, from the face of the judgment, it appears that the clause did not include a waiver of objection to jurisdiction).

[35] [2011] 4 SLR 503.

[36] [2011] 4 SLR 503, [120].

[37] *Industrial & Commercial Bank Limited v Banco Ambrosiano Veneto S.P.A.* [2000] SGHC 188; *UBS AG v Telesto Investments Ltd* [2011] 4 SLR 503; *Dinesh Kishin Kikla v The Hong Kong and Shanghai Banking Corporation Ltd* [2013] SGHCR 06 (High Court Registry). In *Asia-Pacific*

However, the law in this area has been revised by the recent decision of the Court of Appeal in *Shanghai Turbo Enterprises Ltd v Liu Ming* ("*Shanghai Turbo*").[38] The optional choice of court agreement was in these terms: "[E]ach of the parties hereto submits to the non-exclusive jurisdiction of the Courts of Singapore/or People's Republic of China." The Court of Appeal held that where the proper law of the contract is Singapore law and Singapore is a named forum in the optional choice of court agreement, the defendant must show "strong cause" why he should not be bound to his contractual agreement to submit to the Singapore court's jurisdiction. This means that a presumption that the parties have agreed not to object to the exercise of jurisdiction by the Singapore court will be read into the agreement.

In holding that the "strong cause" test applies to optional choice of court agreements for the Singapore court, the Court of Appeal in *Shanghai Turbo* has clarified the state of the Singapore law on this issue. The court's position in *Shanghai Turbo* can be contrasted with its earlier decision in *Orchard Capital I Ltd v Ravindra Kumar Jhunjhunwala* ("*Orchard Capital*").[39] Drawing on work done by Professor Yeo Tiong Min,[40] the Court of Appeal in *Orchard Capital* had canvassed two possible strands of analysis that could be taken in relation to optional choice of court agreements. First, a contractual analysis could be taken where it could be implied that the parties had undertook that the chosen court is the *most appropriate* forum so that it would be a breach of contract for one of the parties to argue that some other court should hear the case.[41] The second strand of analysis is general in nature: an optional choice of court agreement is a factor to be applied *in all cases* pursuant to the *Spiliada* principles.[42] Under the general analysis, the weight to be attached to the optional choice of court agreement would depend on the facts and circumstances concerned; there was "no magic formula as such".[43] The court in *Orchard Capital* appeared to prefer the second strand of analysis, noting that the contractual approach may be impractical to apply at an interlocutory stage and could lead to uncertainty.[44] While it could be said that the contractual approach is a principled one, it ran the risk

Ventures II Ltd v PT Intimutiara Basindo [2001] 2 SLR(R) 371, [22] the court cited *Dicey and Morris on the Conflict of Laws* (13th ed, 2000) to the effect that pursuant to the test in *Spiliada*, in principle, it is not open to either party to object to the court's exercise of its jurisdiction on grounds which should have been foreseeable when the agreement was made. However, the court did not appear to apply this prohibition in its analysis of the facts.

[38] [2019] 1 SLR 779.

[39] [2012] 2 SLR 519.

[40] Yeo (2005).

[41] The Court of Appeal cautioned that it by no means wholeheartedly accepted the contractual approach: [2012] 2 SLR 519, [26].

[42] Emphasis in original: [2012] 2 SLR 519, [25].

[43] [2012] 2 SLR 519, [31].

[44] The court also did not have to grapple with the contractual analysis as it had not been raised by the parties, and further, the court held that the parties had not intended the particular agreement in the case to have a significant effect: see [2012] 2 SLR 519, [27].

of effacing the distinction between optional and exclusive choice of court agreements.[45]

However, in *Shanghai Turbo*, it is clearly the case that the Court of Appeal embraced the contractual strand of analysis. It observed that the court in *Orchard Capital* did not have to decide whether the contractual strand ought to apply as it had not been raised by the parties[46] but that the very issue was presently before the court.[47] It held that the meaning of the word "submit" in the optional choice of court agreement is that "the parties consent to the *exercise* of jurisdiction by the courts of that forum and waive any objection thereto…".[48] Five points ought to be noted. First, despite the focus on the word "submit" in the clause at hand, the court referred to a number of English cases where the optional choice of court agreements were variously worded in support of its decision. Thus, it appears that the presumption of a waiver of objection will apply even if the optional choice of court agreement does not expressly refer to the parties "submitting" to the jurisdiction of the Singapore court.[49] Secondly, the court adopted the contractual strand of analysis notwithstanding that the clause concerned was an optional choice of court agreement which named another court in addition to the Singapore court. Thus, the court stated that any challenge to the exercise of jurisdiction of the Singapore court, whether in the context of an application to set aside an order granting the plaintiff leave to serve the writ out of jurisdiction, or to stay the Singapore proceedings in favour of proceedings abroad would require the defendant to show "strong cause" why he ought to be allowed to break the contractual bargain. Significantly, the court stated that this is so even if the defendant applies to stay the proceedings in favour of a jurisdiction which is also named in the optional choice of court agreement.[50] Thirdly, the court noted that its analysis only applied to "paradigmatic" optional choice of court agreements such as that in the present case and "should not be applied unthinkingly to jurisdiction clauses which do not have the same legal effect."[51] Thus, if party intentions are clearly expressed, the presumption will not apply. Fourthly, this presumption of a waiver against objecting to the exercise of jurisdiction by the court only applies insofar as Singapore law, or a law with similar construction of contract principles, is the proper law of the contract. Of course, in the absence of proof of foreign law, the presumption of similarity with Singapore law will apply. Fifthly, if the defendant brings an anti-suit injunction restraining the plaintiff from seising the Singapore court, there would be a breach of contract by the defendant. If the plaintiff in turn sought an anti-anti-suit injunction from the Singapore court to restrain the foreign

---

[45] *Orchard Capital* [2012] 2 SLR 519, [24].

[46] *Orchard Capital* [2012] 2 SLR 519, [27].

[47] *Shanghai Turbo* [2019] 1 SLR 779, [80].

[48] [2019] 1 SLR 779, [84] (emphasis in original).

[49] For example, the clause provides that: "The contract is subject to the jurisdiction of the Singapore court." See [2019] 1 SLR 779, [89].

[50] [2019] 1 SLR 779, [86].

[51] [2019] 1 SLR 779, [83].

anti-suit application, the defendant would have to show "strong cause" why the anti-anti-suit injunction should not be granted.[52]

The "strong cause" test articulated in *Shanghai Turbo* normally applies to exclusive choice of court agreements outside the context of the SICC and the CCAA. The burden of proof is on the person breaking the agreement. The court in exercising its discretion on whether to grant a stay may have regard to the following matters:

(a) In what country the evidence on the issues of fact is situated or more readily available, and the effect of that on the relative convenience and expense of trial as between the Singapore and foreign courts.
(b) Whether the law of the foreign court applies and, if so, whether it differs from Singapore law in any material respects.
(c) With what country either party is connected and, if so, how closely.
(d) Whether the defendants genuinely desire trial in the foreign country, or are only seeking procedural advantages.
(e) Whether the plaintiffs would be prejudiced by having to sue in the foreign court because they would:

   (i) be deprived of security for their claim;
   (ii) be unable to enforce any judgment obtained;
   (iii) be faced with a time bar not applicable here; or
   (iv) for political, racial, religious or other reasons be unlikely to get a fair trial.[53]

The factors above are culled from *The Eleftheria*.[54] However, in *Vinmar Overseas (Singapore) Pte Ltd v PTT International Trading Pte Ltd*,[55] the Court of Appeal observed that the wording of factor (d) above was infelicitous as it suggests that: (a) the applicant's subjective desire for trial would be a relevant consideration when it is not; and (b) it is improper for the applicant to seek procedural advantages in applying for a stay when there is nothing wrong with a party seeking the procedural advantages of an agreed forum.[56] In an earlier case, *The "Jian He"*,[57] the fact that the defendant did not have a genuine defence on the merits of the claim had been determinative in the refusal of a stay on grounds that the defendant is not really interested in trial in the agreed forum but is merely seeking a procedural advantage. The court in *Vinmar* decisively overruled the *Jian He* position by holding that the merits of the case or lack thereof should not be a relevant consideration in the "strong cause" test. It stated that factor (d) should instead be interpreted as capturing the inquiry: "is the applicant acting abusively in applying for a stay of proceedings?"[58]

---

[52]See below, text following n 103.

[53]*Vinmar Overseas (Singapore) Pte Ltd v PTT International Trading Pte Ltd* [2018] 2 SLR 1271, [71].

[54][1969] 1 Lloyd's Rep 237.

[55][2018] 2 SLR 1271.

[56][2018] 2 SLR 1271, [130].

[57][1999] 3 SLR(R) 432.

[58][2018] 2 SLR 1271, [130].

The above factors were formulated where the Singapore proceedings are commenced in breach of a choice of court agreement for a foreign court. Where the Singapore proceedings are in line with an optional choice of court agreement for Singapore and it is the defendant who is applying to set aside or stay the proceedings, the *Eleftheria* factors will have to be adapted. The defendant who is relying on factor (d) would have to show that the plaintiff's conduct in commencing the Singapore proceedings is abusive.[59] Factor (e) would require showing that the defendant would be prejudiced by having to defend in Singapore.[60] It might be observed that the defendant would be hard pressed to make the last point.

The above list is not a closed one.[61] Further, foreseeable factors, that is, factors known to the parties at the time the agreement was made, will be given less weight compared to unforeseeable factors.[62]

2.3.2 Singapore International Commercial Court

If the optional choice of court agreement is in favour of the SICC,[63] leave need not be obtained to serve the writ outside of Singapore on a party to the written jurisdiction agreement.[64] This is a move away from the traditional notion of service out as being exorbitant in nature.[65] While under the traditional rules, service has a jurisdiction founding function, it can be said that under the SICC framework, service serves a notification function, i.e., to notify parties of the proceedings.[66]

The test for a stay application also differs from the traditional rules under the SICC framework. According to Order 110, rule 8 of the Rules of Court:

(1) Subject to paragraph (2), the Court may decline to assume jurisdiction ... if it is not appropriate for the action to be heard in the Court.
(2) The Court must not decline to assume jurisdiction in an action solely on the ground that the dispute between the parties is connected to a jurisdiction other than Singapore, if there is a written jurisdiction agreement between the parties.
(3) In exercising its discretion under paragraph (1), the Court shall have regard to its international and commercial character.

[59] *Shanghai Turbo* [2019] 1 SLR 779, [95].

[60] *Shanghai Turbo* [2019] 1 SLR 779, [95].

[61] *Trisuryo Garuda Nusa Pte Ltd v SKP Pradiksi* [2017] 2 SLR 814, [85] and [90].

[62] *Golden Shore Transportation Pte Ltd v UCO Bank* [2004] 1 SLR(R) 6, [38]; *The "Hyundai Fortune"* [2004] 4 SLR(R) 548, [30]; *Vinmar Overseas (Singapore) Pte Ltd v PTT International Trading Pte Ltd* [2018] 2 SLR 1271, [72] and [112].

[63] If the optional choice of court agreement is in favour of the "Singapore High Court" and the agreement is concluded on or after 1 October 2016, Order 110, rule 1(2)(*ca*) of the Rules of Court provides that the agreement is to be construed as including an agreement to the jurisdiction of the SICC, unless a contrary intention appears in the agreement. The SICC is a division of the Singapore High Court.

[64] Rules of Court, Order 110, rule 6(2).

[65] Cf. *Abela v Baadarani* [2013] UKSC 44, [2013] 1 WLR 2043, [53].

[66] See further Chong and Yip (2019), pp. 109–110.

It is clear that the test set out in Order 110 rule 8(1) is an eschewing of the *Spiliada* test and is intended to operate more strictly to the question of when jurisdiction may be declined by the SICC. The "not appropriate" test has been interpreted by the High Court Registry[67] to oblige the SICC to apply the Australian "clearly inappropriate forum" test.[68] There are grounds to doubt this.[69] It is more likely that the drafters intended the "not appropriate" forum test to be autonomous in nature.[70]

2.3.3 Parallel Proceedings Abroad and Anti-suit Injunctions

An optional choice of court agreement for Singapore does not restrict the parties' right to pursue proceedings in other jurisdictions. It has been said in the context of an application for an anti-suit injunction that a multiplicity of proceedings is not presumed to be vexatious.[71] However, the courts' approach towards the grant of an anti-suit injunction restraining foreign proceedings differs according to whether Singapore proceedings have or have not been commenced pursuant to an optional Singapore choice of court agreement. It has been held that "the court should be slow to grant an anti-suit injunction where there is no existing *lis* in Singapore."[72]

2.4 *Optional Choice of Court Agreement for a Foreign Court*

In *Shanghai Turbo*, the Court of Appeal held that if the optional choice of court agreement were for a foreign court and Singapore is the proper law of the contract, the defendant may apply for a stay or to set aside service of the writ on the basis that Singapore is *forum non conveniens*. In other words, there is no breach of contract and the *Spiliada* test applies where the optional choice of court agreement is but one factor to be weighed in the *Spiliada* exercise. This is in line with previous decisions on foreign optional choice of court agreements.

In *PT Jaya Putra Kundur Indah v Guthrie Overseas Investments Pte Ltd*,[73] the High Court interpreted an optional choice of court agreement for Indonesia to mean that *prima facie*, the parties had agreed that Indonesia would be an appropriate forum

[67] *IM Skaugen SE v MAN Diesel & Turbo SE* [2016] SGHCR 6, overruled, without consideration of this point [2018] SGHC 123.

[68] *Voth v Manildra Flour Mills Pty Ltd* (1991) 65 ALJR 83.

[69] Yeo (2015), para 32.

[70] See further, Yeo (2015), paras 27–34; Yip (2016), pp. 456–460.

[71] *UBS AG v Telesto Investments Ltd* [2011] 4 SLR 503, [119].

[72] *Morgan Stanley Asia (Singapore) Pte (formerly known as Morgan Stanley Dean Witter Asia (Singapore) Pte) v Hong Leong Finance Ltd* [2013] 3 SLR 409, [71].

[73] [1996] SGHC 285.

and the plaintiffs should not be heard to argue that it would not be an appropriate forum for trial of the action.[74] However, despite this, the applicable test was not "strong cause", rather, Lai J considered the optional choice of court agreement for Indonesia to be a factor, albeit a strong one, in the *Spiliada* test.[75] This can be explained on the basis that the parties only agreed that Indonesia was an appropriate forum and it would not be a breach of contract to argue that Singapore is a *more* appropriate forum.[76]

The modern preference of Singapore courts to adopt a general analysis in relation to foreign optional choice of court agreements is also illustrated by the Singapore High Court decision of *Abdul Rashid bin Abdul Manaf v Hii Yii Ann* ('*Hii Yii Ann*')[77] which involved an optional choice of court agreement for the courts of Queensland. In *Hii Yii Ann*, the court contrasted an optional choice of court agreement (referred to as a non-exclusive jurisdiction clause, or "NEJ"), which denotes "an" appropriate jurisdiction, with a "most appropriate jurisdiction" agreement ("MAJ"), which denotes "the" appropriate jurisdiction. While the court accepted that the use of the word "non-exclusive" in the choice of court agreement did not always mean that it was the former type of clause and not the latter, it favoured giving an ordinary meaning to the word "non-exclusive". Woo J stated:

> ... if a negotiated NEJ clause amounts to an MAJ clause in substance so that the evidential burden shifts to a plaintiff suing in the non-contractual jurisdiction to show strong cause as to why he should be permitted to do so, this will bring the negotiated NEJ clause very close to an EJ clause. Indeed, one may even ask whether there is then any practical difference between a negotiated NEJ clause and an EJ clause because even for an EJ clause, a plaintiff may still show strong cause why he should be permitted to bring an action in a jurisdiction which is not the contractual one. ...[78]

Woo J proceeded to apply the usual *Spiliada* principles, under which the optional choice of court agreement was but one factor to be considered in the balancing exercise. However, the learned judge also accepted that whether the clause could be something more than "an" appropriate choice of court agreement would depend on the context and the rest of the terms.[79]

In sum, an optional choice of court agreement in favour of a foreign court will usually be a factor within the *Spiliada* analysis. That said, if the wording of the choice of court agreement and circumstances of the case indicate that the parties intend an optional choice of court agreement to be more than what it would be in the

---

[74][1996] SGHC 285, [64].

[75]Lai J expressly rejected the approach suggested by Waller J in *British Aerospace v Dee Howard* [1993] 1 Lloyd's Rep 368, 375–377, under which factors which are eminently foreseeable at the time they entered into the contract cannot be relied upon by the parties in the context of the *Spiliada* test, particularly if the choice of court agreement was freely negotiated and is an express term of a detailed agreement.

[76]Yeo (2005), para 81.

[77][2014] 4 SLR 1042.

[78][2014] 4 SLR 1042, [54].

[79][2014] 4 SLR 1042, [53].

ordinary case, the courts would honour party intentions. For example, in *Bambang Sutrisno v Bali International Finance Ltd*,[80] the optional choice of court agreement was for the Indonesian courts. However, the plaintiff reserved the right to sue the defendant in any other competent court in any other jurisdiction and the defendant agreed to waive any objections on the ground of venue or *forum non conveniens* or any similar grounds. Thus, when the plaintiff commenced Singapore proceedings, the defendant was put to "strong cause" why a stay should be allowed, given that the waiver portion of the agreement was not confined merely to proceedings before the Indonesian courts.[81]

It should lastly be noted that if proceedings have been commenced in the nominated foreign court, the existence of parallel proceedings would also be a factor that the court would weigh in the *Spiliada* analysis.

2.5 Comparison Between Forum and Foreign Optional Choice of Court Agreements

If the optional choice of court agreement is for the SICC, it is evident that a different approach is taken compared to optional choice of court agreements for a foreign court. The applicable test on a stay application for the SICC is the arguably autonomous "not appropriate" forum test.[82]

Outside of the SICC, it is established after *Shanghai Turbo* that different approaches would be taken for foreign and forum optional choice of court agreements insofar as Singapore law, or a law with similar principles of construction, apply to the contract.[83] Where Singapore is the named forum or one of the named fora in the optional choice of court agreement, the defendant who is resisting trial in Singapore will have to show "strong cause" as he is breaching the presumption of waiver of objection to the Singapore court's jurisdiction. Conversely, where a foreign court is named, no breach of contract is presumed upon commencement of Singapore proceedings. The foreign optional choice of court agreement is a factor in the *Spiliada* test. In other words, optional choice of court agreements for the forum would be treated more favourably compared to optional choice of court agreements for a foreign court.[84]

[80] [1999] 2 SLR(R) 632.

[81] See also *Baiduri Bank Bhd v Dong Sui Hung* [2000] 2 SLR(R) 271. Cf. *OCBC Capital Investment Asia Ltd v Wong Hua Choon* [2010] 4 SLR 904, where the optional choice of court agreement was for Malaysia and coupled with a waiver of objection on grounds of inconvenient forum. On construction of the agreement, it was held that the waiver portion only applied to proceedings before the Malaysian court. Hence the *Spiliada* test was applied to the stay application.

[82] Rules of Court, Order 110, rule 8(1).

[83] The Court endorsed the Hong Kong Court of Appeal decision of *Noble Power Investments Ltd v Nissei Stomach Tokyo Co Ltd* [2008] 5 HKLRD 631.

[84] Cf. *Hii Yii Ann* [2014] 4 SLR 1042, [25]–[26] and [49].

2.6 Weaker Parties

In *Vinmar Overseas (Singapore) Pte Ltd v PTT International Trading Pte Ltd*, the Court of Appeal tentatively expressed a preference for the view that the same principles ought to apply to negotiated and non-negotiated choice of court agreements.[85] *Vinmar* was a case on exclusive choice of court agreements. The Court of Appeal in *Shanghai Turbo* declined to decide if the waiver of objection to the exercise of jurisdiction of the Singapore courts should similarly be presumed if the optional choice of court agreement was not freely negotiated.[86] However, the court held that if the optional choice of court agreement is for a foreign court, the weight to be attributed to the agreement would depend on circumstances of the case, such as whether the agreement was part of a closely negotiated contract or was a standard term in a contract of adhesion.[87]

2.7 Proceedings Brought in a Non-chosen Court

If proceedings are brought in Singapore when there exists an optional choice of court agreement for another court, the defendant may apply for a stay of the proceedings. Outside the context of the SICC, the test of *forum non conveniens* set out in *Spiliada*[88] will apply. It comprises of two stages. The defendant must show that there is another court which is clearly or distinctly more appropriate than Singapore for trial of the action in the first stage. Under this first stage, factors such as the residence of the parties, the locations of relevant witnesses, facts and evidence, and governing law of the dispute will be considered.[89] The possibility of a transfer of the case from the Singapore High Court to the SICC is also a relevant factor, as certain characteristics of the SICC may render Singapore a more appropriate forum compared to a foreign forum.[90] Further, as mentioned above, the Singapore courts tend to treat an optional choice of court agreement as a factor in the *Spiliada* analysis and the weight to be attributed to the agreement would depend on whether it was part of a negotiated contract or a contract of adhesion. The search is for the forum to which the action has the most real and substantial connection, although the concept of the natural forum is a relative one.[91] If the defendant discharges this burden, ordinarily a

[85][2018] 2 SLR 1271, [138].

[86][2019] 1 SLR 779, [90]. The clause on the facts appeared to have been freely negotiated. Cf. *Hii Yii Ann* [2014] 4 SLR 1042, [51].

[87][2019] 1 SLR 779, [88].

[88][1987] AC 460.

[89]*JIO Minerals FZC v Mineral Enterprises Ltd* [2011] 1 SLR 391, [41]–[42].

[90]*Rappo, Tania v Accent Delight International Ltd* [2017] 2 SLR 265.

[91]"The search is for *a* natural forum, not *the* natural forum": Yeo (2009), para 75.089, cited in *JIO Minerals FZC v Mineral Enterprises Ltd* [2011] 1 SLR 391, [53].

stay will be granted unless the plaintiff shows that there are circumstances by reason of which justice requires that a stay should nevertheless be refused. All circumstances of the case will be considered in the second stage.[92]

The SICC may hear a case which has been transferred to it by the Singapore High Court.[93] In this situation, the SICC may not reconsider whether it has jurisdiction.[94]

Anti-suit injunctions are part of the Singapore court's litigation toolbox. The anti-suit injunction will only be granted where the "ends of justice" require it and the jurisdiction is one which must be exercised with caution lest comity be infringed.[95] The court, in considering whether to grant an anti-suit injunction, will consider the following elements[96]:

(a) whether the defendants are amenable to the jurisdiction of the Singapore court;
(b) the natural forum for resolution of the dispute between the parties;
(c) the alleged vexation or oppression to the plaintiffs if the foreign proceedings are to continue;
(d) the alleged injustice to the defendants as an injunction would deprive the defendants of the advantages sought in the foreign proceedings; and
(e) whether the institution of the foreign proceedings is in breach of any agreement between the parties.

In the specific context of an application for an anti-suit injunction to restrain foreign proceedings commenced in breach of an agreement between the parties, it has been held that the anti-suit injunction would be granted unless there are strong reasons not to and that there would be no need for the applicant to put forward additional evidence of unconscionable conduct.[97] The court need not feel any diffidence in granting the anti-suit injunction if it is sought promptly and the foreign proceedings are not too far advanced.[98] Comity considerations would militate

---

[92] *Eng Liat Kiang v Eng Bak Hern* [1995] 2 SLR(R) 851, [19].

[93] Rules of Court, Order 110, rule 7(2).

[94] Rules of Court, Order 110, rule 12(5)(a). This provides that where a case is transferred, "the court to which the case is transferred must not reconsider whether it has jurisdiction". On the one hand, the original text read: "the court to which the case is transferred must not reconsider whether it has *or will assume* jurisdiction" (emphasis added). The omission of the italicised words in the amended text (2016 amendment) suggests that the SICC retains the discretion to examine the exercise of jurisdiction. On the other hand, the wording of Order 110, rule 8(1), which sets out the 'not appropriate' forum test as the test for exercise of jurisdiction by the SICC was recently amended to be "[s]ubject to … Rule 12(5)(a)" (2018 amendment). On policy grounds, a prohibition on a review of both existence and exercise of jurisdiction in a transfer case would be sound.

[95] *John Reginald Stott Kirkham v Trane US Inc* [2009] 4 SLR(R) 428, [25], citing *Société Nationale Industrielle Aerospatiale v Lee Kui Jak* [1987] AC 871, 892.

[96] *John Reginald Stott Kirkham v Trane US Inc* [2009] 4 SLR(R) 428, [28]–[29].

[97] *Sun Travels & Tours Pvt Ltd v Hilton International Manage (Maldives) Pvt Ltd* [2019] 1 SLR 732, [68].

[98] *Sun Travels & Tours Pvt Ltd v Hilton International Manage (Maldives) Pvt Ltd* [2019] 1 SLR 732, [68].

against grant of the anti-suit injunction the longer the delay and the more advanced the foreign court proceedings are.[99]

The mere commencement of foreign proceedings where there is an optional choice of court agreement for Singapore does not engage element (e) above. The Singapore High Court in *UBS AG v Telesto Investments Ltd*[100] held that there was no breach when the defendants commenced proceedings abroad.[101] There is no presumption that a multiplicity of proceedings is vexatious and the burden will be on the applicant to demonstrate a reason which is independent of the optional choice of court agreement that the foreign proceedings are vexatious or oppressive.[102] The fact that no substantive proceedings have been commenced in Singapore would be a factor militating against the grant of the anti-suit injunction.[103] However, if the plaintiff applies for an anti-anti-suit injunction to restrain the defendant from applying for an anti-suit injunction restraining the plaintiff from commencing Singapore proceedings, the plaintiff need not show that the foreign proceedings are vexatious or oppressive. Instead, the burden will be on the defendant to show strong reasons why the anti-anti-suit injunction should not be granted.

In *Sun Travels & Tours Pvt Ltv v Hilton International Manage (Maldives) Pvt Ltd*,[104] the Court of Appeal considered if an anti-enforcement injunction ought to be granted to restrain a Maldivian judgment procured in breach of an arbitration agreement. Mindful that the effect of such an injunction would be akin to nullifying the foreign judgment, the court held that anti-enforcement injunctions would only be granted in exceptional circumstances that warrant the injunction.[105] This must be over and above the usual requirements for the grant of an anti-suit injunction.[106] The idea of exceptional circumstances was to be tied to the notion of unconscionability.[107] The court gave two examples where an anti-enforcement injunction may be warranted: fraud by the other party and when the applicant had no knowledge of the foreign proceedings until the judgment was rendered.[108]

Under the Reciprocal Enforcement of Foreign Judgments Act ("REFJA"),[109] a foreign judgment which is handed down in breach of a choice of court agreement in

---

[99] *Sun Travels & Tours Pvt Ltd v Hilton International Manage (Maldives) Pvt Ltd* [2019] 1 SLR 732, [82]–[83].

[100] *UBS AG v Telesto Investments Ltd* [2011] 4 SLR 503.

[101] The reasoning used by the court in *UBS*, [2011] 4 SLR 503, [120], which was that to hold otherwise would render the distinction between exclusive and optional choice of court agreements illusory, is no longer good law after *Shanghai Turbo*. The principle remains untouched by *Shanghai Turbo*.

[102] *UBS AG v Telesto Investments Ltd* [2011] 4 SLR 503, [119].

[103] *Morgan Stanley Asia (Singapore) Pte (formerly known as Morgan Stanley Dean Witter Asia (Singapore) Pte) v Hong Leong Finance Ltd* [2013] 3 SLR 409, [71].

[104] [2019] 1 SLR 732.

[105] [2019] 1 SLR 732, [98]–[99].

[106] [2019] 1 SLR 732. [99].

[107] [2019] 1 SLR 732, [105].

[108] [2019] 1 SLR 732, [113].

[109] Cap 265, 2001 Rev Ed.

favour of a court other than that which rendered judgment would be refused enforcement.[110] This would be relevant provided that an optional choice of court agreement can be construed to contain a promise not to sue in other courts. The REFJA is to date restricted to judgments handed down from the courts of Hong Kong SAR. Outside of this context, there is no prohibition against recognising and enforcing a foreign judgment merely because it was handed down by a court other than that which was nominated in an optional choice of court agreement.

In *Tradewaves Ltd v Standard Chartered Bank*,[111] the Singapore court was open to the idea of awarding damages for breach of contract where one party commences proceedings in a court other than that named in an exclusive choice of court agreement. It cited the English Court of Appeal decision of *Union Discount v Zoller*,[112] where the court held that "unusual features" would entitle the plaintiff to an award of damages for breach of an exclusive choice of court agreement. The "unusual features" include where the rules of the foreign court only permitted the recovery of costs in exceptional circumstances and the foreign court had made no adjudication on costs. As no evidence on any exceptional feature had been led, the court in *Tradewaves* dismissed the claim for damages for breach of the exclusive choice of court agreement.[113] The Singapore courts have not considered the same issue in relation to a breach of an optional choice of court agreement, but it stands to reason that the contractual approach post-*Shanghai Turbo* would allow for it.

3 Exclusive Choice of Court Agreements

An exclusive choice of court agreement is considered to have both prorogative and derogative effects. Optional choice of court agreements are generally considered only to have a prorogative effect, although it has been seen above that the agreement may sometimes be construed to have a greater effect than this. Different tests on the exercise of a court's jurisdiction apply depending on whether an agreement is considered to play both prorogative and derogative functions, and when it is considered to play only a prorogative function.

Outside the context of the SICC and the CCAA, a party who seeks to bring an action in Singapore in breach of an exclusive choice of court agreement for another court must show exceptional circumstances amounting to "strong cause" why the court should exercise its discretion to assist him.[114] A party who seeks a stay of

[110] S 5(3)(b). Unless the judgment debtor submitted to that court's jurisdiction.

[111] [2017] SGHC 93.

[112] [2002] 1 WLR 1517.

[113] [2017] SGHC 93, [293].

[114] *The "Jian He"* [1999] 3 SLR(R) 432; *Golden Shore Transportation Pte Ltd v UCO Bank* [2004] 1 SLR(R) 6.

Singaporean proceedings which are commenced pursuant to an exclusive choice of court agreement for Singapore is also put to the same standard. Similarly, if proceedings are commenced in Singapore pursuant to an exclusive choice of court agreement for Singapore, a defendant who applies to set aside service of the writ on him abroad will have to fulfil the "strong cause" test. The starting point in all these cases is that the contractual bargain must be upheld. The "strong cause" test has been elaborated on above.[115] Further, comity considerations are less relevant when an anti-suit injunction to restrain foreign proceedings brought in breach of a Singapore exclusive choice of court agreement is sought,[116] provided that there is no delay in bringing the application for anti-suit relief.[117]

Once an agreement has been identified as being exclusive in nature, its legal effect and the relevant test to be applied to the court's exercise of jurisdiction are clear whether the agreement is for the Singapore court or a foreign court. The only difference is on whom the burden of proof lies. The legal effect of optional choice of court agreements, outside the context of the SICC, would depend on whether the named court is the Singapore court or a foreign court.

In the specific context of proceedings before the SICC,[118] if the SICC assumed jurisdiction on the basis of an exclusive choice of court agreement in its favour, the applicable test when considering whether it ought to decline jurisdiction is the "not appropriate" forum test.[119] If the case has been transferred to the SICC from the High Court[120] in circumstances where the commencement of the High Court action was in breach of an exclusive choice of court agreement for a foreign court, the SICC may not reconsider whether it has jurisdiction.[121]

The CCAA enacts the HCCCA into Singapore law. It only applies in international cases[122] to exclusive choice of court agreements[123] in favour of the courts of Contracting States to the HCCCA in civil and commercial matters.[124] If Singapore is the exclusively chosen forum, it must hear the case unless the choice of court agreement is null and void under Singapore law.[125] Notably, discretionary tests such as *forum non conveniens* and "strong cause" are precluded under the CCAA.[126]

[115]See text to n 53–62.

[116]*John Reginald Stott Kirkham v Trane US Inc* [2009] 4 SLR(R) 428, [29]; *UBS AG v Telesto Investments Ltd* [2011] 4 SLR 503, [109].

[117]*Sun Travels & Tours Pvt Ltd v Hilton International Manage (Maldives) Pvt Ltd* [2019] 1 SLR 732, [81].

[118]The presumptions which apply when there is a choice of court agreement for the SICC have been set out above, text to n 19 above.

[119]Rules of Court, Order 110, rule 8(1). See above, text to n 67–70.

[120]Rules of Court, Order 110, rules 7(2), 12(3B) and 12(4).

[121]See n 94 above.

[122]Defined in CCAA, s 4.

[123]Defined in CCAA, s 3.

[124]A list of matters excluded from the Act are set out in CCAA, s 9.

[125]CCAA, s 11(1).

[126]Hartley and Dogauchi (2005) ("Hartley and Dogauchi Report"), paras 132 and 134.

However, if the defendant is abroad and the case is commenced in the Singapore High Court, leave[127] is still ostensibly required to serve the writ on the defendant although the court is obliged to hear the case. Formally, this can be considered to be anomalous, although in practical terms, leave is usually granted readily even in a non-CCAA case where there is a choice of court agreement for Singapore.

If the parties have chosen a specific court in Singapore in their agreement, the chosen court retains the discretion to transfer the case to another Singapore court pursuant to its internal allocation of jurisdiction rules.[128]

If another Contracting State court to the HCCCA is the exclusively chosen forum, the Singapore court must stay or dismiss the action before it unless one of the following exceptions set out in section 12(1) of the CCAA applies:

(a) the agreement is null and void under the law of the State of the chosen court;
(b) a party to the agreement lacked capacity, under the law of Singapore, to enter into or conclude the agreement;
(c) giving effect to the agreement would lead to a manifest injustice or would be manifestly contrary to the public policy of Singapore;
(d) for exceptional reasons beyond the control of the parties to the agreement, the agreement cannot reasonably be performed; or
(e) the chosen court has decided not to hear the case or proceeding.

4 Asymmetrical Choice of Court Agreements

There appear to be few reported cases dealing expressly with asymmetrical choice of court agreements and of those few, the optional portion of such agreements has not been at issue. In view of the Singapore court's approach towards optional choice of court agreements in general, it seems safe to conclude that the court will enforce the optional portion of the agreement.

In *TMT Co Ltd v The Royal Bank of Scotland*,[129] the clause provided for disputes to be subject to the jurisdiction of the English courts for the defendants' benefit, and further provided that the defendants shall not be prevented from seising the courts of any other competent jurisdiction. The plaintiffs commenced proceedings in England; these proceedings culminated in a settlement agreement. The plaintiffs thereafter commenced proceedings in Singapore. The defendants applied to set aside service of the writ out of the jurisdiction. In determining this application, the Singapore High Court carefully construed the agreement to determine whether the dispute at hand fell within its scope, and the obligations which it imposed on the plaintiff in respect of the disputes. It then applied the *Spiliada* test and concluded that Singapore was *forum non conveniens*. The asymmetric choice of court agreement did not feature in

---

[127] Pursuant to Rules of Court, Order 11.

[128] CCAA, s 11(5): however, "the chosen court must, before exercising that discretion, take into account the parties' choice of court."

[129] [2018] 3 SLR 70.

the *Spiliada* analysis, but this may have been because the claim involved several defendants, not all of whom were a party to that agreement.

The judgment in *Bayerische Landesbank Girozentrale v Kong Kok Keong*[130] is inconclusive as to the relevant test that applies when the jurisdiction of the court is contested. The agreement in *Bayerische* provided for the defendant borrower to submit to the jurisdiction of the Singapore courts, but for the plaintiff bank to retain the right to commence proceedings in the courts of any other country. The Singapore High Court referred to authorities on "strong cause" as well as *Spiliada*, appearing in the end to apply the latter principles in the stay application.[131] One of the main factors relied on by the court when refusing to stay its proceedings was that the parties had expressly submitted to the Singapore court's jurisdiction.[132]

The effect of asymmetrical choice of court agreements does not depend on the relative bargaining strength of the parties. The courts have enforced asymmetrical agreements which favour banks as against borrowers. The only caveat is that the agreements are entered into freely between the parties.[133]

Lastly, it should be noted that the Hartley and Dogauchi Report states that asymmetrical choice of court agreements do not fall within the scope of the HCCCA as they are not exclusive for the purposes of the HCCCA.[134] The English High Court decision of *Commerzbank AG v Liquimar Tankers Management Inc*[135] has thrown some doubt on this proposition. It is unlikely that the Singapore court would follow *Commerzbank*; in the one case to be decided to date under the CCAA, the court quoted copiously from the Hartley and Dogauchi Report.[136] In addition, as a matter of principle, the Hartley and Dogauchi Report ought to be considered authoritative in relation to the interpretation of the HCCCA to ensure a degree of uniformity of application amongst Contracting States.

5 Evaluation and Reform

It can be seen from the above that Singapore law places great emphasis on giving effect to party autonomy. To that end, optional choice of court agreements are enforceable, and at common law, Singapore courts will construe the agreement in accordance with the proper law of the contract to determine its legal effect.

If Singapore law were to be the proper law of the contract, a presumption that the parties have waived their right to object to the exercise of jurisdiction will be read

[130][2002] 1 SLR(R) 485. The court did not refer to its asymmetry as being a special feature and the agreement was dealt with on the basis that it was like any other optional choice of court agreement.
[131]Cf. Lee (2003), pp. 598–599, who is of the view that the court applied the test of "strong cause".
[132][2002] 1 SLR(R) 485, [14].
[133]*TMT Co Ltd v The Royal Bank of Scotland plc* [2018] 3 SLR 70, [74].
[134]Hartley and Dogauchi Report, paras 32, 105–106 and 249.
[135][2017] EWHC 161 (Comm), [2017] 1 WLR 3497, [74].
[136]*Ermgassen & Co Ltd v Sixcap Financials Pte Ltd* [2018] SGHCR 8.

into the agreement if Singapore is the, or a, named forum. The *Shanghai Turbo* approach means that the distinction between exclusive and optional choice of court agreements for the Singapore court is abrogated. It also has the effect that forum and foreign optional choice of court agreements are treated differently, with the former having greater legal effect. This has unwelcome overtones of parochialism. That said, the decision is in line with the use of the presumption of exclusivity under the SICC's rules and the CCAA. The use of the presumption of exclusivity may mean that some agreements which were intended, but not adequately expressed, to be optional in nature would be treated as exclusive choice of court agreements. The overall net effect of the recent common law and legislative developments is to encourage the Singapore courts to exercise jurisdiction. This can be seen as a manifestation of the desire to position Singapore as an international dispute resolution hub. Moving forward, parties to a contract should be careful to make explicit their specific intentions whenever they agree on an optional choice of court agreement as a failure to do so may have an unintended effect.

References

Chong A, Yip M (2019) Singapore as a centre for International Commercial Litigation: party autonomy to the fore. J Private Int Law 15(1):97–129

Hartley T, Dogauchi M (2005) Explanatory report: convention of 30 June 2005 on choice of court agreements. https://www.hcch.net/en/publications-and-studies/details4/?pid=3959. Accessed 29 Jan 2019

Lee J (2003) Non-exclusive jurisdiction clauses – changing approaches? Singapore J Leg Stud, pp 593–600

Yeo TM (2005) The contractual basis of the enforcement of exclusive and non-exclusive choice of court agreements. Singapore Acad Law J 17:306–360

Yeo TM (2009) Halsbury's laws of Singapore, vol 6(2). LexisNexis, Singapore

Yeo TM (2015) Staying relevant: exercise of jurisdiction in the age of the SICC. Eighth Yong Pung How Professorship of Law Lecture 2015. https://law.smu.edu.sg/sites/default/files/law/CEBCLA/YPH-Paper-2015.pdf. Accessed 29 Jan 2019

Yip M (2016) The resolution of disputes before the Singapore International Commercial Court. Int Comp Law Q 65:439–473

Adeline Chong is an Associate Professor at the School of Law, Singapore Management University. She was formerly a lecturer at the School of Law, University of Nottingham. She obtained First Class Honours from the University of Birmingham and subsequently was awarded a scholarship to pursue a PhD in Nottingham. She has published in the *Law Quarterly Review*, *International and Comparative Law Quarterly*, *Lloyd's Maritime and Commercial Law Quarterly* and the *Journal of Private International Law*. She is the co-author of Hill and Chong, *International Commercial Disputes: Commercial Conflict of Laws in English Courts* (Oxford, Hart, 4th edn, 2010). Her work has been cited by the Singapore and New South Wales Court of Appeals, the Singapore and New Zealand High Courts, as well as in leading texts on conflict of laws such as *Dicey, Morris and Collins on the Conflict of Laws* (15th edition, 2012). She has issued declarations on Singapore law for Finnish and US court proceedings and has appeared as an expert on Singapore law before a Finnish court. She was awarded the 2013 School of Law Research Excellence Award and was appointed as a Lee Kong Chian Fellow, which is awarded for research excellence, in 2015.

South Africa: Time for Reform

Elsabe Schoeman

1 Introduction

The South African law of jurisdiction is based on common law, statute law and case law. Due to its history of colonisation by both The Netherlands and Britain, South African law presents as a mixed or hybrid system of law, with Continental civil law, Anglo-common law and African customary/indigenous law as its principal constituents.[1] As far as the assumption of jurisdiction in cross-border disputes is concerned, common law and case law are by far the most important sources. The common-law principles of jurisdiction are derived from Roman Law, Roman-Dutch law, and English law.[2] These principles have been adapted and developed by the courts to resolve cross-border jurisdictional disputes. During the last two decades the Constitution of the Republic of South Africa, 1996, has also started to exert its influence on cross-border jurisdiction.[3]

[1]Hosten et al. (1997), pp. 337ff.

[2]See, in general, Pistorius (2017), Chapter 1.

[3]See, for e.g., *Bid Industrial Holdings (Pty) Ltd v Strang and Another (Minister of Justice and Constitutional Development, Third Party)* 2008 3 SA 355 (SCA), discussed below under Sect. 5.2.

E. Schoeman (✉)
University of Pretoria, Faculty of Law, Pretoria, South Africa
e-mail: elsabe.schoeman@up.ac.za

M. Keyes (ed.), *Optional Choice of Court Agreements in Private International Law*, Ius Comparatum – Global Studies in Comparative Law 37,
https://doi.org/10.1007/978-3-030-23914-5_15

2 The South African Jurisdictional Landscape

There are a number of features regarding the law of jurisdiction in South Africa that have already influenced, or may in future influence, the effect afforded to choice of court agreements, either in favour of South African fora or in favour of foreign fora.

While there has been very limited statutory intervention as far as the common-law principles of jurisdiction are concerned, the Superior Courts Act 10 of 2013,[4] which regulates the jurisdiction of the Superior Courts, including the High Courts, provides a good starting point for a discussion of the main jurisdictional features, relevant to cross-border commercial disputes.[5] According to its long title, the Superior Courts Act 10 of 2013 was enacted

> [t]o rationalise, consolidate and amend the laws relating to the Constitutional Court, the Supreme Court of Appeal and the High Court of South Africa; to make provision for the administration of the judicial functions of all courts; to make provision for administrative and budgetary matters relating to the Superior Courts; and to provide for matters incidental thereto.

Section 21(1) demarcates the jurisdiction of the different Divisions of the High Court as follows:

> A Division has jurisdiction over all persons residing or being in, and in relation to all causes arising . . . within its area of jurisdiction and all other matters of which it may according to law take cognisance . . .

This section was specifically drafted in a general manner to avoid restraining or limiting the role of the common law in the interpretation and application of jurisdictional grounds by the courts.[6]

Jurisdictional grounds or connecting factors (*rationes jurisdictionis*) are used to establish a link between the jurisdictional area of the court and the parties involved in the dispute or the occurrence that gave rise to the dispute.[7] Service of process does not enjoy the prominence in establishing jurisdiction that it does in some Anglo-common law systems—a proper jurisdictional ground must be established in each case. The following are examples of jurisdictional grounds: residence; domicile (*ratione domicilii*); creation, performance or breach of a contract (*ratione contractus*); commission of a delict (*ratione delicti commissi*); *ratione rei gestae*; cohesion of causes (*ratione causae continentia*); location of property (*ratione rei sitae*); and attachment of property.[8] A Division of the High Court will not assume

[4]Its predecessor was the Supreme Court Act 59 of 1959.

[5]Cross-border commercial disputes are normally heard in a Division of the High Court, either at first instance or on appeal from a lower court. For the hierarchy of South African courts and the jurisdictional limits of each court, see http://www.justice.gov.za/about/sa-courts.html.

[6]See *Veneta Mineraria Spa v Carolina Collieries (Pty) Ltd (In Liquidation)* 1987 (4) SA 883 (A), 887I-J, dealing with s 19(1) of the Supreme Court Act 59 of 1959 (the predecessor of the Superior Courts Act 10 of 2013), which was almost identical to s 21(1).

[7]Forsyth (2012), p. 169.

[8]Forsyth (2012), pp. 203ff; Harms (2016), [26].

jurisdiction in a cross-border dispute unless there is a proper connection with the jurisdictional area of the court. This has important implications for choice of court agreements selecting a South African forum as a neutral venue—without a proper *ratio jurisdictionis*, the court will not assume jurisdiction in the matter.[9]

The jurisdiction of the South African High Courts is strictly territorial—each Division presides over its own area of jurisdiction.[10] A litigant is classified as either an *incola* or a *peregrinus* with reference to the jurisdictional area of the Court. An *incola* is a party[11] who is domiciled or resident within the jurisdictional area of the court, while a *peregrinus* is a party who is not domiciled or resident within the jurisdictional area of the court.[12] The question, whether a party is an *incola* or a *peregrinus*, is not determined with reference to South Africa as a whole and, as a result, a party may be an *incola* of one Division of the High Court, while being a *peregrinus* of another. A party who is an *incola* of another Division of the High Court, but a *peregrinus* of the Division of the High Court where proceedings are brought, is called a local *peregrinus*. A party who is not domiciled or resident in any Division of the High Court in South Africa, is called a foreign *peregrinus*.[13] Therefore, it is crucial to determine jurisdiction, not with reference to South Africa as a whole, but with reference to a specific Division of the High Court. This fragmented nature of High Court jurisdiction presents significant challenges on the cross-border level, since jurisdiction cannot be determined generically with reference to 'South African courts'—a choice of court agreement clause in a contract must indicate a specific Division of the High Court and jurisdiction must be established in that Division.

Parties can never oust the jurisdiction of a South African court through a choice of court agreement.[14] The reason for this is that it is not up to the parties to determine the jurisdiction of the court—jurisdiction is determined by the court itself and not the litigants. As such, jurisdiction is a matter of public law and not a matter of contractual freedom.[15] This means that a court will always have a discretion whether to enforce a choice of court agreement or not and this may create tension between the 'public law' power of courts, regarding assumption of jurisdiction, and the 'private

---

[9]See below Sect. 3.5.

[10]Currently there are 13 Divisions of the High Court: https://www.judiciary.org.za/index.php/the-south-african-judicial-system.

[11]A 'party' in this sense denotes a natural person (private individual) or a juristic person (e.g., a company).

[12]Forsyth (2012), p. 213.

[13]Forsyth (2012), p. 223.

[14]There is a presumption against legislative ouster or other interference with the jurisdiction of the High Court: Harms (2016), [23]. See also Pistorius (2017), p. 19; *Astra Furnishers (Pty) Ltd v Arend and Another* 1973 (1) SA 446 (C), 450B; *Butler v Banimar Shipping Co SA* 1978 (4) SA 753 (SE), 762A; *Foize Africa (Pty) Ltd v Foize Beheer BV and Others* 2013 (3) SA 91 (SCA), [21].

[15]*Goldschmidt and Another v Folb and Another* 1974 (1) SA 576 (T), 577A; Roodt and Esser (2006), p. 21.

law' doctrine of party autonomy, in terms of which parties are free to choose a venue for litigation.[16]

It is often said that the doctrine of effectiveness underlies the assumption of jurisdiction by South African courts.[17] According to this view the establishment of jurisdiction involves a two-step process: first, there must be a recognised jurisdictional ground and, secondly, it must be determined whether the defendant is subject to the authority of the court in order for the court to be able to render an effective judgment.[18] Choice of court agreements are treated as submission to jurisdiction by consent,[19] but the relationship between effectiveness and submission to jurisdiction is an ambivalent one. On the one hand, submission may support effectiveness by making it potentially possible for a judgment to be enforced elsewhere—many foreign jurisdictions, similarly to South Africa, recognise submission to jurisdiction as a sufficient ground of international competence when recognising and/or enforcing a foreign judgment.[20] On the other hand, it may be argued that control over a defendant, who has submitted to the jurisdiction of the court, with the result that attachment of property is not permitted,[21] does not guarantee effectiveness in the

---

[16]Nygh (1999), pp. 15, 37.

[17]See, e.g., *Veneta Mineraria Spa v Carolina Collieries (Pty) Ltd (In Liquidation)* 1987 (4) SA 883 (A), 893E, per Viljoen JA (Smallberger JA, Vivier JA, Boshoff AJA and M T Steyn AJA concurring): "A Court can only be said to have jurisdiction in a matter if it has the power not only of taking cognisance of the suit but also of giving effect to its judgment." The rule that the plaintiff should sue the defendant in his place of domicile (*actor sequitur forum rei*) embodies the doctrine of effectiveness, since the court has effective control over a defendant in its area of jurisdiction with greater potential for the enforcement of the judgment.

[18]*Hugo v Wessels* 1987 (3) SA 837 (A), 849H-J; *Bisonboard Ltd v K Braun Woodworking Machinery (Pty) Ltd* 1991 (2) SA 482 (A), 499E-F; but see Pistorius *Pollak on Jurisdiction* (2017), 7: "The two-stage enquiry ... does not mean ... that the court must first decide whether it has jurisdiction and then whether it can enforce any order granted pursuant to that jurisdiction. The question is always whether the court has jurisdiction ... in each case there is only one power, namely, not merely to give judgment but to give effective judgment."

[19]On submission and consent in the cross-border jurisdictional context, see Spiro (1967), Kelbrick (1986), Kahn (1987), Kelbrick (1992), and Kahn (1992).

[20]See *Elscint (Pty) Ltd and Another v Mobile Medical Scanners (Pty) Ltd* 1986 (4) SA 552 (W), 557I-558C, per Goldstone J: "The Courts of most, if not all, Western nations will recognise and enforce a judgment of our Courts sounding in money in cases where our Courts possess and exercise 'international' or 'competent' jurisdiction ... The validity of a submission clause appears to be a well-recognised ground for confirming international or competent jurisdiction ... It follows, in my opinion, that there are good juridical practical grounds for refusing to allow the attachment of a person or property *ad confirmandam jurisdictionem* where the Court, because of a submission or consent to jurisdiction, is already possessed of full and complete jurisdiction." See also, in regard to submission as a recognised ground of international competence, *Purser v Sales; Purser and Another v Sales and Another* 2001 (3) SA 445 (SCA), [12]; *Blanchard, Krasner & French v Evans* 2002 (4) SA 144 (T), [3].

[21]The defendant's property may be attached to found (*ad fundandam jurisdictionem*), or to confirm jurisdiction (*ad confirmandam jurisdictionem*) to comply with the doctrine of effectiveness. However, once a defendant has submitted to the jurisdiction of the court, attachment of property is no longer permitted (*American Flag plc v Great African T-Shirt Corporation* 2000 (1) SA 356 (W),

sense that attachment of property was intended to.[22] However, when considering that the value of attached property is not necessarily commensurate with the value of the claim, the attachment of property provides no guarantee for the enforcement (or effectiveness) of a judgment.[23] Therefore, it is submitted that, while the doctrine of effectiveness still plays a role in the assumption of jurisdiction, it is no longer an essential requirement.[24] The doctrine may be used to justify the assumption of jurisdiction, but it is no longer a prerequisite for it.[25] This shift in thinking may open the door to choice of court agreements being enforced more readily, especially where a South African forum is selected as a neutral venue without any substantial connection to the parties or the dispute.

3 The Current Position in South Africa Regarding Choice of Court Agreements

Choice of court agreements are normally referred to as 'jurisdiction clauses' or 'forum clauses' in South Africa. There is a strong trend to regard choice of court agreements as exclusive rather than optional.[26] There is little evidence of optional choice of court agreements, although the choice of a *domicilium citandi et*

377F; *Tsung v Industrial Development Corporation of SA Ltd* 2006 (4) SA 177 (SCA), [6]) and, therefore, submission often serves the purpose of avoiding attachment of property: see Forsyth (2012), p. 233.

[22]Forsyth (2012), p. 230.

[23]See *Yorigami Maritime Construction Co Ltd v Nissho-Iwai Co Ltd* 1977 (4) SA 682 (C), 697E-G, per Friedman J: "The purpose of an attachment *ad fundandam jurisdictionem* is twofold: firstly, to found jurisdiction, and, secondly, to provide an asset in respect of which execution can be levied in the event of a judgment being granted in favour of the plaintiff. The fact that the value of the article attached is less than the amount claimed by the plaintiff in no way detracts from this principle. An attachment is necessary to render the Court's jurisdiction effective, but the Court's jurisdiction is not rendered ineffective if the value of the article attached is less than the amount of the claim in respect of which it is attached, nor even if the attached article has only a trifling value. The doctrine of effectiveness, from a jurisdictional point of view, does not require that the value of the property attached *ad fundandam jurisdictionem* should be such as would satisfy the judgment in full. In our law, all that is required, is that the article attached should have some value as that would enable the Court to give a judgment which has some effect, even though it cannot be satisfied in full."

[24]Pistorius (2017), p. 5.

[25]See *Bid Industrial Holdings (Pty) Ltd v Strang and Another (Minister of Justice and Constitutional Development, Third Party)* 2008 3 SA 355 (SCA), [57], per Howie P (Nugent JA, Ponnan JA, Maya JA and Malan AJA concurring): "As to the principle of effectiveness, despite its having been described as 'the basic principle of jurisdiction in our law' it is clear that the importance and significance of attachment has been so eroded that the value of attached property has sometimes been 'trifling'. However, as I have said, effectiveness is largely for the plaintiff to assess and to act accordingly."

[26]See Sect. 3.4 below.

executandi[27] could be regarded as a tacit, optional, choice of court agreement through submission to jurisdiction by consent.

3.1 Interpretation of Choice of Court Agreements

Choice of court clauses are interpreted according to the proper law of the contract:[28]

> Whether a provision in a contract contains a submission to the jurisdiction of a foreign court is a question of interpretation which must be approached in accordance with the ordinary canons of construction of the system of law applicable to that contract.

In *MV Spartan-Runner v Jotun-Henry Clark Ltd* this principle was explained in more detail:[29]

> The question is not whether the parties intended that the English Courts should have exclusive jurisdiction, it is whether the English law at the time of the litigation provided for the exclusive jurisdiction of the Courts ... The English Court therefore has exclusive jurisdiction in terms of the contract, which falls to be interpreted according to English law.

However, it appears that a choice of court agreement is often judged on its wording. In *Butler v Banimar Shipping Co SA* a foreign choice of court agreement, using the imperative "shall", was treated as exclusive without it being labelled as such,[30] and in *Foize Africa (Pty) Ltd v Foize Beheer BV and Others* the words "irrevocably consent" also seemed to be indicative of an exclusive choice of court agreement.[31]

3.2 The Legal Effect of a Choice of Court Agreement

The legal effect of a choice of court agreement is determined by the proper law of the contract in which the choice of court agreement is contained.[32]

---

[27] See Sect. 3.5 below.

[28] *Blanchard, Krasner & French v Evans* 2002 (4) SA 144 (T), [9], per Cloete J.

[29] 1991 (3) SA 803 (N), an admiralty case, 805H-I, per Shearer J (Howard JP agreeing and Booysen J concurring).

[30] 1978 (4) SA 753 (SE), 760D-E, 762C-D. It is clear that the choice of court agreement was regarded as exclusive since, with reference to *The Eleftheria* [1969] 2 All ER 641 (PDA), Howie AJ said that the burden of proof was on the breaching party to show why the choice of court agreement should not be complied with.

[31] 2013 (3) SA 91 (SCA), [8], [27]-[28]. Leach JA (Mthiyane DP, Cloete JA, Heher JA and Shongwe JA concurring) referred to *The Eleftheria* [1969] 2 All ER 641 (PDA) in regard to factors relevant to a stay of proceedings ([27]) and went on to hold that "a very strong case [must be] made out for the parties not to be bound by their agreement" ([28]).

[32] *MV Spartan-Runner v Jotun-Henry Clark Ltd* 1991 (3) SA 803 (N), 805H-I; *Blanchard, Krasner & French v Evans* 2002 (4) SA 144 (T), [9].

3.3 *Enforcement of Choice of Court Agreements*

There is a strong policy in favour of enforcing choice of court agreements, especially exclusive choice of court agreements in favour of a foreign court.[33] The two main arguments in support of the enforcement of choice of court agreements are party autonomy and the sanctity of contract.

Parties are free to enter into choice of court agreements:[34]

> This is an aspect of party autonomy. With regard to the choice of law "... where the parties have expressly or impliedly or tacitly agreed upon a governing law, our Courts would give effect to the intention of the parties" ... By the same token the Courts will lean towards the chosen forum of the parties.

South African courts regard the sanctity of contract in a serious light:[35]

> Flowing from the sanctity of contracts, it has often been said that a decision not to enforce either an arbitration or foreign jurisdiction clause should only be made where there is a very strong case made out for the parties not to be bound by their agreement.

3.4 *Exclusive Choice of Court Agreements in Favour of Foreign Courts*

The Eleftheria, the *locus classicus* on exclusive foreign choice of court agreements in Anglo-common law jurisdictions, is widely recognised in South African case law as the authority on foreign choice of court agreements: the breaching party bears the burden of proving why the agreement should not be upheld or why a stay should not be granted by a South African court in order to give effect to the foreign choice of court agreement.[36] The following cases are representative of the approach of the South African courts in this regard.

---

[33]Pistorius (2017), p. 20.

[34]*MV Spartan-Runner v Jotun-Henry Clark Ltd* 1991 (3) SA 803 (N), 806G-H, per Shearer J (Howard JP agreeing and Booysen J concurring). See also *Blanchard, Krasner & French v Evans* 2002 (4) SA 144 (T), [11].

[35]*Foize Africa (Pty) Ltd v Foize Beheer BV and Others* 2013 (3) SA 91 (SCA), where there was an agreement on choice of law (Dutch), choice of court (Dutch) and arbitration in The Netherlands, [28 *(a)*], per Leach JA (Mthiyane DP, Cloete JA, Heher JA and Shongwe JA concurring).

[36][1969] 2 All ER 641 (PDA), 645B-C, per Brandon J: "(I) Where plaintiffs sue in England in breach of an agreement to refer disputes to a foreign court, and the defendants apply for a stay, the English court, assuming the claim to be otherwise within its jurisdiction, is not bound to grant a stay but has a discretion whether to do so or not. (II) The discretion should be exercised by granting a stay unless strong cause for not doing so is shown. (III) The burden of proving such strong cause is on the plaintiffs."

In *Butler v Banimar Shipping Co SA* a foreign choice of court agreement, using the imperative "shall", was treated as exclusive without it being labelled as such. The relevant clause in the contract provided that:[37]

> Any dispute arising under this bill of lading shall be decided in the country where the carrier has his principal place of business . . .

Howie AJ noted that this type of clause is sometimes referred to as a "foreign jurisdiction clause",[38] but did not identify it as an exclusive foreign choice of court agreement. However, he applied the burden of proof criterion from *The Eleftheria*, which indicates that the clause was regarded as an exclusive one.[39]

In *MV Spartan-Runner v Jotun-Henry Clark Ltd*, an admiralty case,[40] the relevant clause stipulated that:[41]

> Any disputes arising from this contract will be subject to English law and the jurisdiction of the English Courts.

Shearer J (Howard JP agreeing and Booysen J concurring) held that "[t]he question is not whether the parties intended that the English Courts should have exclusive jurisdiction, it is whether the English law at the time of the litigation provided for the exclusive jurisdiction of the Courts".[42] Finding that the clause did amount to an exclusive choice of court agreement, Shearer J relied on *The Eleftheria* to decide that the burden was on the plaintiff to show why a stay of proceedings should not be granted, thus giving effect to the choice of court agreement between the parties. The judge also emphasised that choosing a forum was an aspect of party autonomy and, therefore, similar to contractual choice of law clauses, courts would "lean towards the chosen forum of the parties".[43]

In *Mt Fotiy Krylov v Owners of the Mt Ruby Deliverer* the contract contained a clause providing that:[44]

> Any dispute or difference which may arise out of or in connection with this agreement or the services to be performed hereunder shall be referred to the High Court of Justice in London.

---

[37] 1978 (4) SA 753 (SE), 760C.

[38] 1978 (4) SA 753 (SE), 760D.

[39] 1978 (4) SA 753 (SE), 761G and 762D: "It . . . results in the party breaching it having to carry the onus of showing why the clause ought not to be complied with."

[40] See also *MV Achilleus v Thai United Insurance Co Ltd and Others* 1992 (1) SA 324 (N), another admiralty case, where the contract contained a clause providing for jurisdiction in "the courts of Piraeus exclusively", in which case the plaintiff bore the onus to prove why a stay of proceedings should not be granted to uphold the choice of court agreement.

[41] 1991 (3) SA 803 (N), 804G.

[42] 1991 (3) SA 803 (N), 805I-J.

[43] 1991 (3) SA 803 (N), 806E-H.

[44] 2008 (5) SA 434 (C), 442D.

The contract further stipulated that:[45]

> No suit shall be brought in any other State or jurisdiction, except that either party shall have the option to bring proceedings *in rem* to obtain conservative seizure or any similar remedy against any vessel or property owned by the other party in any State or jurisdiction where such vessel or property may be found.

The case proceeded on the basis that there was an exclusive choice of court agreement in favour of the High Court of Justice in London, without any analysis of the clause and without any reference to the derogation clause. In this instance, Davis J made no reference to *The Eleftheria*.

In *Foize Africa (Pty) Ltd v Foize Beheer BV and Others* the contract contained a choice of law, choice of court and arbitration agreement:[46]

> This agreement shall . . . be governed by and executed according to Dutch law . . . The parties irrevocably consent to the jurisdiction of the courts of Holland for any matter arising out of or in connection with this agreement . . . Should any dispute arise out of or in connection with this agreement, that dispute shall be referred to and finally decided by arbitration . . . with the seat of the arbitration being Amsterdam. . .

Leach JA (Mthiyane DP, Cloete JA, Heher JA and Shongwe JA concurring) emphasised the sanctity of contract and applied *The Eleftheria* to both the jurisdiction and the arbitration clauses.[47] Although the choice of court agreement was not labelled "exclusive", the use of the word "irrevocably" might have been conclusive.

From the above it is clear that, even though foreign choice of court agreements may not always be classified or designated as "exclusive", the application of the principles enunciated in *The Eleftheria* by South African courts indicates that foreign choice of court agreements are treated as exclusive in the majority of cases.

3.5 Optional Choice of Court Agreements in Favour of South African Courts

The clearest evidence of optional choice of court agreements in South African law is to be found within the context of submission to jurisdiction by consent. Submission to jurisdiction operates within the context of the fragmented South African High Court jurisdictional structure and, therefore, submission to the jurisdiction of a particular Division of the High Court must be established.[48]

Submission by consent is subject to the normal requirements that apply to submission at common law. Mere submission is not sufficient to establish jurisdic-

[45] 2008 (5) SA 434 (C), 442E.

[46] 2013 (3) SA 91 (SCA), [8].

[47] 2013 (3) SA 91 (SCA), [27]-[28].

[48] See Sect. 2 above.

tion in the absence of a recognised jurisdictional ground (*ratio jurisdictionis*).[49] In actions sounding in money, the general principle is that the plaintiff should sue the defendant in the court of the defendant's residence or domicile—*actor sequitur forum rei*.[50] Where both parties are foreigners (*peregrini*) and the cause of action arose outside the area of the court's jurisdiction, a choice of court agreement in favour of that court will not be given effect, since there is no valid *ratio jurisdictionis*.[51] This is why contractual submission to the jurisdiction of a South African court is properly called 'prorogation'—an extension of an already existing ground of jurisdiction by subjecting her/his (the defendant's) person to the court.[52]

Submission will also not ground jurisdiction in certain types of proceedings where subject matter jurisdiction is required, for example, proceedings involving title to foreign land, or where special jurisdictional connecting factors are required, for example in private-law status matters, such as divorce proceedings.[53]

Submission to jurisdiction by consent may be established through the choice of a *domicilium citandi et executandi*. In *Beverley Building Society v De Courcy and Another*, a case where both parties were *peregrini* but the contract had extensive connections with Southern Rhodesia, Maisels J held that the selection of a *domicilium citandi et executandi* within the area of the jurisdiction of a court, to which the party was not normally subject, could amount to an intention to submit to the jurisdiction of that court.[54] The importance of the intention to submit to the

[49]Pistorius (2017), p. 9. The common law grounds of jurisdiction are domicile (*ratione domicilii*); contract (*ratione contractus*); delict (*ratione delicti commissi*); *ratione rei gestae*; cohesion of causes (*ratione causae continentia*); location of property (*ratione rei sitae*); and jurisdiction based on attachment of property: Harms (2016), [26].

[50]Harms (2016), [33]. See also *Benidai Trading Co Ltd v Gouws & Gouws (Pty) Ltd* 1977 (3) SA 1020 (T), 1038H.

[51]Pistorius (2017), p. 9; Forsyth (2012), pp. 217, 221ff (which contains a table setting out the jurisdictional requirements for claims sounding in money), 230ff.

[52]*Veneta Mineraria Spa v Carolina Collieries (Pty) Ltd* 1987 (4) SA 883 (A), 894A-B, per Viljoen JA (Smalberger JA, Vivier JA, Boshoff AJA and MT Steyn AJA concurring): "By prorogation a defendant subjects his person to the jurisdiction of the Court, but that is not enough. One or more of the traditional grounds of jurisdiction must also be present." But see the earlier case of *Negro v SAR* 1911 TPD 979, 981, per De Villiers JP: "It is well-known that if a person consents to the jurisdiction of a court of a place where he is not domiciled that is a prorogation of jurisdiction which is allowed by our law, because it is a privilege granted to the defendant, to be sued in the court of his domicile, which he may renounce."

[53]Pistorius (2017), p. 9.

[54]1964 (4) SA 264 (SR), 270D, deciding that "it is more probable that the choice of a *domicilium citandi et executandi* in Salisbury was for the purpose and with the intention of submitting to the jurisdiction of the Southern Rhodesian Court than that this choice was made merely in order to facilitate service if the Court otherwise had jurisdiction" (272G).

jurisdiction of the court was emphasised in *Hay Management Consultants (Pty) Ltd v P3 Management Consultants (Pty) Ltd*, where there was an express choice of South African law and the foreign defendant had chosen a *domicilium citandi et executandi* in the area of the court. Heher JA (Scott JA, Cameron JA, Conradie JA and Patel AJA concurring) concluded that the defendant had intended to submit to the jurisdiction of the court, which was "the appropriate Court in the context of the agreement".[55] In this case the plaintiff was an *incola* of the court and, therefore, there was a *ratio jurisdictionis*.[56]

A bare choice of a *domicilium citandi et executandi*, with nothing else to support an intention to submit to jurisdiction, will not amount to tacit submission.[57] In *Standard Bank Ltd v Butlin*, Didcott J emphasised that submission to jurisdiction can be express or tacit.[58] Although the judge used the terms "impliedly" or "tacitly", Forsyth points out that implied submission does not arise here, since implied submission is established by operation of law, based on facts (such as having registered a company in the area of the jurisdiction of the court), and independent of a party's intention. Tacit submission, on the other hand, requires the intention to agree to submit to the jurisdiction of the court.[59]

From the above discussion it is clear that submission to the jurisdiction of a South African court without a *ratio jurisdictionis* is not possible. As a result, a choice of court agreement between two foreigners, choosing a South African court as a neutral venue, will not be enforced.[60]

[55] 2005 (2) SA 522 (SCA), [15].

[56] This case endorsed *American Flag plc v Great African T-Shirt Corporation* 2000 (1) SA 356 (W), where the plaintiff was an *incola* and the defendant a *peregrinus*—submission by the defendant could serve as a ground of jurisdiction. However, in *Veneta Mineraria Spa v Carolina Collieries (Pty) Ltd (In Liquidation)* 1987 (4) SA 883(A), involving a local *peregrinus* as defendant and a foreign *peregrinus* as plaintiff, with no contractual connections with the forum, Viljoen JA (Smalberger JA, Vivier JA, Boshoff AJA and M T Steyn AJA concurring) decided that written consent by the defendant did not suffice (894A-B)—a proper *ratio jurisdictionis* was required to establish jurisdiction.

[57] *Standard Bank Ltd v Butlin* 1981 (4) SA 158 (D), 165D. Didcott J distinguished (164G-H) the case of *Beverley Building Society v De Courcy and Another* 1964 (4) SA 264 (SR), and decided that it was "safe to view the address he selected as one furnished simply for the service of processes" (162H) and, therefore, did not amount to an intention to submit to the jurisdiction of the forum (165B-C). Where a *domicilium citandi et executandi* is selected in response to a court order, it also does not amount to submission to jurisdiction: *JPS Nominees (Pty) Ltd v Binstock and Another* 1993 (1) SA 341 (W), 346G-H, per Lazarus J.

[58] 1981 (4) SA 158 (D), 161E-G.

[59] Forsyth (2012), p. 428.

[60] Forsyth (2012), p. 232: "[T]wo peregrines cannot agree that their disputes should be settled in the local courts. The point may be stressed: submission is not a *ratio jurisdictionis*, it is a substitute for attachment *ad confirmandam*."

4 Relationship Between Foreign Choice of Court Agreements and Foreign Arbitration Agreements in South Africa

South Africa recently introduced a new international arbitration regime, the International Arbitration Act 15 of 2017. This Act incorporates the United Nations Commission on International Trade Law (UNCITRAL) Model Law on International Commercial Arbitration, as well as the New York Convention on the Recognition and Enforcement of Foreign Arbitral Awards (1958), into South African law. South Africa already became a party to the New York Convention in 1976, but the implementing legislation, the Recognition and Enforcement of Foreign Arbitral Awards Act 40 of 1977,[61] did not incorporate the full Convention. It only provided for the enforcement of foreign arbitral awards and omitted the crucial Article II(3) of the Convention, which determines that:

> The court of a Contracting State, when seized of an action in a matter in respect of which the parties have made an agreement within the meaning of this article, shall, at the request of one of the parties, refer the parties to arbitration, unless it finds that the said agreement is null and void, inoperative or incapable of being performed.

As a result of this legislative oversight, South African courts treated foreign arbitration agreements in the same way as exclusive foreign choice of court agreements and applied the principles, enunciated in *The Eleftheria*,[62] to foreign arbitration agreements.[63] Under the new International Arbitration Act 15 of 2017, the courts will no longer have this discretion whether to enforce a foreign arbitration agreement or not—upon request by one of the parties, they must refer the parties to arbitration, unless the arbitration agreement is "null and void, inoperative or incapable of being performed".[64]

5 The Case for Reform of the South African Law Relating to Choice of Court Agreements

In the past two decades South African law has been substantially shaped by its Constitution.[65] Emerging from an apartheid era that saw the country being isolated in almost all spheres of human activity and interaction on a global level—on the

[61] This Act has now been repealed by the International Arbitration Act 15 of 2017.

[62] [1969] 2 All ER 641 (PDA).

[63] *Intercontinental Export Company (Pty) Ltd v MV Dien Danielsen* 1982 (3) SA 534 (N); *Polysius (Pty) Ltd v Tvl Alloys (Pty) Ltd, Tvl Alloys (Pty) Ltd v Polysius (Pty) Ltd* (1983 (2) SA 630 (W); *MV Iran Dastghayb Islamic Republic of Iran Shipping Lines v Terramarine SA* (2010 (6) SA 493 (SCA); *Foize Africa (Pty) Ltd v Foize Beheer BV and Others* (2013 (3) SA 91 (SCA).

[64] International Arbitration Act 15 of 2017, s 16(1); Article II(3) of the New York Convention; Art 8 (1) of the UNCITRAL Model Law on International Commercial Arbitration.

[65] Constitution of the Republic of South Africa, 1996.

political, commercial, economic, cultural, social and sporting front—it is not surprising that cross-border commercial litigation and dispute resolution lacked the structures and systems required to deal with international commercial disputes. As one of the economic powerhouses on the African continent, South Africa plays a leading role in contributing to the development of a secure financial and economic future for the entire continent. This involves major international commercial transactions, not only with the rest of the world, but also with other African countries. Effective cross-border dispute regimes are essential to support international commercial enterprise, and in this regard the enactment of the International Arbitration Act 15 of 2017[66] has been a major step forward. In tandem with the strengthening of South Africa as an international arbitration venue, the development of a sound jurisprudential basis for choice of court agreements in international commercial litigation is of paramount importance.

The Constitution expressly empowers the courts to develop the common law under section 173:

> The Constitutional Court, the Supreme Court of Appeal and the High Court of South Africa each has the inherent power . . . to develop the common law, taking into account the interests of justice.

The power of the courts to develop the common law must be read in conjunction with three sections in Chapter 2 of the Constitution (the Bill of Rights), namely sections 34, 36 and 39.

Section 34 guarantees the right to access to courts and other tribunals:

> Everyone has the right to have any dispute that can be resolved by the application of law decided in a fair public hearing before a court or, where appropriate, another independent and impartial tribunal or forum.

Section 36, known as the 'limitation clause', determines when and how the rights contained in the Bill of Rights, including the right to access to courts, may be limited.[67]

Section 39 provides guidelines for the interpretation of the Bill of Rights:

> (1) When interpreting the Bill of Rights, a court, tribunal or forum:
>
> (a) must promote the values that underlie an open and democratic society based on human dignity, equality and freedom;
> (b) must consider international law; and
> (c) may consider foreign law.

[66] See Sect. 4 above.

[67] "(1) The rights in the Bill of Rights may be limited only in terms of law of general application to the extent that the limitation is reasonable and justifiable in an open and democratic society based on human dignity, equality and freedom, taking into account all relevant factors, including— (a) the nature of the right; (b) the importance of the purpose of the limitation; (c) the nature and extent of the limitation; (d) the relation between the limitation and its purpose; and (e) less restrictive means to achieve the purpose. (2) Except as provided in subsection (1) or in any other provision of the Constitution, no law may limit any right entrenched in the Bill of Rights."

(2) When interpreting any legislation, and when developing the common law or customary law, every court, tribunal or forum must promote the spirit, purport and objects of the Bill of Rights.
(3) The Bill of Rights does not deny the existence of any other rights or freedoms that are ecognised or conferred by common law, customary law or legislation, to the extent that they are consistent with the Bill.

Section 39(2) was invoked by the Supreme Court of Appeal in *Bid Industrial Holdings (Pty) Ltd v Strang and Another (Minister of Justice and Constitutional Development, Third Party)* to declare the common-law principle of arrest of the person to found or confirm jurisdiction unconstitutional:[68]

> Section 173 of the Constitution empowers the court to develop the common law and s 39 (2) requires the court, when interpreting s 19(1) of the Supreme Court Act and developing the common law, to promote the objects of the Bill of Rights.

Section 39(1)(b) and (c), in particular, open up the possibility for international and comparative reference to international legal instruments and comparable foreign legal systems/legal instruments. There is, as yet, no case authority on the application of these two subsections in respect of cross-border jurisdiction, but it is submitted that there is now a strong constitutional incentive for the development of cross-border jurisdictional rules, including rules governing choice of court agreements, to better support international commercial litigation.

5.1 Defining Exclusive and Optional Choice of Court Agreements

Exclusive and optional choice of court agreements are not clearly defined and distinguished in South African law. An interesting feature of the current position is that jurisprudence in regard to exclusive choice of court agreements is entirely focused on *foreign* exclusive choice of court agreements,[69] while exclusive choice of court agreements in favour of South African courts have not received any attention at all. In this regard it must be asked whether no distinction is drawn between exclusive and optional choice of court agreements, in other words, are all choice of court agreements considered to be exclusive? This does not seem to be the case, since choice of court agreements in favour of South African courts, within the context of submission to jurisdiction by consent, can definitely not be regarded as exclusive.

Submission to jurisdiction by consent is often evidenced by a contractual designation of a *domicilium citandi et executandi*, and the courts have emphasised the importance of the intention to submit to the jurisdiction of the court in order to

[68] 2008 (3) SA 355 (SCA), [50], per Howie P (Nugent JA, Ponnan JA, Maya JA and Malan AJA concurring): see further discussion under Sect. 5.2 below.

[69] See Sect. 3.4 above.

establish tacit submission to jurisdiction.[70] The focus of these 'choice of court agreements' is on the submission of the defendant to the jurisdiction of the court. In this regard, submission to jurisdiction is not unfettered—apart from certain categories of cases where submission to jurisdiction is not permitted (for example, disputes concerning title to foreign immovable property and matters concerning private-law status),[71] a *ratio jurisdictionis* is required for claims sounding in money in order for submission to be effective. In these cases it would seem that submission becomes a substitute for attachment of property *ad confirmandam jurisdictionem*, and that submission is not a ground of jurisdiction *ad fundandam jurisdictionem*.[72] This means that two *peregrini* cannot choose a South African court as a completely neutral forum for litigation.

The current position in South African law appears to be as follows: the focus of exclusive choice of court agreements is on *foreign* exclusive choice of court agreements, while the focus of *optional* choice of court agreements is on choice of court agreements in favour of South African courts. The *lacunae* in regard to exclusive choice of court agreements in favour of South African courts and optional choice of court agreements in favour of foreign courts must be addressed. Within this context, a number of underlying issues also need to be addressed, namely:

- The current paradox regarding submission as a ground of jurisdiction: while submission is recognised as a ground of international competence in respect of the recognition and enforcement of foreign judgments, it is not recognised as an independent ground of jurisdiction in cross-border litigation in South Africa.[73]
- The territorial jurisdiction of the Divisions of the South African High Court: the number of different permutations regarding *incolae* and *peregrini* in respect of submission to jurisdiction complicate the assumption of jurisdiction in cross-border scenarios unnecessarily.[74]
- The uneasy relationship between party autonomy and jurisdiction: currently the power of jurisdiction lies with the courts and party autonomy has to give way to domestic jurisdictional requirements.[75]

[70]See Sect. 3.5 above.

[71]Pistorius (2017), p. 9.

[72]Forsyth (2012), p. 232.

[73]See *Elscint (Pty) Ltd and Another v Mobile Medical Scanners (Pty) Ltd* 1986 (4) SA 552 (W), 557I-558C, per Goldstone J: "The Courts of most, if not all, Western nations will recognise and enforce a judgment of our Courts sounding in money in cases where our Courts possess and exercise 'international' or 'competent' jurisdiction ... The validity of a submission clause appears to be a well-recognised ground for confirming international or competent jurisdiction ..." See also, in regard to submission as a recognised ground of international competence, *Purser v Sales; Purser and Another v Sales and Another* 2001 (3) SA 445 (SCA), [12]; *Blanchard, Krasner & French v Evans* 2002 (4) SA 144 (T), [3].

[74]See Sect. 2 above.

[75]Roodt and Esser (2006), p. 21.

5.2 *The Doctrine of* forum non conveniens

South African courts have embraced the authority of *The Eleftheria*[76] in respect of exclusive foreign choice of court agreements.[77] The logical step would be to adopt the *forum non conveniens* doctrine in regard to optional choice of court agreements in favour of South African courts or foreign courts. This will provide the courts with the necessary discretion to decide whether to stay proceedings in favour of another, distinctly more appropriate foreign forum.[78]

The *forum non conveniens* doctrine is not completely foreign to South African law. Section 7(1)*(a)* of the Admiralty Jurisdiction Regulation Act 105 of 1983, which deals with disputes regarding venue and jurisdiction, provides for a stay of proceedings in favour of a "more appropriate court":

> A court may decline to exercise its admiralty jurisdiction in any proceedings instituted or to be instituted, if it is of the opinion that any other court in the Republic or any other court or any arbitrator, tribunal or body elsewhere will exercise jurisdiction in respect of the said proceedings and that it is more appropriate that the proceedings be adjudicated upon by any such other court or by such arbitrator, tribunal or body.

This section, which only applies in respect of admiralty jurisdiction, allows for a *forum non conveniens* inquiry and *Spiliada Maritime Corp v Cansulex Ltd*[79] has been accepted as authority in this regard.[80]

The doctrine of *forum non conveniens* might just have found its way into non-admiralty cross-border cases in South Africa in recent times. This was sparked by a successful constitutional challenge to the common-law rule of arrest of the person to found or confirm jurisdiction in *Bid Industrial Holdings (Pty) Ltd v Strang and Another (Minister of Justice and Constitutional Development, Third Party)*.[81] The case concerned a claim by a South African plaintiff against two peregrine defendants (Australians), who refused to submit to jurisdiction and who had no assets in South Africa at the time that could be attached to found or confirm

[76] [1969] 2 All ER 641 (PDA).

[77] See Sect. 3.4 above.

[78] *Spiliada Maritime Corp v Cansulex Ltd* [1987] AC 460 (HL), where Lord Goff set out the parameters of the *forum non conveniens* doctrine. Significantly, the burden is on the defendant to prove that another competent court is clearly more appropriate (476D). This is different from the burden of proof in regard to exclusive foreign choice of court agreements, where the burden is on the plaintiff to prove why a stay should not be granted: *The Eleftheria* [1969] 2 All ER 641 (PDA), 645B-C.

[79] [1987] AC 460 (HL).

[80] *MV Spartan-Runner v Jotun-Henry Clark Ltd* 1991 (3) SA 803 (N), 807E-808E; *Great River Shipping Inc v Sunnyface Marine Ltd* 1992 (4) SA 313 (C), 316D-317I; *MT Tigr Bouygues Offshore SA and Another v Owners of the MT Tigr and Another* 1998 (4) SA 740 (C), 741H-742B.

[81] 2008 (3) SA 355 (SCA).

jurisdiction. The Court decided that the common-law rule of arrest of the defendant was unconstitutional:[82]

> For all these reasons the common-law rule that arrest is mandatory to found or confirm jurisdiction cannot pass the limitations test set by s 36(1) [of the Constitution]. It is contrary to the spirit, purport and objects of the Bill of Rights. The common law must be, and is hereby, developed by abolition of the rule and the adoption in its stead, where attachment is not possible, of the practice according to which a South African High Court will have jurisdiction if the summons is served on the defendant while in South Africa and there is sufficient connection between the suit and the area of jurisdiction of the court concerned so that disposal of the case by that court is appropriate and convenient. It goes without saying that the new practice could itself be subject to development with time.

Although the Court did not adopt the *forum non conveniens* doctrine by name, the requirement of a "sufficient connection between the suit and the area of jurisdiction of the court concerned so that disposal of the case by that court is appropriate and convenient", is a definite indication in that direction. This is supported by the following statement earlier on in the judgment, which embodies the burden of proof resting on the defendant in the case of *forum non conveniens*[83] to prove that there is another competent court that is a distinctly more appropriate forum to hear the matter:[84]

> And if the plaintiff decides in favour of suing here it is open to the defendant to contest, among other things, whether the South African court is the *forum conveniens* and whether there are sufficient links between the suit and this country to render litigation appropriate here rather than in the court of the defendant's domicile.

If this represents the beginnings of the *forum non conveniens* doctrine for cross-border commercial litigation in South Africa,[85] it should be embraced and further developed to play its role in regard to optional choice of court agreements in respect of South African courts or foreign courts. Where a choice of court agreement is based on submission to jurisdiction by consent, very often by way of the choice of a *domicilium citandi et executandi*,[86] the *forum non conveniens* doctrine can operate as an efficient check on the appropriateness of the South African forum. Taken one step further, the choice of a South African court as a completely neutral forum should also then be allowed, with the *forum non conveniens* doctrine operating as a check on the appropriateness of the South African forum to hear the matter.

[82] 2008 (3) SA 355 (SCA), [59], per Howie P (Nugent JA, Ponnan JA, Maya JA and Malan AJA concurring).

[83] See *Spiliada Maritime Corp v Cansulex Ltd* [1987] AC 460 (HL), 476D.

[84] 2008 (3) SA 355 (SCA), [55].

[85] See, e.g., *Multi-Links Telecommunications Ltd v Africa Prepaid Services Nigeria Ltd* 2014 (3) SA 265 (GP), [17]-[19]. See also Forsyth (2012), pp. 184ff, for a thorough discussion of *forum non conveniens* in the South African jurisdictional context.

[86] See Sect. 3.5 above.

5.3 The Hague Convention on Choice of Court Agreements (2005)

The "Choice of Court Convention", as it is commonly known, applies in international cases to *exclusive*[87] choice of court agreements "concluded in civil or commercial matters".[88] The Convention is based on three basic rules: in principle, the chosen court should hear the case,[89] any court not chosen must decline to hear the case,[90] and the judgment rendered by the chosen court must be recognised and enforced in other contracting states.[91]

The Choice of Court Convention is intended to be the "litigation" counterpart of the New York Convention on the Recognition and Enforcement of Foreign Arbitral Awards (1958), in terms of which foreign arbitration agreements must, at the request of one of the parties, be enforced, unless the agreement is "null and void, inoperative or incapable of being performed".[92] Since South Africa is already a member of the New York Convention,[93] it would make good commercial and legal sense to accede to the Choice of Court Convention in order to provide the certainty in respect of exclusive choice of court agreements that the New York Convention provides in regard to arbitration agreements.[94] In addition, accession to the Choice of Court Convention will provide the impetus for South African courts and scholars to re-evaluate the existing South African jurisprudence on choice of court agreements, exclusive and optional, and to bring it into step with prevailing international commercial best practice.

6 Conclusion

The South African law relating to jurisdiction in cross-border commercial litigation is complex. Several factors contribute to this: the fragmented nature of High Court jurisdiction, common-law rules that are subject to interpretation by the courts and strict grounds of jurisdiction.[95] In addition, choice of court agreements are not well

[87]Defined in Art 3.

[88]Art 1(1). Art 2 excludes certain matters and exclusive choice of court agreements from the scope of the Convention.

[89]Art 5.

[90]Art 6.

[91]Art 8. Art 9 contains grounds of refusal.

[92]Art II(3) of the New York Convention. This has now been reinforced by the adoption of the UNCITRAL Model Law on International Commercial Arbitration by the International Arbitration Act 15 of 2017: see Sect. 4 above.

[93]Since 1976.

[94]Schulze (2007), p. 149.

[95]See Sect. 2 above.

defined and no clear distinction is drawn between exclusive and optional choice of court agreements. While the position regarding the treatment of exclusive foreign choice of court agreements is reasonably clear and settled,[96] the same cannot be said of optional choice of court agreements. Optional choice of court agreements in favour of South African courts are based on submission to jurisdiction by consent; however, mere submission without a recognised *ratio jurisdictionis* will not suffice. As a result, two foreigners cannot choose a South African court as a neutral venue for litigation.[97] Considering that the International Arbitration Act 15 of 2017 was enacted to establish South Africa as an international arbitration venue of choice, with full effect being given to party autonomy, a choice of court agreement in favour of a South African court, as a neutral forum, should be possible.[98] Therefore, the law regarding choice of court agreements must be reviewed and reformed. To this end, a number of issues, which need to be addressed, have been identified in this contribution. Reform should be undertaken adopting an international and comparative approach. In this regard, the constitutional empowerment of the Superior Courts to develop the common law,[99] as well as the constitutional imperative to refer to international law and the constitutional incentive to refer to comparable foreign legal systems,[100] will be crucial in driving reform of this area of South African law.

References

Books and Encyclopedias

Forsyth CF (2012) Private International Law, 5th edn. Juta, Cape Town

Harms DR (2016) Civil Procedure: Superior Courts in Joubert WA (founding ed) The Law of South Africa, vol 4, 3rd edn. Butterworths, Durban

Hosten WJ, Edwards AB, Bosman F, Church J (1997) Introduction to South African Law and Legal Theory, 2nd edn. Butterworths, Durban. 1995, Reprint, 1997

Nygh PE (1999) Autonomy in International Contracts. Clarendon Press, Oxford

Pistorius D (2017) Pollak on Jurisdiction, 2nd edn. 1993, Reprint, 2017, Juta, Cape Town

Journal Articles

Kahn E (1987) Conflict of laws. Ann Surv S Afr Law, 472–481

Kahn E (1992) Conflict of laws. Ann Surv S Afr Law, 673–692

[96]See Sect. 3.4 above.

[97]See Sect. 3.5.

[98]See also Forsyth (2012), p. 231: "The judicial policy should not be 'Peregrines go home' but 'Peregrines welcome'."

[99]Section 173 of the Constitution.

[100]Section 39(2) of the Constitution.

Kelbrick R (1986) The doctrine of consent. Comp Int Law J South Afr 19:130–136
Kelbrick R (1992) The *incola* plaintiff, consent and arrest or attachment to found jurisdiction. Comp Int Law J South Afr 25:332–342
Roodt C, Esser I-M (2006) Venue in transnational litigation: party autonomy adds new impetus to the 'judgment project'. S Afr Mercantile Law J 18:13–30
Schulze C (2007) The 2005 Hague Convention on choice of court agreements. S Afr Mercantile Law J 19:140–150
Spiro E (1967) Jurisdiction by consent. S Afr Law J 84:295–307

Cases

South Africa

American Flag plc v Great African T-Shirt Corporation 2000 (1) SA 356 (W)
Astra Furnishers (Pty) Ltd v Arend and Another 1973 (1) SA 446 (C)
Benidai Trading Co Ltd v Gouws & Gouws (Pty) Ltd 1977 (3) SA 1020 (T)
Beverley Building Society v De Courcy and Another 1964 (4) SA 264 (SR)
Bid Industrial Holdings (Pty) Ltd v Strang and Another (Minister of Justice and Constitutional Development, Third Party) 2008 3 SA 355 (SCA)
Bisonboard Ltd v K Braun Woodworking Machinery (Pty) Ltd 1991 (2) SA 482 (A)
Blanchard, Krasner & French v Evans 2002 (4) SA 144 (T)
Butler v Banimar Shipping Co SA 1978 (4) SA 753 (SE)
Elscint (Pty) Ltd and Another v Mobile Medical Scanners (Pty) Ltd 1986 (4) SA 552 (W)
Foize Africa (Pty) Ltd v Foize Beheer BV and Others 2013 (3) SA 91 (SCA)
Goldschmidt and Another v Folb and Another 1974 (1) SA 576 (T)
Great River Shipping Inc v Sunnyface Marine Ltd 1992 (4) SA 313 (C)
Intercontinental Export Company (Pty) Ltd v MV Dien Danielsen 1982 (3) SA 534 (N)
Hay Management Consultants (Pty) Ltd v P3 Management Consultants (Pty) Ltd 2005 3 All SA 119 (SCA); 2005 2 SA 522 (SCA)
Hugo v Wessels 1987 (3) SA 837 (A)
J P S Nominees (Pty) Ltd v Binstock and Another 1993 (1) SA 341 (W)
MV Achilleus v Thai United Insurance Co Ltd and Others 1992 (1) SA 324 (N)
Mt Fotiy Krylov v Owners of the Mt Ruby Deliverer 2008 (5) SA 434 (C)
MT Tigr Bouygues Offshore SA and Another v Owners of the MT Tigr and Another 1998 (4) SA 740 (C)
Multi-Links Telecommunications Ltd v Africa Prepaid Services Nigeria Ltd 2014 (3) SA 265 (GP)
MV Iran Dastghayb Islamic Republic of Iran Shipping Lines v Terramarine SA 2010 (6) SA 493 (SCA)
MV Spartan-Runner v Jotun-Henry Clark Ltd 1991 (3) SA 803 (N)
Negro v SAR 1911 TPD 979
Polysius (Pty) Ltd v Tvl Alloys (Pty) Ltd, Tvl Alloys (Pty) Ltd v Polysius (Pty) Ltd 1983 (2) SA 630 (W)
Purser v Sales; Purser and Another v Sales and Another 2001 (3) SA 445 (SCA)
Standard Bank Ltd v Butlin 1981 (4) SA 158 (D)
Tsung v Industrial Development Corporation of SA Ltd 2006 (4) SA 177 (SCA)
Veneta Mineraria Spa v Carolina Collieries (Pty) Ltd (In Liquidation) 1987 (4) SA 883 (A)
Yorigami Maritime Construction Co Ltd v Nissho-Iwai Co Ltd 1977 (4) SA 682 (C)

United Kingdom

The Eleftheria [1969] 2 All ER 641 (PDA)
Spiliada Maritime Corp v Cansulex Ltd [1987] AC 460 (HL)

Legislation

Supreme Court Act 59 of 1959
Recognition and Enforcement of Foreign Arbitral Awards Act 40 of 1977
Constitution of the Republic of South Africa, 1996 (Constitution)
Superior Courts Act 10 of 2013
International Arbitration Act 15 of 2017

Conventions

New York Convention on the Recognition and Enforcement of Foreign Arbitral Awards (1958)
Hague Convention on Choice of Court Agreements (2005)

Internet Resources

http://www.justice.gov.za/about/sa-courts.html (accessed 16 September 2018)
https://www.judiciary.org.za/index.php/the-south-african-judicial-system (accessed 16 September 2018)

Elsabe Schoeman holds the degrees BLC (UP) LLB LLD (Unisa). She is a Professor in the Department of Private Law, Faculty of Law, at the University of Pretoria, South Africa.

Previously, she was a Professor in the Department of Jurisprudence, College of Law, at the University of South Africa, and an Associate Professor in the Faculty of Law at the University of Auckland, New Zealand. She is an Alexander von Humboldt Fellow and spends significant periods of time researching at the Institut für internationales und ausländisches Privatrecht at the University of Cologne, Germany.

Her main areas of research are jurisdiction in cross-border commercial litigation and choice of law in contract, delict/tort and selected areas of family law. She has published widely in her areas of interest and has also made contributions to international legal encyclopaedias, as well as submissions to law commissions (in South Africa and New Zealand), and she regularly advises law firms on transnational litigation.

Switzerland: Choice of Court Agreements According to the Code on Civil Procedure, the Private International Law Act and the Lugano Convention

Eliane Haas and Kevin MacCabe

1 Introduction

Choice of court agreements can be found in almost every international commercial contract.[1] While they formally only determine which courts are prorogated and which courts are derogated, they do in fact often have a direct impact on the outcome of the proceedings.[2] This chapter intends to give a short overview of the legal sources, requirements, limitations and effects of optional choice of court agreements in Switzerland.

2 Legal Sources

Being located in continental Europe, Switzerland is a traditional Civil Law country.[3] As such, the primary sources of law are the laws enacted by the legislator.[4] Among those laws are the Code on Civil Procedure (CCP)[5] and the Private International Law

The bibliography of this paper is considered until April 2018.

[1]Dasser (2015), p. 89.

[2]Dasser (2015), p. 89.

[3]Müller-Chen et al. (2015), p. 151 et seq.

[4]Müller-Chen et al. (2015), p. 161 et seq. This contrasts with common law systems, where case law is the typical starting point for legal reasoning: Müller-Chen et al. (2015), p. 222 et seq.

[5]Schweizerische Zivilprozessordnung vom 19. Dezember 2008, SR 272.

E. Haas (✉) · K. MacCabe
University of Basel, Faculty of Law, Basel, Switzerland
e-mail: kevin.maccabe@unibas.ch

M. Keyes (ed.), *Optional Choice of Court Agreements in Private International Law*,
Ius Comparatum – Global Studies in Comparative Law 37,
https://doi.org/10.1007/978-3-030-23914-5_16

Act (PILA).[6] They both contain rules on jurisdiction and are therefore relevant legal sources for choice of court agreements. In addition to laws enacted by the Swiss legislator (such as the above-mentioned examples), Swiss courts also rely heavily on international law. This is especially true regarding Switzerland's relationship with the European Union. One of the many contracts governing this relationship is the Lugano Convention (LC),[7] a contract based on the European Union's Brussels I Regulation (EuGVVO).[8] It includes, among other things, rules on jurisdiction and is, therefore, also a relevant legal source when it comes to choice of court agreements.

3 Agreements About Jurisdiction

3.1 In General

Choice of court agreements are generally permitted and are very common in Switzerland.[9] When determining whether a choice of court agreement is permitted and what the requirements and limitations of its validity as well as its effects are, a distinction must be made between the above-mentioned three legal sources: The Code on Civil Procedure, the Private International Law Act and the Lugano Convention. Each of these legal sources has its own scope of application. Therefore, determining the validity of a choice of court agreement presupposes the determination of the applicable legal source.

The applicable legal source can be determined by following two steps: The first step is to determine whether the choice of court agreement concerns a cross-border transaction.[10] In contract law, a cross-border transaction is usually assumed when one of the following attributes of the parties or the contract involves a cross-border component: Domiciles of the contracting parties, place of performance or place of conclusion of the contract.[11] If none of these criteria involves a cross-border component, the applicable legal source is usually the Code on Civil Procedure. Its scope of application is limited to national transactions.[12]

The second step is only relevant in cross-border transactions. In cross-border transactions, a distinction must be made between the scope of application of the

[6]Bundesgesetz über das Internationale Privatrecht vom 18. Dezember 1987, SR 291.

[7]Convention of 30 October 2007 on jurisdiction and the recognition and enforcement of judgments in civil and commercial matters, SR 0.275.12.

[8]Council Regulation (EC) No 44/2001 of 22 December 2000 on jurisdiction and the recognition and enforcement of judgments in civil and commercial matters.

[9]See Dasser (2015), p. 89.

[10]Grolimund and Bachofner In: Honsell et al. (2013), art. 5 N 5; Killias In: Dasser and Oberhammer (2011), art. 23 N 15.

[11]Schnyder and Liatowitsch (2017), p. 4 et seq.; Kren Kostkiewicz (2018), p. 86.

[12]Grolimund and Bachofner In: Honsell et al. (2013), art. 5 N 7.

Private International Law Act and the Lugano Convention. The Lugano Convention is only applicable in civil and commercial matters if at least one of the parties has his/her domicile in a member state and the parties select a court of one (or more) of those states.[13] If one of those three conditions is not met, the validity of the choice of court agreement is determined by the Private International Law Act.

3.2 *Requirements*

3.2.1 Form

While it is safe to say that a written choice of court agreement signed by both parties is formally valid according to all three legal sources, the same cannot be said for other forms of contract.[14]

According to art. 17 para. 2 CCP "the agreement must be in writing or in any other form allowing it to be evidenced by text." This does not mean that the agreement must be contained in one document. The exchange of two separate documents each containing a choice of court clause is sufficient if the parties' consent is clearly expressed thereby.[15] According to the prevailing legal opinion, signature of the written document is not necessary.[16] Other forms allowing evidence by text are email and fax. According to the nature of these electronic forms of contracting, the parties' signature is not required.[17] A mere oral agreement—even if it is confirmed in writing by one party—is, however, not sufficient.

The form required by art. 5 para. 1 PILA is identical to the form required by art. 17 para. 1 CCP.[18]

A more liberal approach is taken by art. 23 LC. As in transactions governed by the Code on Civil Procedure and the Private International Law Act, a written choice of court agreement is valid under the Lugano Convention. Written form does not require the parties' signature.[19] According to art. 23 para. 2 LC "any communication

[13]Grolimund and Bachofner In: Honsell et al. (2013), art. 5 N 8 et seq; Furrer et al. (2013), p. 196.

[14]Hedinger and Hostettler In: Sutter-Somm et al. (2016), art. 17 N 17; Grolimund and Bachofner In: Honsell et al. (2013), art. 5 N 21; Killias In: Dasser and Oberhammer (2011), art. 23 N 93.

[15]Hedinger and Hostettler In: Sutter-Somm et al. (2016), art. 17 N 17; Füllemann In: Brunner et al. (2016), art. 17 N 14.

[16]Kramer et al. (2016), p. 152; Hedinger and Hostettler In: Sutter-Somm et al. (2016), art. 17 N 17; Füllemann In: Brunner et al. (2016), art. 17 N 14; Haas and Schlupmf In: Oberhammer et al. (2014), art. 17 N 17; signature is however recommended to facilitate proof of the parties' consent.

[17]Hedinger and Hostettler In: Sutter-Somm et al. (2016), art. 17 N 18.

[18]Füllemann In: Brunner et al. (2016), art. 17 N 32.

[19]Killias In: Dasser and Oberhammer (2011), art. 23 N 94; as mentioned above, signature is recommended as evidence.

by electronic means which provides a durable record of the agreement shall be equivalent to writing." Therefore, contracts concluded via email or fax containing a choice of court agreement are equivalent to written contracts and are formally valid. In addition to these two options, the Lugano Convention provides three further forms of contract with which a choice of court agreement can be validly concluded.

First, an oral agreement confirmed in writing by one party.[20] In this case the parties must orally agree on either the choice of court clause itself or on general terms and conditions containing such a clause.[21] The written confirmation following the oral agreement must be in writing or in an electronic form in accordance with art. 23 para. 2 LC.[22]

Second, "a form which accords with practices which the parties have established between themselves." This form requires a business relationship between the parties of a certain duration and intensity in which the parties have always concluded their contracts based on a specific choice of court agreement.[23] This form of contract is mainly applicable in cases in which a party sends its general terms and conditions to the recipient *after* the conclusion of the contract (for example with the order confirmation or bill) and the recipient does not object.[24] If the parties have used the same choice of court clause in the course of their business relationship, it can be assumed that the recipient was aware that the contract would be based on general terms and conditions containing such a clause.[25]

Third, "in international trade or commerce, in a form which accords with a usage of which the parties are or ought to have been aware and which in such trade or commerce is widely known to, and regularly observed by, parties to contracts of the type involved in the particular trade or commerce concerned." It is not necessary that the usage in question entails a specific choice of court agreement.[26] Art. 23 para. 1 lit. c LC merely refers to the *form* of contract which accords with a certain usage.[27] If the contract containing a choice of court agreement was concluded in such a form and the parties were or ought to have been aware of the usage in question, the choice of court agreement was validly agreed upon. A party's awareness of a usage is generally assumed when it has previously conducted business in the respective trade with either its current partner or a third party.[28]

[20]Furrer et al. (2013), p. 199 et seq.; Killias In: Dasser and Oberhammer (2011), art. 23 N 103.

[21]Furrer et al. (2013), p. 200 et seq.; Killias In: Dasser and Oberhammer (2011), art. 23 N 104.

[22]Killias In: Dasser and Oberhammer (2011), art. 23 N 107.

[23]Killias In: Dasser and Oberhammer (2011), art. 23 N 120.

[24]Furrer et al. (2013), p. 200; Killias In: Dasser and Oberhammer (2011), art. 23 N 121.

[25]Killias In: Dasser and Oberhammer (2011), art. 23 N 121.

[26]Killias In: Dasser and Oberhammer (2011), art. 23 N 128.

[27]Schnyder and Liatowitsch (2017), p. 316.

[28]Killias In: Dasser and Oberhammer (2011), art. 23 N 132.

3.2.2 Consent

A choice of court agreement is a contract. Its conclusion, therefore, requires consent of the parties involved.[29] The question of consent is very closely linked to the question of the required form. If the parties have expressed their intent in one of the forms required (as mentioned above), their consent can often be ascertained from the written documents.[30] However, this is not always the case. Certain aspects of the parties' consent go beyond the mere expression of intent. Questions may arise regarding time limits for offer and acceptance, the interpretation of the contract or defects in consent such as error, duress or fraud to name only a few.[31] This raises the question of the law applicable to such aspects of consent.

Regarding art. 5 PILA, the discussion of this highly controversial question amongst legal scholars has led to three different approaches: According to the first approach, the choice of court agreement is subject to the *lex fori*.[32] According to the second approach, the *lex causae* is relevant.[33] The third approach is based on an analogy with the rules set out for arbitration agreements in art. 178 para. 2 PILA.[34] According to art. 178 para. 2 PILA, an arbitration agreement is valid if it complies with the law chosen by the parties, the law governing the object of the dispute, in particular the law applicable to the principal contract, or with Swiss law. In this case, the choice of court agreement needs to comply with only one of the three laws stated in art. 178 para. 2 PILA in order to be valid. It is unclear whether the *lex fori*, the *lex causae* or the analogy with arbitration agreements-approach applies. The Swiss Supreme Court has not yet decided the issue.[35]

Regarding the scope of application of art. 23 LC, the situation is much clearer: The law applicable to the choice of court agreement is determined by the private international law of the forum state.[36]

---

[29]BGE 132 III 268, 274; BGE 122 III 439, 443.

[30]Grolimund and Bachofner In: Honsell et al. (2013), art. 5 N 37.

[31]Grolimund and Bachofner In: Honsell et al. (2013), art. 5 N 39; Killias In: Dasser and Oberhammer (2011), art. 23 N 139.

[32]Furrer et al. (2013), p. 195.

[33]Walter and Domej (2012), p. 127; Grolimund and Bachofner In: Honsell et al. (2013), art. 5 N 39.

[34]Reiser (1989), p. 66 et seq.

[35]However, the Swiss Supreme Court (BGer 4C.189/2001 of 1 February 2002, Cons. 5. et seq.) has stated that it does not consider applying the *lex fori* to be arbitrary.

[36]ECJ, 3.7.1997, C-269/95, Benincasa v. Dentalkit Srl., No 25; Furrer et al. (2013), p. 200 et seq., Killias In: Dasser and Oberhammer (2011), art. 23 N 140.

3.3 Limitations

Choice of court agreements are not permitted in all fields of law. To determine the limitations of the parties' freedom of contract, once again, a distinction must be made between the three relevant legal sources.

Art. 17 para. 1 CCP states that a choice of court agreement is permitted unless the law provides otherwise. Freedom of contract is considered the rule, limitations thereof the exception.[37] Exceptions can be found throughout the chapter of the Code on Civil Procedure regulating jurisdiction. They concern various fields of law such as family law (art. 23 et. seq. CCP), consumer contracts (art. 32 CCP), rental contracts (art. 33 CCP) and employment contracts (art. 34 CCP).

A slightly different approach is taken by art. 5 PILA. According to art. 5 para. 1 and 2 PILA, choice of court agreements are limited to disputes concerning pecuniary claims and are void if one party is denied in an abusive manner a court to which that party is entitled under Swiss law (see below Sect. 8. re. art. 5 para. 2 PILA). In addition to these two general limitations, further limitations for various fields of law can be found throughout the entire Private International Law Act, such as for consumer contracts (art. 114 para. 2 PILA) or real estate (art. 97 PILA).[38]

Unlike the Private International Law Act, art. 23 LC does not set any general limitations to choice of court agreements. The general limitations are already given by the scope of application of the Lugano Convention which is limited to civil and commercial matters.[39] Like the Code on Civil Procedure and the Private International Law Act, the Lugano Convention does, however, name certain fields of law in which freedom of contract regarding choice of court agreements is limited, such as employment contracts, insurance contracts or consumer contracts.

Although the limitations to choice of court agreements vary among the different legal sources, there are certain similarities between them (for details see below Sect. 10).

4 Recent Changes

The legal treatment of choice of court agreements has changed considerably in the past few decades for numerous reasons. On the one hand, new laws were enacted; the Private International Law Act in 1989 and the Code on Civil Procedure in 2011. On the other hand, Switzerland signed the revised Lugano Convention in 2007 which came into effect in 2011.[40]

[37] Sutter-Somm et al. (2016), art. 17 N 13.

[38] Grolimund and Bachofner In: Honsell et al. (2013), art. 5 N 17.

[39] Schnyder and Liatowitsch (2017), p. 315.

[40] Botschaft zum Bundesbeschluss über die Genehmigung und die Umsetzung des revidierten Übereinkommens von Lugano über die gerichtliche Zuständigkeit, die Anerkennung und die

Before 1989, there was no single codification of private international law. Rules on private international law were spread out[41] over various laws such as the Code of Obligations (CO),[42] the Civil Code (CC)[43] and the Code regarding the private law affairs of settled persons and foreign residents.[44] In addition to this, there was no federal law on civil procedure at the time. Until the enactment of the federal Code on Civil Procedure in 2011, civil procedure was governed by cantonal[45] laws.[46] This meant that the rules governing private international law were not only spread out over various federal laws, but also over different levels of government.[47] With international trade increasing constantly, the necessity to find a solution to the complex legal situation became apparent.[48] The solution was the Private International Law Act, which was enacted on 1 January 1989.

Before 1989, choice of court agreements were mainly governed by the cantonal laws on civil procedure.[49] According to many of those laws, choice of court agreements could only be concluded in writing. Written form in this case meant a written document signed by the parties, as prescribed by art. 13 para. 1 CO.[50] The formal requirements prescribed today by art. 5 para. 1 PILA and art. 17 para. 2 CCP are more liberal, since they allow other forms of contract as long as they can be evidenced by text.

The most recent change was the signature of the revised Lugano Convention by Switzerland in 2007. It was enacted on 1 January 2011 together with the Code on Civil Procedure. The most notable change regarding choice of court agreements is the new art. 23 para. 2 LC which states that "any communication by electronic means which provides a durable record of the agreement shall be equivalent to writing."[51] Like the Code on Civil Procedure and the Private International Law Act, the revised Lugano Convention led to somewhat more liberal formal requirements.

Vollstreckung gerichtlicher Entscheidungen in Zivil- und Handelssachen, BBl 2009, 1777, 1778 et. seq.

[41]Botschaft zum Bundesgesetz über das internationale Privatrecht vom 10. November 1982, BBl 1983 I 263, 265.

[42]Bundesgesetz betreffend die Ergänzung des Schweizerischen Zivilgesetzbuches (Fünfter Teil: Obligationenrecht) vom 30. März 1911, SR 220.

[43]Schweizerisches Zivilgesetzbuch vom 10. Dezember 1907, SR 210.

[44]Bundesgesetz vom 25. Juni 1891 betreffend die zivilrechtlichen Verhältnisse der Niedergelassenen und Aufenthalter (BS 2 737), SR 211.435.1.

[45]Cantons are administrative subdivisions of the Swiss Confederation.

[46]Sutter-Somm (2017), p. 9. Before the enactment of the federal Code on Civil Procedure, there was, however, a federal Code on Jurisdiction in Civil Matters (so-called *Gerichtsstandsgesetz* from 24 March 2000, former SR 272) which contained provisions on choice of court agreements.

[47]Botschaft IPRG (Fn 41), 265.

[48]Botschaft IPRG (Fn 41), 270.

[49]Vogel (1988), p. 85.

[50]Vogel (1988), p. 85; art. 13 para. 1 CO: "A contract required by law to be in writing must be signed by all persons on whom it imposes obligations."

[51]Killias In: Dasser and Oberhammer (2011), art. 23 N 134.

Unlike the European Union, Switzerland has not signed the Hague Choice of Court Agreements Convention of 2005. At this point it is unclear whether Switzerland intends to sign this convention at some point in the future or not. So far, no steps towards signing the convention have been initiated in Switzerland.[52]

5 The Effect of Choice of Court Agreements

Choice of court agreements can be divided into two types of agreements: optional choice of court agreements and exclusive choice of court agreements. The Code on Civil Procedure, the Private International Law Act and the Lugano Convention distinguish between optional and exclusive choice of court agreements and, therefore, acknowledge the two possible effects of the agreements; however, none of these three legal sources contain separate provisions for the two types of agreements. Hence, all provisions relevant to exclusive choice of court agreements apply to its optional counterpart likewise. A distinction is, therefore, only (but nevertheless) necessary with regard to the effects of the agreements.

Under the Code on Civil Procedure, the Private International Law Act and the Lugano Convention, all choice of court agreements are presumed to be exclusive unless otherwise stated (see art. 17 para. 1 CCP; art. 5 para. 1 PILA; art. 23 para. 1 LC).[53] Hence, if the parties do not agree to the contrary, the choice of court agreement is exclusive. This rule on the effect of the agreement enables a high degree of clarity already at the time of conclusion of the agreement.[54] If a party wishes to challenge the exclusive effect presumed by law (by suing in front of a presumptively derogated court), it needs to prove that an optional effect was agreed upon.[55]

In order for the choice of court agreement to be optional, it is not necessary to state the intended optional effect explicitly; however, the intention of the parties needs to be clearly expressed in the agreement.[56] Thus, it is sufficient to say that "party A can bring action in front of court X in addition to the courts designated by law" or that "court X is competent in addition to the courts designated by law".[57] It is, however, not sufficient to say that "action can be brought before court X or Y", as it is not clear that the courts designated by law remain in place.

---

[52]Dasser (2015), p. 95.

[53]Infanger In: Spühler et al. (2017), art. 17 N 20; Grolimund and Bachofner In: Honsell et al. (2013), art. 5 N 43; Berger In: Oetiker and Weibel (2016), art. 23 N 2, 61; Killias In: Dasser and Oberhammer (2011), art. 23 N 145.

[54]Berger In: Oetiker and Weibel (2016), art. 23 N 61; Hausmann In: Reithmann and Martiny (2015), recital 8.113.

[55]Hausmann In: Reithmann and Martiny (2015), recital 8.115; Berger In: Oetiker and Weibel (2016), art. 23 N 62.

[56]Hausmann In: Reithmann and Martiny (2015), recital 8.115.

[57]Grolimund and Bachofner In: Honsell et al. (2013), art. 5 N 43a.

If the choice of court agreement has an optional effect, the agreement operates as prorogation to the court(s) designated by agreement; however, it does not derogate the court(s) designated by law.[58] Based on the optional choice of court agreement, the parties can, hence, bring an action before the court(s) designated by agreement or before the court(s) designated by law.

If, however, the choice of court agreement is exclusive, it operates as prorogation to the court(s) designated by agreement and, simultaneously, as derogation of the court(s) designated by law.[59] Based on the exclusive choice of court agreement, the parties can, therefore, only bring action before the court(s) designated by agreement.

6 Jurisdictional Competence of Prorogated Swiss Courts

6.1 Local or Factual Proximity

Whether or not a Swiss court prorogated by choice of court agreement, regardless of its status as exclusive or optional, will deem itself jurisdictionally competent and consequently take on the case, used to be (and partially still is) dependent on the local and factual proximity of the court.[60] Under the former Code on Jurisdiction in Civil Matters,[61] courts prorogated by choice of court agreement had the right to decline the submission to their jurisdiction if the necessary local or factual proximity was missing (*forum non conveniens*).[62] This right of refusal was problematic for two reasons: First, it was impossible to choose a court that was neutral, even though neutrality can make a court particularly suitable. Second, it led to reverse discrimination, since equivalent provisions on the international level (art. 23 LC; art. 5 PILA) were less restrictive. As a consequence, the new Code on Civil Procedure refrains from requiring such local or factual proximity, which is why, under art. 17 CCP, the courts prorogated by agreement have an obligation to accept the submission to their jurisdiction.

The same is true if the Lugano Convention applies.[63] Consequently, a Swiss court prorogated by agreement has the obligation to accept the submission to its jurisdiction based on art. 23 LC if (1) it is a civil or commercial matter; and if (2) at least one

[58] Killias In: Dasser and Oberhammer (2011), art. 23 N 146.

[59] Infanger In: Spühler et al. (2017), art. 17 N 20; Grolimund and Bachofner In: Honsell et al. (2013), art. 5 N 43; Berger In: Oetiker and Weibel (2016), art. 23 N 61; Killias In: Dasser and Oberhammer (2011), art. 23 N 145.

[60] Cp. Infanger In: Spühler et al. (2017), art. 17 N 2; Honsell et al. (2013), art. 5 N 49.

[61] See footnote 46.

[62] Infanger In: Spühler et al. (2017), art. 17 N 2.

[63] Cp. Berger In: Oetiker and Weibel (2016), art. 23 N 57.

party to the agreement has his/her domicile in a member state of the Lugano Convention.[64]

If one of these two conditions is not met, hence, if the Lugano Convention does not apply, a Swiss court will decide if it will deem itself jurisdictionally competent based on the Private International Law Act. Unlike the Code on Civil Procedure and the Lugano Convention, the Private International Law Act requires local or factual proximity of the court designated by agreement.[65] According to art. 5 para. 3 PILA, the court designated by agreement must accept the submission to its jurisdiction if at least one party to the agreement has (1) his/her domicile; (2) his/her main whereabouts; or (3) his/her place of business at the location of the court, or (4) if Swiss law applies to the matter in dispute.[66] As for the latter, the application of Swiss law can be derived from objective conflict of law rules or from subjective choice of law agreements.[67] If none of these four conditions apply, the required local or factual proximity is missing and, hence, a Swiss court can—but is not required to—decline the submission to its jurisdiction (*forum non conveniens*).[68] The court applies its discretionary power to make such a decision.[69] This right of refusal of art. 5 para. 3 PILA aims to protect Swiss courts from overloading.[70] Critics of art. 5 para. 3 PILA primarily point out that the right of refusal leads to legal uncertainty and is, therefore, to be interpreted restrictively.[71]

6.2 *Lis Pendens*

If the prorogated court is the first to be concerned with the proceeding, it will be able to rule on the validity of the choice of court agreement right away. If, however, the proceeding is initially brought before a derogated court and the prorogated court gets involved with the proceeding only later on, the question arises whether the prorogated court needs to await the decision of the derogated court (*lis pendens*).

Under all three legal sources—the Code on Civil Procedure (art. 59 para. 2 lit. d CCP, art. 126 para. 1 CCP), the Lugano Convention (art. 27 LC) and the Private International Law Act (art. 9 para. 1 PILA)—the prorogated court, that gets involved

---

[64]See Berger In: Oetiker and Weibel (2016), art. 23 N 11 et seq., with further notes on the issue of interpretation regarding art. 23 para. 1.

[65]Grolimund and Bachofner in: Honsell et al. (2013), art. 5 N 49.

[66]See also Grolimund and Bachofner in: Honsell et al. (2013), art. 5 N 49.

[67]Botschaft 1983 I 263, 302; see also Buhr, Gabriel, Schramm In: Furrer et al. (2016), art. 5 N 40.

[68]Grolimund and Bachofner in: Honsell et al. (2013), art. 5 N 49; Buhr, Gabriel, Schramm In: Furrer et al. (2016), art. 5 N 40.

[69]Grolimund and Bachofner in: Honsell et al. (2013), art. 5 N 49.

[70]Botschaft 1983 I 263, 302; Grolimund and Bachofner in: Honsell et al. (2013), art. 5 N 49; Buhr, Gabriel, Schramm In: Furrer et al. (2016), art. 5 N 40.

[71]Grolimund and Bachofner in: Honsell et al. (2013), art. 5 N 49; dissenting opinion see Reiser (1989), p. 136.

with the proceeding only later on, will as a general principle need to stay the proceeding until the derogated court rules on its jurisdiction.[72] It needs to do so *ex officio*.[73] Under the Code on Civil Procedure that applies to national transactions only, both the derogated and the prorogated courts are Swiss courts; thus, there will be no issue with regard to the duration of the proceeding and the recognition of the decision of the derogated court.

Under the Lugano Convention that applies to cross-border transactions, the prorogated Swiss court will need to stay the proceeding until the foreign court rules on its jurisdiction (art. 27 LC), even if the proceedings of the foreign court are known to be unreasonably long.[74] The parties to the choice of court agreement have, therefore, no guarantee that the court designated by agreement will be the first to concern itself with the proceedings; thus, so-called *torpedo law-suits*[75] are still possible.[76]

Under the Private International Law Act that applies to cross-border transactions too, the general principle that the prorogated Swiss court must stay proceedings due to *foreign lis pendens* contains a limitation: If the foreign court will not likely and within a reasonable amount of time make a decision that is recognizable under Swiss law (art. 25 PILA), *foreign lis pendens* must be ignored and the Swiss court must take on the case right away (art. 9 para. 1 PILA).[77] Due to this rule, *torpedo law-suits* can be avoided.[78]

---

[72]Gehri In: Spühler et al. (2017), art. 59 N 17; Müller In: Brunner et al. (2016), art. 59 N 42; Berger In: Oetiker and Weibel (2016), art. 27 N 55; vgl. Grolimund and Bachofner in: Honsell et al. (2013), art. 5 N 50a; vgl. Berti and Droese In: Honsell et al. (2013), art. 9 N 24. This is also true under the former Brussels I Regulation, paralleling the provisions of the Lugano Convention, see Berger In: Oetiker and Weibel (2016), art. 23 N 58.

[73]Gehri In: Spühler et al. (2017), art. 59 N 14; Berger In: Oetiker and Weibel (2016), art. 23 N 58; cp. Grolimund and Bachofner In: Honsell et al. (2013), art. 5 N 50a; vgl. Berti and Droese In: Honsell et al. (2013), art. 9 N 24.

[74]Berger In: Oetiker and Weibel (2016), art. 23 N 58; cp. ECJ, 9.12.2003, C-116/02, Gasser v. MISAT Srl., No 73 et seq. Cases of the ECJ are relevant for Switzerland within the application of the Lugano Convention, since the Lugano Convention is to be interpreted like the former Brussels I Regulation; see hereto the preamble of the LC.

[75]I.e. law-suits that are intentionally brought before a derogated court in order to protract the proceedings; cp. Berger In: Oetiker and Weibel (2016), art. 23 N 58.

[76]Under the Brussels I Recast Regulation, however, such *torpedo law-suits* are not possible anymore, since any derogated court that is concerned with the case will need to stay their proceeding until the prorogated court decides on its jurisdiction (art. 31 para. 2 nEuGVVO). See Berger In: Oetiker and Weibel (2016), art. 23 N 58.

[77]Grolimund and Bachofner In: Honsell et al. (2013), art. 5 N 50a; Berti and Droese In: Honsell et al. (2013), art. 9 N 10, 20, 22 et seq.

[78]Buhr, Gabriel, Schramm In: Furrer et al. (2016), art. 9 N 18.

6.3 Anti-Suit and Anti-Enforcement Injunctions

Anti-suit injunctions are a means used by courts to restrain the commencement or continuation of proceedings in front of another court. In the context of choice of court agreements, such injunctions are of particular interest, as they could serve the enforcement of the agreement. While such anti-suit injunctions are particularly widespread in Anglo-American jurisdictions, they are not granted under Swiss law. The Code on Civil Procedure and the Private International Law Act do not hold respective provisions; however, they hold provisions on *foreign lis pendens* and the actions Swiss courts must take *ex officio* if *foreign lis pendens* applies (art. 59 para. 2 lit. d CCP, art. 126 para. 1 CCP and art. 9 para. 1 PILA).[79] Thus, it can be implicitly derived from these provisions that anti-suit injunctions are prohibited under the Code on Civil Procedure and the Private International Law Act.[80] As for the Lugano Convention, there is no explicit provision, either; however, the European Court of Justice addressed the issue explicitly and held that anti-suit injunctions cannot be granted.[81] Thus, a Swiss court cannot grant an anti-suit injunction in order to strengthen the prorogation.

Anti-enforcement injunctions are a means to restrain an application for enforcement of a judgment made by specific courts. Like anti-suit injunctions, anti-enforcement injunctions can be of particular interest in the context of choice of court agreements as such injunctions could be granted to restrain an application for enforcement of a judgment given by a court other than those nominated in the agreement. Under Swiss law, there is no tradition of issuing anti-enforcement injunctions as there is no legal basis to do so. Thus, anti-enforcement injunctions cannot be granted.

6.4 Decisions of Foreign Courts

If a foreign court renders a decision despite the fact that a Swiss (or any other) court was prorogated by agreement, it is questionable whether such decision will be recognized and enforced in Switzerland. The answer to this question is fairly simple: The fact that the decision was rendered by a court other than that prorogated by agreement does not necessarily limit its recognition and enforcement since choice of

---

[79]Cp. Stacher (2006), p. 61, 65 et seq.

[80]Cp. Stacher (2006), p. 61, 65 et seq.

[81]ECJ, 27 April 2004, C-159/02, Turner v. Grovit, nr. 31; see also Berger In: Oetiker and Weibel (2016), art. 23 N 58. According to Berger, it, consequently, needs to be prohibited to start an action in front of a prorogated or derogated court for a declaratory judgment regarding the validity of a choice of court agreement. See Berger In: Oetiker and Weibel (2016), art. 23 N 58. However, such prohibition is not necessary as the action would lack the necessary legitimate interest in the proceeding anyway. See Berger In: Oetiker and Weibel (2016), art. 23 N 58; dissenting opinion to the latter: Geimer and Schütze (2010), art. 23 EuGVVO N 131.

court agreements can be altered. Thus, if the lawsuit is brought in front of a court other than that prorogated by agreement, it is considered an offer to alter the agreement.[82] If the opposing party responds to such proceedings by pleading to the charge, then the jurisdiction of such court is established; hence, the offer to alter the agreement is accepted (so-called *Einlassung*, art. 18 CCP, art. 24 LC, art. 6 PILA).[83] As a consequence, the Swiss court will recognize and enforce the foreign decision as long as all further requirements for recognition and enforcement are given (art. 25 et seq. PILA, art. 32 et seq. LC).

If the opposing party does not respond by pleading to the charge but rather by raising the *exceptio fori prorogati,* the jurisdiction of the foreign court is not established. Hence, the Swiss court will not recognize and enforce its decision (art. 25 lit. a PILA).[84]

If the foreign court applied the Lugano Convention when rendering its decision, the Swiss court will be bound by the decision of the foreign court; it will, hence, skip the process of recognition and enforce the decision right away.[85]

7 Jurisdictional Competence of Derogated Swiss Courts

If a Swiss court is competent by law but its competence is derogated by choice of court agreement (i.e. by exclusive choice of court agreement), the question arises whether or not the Swiss court is bound by the derogation of such agreement. If, despite the choice of court agreement, the case is brought before the derogated Swiss court, such Swiss court cannot stay the proceedings but needs to rule on its competence to take on the case. The court will do so based on the statutory provisions on jurisdiction (CCP, LC, PILA). Only if the opposing party raises the *exceptio fori prorogati* will the court take into consideration the choice of court agreement.[86] In the latter case, the Swiss court needs to rule on the choice of court agreement comprehensively; therefore, it cannot limit itself to a summary inspection as to whether the prorogated foreign court is competent. If the Lugano Convention applies and the prorogated foreign court is from a member state of the Convention, such court will even be bound to the finding of the Swiss court. If, however, the prorogated foreign court is not from a member state of the Convention, such court will not be bound by the finding of the Swiss court; rather, it will rule on the choice

[82]Hence, no damages for breach of agreement can be awarded.

[83]See Infanger In: Spühler et al. (2017), art. 18 N 1 et seq.; Vasella In: Honsell et al. (2013), art. 6 N 1 et seq.; Berger In: Oetiker and Weibel (2016), art. 24 N 1 et seq.

[84]Däppen and Mabillard In: Honsell et al. (2013), art. 25 N 30.

[85]See Däppen and Mabillard In: Honsell et al. (2013), art. 29 N 8; Schuler and Marugg in: Oetiker and Weibel (2016), art. 33 N 1 et seq.

[86]Berger In: Oetiker and Weibel (2016), art. 23 N 60. Only if another court is exclusively competent by law can the court dismiss the case *ex officio*; in such case, it is even obliged to do so.

of court agreement based on its own national law (including private international law).[87]

8 Discrepancy Between Prorogated and Derogated Swiss Courts

Under Swiss law, choice of court agreements in favour of Swiss courts and choice of court agreements in favour of foreign courts are treated equally in the sense that they need to fulfill the same requirements in order to be valid. Hence, a choice of court agreement in favour of foreign courts is valid if the subject matter at hand qualifies for choice of court agreements, if all formal requirements for entering a choice of court agreement are met and if the agreement is concluded validly (see above Sect. 3.2).

There is, however, one difference between choice of court agreements in favour of Swiss courts and choice of court agreements in favour of foreign courts that applies under the Private International Law Act: According to art. 5 para. 2 PILA, choice of court agreements in favour of foreign courts are considered invalid if a Swiss court is derogated in an abusive fashion (art. 5 para. 2 PILA); the agreement is, therefore, subject to control against abuse.[88] This provision only applies to exclusive choice of court agreements, as their optional counterparts do not lead to a derogation of courts. Derogation in an abusive fashion is likely given if e.g. the agreement is deemed to be unconscionable.[89] The provision of art. 5 para. 2 PILA is, however, to be interpreted restrictively as the legislator shall protect presumptively weaker parties by exclusive jurisdiction.[90]

9 Proceedings Before Courts Not Designated by Agreement

Even if the choice of court agreement is permissible, all formal requirements are met and the agreement was concluded validly, the parties can start proceedings in front of another court than that prorogated by agreement. This is not considered a breach of the agreement; rather it is considered an offer to alter it.[91] If the opposing party responds to such proceedings by pleading to the charge, then the jurisdiction of such court is established and the offer to alter the agreement is accepted (so-called

[87] See Berger In: Oetiker and Weibel (2016), art. 23 N 58 et seq.

[88] Grolimund and Bachofner In: Honsell et al. (2013), art. 5 N 48.

[89] Grolimund and Bachofner In: Honsell et al. (2013), art. 5 N 48; Dutoit (2016), art. 5 N 13.

[90] Grolimund and Bachofner In: Honsell et al. (2013), art. 5 N 48.

[91] Hence, no damages for breach of agreement can be awarded.

Einlassung, art. 18 CCP, art. 24 LC, art. 6 PILA, see above Sect. 6.4).[92] If, however, the opposing party responds to the proceedings by raising the *exceptio fori prorogati*, the court needs to examine whether a valid choice of court agreement was entered into, and if so, it needs to dismiss the case and the parties need to start proceeding in front of the court prorogated by agreement. If a valid choice of court agreement was concluded and the case is, indeed, brought before the prorogated court, the jurisdiction of such court is established and, consequently, the parties cannot contest the jurisdiction of such court (see however above Sect. 6.1 re. *forum non conveniens*).

10 Choice of Court Agreements Involving Presumptively Weaker Parties in Switzerland

Under Swiss Law, optional choice of court agreements involving presumptively weaker parties (such as employees, consumers, tenants and insureds; see art. 35 CCP; art. 8 et seq., 15 et seq., 18 et seq. LC; and art. 114 PILA) are treated differently to optional choice of court agreements in commercial contracts in that prior to the dispute, presumptively weaker parties cannot waive the competence of a court that is competent by law; only the presumptively stronger party can.[93] In commercial contracts, all parties can effectively undertake such waiver prior to the dispute. Such difference is legitimized by the need of presumptively weaker parties to be protected against giving up a jurisdiction that is favourable to them.

The definition of the presumptively weaker party depends on the applicable law: Under the Code on Civil Procedure, consumers (art. 35 para. 1 lit. a CCP), tenants (art. 35 para. 1 lit. b, c CCP) and employees (art. 35 para. 1 lit. d CCP) are considered weak; under the Lugano Convention, insureds (art. 13 LC), consumers (art. 17 LC) and employees (art. 21 LC) are considered weak; and under the Private International Law Act, consumers (art. 114 para. 2 PILA) are considered weak.

As for the effect of choice of court agreements, the presumption that all agreements are considered exclusive unless otherwise stated (see above Sect. 5) is put into perspective: Killias states that choice of court agreements that involve presumptively weaker parties and appear to be exclusive shall only be exclusive for the presumptively stronger party. As for the presumptively weaker party, the agreement shall be

[92] See Infanger In: Spühler et al. (2017), art. 18 N 1 et seq.; Vasella in: Honsell et al. (2013), art. 6 N 1 et seq.; Berger In: Oetiker and Weibel (2016), art. 24 N 1 et seq.

[93] Kaiser Job in: Spühler et al. (2017), art. 35 N 2; Oetiker and Jenny In: Oetiker and Weibel (2016), art. 13 N 18; Gehri In: Oetiker and Weibel (2016), art. 17 N 9; BSK Meyer and Stojilikovic In: Oetiker and Weibel (2016), art. 21 N 5.

optional, so that the court(s) designated by agreement and the courts designated by law shall both be competent.[94]

11 Asymmetrical Choice of Court Agreements

Asymmetrical choice of court agreements are optional choice of court agreements in which the option is drafted only in favour of one of the parties.[95] As Swiss law provides no specific legal treatment for optional choice of court agreements, there is no specific legal treatment of asymmetrical choice of court agreements either. Nevertheless, asymmetrical choice of court agreements are permitted within the above-mentioned boundaries (see Sect. 3.3).[96] These boundaries are especially relevant for contracts that involve a presumptively weaker party (see Sect. 10).

12 Evaluation and Reform

The main issue to be considered when determining whether the legal treatment of optional choice of court agreements is appropriate is the protection of the presumptively weaker parties. As already mentioned, Swiss law does not provide specific provisions for optional choice of court agreements. The limitations applicable to exclusive choice of court agreements also apply to optional ones. In our view, this identical treatment of optional and exclusive choice of court agreements is justified. Specific provisions would only be necessary if optional choice of court agreements put the presumptively weaker parties at a greater risk of being denied a jurisdiction favourable to them. This is, however, not the case. The presumptively weaker party cannot waive the competence of a court that is competent by law regardless of the qualification of the choice of court agreement. Therefore, the protection of presumptively weaker parties is ensured without the need for a distinction between optional and exclusive choice of court agreements.

One of the main problems that arises regarding choice of court agreements is the treatment of so-called "torpedo law-suits" in the Lugano Convention.[97] Within the European Union, this problem has been partially solved by the introduction of the new art. 31 para. 2 EuGVVO.[98] A similar provision has not been introduced into the Lugano Convention. For the time being, there is no indication that the contracting

[94]Killias In: Dasser and Oberhammer (2011), art. 23 N 147, 149.

[95]Killias In: Dasser and Oberhammer (2011), art. 23 N 147.

[96]Grolimund and Bachofner in: Honsell et al. (2013), art. 5 N 43a; Killias In: Dasser and Oberhammer (2011), art. 23 N 145.

[97]See footnote 76.

[98]Berger In: Oetiker and Weibel (2016), art. 23 N 58; Schlosser (2015), 598.

parties intend to adapt the Lugano Convention to the revised Brussels I Regulation. Should a reform take place in the foreseeable future, it will most likely be initiated by Swiss courts rather than the Swiss legislator.[99]

References

Brunner A, Gasser D, Schwander I (eds) (2016) Schweizerische Zivilprozessordnung – Kommentar, 2nd edn. Zurich

Dasser F (2015) Bern, Lugano, Brüssel oder doch lieber Den Haag? – Ein Ausflug zu den Rechtsquellen für Gerichtsstandsvereinbarungen. In: Breitschmid P, Jent-Sorensen I, Schmid H, Sogo M (eds) Tatsachen – Verfahren – Vollstreckung, Festschrift für Isaak Meier, Zurich

Dasser F, Oberhammer P (eds) (2011) Stämpfli Handkommentar zum Lugano-Übereinkommen, 2nd edn. Bern

Dutoit B (2016) Droit international privé suisse, 5. updated edn. Basel

Furrer I, Girsberger D, Müller-Chen M, Schramm D (2013) Internationales Privatrecht, 3. updated edn. Zurich

Furrer I, Girsberger D, Müller-Chen M (eds) (2016) Handkommentar zum Schweizer Privatrecht, Internationales Privatrecht, 3rd edn. Zurich

Geimer R, Schütze RA (2010) Europäisches Zivilverfahrensrecht, Kommentar zur EuGVVO, EuEheVO, EuZustellungsVO, EuInsVO, EuVTVO, zum Lugano-Übereinkommen und zum nationalen Kompetenz- und Anerkennungsrecht, 3rd edn. Munich

Honsell H, Vogt NP, Schnyder AK, Berti SV (eds) (2013) Basler Kommentar zum internationalen Privatrecht, 3rd edn. Basel

Kramer EA, Probst T, Perrig R (2016) Schweizerisches Recht der Allgemeinen Geschäftsbedingungen, Bern

Kren Kostkiewicz J (2018) Schweizerisches Internationales Privatrecht, 2nd edn. Bern

Müller-Chen M, Müller C, Widmer Lüchinger C (eds) (2015) Comparative Private Law, Zurich

Oberhammer P, Domej T, Haas U (eds) (2014) Kurzkommentar – Schweizerische Zivilprozessordnung, 2nd edn. Basel

Oetiker C, Weibel T (eds) (2016) Basler Kommentar zum Lugano-Übereinkommen, 2nd edn. Basel

Reiser H (1989) Gerichtsstandsvereinbarungen nach dem IPR-Gesetz, Zurich

Reithmann C, Martiny D (eds) (2015) Internationales Vertragsrecht, 8th edn. Cologne

Schlosser P (2015) Brüche im EuGVVO-LugÜ-Gefüge? In: Breitschmid P, Jent-Sorensen I, Schmid H, Sogo M (eds) Tatsachen – Verfahren – Vollstreckung, Festschrift für Isaak Meier, Zurich

Schnyder AK, Liatowitsch M (2017) Internationales Privat- und Zivilverfahrensrecht, 4th edn. Zurich

Spühler K, Tenchino L, Infanger D (eds) (2017) Basler Kommentar zur Zivilprozessordnung, 3rd edn. Basel

Stacher M (2006) Prozessführungsverbote zur Verhinderung von sich widersprechenden Entscheiden, ZZZ, pp 61–87

Sutter-Somm T (2017) Schweizerisches Zivilprozessrecht, 3rd edn. Zurich

Sutter-Somm T, Hasenböhler F, Leuenberger C (eds) (2016) Kommentar zur Schweizerischen Zivilprozessordnung (ZPO), 3rd edn. Zurich

Vogel O (1988) Grundriss des Zivilprozessrechts, 2nd edn. Bern

Walter G, Domej T (2012) Internationales Zivilprozessrecht der Schweiz, 5th edn. Bern

[99] See Schlosser (2015), 601 et seq.

Eliane Haas studied at the University of Basel and at Boston University. She earned her Master's Degrees in 2013 (LL M) and 2014 (M Law), and her doctorate in 2018. In her doctoral research, she focused on sequential innovation in copyright law. She is currently working towards the bar exam.

Kevin MacCabe studied Law at the University of Basel. He earned a Master's Degree in 2015 and was admitted to the bar of the Canton of Basel-Stadt in 2017. He is currently working as a research and teaching assistant at the University of Basel and is completing a doctoral thesis on the topic of distributed ledger technology.

Taiwan: Legislation and Practice on Choice of Court Agreements in Taiwan

Rong-Chwan Chen

1 Legislation on Freedom of Procedural Options

1.1 The Party Autonomy Principle

In Taiwan,[1] choice of court agreements are legally acknowledged as an aspect of the party autonomy principle. The freedom to form contracts is embodied in Articles 71, 72 and 153 of the Taiwanese Civil Code (Min-Fa),[2] while the freedom of choosing the law applicable to contractual obligations is embodied in Article 20 of the Act Governing the Application of Laws in Civil Matters Involving Foreign Elements (She-Wai-Min-Shi-Fa-Lü-Shi-Yong-Fa, henceforth Taiwanese PILA).[3] With regard to the resolution of disputes, the parties' freedom to resort to arbitration

[1]Taiwan bears the "Republic of China" (henceforth ROC) as its official name and coexists with the "People's Republic of China" on the Chinese Mainland. The geographic territory under its effective jurisdiction includes islands of Taiwan (formerly known as Formosa), Penghu, Kinmen, Matsu and their surrounding islands, as well as two major islands of Dongsha Island and Nansha Island.

[2]Civil Code (Min- Fa), adopted in 1929 (174 Guo-Min-Zheng-Fu-Gong-Bao 2) and last revised in 2015 (7197 POG 27).

[3]Act Governing the Choice of Law in Civil Matters Involving Foreign Elements (She-Wai-Min-Shi-Fa-Lü-Shi-Yong-Fa), promulgated on 6 June 1953 (403 POG 1), last revised in 2010 (6923 POG 24). For its English translation, see Chen (2014c), pp. 453–465; Chen (2017b), pp. 3880–3889.

R.-C. Chen (✉)
National Taipei University, College of Law, Taipei City, Taiwan
e-mail: ronchen@gm.ntpu.edu.tw

M. Keyes (ed.), *Optional Choice of Court Agreements in Private International Law*,
Ius Comparatum – Global Studies in Comparative Law 37,
https://doi.org/10.1007/978-3-030-23914-5_17

instead of litigation in courts is recognized in Article 1 of the Arbitration Act (Zhong-Cai-Fa).[4]

1.2 Freedom to Contract About Jurisdiction

1.2.1 Legislative Provisions

As a part of the right of procedural option, the parties' freedom to contract about jurisdiction is explicitly recognized and stipulated in Article 24 of the Taiwanese Code of Civil Procedure (Min-Shi-Su-Song-Fa, henceforth Taiwanese CCP).[5] It provides: "1. Parties may, by agreement, designate a court of first instance to exercise jurisdiction, provided that such agreement relates to a particular legal relation." "2. The agreement provided in the preceding paragraph shall be evidenced in writing."

1.2.2 Limits to the Freedom to Agree Upon Jurisdiction

Under these provisions, the parties' freedom to agree upon jurisdiction of a court is limited in the following respects:

(1) The agreement is required to be explicitly concluded. The defendant's implicit consent or the parties' implied agreement about jurisdiction is unenforceable if no other additional explicit legal prescription is provided to grant the chosen court jurisdiction. If an action was brought before a court which has no statutory jurisdiction, and the defendant proceeds orally on the merits without contesting lack of jurisdiction, such procedural facts indicate that the defendant agreed not to raise any jurisdictional issues and rather to proceed to the merits of the dispute. Article 25 of the Taiwanese CCP provides that the court thereby obtains jurisdiction over such action. This jurisdiction relates somehow to the defendant's fictional or implied consent to resolve the parties' dispute in such court. This is an exception to the principle of explicitness embodied in Article 24 of the Taiwanese CCP.

(2) The agreement is required to confer jurisdiction on a court of first instance. Courts of appeal are not within the scope of the parties' choice. The agreement shall therefore be concluded before the lawsuit is initiated. Once a court is seized with the dispute, according to the rule established by the ROC Supreme Court in

[4]Arbitration Act (Zhong-Cai-Fa), adopted in 1998 (6224 POG 40) and last revised in 2015 (7222 POG 31) to replace the Commercial Arbitration Act (Shang-Wu-Zhong-Cai-Tiao-Li) promulgated in 1961 (1194 POG 1).

[5]Taiwanese Code of Civil Procedure (Min-Shi-Su-Song-Fa), adopted in 1930 (659 Guo-Min-Zheng-Fu-Gong-Bao 15) and last revised in 2018 (7638 POG 38).

its Decision # Kang-16 of 1930, the parties can only follow or enforce the previous agreement, no further choice or alteration to it is permitted. Such freedom is obviously limited by the time element.

(3) The agreement is required to relate to a particular legal relation. The explanatory comment for the Taiwanese CCP mentioned in 1936 that the scope of choice shall basically be defined and limited to "a particular legal relation" such as a contract of sale or a contract of gift. The designated court is competent to decide disputes relating to damages for breach of contracts. The freedom of choice is thus limited in terms of contents as it requires the specification of definite scope of subject matters covered by the parties' choice. The disputes arising from the prescribed legal relation are all subject to the jurisdiction of the designated court. A general agreement on a court to exercise jurisdiction over all future disputes between the parties is unenforceable, as is an agreement on jurisdiction over disputes about unidentified legal relations.

(4) The agreement is limited to actions not subject to a Taiwanese court's exclusive jurisdiction. Under Article 26 of the Taiwanese CCP, the provisions on choice of court do not apply to an action that is subject to another court's exclusive jurisdiction under the CCP. The underlying principle is that the public interest to grant a court statutory exclusive jurisdiction shall not be infringed by the parties' exercise of procedural right of disposition.[6]

1.2.3 The Form of Writing

Whether the choice of court agreement is required to be in writing is not beyond scholarly debate. The root of this problem is that the phrase adopted in Article 24 Sec 2 of the CCP is "evidenced in writing" instead of "concluded in writing". No matter what view is taken, the relevant "writing" is required in the court proceedings. With regard to the meaning or forms of "writing", Article 3 of the Taiwanese Civil Code provides that when a juridical act is required by law to be in "writing", it is not necessary that it was written by the person himself, but it must be signed by him; if the person uses a seal instead of his signature, the affixing of such seal has the same

[6]An exception is provided in Article 52 Sec 2 of the Family Matters Act 2012 (adopted in 2012, 7012 POG 35, and last revised in 2015, 7226 POG 106). Sec 1 provides: "With regard to matters concerning determination of the invalidity of a marriage, annulment of a marriage, divorce, or determination of the existence or non-existence of a marriage, the jurisdiction to hear the proceedings exclusively belongs to the courts listed in the following: 1. the court for the place of the domicile of the husband and wife; 2. the court for the place of the joint habitual residence of the husband and wife; or 3. the court for the place of the habitual residence of the husband or the wife from whom the transactions or occurrences that gives rise to the claim take place." Sec 2 provides: "Notwithstanding the provisions in the preceding paragraph, the parties may, by a written agreement, agree on the court that shall hear the proceedings." It is argued that the "exclusive" jurisdiction prescribed in Sec 1 is not a genuine exclusive jurisdiction in nature, since some courts, instead of only one court, possess statutory jurisdiction under it. The choice of court agreement is required to be concluded, instead of evidenced, in writing.

effect as his signature. Such a flexible attitude toward interpretation had easily adapted to the circumstances when the Taiwanese CCP was promulgated, but it has been superseded as the science and technology of information has created new forms to conclude contracts.

A signature is characterized as evidence of a party's consent. Two signatures are required to prove the mutual consent of the offeror and offeree to conclude a bilateral contract. However, there is no signature on an electronic contract which has been accepted by both parties, and only one signature exists on a ticket or waybill. A standard contract or contract of adhesion is usually the evidence of unilateral promise of its preparer. The other party's signature sometimes is found to be just evidence of accepting some portion of that contract while leaving other portions untouched. To cope with the evolution of communication technology, the requirement of "writing" shall be flexibly interpreted so as to include agreements evidenced by telegraph, fax, email or other electronic records.

1.3 The Trend in Legal Treatment of Choice of Court Agreements

1.3.1 Legislative Development

The development of the law on arbitration has some influence on the trend in legal treatment of choice of court agreements. The parties' freedom to contract about jurisdiction has been explicitly acknowledged in the Taiwanese CCP. Choice of court agreements are widely used in commercial contracts. The original provisions on enforcing choice of court agreements are unchanged since the promulgation of the CCP in 1930 (although Article 23 has been renumbered to Article 24).

1.3.2 Influence of Arbitration Legislation

Due to its unique status in the international arena, Taiwan is not a UN member and thus is neither accepted as a member state of the Hague Conference on Private International Law nor allowed to accede to any of its conventions, or to the United Nations Convention on the Recognition and Enforcement of Foreign Arbitral Awards 1958 (the New York Convention).[7] Article 1 Section 2 of the Commercial Arbitration Act[8] of 1961 provides that arbitration agreements shall be "in writing". This requirement was interpreted in the same way as in the context of the writing requirement for court choice agreements. Such provisions remain unchanged and were moved to Article 1 Section 3 when the Commercial Arbitration Act was

[7] See Chen (2017c), pp. 945–962.

[8] Commercial Arbitration Act (Shang-Wu-Zhong-Cai-Tiao-Li) promulgated in 1961 (1194 POG 1).

replaced by the Arbitration Act (Zhong-Cai-Fa)[9] of 1998, while Section 4 was added to cope with the modern development of communication technology. Section 4 provides: "An arbitration agreement is deemed to be concluded if the parties' written documents, documentary instruments, correspondence, facsimiles, telegrams or any other similar types of communications are sufficient to evince that they agreed on it." There is no such provision concerning choice of court agreements although the situation of need is quite similar. In judicial practice, the above provision shall also be applied in analogy to the choice of court agreements to fill the legislative gap. Article 3 of Arbitration Act can also be applied in analogy to explain the severance of the jurisdiction clause from the principal contract within which it is included.[10]

1.3.3 Influence of International Instruments

As mentioned earlier, Taiwan is currently not allowed to sign or to accede to many international conventions for which a state's membership of the UN is required. The Hague Choice of Court Agreements Convention 2005 is just one among them. Currently, no multilateral, regional, and bilateral instruments concerning jurisdiction that directly affect the Taiwanese law on choice of court agreements have been signed. However, the Hague Choice of Court Agreements Convention 2005 and the European Union instruments relevant to jurisdiction (the Brussels Convention, the Brussels I Regulation, and the Brussels I Recast Regulation) are highly valued and referred to by Taiwanese courts in some cases. It is certain that legislative preparation in the future will adopt the policy and the rules of the multilateral conventions and cite them in the explanatory comments as the drafters did for the Taiwanese PILA.[11] Such instruments about jurisdiction will undoubtedly have great indirect effects on interpreting the current law and its reform in the future.

2 Optional Choice of Court Agreements

2.1 Legal Sources

According to Article 24 Section 1 of the Taiwanese CCP, the parties "may, by agreement, designate a court of first instance to exercise jurisdiction". This consensual designation of court applies to both exclusive and optional choice of court

[9]Arbitration Act (Zhong-Cai-Fa), adopted in 1998 (6224 POG 40) and last revised in 2015 (7222 POG 31).

[10]Article 3 of the Arbitration Act provides that "The validity of an arbitration clause which forms part of a principal contract between the parties may be determined separately from the rest of the principal contract. A decision that the contract is nullified, invalid, revoked, rescinded or terminated shall not affect the validity of the arbitration clause."

[11]Chen (2017a), p. 2559.

agreements. No provisions on the effects of exclusive or optional choice of court agreements are prescribed in the CCP. The questions are left to the judicial practice.

2.2 *Characterization of a Choice of Court Agreement*

2.2.1 Choice of Law Rule

In Taiwan, the choice of law rules are embodied in the Taiwanese PIL Act. Modernized and amended in 2010, it deals basically with substantive international legal relationships, rather than procedural questions. Characterization of the legal relation at issue is necessary to identify the relevant choice of law rule to determine the law applicable to it. The standard of characterization is left open in the PIL Act to allow the courts to decide on a case-to-case basis.[12] There is no specific choice of law rule for choice of court agreements either in the PIL Act or the CCP. This gap is left for the courts to fill with a principle refined from the theory of private international law.[13]

In such process, the nature of a choice of court agreement is essential in finding a principle to fill the gap. The effects of a choice of court agreement are that the designated court can thereby exercise its optional or exclusive jurisdiction over the prescribed dispute and the domestic court's jurisdiction under the domestic rules is thus co-shared or excluded. These effects indicate that such an agreement is procedural in nature. It is a general principle in private international law that procedural problems are governed by the *lex fori*, and no choice of law rule is necessary to determine the law applicable to them. But a choice of court agreement is different from other purely procedural activity at court in many respects. Besides the procedural effects, it is similar to an obligatory contract.

This author is thus of the opinion that a choice of court agreement is a non-obligatory contract which does not fall into the category of "obligatory acts" in Article 20 of the PIL Act, yet the applicable law for its validity shall be decided under the "legal rationale" of conflict of laws. It is thus reasonable to apply Article 20 of the PIL Act in analogy to this question.[14] It can resort first to the parties' express intention and then to the law of the place which is most closely connected with the choice of court agreement.[15]

---

[12]Chen (2017a), p. 2563; Chen (2014a), pp. 77–80.

[13]Article 1 of the PILA states that "Civil matters involving foreign elements are governed, in the absence of any provisions in this Act, by the provisions of other statutes; in the absence of applicable provisions in other statutes, by the principles of law."

[14]Liu and Chen (2018), p. 639; Chen (2015), p. 28.

[15]Article 20 of the PIL Act provides that "(1) The applicable law regarding the formation and effect of a juridical act which results in a relationship of obligation is determined by the intention of the parties.

2.2.2 Principles to Characterize a Choice of Court Agreement

The characterization of a choice of court agreement relates to exploration of the parties' real intent—whether to grant jurisdiction exclusively to the designated court or just nominate it as one of the jurisdictionally competent courts. This can be categorized as construction of the parties' expressed intent. The construction of the choice of court agreement sometimes was treated as the ascertainment of facts about the agreement. The forum law (*lex fori*) is thus applicable to its construction either under the idea that it is within the scope of the court's fact-finding authority or that such a procedural agreement is governed by the forum law under the Taiwanese PILA. The law of the designated forum competes with the law of seized forum when the action is initiated in a court other than the chosen or designated court. The problem which forum law shall be decisive to the construction of the parties' intent remains to be solved.

2.2.3 Illustrative Court Decisions

It is apparent that the law of the designated court is more closely connected with the choice of court agreement than the law of the court seised, for deciding the validity and construction of the parties' agreement. The Supreme Court's Decision # Tai-Kang 259 of 2012 expressed well the judicial reasoning and illustrated the related problems.

In this Decision, X (a Taiwanese company) and Y (a Japanese company) signed a patent license contract in which the following jurisdictional clause was included: "Any United States District Court will have jurisdiction over any claim or controversy arising under or in relation to this Agreement." X terminated the contract and stopped paying the licensing fee. Y first filed a lawsuit claiming damages for breach of contract in the US District Court for the Northern District of California. Then, Y withdrew this claim, and filed on the same day for the same purpose in the Superior Court of the State of California, County of San Francisco. A ruling against Y was granted after X contended that the US court is a forum *non conveniens* and an alternative Taiwanese court is appropriate to determine the dispute. X filed a lawsuit in the Taiwanese Court of Intellectual Property (of first instance). Y contended that Taiwanese courts' jurisdiction was excluded by the choice of court agreement.

---

(2) Where there is no express intention of the parties or their express intention is void under the applicable law determined by them, the formation and effect of the juridical act are governed by the law which is most closely connected with the juridical act.

(3) Where among the obligations resulting from a juridical act there is a characteristic one, the law of the domicile of the party obligated under the characteristic obligation at the time he/she undertook the juridical act is presumed to be the most closely connected law. However, where a juridical act concerns immovable property, the law of the place where the immovable property is located is presumed to be the most closely connected law."

In this case, the Taiwanese courts of three instances addressed their opinions in relation to several questions relating to the effect of the jurisdictional agreement. They all agreed that it is well established that the provisions of jurisdiction in the Taiwanese CCP shall be applicable by analogy to the choice of court agreement at issue. The enforceability of such an agreement was confirmed, while the three levels of court reached different conclusions about its nature and effects. With regard to the optional or exclusive nature of such agreement, their opinions differed in an interesting way. The Court of First Instance referred to the Hague Convention on Choice of Court Agreements 2005 and the Principles for Conflict of Laws in Intellectual Property 2010 (CLIP) and ruled that it is an exclusive agreement by which the Taiwanese court's jurisdiction was excluded. The Court of Appeal looked into the wording of the choice of court clause and ruled that it is an optional agreement so that the Taiwanese courts can exercise their statutory jurisdiction. The Supreme Court upheld the Court of Appeal's decision in its Decision # Tai-Kang 259 of 2012 and ruled that an agreement shall be presumed to be optional unless it has been proved to be exclusive.

The Supreme Court reiterated some principles in this Decision. First, the court stated that

> If the designated court has no jurisdiction over such international litigation, unless otherwise provided by the *lex fori*, the choice of court agreement is not necessarily binding on such designated court. As there is no rule on international transfer of jurisdiction in legislation or judicial practice, the effects of choice of court agreements are not necessarily exclusive.

The judgment goes on to say that

> The disputes on international jurisdiction by agreement shall be settled by contract construction case by case. The elements that shall be taken into account include the factual background, usage of trade, economic purpose, reasonable and objective notice of common society, principles of experience, and the effects intended by the parties when they expressed their willingness. The result of construction shall be reviewed by weighing the above elements in order to pursue fairness and justice.

The Supreme Court ruled that the parties' agreement on court jurisdiction, if any, is only valid in relation to disputes about patent infringements, noting that

> This action on non-existence of obligation has nothing to do with patent. There is no federal element or federal interest in it, so it is not under jurisdiction of the US federal courts. The agreement on jurisdiction over patent infringements is therefore unenforceable over this action.

Since this action is not covered by the parties' agreement on jurisdiction, the jurisdiction of the ROC courts over it, if any, is not excluded by it. Article 3 Section 1 of the Taiwanese CCP provides: "In matters relating to proprietary rights, an action may be initiated against a defendant who either does not have a place of domicile in the R.O.C. or whose domicile is unknown, in the court for the location of the defendant's attachable property or the subject matter of the claim."

The Supreme Court held that, by analogy to such provision, the ROC courts' jurisdiction over this action was confirmed.

In this Decision, the law of the designated court was taken into account to evaluate the effects on jurisdiction of the court in which the action was initiated. The Supreme Court characterized the agreement as an optional choice of court without mentioning the applicable law in this case. Apparently the standards adopted to construe and characterize the agreement are some criteria evolved from the practice in the domestic courts. It seems a two-tier method underlies in this judicial thinking: the validity is governed by the law of the designated court, and the construction or characterization is governed by the forum law. The Supreme Court ruled in this decision that a choice of court agreement is characterized as optional if the parties' intentions are not established as exclusive. The fact that the word "shall" or "must" is used in the forum selection clause is not sufficient to indicate the exclusiveness of the selection.

When a choice of court agreement is characterized as exclusive, the Taiwanese courts often interpret its words so as to limit its scope of application. The Supreme Court's Decision # Tai-Shang 592 of 1989 illustrates this attitude. In this decision, the Supreme Court ruled that the Taiwanese courts are jurisdictionally competent to decide the dispute between a Swiss corporation and the manager of its Taiwanese branch who is a Swiss citizen. The Taiwanese branch sued the Swiss manager in Shi-Lin District Court where he had a residence provided by the former at the time the lawsuit commenced. The Swiss manager contended that Taiwanese courts have no jurisdiction because it was prescribed in the employment contract that the related disputes should be subject to the jurisdiction of the court at Zurich. The Supreme Court ruled that Taiwanese courts are jurisdictionally competent according to Article 1 Sections 1 & 2 of the Taiwanese CCP. The legal relationships that the Taiwan branch asserted are based on the tortious act and unjust enrichment which occurred after the employment contract was terminated, which the court said were beyond the scope of the choice of court clause. Therefore, the Taiwanese courts' jurisdiction was not affected by the choice of court agreement in favour of a foreign court at Zurich.

2.3 Applicable Law to the Legal Effect of an Optional Choice of Court Agreement

2.3.1 Choice of Law Principle

If the forum is not the court designated in an optional choice of court agreement, different aspects of the legal effects of such agreement will be considered under the laws of the places of the forum and of the selected forum. The Supreme Court thus ruled in its Decision # Tai-Shang 96 of 1975 that for the validity of a choice of court agreement, we have to look first to its effect under the law of the designated court, then to characterize it as optional or exclusive. The effect in the forum state is apparently governed by forum law.[16] The Supreme Court did not specifically determine the law applicable to the effect of an optional choice of court agreement.

Such principle referring to the *lex fori* is not expressly provided for in the Taiwanese CCP or Taiwanese PILA. The underlying doctrine is that the legal effect of a jurisdictional agreement is purely procedural, so the *lex fori* is applicable to it. Unlike the exclusive choice of court agreement, it is established that the parties to an optional choice of court agreement are not bound to initiate proceedings in the designated court even if it is otherwise jurisdictionally incompetent.

2.4 *Effect of an Optional Choice of Court Agreement in Favour of the Courts of the Forum*

2.4.1 Waiver of the Parties' Rights to Contest Jurisdiction

According to Article 24 of the Taiwanese CCP, an optional choice of court agreement is effective if it meets the qualification set by the law applicable to it. If it is valid, whether it is in favour of the courts of Taiwan or other country, the legal effect is to prorogate the jurisdiction to the chosen court under the CCP. When the Taiwanese courts are chosen, they can exercise either the statutory jurisdiction under the CCP or the selected jurisdiction under the choice of court agreement. The main effect is that the jurisdiction which a court can exercise to decide the consented dispute is widened to include statutory jurisdiction as well as the consented jurisdiction. The courts with statutory jurisdiction will not be affected by the optional choice of court agreement. The defendant can challenge the validity of the agreement or the legal ground on which the forum's jurisdiction stands. It has nothing to do with waiver of contention to the jurisdiction or voluntary submission to the forum. Article 25 of the Taiwanese CCP is thus inapplicable to an optional choice of court agreement.[17]

2.4.2 Exercise of the Option and Its Legal Effect

As mentioned above, it is established that an optional choice of court agreement does not derogate the jurisdiction of any court. Litigants can choose one among the jurisdictionally competent courts in which to initiate the lawsuit. If the option has been exercised by commencing proceedings in one court and the dispute or subject matter is seized with that court, the litigants are not prohibited by the Taiwanese law from instituting a new lawsuit in a foreign jurisdictionally competent court. In other

[16] Chen (2015), pp. 30–32.

[17] Article 25 of the Taiwanese CCP provides that "A court obtains jurisdiction over an action where the defendant proceeds orally on the merits without contesting lack of jurisdiction."

words, the exercise of the option by a litigant does not affect the jurisdiction of the courts of other countries. Although parallel litigation in different domestic courts within Taiwan is not permitted, parallel litigation in courts of different countries is tolerated under the Taiwanese CCP. If one of the courts in which parallel litigation has been initiated is Taiwanese, it is stipulated in Article 182-2 of the Taiwanese CCP that the domestic forum can basically stay the proceeding and wait for a judgment from a foreign court.

2.5 Legal Effect of an Optional Choice of Court Agreement in Favour of Foreign Courts

An optional choice of court agreement in favour of foreign courts does not affect the jurisdiction the Taiwanese courts have under the Taiwanese CCP. The parallel jurisdiction will not change even if the option has been exercised by commencing proceedings in the nominated foreign court. The seized Taiwanese court will handle the problem of parallel litigation by staying proceeding and waiting for the foreign judgment.

In the Supreme Court's Judgment # Tai-Shang 2477 of 2003, a foreign corporation sued two Taiwanese corporations in Taiwan for performance of a contract which the parties agreed to subject to the jurisdiction of courts in London. The Supreme Court ruled that the principle of *Actor Sequitur Forum Rei* adopted by the CCP is to protect defendants from being sued in a distant court, and that if the plaintiff waived the jurisdiction of the chosen court in London, the Taiwanese courts are convenient for the defendants and have jurisdiction under the Taiwanese CCP despite the choice of court agreement.

2.6 Treatment of Optional Choice of Court Agreements

As mentioned above, an optional choice of court agreement only prorogates jurisdiction of the chosen court; no court will thus be derogated from exercising its jurisdiction. Under such circumstances, the jurisdiction of Taiwanese courts is parallel with courts of other countries, irrespective of whether the agreement is in favour of forum courts or foreign courts. Unless a judgement rendered by a foreign court is sought to be recognised and enforced in Taiwan, it is beyond the power of the Taiwanese courts to address the jurisdiction of courts of foreign countries. They can exercise jurisdiction either under the Taiwanese CCP or on the basis of the parties' agreements, so the agreements are basically treated consistently irrespective of which country the nominated court belongs to.

2.7 *Protection of Weaker Parties*

Article 28 Section 2 of the Taiwanese CCP plays a role in protecting weaker parties from adhesive choice of court agreement made by stronger parties. Based on the idea of equality of bargaining power and substantial fairness to both parties, it provides that choice of court agreements between legal persons and merchants are binding and enforceable, but the validity of such a choice of court clause in a standard contract shall be further examined.

Article 28 Section 2 states:

> Before proceeding orally on the merits, a party may move the court to transfer the action to another court with jurisdiction when the court in which the action is pending obtains jurisdiction in accordance with the provision of Article 24 and such an agreement is part of a standard contract prepared by the opposing party which is either a juridical person or a merchant, and the contract is manifestly unfair under the circumstances.

In other words, the weaker party is protected from abuse of bargaining power by moving the action to a court that otherwise has jurisdiction. Such principle is also embodied in the Small-Claim Proceedings.[18]

In Supreme Court's Decision # Tai-Shang 58 of 2016, an employee sued his employer, a computer chip corporation, and argued that the employment contract between them was still effective in the Taipei District Court. A clause in the standard employment contract stated that related disputes shall be subject to the jurisdiction of Shin-Chu District Court. The Supreme Court ruled that the employee is a weaker party relative to the corporate employer and it is not inconvenient for the corporation to go out of its domicile to litigate in Taipei. The employee was therefore not bound to the adhesive choice of law clause.

2.8 *Possible Consequences of a Breach of an Optional Choice of Court Agreement*

2.8.1 Stay of Proceedings

As mentioned above, the court nominated in an optional choice of court agreement does not have a superior position to other courts in exercising jurisdiction over the dispute. However, in dealing with problem of parallel litigation initiated in the courts of Taiwan and foreign countries, the nominated Taiwanese court's proceeding

[18]Article 436-9 of the Taiwanese CCP states that "In cases where a party to a Small-Claim Proceeding is a juridical person or a merchant and it has, by the standard contract that it uses, designated either the place of performance of obligations or a court of the first instance to exercise jurisdiction, the provisions of Article 12 or Article 24 shall not apply, except when both parties to such action are legal persons or merchants."

outweighs exceptionally the foreign court proceedings. Article 182-2 Section 1 of the Taiwanese CCP provides:

> In cases where a party has initiated an action with regard to a subject matter for which an action is pending in a foreign court, if reasons exist for the court reasonably to believe that the foreign court's judgment on the action may be recognized in the R.O.C., and it is not substantially inconvenient for the defendant to litigate in such foreign country, then the court by a ruling may stay the proceeding until the entry of a final and binding judgment on the action in that foreign country, except where the parties have otherwise consented to have the subject matter adjudicated by the R.O.C. court. . . .Before deciding on the ruling provided in the preceding paragraph, the court shall accord the parties an opportunity to be heard.

It is clear that if the Taiwanese court is seized in advance, it is not required to stay proceedings. If the Taiwanese court is nominated in the choice of court agreement, even though the foreign court is seized in advance, the proceedings in the Taiwanese court will not be affected.

2.8.2 Damages for Breach

As the choice of court agreement is only procedural in nature, no substantive effect is conferred on it. Parties to an optional choice of court agreement are not obliged to sue in the nominated court. Instead, they are allowed to sue in any jurisdictionally competent court. Therefore, unless otherwise agreed, it cannot be treated as breach of an obligatory contract when one party commences proceedings in a court other than that nominated in the optional choice of court agreement. The legal effects of breach of such an agreement are purely procedural. As there is no legal ground for a claim of damages, the opposite party can only contest the jurisdictional basis and assert the limited procedural interest created by the agreement.

2.8.3 Anti-suit Injunctions

The Taiwanese CCP deals only with the procedure and court activities in Taiwanese courts. It is beyond the authority of the Taiwanese forum to restrain courts of foreign countries from hearing related proceedings. No anti-suit injunction can be granted to restrain the commencement or continuation of foreign proceedings even if the other party was in breach of the choice of court agreement, not to mention that the other party commenced the proceeding in a jurisdictionally competent court other than the nominated one.

2.8.4 Anti-enforcement Injunctions

The judgments given by foreign courts are generally recognized and enforceable in Taiwan unless they fall into any one of the four negative categories provided in Article 402 Section 1 of the Taiwanese CCP. This states that:

> A final and binding judgment rendered by a foreign court shall be recognized, except in case of any of the following circumstances: 1. Where the foreign court lacks jurisdiction pursuant to the R.O.C. laws; 2. Where a default judgment is rendered against the losing defendant, except in the case where the notice or summons of the initiation of action had been legally served in a reasonable time in the foreign country or had been served through judicial assistance provided under the R.O.C. laws; 3. Where the performance ordered by such judgment or its litigation procedure is contrary to R.O.C. public policy or morals; 4. Where there exists no mutual recognition between the foreign country and the R.O.C.

In light of the limited legal effects of an optional choice of court agreements mentioned earlier, a court other than that nominated in it does not necessarily lack jurisdiction. A judgment given by that court does not automatically fall into the first category of the above provisions. It might still be recognized and enforced. The parties can bring a suit to ask the court to declare whether the conditions to the four categories are satisfied. No power to grant anti-enforcement injunctions is provided in the Taiwanese CCP.

2.8.5 Judgment Rendered by a Non-nominated Foreign Court

As mentioned above, suing in a court which is not nominated in an optional choice of court agreement in disputes within the scope of the agreement is not treated as breach of agreement or violation of law. The non-nominated court can exercise its jurisdiction under its own rules. A judgment rendered by a foreign court that is not nominated in an optional choice of court agreement will be recognized and enforced by the courts of Taiwan if there is no other bar to its recognition and enforcement.

2.9 Sub-national Units and the Law on Optional Choice of Court Agreements

In terms of Article 10 of the Additional Articles of the ROC Constitution (Zhong-Hua-Min-Guo-Xian-Fa Zeng-Xiu-Tiao-Wen)[19] of 1991, Taiwan, mainland China, Hong Kong and Macao are different and separate regions of a single country ("one China"). The legal system differs from region to region. The inter-regional conflict of laws problems between these four territories are dealt with in the Act on Relations between the People of the Taiwan Area and the Mainland Area (Tai-Wan-Di-Qu Yu Da-Lu-Di-Qu Ren-Min-Guan-Xi Tiao-Li)[20] and the Act Governing Relations with

[19] Additional Articles of the ROC Constitution (Zhong-Hua-Min-Guo-Xian-Fa Zeng-Xiu-Tiao-Wen) of 1991, 5403 POG 2 (1991).

[20] Act on Relations between the People of the Taiwan Area and the Mainland Area (Tai-Wan-Di-Qu Yu Da-Lu-Di-Qu Ren-Min-Guan-Xi Tiao-Li), adopted in 1992 (5601 POG 1) and last revised in 2015 (7192 POG 11).

Hong Kong and Macau (Xiang-Gang-Ao-Men-Guan-Xi Tiao-Li).[21] It is a unique framework which differentiates inter-regional relations from international relations. However, unlike the sub-national units in a federation, there is no single constitution which applies to all four regions and regulates their links with each other. The Taiwanese CCP applies as a unified law wholly and only to Taiwan. The other three regions apply their own autonomous relevant statutes and rules.[22]

2.10 *Optional Choice of Court Agreements in Intranational Cases and International Cases*

As mentioned earlier, an optional choice of court agreement only widens the range of courts with jurisdiction to decide the consented dispute. The jurisdiction of the nominated court is not exclusive. The non-nominated Taiwanese or foreign court's statutory jurisdiction is not thus derogated. Such a principle applies to intranational, interregional and international cases.

2.11 *Effect of an Exclusive Choice of Court Agreement*

2.11.1 Different Treatments of Domestic and International Exclusive Choice of Court Agreements

An exclusive choice of court agreement is derogative in nature. Basically, the nominated court has exclusive jurisdiction over actions arising from the subject matters covered in the agreement. If a court has exclusive jurisdiction over the action under the Taiwanese CCP, such jurisdiction will not be derogated or excluded by a choice of court agreement. The treatment of exclusive choice of court agreement in intranational litigation differs from their treatment in international litigation as mentioned earlier. Where a Taiwanese court is nominated as the sole and exclusive court to decide the dispute, unless otherwise provided in Taiwanese law, all other Taiwanese and foreign courts are derogated from exercising jurisdiction over it. However, the statutory jurisdiction of Taiwanese courts will not necessarily be excluded where a foreign court was selected as the exclusive court to decide the dispute at issue. Some additional conditions were required in judicial practice to derogate the statutory jurisdiction of Taiwanese courts. The scope of an effective

[21] Act Governing Relations with Hong Kong and Macau (Xiang-Gang-Ao-Men-Guan-Xi Tiao-Li), adopted in 1997 (6146 POG 14) and last revised in 2017 (7340 POG 4).

[22] See Tu and Huang, in this collection, for further information on the law of the PRC.

exclusive choice of court agreement is often strictly confined to cover only very limited disputes.[23]

2.11.2 Effects of an Optional and Exclusive Choice of Court Agreement

The effects of an optional choice of court agreement are quite different from those of an exclusive one. The former can only add the nominated court to the list of courts with jurisdiction, while the latter can make the nominated court the only court with jurisdiction and exclude the other courts from the list. For this reason, when Taiwanese courts are excluded from the list, the future recognition and enforcement of the judgment given by the nominated court shall be taken into account in deciding whether the Taiwanese courts shall exceptionally reserve their jurisdiction to protect the party's right to access the courts.

2.12 *Law on Treatment of Choice of Court Agreements*

2.12.1 Exclusive Choice of Court Agreements in Direct and Indirect Jurisdiction

Article 24 of the Taiwanese CCP deals with choice of court agreements as a whole and treats optional and exclusive agreements together in a single article. Once a specific court is nominated by the parties, this Article provides that the jurisdiction of other courts is basically excluded. The nominated domestic court's jurisdiction is apparently presumed to be exclusive. In international litigation, the Taiwanese courts encounter two types of issues. The first is whether they have direct jurisdiction to hear the case, the other is whether the foreign rendering court had indirect jurisdiction to give the judgment. For some reason, most cases concern the first type. The core disputed problem is whether the Taiwanese courts' jurisdiction is excluded. The issues included in this problem are, *inter alia*, characterization of the choice of court agreement, the scope of disputes covered by the choice, and the effects of the choice of court agreement. The ROC Supreme Court ruled in its Decision # Tai-Shang 96 of 1975 that an international choice of court agreement can only exclude Taiwanese courts' jurisdiction under two conditions: first, the nominated foreign court is

[23]In Supreme Court's Decision # Tai-Kang 165 of 2005, a Japanese company and a Taiwanese company agreed in their "contract of development, manufacture and sales" that "all the litigations related to this contract or litigations of disputes incidental to it shall be subject to the exclusive jurisdiction of Osaka District Court in Japan for their first instance trials," and that "Japanese Law is the law applicable to this contract and its interpretation." The Japanese company sued the Taiwanese company for infringement of copyright after the contract was terminated. The Supreme Court ruled in this case that the problem of jurisdiction should be decided separately because the case at issue may stand beyond the scope of that contract. *See* Chen (2014b), p. 29.

jurisdictionally competent under the law of the designated forum; and secondly, its judgment will be recognized in Taiwan.

2.12.2 Optional Choice of Court Agreements

Comparatively, optional choice of law agreements seldom caught the judicial attention. To cope with the need for judicial practice, scholars gave greater attention to exploring problems of exclusive choice of court agreements than to those of optional choice of court agreements. It is beyond doubt that the pragmatic diversity and academic significance of optional choice of court agreements are still to be explored.

3 Asymmetrical Choice of Court Agreements

3.1 Validity and Effectiveness of an Asymmetrical Choice of Court Agreement

In an asymmetrical choice of court agreement, the parties are subject to different conditions of initiating actions against the other party. The agreement on designated courts is binding on one party while the other party enjoys greater freedom to institute suits in convenient courts. Such an agreement is not invalid merely because it is asymmetrical. As a reflection of the principle of party autonomy, its validity shall be decided pursuant to Articles 24 and 28 of the Taiwanese CCP. It is generally valid if the requirements of Article 24 are satisfied. However, when "such an agreement is part of a standard contract prepared by the opposing party which is either a juridical person or a merchant, and the contract is manifestly unfair under the circumstances", it is ineffective under Article 28 Section 2, which is designed to protect the weaker party.

3.1.1 Effect of the Optional Component of an Asymmetrical Agreement

The legal effects of an asymmetrical choice of court agreement depend on the intention expressed by the parties. Interpretation and construction of the relevant intention are essential at this stage. The optional component allows one party to optionally sue in two or more designated courts. In this respect, the consented submission to jurisdiction is as valid as other optional choice of court agreements. Such party therefore has the option of commencing proceedings in any court with jurisdiction.

3.1.2 Exercise of the Option

Asymmetric choice of court agreements require one party to sue in the courts of a specified jurisdiction only whilst allowing the other party to sue in any court with jurisdiction. The party with the option is not restricted to sue in a designated court. If the option has not been exercised, the only problem is whether the exclusive component restricts the plaintiff to sue in the designated court. If it has been exercised by commencing proceedings in a court, the jurisdictional dispute is whether such option is legally granted to the plaintiff, or whether the parties are equally bound by the exclusive designation of that court. It is also possible that the other party institutes parallel litigation in the designated court. The root of the problem in such situations is whether the drafted option is unfair to the other party and should therefore be invalidated. If so, the issue whether the exclusive component is also binding on this party will automatically arise.

The Supreme Court's Decision # Tai-Kang 571 of 2014 illustrates the situation in which the option was not exercised. In this case, a Taiwanese corporation purchased a machine from a German corporation under a contract of sale. The asymmetrical choice of court agreement in their contract includes the following sentences:

> If the customer is a merchant ('Kaufmann')…the exclusive venue for all disputes arising from the Contract shall be Stuttgart, Germany. … The same shall apply if the customer has no general venue in the Federal Republic of Germany or moved its ordinary residence to a country outside Germany after the conclusion of the Contract. … MAYER & CIE shall be entitled, however, to sue the customer at any other court having statutory jurisdiction.

The Taiwanese corporation commenced court proceedings in Taiwan, while the German corporation contended that the action was subject to the exclusive jurisdiction of courts in Stuttgart, Germany because of their agreement, and that the Taiwanese courts were without jurisdiction. The Supreme Court focused on the validity of the exclusive component and did not address the optional component. It ruled that the Taiwanese corporation was not a weaker party during their negotiation process, and that the asymmetrical choice of court agreement was far from unfair. "As the parties had agreed on exclusive jurisdiction, the jurisdiction of courts other than the designated one is derogated accordingly to make it exclusive. The non-designated courts lost their statutory jurisdiction due to that exclusive choice of court agreement."

3.2 *Party in Whose Favour the Option Is Drafted*

As asymmetrical choice of court agreements are subject to provisions on scrutiny of adhesive contracts or standard clauses, the test in Article 28 Section 2 of the Taiwanese CCP applies. Instead of judging which party is weaker or stronger, the criteria are: (1) whether only one party is a legal person or merchant, (2) whether the choice of law clause is included in a standard contract prepared by one party, and

(3) whether the agreement is manifestly unfair under the circumstances. The party in whose favour the option is drafted is, as a matter of fact, quite often the stronger party to the transaction. But that imbalance of bargaining power is not presumed in Taiwanese law or judicial practice. Taiwanese courts emphasize evaluating the parties' substantial bargaining power and fairness of the agreement on a case-to-case basis. In its Decision # Tai-Kang 571 of 2014, the Supreme Court took a serious look at the Taiwanese corporation's substantial bargaining power, and ruled that it is not unfair to enforce their asymmetrical choice of court agreement.

4 Conclusion

The effectiveness of a choice of court agreement was envisaged and recognized in the Taiwanese CCP. The provisions are basically designed for exclusive choice of court agreements. Optional choice of court agreements are subject to the same provisions unless otherwise indicated by legal theory. The legal treatment is too unrefined to deal with all related problems. The effects of optional choice of court agreements can differ from case to case, dependent on the intent of the parties. Asymmetrical choice of court agreements just illustrate the diversity of optional choice of court agreements.

It is foreseeable that the problems of several other kinds of optional choice of court agreements and their diverse effects may be disputed in the future judicial practice. Without concrete provisions to rely on, the parties to such agreements will face uncertainties and cost in enforcing their agreements to resolve the disputes. There is currently no governmental plan or proposal to reform the related laws on choice of court agreements, yet the experiences of the Hague Convention of 30 June 2005 on Choice of Court Agreements and the Brussels Ibis Regulation of European Union will somehow affect the legal treatment. It is expected the problems mentioned above will all be well addressed both in legislative reform and judicial practice.

References

Chen R-C (2014a) General provisions in the Taiwanese private international law enactment 2010. In: Basedow J, Pissler KB (eds) Private international law in Mainland China, Taiwan and Europe. Mohr Siebeck, Tübingen, pp 77–80

Chen R-C (2014b) Jurisdiction, choice of law and the recognition of foreign judgments in Taiwan. In: Basedow J, Pissler KB (eds) Private international law in Mainland China, Taiwan and Europe. Mohr Siebeck, Tübingen, pp 17–38

Chen R-C (2014c) Taiwanese PIL Act 2010. In: Basedow J, Pissler KB (eds) Private international law in Mainland China, Taiwan and Europe. Mohr Siebeck, Tübingen, pp 453–465

Chen R-C (2015) Private international law in practice: analytical study on civil cases with foreign elements (Guo-ji Si-fa Shi-yong) (in Chinese). Wu-nan Publisher, Taipei

Chen R-C (2017a) Taiwan. In: Basedow J, Rühl G, Ferrari F, Asensio PM (eds) Encyclopedia of private international law, vol 3. Edward Elgar, Cheltenham, pp 2559–2569
Chen R-C (2017b) Act governing the choice of law in civil matters involving foreign elements. In: Basedow J, Rühl G, Ferrari F, Asensio PM (eds) Encyclopedia of private international law, vol 4. Edward Elgar, Cheltenham, pp 3880–3889
Chen R-C (2017c) Interpretation and application of the New York Convention in Taiwan. In: Bermann GA (ed) Recognition and enforcement of foreign arbitral awards – the interpretation and application of the New York Convention by National Courts. Springer, Cham, pp 945–962
Liu T-C, Chen R-C (2018) Liu and Chen on private international law (Guo-ji Si-fa Lun) (in Chinese), 6th edn. San-Ming, Taipei

Legislation

Act Governing Relations with Hong Kong and Macau (Xiang-Gang-Ao-Men-Guan-Xi-Tiao-Li), adopted in 1997, 6146 Presidential Office Gazette (Zong-tong-fu Gong-bao) 14 (1997), and last revised in 2017, 7340 Presidential Office Gazette (Zong-tong-fu Gong-bao) 4 (2017)
Act Governing the Choice of Law in Civil Matters Involving Foreign Elements (She-Wai-Min-Shi-Fa-Lü-Shi-Yong-Fa), adopted in 1953, 403 Presidential Office Gazette (Zong-tong-fu Gong-bao) 1 (1953), and last revised in 2010, 6923 Presidential Office Gazette (Zong-tong-fu Gong-bao) 24 (2010)
Act on Relations between the People of the Taiwan Area and the Mainland Area (Tai-Wan-Di-Qu-Yu-Da-Lu-Di-Qu-Ren-Min-Guan-Xi-Tiao-Li), adopted in 1992, 5601 Presidential Office Gazette (Zong-tong-fu Gong-bao) 1 (1992), and last revised in 2015, 7192 Presidential Office Gazette (Zong-tong-fu Gong-bao) 11 (2015)
Additional Articles of the ROC Constitution (Zhong-Hua-Min-Guo-Xian-Fa-Zeng-Xiu-Tiao-Wen) of 1991, 5403 Presidential Office Gazette (Zong-tong-fu Gong-bao) 2 (1991)
Arbitration Act (Zhong-Cai-Fa), adopted in 1998, 6224 Presidential Office Gazette (Zong-tong-fu Gong-bao) 40 (1998), and last revised in 2015, 7222 Presidential Office Gazette (Zong-tong-fu Gong-bao) 31 (2015)
Civil Code (Min- Fa), adopted in 1929, 174 Guo-Min-Zheng-Fu-Gong-Bao 2 (1929), and last revised in 2015, 7197 Presidential Office Gazette (Zong-tong-fu Gong-bao) 27 (2015)
Commercial Arbitration Act (Shang-Wu-Zhong-Cai-Tiao-Li), adopted in 1961, 1194 Presidential Office Gazette (Zong-tong-fu Gong-bao) 1 (1961), replaced by Arbitration Act (Zhong-Cai-Fa), adopted in 1998, 6224 Presidential Office Gazette (Zong-tong-fu Gong-bao) 40 (1998)
Family Matters Act (Jia-shi Shi-jian Fa), adopted in 2012, 7012 Presidential Office Gazette (Zong-tong-fu Gong-bao) 35 (2012), and last revised in 2015, 7226 Presidential Office Gazette (Zong-tong-fu Gong-bao) 106 (2015)
Supreme Court Decisions and Judgments: Supreme Court's Decision # Tai-Kang 165 of 2005, Decision # Kang-16 of 1930, Decision # Tai-Kang 259 of 2012, Decision # Tai-Shang 592 of 1989, Decision # Tai-Shang 96 of 1975, Judgment # Tai-Shang 2477 of 2003, Decision # Tai-Shang 58 of 2016 and Decision # Tai-Kang 571 of 2014
Taiwanese Code of Civil Procedure (Min-Shi-Su-Song-Fa), adopted in 1930, 659 Guo-Min-Zheng-Fu-Gong-Bao 15 (1930), and last revised in 2018, 7638 Presidential Office Gazette (Zong-tong-fu Gong-bao) 38 (2018)

Rong-Chwan Chen (PhD in Law, National Cheng-chi University, Taiwan) is a University Distinguished Professor at National Taipei University, where he served as the Chairperson of Department of Judicial Studies from 2005 to 2007 and Chairperson of Department of Law from 2010 to 2012. Before joining National Taipei University in 2004, he was a Professor at Soochow University School of Law, Taiwan. His work focuses on the private international law and law of property, and is published in several books and more than 150 articles and chapters. In particular he was appointed as the key drafter to prepare the comprehensive revising draft of Taiwan's Act on Choice of Law in Civil Matters Involving Foreign Elements and its explanatory comments. After the Congress passed the enactment in 2010, he prepared its English translation which is now widely accessed on the government website and internationally circulated. Professor Chen was appointed as a Commissioner of Fair Trade Commission to enforce Taiwan's antitrust law in 2009. He was elected as Secretary General of Taiwan Jurists Association and an associate member of the International Academy of Comparative Law.

Turkey: Optional Choice of Court Agreements

Zeynep Derya Tarman and Meltem Ece Oba

1 Introduction

The increasing globalization of markets has resulted in cross-border disputes becoming a common feature of practice for most lawyers. Consequently, jurisdiction agreements have been very frequently utilized by parties who are subjected to different legal systems, in order to find the most convenient forum to resolve their disputes. In line with the widely recognized doctrine of freedom of contract, Turkish private international law allows parties to grant jurisdiction to foreign courts or to Turkish courts for the resolution of their legal disputes. Jurisdiction agreements can be in the form of a separate agreement or a clause in a contract. There are certain requirements under the law that shall be fulfilled in order to form a valid jurisdiction agreement. The rules regarding agreements granting jurisdiction to foreign courts and those granting jurisdiction to Turkish courts differ and are regulated under different legal codes.

The main focus of this study is to examine the Turkish legal rules regarding jurisdiction agreements.[1] In elaborating this issue, first the relevant sources of law in this area will be introduced (Sect. 2). Following that, agreements granting jurisdiction to foreign courts will be examined mainly through the requirements and consequences of forming such an agreement (Sect. 3). Next, agreements granting jurisdiction to Turkish courts will be examined (Sect. 4). Following that, asymmetrical jurisdiction agreements will be discussed (Sect. 5). Subsequently, the recognition and enforcement of a foreign judgment rendered by a court authorized under a

[1]In this chapter, "choice of court agreement" is used interchangeably with "jurisdiction agreement".

Z. D. Tarman (✉) · M. E. Oba
Department of Private International Law, Koç University Law School, Istanbul, Turkey
e-mail: ztarman@ku.edu.tr; meoba@ku.edu.tr

M. Keyes (ed.), *Optional Choice of Court Agreements in Private International Law*,
Ius Comparatum – Global Studies in Comparative Law 37,
https://doi.org/10.1007/978-3-030-23914-5_18

jurisdiction agreement will be elaborated upon (Sect. 6). Finally, co-existing jurisdiction and arbitration clauses will be examined (Sect. 7).

2 Sources of Law Relating to Jurisdiction Agreements

Turkey is a unitary state so the relevant law on the requirements and consequences of a choice of court agreement are identical within the Turkish jurisdiction. The Turkish legal system is a part of the continental system.[2] Thus, unlike the common law system, in principle judicial precedent is not binding and the judges apply the statutory sources of law. Court decisions are utilized only to interpret the existing statutory law and are not traditionally considered a source of law. Although prior decisions may guide the judge to arrive at a conclusion, in principle the judges are not bound by the previous decisions.

The principal statutory sources of law in dealing with jurisdiction agreements are as follows: (1) relevant international conventions to which Turkey is a party, (2) the Turkish Private International Law and International Civil Procedure Code[3] (hereafter: "PIL Code") and (3) Turkish Code of Civil Procedure[4] (hereafter: "CCP"). Besides the statutory sources (4) court decisions regarding jurisdiction agreements are also applied in interpreting and filling the internal gaps of the statutory law.

There is an order in the application of the abovementioned sources of law regarding jurisdiction agreements. Accordingly, international conventions to which Turkey is a party prevail over the domestic rules. Thus, the domestic rules apply only when there are no rules regarding jurisdiction agreements under international conventions that Turkey has ratified. Within the domestic rules, the PIL Code is the special code (*lex specialis*) in relation to the CCP, and therefore the rules under the PIL Code prevail over the CCP rules. Therefore, CCP rules are applied only to the issues which the PIL Code does not cover. For example, in relation to jurisdiction agreements, the PIL Code only regulates agreements that authorize foreign courts. On the other hand, the CCP encompasses rules regarding jurisdiction agreements that authorize only Turkish courts. Thus, the validity of a jurisdiction agreement that authorizes a foreign court is evaluated in light of the PIL Code, while the validity of a jurisdiction agreement that authorizes a Turkish court is governed by the CCP.

As regards rules of civil procedure Turkish private international law recognizes the principle of *lex fori*.[5] In other words, domestic civil procedural rules such as the functioning of the court, means and burden of proof, time limits etc. are applied as

---

[2]For further information on Turkish law see: Ansay and Wallace (2011).

[3]Law No. 5718. Official Gazette 12.12.2007/26728.

[4]Law No. 6100. Official Gazette 04.02.2011/27836.

[5]Nomer (2017), pp. 392–393; Şanlı et al. (2018), pp. 338–339; Çelikel and Erdem (2017), pp. 481–482.

stipulated under the CCP even where the proceedings contain a foreign element; unless international conventions or the PIL Code exceptionally stipulate otherwise.

2.1 International Conventions

The Turkish Constitution[6] Art. 90, reads in part that international agreements duly put into effect have the force of law. Besides, pursuant to Art. 1(2) of the PIL Code, provisions of international conventions to which the Republic of Turkey is a signatory are reserved. When the said provisions are read together the conclusion is that the rules under the international conventions to which Turkey is a party shall prevail over the domestic rules. Thus, in the instances where an issue is not regulated by an international convention, domestic rules and more specifically the PIL Code and the CCP shall apply.

Turkey is a signatory to many international conventions that contain conflict of laws rules, international procedural rules and/or rules regarding recognition and enforcement of foreign decisions and arbitral awards. Turkey is also a member of the Hague Conference on Private International Law and a party to a total of 14 international conventions drafted by the Hague Conference.[7] Examples of such conventions are the Convention Relating to Civil Procedure; Convention on the Civil Aspects of International Child Abduction; Convention on the Law Applicable to Maintenance Obligations; Convention on the Recognition and Enforcement of Decisions Relating to Maintenance Obligations and Convention on the Taking of Evidence Abroad in Civil or Commercial Matters. Nevertheless, Turkey is not a party to the Hague Convention of 30 June 2005 on Choice of Court Agreements. Regarding the enforcement of foreign arbitral awards, Turkey is a party to the New York Convention on the Recognition and Enforcement of Foreign Arbitral Awards.[8]

2.2 PIL Code

The PIL Code is composed of three main sections which respectively encompass rules related to the conflict of laws, international jurisdiction of Turkish courts, and the recognition and enforcement of foreign court decisions and arbitral awards.

The formation of a jurisdiction agreement authorizing a foreign court is regulated by the PIL Code. Besides, the rules pertaining to the recognition and enforcement of

[6] Law No. 2709. Official Gazette 09.11.1982/17863.

[7] For the whole list of conventions see: http://www.uhdigm.adalet.gov.tr/sozlesmeler/coktaraflisoz/lahey.html.

[8] Law no. 3731. Official Gazette no. 21.05.1991/20877.

a foreign court decision rendered by a court authorized through a jurisdiction agreement are also regulated by the PIL Code. Nevertheless, the PIL Code regulates only such specific issues and the more comprehensive and general rules regarding the functioning and jurisdiction of the Turkish courts are stipulated under the CCP. In other words, the PIL Code is the special code (*lex specialis*) in relation to the CCP. Thus, the rules under the PIL Code prevail over the CCP rules and only where an issue is not covered by the PIL Code, CCP is applied.

2.3 CCP

The principal domestic code that regulates Turkish civil procedural rules is the CCP. The CCP, as the general law, applies to issues pertaining to civil procedure such as rules of evidence, structure of trials and pleadings, competence and the jurisdiction of Turkish courts. The CCP rules are applied to issues regarding jurisdiction agreements containing a foreign element that are regulated by neither an international convention ratified by Turkey nor the PIL Code. For example, the PIL Code only regulates jurisdiction agreements that authorize foreign courts. Thus, if parties have authorized a Turkish court, CCP rules regarding jurisdiction agreements will be applied. Determination of the Turkish courts' jurisdiction is another example of the prevalence of the international conventions and the PIL Code over the CCP. The PIL Code stipulates jurisdiction of Turkish courts only in relation to particular disputes such as lawsuits related to personal status of foreigners and Turkish citizens, inheritance, employment contracts/relations, consumer contracts and insurance contracts. For other lawsuits, according to Art. 40 of the PIL Code, the international jurisdiction of Turkish courts shall be determined pursuant to the domestic jurisdiction rules which are principally stipulated under the CCP. Thus, excluding disputes where exceptionally the PIL Code stipulates special jurisdiction rules; the CCP shall determine whether a Turkish court has an international jurisdiction or not.

2.4 Court Decisions

The Turkish court system is structured into three categories of courts, namely military courts, administrative courts and judicial courts. Judicial courts are composed of civil courts and criminal courts.[9] As regards private international law disputes, civil courts have competence to review disputes.

Civil courts are composed of a three-degree court system, namely first instance courts, regional courts of appeal and the Court of Cassation. The Court of Cassation

[9]For further information on Turkish law of procedure and court structure see: Budak et al. (2011), pp. 213–236.

is the last instance court for reviewing decisions rendered by the first instance courts and regional courts of appeal. The Court of Cassation is composed of chambers and the civil law chambers of the court of cassation deal with issues arising from private law.

Under Turkish law, in principle, court judgments are not binding. When there is a contradiction between the decisions of a chamber of Court of Cassation or between different chambers, the General Assembly on the Unification of Judgments is gathered.[10] The decisions rendered in such instances by the General Assembly on the Unification of Judgments are binding on all other first instance courts and the Court of Cassation itself.

3 Agreements Granting Jurisdiction to Foreign Courts

In this section, jurisdiction agreements that authorize foreign courts will be elaborated upon. Accordingly, first the requirements for a valid agreement granting jurisdiction to a foreign court will be explained (a). Following that, the restrictions under the PIL Code, regarding jurisdiction agreements pertaining to disputes arising from employment, consumer and insurance contracts will be examined (b). Following this issue, instances where the jurisdiction of Turkish courts is established despite a jurisdiction agreement authorizing a foreign court will be elaborated upon (c). Within this section, the substantive validity of jurisdiction agreements, objection before Turkish courts and the Turkish courts' competence to grant interim measures will be discussed.

3.1 Requirements for a Valid Agreement Granting Jurisdiction to a Foreign Court

The PIL Code is the main legal source for the rules regulating jurisdiction agreements that authorize a foreign court. Art. 47 of the PIL Code stipulates the validity requirements as regards agreements granting jurisdiction to foreign courts. According to the first paragraph of the said article, except where the jurisdiction of a court is determined as exclusive jurisdiction, the parties may agree on authorizing a foreign court in a dispute that contains a foreign element and arises from obligatory relations. The agreement shall be invalid unless it is proved by written evidence. Accordingly, pursuant to Art. 47(1), the grounds for a valid agreement that grants jurisdiction to a foreign court are listed below.

---

[10]For further information on sources of Turkish law see: Güriz (2011), pp. 1–18.

3.1.1 The Dispute Shall Involve a Foreign Element

The first requirement to conclude a valid jurisdiction clause authorizing a foreign court is that the dispute shall involve a foreign element.[11] Turkish statutory law does not stipulate a clear, descriptive explanation for what constitutes a foreign element. The court of cassation makes a broad interpretation in examining what may constitute a foreign element in a given dispute.[12] Elements such as the nationalities or domiciles of the parties, the place of performance or formation of the contract, and the place where the tortious act was committed are taken into account.[13] As long as the dispute has some sort of contact with a non-Turkish jurisdiction, it is considered as having a foreign element.

3.1.2 The Subject Matter of the Dispute Shall Not Be Within the Exclusive Jurisdiction of the Turkish Courts

The law neither codifies a definition of exclusive jurisdiction nor stipulates an exhaustive list of the types of disputes that fall under the exclusive jurisdiction of the Turkish courts. When a legal matter is within the exclusive jurisdiction of Turkish courts, all disputes arising out of the relevant matter are to be resolved by the Turkish courts only. In line with this finding, the parties shall always be able to find a competent Turkish court to resort to for the resolution of a matter that is within the exclusive jurisdiction of Turkish courts.[14]

The concept of exclusive jurisdiction in private international law is different from and narrower than the concept of exclusive jurisdiction regarding domestic civil procedure rules.[15] Doctrine establishes that Turkish courts have exclusive jurisdiction regarding disputes concerning rights *in rem* in immovable properties situated in

[11] Nomer (2017), p. 491; Şanlı et al. (2018), p. 413; Çelikel and Erdem (2017), p. 616.

[12] In one of its decisions, the Civil General Assembly of Court of Cassation examined a choice of court agreement under a credit contract involving a foreign element: Case no. 1998/12-287, Decision no. 1998/325, Date 06.05.1998 (www.kazanci.com). In another decision, the Court of Cassation decided on the presence of a foreign element due to the fact that the company where the claimant was working was registered in a foreign state. 9th Civil Chamber of Court of Cassation, Case no. 2016/28517, Decision no. 2016/20723, Date 24.11.2016 (www.kanunum.com).

[13] Nomer (2017), p. 490.

[14] Nomer (2017), p. 486; Çelikel and Erdem (2017), p. 618; Şanlı et al. (2018), pp. 417–419 and 534–535. For exemplary decisions supporting this finding see: 23th Civil Chamber of Court of Cassation, Case no. 2015/8353, Decision no. 2017/2320 Date 21.09.2017; General Assembly of Court of Cassation, Case no. 2015/894, Decision no. 2013/18-1628, Date 04.03.2015 (www.kazanci.com).

[15] Nomer (2017), p. 485; Şanlı et al. (2018), p. 417, fn 172; Çelikel and Erdem (2017), pp. 583 and 617–618.

Turkey, infringement of intellectual property rights, and cancellation of a general assembly decision of a company whose center is located in Turkey.[16]

3.1.3 The Dispute Shall Be Grounded on an Obligatory Relationship

The third requirement for the conclusion of a valid jurisdiction agreement authorizing a foreign court concerns the type of the legal relationship between the parties. The dispute regarding which the parties conclude a jurisdiction agreement shall arise from an obligatory relationship. Thus, the dispute shall be grounded on a contractual relationship, tortious liability or an unjust enrichment.[17] In other words, the parties cannot conclude a valid agreement that grants jurisdiction to a foreign court in relation to issues of family law, the law of persons or inheritance.[18] For example, if the parties enact a jurisdiction agreement regarding their divorce that grants jurisdiction to a foreign court, such an agreement is invalid from the Turkish law perspective. If the foreign court invalidly designated under this contract finds itself competent according to its own national rules and renders a judgment on the case, the fact that the proceedings were held at a foreign court authorized by an invalid jurisdiction agreement under Turkish law does not interfere with the recognition of this decision in Turkey. The requirements for the recognition and enforcement of a foreign court decision are listed under the PIL Code and cannot be extended by way of interpretation. The effect on the recognition and enforcement of a decision by a foreign court that was authorized by an invalid jurisdiction agreement shall be explained in further detail under Sect. 4 of this chapter.

3.1.4 The Agreement Is Invalid Unless It Is Proved by Written Evidence

Art. 47 of the PIL Code does not require a special form for the validity of the jurisdiction agreement. However, for reasons of evidence, it is required that the agreement is made in writing. It is not required that the parties sign the jurisdiction agreement.[19] As long as the agreement is concluded through any communication devices such as e-mails, letters, or exchange of documents that show the content of the agreement, the writing requirement is deemed as fulfilled.

---

[16] Nomer (2017), pp. 485–486; Şanlı et al. (2018), pp. 417–419; Çelikel and Erdem (2017), pp. 583–588.

[17] Nomer (2017), p. 491; Şanlı et al. (2018), p. 413; Çelikel and Erdem (2017), p. 618. In a recent decision, the Court of Cassation explicitly explains the requirements of a valid jurisdiction agreement under Art. 47 of the PIL Code and in carrying out this evaluation examines the agreement to understand if it is rooted in a contractual relationship: 11th Civil Chamber of Court of Cassation, Case no. 2015/7244, Decision no. 2016/1657, Date 17.02.2016 (www.kanunum.com).

[18] Çelikel and Erdem (2017), p. 588.

[19] Nomer (2017), p. 490; Şanlı et al. (2018), p. 421, fn 179; Çelikel and Erdem (2017), p. 621.

3.1.5 Assigning a Particular Court

Although not explicitly stipulated under Art. 47 of the PIL Code, there is a doctrinal debate as to whether there is an additional requirement that the chosen court has to be specifically indicated. In other words, it is not clear if a general clause authorizing the courts of a foreign state is sufficient or if the specific place of the court within the chosen jurisdiction must be designated. One view[20] argues that indication of a foreign court in a general way is sufficient to conclude a valid jurisdiction agreement. For instance, a clause such as "*German* Courts have jurisdiction to review any disputes that may arise from this sales contract" would be a valid clause according to this view. The conflicting view[21] argues that for practical reasons such a general authorization of foreign courts is not sufficient. According to this view, instead of a general clause authorizing the foreign courts, a clause such as "*Berlin* Courts have jurisdiction to review any disputes that may arise from this sales contract" is a valid clause.

Decisions of the Court of Cassation in this area are not clear either. In one decision[22] it was concluded that in order to have a valid jurisdiction agreement that authorizes a foreign court, the competent foreign court shall be clearly stated in the agreement. In the dispute that led to this decision, the parties had made an agreement authorizing English courts to have jurisdiction. The Court of Cassation ruled that, instead of a general reference to the courts of England, the parties should have specifically indicated which particular court they wish to grant jurisdiction to. The same chamber of the Court of Cassation in another decision[23] ruled that a jurisdiction clause authorizing the Federal Courts of the United States of America was valid.

Another question that may be asked regarding the designation of a foreign court is whether the parties are allowed to choose one court only, or if they may assign alternative courts under their jurisdiction agreement. The doctrine[24] interprets Art. 47 of the PIL Code in such a way that the parties have the right to assign more than just one foreign court. Accordingly, the parties to a jurisdiction agreement may authorize multiple courts to review their cases.

Although it is not explicitly codified under the PIL Code, it is required that jurisdiction agreements authorizing foreign courts shall not be contrary to morals and the principle of good faith.[25] In the instances where the jurisdiction clause was

[20] Nomer (2017), p. 491; Çelikel and Erdem (2017), p. 589; Sargın (1996), p. 171.

[21] Ekşi (1998), p. 873; Şanlı et al. (2018), p. 414; Çelikel and Erdem (2017), p. 619.

[22] 11th Chamber of the Court of Cassation Case no. 2006/8585, Decision no. 2006/12877, Date 07.12.2006 (www.kazanci.com).

[23] 11th Chamber of the Court of Cassation Case no. 2008/10853, Decision no. 2010/1688, Date 15.02.2010 (www.kazanci.com).

[24] Şanlı et al. (2018), p. 415, fn 166; Çelikel and Erdem (2017), p. 619.

[25] Nomer (2017), p. 490; Şanlı et al. (2018), p. 415. For an illustrative decision supporting this view see: Civil General Assembly of Court of Cassation, Case no. 1998/12-287, Decision no. 1998/325, Date 06.05.1998 (www.kazanci.com).

stipulated under a general terms and conditions agreement by one of the parties which was not drawn to the counter party's attention, such jurisdiction clauses may be deemed as invalid.[26]

3.2 *Disputes Regarding Employment, Consumer and Insurance Contracts*

The second paragraph of Art. 47 of the PIL Code which regulates the requirements for a valid jurisdiction agreement that authorizes foreign courts, stipulates a rule that restricts parties' freedom to draft a jurisdiction agreement regarding employment contracts/relations, consumer contracts and insurance contracts. Accordingly, international jurisdiction of the Turkish courts regarding disputes arising from employment contracts or relations, consumer contracts and insurance contracts which are stipulated under Art. 44, 45, 46 of the PIL Code cannot be removed by the parties' jurisdiction agreement. The lawmaker, in enacting such a provision, aims at protecting the financially weaker party. The said jurisdiction rules are as follows.

3.2.1 Employment Contracts/Relations

International jurisdiction of Turkish courts regarding disputes arising from employment contracts and employment relations is regulated under Art. 44 of the PIL Code.[27] Accordingly, the court of the place where the employee habitually performs his work in Turkey is competent. In lawsuits filed by the employee, the Turkish courts in places of the domicile of the employer or the domicile or habitual residence of the employee are competent as well.

3.2.2 Consumer Contracts

Conflicts arising from consumer contracts are regulated under Art. 45 of the PIL Code. Pursuant to this provision, according to the preference of the consumer, the Turkish courts in the places where the consumer is domiciled or habitually resident or the counter-party's work place, domicile or habitual residence is located are competent. However, regarding suits filed against the consumer, only the Turkish courts in the place where the consumer habitually resident shall have jurisdiction.

---

[26]Nomer (2017), p. 490.

[27]For further information on international jurisdiction of Turkish courts regarding disputes arising from employment contracts and employment relations see Çörtoğlu Koca (2016).

3.2.3 Insurance Contracts

Finally, the court of the principal place of business of the insurer or of the place where the branch concluding the insurance contract or its agency is situated in Turkey shall have jurisdiction in conflicts arising from insurance contracts. However, in suits filed against the policy owner, the insured and the beneficiary, the court having jurisdiction shall be the court of their domicile or habitual residence in Turkey.

Views from academic commentary[28] argue that a jurisdiction agreement concluded regarding disputes arising from employment, consumer or insurance contracts shall be valid as long as such an agreement provides alternative courts to the weaker party, that is, the employee, consumer or the insured, while not eliminating those courts authorized under the PIL Code. The Court of Cassation decisions[29] do not support this view. Court decisions are in the direction that any jurisdiction agreements pertaining to employment, consumer and insurance contracts are invalid, regardless of whether they eliminate or provide alternatives to the weaker party regarding the international jurisdiction of Turkish courts stipulated under the PIL Code.

3.3 Jurisdiction of Turkish Courts Despite an Agreement Authorizing a Foreign Court

During the application of the former code no. 2675 on International Private Law and Procedural Law, there was ambiguity as to whether it was possible to bring a lawsuit before a Turkish court despite a jurisdiction agreement authorizing foreign courts. The reason for this ambiguity was the interpretation of the provision on jurisdiction agreements, namely Art. 31 of the former code no. 2675. Decisions of the Court of Cassation were contradictory. Some decisions reasoned that a jurisdiction agreement does not provide alternatives to Turkish courts but exclusively authorizes the designated foreign court so that the Turkish courts lack jurisdiction.[30] Other decisions ruled that Turkish courts continue to have jurisdiction despite an agreement authorizing a foreign court. The reasoning in such decisions was that a refusal of jurisdiction by the Turkish courts due to a jurisdiction agreement would indicate a

[28] Şanlı et al. (2018), pp. 420–421; Çelikel and Erdem (2017), pp. 626–627.

[29] 9th Chamber of Court of Cassation Case no: 2010/7381, Decision no: 2010/16168, Date 03.06.2010. For the decision see Ekşi (2016), pp. 123–129. 9th Chamber of Court of Cassation Case no: 2007/12043, Decision no. 2007/17765 Date 04.06.2007 (www.kazanci.com). Nomer's view is parallel to the interpretation of the Court of Cassation: Nomer (2017), p. 492, fn 212.

[30] Şanlı et al. (2018), pp. 424–425; Çelikel and Erdem (2017), pp. 615–616; Civil General Assembly of Court of Cassation Case no. 1998/12-287, Decision no. 1998/325, Date 06.05.1998 (www.kazanci.com).

mistrust of adjudication by the Turkish courts and would be contrary to public order.[31]

With the entry into force of the PIL Code no. 5718, to clarify this ambiguity, the rule under Art. 31 of the former code no. 2675 was replaced by Art. 47 which has a slightly different wording.[32] Consequently, under the current law, where a valid jurisdiction agreement authorizes a foreign court, Turkish courts shall decline jurisdiction in favor of that court.[33] According to the third sentence of the second paragraph of Art. 47 of the PIL Code, in two exceptional cases Turkish courts may assume jurisdiction despite the existence of a jurisdiction agreement authorizing foreign courts. These exceptional cases are (1) if the competent foreign court decides on its non-competence for some reason; or (2) the respondent does not object to the jurisdiction of the Turkish court. Besides, these two exceptional cases, Turkish courts may still be held competent in relation to (3) granting interim measures despite a jurisdiction agreement authorizing a foreign court.

3.3.1 Non-Competence of the Foreign Court

A foreign court is deemed to have jurisdiction based on a choice of court agreement only when the agreement meets the validity requirements under the law of the foreign state whose courts are authorized under the jurisdiction agreement.[34] A jurisdiction agreement that fulfils the requirements envisaged under Art. 47 of the PIL Code may not meet the requirements of the state whose courts are authorized by the jurisdiction agreement. The substantive validity of a choice of court agreement is subjected to the law of the state of the court or courts authorized in the agreement. Therefore, it is advisable at the stage of contract drafting to make sure that the choice of court agreement is valid under the law of the chosen court. Additionally, the *forum non-conveniens* doctrine[35] may prevent a foreign state from establishing jurisdiction even where there is a valid jurisdiction under the law of that foreign state.

[31]Civil General Assembly of Court of Cassation Case no. 1988/11-246, Decision no. 1998/476, Date 15.06.1988 (www.kazanci.com); 19th Chamber of Court of Cassation Case no. 1995/1632, Decision no. 1995/9151, Date 02.11.1995. For further information on the evolution of case law regarding this issue see: Şanlı et al. (2018), p. 423; Çelikel and Erdem (2017), pp. 622–625.

[32]In the case where there is a valid jurisdiction agreement authorizing foreign courts, Art. 31 of the former code no. 2675 stipulated that "Turkish courts shall have jurisdiction if the foreign court decides that it has no jurisdiction". On the other hand, the relevant wording under Art. 47 of the PIL Code is as follows: "The competent Turkish court shall have jurisdiction *only* if the foreign court decides that it has no jurisdiction".

[33]Nomer (2017), p. 486; Şanlı et al. (2018), p. 426; Çelikel and Erdem (2017), p. 625.

[34]Nomer (2017), p. 489; Şanlı et al. (2018), p. 427; Çelikel and Erdem (2017), p. 617.

[35]The doctrine of *forum non conveniens* originated from the Scottish law and is currently applied in the United States of America, England, and other common law countries. According to this doctrine, a court which has jurisdiction to hear a case may decide not to hear the case, if there is another court which is more closely related to the dispute and so is capable to render a better judgment. See: Nomer (2017), p. 495; Şanlı et al. (2018), pp. 368–369.

If a jurisdiction agreement which is valid pursuant to Art. 47 of the PIL Code does not fulfill the requirements under the law of the chosen foreign court, and so the foreign judge refuses to establish jurisdiction, Turkish courts shall have jurisdiction to resolve the dispute. Where the foreign court authorized under the jurisdiction agreement has not yet made a judgment on refusal of jurisdiction but the parties have presented concrete evidence before the Turkish courts showing that the foreign court will definitely refuse to establish jurisdiction, Turkish courts shall also have jurisdiction to resolve the dispute.[36]

Besides, if the dispute between the parties is resolved by the foreign court as authorized under the jurisdiction agreement but the foreign decision cannot be recognized or enforced in Turkey, then Turkish courts will also have jurisdiction.[37] One view[38] from the doctrine argues that if the debtor's assets are exclusively situated in Turkey and if it is proven that the decision to be rendered by the foreign court authorized under the jurisdiction agreement will not be recognized or enforced before the Turkish courts, Turkish courts shall have jurisdiction to resolve the dispute.

3.3.2 Objection to International Jurisdiction of Turkish Courts and Plea of Lis Alibi Pendens

Under Turkish private international law, rules pertaining to procedure are always subjected to the law of the forum. Pursuant to the principle of *lex fori*, the domestic rules on local jurisdiction are resorted to as rules of international jurisdiction.[39] Thus, objections on grounds that a court lacks jurisdiction to hear the case are subject to the provisions in the CCP.

Before the Lawsuit Is Filed at the Authorized Foreign Court

If one of the parties to the jurisdiction agreement files a lawsuit before a Turkish court contrary to the jurisdiction agreement, the opposing party shall raise the objection to jurisdiction. Pursuant to Art. 19(2) of the CCP, the absence of jurisdiction of Turkish courts may be asserted only as a primary objection, in the initial rebuttal petition.[40] Upon such objection, if the court considers that it does not have international jurisdiction, it shall reject the case on lack of competence grounds.

[36] Şanlı et al. (2018), p. 431.

[37] Nomer (2017), p. 494.

[38] Şanlı et al. (2018), p. 431.

[39] Nomer (2017) p. 489; Şanlı et al. (2018), pp. 338–339 and 369; Çelikel and Erdem (2017), pp. 481–482.

[40] Nomer (2017), p. 482; Şanlı et al. (2018), p. 432; Çelikel and Erdem (2017), p. 624.

If such an objection to jurisdiction is not made by the respondent, the court shall not consider the respondent's claim regarding jurisdiction at a later stage or *ex officio*. Indeed, Art. 19(4) explicitly provides that where there is no objection to the jurisdiction, the court will automatically gain jurisdiction over the case. Where the defendant does not assert his primary objection concerning the absence of international jurisdiction, s/he is considered to have implicitly consented to the international jurisdiction of the Turkish court and the case shall be heard before the Turkish court.[41]

This rule is applied in all cases including where the defendant is domiciled abroad and is unfamiliar with Turkish law. One could take the example of a contract between a German party and a Turkish party containing a jurisdiction clause referring to the competence of the courts in Berlin, Germany. In our example, the Turkish party may opt to file a lawsuit against the German party in a Turkish court notwithstanding the valid jurisdiction clause under Turkish law. Under these circumstances, the German party must assert objection concerning the absence of international jurisdiction within 2 weeks in accordance with Art. 19 of the CCP, otherwise the Turkish courts will assert jurisdiction and hear the case.

Under certain circumstances, despite a valid jurisdiction agreement and an objection duly made in time, the Court of Cassation may take into account the principle of good faith and establish a Turkish court's jurisdiction. Such a situation occurs when the respondent's domicile is in Turkey and the claimant files a lawsuit against the respondent in Turkey before the courts situated in the domicile of the respondent. Under such circumstances, if the respondent raises an objection to the jurisdiction of the Turkish court of his/her domicile based on the jurisdiction agreement that authorizes foreign courts, the Court of Cassation may disregard objection and establish the Turkish court's jurisdiction.[42] The reasoning of the Court of Cassation is that the respondent can best defend itself in his/her domicile and so raising an objection despite the valid jurisdiction agreement would be contrary to the principle of good faith. This reasoning is heavily criticized in the academic commentary.[43]

Despite the recognition of the *lex fori* principle in relation to the civil procedural rules, there may be certain exceptional deviations from CCP rules in relation to proceedings having a foreign element. As regards objection to international jurisdiction of Turkish courts, the second and third paragraphs of the relevant CCP provision, namely Art. 19(2) and (3), are not applicable. According to Art. 19(2), the party who files the objection must state the competent court as the basis of the claim. Otherwise, the objection will not be taken into account by the judge. Art. 19

[41]Nomer (2017), p. 485; Şanlı et al. (2018), pp. 427 and 432; Çelikel and Erdem (2017), p. 624.

[42]Nomer (2017), p. 493, fn 215; Şanlı et al. (2018), pp. 427–428; 11th Chamber of the Court of Cassation Case no. 2008/5454, Decision no: 2009/2604, Date 06.03.2009; 11th Chamber of the Court of Cassation Case no. 2015/9758, Decision no. 2016/4646, Date 25.04.2016; 11th Chamber of the Court of Cassation Case no. 015/11534, Decision no. 2016/8512, Date 31.10.2016, and 11th Chamber of the Court of Cassation Case no. 2015/5517 Decision no. 2015/12591, Date 25.11.2015 (www.kazanci.com).

[43]Şanlı et al. (2018), p. 428; Esen (2001), p. 203.

(3) indicates that the court shall also declare which Turkish court has jurisdiction after the party's objection. While domestic rules are stipulated as such, as regards objection to international jurisdiction of Turkish courts the parties are not required to indicate the foreign court that has jurisdiction. Besides, the court shall not determine which foreign court has jurisdiction either. This deviation was based on the understanding that every state has its own sovereignty rights and so the jurisdiction rules of each state shall be determined within their legislative powers. Turkish judges cannot make a ruling on the jurisdiction of a foreign state, they can only rule on their lack of competence based on a jurisdiction agreement.[44]

After the Lawsuit Is Filed Before the Authorized Foreign Court

If one of the parties to the jurisdiction agreement files a lawsuit before a Turkish court contrary to what is determined under the jurisdiction agreement, while the lawsuit is ongoing before that authorized foreign court, then the opposing party shall raise the plea of another action pending, instead of objecting to jurisdiction.[45] The plea of another action pending is raised when there is an ongoing lawsuit before another court between the same parties, on the same dispute and cause of action. Under Turkish private international law, the plea of another action pending is taken into account by the Turkish courts only under exceptional circumstances, one of which is the situation where the parties have signed a jurisdiction agreement and the case is being heard by that court. The important point in the distinction between a plea of another action pending and objection to jurisdiction is that a plea of another action pending is a condition to commence an action under Art. 114 of the CCP. Thus, the parties can assert a plea of another action pending at any time during the proceedings. Besides, pursuant to Art. 115 of the CCP, the judge upon understanding from the case file that there is an ongoing lawsuit before the foreign court authorized under the jurisdiction agreement between the same parties and regarding the same dispute, shall *ex officio* take this into account and dismiss the case.[46]

---

[44]Şanlı et al. (2018), p. 434; Çelikel and Erdem (2017), pp. 589–591. For exemplary decisions supporting this finding see: 8th Civil Chamber of the Court of Cassation, Case no. 2013/219, Decision no. 2013/10820, Date 10.07.2013; 11th Civil Chamber of the Court of Cassation, Case no. 2007/12254, Decision no. 2009/1912, Date 20.02.2009 (www.kazanci.com).

[45]Nomer (2017), pp. 492–493; Şanlı et al. (2018), pp. 438–439; Çelikel and Erdem (2017), p. 596. For further information see: Bayraktaroğlu Özçelik (2016/2017), pp. 393–422.

[46]For a decision supporting this view see: 11th Civil Chamber of Court of Cassation, Case no. 2016/4200, Decision no. 2016/5291, Date 11.5.2016 (www.kazanci.com). On the other hand, there is an opposing view within academic commentary with regards to the process of raising the plea of *lis alibi pendens*. Accordingly, the plea of *lis alibi pendens* shall be raised as a primary objection for the reason that a Turkish judge may not be able to examine whether there is an ongoing action in a foreign forum. Authors argue that this rule under the CCP was stipulated for domestic cases where it is convenient for the Turkish judge to examine ex officio whether there is an ongoing action before another Turkish court. For this view see: Çelikel and Erdem (2017), p. 640.

3.3.3 Turkish Courts' Jurisdiction Regarding Interim Measures

Problems may arise in relation to the Turkish courts' competence to render interim measures in the instances where the parties have agreed to grant jurisdiction to a foreign court. The disputed legal issues differ depending on whether the interim measure is demanded prior to or after the filing of the lawsuit at the competent foreign court. Under the PIL Code, there are no provisions pertaining to the Turkish courts' competence to grant interim measures in the instances where the parties have signed a jurisdiction agreement that grants jurisdiction to a foreign court. Thus, relevant CCP rules shall apply to this issue.

Prior to Filing of the Lawsuit Before a Foreign Court

According to the CCP Art. 390(1), prior to the filing of a lawsuit, the court which has jurisdiction to decide on the merits of the case has also jurisdiction to grant an interim measure. Pursuant to Art. 397 of the CCP, following the granting of the interim measure, the claimant shall file the actual lawsuit at the competent court within 2 weeks, otherwise the interim measure is automatically annulled. This 2-week time limit causes problems in the instances where the party who holds an interim measure rendered by a Turkish court has also agreed on the authorization of a foreign court to review his/her case on the merits. In such an instance, the question arises as to whether filing of the lawsuit at the foreign court authorized by the parties within 2 weeks fulfils the requirement under Art. 397. If the court before which the parties have to file the actual lawsuit within 2 weeks following the granting of interim measure has to be a Turkish court; interim measures shall always be automatically annulled after 2 weeks where there is a jurisdiction agreement authorizing a foreign court. If one of the parties applies to the Turkish courts for interim measures, the opposing party will, in principle, always raise an objection against the Turkish courts' jurisdiction due to the jurisdiction agreement authorizing foreign courts. Such an interpretation would deprive the parties of their right to legal protection. The doctrine[47] argues that in such instances, documentation of commencement of the legal action within 2 weeks at the foreign court that was authorized by the jurisdiction agreement shall fulfill the requirement under Art. 397. However, the case law[48] regarding this issue does not support the view of the doctrine.

[47]Nomer (2017), p. 487; Şanlı et al. (2018), p. 501; Çelikel and Erdem (2017), pp. 627–629.

[48]The Turkish courts' approach in relation to grant interim measures where the parties have authorized a foreign court through a jurisdiction agreement contrasts with the view of the doctrine. In a dispute where the parties had signed an arbitration clause and the arbitral process had begun, one of the parties wanted to obtain an interim measure. First Instance Civil Court of Şanlıurfa (which is a city in south eastern Turkey) decided that due to the arbitration agreement between the parties authorizing International Cotton Association Arbitration as the competent authority to decide on the merits of the case, Turkish courts did not have jurisdiction to render interim measures

After Filing of the Lawsuit Before a Foreign Court

According to Art. 390(1) of the CCP, after the filing of a lawsuit, only the court before which the lawsuit was filed has jurisdiction to grant interim measures. The application of this rule is problematic as regards instances where the parties have already filed a lawsuit outside of Turkey based on a jurisdiction agreement that authorizes a foreign court. Since a Turkish domestic rule cannot authorize a foreign court to grant an interim measure, it is argued that Art. 390(1) was stipulated in relation to purely domestic cases. Thus, it is interpreted that in cases where the parties have designated a foreign court to decide on their dispute and commenced an action before that court, they shall nevertheless be able to apply to Turkish courts for interim measures. A contrary interpretation would deprive the parties of having an interim measure and would be against the purpose of the said provision. As the parties cannot be denied of their right to legal protection, doctrine supports the aforementioned interpretation of Art. 390(1).[49]

In conclusion, the existence of a jurisdiction agreement between the parties that grants jurisdiction to a foreign court regarding an existing or a future dispute does not eliminate the competence of the Turkish courts to render an interim measure.[50] This statement, however, reflects the dominant view from the doctrine and there clearly is a need to reform the PIL Code to ensure the positive legal basis for this interpretation.

This problem is resolved with regards to Turkish courts' competence to grant interim measures during international arbitration disputes.[51] According to Art. 6 (1) of the Turkish International Arbitration Code, existence of an arbitration agreement does not deprive the Turkish courts of competence to issue an interim measure either prior to or after the commencement of arbitration proceedings. Besides, according to Art. 6(5) of the said act, the court decision on interim measures is automatically annulled when the arbitral award becomes enforceable or when the dispute is dismissed by the arbitral tribunal.

4 Agreements Granting Jurisdiction to Turkish Courts

As stated above in Sect. 2, if the PIL Code, as the *lex specialis*, does not contain specific provisions pertaining to a certain jurisdictional matter, the CCP as the general law applies. Since the PIL Code regulates solely the rules pertaining to agreements granting jurisdiction to foreign courts, the rules regulating jurisdiction

(Case no. 2012/190 Decision no. 2012/189 Date 9.11.2012). The case is not published. For further information on this case see: Arslan (2016), pp. 691–727.

[49]Nomer (2017), p. 487; Şanlı et al. (2018), p. 494; Çelikel and Erdem (2017), pp. 627–628.

[50]Nomer (2017), p. 487; Çelikel and Erdem (2017), p. 629.

[51]Nomer (2017), p. 488.

agreements authorizing Turkish courts are governed by the CCP. The requirements for enacting a jurisdiction agreement that authorizes Turkish courts are regulated under Art. 17 and 18 of the CCP. Such requirements are listed below.

4.1 The Parties Shall Either Be Merchants or Public Legal Entities

According to CCP Art. 17, only merchants and public legal entities are allowed to choose a Turkish court in their jurisdiction agreement.[52] In other words, the law allows for the signing of a jurisdiction agreement that grants jurisdiction to a Turkish court only between or among merchants and public entities. With this restriction, the lawmaker aims at protecting consumers by trying to prevent financially stronger parties such as merchants from enforcing jurisdiction clauses which may be to the disadvantage of consumers. There is no restriction as regards the parties to a jurisdiction agreement that grants jurisdiction to foreign courts pursuant to Art. 47 of the PIL Code. In other words, while a real person, for instance an architect, cannot validly conclude a jurisdiction agreement that authorizes a Turkish court, s/he can do if the agreement grants jurisdiction to a foreign court.

4.2 The Chosen Court(s) Should Be Specific

The parties in their jurisdiction agreement must specify which particular Turkish court they are willing to grant jurisdiction to. For instance, a jurisdiction clause that states "Istanbul Commercial Courts shall have jurisdiction to review the disputes arising from this sales contract" satisfies this condition. But a jurisdiction clause or an agreement which grants jurisdiction generally to all Turkish courts would be invalid. For example, a jurisdiction clause that states "Any court situated in Turkey shall have jurisdiction to review the disputes arising from this sales contract" does not satisfy this condition.[53]

---

[52]Nomer (2017), p. 483; Şanlı et al. (2018), p. 406; Çelikel and Erdem (2017), p. 632. For illustrative decisions applying this rule see: 12th Civil Chamber of the Court of Cassation, Case no. 2016/22765, Decision no. 2017/14559, Date 23.11.2017; 12th Civil Chamber of the Court of Cassation, Case no. 2016/21765, Decision no. 2017/13784, Date 8.11.2017.

[53]Şanlı et al. (2018), p. 408; Çelikel and Erdem (2017), p. 633.

4.3 *The Dispute Shall Not Be on a Subject of Which the Parties May Not Freely Dispose*

According to the CCP Art. 18(1), for a jurisdiction agreement that authorizes a Turkish court to be valid, the dispute between the parties shall be on a matter which they can freely dispose of.[54] Unlike the requirements for a valid jurisdiction agreement authorizing a foreign court; the dispute need not necessarily be grounded on an obligatory relationship. Under Turkish law, the disputes which the parties may not freely dispose of are disputes relating to family law, law of persons, inheritance, and insolvency.

4.4 *The Dispute Shall Not Fall Under the Exclusive Jurisdiction of a Turkish Court*

Certain disputes are exclusively within the jurisdiction of Turkish courts. There does not exist a comprehensive list of disputes that fall under the exclusive jurisdiction of Turkish courts. Through verbal interpretation of the relevant provisions under different codes, the exclusive jurisdiction of Turkish courts can be detected. Art. 12 of the CCP constitutes an example of a rule that stipulates exclusive jurisdiction. Accordingly, if there is a dispute regarding rights *in rem* in immovable properties located in Turkey, only the courts where the immovable property is located shall have jurisdiction. Another example is stipulated under Art. 14 of the CCP. Accordingly, regarding disputes concerning a legal entity, between the shareholders and the legal entity, only the courts at the place where the relevant legal entity is located shall have jurisdiction.

4.5 *The Parties Are Allowed to Grant Jurisdiction to More Than One Turkish Court*

The parties are allowed to authorize more than one Turkish court; there is no restriction under the law. However, a jurisdiction clause that allows the parties to start proceedings in any court in Turkey shall be invalid.[55]

[54] Nomer (2017), p. 483; Şanlı et al. (2018), p. 409; Çelikel and Erdem (2017), p. 633.

[55] Kuru et al. (2014), p. 115.

4.6 The Legal Relationship Shall Be Identified or Identifiable

According to Art. 18(2) of the CCP, the dispute over which a Turkish court is authorized must be identified or identifiable. A jurisdiction clause such as "from now on all the disputes that might arise from any sales contract between the parties shall be resolved by Istanbul courts" would not fulfill this criterion and would be deemed as invalid. On the other hand, the parties can authorize a Turkish court regarding all disputes that might arise from a particular legal relationship between them. For instance, a jurisdiction clause such as "Courts of Istanbul shall have jurisdiction to resolve all of the disputes arising from the agreement hereby" would fulfill this criterion and thus be deemed as valid. Besides, the jurisdiction should be granted to the chosen courts regarding an existing or a possible dispute.

4.7 The Agreement Shall Be Made in Writing

According to Art. 18 of the CCP, a jurisdiction agreement that authorizes Turkish courts shall be made in writing to be deemed as valid.

For a jurisdiction agreement authorizing Turkish courts to be considered as valid, a connection with Turkey is not required.[56] Parties, regardless of their nationalities and the facts of their dispute, can choose Turkish courts in their jurisdiction agreement. Turkish law does not accept the forum *non-conveniens* doctrine. Besides, whether the decision by the Turkish court authorized under a jurisdiction agreement will be recognized or enforced in the respondent's jurisdiction is irrelevant to the validity of the jurisdiction agreement.[57]

5 Asymmetrical Jurisdiction Agreements

An asymmetric jurisdiction clause provides one of the parties with alternative options in terms of the fora in which they may sue the other party, while not providing as many options to the other party. It is disputable whether unilateral jurisdiction agreements are valid under Turkish law. One view from the doctrine argues that asymmetrical jurisdiction clauses tilt the balance between the parties against the financially weaker party while violating the right to fair trial and right to justice of the weaker party. This view claims that in such instances asymmetrical agreements shall be invalid.[58]

[56] Nomer (2017), p. 484; Şanlı et al. (2018), pp. 409–410.

[57] Nomer (2017), pp. 484–485; Şanlı et al. (2018), p. 410.

[58] Nomer (2017), p. 490; Çelikel and Erdem (2017), pp. 620–621.

This doctrinal view is rooted in the former code of civil procedure no. 1086, which did not stipulate any restriction as regards the parties to a jurisdiction agreement that authorizes Turkish courts. Thus, the aforementioned view is rather obsolete for the CCP now only allows merchants and legal entities to authorize a Turkish court in their jurisdiction agreement. Consequently, the said doctrinal view may only be relevant where the parties assign a foreign court, since the PIL Code Art. 47 does not envisage a restriction regarding the parties to a jurisdiction agreement that authorizes foreign courts.

The approach of the Court of Cassation is not clear on the issue of the validity of asymmetrical jurisdiction agreements. A recent Court of Cassation decision[59] may be interpreted in such a way that asymmetrical jurisdiction clauses are considered as valid. In the said decision, parties who are merchants had concluded an asymmetrical jurisdiction clause, which provided the claimant with an additional choice to bring legal action at the courts of the defendant's domicile. The Court of Cassation reasoned that there were no obstacles against the commencement of a lawsuit against the defendant at the courts of his/her domicile. It may be interpreted that the Court of Cassation considered an asymmetrical jurisdiction clause as valid. Nevertheless, the dominant view of the doctrine still considers asymmetrical jurisdiction clauses as invalid.

6 Recognition and Enforcement of Court Decisions Under Turkish Law

As explained above in Sect. 3.3.1, each State shall determine pursuant to its own law whether a jurisdiction agreement is capable of granting jurisdiction to its courts. A jurisdiction agreement that is valid under Turkish law may not be valid under a foreign law; or visa versa. Thus, in some instances, the foreign court may refuse to establish jurisdiction despite a jurisdiction agreement which is valid according to Turkish law. Or a foreign court may establish jurisdiction based on a jurisdiction agreement that is invalid under Turkish law and decide on the merits of the case.

A decision rendered by a foreign court that established jurisdiction based on a jurisdiction agreement which is invalid under Turkish law can still be recognized and enforced in Turkey.[60] For example, pursuant to Art. 47(1) of the PIL Code, a valid jurisdiction agreement shall be on a dispute grounded on an obligatory relationship. If a couple authorizes a court of a foreign state to decide on their divorce, such an agreement would be invalid from the perspective of Turkish law. However, if the authorized court of the foreign state decides on the case, this foreign decision may be recognized in Turkey. In other words, invalidity of a jurisdiction agreement based on

[59] 11th Chamber of the Court of Cassation Case no. 2015/9758, Decision no. 2016/4646; Date 25.04.2016 (www.kazanci.com).

[60] Nomer (2017), p. 489; Çelikel and Erdem (2017), p. 617.

which a foreign decision was given, is not a ground for non-recognition or non-enforcement of that foreign decision. However, there is an exception to this finding. If the invalidity of the jurisdiction agreement is due to the fact that the parties have authorized a foreign court on a subject concerning which the Turkish courts have exclusive jurisdiction, then the decision by the foreign court authorized by this invalid agreement will not be recognized or enforced in Turkey under Art. 54(b) of the PIL Code.

Rules regarding recognition and enforcement of court decisions are regulated under Art. 50–59 of the PIL Code. Art. 50 stipulates the preconditions for recognition and enforcement of court decisions; whereas Art. 54 regulates the grounds absence of which results in non-recognition or non-enforcement.[61]

6.1 General Remarks

Fulfilment of the grounds set forth under Art. 54 is sufficient for the recognition and enforcement of the foreign court decisions, leaving the Turkish judge with no discretion or any rights to make further inquiries as to the merits of the case (prohibition of *révision au fond*).[62] The party against whom enforcement is sought may not submit any objections concerning the content of the foreign judgment or the merits of the dispute. The Second Civil Chamber of the Court of Cassation, in its decision dated 16 June 2008,[63] clearly stated that the "non-application of the competent law" may not constitute a valid objection against the enforcement of a foreign judgment and may not be taken into account by the Turkish court.

In principle, the Turkish court shall *ex officio* review the existence of grounds of non-recognition and non-enforcement. However, there are two grounds that the court shall not review *ex officio*. These grounds are that (1) the foreign court has exercised an exorbitant ground of jurisdiction as prescribed in Article 54(b) and that (2) the right of defense of the party against whom enforcement is sought has been violated as prescribed in Article 54(ç). The said two grounds need to be raised by the party against whom enforcement is sought.

[61] For further information on the recognition and enforcement of foreign judgments in Turkey see: Süral and Tarman (2013/2014), pp. 485–508.

[62] Nomer (2017), p. 516; Şanlı et al. (2018), pp. 511–512; Çelikel and Erdem (2017), p. 690.

[63] 2nd Chamber of the Court of Cassation, Case no. 2008/5111, Decision no. 2008/8673, Date 16.06.2008 (www.legalbank.net).

6.2 *Prerequisites*

6.2.1 The Judgement Shall Be on a Civil or Commercial Matter

Art. 50 of the PIL Code requires that the decision subjected to recognition or enforcement should be related to either civil or commercial matters. Whether an action is a civil action is determined pursuant to classifications under Turkish law.[64] Thus, court judgments regarding administrative and criminal matters shall not be subjected to recognition and enforcement. Besides, court judgments rendering punitive damages that are issued in common law jurisdictions will not be enforced in Turkey due to their punitive character.[65]

6.2.2 The Decision Shall Be Rendered by a State Court

The decision which will be subjected to the recognition or enforcement proceedings should have been rendered by a foreign court.[66] Thus, in principle,[67] decisions issued by administrative bodies such as the municipality, governorship or notary cannot be enforced in Turkey pursuant to the PIL Code. Whether the foreign decision is a court decision or not shall be determined in accordance with the law of the country where it was rendered. For instance, the Second Civil Chamber of the Court of Cassation[68] in its decision dated 13 April 1995, decided that a foreign divorce decision issued by the Copenhagen municipality could not be recognized in Turkey because the aforementioned divorce decision was not rendered by a court under Danish law.

There are certain exceptions to this requirement. First, where an international convention to which Turkey is a party envisages a rule as to the recognition and enforcement of a decision by a non-judicial body, then that decision shall be recognized or enforced. For example, the Convention of 2 October 1973 on the Recognition and Enforcement of Decisions Relating to Maintenance Obligations[69] allows the enforcement of decisions issued by administrative bodies. Secondly, there may be domestic rules which set an exception to the PIL Code. For example, the

---

[64]Nomer (2017), p. 509; Şanlı et al. (2018), p. 517; Çelikel and Erdem (2017), p. 685.

[65]Nomer (2017), p. 510; Şanlı et al. (2018), p. 518; Çelikel and Erdem (2017), pp. 685–686.

[66]Nomer (2017), p. 508; Şanlı et al. (2018), pp. 513–515; Çelikel and Erdem (2017), pp. 685–686. 8th Chamber of the Court of Cassation, Case no. 2017/6212, Decision no. 2017/13546, Date 24.10.2017 (www.kanunum.com).

[67]There are certain exceptions to this requirement stipulated under international conventions to which Turkey is a party or domestic laws. The exceptions are regarding the recognition of decisions pertaining to maintenance obligations, adoption and divorce. For further information see: Süral and Tarman (2013/2014), p. 220.

[68]2nd Chamber of the Court of Cassation, Case no. 3612, Decision no.4567, Date 13.4.1995 (www.kazanci.com).

[69]Official Gazette 06.11.1980/17152.

Code of Civil Registry stipulates two exceptions to the requirement that the decision which is subjected to recognition and enforcement shall be a court decision. The exceptions are regarding the recognition of decisions pertaining to adoption and divorce. As regards adoption, Art. 30(2) of the Code of Civil Registry stipulates that decisions regarding adoption that are final and duly rendered by both judicial and administrative authorities can be subjected to enforcement proceedings in Turkey. Another exception is stipulated under Art. 27(A) of the Code of Civil Registry. Accordingly, decisions given by the judicial or administrative authorities of foreign countries regarding divorce, nullity, annulment, presence or absence of marriage are registered on the civil register on condition that the parties make their application together in person or by attorney, the decision was given by the competent judicial or administrative authority pursuant to the laws of the state and procedurally finalized, and it is not explicitly contrary to Turkish public order.

6.2.3 The Court Decision Shall Be Final

In order to be recognised or enforced in Turkey, a foreign judgment shall be final and enforceable under the law of the state where the judgment was rendered.[70] Thus, except where it is exceptionally allowed under international agreements, foreign provisional and protective measures cannot be recognized or enforced under Turkish private international law.

6.3 Conditions

Art. 54 of the PIL Code provides four requirements for enforcement of the foreign judgment. Pursuant to Art. 58(1) of the PIL Code, except for the condition regarding reciprocity, the same conditions listed under Art. 54 apply to the recognition of awards. The grounds listed under Art. 54 are as follows.

6.3.1 Reciprocity

Pursuant to Article 54(a), for a foreign judgment to be enforced in Turkey, there needs to be reciprocity between Turkey and the foreign state from whose courts the

[70]Nomer (2017), pp. 513–514; Şanlı et al. (2018), p. 519; Çelikel and Erdem (2017), pp. 687–689. For exemplary decisions regarding this requirement under the PIL Code Art. 50 see 3rd Chamber of the Court of Cassation, Case no. 2016/9464, Decision no. 2016/12221, Date 27.10.2016; 11th Chamber of the Court of Cassation, Case no. 2015/1049, Decision no. 2015/2238, Date 19.02.2015 (www.kazanci.com).

foreign judgment is rendered.[71] Thus, the nationality of the parties is of no significance. The reciprocity requirement can be established in three ways. (1) There may be a multilateral or bilateral agreement providing for the mutual enforcement of foreign judgments between Turkey and the state from whose courts the foreign judgment was given. (2) If no such agreement is in place, a statutory provision may be in place in the relevant foreign state enabling the enforcement of Turkish court decisions in the relevant foreign state. Reciprocity shall be deemed as evident if the foreign court judgment may be enforced in the relevant foreign state with similar conditions as Turkish law. In other words, where the foreign state does not require the existence of further conditions and burdens in order to enforce Turkish judgments, it is considered that there is reciprocity.[72] For example, if the relevant State does not apply the prohibition of the *révision au fond* principle, reciprocity will be deemed not to exist. (3) If no such statutory provisions exist, Turkish court decisions shall *de facto* be enforced in that state.

However, statutory reciprocity will not be sufficient in certain cases where, despite the existence of statutory provisions in the foreign law enabling enforcement of Turkish court judgments in that foreign country, the Turkish court decisions are not being enforced in practice.[73] For example, the Eleventh Civil Chamber of the Court of Cassation, in its decision of 30 January 2009,[74] stated that the court should also have inquired with the Ministry of Justice General Directorate of International Law and Foreign Relations whether the Syrian courts currently enforce Turkish court decisions in practice and the court should have not limited itself to the existence of certain statutory provisions concerning enforcement of foreign judgments in Syrian law.

The requirement of reciprocity with regards to the enforcement of foreign judgments has long been criticized in the Turkish doctrine.[75] Some authors are of the opinion that reciprocity does not serve the interests of persons; that, it is an entirely political criterion where most states would first expect the other state to start enforcing its judgments; and thus, reciprocity should not be required for the

[71]For illustrative decisions regarding this requirement under Art. 54 of the PIL Code see: 11th Civil Chamber of the Court of Cassation, Case no. 2014/4148, Decision no. 2014/10274, Date 02.06.2014; 11th Civil Chamber of the Court of Cassation, Case no. 2013/17269, Decision no. 2014/1375, Date 22.01.2014; 2nd Civil Chamber of the Court of Cassation, Case no. 2010/11237, Decision no. 2011/2718, Date 16.02.2011; 11th Civil Chamber of the Court of Cassation, Case no. 2003/1872, Decision no. 2003/7813, Date 15.09.2003 (www.kanunum.com).

[72]Nomer (2017), p. 520; Şanlı et al. (2018), p. 529, fn 375; Çelikel and Erdem (2017), pp. 705–707.

[73]Nomer (2017), p. 519; Şanlı et al. (2018), p. 533; Çelikel and Erdem (2017), p. 710. For a decision supporting this view see: 11th Chamber of the Court of Cassation, Case no. 2008/1284, Decision no. 2009/980, Date 30.01.2009 (www.kazanci.com).

[74]Nomer (2017), p. 519; Şanlı et al. (2018), p. 535; Çelikel and Erdem (2017), pp. 714–719. For illustrative decisions regarding this requirement under Art. 54 of the PIL Code see: 8th Civil Chamber of the Court of Cassation, Case no. 2017/6212, Decision no. 2017/13546, Date 24.10.2017; 8th Civil Chamber of the Court of Cassation, Case no. 2016/4772, Decision no. 2016/5813, Date 30.03.2016 (www.kanunum.com).

[75]Nomer (2017), pp. 519–520; Çelikel and Erdem (2017), p. 673; Sarıöz Büyükalp (2018), p. 162.

enforcement of foreign judgments.[76] It is also argued that ensuring the existence of reciprocity puts a great burden on the Turkish judges who decide on enforcement; since the information provided by Turkish authorities may not be reliable on this matter and the application in different countries may rapidly change.[77] On the other hand, other authors argue that reciprocity does serve a purpose, especially in enforcing foreign judgments concerning property rights. This view claims that the exercise of jurisdiction and execution of judgments are a part of the sovereignty of the state; and that all states are free to exercise such power only with respect to judgments of foreign states which would mutually exercise the same power.[78]

6.3.2 Exclusive Jurisdiction

According to Art. 54(b) of the PIL Code, the foreign judgment must have been given on matters not falling within the exclusive jurisdiction of the Turkish courts. As explained above, what constitutes exclusive jurisdiction is not codified in the PIL Code. The case law establishes that decisions pertaining to *rights in rem* in immovable property situated in Turkey, decrees relating to intellectual property rights and decrees regarding appointment of a conservator are among the issues over which Turkish courts have exclusive jurisdiction.[79]

6.3.3 Exorbitant Jurisdiction

The judgment must not have been given by a state court which has accepted itself as competent even though there was not a real relation between the court and the subject or the parties of the lawsuit (*exorbitant jurisdiction*).[80] For this condition to be taken into account by the judge, it should have been contested by the defendant. In other words, the court shall not take into account this condition on its own motion.

6.3.4 Public Order

The court decree shall not manifestly be contrary to public order. The definition of public order is not regulated under the law. The concept of public order is not clear

[76] Nomer (2017), p. 520; Sargın (2008), p. 355; Sakmar (1990), p. 399; Ekşi (2013), p. 174.

[77] Nomer (2017), p. 519; Şanlı et al. (2018), p. 526.

[78] Çelikel and Erdem (2017), p. 705; Güven (2013), p. 86.

[79] Nomer (2017), p. 521; Şanlı et al. (2018), p. 535; Çelikel and Erdem (2017), pp. 714–719. For illustrative decisions regarding this requirement under Art. 54 of the PIL Code see: 8th Civil Chamber of the Court of Cassation, Case no. 2017/6212, Decision no. 2017/13546, Date 24.10.2017; 8th Civil Chamber of the Court of Cassation, Case no. 2016/4772, Decision no. 2016/5813, Date 30.03.2016 (www.kanunum.com).

[80] Nomer (2017), pp. 524–527; Şanlı et al. (2018), p. 541; Çelikel and Erdem (2017), pp. 719–722.

either. According to Art. 54(c) of the PIL Code, the contradiction to public order must be "manifest". This wording aims at a strict application of the intervention of public order in practice by judges. In examining whether the foreign court decision is manifestly contrary to public order, the judge shall decide whether the results of the implementation of such a judgment in Turkey would give rise to any public policy infringement.[81] In other words, for public order to be considered as a ground for non-recognition or non-enforcement, the effects or consequences of foreign judgments should be manifestly incompatible with the fundamental principles of Turkish law, human rights and ethics of Turkish society. A foreign court decision contrary to the provisions of European Convention on Human Rights as well as other rights secured by the European Court of Justice are deemed to be against Turkish public order, and thus cannot enforced in Turkey.[82]

The public order argument can only be exceptionally raised against the enforcement of the foreign court decision. The Court of Cassation used to consider that certain issues such as guardianship[83] and custody[84] fell categorically under the Turkish public order and so the enforcement of such decisions were to be automatically rejected in Turkey. Nevertheless, in its recent decisions the Court of Cassation has shifted from this view. In a recent judgement, the Court of Cassation has taken Art. 6 of the European Convention on Human Rights as its ground and recognized a foreign court decision on guardianship.[85,86] Similarly, in another recent judgement[87] Turkish Court of Cassation recognized a foreign divorce decree granting parental

[81] Nomer (2017), p. 527; Şanlı et al. (2018), p. 542; Çelikel and Erdem (2017), p. 722.

[82] Nomer (2017), p. 528.

[83] Foreign court decisions regarding guardianship used to be categorically regarded as an issue of Turkish public policy. See: Civil General Assembly of the Turkish Court of Cassation, Case no. 2009/2-557, Decision no. 2009/527, Date 18.11.2009; Civil General Assembly of the Turkish Court of Cassation, Case no. 2009/2-280, Decision No 2009/326, Date 08.07.2009 (www.kazanci.com). The Turkish Court of Cassation has changed its view regarding this issue.

[84] 2nd Chamber of the Turkish Court of Cassation, Case no. 2003/3784, Decision no. 2003/4670, Date 02.04.2003 (www.kazanci.com). For a criticism of this judgement see Şanlı et al. (2018), pp. 553–554.

[85] 18th Chamber of the Turkish Court of Cassation, Case no. 2012/12365, Decision no. 2013/483, Date 17.01.2013. For further information on the relationship between recognition and enforcement of foreign judgments in Turkey with the right to fair trial pursuant Art. 6 of the European Convention on Human Rights see Sarıöz Büyükalp (2018), pp. 123–205.

[86] On the other hand, decisions on the administration of guardianship cannot be enforced in Turkey as they cannot realize the prerequisite that foreign judgement subjected to enforcement shall be on a civil or commercial matter. Civil General Assembly of the Turkish Court of Cassation, Case no. 2013/18-1628, Decision no. 2015/894, Date 04.03.2015; 18th Chamber of the Turkish Court of Cassation, Case no. 2015/5194, Decision no. 2015/18432, Date 14.12.2015; 18th Chamber of the Turkish Court of Cassation, Case no. 2013/16914, Decision no. 2014/5145, Date 20.03.2014; 18th Chamber of the Turkish Court of Cassation, Case no. 2016/3763, Decision no. 2016/6542, Date 25.04.2016 (www.kazanci.com).

[87] 2nd Chamber of the Turkish Court of Cassation, Case no. 2016/15771, Decision no. 2017/1737, Date 20.02.2017 (www.kazanci.com).

authority to both parents and so radically changed its established case law that a common parental right after divorce is contrary to Turkish public policy.

6.3.5 Requirements Pertaining to the Respondent's Rights of Defense

According to the last paragraph of Art. 54 of the PIL Code, if the person against whom enforcement is requested was not duly summoned pursuant to the laws of that foreign state or to the court that has given the judgment, or was not represented before that court, or the court decree was not pronounced in his/her absence or by a default judgment in a manner contrary to these laws, and the person has objected to the exequatur based on the foregoing grounds before the Turkish court, then such a foreign decision shall not be recognized or enforced in Turkey. The principle of *révision au fond* does not prevent an examination by the Turkish court upon an assertion by the respondent, as to whether the respondent's rights of defense were violated by the foreign court.[88]

7 Arbitration and Jurisdiction Agreements

Parties to international commercial contracts may choose different methods for the resolution of disputes arising from contractual relations. The parties may prefer litigation and file lawsuits in national courts, or select alternative dispute resolution methods, including arbitration and/or mediation. Problems might arise in relation to the validity of the arbitration agreement, where the parties have agreed on both a jurisdiction agreement and an arbitration clause.

7.1 General Remarks on Turkish Law Regarding Arbitration

The Turkish International Arbitration Code[89] is based on the UNCITRAL Model Law and the international arbitration sections of the Swiss Federal Private International Law of 1987. Therefore, it contains regulations generally accepted in the arena of international arbitration. The parties have equal rights and competence in arbitral proceedings and both parties must be given the opportunity to submit their claims and defenses in full. Party autonomy is encouraged and the intervention of the state courts in arbitral proceedings is limited to specific circumstances. Arbitration rules in Turkey are at an international level which creates a positive legal framework for foreign parties.

[88]Nomer (2017), p. 439; Şanlı et al. (2018), p. 557, fn 426; Çelikel and Erdem (2017), p. 740.

[89]Law No. 4686. Official Gazette no. 05.07.2001/24453.

The recognition and enforcement of foreign arbitral awards is regulated separately under the PIL Code. As explained in Sect. 2, international agreements duly put into force have the force of law and are applied prior to the domestic rules. In other words, if an issue falls within the scope of an international convention, the international convention takes precedence over provisions of the national law. Turkey is a party to the Washington Convention on the Settlement of Investment Disputes between States and Nationals of Other States (1965),[90] to the New York Convention on the Recognition and Enforcement of Foreign Arbitral Awards (1958),[91] and to the Geneva Convention on International Commercial Arbitration (1961).[92] These conventions constitute a major part of Turkish arbitration legislation. Thus, the rules under the PIL Code apply only when there is an arbitral award rendered at a state not a party to an international agreement. This is the reason why, in practice, Art. V of the New York Convention which stipulates the conditions for the recognition and enforcement of arbitral awards is applied more frequently than the PIL Code.

7.2 *Coexisting Jurisdiction and Arbitration Clauses*

One of the principal elements of the validity of an arbitration agreement is the clear intent of the parties to arbitrate.[93] In the event the parties choose arbitration as an alternative dispute resolution method, it is crucial to precisely express that intention to resolve any related dispute by arbitration within a contract and avoid any contradictory statements. The Court of Cassation has stated that there should be no doubt concerning the parties' intent to arbitrate for there to be a valid arbitration agreement.[94] If the parties have not eliminated the possibility to resort to national courts, it is very probable that the arbitration agreement will be deemed invalid.[95]

Coexisting jurisdiction and arbitration clauses in a contract may raise a question as to the intent of the parties to arbitrate. In other words, where an agreement includes both a jurisdiction clause authorizing national courts and an arbitration clause, it is very likely that the arbitration agreement will be deemed invalid. Parallel to this finding, in a dispute[96] brought before the Court of Cassation, it was decided

[90]Law No. 3460 of 27 May 1988. Official Gazette 02.06.1988/19830.

[91]Law No. 3731 of 8 May 1991. Official Gazette 21.05.1991/20877.

[92]Law No. 3730 of 8 May 1991. Official Gazette 21.05.1991/20877.

[93]Akıncı (2016), p. 98. For further information on Turkish arbitration law see Tarman (2014), pp. 245–255.

[94]9th Chamber of the Court of Cassation Case no. 2013/1773, Decision no. 2013/6664, Date 25.02.2013; 15th Chamber of the Court of Cassation Case no. 2007/2680, Decision no. 2007/4137, Date 18.06.2007 (www.kazanci.com).

[95]See the dissenting opinion in 15th Chamber of the Court of Cassation Case no. 2014/3330, Decision no. 2014/4607, Date 01.07.2014 (emsal.yargitay.gov.tr).

[96]15th Chamber of the Court of Cassation Case no. 2009/1438, Decision no. 2013/2153, Date 13.04.2009 (www.kazanci.com).

that the arbitration agreement in question was void since the contract between the parties both stipulated an arbitration clause and a jurisdiction clause authorizing the courts of Istanbul.

In another decision[97] the Court of Cassation held that the arbitration agreement was invalid since the arbitral tribunal was not the only body which was authorized to resolve the dispute between the parties. In the said case, the agreement between the parties envisaged that any dispute regarding the contract shall be resolved by an arbitral tribunal. Nevertheless, the agreement also stipulated that if the parties could not reach a consensus within 30 days upon the submission of the case to the arbitral tribunal, Istanbul Courts shall have jurisdiction to resolve the dispute; which caused uncertainty regarding the parties' intent to arbitrate.

In another dispute where the parties through an asymmetrical agreement granted only one of the parties the right to apply to arbitration, the Court of Cassation held that the agreement was void. It was reasoned that the party who was deprived of the option to apply to arbitration still had the right to commence a legal action before a national court. Thus, such an asymmetrical arbitration agreement indirectly resulted in providing for both arbitral and judicial adjudication regarding the same dispute, which cast doubt on the parties' intent to arbitrate and rendered the arbitration clause as invalid.[98]

In conclusion, the dominant approach in Turkish private international law supports the view that where there is a jurisdiction clause co-existing with an arbitration clause, the arbitration clause is deemed as invalid.[99] The reason for the invalidity is the lack of certainty and clarity pertaining to the intent of the parties to arbitrate. Thus, it is recommended that the parties avoid drafting clauses that provide options to the parties so that adjudication by national courts becomes an alternative to arbitration. Since the clear and absolute intent of the parties to arbitrate is a principal element for the validity of the arbitration agreement, it is recommended that the parties avoid co-existing jurisdiction and arbitration clauses in their agreements.

7.3 *Arbitration Objection as a Primary Objection*

Under Turkish law, where a valid arbitration agreement[100] is present, the Turkish courts shall decline jurisdiction in favor of arbitration upon objection by a party

[97]15th Chamber of the Court of Cassation Case no. 2015/2198, Decision no. 2015/2758, Date 22.05.2015 (www.kazanci.com).

[98]11th Chamber of the Court of Cassation Case no. 2009/3257, Decision no. 2011/1675, Date 15.02.2011 (www.kazanci.com). For further analysis on this decision see: Esen (2010), pp. 145–155.

[99]For further information on Turkish case law regarding coexisting arbitration and jurisdiction agreements see: Kocasakal (2017), pp. 509–535; Özçelik (2016), pp. 53–81.

[100]Where the place of arbitration is Turkey and the dispute involves a foreign element, the Turkish International Arbitration Act determines the validity of an arbitration agreement. According to Art.

seeking to enforce the arbitration agreement. If one of the parties files a lawsuit before state courts despite a valid arbitration agreement, the other party can raise an arbitration objection. Pursuant to Art. 116 and 117 of the CCP, an arbitration objection must be made as a first objection in the response petition. The judge cannot *ex officio* take into account the arbitration clause.

8 Conclusion

With the increase in cross-border trade, the number of jurisdiction agreements concluded has also increased. Turkish law has also responded to this legal trend. At the time when the former Code on International Private Law and Procedural Law numbered 2675 was in force, there was ambiguity as to whether it was possible to bring a lawsuit before a Turkish court despite a jurisdiction agreement authorizing a foreign court to resolve the dispute. Former decisions of the Court of Cassation used to uphold the jurisdiction of Turkish courts despite a valid jurisdiction agreement on the grounds of public order and reliance of the Turkish courts. The approach of the Court of Cassation has evolved in a way to interpret jurisdiction agreements as granting exclusive jurisdiction to the foreign court authorized under the relevant jurisdiction agreement. The lawmaker has recognized this issue and amended the law so that where a valid jurisdiction agreement confers jurisdiction on a foreign court, in principle, the Turkish court shall decline jurisdiction in favor of that court.

As explained above, the law applicable to the validity of a jurisdiction agreement differs depending on which courts are authorized by the parties. If the parties designate a foreign court to resolve their dispute, the validity of the jurisdiction agreement is subject to the PIL Code. On the other hand, if the parties designate a Turkish court, they must abide by the rules under the CCP. Since the parties are allowed to assign more than one court under their jurisdiction agreements, in the instances where the parties authorize both foreign and Turkish courts, the jurisdiction agreement shall be subjected to a dual inquiry. The conditions for the validity of the authorization of the Turkish courts will be evaluated in light of the CCP while the evaluation for foreign courts shall be done following the rules under the PIL Code.

One of the major discussions that still remains regarding jurisdiction agreements boils down to the question of whether the parties are obliged to specify which particular court of a foreign state they want to authorize under their jurisdiction agreement or whether it is sufficient to generally authorize the courts of a foreign state. While there are conflicting decisions from the Court of Cassation, there is no consensus among academics on this issue either. Until the issue is clarified through an amendment of law or a unification judgment it is recommended that the parties

4 of the Turkish International Arbitration Act, the validity of an arbitration agreement is determined in line with the chosen law by the parties to apply to the arbitration agreement or where there is no such choice made, by Turkish law.

indicate the particular courts by drafting their jurisdiction clauses to be on the safe side. Besides this discussion, the question of whether asymmetrical jurisdiction agreements are valid is still unresolved.

One other point that might create uncertainty for the parties is the intervention of the doctrine of good faith in the establishment of Turkish courts' jurisdiction by the Court of Cassation. The court tends to establish jurisdiction at the instances where the claimant files a lawsuit at the residence of the respondent contrary to the jurisdiction agreement between the parties, on the grounds that the respondent can best defend itself at its residence. There is a clear need for the shift of the court's approach in favor of party autonomy regarding this issue. Besides, the Turkish courts' jurisdiction to render an interim measure is also a problematic issue when there is a jurisdiction agreement authorizing a foreign court. There is a need for drafting of a special rule on interim measures which takes into account the legal actions with a foreign element.

It is also extremely important to note that Turkish civil procedural law considers the objection to jurisdiction as a primary objection that must be raised by the respondent; the judge cannot consider the existence of a jurisdiction clause *ex officio*. Thus, it is of extreme importance for the parties to object to jurisdiction within the time provided by law for the primary objections, or else the Turkish court where the proceedings have been commenced is deemed to be implicitly authorized by the parties.

Despite the doctrinal debates regarding particular aspects of jurisdiction agreements, it must be said that the legal treatment of choice of court agreements in Turkey is effective and well-justified. While, there may be the need to reform the law to clarify certain points pertaining to the validity of the jurisdiction agreements, the Turkish legal framework in this area is sufficient for the parties to securely conclude jurisdiction agreements.

References

Akıncı Z (2016) Milletlerarası tahkim (International arbitration). Vedat Yayıncılık, Istanbul

Ansay T, Wallace D (eds) (2011) Introduction to Turkish law. Wolters Kluwer, Ankara

Arslan İ (2016) Milletlerarasi ticari tahkimde Türk mahkemelerinin ihtiyati tedbir ve ihtiyati haciz kararı verme yetkisi. Türkiye Adalet Akademisi Dergisi 7(27):691–727

Bayraktaroğlu Özçelik (2016/2017) International Lis Pendens as a contemporary problem of Turkish international civil procedure. Yearb Private Int Law 18:393–422

Budak AC, Kuru B, Ansay T, Konuralp H (2011) Law of procedure. In: Ansay T, Wallace D (eds) Introduction to Turkish law, 6th edn. Wolters Kluwer, Ankara, pp 213–236

Çelikel A, Erdem B (2017) Milletlerarası özel hukuk (International private law). Beta Yayıncılık, Istanbul

Çörtoğlu Koca S (2016) Zayıf tarafın korunduğu sözleşmelerde mahkemelerin milletlerarası yetkisi (International jurisdiction of courts regarding contracts that protect the weaker party). Yetkin Yayınları, Ankara

Ekşi N (1998) Uluslararası ticarete ilişkin iki güncel sorun: sözleşme bedelinin yabancı para olarak ödenmesi ve yabancı mahkemenin yetkisinin tesisi (Two current issues regarding international

trade: payment of the consideration through foreign currency and granting jurisdiction to a foreign court). İstanbul Barosu Dergisi 72(10-11-12):864–882
Ekşi N (2013) Yabancı mahkeme kararlarının tanınması ve tenfizi (Recognition and enforcement of foreign court decisions). Beta Yayıncılık, İstanbul
Ekşi N (2016) Milletlerarası özel hukuk I pratik çalışma kitabı: kanunlar ihtilâfı kurallarına ve milletlerarası usul hukukuna ilişkin seçilmiş mahkeme kararları (International private law I practice questions: chosen court decisions on conflict of laws rules and international procedural law). Beta Yayıncılık, İstanbul
Esen E (2001) Yabancı mahkeme lehine yapılan yetki anlaşmasına dayanan yetki itirazının değerlendirilmesinde dürüstlük kuralının etkisi ve Yargıtay 11. Hukuk Dairesinin 6.3.2009 tarihli içtihadının eleştirisi (The effect of the principle of good faith in evaluating the opposition to jurisdiction based on a jurisdiction agreement designating a foreign court and a critique of the Decision dated 6.3.2009 by the Court of Cassation). Milletlerarası Hukuk ve Milletlerarası Özel Hukuk Bülteni 31(1):191–207
Esen E (2010) Taraflardan sadece birine tahkime müracaat hakkı tanıyan tahkim anlaşmalarının ve özellikle Kıyı Emniyeti Genel Müdürlüğü'nün Kurtarma Yardım Sözleşmesi'nde yer alan tahkim şartının geçerliliği (Validity of arbitration clauses that grant only one of the parties the right to apply to arbitration: in particular the validity of the arbitration clause under the General Directorate of Coastal Safety Rescue Assistance Contract). İstanbul Kültür Üniversitesi Hukuk Fakültesi Dergisi 9(2):145–155
Güriz A (2011) Sources of Turkish law. In: Ansay T, Wallace D (eds) Introduction to Turkish law, 6th edn. Wolters Kluwer, Ankara, pp 1–18
Güven P (2013) Tanıma-tenfiz: yabancı mahkeme kararlarının tanınması ve tenfizi (Recognition-enforcement: recognition and enforcement of foreign court decisions). Yetkin Yayınları, Ankara
Kocasakal HÖ (2017) Yargıtay 15. Hukuk Dairesi'nin bir kararı çerçevesinde mahkemelere de yetki veren tahkim anlaşmalarının geçerliliği ve bu geçerliliğin tespitinin mahkemeler tarafından yapılıp yapılamayacağı (In the framework of a decision by the 15th Chamber of the Court of Cassation the validity of arbitration agreements that also grant jurisdiction to national courts and whether this validity assessment shall be made by national courts). In: Erdem E et al (eds) Prof. Dr. Hamdi Yasaman'a Armağan, 1st edn. On İki Levha Yayıncılık, İstanbul, pp 509–535
Kuru B, Arslan R, Yılmaz E (2014) Medeni usul hukuku (Civil procedural law). Yetkin Yayınları, Ankara
Nomer E (2017) Devletler hususi hukuku (International private law). Beta Yayıncılık, Istanbul
Özçelik NŞ (2016) Resmi yargı ve tahkimin ayrı ayrı ve birlikte yetkilendirildiği anlaşmaların geçerliliği (Validity of arbitration agreements in which arbitration and national courts are jointly or separately designated). Milletlerarası Hukuk ve Milletlerarası Özel Hukuk Bülteni 36 (2):53–81
Sakmar A (1990) Le nouveau droit international privé turc (The new Turkish private international law). Recueil des Cours de l'Académie de Droit International 223:315–416
Şanlı C, Esen E, Ataman-Figanmeşe İ (2018) Milletlerarası özel hukuk (International private law). Vedat Kitapçılık, Istanbul
Sargın F (1996) Milletlerarası usul hukukunda yetki anlaşmaları (Jurisdiction agreements in international procedural law). Yetkin Yayınları, Ankara
Sargın F (2008) A critical analysis of the requirements of recognition and enforcement of foreign judgments under Turkish law. IPRax-Hafts 4:354–359
Sarıöz Büyükalp İ (2018) Adil yargılanma hakkının Türk tanıma ve tenfiz hukukuna etkileri (Effects of right to a fair trial on the Turkish recognition and enforcement law). In: Tarman ZD (ed) Genç milletlerarası özel hukukçular konferansı II (Young international private law academics Conference II). On İki Levha Yayıncılık, İstanbul
Süral C, Tarman ZD (2013/2014) Recognition and enforcement of foreign court judgments in Turkey. Yearb Private Int Law 15:218–240
Tarman ZD (2014) International commercial arbitration in Turkey. In: Ansay T, Schneider EC (eds) Introduction to Turkish business law, 2nd edn. Wolters Kluwer, Ankara, pp 245–255

Zeynep Derya Tarman is a professor at Koç University Law School, which is one of the top law schools in Turkey. She earned a doctoral degree in law in 2007 from the University of Konstanz School of Law in Germany (*magna cum laude*), previously having earned a Master's in Law and a Bachelor degree in Law from Istanbul University, Turkey. She joined Koç University in 2007 as an assistant professor and was promoted to associate professor in June 2014 and to professor in June 2019. Her areas of research and specialization include International Private Law, International Commercial Arbitration, Foreign Law and Foreign Investment Law.

Meltem Ece Oba is a research and teaching assistant at Koç University Law School in Istanbul, Turkey. She earned a Master of Laws degree in private law in July 2018 from Koç University where she previously obtained her Bachelor of Laws degree (*magna cum laude*). Her areas of research include Conflict of Laws, International Civil Procedure Law, Law of Foreigners and Law of Refugees.

United Kingdom: Giving Effect to Optional Choice of Court Agreements—Interpretation, Operation and Enforcement

Louise Merrett and Janeen Carruthers

1 Introduction and the Recognition of Party Autonomy

1.1 The Attitude to Party Autonomy

The recognition of party autonomy is an important feature of both the national rules and the European rules[1] which together govern jurisdiction in civil and commercial matters in the UK.

As will be explained in detail in Sect. 2.3.2 below, in the European regime respect for party autonomy is achieved through a series of provisions which both confer

This chapter is written principally from an English law perspective, but addresses also aspects of Scots law. The position under Scots law should be taken to be the same as that under English law, except where the contrary is stated. The chapter describes the law as it applies in the UK pre-Brexit. However, the potential impact of Brexit and possible ways forward are discussed in Sect. 4 below.

[1]See e.g. Recital (19) to Regulation (EC) No 1215/21012 on jurisdiction and the recognition and enforcement of judgments in civil and commercial cases (the "BIR recast"): "The autonomy of the parties to a contract, other than an insurance, consumer or employment contract, where only limited autonomy to determine the courts having jurisdiction is allowed, should be respected subject to the exclusive grounds of jurisdiction laid down in this Regulation". See also, in the context of choice of law, Regulation (EC) No 593/2008 on the law applicable to contractual obligations ("RIR"), Recital (11) "The parties' freedom to choose the applicable law should be one of the cornerstones of the system of conflict-of-law rules in matters of contractual obligation".

L. Merrett (✉)
University of Cambridge, Faculty of Law, Cambridge, UK
e-mail: lm324@cam.ac.uk

J. Carruthers
University of Glasgow, School of Law, Glasgow, UK
e-mail: Janeen.Carruthers@glasgow.ac.uk

M. Keyes (ed.), *Optional Choice of Court Agreements in Private International Law*, Ius Comparatum – Global Studies in Comparative Law 37,
https://doi.org/10.1007/978-3-030-23914-5_19

jurisdiction on a chosen court and require other courts to decline jurisdiction in favour of that court.

The English common law rules, which are described in detail in Sect. 2.3.3 below, are more complex because of the adjudicatory discretion which is a key feature of the English common law rules. However, although the exercise of jurisdiction in a particular case remains discretionary:

> contractual pre-management of [international commercial litigation] is respected in several ways. The law strongly favours upholding jurisdiction agreements, and recognises the validity of provisions requiring a party which ignores such a provision to indemnify the other party. It also recognizes the existence of a claim in damages against a party ignoring a jurisdiction agreement.[2]

Thus, "[t]he English court does not automatically follow the will of the parties expressed in their agreement on jurisdiction but takes into account a range of other factors. However, the jurisdiction agreement, especially if exclusive, will almost always be upheld".[3]

The residual, national rules of jurisdiction in Scotland, *per* section 20 of the Civil Jurisdiction and Judgments Act 1982 (as amended) ('CJJA 1982'), are set out in Schedule 8 to that Act.[4] The introduction of this set of rules for Scotland was advocated by the Maxwell Committee,[5] which recommended that the grounds of jurisdiction in use in Scotland should be rationalised and set out in a single code.[6] The scheme of jurisdiction for Scotland introduced by the CJJA 1982 supersedes all pre-existing rules of jurisdiction in matters covered by the Act, subject to retention of the *nobile officium* of the Court of Session. The rules in Schedule 8 are identical *in substance* to their counterpart in BIR recast; some rules in Sch 8 remain in the original Brussels Convention form, unamended to reflect the modifications effected subsequently by the Brussels I Regulation and BIR recast,[7] and some rules in Sch 8 are similar to those in BIR recast, though are not identical in formulation. Notably, Sch 8, rule 6 (prorogation) does not include a presumption of exclusivity, and parties are not required to choose the court of an EU Member State.

The leading and influential practitioner text, *Dicey, Morris & Collins*,[8] which is often referred to in English cases, includes the following rule:

> Rule 39 (1) Where a contract provides that all disputes be referred to England, the court normally has jurisdiction.

---

[2]Fentiman (2015), para 1.38.

[3]Rogerson (2013), p. 179.

[4]Schedule 8 takes effect subject to Brussels I Recast, the Lugano II Convention, and Schedule 4 of the 1982 Act (the "Modified Convention", which allocates jurisdiction within the UK).

[5]Scottish Committee on Jurisdiction and Enforcement, *Report of the Scottish Committee on Jurisdiction and Enforcement* (HMSO, 1980) ('Maxwell Report').

[6]Maxwell Report, paras 2(16)(h), 2.23, and 2.24. Crawford and Carruthers (2015), para 7-78.

[7]e.g. Sch 8 r 2(b) (special jurisdiction in matters relating to a contract).

[8]*Dicey, Morris & Collins* (2012), Rule 39.

(2) Where a contract contains an exclusive jurisdiction agreement in favour of a foreign tribunal, the English court will stay or refuse service unless there is strong cause;

...

(4) An English court may restrain a party over whom it has personal jurisdiction from instituting or continuing proceedings in a foreign court in breach of a contract to refer to the English court.

Statements confirming that effect will generally be given to parties' agreements about jurisdiction can be found in numerous cases concerning both foreign jurisdiction agreements and agreements in favour of the English courts. For example:

- The Court of Appeal in *The El Amria*,[9] upholding the judge's first instance decision concerning a foreign jurisdiction clause, held:

  He directed himself, correctly... that the court will generally enforce an exclusive jurisdiction agreement, and that the plaintiffs had to show strong reasons why it should not do so.

- Similarly, in *The Sennar (No 2)*, Kerr LJ stated:[10]

  Approaching the matter on the basis that the Court has a residual discretion, both parties were in agreement that the relevant considerations have been authoritatively stated in the judgment of Lord Justice Brandon in *The El Amria*, [1981] 2 Lloyd's Rep. 119 at p. 123, 124, as follows:

  (1) Where plaintiffs sue in England in breach of an agreement to refer disputes to a foreign Court, and the defendants apply for a stay, the English Court, assuming the claim to be otherwise within its jurisdiction, is not bound to grant a stay but has a discretion whether to do so or not.
  (2) The discretion should be exercised by granting a stay unless strong cause for not doing so is shown.
  (3) The burden of proving such strong cause is on the plaintiffs.

- The House of Lords in *Donohue v Armco Inc*[11] summarised the position as follows:

  If contracting parties agree to give a particular court exclusive jurisdiction to rule on claims between those parties, and a claim falling within the scope of the agreement is made in proceedings in a forum other than that which the parties have agreed, the English court will ordinarily exercise its discretion (whether by granting a stay of proceedings in England, or by restraining the prosecution of proceedings in the non-contractual forum abroad, or by such other procedural order as is appropriate in the circumstances) to secure compliance with the contractual bargain, unless the party suing in the non-contractual forum (the burden being on him) can show strong reasons for suing in that forum. I use the word "ordinarily" to recognise that where an exercise of discretion is called for there can be no absolute or inflexible rule governing that exercise, and also that a party may lose his claim to equitable relief by dilatoriness or other unconscionable conduct. But the general rule is clear: where parties have bound themselves by an exclusive jurisdiction clause effect should ordinarily be given to that obligation in the absence of strong reasons for departing from it. Whether a party can show strong reasons, sufficient to displace the other party's prima facie entitlement to enforce the contractual bargain, will depend on all the facts and circumstances of the particular case.

[9] [1981] 2 Lloyd's Rep 119.

[10] [1984] 2 Lloyd's Rep 142, 154.

[11] [2001] UKHL 64 at [24].

In the English common law cases, and in Scots law, the terminology used in connection with jurisdiction agreements is usually "exclusive" or "non-exclusive" jurisdiction agreements; rather than "optional" choice of court agreement. However, the term "optional choice of court agreement" will be used where possible in this chapter.

1.2 Multilateral, Regional, and Bilateral Instruments Applicable to Choice of Court Agreements

There are broadly currently four main regimes which apply to choice of court agreements in the UK:[12]

(a) the Brussels I Regulation recast;[13]
(b) the Hague Convention;
(c) the Lugano II Convention; and
(d) the residual national rules, i.e. the English common law, and the rules contained, for Scotland, in CJJA 1982, Sch 8.

This chapter will focus on the regime introduced by the BIR recast which are the rules currently in force in most European cases.

1.2.1 The Brussels I Regulation Recast

In cases within its scope, the Regulation rules apply to the exclusion of any residual national law rules (Art 6).

The Regulation rules engage where the case falls within the material scope of the Regulation (Art 1) and the defendant is domiciled in a Member State (Art 6). However, Art 6 is also subject to Art 25 which deals with choice of court agreements. The BIR recast rules relating to choice of court agreements are set out in Art 25 which provides:

> 1. If the parties, regardless of their domicile, have agreed that a court or the courts of a Member State are to have jurisdiction to settle any disputes which have arisen or which may arise in connection with a particular legal relationship, that court or those courts shall have jurisdiction, unless the agreement is null and void as to its substantive validity under

[12]The position in relation to intra-UK disputes is discussed in Sect. 2.6 below.

[13]The BIR recast applies where proceedings are commenced on or after 10 January 2015 replacing the BIR and the Brussels Convention. A parallel scheme applies as between Denmark (which is not bound directly by the BIR recast) and the other Member States, including the UK.

the law of that Member State. Such jurisdiction shall be exclusive unless the parties have agreed otherwise. The agreement conferring jurisdiction shall be either:

(a) in writing or evidenced in writing;
(b) in a form which accords with practices which the parties have established between themselves; or
(c) in international trade or commerce, in a form which accords with a usage of which the parties are or ought to have been aware and which in such trade or commerce is widely known to, and regularly observed by, parties to contracts of the type involved in the particular trade or commerce concerned.

2. Any communication by electronic means which provides a durable record of the agreement shall be equivalent to 'writing'.
3. The court or courts of a Member State on which a trust instrument has conferred jurisdiction shall have exclusive jurisdiction in any proceedings brought against a settlor, trustee or beneficiary, if relations between those persons or their rights or obligations under the trust are involved.
4. Agreements or provisions of a trust instrument conferring jurisdiction shall have no legal force if they are contrary to Articles 15, 19 or 23, or if the courts whose jurisdiction they purport to exclude have exclusive jurisdiction by virtue of Article 24.
5. An agreement conferring jurisdiction which forms part of a contract shall be treated as an agreement independent of the other terms of the contract.
   The validity of the agreement conferring jurisdiction cannot be contested solely on the ground that the contract is not valid.

The effect of Art 25 is that, provided the choice of court agreement complies with the formality requirements, the BIR recast rules will engage if the parties, *regardless of their domicile*, have agreed that a court or the courts of a Member State are to have jurisdiction.

In this regard, Art 25 of the recast Regulation has expanded the scope of the Regulation. Article 25 now applies to all choice of court agreements in favour of a Member State; previously the rules engaged only when at least one of the parties was also domiciled in a Member State[14] (BIR Art 23.1).[15] This means that cases involving English choice of court agreements will now usually be subject to the European regime. This has significantly narrowed the application of the residual common law rules.

1.2.2 Hague Choice of Court Convention

As a Member State of the EU, the UK is subject to the Hague Convention on Choice of Court Agreements (which the EU signed on behalf of all Member States save Denmark on 1 October 2015) (the Hague Convention). Under this Convention,

[14]Cf. Lugano II Convention, Art 23, which applies if one or more of the contracting parties is domiciled in a Lugano-Contracting State (Art 23.1).

[15]Subject to Art 23.3 which provided: where such an agreement is concluded by parties, none of whom is domiciled in a Member State, the courts of other Member States shall have no jurisdiction over their disputes unless the court or courts chosen have declined jurisdiction.

Contracting States[16] must give effect to exclusive jurisdiction agreements in favour of other Contracting States and "suspend or dismiss" any proceedings brought before them in breach of such clauses (Article 6). As between the courts of the Member States, the BIR recast generally takes precedence.[17]

1.2.3 Lugano II Convention

The Lugano II Convention on Jurisdiction and the Enforcement of Judgments in Civil and Commercial Matters applies between the UK and other Member States and Iceland, Norway and Switzerland.[18] It was adopted in 2007 to mirror rules in force in the BIR, but has not yet been amended to mirror the changes made in the recast Regulation. Art 23 addresses prorogation of jurisdiction, providing that,

Article 23

1. If the parties, one or more of whom is domiciled in a State bound by this Convention, have agreed that a court or the courts of a State bound by this Convention are to have jurisdiction to settle any disputes which have arisen or which may arise in connection with a particular legal relationship, that court or those courts shall have jurisdiction. Such jurisdiction shall be exclusive unless the parties have agreed otherwise. Such an agreement conferring jurisdiction shall be either:
   (a) in writing or evidenced in writing; or
   (b) in a form which accords with practices which the parties have established between themselves; or
   (c) in international trade or commerce, in a form which accords with a usage of which the parties are or ought to have been aware and which in such trade or commerce is widely known to, and regularly observed by, parties to contracts of the type involved in the particular trade or commerce concerned.
2. Any communication by electronic means which provides a durable record of the agreement shall be equivalent to 'writing'.
3. Where such an agreement is concluded by parties, none of whom is domiciled in a State bound by this Convention, the courts of other States bound by this Convention shall have

[16]Which include Mexico, Montenegro, Singapore and Denmark. The People's Republic of China, the Ukraine and the USA have signed, but not yet ratified, the Convention.

[17]Article 26(6) provides "This Convention shall not affect the application of the rules of a Regional Economic Integration Organization that is a Party to this Convention, whether adopted before or after this Convention (a) where none of the parties is resident in a Contracting State that is not a Member State of the Regional Economic Integration organization; (b) as concerns the recognition or enforcement of judgments as between member States of the Regional Economic Integration Organization."

[18]Decision 2007/712/EC on the signing, on behalf of the Community, of the Convention on jurisdiction and the recognition and enforcement of judgments in civil and commercial matters [2007] OJ L339/1; and Decision 2009/430/EC concerning the conclusion of the Convention on jurisdiction and the recognition and enforcement of judgments in civil and commercial matters [2009] OJ L147/1. See Civil Jurisdiction and Judgment Act 1982, as amended by the Civil Jurisdiction and Judgments Regulations 2009 (SI 2009/3131).

no jurisdiction over their disputes unless the court or courts chosen have declined jurisdiction.
4. The court or courts of a State bound by this Convention on which a trust instrument has conferred jurisdiction shall have exclusive jurisdiction in any proceedings brought against a settlor, trustee or beneficiary, if relations between these persons or their rights or obligations under the trust are involved.
5. Agreements or provisions of a trust instrument conferring jurisdiction shall have no legal force if they are contrary to the provisions of Articles 13, 17 or 21, or if the courts whose jurisdiction they purport to exclude have exclusive jurisdiction by virtue of Article 22.

1.2.4 The Residual National Law

The residual national rules, for English and Scots law, respectively, can be applied only in cases not governed by any of the regimes outlined above.

2 Optional Choice of Court Agreements

2.1 The Law Applicable to Choice of Court Agreements

2.1.1 Common Law Choice of Law Rules

At common law, English and Scots courts proceed on the basis that a choice of court agreement is an agreement between the parties capable of generating private law contractual rights and encompassing contractual promises. It is severable from any underlying contract of which it forms a part, due to the doctrine of severability.[19]

The law applicable to a choice of court agreement is determined by applying contractual choice of law rules. That applicable law will apply to determine questions of interpretation, including the construction of express terms and whether terms should be implied. It is also often said that the applicable law will determine whether a clause is exclusive or optional.[20] However, while this might be a useful shorthand way to describe the process of construction, this is a question of construction rather than characterisation; an agreement can contain positive and negative obligations which can be different depending on the party and circumstances.

[19]Confirmed at common law by *Fiona Trust & Holding Corp v Privalov* [2007] UKHL 40 and, under the BIR, by *Benincasa v Dentalkit srl* Case C-269/95 and now by Art 25.5 of the recast Regulation. See, for Scotland, *Belgian International Insurance v McNicoll* 1999 GWD 22-1065, reversing single judge decision reported at 1999 GWD 13-622.

[20]*Dicey, Morris & Collins* (2012), para 12-105: "It is a question of interpretation, governed by the law applicable to the contract or, more accurately, the law governing the jurisdiction agreement, whether a jurisdiction clause is exclusive or non-exclusive". See, in Scots law, Maher and Rodger (2010), para 17-17; and, by way of example, *Breitenbucher v Wittke* [2008] CSOH 145.

Choice of law in contract in the UK is governed by the Rome I Regulation[21] ("RIR").[22] However, Art 1.2 excludes certain matters from the scope of the Regulation including, at (e), arbitration agreements and agreements on choice of court. This means that the law applicable to a choice of court agreement must be determined using common law choice of law rules.[23] At common law, although a choice of court agreement is a severable agreement, there is a presumption that it is governed by the same law as that which applies to the underlying agreement. As the court explained in *Mauritius Commercial Bank v Hestia*:[24]

> The governing law of a jurisdiction agreement is, like any other contractual provision, to be determined by the parties' express choice if they have made one, and in general the parties' intention will be taken to be that it is to be governed by the law applicable to the contract of which it forms part.

The law of the underlying agreement will itself be determined by the RIR; this means that although choice of court agreements are excluded from the scope of the Regulation, at common law those rules are likely to have an important indirect effect. Very often a choice of court agreement is accompanied by an express choice of law clause.[25] Otherwise, absent an express choice of a different law in the underlying contract, the law of the chosen court will often apply through this indirect route because a choice of jurisdiction is often said to lead to an implied choice of the same law.[26]

As well as questions of interpretation, the law applicable to the choice of court agreement will also determine questions of contractual validity, e.g. duress, misrepresentation, undue influence etc.[27] However, how a promise, either to submit to the jurisdiction of the English court or not to sue elsewhere, takes effect on the court's jurisdiction cannot be solely a matter of agreement between the parties themselves. Questions which go to the jurisdiction of the court can be answered only by applying

[21]Regulation (EC) No 593/2008 on the law applicable to contractual obligations.

[22]Provided the relevant contract was entered into after 17 December 2009 (Art 28 RIR). Although a European Regulation, the RIR applies in all cases before a UK court regardless of the domicile of the parties or any other connections to the EU and regardless of whether the law identified is the law of a Member State.

[23]See *Mauritius Commercial Bank v Hestia* [2013] EWHC 1328 (Comm), [15] and [16].

[24][2013] EWHC 1328 (Comm).

[25]Cf. recital (12), RIR, viz.: "An agreement between the parties to confer on one or more courts or tribunals of a Member State exclusive jurisdiction to determine disputes under the contract should be one of the factors to be taken into account in determining whether a choice of law has been clearly demonstrated."

[26]See Rogerson (2013), p. 180. Cf. Joseph (2015), para 6.21 "by itself, a non-exclusive jurisdiction agreement will only amount to a weak inference of choice of governing law".

[27]Because the doctrine of severability says that invalidity in the underlying agreement does not invalidate a choice of court agreement, those defences are likely to be limited: *Fiona Trust& Holding Corp v Privalov* [2007] UKHL 40.

the procedural law of the forum.[28] The effect of optional jurisdiction agreements is considered further in Sect. 2.3 below.

2.1.2 Choice of Law Under the BIR Recast

The dual nature of choice of court agreements is also reflected in Art 25 BIR recast.[29] The contractual basis is confirmed by Art 25(5): "An agreement conferring jurisdiction which forms part of a contract shall be treated as an agreement independent of the other terms of the contract". It is also apparent from the addition in the recast regulation of the proviso in Art 25.1 that Art 25 will not operate if "the agreement is null and void as to its substantive validity under the law of [the chosen] Member State". The CJEU has confirmed that contractual questions, such as interpretation, are governed by the applicable national law.[30] Thus, as is the case at common law, the starting point in cases governed by the BIR recast is that the relevant contractual applicable law will apply to determine interpretation and, to the extent provided in Art 25, the validity of the clause.[31] The difference comes at the final stage; determining the effect of those promises on jurisdiction. In cases governed by the Regulation, that will be a matter for the rules of the Regulation itself. The effect of optional jurisdiction agreements under the Regulation will be considered further in Sect. 2.3.2 below.

---

[28]Briggs (2008), para 1.17: "a contractual term which specifies the jurisdiction of a court . . . may be regarded as a part of procedural or public law, on the basis that whether a court has jurisdiction is always a matter of public law which lies beyond the control or autonomy of the parties".

[29]See Fentiman (2015), para 2.169: "jurisdiction agreements are severable from their host contracts, and have a procedural effect for jurisdictional purposes independent of their contractual effect between the parties".

[30]*Powell Duffryn plc v Wolfgang Petereit* Case C-214/89 and see *Roche Products Ltd v Provimi* [2003] All ER (Comm) 683. See also *British Sugar plc v Fratelli Babbini* [2005] 1 All ER 55, 72 para [40]: "the starting point, at any rate, in the process of construction, is to consider the meaning of the relevant clause under the law which is the proper law of the contract. In formulating its opinion in the terms that "the concept of 'agreement conferring jurisdiction' should not be interpreted simply as referring to the national law of one or other of the States concerned', I do not think that the European Court of Justice was intending to indicate that those national laws should be excluded from consideration or that it was inappropriate to consider the proper law of the relevant agreement".

[31]Cf. Magnus and Mankowski (2016), p. 656, [143]: "it is submitted here that as far as possible an autonomous method of interpretation should be developed and applied. For this purpose any interpretation of a jurisdiction agreement should first make use of the rules enshrined in Art. 25 itself, namely, the wording of the jurisdiction clause as the starting point, the precedence of the parties' intentions and the presumed exclusive effect of a jurisdiction agreement. . . . Only if the Regulation does not provide any assistance then in cases of doubt the interpretation rules of the law (including the conflicts rules) apply that governs the jurisdiction agreement. Insofar it is suggested here that the applicable law is to be determined in applying the provisions of the Rome I Regulation by analogy."

2.2 *Characterising a Choice of Court Agreement as Optional or Exclusive*

2.2.1 Common Law Rules of Construction

It has become commonplace in English cases and commentary to start any analysis of jurisdiction agreements by noting that jurisdiction agreements can have positive and negative elements.[32] The agreement has a positive effect if it seeks to confer jurisdiction on a particular court or courts. However, as has been discussed above, whether an agreement between the parties results in a court having jurisdiction is a matter for the forum applying its own law, not a matter for the parties themselves.[33]

A jurisdiction agreement which has a negative effect[34] also contains an obligation not to sue in any other or certain other jurisdictions.[35] Again, the parties themselves cannot prohibit a court from taking jurisdiction. But the existence of a promise not to sue may well lead another court to decline to hear the case. Furthermore, if one of the parties does sue in a jurisdiction which is not permitted under the agreement, that will constitute a breach of the promise not to sue elsewhere and may lead to remedies based on breach of contract, including damages or an anti-suit injunction.

The first type of agreement, which contains only a positive obligation to submit, is often referred to in the UK as a non-exclusive (or "permissive" or "optional") jurisdiction agreement, whereas an agreement which contains both a negative and positive obligation is referred to as an exclusive (or "mandatory" or "binding") jurisdiction agreement.[36]

However, the distinction is neither as clear-cut nor as simple as that simple binary classification might imply.[37] For example, a clause could positively confer jurisdiction on two named courts, say France and Germany, and only those courts. Such an agreement is exclusively non-exclusive.[38] The obligations may also be different for each party (as in an asymmetric clauses discussed in Sect. 3 below). Moreover, a party may have promised different things, expressly or impliedly, in different contexts, for example, never to sue anywhere other than England; not to object to English jurisdiction; that England is the appropriate forum; or not to start proceedings

[32]See Joseph (2015), para 4.02; Magnus and Mankowski (2016), Art 25 [28] referring to a prorogation effect and a derogation effect. The same terminology is used in Dickinson and Lein (2015), para 9.06. Cf., in Scots law, *Anton's Private International Law* (2011), para 8.131.

[33]Effectively a unilateral submission in advance to the jurisdiction of the named court: Briggs (2012), pp. 378. Cf., in Scots law, Maher and Rodger (2010), para 17-17.

[34]See Lord Mance in *Hydropower v AES* [2013] 2 Lloyd's Rep 201 referring to the "negative promise" in an exclusive jurisdiction agreement.

[35]A unilateral renunciation of jurisdiction which would otherwise have been found in other courts: Briggs (2012), p. 378.

[36]For a detailed discussion see Keyes and Marshall (2015).

[37]See e.g. *Dicey, Morris & Collins* (2012), para 12-102: a rigid division into exclusive and non-exclusive agreements may sometimes be misleading.

[38]Or, as Keyes and Marshall prefer, "non-uniquely exclusive agreements." (2015) pp. 355–356.

elsewhere once proceedings have been commenced in England.[39] Furthermore, apparently optional agreements may also contain express or implied obligations of a negative nature, for example, not to seek an anti-suit injunction from another court. That is why the question must be conceptualised as what a particular party promises to do or not to do in a particular agreement. It is only once those promises have been identified and construed that consideration can be given to the effect of those promises on jurisdiction. The crucial difference between exclusive and optional agreements comes down to whether "the commencement and pursuit of the foreign proceedings in question are things which a party has promised not to do".[40]

First a court will consider whether a clause is expressly exclusive or non-exclusive, or, perhaps more likely, whether it uses the words exclusive or non-exclusive.

A jurisdiction clause may expressly spell out what obligations it contains; for example, party A agrees to submit to the jurisdiction of the English court and promises not to sue anywhere else. That does not usually happen. But if Party A agrees to the "exclusive jurisdiction of the English courts" that will usually be construed as a promise to submit and not to sue elsewhere. Conversely if Party A agrees to the "non-exclusive jurisdiction of the English courts" that will usually be construed as a promise to submit, but not including a promise not to sue elsewhere. The parties also sometimes include express terms which confirm or extend those basic promises. For example, in *Deutsche Bank v Sebastian Holdings*[41] a series of related contracts contained a variety of jurisdiction clauses. Some were expressly stated to be exclusive and some non-exclusive; others contained an "other jurisdiction acceptance clause" i.e. underlining the optional jurisdiction of the English courts by confirming the availability of other relevant jurisdictions;[42] other clauses contained an express *forum non-conveniens* waiver, i.e. a clause providing that the parties would not object to the jurisdiction of the English court on the basis that it was an inappropriate forum.

Even if there is no express promise not to sue elsewhere and the parties have not used the word "exclusive," English courts have sometimes found an implied obligation not to sue elsewhere, in other words, have construed a clause as being exclusive. They have done so by construing jurisdiction clauses in a very sophisticated manner.[43] A well-known example is the decision in *British Aerospace plc v Dee Howard Co.*[44]

[39]See *Sabah Shipyard (Pakistan) Ltd v Islamic Republic of Pakistan* [2003] 2 Lloyds Rep 511 and Joseph (2015), para 4.04.

[40]*BNP Paribas SA v Anchorage Capital Europe LLP* [2013] EWHC 3073 (Comm) at [88] and Fentiman (2015), para 2.61.

[41][2009] EWHC 3069 (Comm).

[42]Burton J at [17] said "this addition would seem only to make explicit what would, in any event, be implicit from the very fact that the chosen jurisdiction is not exclusive".

[43]See Rogerson (2013), p. 181.

[44][1993] 1 Lloyd's Rep 368.

The contract in that case provided:

> This agreement shall be governed by and construed and take effect according to English law and the parties hereto agree that the courts of law in England shall have jurisdiction to entertain any action in respect hereof.

In deciding that the agreement conferred exclusive jurisdiction on the English courts, Waller J took into account a number of considerations:

(1) Because the English court would have had jurisdiction in any event (because the express choice of law clause would have provided a ground of jurisdiction) some further effect must have been intended (otherwise the clause would have been redundant).[45]
(2) Linked to this was the fact that the clause additionally required the parties to provide an address for service in England.
(3) The language of the clause was transitive as it submitted the disputes rather than simply the parties to the jurisdiction of the English courts. A linked point was that the use of the word "shall" imposed an obligation as to jurisdiction.[46] However, as has been made clear in subsequent cases, simply saying language is "transitive" does not really take matters any further as it simply states a conclusion and does not explain why the conclusion is reached. See, for example, *BNP Paribas SA v Anchorage Capital Europe LLP*:[47]

> . . . the distinction in the present case between submitting to the jurisdiction in respect of certain matters (intransitive and therefore, so the argument goes, non-exclusive) and submitting disputes in respect of certain matters to the jurisdiction of the court (transitive, and therefore exclusive) is so elusive that it escapes me altogether.
>
> In the end all of these factors are only signposts which may sometimes assist in determining the intention of the parties, while the terms 'exclusive' and 'non-exclusive' themselves are merely convenient labels. In agreement with *Dicey* at para 12-105 ('the true question is whether on its proper construction the clause obliges the parties to resort to the relevant jurisdiction, irrespective of whether the word "exclusive" is used'), I prefer to ask the question whether the commencement and pursuit of the foreign proceedings in question are things which a party has promised not to do.

Special principles may also apply to asymmetric jurisdiction agreements. The fact that one party only is given an option to sue elsewhere "brings into play the *expressio unius exclusio alterius* canon of construction", i.e. the assumption that in relation to

[45]This presumption was applied in *Sohio Supply Co v Gatoil* [1989] 1 Lloyd's Rep 580 and explained in *Starlight Shipping Co v Allianz Marine & Aviation Versicherungs AG* [2011] EWHC 3381 (Comm); at first instance (the first instance decision was reversed by the Court of Appeal but not on this point). Cf. Fentiman (2015), para 2.63: there are good reasons to agree even to a court's optional jurisdiction when a court already has jurisdiction since it has contractual effects and may significantly affect the exercise of a court's discretion to stay and once activated may become exclusive.

[46]See Fentiman (2015), para 2.66. The question is whether the language used suggests anything about whether it is possible to imply a promise not to sue in any other jurisdiction.

[47][2013] EWHC 3073 (Comm) at [87] and [88].

the other party that was not intended so the jurisdiction against that party is exclusive.[48]

2.2.2 Construction Under BIR Recast Art 25

Art 25 provides that agreements within its scope "shall be exclusive unless the parties have agreed otherwise".

The precise effect of this provision is uncertain. In particular, it is unclear whether this rule applies unless the parties have expressly agreed otherwise. The views expressed in English commentaries differ:

- Briggs[49]notes that "it is occasionally said that art. 25 contains a presumption of exclusivity. This is questionable. Simply states the obvious and makes it clear that can have non-exclusive agreements."
- Garcimartín[50] states that Art 25 establishes a rebuttable presumption on the nature of choice of court agreements: they are taken to be exclusive, absent contrary agreement between the parties.
- Fentiman states that "an agreement, silent as to its effect, might properly be construed as non-exclusive in English law, but unless its non-exclusive character is explicitly stated, it is likely that it is subject to the presumption in Article 25 that such agreements are exclusive unless otherwise agreed."[51]

It is also unclear what effect the presumption has on private law rights. The presumption, if that is what it is, applies to determine the effect given to the agreement under the BIR recast. It has already been stated that matters of construction are for the relevant national law. Thus, it may be possible to have an optional agreement so construed under the relevant national law, but that creates exclusive jurisdiction under the BIR recast. To put it another way, the presumption relates to the effect of the agreement under the Regulation, but may not alter the private law rights created by the agreement according to the relevant contractual applicable law.

2.2.3 Interpretation Under the Hague Convention

Art 3(b) provides that a jurisdiction agreement which designates the courts of a Contracting State "shall be deemed to be exclusive unless the parties have expressly provided otherwise".

---

[48]See *Continental Bank v Aeakos* [1994] 1 WLR 588 applied in *Credit Suisse First Boston (Europe) Ltd v MLC (Bermuda) Ltd* [1999] CLC 579.

[49]Briggs (2014), para 4.186.

[50]F Garcimartín, ch 9 in Dickinson and Lein (2015), para 9.83.

[51]Fentiman (2015), para 2.52.

2.2.4 Interpretation Under the Lugano II Convention

Art 23.1 provides that a jurisdiction agreement which designates the courts of a Contracting State "shall be exclusive unless the parties have agreed otherwise".

2.3 *Determining the Legal Effect of an Optional Choice of Court Agreement*

The effect of a jurisdiction agreement on the jurisdiction of a court is a matter for the procedural law of the forum. Thus, the effect of an optional choice of court agreement on the English court's jurisdiction is a matter for English procedural law and depends on which regime applies.

2.3.1 Overview of Residual National Jurisdiction Rules

The two key features of the English common law jurisdiction rules are that in general the basis of jurisdiction is service, but the exercise of jurisdiction is discretionary. Initiating process can be served on a defendant as of right if that party is present in the jurisdiction.[52] But a defendant can apply for a stay of those proceedings on the basis that there is another clearly more appropriate forum. If the defendant is not present and so cannot be served as of right, the claimant will have to seek permission to serve out of the jurisdiction.[53] At common law, the mere agreement of the parties that the English court has jurisdiction is not sufficient by itself to give the court jurisdiction. In order to get permission to serve out of the jurisdiction, the claimant will need to identify a ground (Civil Procedure Rules Practice Direction 6B). One of those grounds is that a claim is made in respect of a contract where the contract contains a term to the effect that the court shall have jurisdiction to determine any claim in respect of the contract.[54] The claimant must also show that that England is the most appropriate forum. Together the exercise of discretion in the case of a stay and applications for service out is referred to as the doctrine of *forum conveniens*.

The test to be applied in relation to both aspects of the *forum non conveniens* discretion was set out by Lord Goff in *Spiliada Maritime Corporation v Cansulex Limited.*[55] The defendant must show not only that England is not the natural or appropriate forum for the trial, but also that there is another available forum which is clearly or distinctly more appropriate. "The question in both groups of cases must be,

---

[52]Temporary presence is enough: *Maharanee of Baroda v Wildenstein* [1972] 2 QB 283. The methods of service are set out in the Civil Procedure Rules (CPR) r 6.9(2).

[53]Under CPR rr 36 and 37.

[54]CPR Practice Direction 6B 3.1(6)(d).

[55][1987] AC 460, 476–477.

at bottom, . . . to identify the forum in which the case can be suitably tried for the interests of all the parties and for the ends of justice”.[56]

The factors which the court is entitled to take into account in considering whether one forum is more appropriate than another are numerous and the weight to be given to the same connecting factor may vary from case to case. However, agreements on jurisdiction are crucial because they fundamentally alter the normal *Spiliada forum conveniens* exercise. Although the parties’ promises as to jurisdiction will not be automatically or specifically enforced because jurisdiction is ultimately a matter for the court, they will be upheld unless there is a strong or overwhelming reason not to do so. In relation to exclusive jurisdiction agreements, the House of Lords in *Donohue v Armco Inc*[57] stated:

> If contracting parties agree to give a particular court exclusive jurisdiction to rule on claims between those parties, and a claim falling within the scope of the agreement is made in proceedings in a forum other than that which the parties have agreed, the English court will ordinarily exercise its discretion (whether by granting a stay of proceedings in England, or by restraining the prosecution of proceedings in the non-contractual forum abroad, or by such other procedural order as is appropriate in the circumstances) to secure compliance with the contractual bargain, unless the party suing in the non-contractual forum (the burden being on him) can show strong reasons for suing in that forum. I use the word “ordinarily” to recognise that where an exercise of discretion is called for there can be no absolute or inflexible rule governing that exercise, and also that a party may lose his claim to equitable relief by dilatoriness or other unconscionable conduct. But the general rule is clear: where parties have bound themselves by an exclusive jurisdiction clause effect should ordinarily be given to that obligation in the absence of strong reasons for departing from it.

Thus, a contractual promise as to jurisdiction will be enforced unless strong cause is shown why not. The approach in cases of exclusive jurisdiction agreements is clear; the position in relation to optional agreements is more complex and is considered in Sect. 2 below.

In Scotland, use of residual national rules opens the way to the plea of *forum non conveniens*. Schedule 8 to the CJJA 1982 contains those native or idiosyncratic rules of Scots law which are capable of being utilised against persons not domiciled in an EU or EFTA Member State. A defence which can be offered for retention of these native grounds is that their effect may be mitigated by the plea of *forum non conveniens*, where it remains available and competent.[58]

2.3.2 BIR Recast Jurisdiction Rules

All jurisdiction agreements in favour of a Member State are now governed by Art 25 BIR recast: as has been described in Sect. 1.2.1 above, under BIR recast it does

[56][1987] AC 460, 480.

[57][2001] UKHL 64, [24].

[58]See, for detail, Crawford and Carruthers (2015), paras 7-80 et seq.

not matter if neither party is domiciled in a Member State, which means that all cases where there is a jurisdiction agreement in favour of England are governed by the BIR recast.

Art 25 BIR recast does not apply to jurisdiction agreements which purport to confer jurisdiction on a third state. Thus, the effect of these agreements on the English courts' jurisdiction will be determined by national rules. However, where the English court itself has jurisdiction under the BIR recast, it is unclear whether and in what circumstances those proceedings can be stayed in favour of a non-Member State. This aspect of the interface between the BIR rules and the common law is considered further in Sect. 2.3.4 below.[59]

2.3.3 Legal Effect of an Optional Choice of Court Agreement at Common Law

In an optional jurisdiction agreement the parties have (1) agreed (2) in advance (3) to submit to the jurisdiction of the named court.

By agreeing to a named court's jurisdiction, the parties are agreeing that that court should have international jurisdiction to hear the merits of the case, even if it would not otherwise have had jurisdiction under its rules absent prorogation. It should follow that once proceedings are commenced in the chosen jurisdiction, the other party promises to accept that the chosen court has international jurisdiction over those proceedings. It does not mean that the party has to appear and argue the merits of the case. Rather, the party is agreeing that it will not take any point or rely on any argument which disputes the jurisdiction of the court to hear the case.[60]

This promise to submit will be enforced unless there is a strong reason for departing from it.[61] In English cases where service out is required, this obligation will include either an obligation to accept service,[62] or not to seek to set aside service out of the jurisdiction.

Furthermore, if a party has agreed to submit, that agreement is inconsistent with applying for a stay of proceedings on jurisdictional grounds. This is very important. Applying for a stay in favour of another jurisdiction is simply inconsistent with submitting to the jurisdiction regardless of what facts or grounds are relied on as indicating the relative appropriateness of another court.

[59]On the *Owusu* point see e.g. Baatz and Sandiforth (2010); *Skype Technologies SA v Joltid Ltd* [2009] EWHC 2783 (Ch); [2011] I.L.Pr. 8 (Ch D); *Equitas Ltd v Allstate Insurance Co* [2008] EWHC 1671 (Comm); [2009] 1 All E.R. (Comm) 1137 (QBD (Comm)); *Owusu v Jackson (t/a Villa Holidays Bal Inn Villas)* (C-281/02) [2005] Q.B. 801; Times, March 9, 2005 (ECJ).

[60]An analogy can be drawn with the general test for submission i.e. not doing anything which is inconsistent with disputing the court's jurisdiction (*Marc Rich & Co AG v Società Italiana Impianti PA (The Atlantic Emperor) (No 2)* [1992] 1 Lloyd's Rep 624).

[61]See *Donohue v Armco* [2001] UKHL 64 (Sect. 2.3.1 above).

[62]Although probably not an obligation to nominate an address for service because that is a slightly different point and sometimes addressed by an express clause.

A promise to submit also includes an implied promise not to interfere with the submission to the designated court. For example, in *Sabah Shipyard (Pakistan) Ltd v Pakistan*[63] Christopher Clarke J held that by agreeing to the non-exclusive jurisdiction of the English court, the parties had impliedly agreed not to prevent proceedings in the chosen forum by seeking an anti-suit injunction in another court.[64]

The starting point, suggested by the analysis set out above, is accordingly that once there is a promise to submit to the English court's jurisdiction, should in due course proceedings be commenced, that promise will be enforced unless there is a strong reason not to do so. The promise to submit is the same in exclusive and optional agreements and should mean that permission to serve will be granted and a stay refused unless there is a strong reason not to do so.

This was the approach taken, for example, by Moore-Bick J in *Mercury Communications Ltd v Communication Telesystems International* [65] which involved an optional jurisdiction clause in favour of England where there were proceedings already in place in California. The judge refused a stay, stating that "particular weight should attach to the fact that the defendant has freely agreed as part of his bargain to submit to the jurisdiction. In principle he should be held to that bargain unless there are overwhelming reasons to the contrary".

However, many English cases take a slightly different approach. Although the result may often be the same, the reasoning is slightly different in treating an optional jurisdiction agreement as part of the normal *Spiliada* discretion which is relevant to identifying the appropriate forum. There are a very large number of cases and it is not possible to discuss them all in detail.[66] One of the first and most well known cases adopting this approach is *British Aerospace Plc v Dee Howard Co.*[67] The agreement in that case contained an *exclusive* jurisdiction clause in favour of England. Despite that clause, the defendant sued British Airways in Texas and applied for a stay of the English proceedings. Waller J held that *whether the clause was exclusive or non-exclusive*, it had been freely negotiated and it was not open to the defendant to argue the relative merits of suing in Texas rather than England. Waller J took as his starting point a passage from Hobhouse J in *S&W Berisford Plc v New Hampshire Insurance Co Ltd*, where he said:

> the fact that the parties have agreed in their contract that the English courts shall have jurisdiction (albeit a non-exclusive jurisdiction) creates a strong prima facie case that that jurisdiction is an appropriate one; it should in principle be a jurisdiction to which neither

---

[63][2002] EWCA Civ 1643.

[64]See also Fentiman (2015), para 2.237: a non-exclusive jurisdiction agreement contains a contractual obligation to accept the jurisdiction of the agreed court if the other party elects to sue there and it is a breach of contract to prevent proceedings in the designated forum by seeking an anti-suit injunction in another court.

[65][1999] 2 All ER (Comm) 33, 40.

[66]In *Deutsche Bank v Sebastian Holdings* [2009] EWHC 3069 (Comm), [14] Burton J referred to the fact that he had been provided with a positive bible of some 38 of the leading authorities.

[67][1993] 1 Lloyd's Rep 368.

> party to the contract can object as inappropriate; they have both implicitly agreed that it is appropriate.[68]

Here the analysis proceeded on the basis that the parties had agreed that England was "an appropriate forum" which, it was said, created a strong prima facie case that that jurisdiction was an appropriate one. Having construed a non-exclusive agreement in this way, Waller J then relied on an estoppel-based analysis, stressing that a party cannot rely on foreseeable factors to argue against English jurisdiction because they have agreed that England was an appropriate forum in the light of or indeed irrespective of those factors: "it simply should not be open to start arguing about relative merits where factors would have been eminently foreseeable."[69]

This approach, which starts by asserting that in an optional agreement the parties have agreed that England is an appropriate forum or the appropriate forum, and proceeds by arguing that as a consequence a party cannot rely on foreseeable factors to apply for a stay or resist permission to serve, has been followed in many of the subsequent cases.[70] It means that absent some exceptional factor, where there is an optional jurisdiction agreement in favour of the English courts, a stay will be refused and permission to serve outside the jurisdiction granted.

For example, in *Highland Crusaders Offshore Partners LP v Deutsche Bank AG*[71] the Court of Appeal stated that an optional jurisdiction agreement precludes either party from later arguing that the forum identified is not an appropriate forum on grounds foreseeable at the time of the agreement, for the parties must be taken to have been aware of such matters at the time of the agreement.

In *Breams Trustees Ltd v Upstream Downstream Simulation Services Inc*[72] having analysed the existing case law, Patten J concluded

> It is clear from the authorities I have referred to that even a non-exclusive jurisdiction clause ... binds the defendant to accept England as the appropriate forum. The Court will not relieve him of that obligation by granting a stay of English proceedings or by setting aside service out of the jurisdiction unless there are strong reasons for doing so. What the first instance decisions ... show is that strong reasons do not include the mere existence of *lis alibi pendens* ... If that were so, a party to a non-exclusive jurisdiction clause could avoid its agreement at will by commencing proceedings in another jurisdiction of its choice.

[68][1990] 2 QB 631, 646.

[69][1993] 1 Lloyd's Rep 368, 376.

[70]For example, *Marubeni Hong Kong and South China Ltd v Mongolia* [2002] All ER (Comm) 873 and *Ace Insurance SA v Zurich Insurance Co Ltd* [2001] EWCA Civ 173; [2001] 1 All ER (Comm) 802. See also, *Dicey Morris & Collins* (2012), para 12-106 Where the court finds that the agreement confers non-exclusive jurisdiction on the designated court (whether an English or a foreign court) it is more difficult to argue that the institution of proceedings is a breach of contract; and on that footing, an application for a stay of proceedings in favour of that foreign court will be determined on the basis of *Spiliada*. See also Rogerson (2013), p. 182: "By entering into even a non-exclusive jurisdiction agreement a party accepts that the chosen court is appropriate ... That leaves rather little room for the party to argue that a court other than one identified in the jurisdiction agreement is a more appropriate court".

[71][2009] EWCA Civ 725; [2010] 1 WLR 1023.

[72][2004] EWHC 211 (Ch), [27].

The law was restated by Gloster J in *Antec International Ltd v Biosafety USA Inc.*[73] A contract contained an expressly "non-exclusive" jurisdiction agreement in favour of England.[74] Proceedings were commenced in England, but the defendant sought a stay in favour of Florida. Gloster J set out a series of principles which have been subsequently applied in a number of cases. In summary,

i) The fact that the parties have freely negotiated a contract providing for the non-exclusive jurisdiction of the English courts and English law, creates a strong prima facie case that the English jurisdiction is the correct one.
ii) Although, in the exercise of its discretion, the court is entitled to have regard to all the circumstances of the case, the general rule is that the parties will be held to their contractual choice of English jurisdiction unless there are overwhelming, or at least very strong, reasons for departing from this rule.
iii) Such overwhelming or very strong reasons do not include factors of convenience that were foreseeable at the time that the contract was entered into (save in exceptional circumstances involving the interests of justice); and it is not appropriate to embark upon a standard *Spiliada* balancing exercise. The defendant has to point to some factor which it could not have foreseen at the time the contract was concluded.
iv) In particular, the fact that the defendant has instituted proceedings or is about to commence proceedings in another jurisdiction, not contemplated by the non-exclusive jurisdiction clause, is not a strong or compelling reason to relieve a party from his bargain, notwithstanding the undesirability of parallel proceedings. Otherwise a party to a non-exclusive jurisdiction clause could avoid its agreement at will by commencing proceedings in another jurisdiction…

Under this *Spiliada* approach, there is some uncertainty in the English case law as to whether there is any difference between exclusive and optional agreements in this regard. In *BP Plc v AON*[75] the relationship between exclusive and non-exclusive agreements was referred to in the following way:

> There can be no doubt that it is implicit in a non-exclusive jurisdiction clause that both parties accept when they agree to it that it will be appropriate for that court in the interests of justice, as distinct from obligatory to exercise jurisdiction over all disputes which may reasonably be envisaged as arising in relation to their agreement. That, however, does not go as far as saying that it is agreed that in all circumstances that may in future arise the designated court will necessarily be the court where the case may most suitably be tried for the interests of all parties and the ends of justice. If that were so, the effect of such a clause would be indistinguishable from that of an exclusive jurisdiction clause.

[73] [2006] EWHC 47 (Comm).

[74] The clause provided: "This agreement shall be governed by and construed in all respects in accordance with the Laws of England and each party hereunder submits to the non-exclusive jurisdiction of the English Courts".

[75] [2005] EWHC 2554 (Comm), [23]. The case actually involved the opposite situation, i.e. a non-exclusive jurisdiction clause in favour of the courts of Illinois.

In *Highland Crusader Offshore Partners LP v Deutsche Bank AG*[76] the court stated:

> [B]y agreeing to non-exclusive jurisdiction of state X, parties have implicitly agreed that X is an appropriate jurisdiction ... On the other hand, a non-exclusive jurisdiction clause self evidently leaves open the possibility that there may be another appropriate jurisdiction. The degree of appropriateness of an alternative jurisdiction must depend on all the circumstances of the case. In addition to the usual factors, the wording of the non-exclusive jurisdiction clause may be relevant, because of the light which it may throw on the parties' intentions. Another possibly relevant factor (to which Waller J drew attention in *Dee Howard*) may be whether the choice of non-exclusive jurisdiction was specially negotiated or was contained in a standard form of contract.

An analysis that starts with the promise to submit being inconsistent with applying for a stay emphasises that in this respect an optional and exclusive agreement should have the same effect.

2.3.4 Legal Effect of an Optional Choice of Court Agreement Under BIR Recast

Choice of court agreements under the BIR recast have both a negative and positive effect.

First, Art 25 (1) provides a ground of jurisdiction; if the parties have agreed that courts of a Member State are to have jurisdiction that court shall have jurisdiction. According to the English case law this provision applies to optional as well as exclusive jurisdiction agreements.[77] Thus, if there is an optional choice of court agreement in favour of England, the English courts will have jurisdiction under Art 25 BIR recast. Previously, Art 23 only operated where one of the parties was also domiciled in a Member State but Art 25 is wider as explained in Sect. 1.2.1 above.

Choice of court agreements also have a negative effect under the BIR recast Art 31 by way of an exception to the normal *lis pendens* provisions. The general rule, under Art 29, is that where proceedings involving the same cause of action and between the same parties are brought in the courts of different Member States, any court other than the court first seised shall of its own motion stay its proceedings. However, that provision is subject to Art 31(2), which provides: "where a court of a Member State on which an agreement as referred to in Art 25 confers *exclusive* jurisdiction is seised, any court of another Member State shall stay the proceedings until such time as the court seised on the basis of the agreement declares that it has no jurisdiction under the agreement" (emphasis added). This is a new provision introduced to the BIR recast to reverse the effect of the decision of the CJEU in *Erich Gasser.*[78] However, it applies only to exclusive jurisdiction agreements (and

[76] [2009] EWCA Civ 725, [64].

[77] See e.g. *Antec v Biosafety* discussed above.

[78] Case C-116/02. The Lugano II Convention, not having been revised in light of BIR recast, does not contain any mechanism equivalent to Art 31.2.

possibly the exclusive element of a unilateral jurisdiction agreement, as to which see below).

There is one respect in which the interface between the BIR recast rules and the common law is unclear. If proceedings are commenced under the BIR recast rules, is it possible for those proceedings to be stayed in favour of a non-Member State? Jurisdiction agreements are potentially relevant in two ways.

First, if proceedings are commenced in England by virtue of a jurisdiction agreement in favour of the English courts, i.e. under Art 25, will it be possible to stay proceedings in favour of a non-Member State or is the usual *Spiliada* stay excluded?

It is unclear whether—once proceedings are commenced under Art 25—that jurisdiction is mandatory in the sense that no stay under national procedural rules is possible. The CJEU in *Owusu* held that if proceedings are commenced under Art 2 (now Art 4), on the basis that the defendant is domiciled in a Member State, a stay on *forum conveniens* grounds is not possible. English courts have suggested that the same reasoning would apply to proceedings commenced under Art 25.[79] It is important to note that while Arts 33 and 34 of the BIR recast introduced a limited answer to this problem they do not apply where proceedings are commenced on the basis of Art 25. Accordingly, the question is whether the doctrine of reflexive effect applies.

The other situation in which a jurisdiction agreement may be relevant is where proceedings are commenced under the BIR recast, e.g. under Art 4, Arts 7(1)(2) etc., and a stay is sought on the basis of a jurisdiction agreement in favour of a non-Member State. In certain circumstances a stay may be possible under Arts 33 and 34 of the BIR recast. If those provisions do not apply, e.g. because proceedings were commenced in the Member State first, it is unclear whether the court can fall back on the doctrine of reflexive effect.

2.3.5 Legal Effect of an Optional Choice of Court Agreement Under Hague Convention

The Hague Convention also contains rules covering both the positive and negative aspects of choice of court agreements. Article 5(1) provides:

> The court or courts of a Contracting State designated in an exclusive choice of court agreement shall have jurisdiction to decide a dispute to which the agreement applies, unless the agreement is null and void under the law of that State.

[79] See, e.g. *Konkola Copper Mines Plc v Coromin Ltd* [2006] EWCA Civ 5, per Rix LJ at [71]–[73]. Cf. *Oceanfix International Ltd v AGIP Kazakhstan North Caspian Operating Co NV*, 2009 G.W.D. 17-266; and see also *Skype Technologies SA v Joltid Ltd* [2009] EWHC 2783 (Ch); *Equitas Ltd v Allstate Insurance Co* [2009] Lloyd's Rep. I.R. 227; and *Jefferies International Ltd v Landesbanki Islands HF* [2009] EWHC 894 (Comm).

Under Article 6 the negative effect of an exclusive jurisdiction agreement is confirmed:

> A court of a Contracting State other than that of the chosen court shall suspend or dismiss proceedings to which an exclusive choice of court agreement applies unless -
>
> a) the agreement is null and void under the law of the State of the chosen court;
> b) a party lacked the capacity to conclude the agreement under the law of the State of the court seised;
> c) giving effect to the agreement would lead to a manifest injustice or would be manifestly contrary to the public policy of the State of the court seised;
> d) for exceptional reasons beyond the control of the parties, the agreement cannot reasonably be performed; or
> e) the chosen court has decided not to hear the case.

However, both of these provisions apply only to exclusive agreements. As to whether the provisions apply to the exclusive part of an asymmetric agreement see Sect. 3 below.

2.4 *Optional Choice of Court Agreements Involving Presumptively Weaker Parties*

Under the residual national rules no distinction is made in relation to the enforcement of choice of court agreements involving weaker parties.

Under the BIR recast different rules apply to consumers, employees and holders of insurance policies. As is noted in recital (14) of the recast Regulation: "in order to ensure the protection of consumers and employees . . . certain rules of jurisdiction in this Regulation should apply regardless of the defendant's domicile." The rules of protective jurisdiction which apply in relation to weaker parties share the common characteristic of restricting parties' ability to contract out of those rules to their detriment.

With regard to matters relating to insurance, Art. 15 sets out rules concerning the extent to which the "beneficiaries" of the provisions of Section 3 may depart from them,[80] namely, only by an agreement which:

> 1. . . . is entered into after the dispute has arisen; or
> 2. . . . allows the policyholder, the insured or a beneficiary to bring proceedings in courts other than those indicated in this Section; or
> 3. . . . is concluded between a policyholder and an insurer, both of whom are at the time of conclusion of the contract domiciled or habitually resident in the same Member State, and . . . has the effect of conferring jurisdiction on the courts of that Member State even if the harmful event were to occur abroad, provided that such an agreement is not contrary to the law of that Member State; or

[80] *Societe Financiere et Industrielle du Peloux v Axa Belgium* [2006] QB 251 ECJ.

4. . . . is concluded with a policyholder who is not domiciled in a Member State, except in so far as the insurance is compulsory or relates to immoveable property in a Member State; or
5. . . . relates to a contract of insurance in so far as it covers one or more of the risks set out in Article 16.

Article 16 excludes certain categories of risk, such as loss to seagoing ships, and "large" risks,[81] because certain specific risks are governed by sector-specific instruments.

In relation to consumers, Art 19 provides that,

The provisions of . . . Section [4] may be departed from only by an agreement:

1. which is entered into after the dispute has arisen;
2. which allows the consumer to bring proceedings in courts other than those indicated in this Section; or
3. which is entered into by the consumer and the other party to the contract, both of whom are at the time of conclusion of the contract domiciled or habitually resident in the same Member State, and which confers jurisdiction on the courts of that Member State, provided that such an agreement is not contrary to the law of that Member State.

Likewise, in relation to individual contracts of employment, Art 23 provides that,

The provisions of . . . Section [5] may be departed from only by an agreement:

1. which is entered into after the dispute has arisen; or
2. which allows the employee to bring proceedings in courts other than those indicated in this Section.

The Hague Convention expressly excludes consumer and employment contracts from its scope (Art 2(1)).

2.5 The Consequences of Bringing Proceedings in a Forum Other Than That Nominated in an Optional Choice of Court Agreement

2.5.1 Damages for Breach of a Choice of Court Agreement

A claim for damages arising from breach of a jurisdiction agreement can arise in two different circumstances. First, the party who sues abroad loses those proceedings. In these circumstances a claim for damages would seek to recoup the costs wasted in these proceedings. Alternatively, proceedings brought in breach of a jurisdiction agreement could be successful. A claimant may allege that if the proceedings had been brought in the agreed forum they would have failed. A claim for damages in such a case may include a claim in relation to costs, but also may include a claim for

[81] As defined in Directive 73/239/EEC on the coordination of laws, regulations and administrative provisions relating to the taking-up and pursuit of the business of direct insurance other than life insurance [1973] OJ L228/3, as amended.

substantial damages effectively to reverse the judgment which should not have been given.

At common law, the availability in principle of an action for damages for breach of a jurisdiction agreement has been confirmed by a number of cases.[82] In *Donohue v Armco*[83] the defendant's counsel conceded that damages were in principle available for any loss flowing from breach of a jurisdiction agreement, whether represented by the claimant's costs or any damages awarded in the foreign proceedings. More recently, the Supreme Court in *Starlight Shipping Company v Allianz Marine & Aviation (The Alexandros T)*,[84] accepted the possibility of such a claim in principle.

The availability of damages under the BIR recast is less clear cut. It is not certain that the CJEU would support a claim for damages for breach of a jurisdiction agreement, at least where the courts of another Member State are involved. There may be difficulties of issue estoppel if the other Member State's court has made findings about the scope or validity of the agreement. There may also be an argument that an award of damages, which in effect undoes the judgment of another Member State's court, would breach the principle of mutual trust and confidence. There are two reasons why it might be argued that damages should not be available in this situation. First, the combined effect of the decisions in *Turner v Grovit*[85] and *Erich Gasser* is that there is no *competence competence* for the chosen court: the policy of the Regulation is to allow the court first seized to test the validity of a jurisdiction agreement. It would be inconsistent with this principle to award damages for breach. However, there are two counter arguments: first (a) it could be argued that the procedural consequences of a jurisdiction agreement under the Regulation are different from contractual questions; and that (b) furthermore, the effect of *Erich Gasser* has been reversed by Art 31(2) which does give *competence competence* to the chosen court. Analogous arguments may also arise under the Hague Convention.[86]

The *Alexandros T*[87] litigation illustrates a number of the issues. The background was an insurance dispute following the loss of a vessel, the Alexandros T. Insurers refused to pay and the ship-owners sued in England alleging deliberate refusal and other allegations of misconduct. Those proceedings were eventually settled under settlement agreements which also contained an indemnity in relation to any other claim brought in connection with the loss of the Alexandros T. The agreements were expressly subject to English law and contained exclusive jurisdiction agreements in favour of the English courts. More than 3 years later new proceedings were commenced in Greece alleging breaches of the Greek civil and criminal codes, but based on substantially the same facts. The insurers then brought proceedings in England

---

[82] See Fentiman (2015), para 2.249.

[83] [2002] 1 Lloyd's Rep 425 (HL).

[84] [2013] UKSC 70.

[85] [2005] 1 AC 101; [2004] 3 WLR 1193.

[86] See Ahmed and Beaumont (2017).

[87] *Starlight Shipping Co v Allianz Marine and Aviation* [2013] UKSC 70.

claiming: (1) a declaration that the Greek claims fell within the terms of the release in the settlement agreement; (2) a declaration that the bringing of the Greek claims was a breach of the release in the settlement agreement; (3) damages for breach of the release in the settlement agreement; (4) a declaration that the bringing of the Greek claims was a breach of the jurisdiction clauses in the settlement agreement and the policies; (5) damages for breach of the jurisdiction clauses in the policies and settlement agreement; and (6) an indemnity under clause 3 of that agreement in respect of claims brought by Starlight and/or its associated companies in the various Greek proceedings.

The Supreme Court decision[88] concerned the application of Arts 27 and 28 BIR to these parallel sets of proceedings, in particular, whether the substantive claims in Greece constituted the same cause of action as the English proceedings. In relation to the claims relating to breach of the jurisdiction agreements the justices of the Supreme Court were in agreement.[89] Article 27 and 28 did not apply.

As to the availability of claim for damages itself Lord Clarke commented:

> I understand that this point has been reserved for decision by the Court of Appeal but, as I see it at present, nothing in the relief sought by the CMI offends the principle of mutual trust and confidence which underlies the Regulation: see e.g. *Erich Gasser GmbH v MISAT Srl (Case C-116/02) [2005] QB 1*. The CMI do not seek to stop the Greek proceedings or to restrain Starlight and OME from pursuing them. They merely seek declarations as to the true position under the settlement agreements which are both governed by English law and subject to the exclusive jurisdiction of the English courts and under the clauses in the insurance contracts which also provide for the exclusive jurisdiction of the English courts. This has the advantage that the courts with exclusive jurisdiction decide what is the true meaning of the settlement agreements and the jurisdiction clauses.[90]

Lord Neuberger stated that

> The difference between the English declaration claims and CMI's and LMI's claims in England for an indemnity and damages for breach of the settlement agreements ("the English indemnity and damages claims", ... may appear to be relatively small, but I believe that there is a crucial distinction, as a result of which it is *acte clair* that the English damages and indemnity claims do not fall foul of Article 27. The crucial difference is that, if those claims were successful, they could not lead to inconsistent judgments in England and Greece.
>
> I accept that, if they were successful, the English indemnity and damages claims could be fairly said to neutralise, at any rate in commercial terms, any benefit to Starlight and OME of a judgment in the Greek claims. However, crucially in my view, success for LMI and CMI in the English indemnity and damages claims would not be logically inconsistent in any way with success for Starlight in the Greek claims. It is not inconsistent (although it is commercially pointless) to say that a defendant is liable to pay a claimant a sum by way of damages, while the claimant is bound to indemnify the defendant in respect of the whole of that sum (or is bound to pay an equivalent sum to the defendant). Indeed, the indemnity is not merely logically consistent with the liability: it is positively meaningless without the liability for

[88][2013] UKSC 70.

[89]Lord Mance and Lord Neuberger took a different view in relation to the allegation that the claims had been settled.

[90][2013] UKSC 70, [39].

> damages, and the liability for damages, though rendered nugatory by the indemnity, is not logically inconsistent with the indemnity.[91]

Following the decision of the Supreme Court on the *lis pendens* points, the Court of Appeal heard the appeal on the substantive claims themselves. Having held that the Greek proceedings fell within the settlement and indemnity provisions, it followed that they fell within the exclusive jurisdiction clause in each agreement and the Greek proceedings accordingly breached that clause. However, the defendants asserted that a claim for damages interfered with the jurisdiction of the Greek court to determine its own jurisdiction—relying on *Turner v Grovit*. The Court of Appeal held that reliance was misplaced because *Turner v Grovit* related to anti-suit injunctions. The Greek court remained free to consider the Greek claims. It would have to decide whether to recognise any judgment of the English court, but that was not an interference with the jurisdiction of the Greek court but rather an acknowledgment of the Greek court's jurisdiction: accordingly there was no infringement of EU law.

The Court of Appeal accordingly gave summary judgment, with damages to be assessed.[92]

This reasoning was followed in *Barclays Bank v Ente Nazional de Presidenza*.[93] It was not disputed that proceedings in Milan fell within the language of an English exclusive jurisdiction clause. The first question was as to the applicability of Arts 27 and 28 BIR. The defendant (claimant in the proceedings in Milan) sought to distinguish *The Alexandros T* because the validity of the contract, including the jurisdiction agreement, was at issue in the proceedings in Milan. The judge disagreed and held that the reasoning applied and that these were not the same proceedings.

There was *prima facie* a breach of the jurisdiction agreement, however, the defendant raised as a defence to the claim for summary judgment for damages the argument that to award damages would be contrary to EU law. Again the judge rejected the attempt the distinguish *The Alexandros T* and the judge's decision was approved by the Court of Appeal:[94]

> In my view this proposition is not only unsupported by authority, it is impossible to reconcile with the decision of this court in *The 'Alexandros T'*. As the judge noted, the suggested analogy between ordering summary judgment and granting an anti-suit injunction was

[91] [2013] UKSC 70, [131]–[132].

[92] In relation to damages the question arose as to whether, if the claimant could recover the sums awarded by Greek court, account had to be taken of the fact that if sued in England (in accordance with the EJA) might have still be ordered to pay damages. The Court of Appeal said that it did not need to take this into account [2014] EWCA Civ 1010, [20]: "It is suggested by the owners that any claim for damages is premised on the assumption that the Greek claims would have failed on the merits if they had been advanced in England. But, quite apart from the fact that Tomlinson J refused permission to advance the claims in England (with the result that they have failed in England), the owners' breach of contract lies in the bringing of the claims. Whether they succeed in Greece or would have failed in England is irrelevant."

[93] [2015] EWHC 2857 (Comm).

[94] [2016] EWCA Civ 1261 at [35].

> specifically considered and rejected by Longmore L.J. in paragraphs 15–16 of his judgment. I am unable to accept that there is any material distinction between the present case and *The 'Alexandros T'* and in those circumstances it seems to me that we are bound to take the same view and hold that the judge was not precluded from granting summary judgment by considerations of that kind.

English authority accordingly supports the proposition that a claim for damages in these circumstances does not infringe the principle of mutual trust and confidence, although there is no decision of the CJEU supporting this.[95]

There may also be a further problem of issue estoppel if the Member State's court has made a finding that the jurisdiction agreement does not apply. That decision is binding under the BIR.[96] At common law a judgment is not binding if it is given in breach of a jurisdiction agreement (s 32 CJJA; see Sect. 2.5.5 below), but there is no equivalent in the BIR recast. However, it could be argued that a court in another Member State which finds that Art 25 does not exclude its jurisdiction is not thereby determining the contractual effect of the agreement, but only its procedural effect under the Regulation. The foreign court's finding that it has jurisdiction has a certain procedural effect that may be binding on that exact procedural question, but creates no issue estoppel as to any further private law consequences.[97]

The basis of such a claim for damages for breach of a jurisdiction agreement is breach of a promise, namely, that the defendant promised not to sue in a particular court, and in breach of that promise has done so. If the claimant can establish he has suffered loss as a result (whether wasted costs or sums he has been ordered to pay), he can claim damages for breach of that promise. The cases reflect and confirm the common law view of the private law consequences which flow from a choice of court agreement. Once an agreement, properly construed, includes a promise not to sue, if the borrower in breach of the promise sues elsewhere, there is no reason why a claim for damages should not be available. However, as discussed above, generally speaking the whole point about an optional choice of court agreement is that there is no promise not to sue elsewhere. Accordingly, if it is not a breach of contract to sue in the non-chosen forum there can be no claim for damages. As discussed in Sect. 2.5.3 below, some of the anti-suit injunction cases suggest that there might be an implied promise not to start or continue parallel proceedings in the non-chosen forum. There may also be a promise not to apply for a stay or not to apply for an anti-suit injunction from another court. If losses have been suffered as a result of a breach of such a promise damages may be recoverable.

In relation to the exclusive part of an asymmetric agreement, damages should be available. This was the view of the judge in *Barclays Bank PLC v Ente Nazionale de*

[95]There was discussion in the Court of Appeal judgment in *Barclays Bank v Ente* [2015] EWHC 2857 (Comm) (at [36]) of the fact that there were exchanges in *AMT v Marzillier* [2017] UKSC 13 which suggested that the Supreme Court would have made such a reference.

[96]*Gothaer v Samskip* Case 456/11.

[97]However, it may be difficult to say what loss has been caused in such a situation: see Fentiman (2015), para 2.269.

Previdenza dei Medici degli Odontoiatra.[98] The judge noted that, as is frequently agreed for good practical reasons in financing transactions, the clause in question stipulated that exclusivity in favour of one court did not prevent the financing institution from bringing an action in the courts of any other jurisdiction. The judge continued by noting that there had been a short debate in the skeleton arguments as to whether such a clause can be regarded as "exclusive". While the judge would have accepted the submission that it was exclusive, he noted that:

> [T]he issue for decision in the present case is a more limited one. Regardless of how the clause is characterised in terms of exclusivity, the issue is whether ENPAM is right to say that it is not in breach of it by pursuing proceedings in the Milan courts. In the *Continental Bank*[99] case the court concluded that the clause at issue there evinced a clear intention that the defendant (though not the bank) was obliged to submit disputes in connection with the loan facility at issue to the English courts. I consider that the same construction should be placed upon the jurisdiction clause in the PCA. I do not accept ENPAM's submission that the supposed 'non-exclusivity' of the clause means that the bringing of proceedings relating to the PCA by ENPAM in the Milan court is not a breach of the jurisdiction agreement. In my view, it clearly is a breach.

2.5.2 Damages Against a Claimant's Advisers

Breach of a promise not to sue in a non-chosen forum might also provide the basis for a claim in tort against the parties' advisers for inducing breach of contract. The possibility of such a claim was raised although not decided in *AMT Futures Ltd v Marzillier*.[100] AMTF was a derivatives broker. About 70 former clients commenced proceedings in Germany. The agreements between AMTF and each client contained a clause providing for English law and that the English courts would have exclusive jurisdiction. As well as suing its former clients for damages, AMTF also alleged that Marzillier, a German firm of lawyers, had induced its former clients to breach the jurisdiction agreement by issuing proceedings in Germany. AMTF commenced proceedings in London based on the tort of inducing breach of contract, and claimed damages and an injunction. The judge at first instance found that the English court had jurisdiction under Art 5.3 BIR. The Court of Appeal disagreed and held the BIR did not give jurisdiction to the English courts over AMTF's claim. Accordingly, it

[98] [2015] EWHC 2857 (Comm), [127]–[128]. The clause at issue provided: "... each of the parties irrevocably:

(a) agrees for [C's] benefit that the courts of England shall have jurisdiction to settle any suit, action or other proceedings relating to this Agreement ('Proceedings') and irrevocably submits to the jurisdiction of such courts (provided that this shall not prevent us from bringing an action in the courts of any other jurisdiction); and

(b) waives any objection which it may have at any time to the laying of venue of any Proceedings brought in any such court and agrees not to claim that such Proceedings have been brought in an inconvenient forum or that such court does not have jurisdiction over it."

[99] *Continental Bank v Aeakos* [1994] 1 WLR 588.

[100] [2017] UKSC 13.

did not need to address the issue which had been raised as to whether the English claim breached EU law by impermissibly interfering with the judgments of the German courts.

However, again the problem with an optional agreement is whether there has been breach of a promise at all? If such a claim was available for breach of the agreement not to sue in an exclusive jurisdiction agreement, for the reasons discussed above, there is no reason why such a claim should not be available against the advisers of the borrower under an asymmetric agreement.

2.5.3 Anti-suit Injunctions at Common Law

An anti-suit injunction is an order of the English court restraining a party over which it has jurisdiction from commencing or continuing proceedings abroad. An anti-suit injunction is an equitable injunction, now granted in England under s 37 of the Senior Courts Act 1981.[101] The power is wide and "the injunction can be granted against a party properly before the court where it is appropriate to avoid injustice".[102]

Outside the scope of operation of the BIR recast and the Lugano II Convention, Scottish courts have an equivalent power (traditionally referred to as "restraint of foreign proceedings") to interdict any person who is subject to their jurisdiction, preventing that party from raising, or proceeding with, an action in a foreign court between the same parties and relating to the same subject matter as that before the Scots court. Although a Scots court has no power to restrain a foreign court from proceeding to hear any action, it has power to restrain a person subject to its jurisdiction from proceeding with an action in a foreign court. Scots courts, however, have been less enthusiastic in their use of the remedy than have courts in England.[103]

An anti-suit injunction will not be granted merely because the English court is the *forum conveniens*. An anti-suit injunction is not a corollary to a refusal to stay;[104] furthermore, relief will not be granted merely to prevent parallel proceedings. The injunction will be granted only where the applicant shows that it would be unconscionable, vexatious or oppressive to pursue the proceedings before the foreign court.

[101]This provides that "(1) The High Court may by order (whether interlocutory or final) grant an injunction or appoint a receiver in all cases in which it appears to the court to be just and convenient to do so. (2) Any such order may be made either unconditionally or on such terms and conditions as the court thinks just".

[102]*Castanho v Brown & Root* [1981] AC 557, 573.

[103]See Crawford and Carruthers (2015), paras 7-83 et seq.

[104]*Royal Bank of Canada v Cooperative Centrale Raiffeisen Borenleenbank BA* [2004] EWCA Civ 7; [2004] 2 All ER (Comm) 847: Stricter rules apply to the grant of an anti-suit injunction: in *Donohue v Armco*, Lord Bingham stated: "I am mindful that the principles governing the grant of injunctions and stays are not the same [as those governing the grant of anti-suit injunctions]. . . . Considerations of comity arise in the one case but not in the other.": [2001] UKHL 64 at [24].

However, the position is different where the court is protecting a substantive right. Although an injunction restraining a breach of contract is not granted automatically, it will be granted unless there is a strong reason not to do so. The most common example is an injunction to protect the right to an agreed venue. In the case of an exclusive jurisdiction agreement, there is a promise not to sue in the other jurisdiction and relief will readily be granted.[105]

However, it is only in the case of an exclusive jurisdiction agreement that the parties have agreed not to sue in another jurisdiction. Accordingly, one would expect that one of the key practical or commercial differences between exclusive and optional clauses would be that an anti-suit injunction will be routinely available to enforce an exclusive, but not an optional agreement. However, the cases are inconsistent and the principles far from clear. There are two reasons for this:

(1) First, the willingness of the courts to imply terms concerning parallel proceedings into an optional agreement, in particular, an implied promise that once proceedings are commenced in the chosen forum, the other party will not commence proceedings elsewhere or will discontinue proceedings elsewhere if they had already started.
(2) Second, there are cases where, even if there is no implied term, courts have said that an optional jurisdiction clause means that proceedings can be assumed to be vexatious or oppressive so that an anti-suit injunction can be granted even if there is no breach of contract.

Both of these arguments are based on the same underlying assumption, namely, that the parties would not have intended to allow parallel proceedings.[106] However, as to whether this is a legitimate assumption in cases where there is an optional jurisdiction agreement, there are cases going both ways and some appear to be inconsistent.

An anti-suit injunction was granted in the case of *Sabah Shipyard (Pakistan) Ltd v Pakistan*.[107] A guarantee contained the following jurisdiction agreement: "Each party consents to the jurisdiction of the Courts of England for any action filed by the other party under this agreement" (clause 1.9). The claimant sought an anti-suit injunction restraining the Government of Pakistan ("GOP") from continuing

---

[105]See the passage from *Donohue v Armco* quoted in Sect. 2.3.1 above.

[106]For example, in *Dicey, Morris & Collins* (2012), para 12-107, it is said: "It may be that, on its true construction, though the court was given non-exclusive jurisdiction, the parties agreed that if either were to invoke it, the other would submit to the jurisdiction of the named court *for the sole determination of the dispute* [emphasis added]. It would follow that proceedings taken in a foreign court would breach such a jurisdiction agreement if they sought to prevent the other party from invoking the jurisdiction agreement, or if they aimed to frustrate or prevent the other party having recourse to it." See also Briggs (2014), para 4.423: "[I]f the court finds that the parties did not intend, or cannot have intended, that there should be parallel litigation in separate countries, this may encourage it to see the jurisdiction clause as exclusive. Another possibility is that the clause was non-exclusive until one party invoked it, rather as is the case with an option, which imposes no obligation until the party who is entitled to exercises the option".

[107][2002] EWCA Civ 1643.

proceedings in Pakistan. As part of the proceedings in Pakistan, the GOP had obtained an injunction restraining Sabah from making any demand under the guarantee: it was common ground that this had the effect of preventing Sabah from commencing proceedings in England.

Before the judge at first instance it was not argued that the clause was exclusive. However, this was at issue in the Court of Appeal where it was held that clause 1.9. did not lend itself to a transitive construction and was not exclusive in the sense of making it a breach to commence proceedings other than in England. Despite this, the Court of Appeal upheld the grant of an anti-suit injunction. Waller LJ held that if proceedings had been commenced in England before the GOP commenced their proceedings in Pakistan, then the commencement of such proceedings in Pakistan would have been vexatious and oppressive unless the GOP could show some exceptional reason why parallel proceedings were justified. The fact that the GOP commenced their proceedings first could not change the position. Similarly, Pill LJ put it in the following way:

> Whatever label is attached to it the intention and effect of clause 1.9 [the jurisdiction clause] is that, if proceedings were commenced in England, parallel proceedings could not, in the absence of exceptional reasons be pursued elsewhere. Moreover that intention is not defeated by the government of Pakistan having commenced proceedings in Pakistan first. Once the English proceedings were commenced clause 1.9 operated to confer a jurisdiction on the English court which requires the court in the present circumstances to act by way of injunction to give effect to the agreement of the parties.[108]

This analysis adopts the second of the two approaches referred to above: even if there was no breach of contract, parallel proceedings where there was an optional jurisdiction agreement were presumed to be vexatious or oppressive. However, Waller LJ also relied on the fact that the GOP's conduct in seeking an anti-suit injunction against the English proceedings also demonstrated that its conduct was vexatious and oppressive. As will be described below, later cases have distinguished *Sabah*, and explained it more narrowly on the basis that the proceedings were vexatious and oppressive because they also included a claim for an anti-suit injunction which was clearly in breach of the submission to English jurisdiction.

The first of the cases which took a narrower view and distinguished *Sabah* was *Royal Bank of Canada v Cooperative Centrale*[109] where there was an optional jurisdiction agreement in favour of England. Claims were brought in New York, but the Court of Appeal refused to grant an anti-suit injunction to restrain the continuation of those proceedings. In this case, the jurisdiction clause expressly contemplated the possibility of parallel proceedings. The court held that this jurisdiction agreement could not be said to make England the "primary forum" for the trial of the action because the parties clearly contemplated other proceedings.

An injunction was refused in *Highland Crusader Offshore Partners LP v Deutsche Bank AG.*[110] The agreement at issue contained a clause whereby the parties

[108] [2002] EWCA Civ 1643, [52].

[109] [2004] EWCA Civ 7.

[110] [2009] EWCA Civ 725.

"hereby irrevocably submit for all purposes of or in connection with this Agreement to the jurisdiction of the courts of England". The clause also expressly provided "Nothing in this paragraph shall limit the right of any party to take proceedings in the courts of any other country of competent jurisdiction".

At first instance, the judge had granted an anti-suit injunction to prevent proceedings in Texas, relying on a broad reading of the decision in *Sabah* discussed above. The judge held that even if there was no breach of contract, if either contracting party took proceedings elsewhere, "the policy of the law must be to favour the litigation of issues only once in the most appropriate forum"[111]. Accordingly, the judge held that "where there is a contractual non-exclusive jurisdiction clause, a party will ordinarily act vexatiously and oppressively in pursing proceedings in the non-contractual jurisdiction unless there are exceptional reasons not foreseeable at the time."[112]

The Court of Appeal overturned this decision. The court referred to and adopted the criticism of *Sabah* by commentators,[113] and the view of Andrew Smith J in *Evialis SA v SIAT*,[114] where he adopted a narrow explanation of *Sabah* as being based on the breach of contract in obtaining an anti-suit injunction. The Court of Appeal refused to apply a presumption that proceedings brought in a non-chosen venue could be presumed to be vexatious or oppressive. [115] The Court of Appeal concluded that:

> The starting point for considering the effect of a non-exclusive jurisdiction clause must be the wording of the clause. In terms of contract law, I cannot see how a party could ordinarily be said to be in breach of a contract containing a non-exclusive jurisdiction clause merely by pursuing proceedings in an alternative jurisdiction. It is conceivable that a jurisdiction clause which is not fully exclusive may nevertheless be drafted in such a way as to have the effect of barring parallel proceedings in certain circumstances, but that is a matter of individual contractual interpretation. Looking at the matter in general terms, I agree with Raphael's suggestion in The Anti-Suit Injunction at para 9.12 that
>
> 'where a non-exclusive jurisdiction clause does not clearly indicate whether prior or subsequent parallel proceedings in a non-selected forum are permitted or prohibited, the best interpretation will usually be that, by contracting for non-exclusive jurisdiction, the parties have anticipated and accepted the possibility of some parallel proceedings, and as a result, only foreign proceedings which are vexatious and oppressive for some reason independent of the mere presence of the non-exclusive clause will be restrained by injunction.'[116]

The Court of Appeal accordingly disagreed with the underlying assumption that parties would not have anticipated parallel proceedings. Duplication of litigation

[111][2009] EWCA Civ 725, [40].

[112][2009] EWCA Civ 725, [40].

[113][2009] EWCA Civ 725, [85] and [86] noting that "normally, a non-exclusive jurisdiction agreement will contemplate the possibility of simultaneous trials and if a trial is pursued abroad, there will not only be no breach of agreement but also no vexatious or oppressive conduct."

[114][2003] EWHC 863 (Comm); [2003] 2 Lloyd's Rep. 377.

[115][2003] EWHC 863 (Comm); [2003] 2 Lloyd's Rep. 377, [112].

[116][2003] EWHC 863 (Comm); [2003] 2 Lloyd's Rep. 377, [105]–[106].

through parallel proceedings is undesirable, but it is an inherent risk where the parties use an optional jurisdiction clause. The Court of Appeal also emphasised that such a presumption would come close to treating an optional clause as an exclusive jurisdiction clause once proceedings were commenced under it, whereas there was an important difference. The same view was taken by Andrew Smith J in *SwissMarine Corp Ltd v OW Supply & Trading A/S (in Bankruptcy).*[117] He refused to grant an anti-suit injunction in support of a clause which provided expressly for non-exclusive jurisdiction in England and also contained another jurisdiction provision. There was no room to infer that proceedings brought other than in England were in breach of the agreement to submit to the English courts because they would deprive the claimant of a right to litigate in a chosen non-exclusive jurisdiction, or they would render it worthless. He stated that "The express agreement that the jurisdiction was not exclusive means that the parties have the right to bring proceedings elsewhere, and [the other jurisdiction provision] means that that right is not lost to one party if the other brings proceedings in the chosen non-exclusive jurisdiction".[118]

Although ultimately it is a question of construction in each case what the parties have or have not agreed, so that apparently inconsistent cases are not necessarily wrong, there are cases where the reasoning seems inconsistent with the approach set out above. In *BNP Paribas SA v Anchorage Capital Europe LLP*,[119] the contract contained a term which provided: "This Agreement shall be governed by, and construed in accordance with, English Law and you irrevocably submit to the jurisdiction of the English courts in respect of any matter arising out of this Agreement."

Males J correctly started with the question of construction, asking whether "on its proper construction the clause obliges the parties to resort to the relevant jurisdiction, irrespective of whether the word 'exclusive' is used"; in other words, whether the commencement and pursuit of the foreign proceedings in question were things which a party had promised not to do. However, although that was not the case, he continued: "it is clear that the jurisdiction clause in this case constitutes a promise by Anchorage to submit to the jurisdiction... *and thus gives BNPP the right to litigate in England*, ...if BNPP chooses to litigate here."[120] (emphasis added). He continued:

> Since it is clear that BNPP wishes to exercise its right to litigate these issues in England, the next question is whether by seeking to litigate them in New York Anchorage is in breach of its promise to submit to the jurisdiction of the English court in respect of those matters. That question must be addressed with a measure of common sense. The clause provides that BNPP is entitled to litigate its claim here if it wishes to. It is entitled to require Anchorage to honour its promise to submit to the jurisdiction of the English court. By attempting to litigate in New York, Anchorage is seeking to deprive BNPP of that right or, at the least, to render it

[117][2015] EWHC 1571 (Comm); [2016] 1 All ER (Comm) 1144.

[118][2015] EWHC 1571 (Comm); [2016] 1 All ER (Comm) 1144, [37]–[38].

[119][2015] EWHC 3077. Andrew Smith J in *SwissMarine Corporation Limited* [2015] EWHC 1571 refused to apply the same reasoning.

[120][2015] EWHC 3077, [89].

> worthless. It would make no sense, in my judgment, to construe the clause as permitting Anchorage, so long as it submits to the jurisdiction of the English court, also to bring a claim of its own in New York in respect of essentially the same matters as arise here. It cannot sensibly be supposed that the parties would have regarded such a prospect as acceptable. On the contrary they would rightly have regarded it as a procedural nightmare.[121]

The reasoning in *BNP Paribas* was followed by Teare J in *Global Maritime Investment Cyprus Ltd v OW Supply & Trading NS*.[122] However, there are two problems with this reasoning. First, while the court correctly started by saying that the clause required the defendant to submit, the judge continued by implying that this gave the claimant the *right to litigate in England*. Furthermore, it is clear from the reasoning which followed, that the judge meant a right to litigate *solely* in England. This may be what the parties bargained for, but it does not follow from an agreement to submit in advance that there is also a promise that England will be the sole country with jurisdiction to hear the claim; if it did, it would be hard to see how an optional clause could be distinguished from an exclusive clause. It seems difficult to reconcile an agreement which gives one a right to sue abroad (because it is said to be a non-exclusive clause), but conversely gives the other party a right to be sued solely in England.

Second, the reasoning relies on the underlying assumption that the parties would not have allowed proceedings in two jurisdictions simultaneously. As has been described, this assumption was doubted and not followed by the Court of Appeal in *Highland Crusaders*. Where there is an optional clause, the best interpretation will usually be that, by contracting for non-exclusive jurisdiction, the parties have anticipated and accepted the possibility of some parallel proceedings. While undesirable, there is always a risk of parallel proceedings unless the parties agree on a venue with exclusive jurisdiction.

Although the clauses at issue in *Royal Bank of Canada*, *Highland Crusaders* and *SwissMarine* (which were all cases where the court took a strict view) all contained an express other jurisdiction provision, the reasoning should not turn on that. The key point is that in any optional jurisdiction agreement there is no promise not to sue in another jurisdiction, thus no agreement that England is the sole forum, and accordingly there is an inherent risk of parallel proceedings. This should be the default position unless the parties have provided otherwise. As Burton J noted in *Deutsche Bank v Sebastian Holdings*,[123] an express other jurisdiction clause merely makes express the assumption behind all non-exclusive jurisdiction agreements, i.e. that, saying it is a non-exclusive clause means the parties are free to sue elsewhere.

This point was also made in *Cuccolini SRL v Elcan Industries Inc*:[124] Elcan submitted that, when considering the relative appropriateness of competing fora, the

---

[121] [2015] EWHC 3077, [91]–[92].

[122] [2015] EWHC 2690 (Comm), [53]. Although technically the decision could be said to be *obiter* as the judge had decided that the clause was an exclusive jurisdiction clause.

[123] [2009] EWHC 3069 (Comm); [2010] 1 All E.R. (Comm) 808.

[124] [2013] EWHC 2994.

precise terms of the relevant jurisdiction clause should be considered. That may be right in theory, but in practice there seems to be little difference between an agreement such as the present which expressly recognises the right of the parties to bring proceedings in other courts having jurisdiction and an agreement which merely vests the English courts with non-exclusive jurisdiction. In either event, the possibility of proceedings in other jurisdictions must have been in the parties' reasonable contemplation when making their agreement, and they have vested the English courts with jurisdiction in that knowledge and contemplation.

2.5.4 Anti-suit Injunctions Under the BIR Recast

The CJEU in *Turner v Grovit* [125] held that the grant of an anti-suit injunction against the court of another Member State was not allowed since it breached the mutual trust and confidence between the courts of Member States and the *effet utile* of the Regulation. Thus anti-suit injunctions are not available against proceedings in another Member State.

2.5.5 Recognising a Judgment Given in Breach of a Choice of Court Agreement at Common Law

In the UK, the rules which apply to the enforcement of foreign judgments depend on which court gave the judgment.

Where the judgment is of a non-Member State court, there are two statutory enforcement regimes.[126] However, the substantive rules mirror the common law rules so do not need to be considered separately for this purpose.

At common law, a judgment will not be recognised or enforced if obtained in proceedings in breach of a valid jurisdiction agreement unless the judgment debtor submitted to the foreign court's jurisdiction. Section 32 of the CJJA 1982[127] provides:

32 **Overseas Judgments Given in Proceedings Brought in Breach of Agreement for Settlement of Disputes**

(1) Subject to the following provisions of this section, a judgment given by a court of an overseas country in any proceedings shall not be recognised or enforced in the United Kingdom if—

[125] [2005] 1 AC 101; [2004] 3 WLR 1193.

[126] The Reciprocal Enforcement of Judgments (Administration of Justice) Act 1920 and the Foreign Judgments (Reciprocal Enforcement) Act 1933.

[127] There is a similarly worded provision under the Foreign Judgments (Reciprocal Enforcement) Act 1933.

(a) the bringing of those proceedings in that court was contrary to an agreement under which the dispute in question was to be settled otherwise than by proceedings in the courts of that country; and
(b) those proceedings were not brought in that court by, or with the agreement of, the person against whom the judgment was given; and
(c) that person did not counterclaim in the proceedings or otherwise submit to the jurisdiction of that court.

(2) Subsection (1) does not apply where the agreement referred to in paragraph (a) of that subsection was illegal, void or unenforceable or was incapable of being performed for reasons not attributable to the fault of the party bringing the proceedings in which the judgment was given.
(3) In determining whether a judgment given by a court of an overseas country should be recognised or enforced in the United Kingdom, a court in the United Kingdom shall not be bound by any decision of the overseas court relating to any of the matters mentioned in subsection (1) or (2).
(4) Nothing in subsection (1) shall affect the recognition or enforcement in the United Kingdom of—

(a) a judgment which is required to be recognised or enforced there under the 1968 Convention [or the Lugano Convention][or the Regulation];
(b) a judgment to which Part I of the Foreign Judgments (Reciprocal Enforcement) Act 1933 applies by virtue of section 4 of the Carriage of Goods by Road Act 1965, section 17(4) of the Nuclear Installations Act 1965, . . . [section 6 of the International Transport Conventions Act 1983], section 5 of the Carriage of Passengers by Road Act 1974 or [section 177(4) of the Merchant Shipping Act 1995].

Thus, the question is whether the bringing of the proceedings in the judgment court was "contrary to an agreement under which the dispute in question was to be settled otherwise than by proceedings in the courts of that country". In relation to optional agreements, the application of section 32 turns on the issues of construction and whether a particular optional agreement can be read as including a positive obligation not to sue other than in the designated forum, issues which have been discussed above.

2.5.6 Enforcement Under BIR Recast

Where the judgment is from a court of a Member State, enforcement is under the BIR recast.[128]

It is not a defence to enforcement under the BIR recast that the judgment was given in breach of a jurisdiction agreement.

It would have been open to the drafters of the Regulation expressly to provide that judgments given in breach of an exclusive jurisdiction clause valid under Art 25 are not to be recognised in any Member State; they did so in relation to judgments given in breach of Article 24 (Art 45(1)(e)(ii)). They chose not to do so. Article 45(1)(e) provides that jurisdictional error may be a defence on restricted grounds,

[128]The Lugano II Convention applies in relation to judgments handed down by courts in EFTA states.

principally when a judgment is obtained contrary to a court's exclusive subject-matter jurisdiction under Art 24. However, this provision does not apply to Art 25. "A judgment may not be denied effect because in the opinion of the enforcing court it was obtained in breach of an exclusive jurisdiction agreement."[129] On the contrary, under Art 45(3) the jurisdiction of the judgment court cannot be reviewed and the test of public policy may not be applied to the rules relating to jurisdiction. Therefore, the general rule must be that judgments given by the court first seised are binding and enforceable in all other Member States. It may still be possible to argue that, in an extreme case, given other factors, the judgment is inconsistent with public policy, but it is difficult to think of many situations where that is likely to be the case[130] and breach of Art 25 will not, in itself, be enough. If this is the case for an exclusive jurisdiction agreement, *a fortiori* an optional agreement.

It should also be noted that in the context of arbitration agreements, Recital 12 of the BIR recast provides that where a court exercising jurisdiction under the Regulation or national law has determined that an arbitration agreement is null and void, inoperative or incapable of being performed, this should not preclude that court's judgment on the substance of the matter from being recognised or, as the case may be, enforced in accordance with the Regulation.

2.6 The Effect of Optional Choice of Court Agreements in Intra-UK Disputes

In the UK, there may be a choice among the jurisdictions of Scotland, Northern Ireland, England and Wales.

Allocation of jurisdiction among the legal systems of the UK is governed by the Civil Jurisdiction and Judgments Act 1982 (CJJA), on the basis of similar rules to those set out in the Regulation.

Part II of CJJA 1982 is headed "Jurisdiction, and recognition and enforcement of judgments, within United Kingdom". By section 16, the provisions set out in Schedule 4, which contain a modified version of BIR recast,[131] have effect for determining, for each part of the UK, whether the courts of that part, or any particular court in that part, have or has jurisdiction, where (a) the subject-matter of the proceedings is within

[129]Fentiman (2015), para 18.84.

[130]An obvious example might be where the parties have obtained judgment by ignoring an injunction against the continuing of proceedings as in *Philip Alexander Securities and Futures Ltd v Bamberger* [1997] IL Pr 72, where the court indicated that a judgment given in the face of an interlocutory injunction granted by the commercial court should not, as a matter of public policy, be recognised in the UK. But for the reasons explained in Sect. 2.5.4 above, given that it is no longer open to the court to grant an anti-suit injunction in these circumstances, it is unlikely that such a situation would arise in practice.

[131]Civil Jurisdiction and Judgments Act 1982, s 1, as amended by Civil Jurisdiction and Judgments (Amendment) Regulations 2014 (SI 2014/2947), Sch 1, para 2.

the scope of BIR recast, per Art 1 thereof; and (b) the defendant or defender is domiciled in the United Kingdom or the proceedings are of a kind mentioned in Art 24 of BIR recast (i.e. exclusive jurisdiction regardless of domicile).

Schedule 4, therefore, has two main functions: first, where, under BIR recast, jurisdiction is allotted to the "UK" generally, but not to a particular territorial unit thereof,[132] Schedule 4 supplies the lack. Secondly, it is utilised in cases which arise within the UK, but are related to more than one territorial unit within the UK.

The provisions of Schedule 4 follow those of the BIR recast, and in approach and detail are frequently the same, or similar. However, there are certain differences between the detail of BIR recast and Schedule 4. For example, while protective rules for consumers and employees are contained in Schedule 4, provisions for insured parties and beneficiaries equivalent to those found in BIR recast are not present in Schedule 4. Notably, the presumption of exclusivity of choice of court clauses, found in the prorogation provision of Art 25 of BIR recast, is not found in Schedule 4 rule 12 (prorogation).

Rule 12 provides that—

(1) If the parties have agreed that a court or the courts of a part of the United Kingdom are to have jurisdiction to settle any disputes which have arisen or which may arise in connection with a particular legal relationship, and, apart from this Schedule, the agreement would be effective to confer jurisdiction under the law of that part, that court or those courts shall have jurisdiction.
(2) The court or courts of a part of the United Kingdom on which a trust instrument has conferred jurisdiction shall have jurisdiction in any proceedings brought against a settlor, trustee or beneficiary, if relations between these persons or their rights or obligations under the trust are involved.
(3) Agreements or provisions of a trust instrument conferring jurisdiction shall have no legal force if they are contrary to the provisions of rule 9, or if the courts whose jurisdiction they purport to exclude have exclusive jurisdiction by virtue of rule 11.

There has been conflicting authority at shrieval level on the interpretation of this provision, and, specifically, the absence of the adjective "exclusive".[133] The Court of Session in *McGowan v Summit at Lloyds No 56*[134] concluded that the question whether the jurisdiction arising under a jurisdiction agreement is exclusive or non-exclusive depends on the law governing the agreement and not upon art

---

[132]e.g. for the provision of jurisdiction on the basis of the defendant's domicile under art. 4 of BIR recast, the international allocation of jurisdiction per the regulation is satisfied by a finding that the defendant is domiciled in the UK. Thereafter, identification of the domicile of the defendant as, e.g. between Scotland, and England and Wales, is determined by Sch. 4: *Daniel v Foster*, 1989 SCLR 378.

[133]See *Jenic Properties Ltd v Andy Thornton Architectural Antiques* 1992 SLT (Sh Ct) 5, and *British Steel Corporation v Allivane International Ltd.* 1989 SLT (Sh Ct) 57.

[134]2002 SC 638. See also *Douglas v Glenvarigill Co Ltd* [2009] CSOH 17; 2009 SCLR 379.

17 [now rule 12] of Schedule 4. Lord Reed, delivering the opinion of the Court, stated that,[135]

> The only general principle of interpretation to be extracted from the authorities, in our view, is that which was stated by Hobhouse J in *Berisford* (at p. 637): '[T]he same canons of construction are to be applied in relation to this type of clause as any other mutual contractual provision. It is a matter of construing the words used in accordance with their natural meaning and in the light of the surrounding circumstances in which the contract was made.' There is however nothing new about that principle in Scots law.
>
> All the cases cited are, we think, simply illustrations of an application of that principle, albeit a comparison between them demonstrates the obvious importance of the actual words used. As Hobhouse J observed in *Cannon Screen*: 'Words are an accurate tool and relatively small differences in wording will produce different contractual effects.' Such a comparison also demonstrates the importance of reading the contract as a whole: for example, a provision for an address for service only within the chosen jurisdiction, or the conferring of an option on only one party to bring proceedings elsewhere, may be important. The surrounding circumstances may also colour the interpretation to be placed upon the words used; and it is possible to identify, in the cases which we have cited, particular circumstances which have been regarded as tending to point towards, or away from, the conferring of an exclusive jurisdiction. For example, the fact that a clause selecting a jurisdiction has been specifically agreed, and that the clause is apt to be invoked by either party to the contract, are factors which, *ceteris paribus*, may tend to point towards agreement on an exclusive jurisdiction. On the other hand, the fact that the clause appears in a printed form issued by one party to the other, and the considerations that exclusivity will in practice impose an obligation falling substantially on the party to whom such a form has been issued, and that the clause has (or could have, to other person to whom such a form might be issued) a commercial or legal significance even if construed as only declaratory, are factors which ceteris paribus may tend to point away from agreement of an exclusive jurisdiction. This of course is not intended as an exhaustive list, nor does it purport to lay down any rule of law.

Direct recourse cannot be had to the CJEU for interpretation of the provisions of Schedule 4.[136]

3 Asymmetric Choice of Court Agreements

3.1 Asymmetric Choice of Court Agreements at Common Law

Asymmetric clauses take different forms and their proper construction may depend on their exact wording. But some general points can be made assuming a typical borrower/lender situation.

The most extreme pro-bank construction would be an agreement whereby the borrower agrees to submit to the exclusive jurisdiction of the English court and any

---

[135] 2002 SC 638, [51]–[52].

[136] TFEU art 267 (ex-EC Treaty art 234). See also *Kleinwort Benson Ltd v Glasgow City Council (No. 2)* [1997] 4 All ER 641.

other court in which the bank chooses to sue.[137] If that was the correct construction, it would be entirely one sided and extremely wide:

(1) The borrower would be positively agreeing to submit to the courts of any possible country depending on where the bank chose to sue.
(2) The borrower would also negatively promise only to sue the bank in England and in no other jurisdiction.
(3) The bank would not be agreeing anything.

However, under English law, clauses tend not to be construed in that way.

(1) The first aspect of the clause is usually construed as meaning that the bank can sue *in any court of competent jurisdiction*.[138] The borrower submits to the jurisdiction of the chosen court, but does not agree positively to give any other court jurisdiction. Rather, this part of the clause makes it clear that from the bank's point of view the clause is optional, i.e. the bank can sue elsewhere, but only if that court would otherwise have jurisdiction under its relevant jurisdictional rules.
(2) Second, even if the jurisdiction is not expressly said to be exclusive as against the borrower the court will usually imply a promise not to sue elsewhere. The juxtaposition of a submission to the English court's jurisdiction, plus a provision for the benefit of one party only permitting proceedings to be commenced elsewhere, will usually lead the court to construe the obligation as against the borrower as being exclusive.[139] In other words, such clauses are usually construed as including a promise by the borrower, but not the lender, not to sue anywhere other than in England.
(3) Thirdly, such clauses tend to be construed as also constituting a submission by the bank to the English court's jurisdiction.[140] The fact that the bank at least promises to be sued in a particular forum may be important as otherwise the clause would be entirely one-sided.[141] The bank is usually held to have promised to submit to the jurisdiction of the English court even if it would not otherwise have jurisdiction, but nothing else.

Three arguments have been suggested as to why asymmetric agreements may not be valid at common law:

(1) imbalance between the parties;
(2) article 6 ECHR; and
(3) uncertainty.

[137] Fentiman (2015), para 2.127, describes this as a "unilateral floating jurisdiction agreement".

[138] See *Mauritius Commercial Bank v Hestia* [2013] EWHC 1328 (Comm).

[139] See *Continental Bank v Aekos* [1994] 1 WLR 588 applied in *Credit Suisse First Boston (Europe) Ltd v MLC (Bermuda) Ltd* [1999] CLC 579.

[140] See, for example, *Mauritius Commercial Bank v Hestia* [2013] EWHC 1328 (Comm).

[141] And may fail for lack of consideration: see, for example, Draguiev (2014), p. 27.

3.1.1 Imbalance Between the Parties

The starting point at common law is the principle of party autonomy. The fact that a contractual provision gives better rights to one party than the other does not matter: if the intention is clear it will be upheld and the courts will not rewrite the agreement.

Unless an asymmetric jurisdiction agreement falls into a species of agreement which the common law considers, by its very nature, to be contrary to the policy of the law (like the penalty clause doctrine),[142] a mere imbalance between the parties will make no difference to enforcement.

English case law overwhelmingly supports the view that there is no reason why the imbalance in a jurisdiction clause should make any difference to its enforcement; on the contrary, party autonomy should be respected.[143] For example, in *NB Three Shipping Ltd v Harebell Shipping Ltd*,[144] which concerned a one-sided option to arbitrate, the judge held that the fact that the clause was designed to give "better rights" to one party was no bar to its enforcement. Any other result would "contradict the commercial sense of the clause as a whole". This reasoning was applied in *Law Debenture Trust Corporation PLC v Elektrim Finance BV* [145] which concerned a similar clause, although the other way round (that is, a one-sided option to bring court proceedings). The judge commented that it was not "correct so say that the provisions are somehow less than even handed in any relevant way. They give an additional advantage to one party, but so do many contractual provisions…".

Thus, generally imbalance between the parties will not be a reason not to enforce the contractual promises in an asymmetric agreement.

3.1.2 Article 6 European Convention on Human Rights

An argument sometimes relied on in the context of choice of court agreements is that asymmetric clauses infringe Art 6 ECHR. However, this argument was expressly rejected in *Mauritius Commercial Bank Ltd v Hestia Holdings Limited*:[146]

> The public policy to which [the enforcement of asymmetric agreements] was said to be inimical was 'equal access to justice' as reflected in Article 6 of the ECHR. But Article 6 is directed to access to justice within the forum chosen by the parties, not to choice of forum.

[142]See *Cavendish Square Holding BV v Makdessi* Joined with the appeal in *Parking Eye Limited v Beavis* [2015] UKSC 67 per Lord Neuberger and Lord Sumption at [9].

[143]English cases upholding asymmetric clauses include: *NB Three Shipping Ltd v Harebell Shipping Ltd* [2004] EWHC 2001 (Comm); *Law Debenture Trust Corporation PLC v Elektrim Finance BV* [2005] EWHC 1412 (Ch); *Lornamead Acquisitions Limited v Kaupthing Bank HF* [2011] EWHC 2611 (Comm); *Mauritius Commercial Bank Ltd v Hestia Holdings Limited* [2013] EWHC 1328 (Comm); *Barclays Bank PLC v Ente Nazionale* [2015] EWHC 2857 (Comm).

[144][2014] EWHC 2001 (Comm).

[145][2005] EWHC 1412 (Ch), [46].

[146][2013] EWHC 1328 (Comm), [43].

> No forum was identified in which the Defendant's access to justice would be unequal to that of [the bank] merely because the bank had the option of choosing the forum.

An analogous argument has been relied on to explain why anti-suit injunctions do not infringe Art 6. In particular, in *OT Africa Line Ltd v Hijazy (The Kribi)(No 1)*,[147] the court explained that Art 6 of the ECHR does not deal at all with *where* the right to a "fair and public hearing before an independent and impartial tribunal established by law" is to be exercised by a litigant. The crucial point is that civil rights must be determined *somewhere* by a hearing and before a tribunal in accordance with the provisions of Art 6.[148]

3.1.3 Uncertainty

An argument that a jurisdiction agreement is too uncertain to be enforced is not specific to asymmetric agreements; similar arguments might apply to other choice of court agreements particularly those which do not clearly identify a single forum. It is always necessary to construe agreements and if they are uncertain they cannot be enforced. But construing the agreement involves identifying specific contractual promises: if that can be done, there is no reason why the fact that the promises differ for each party should make any difference. In other words, there is nothing inherent in asymmetric agreements which mean they are likely to fail a certainty test. Furthermore, as discussed in Sect. 3.1, such clauses can usually be construed to create certain albeit one-sided obligations.

For example, in *Hestia*[149] the judge noted that there was a dispute about the proper construction of the clause. It had been contended that it conferred a power to sue in any court of the world, rather than those courts which would otherwise regard themselves under their own rules of private international law as having competent jurisdiction. The judge held that this was an erroneous reading of the clause. Second, on a further question of construction, it had been argued that the clause was entirely one-sided because it conferred no rights on the defendant to sue in any forum. That too was an erroneous reading. The lender was agreeing to be sued in England (subject to its right to bring proceedings abroad). Thus, the judge adopted the construction of asymmetric clauses set out in Sect. 3.1 above and held that was sufficient to dispose of the defendant's application because it was accepted that there was no basis for challenging the clause if it was to be construed in that way.[150]

---

[147] [2001] Lloyds Rep 76, [42].

[148] "The principle of equality of arms concerns the position of the parties before a court, not whether the parties have an equal choice of forum": Fentiman (2015), para 2.149.

[149] [2013] EWHC 1328 (Comm), [37].

[150] A similar construction was adopted in *Commerzbank v Liquimar* [2017] EWHC 161 (Comm) and the same conclusion reached. Furthermore, the judge also commented *obiter* that he would not have acceded to the defendant's argument that the clause was invalid even if it bore the construction for which the defendant contended. "If, improbably, the true intention of the parties expressed in the clause was that [the bank] should be entitled to insist on suing or being sued anywhere in the world,

3.2 *Asymmetric Jurisdiction Agreements Under Brussels I Regulation Recast*

Under the BIR recast, two distinct questions arise in connection with asymmetric agreements. First, is an asymmetric agreement valid under Art 25 to confer jurisdiction on the chosen court and will that jurisdiction be exclusive as against the borrower? Second, does an asymmetric agreement engage Art 31(2) BIR recast and accordingly avoid the normal "first in time" *lis pendens* rule?

3.2.1 Asymmetric Jurisdiction Agreements Under Article 25 BIR Recast

Before the Brussels I Regulation ('BIR') came into effect,[151] there seemed to be little doubt that asymmetric clauses were valid. Article 17 of the Brussels Convention specifically referred to one-way clauses providing: "If an agreement conferring jurisdiction was concluded for the benefit of only one of the parties, that party shall retain the right to bring proceedings in any other court which has jurisdiction by virtue of this Convention." The CJEU in *Anterist v Crédit Lyonnais*[152]confirmed that this provision[153] of the Brussels Convention applied to expressly asymmetric clauses. Furthermore, in *Meeth v Glacetal*[154] the CJEU also confirmed that a clause which named two different courts could fall within Art 17 [155] despite the fact that Art 17, as it was worded, referred to the choice by the parties to the contract of a single court or the courts of a single state. In both cases, the CJEU reasoning confirmed and emphasised respect for party autonomy.[156]

The wording of Art 25 BIR recast, and before that Art 23 BIR, differs from the wording of Art 17 in that the express provision dealing with clauses for the benefit of one party is omitted. On the other hand, Art 25 (and previously Art 23) expressly

---

that is the contractual bargain to which the court should give effect" [2013] EWHC 1328 (Comm), [43]. Cf. Fentiman (2015), para 2.141 arguing that a wider construction would not be valid under Art 25.

[151]Regulation 44/2001, which was replaced by the BIR recast. The Regulation itself replaced the Brussels Convention 1968.

[152]Case C-22/85.

[153]Article 17(3) of the version of the Convention in force at the time.

[154]Case C-23/78.

[155]The clause was asymmetric in that the obligations on each party differed (although it was not for the benefit of one particular party) and also was not exclusive in that it named two different courts.

[156]See in *Anterist* Case 22/85 at [14]: "Since Article 17 of the convention *embodies the principle of the parties' autonomy to determine the court or courts with jurisdiction*, the third paragraph of that provision must be interpreted in such a way as to respect the parties' common intention when the contract was concluded." (emphasis added). In *Meeth* Case 23/78 [5]: "This interpretation is justified on the ground that *Article 17 is based on a recognition of the independent will of the parties to a contract in deciding which courts are to have jurisdiction to settle disputes falling within the scope of the convention* ...'(emphasis added).

envisage the possibility of non-exclusive agreements. It was widely believed that the reference to clauses for the benefit of one party was not necessary given that non-exclusive agreements were now expressly envisaged.[157]

The controversy surrounding the enforcement of asymmetric agreements under the BIR flows from a series of decisions of the French Cour de cassation, starting with *Mme X v Banque Privee Edmund de Rothschild Europe (Societe).*[158] Mme X (a Spanish national domiciled in Paris) opened a private bank account with a Luxembourg bank. Mme X blamed the bank for the poor performance of her investments and issued proceedings in Paris. The standard terms and conditions of the bank included the following jurisdiction clause:

> The relations between the bank and the client are governed by Luxembourg law. The potential disputes between the client and the bank shall fall within the exclusive jurisdiction of the Luxembourg courts. However, the bank reserves the right to sue before the courts of the domicile of the client or before any other court having jurisdiction in the absence of selection of any of the courts previously referred to.:

The bank disputed the jurisdiction of the Paris court, arguing that under Art 23 BIR the Luxembourg courts had exclusive jurisdiction against Mme X. The French Court of Appeal decided that it did have jurisdiction despite the wording of the clause. The bank appealed.[159] The Cour de cassation dismissed the appeal and upheld the jurisdiction of the French court:

> [H]aving found that the clause, under the terms of which the bank reserved for itself the right to sue at the domicile of Mme X . . . or before 'any other court having jurisdiction' was only binding on Mme X . . . who was alone bound to sue before the Luxembourg courts, the Court of Appeal correctly deduced that it had an optional character (*caractère potestatif*) only for the bank, so that it was contrary to the object and purpose of the prorogation of jurisdiction provided for by article 23 of the Brussels I Regulation.[160]

The decision left at least three issues open:

(1) The extent to which it depended on the *caractère potestatif* doctrine of French law.
(2) The significance of the fact that the borrower was an individual.[161]

---

157 Fentiman (2013), p. 26. See also Financial Markets Law Committee (2016), [1.4].

158 French Cour De cassation (Supreme Court) (First Civil Chamber) [2013] I L Pr 12.

159 A claim was also brought against a French financial company based on Art 6.

160 Translation from [2013] I L Pr 12 at [9]. The Cour de cassation appeared to strike the clause down in its entirety. Whether it is possible to sever the unilateral part of the clause and salvage the rest (as to which see Garvey 2016, p. 8) should depend on the parties' intentions, in particular, whether the separate obligations contained in the agreement were intended to be conditional on one another.

161 Keyes and Marshall (2015), p. 367, note that although Madame X was plainly a consumer according to the Regulation, because the Bank seemingly did not direct its activities towards Madame X's place of domicile, the Regulation's jurisdictional rules that protect consumers did not apply. See also Petch (2016), p. 319, referring to two decisions in Luxembourg relying on her status as a consumer.

(3) To what extent the decision of the Cour de cassation depended on the very wide interpretation of the clause adopted by the court below, that is, that the borrower was submitting to any court the bank should choose to sue in.

In the next of the series of cases, *Société Danne v Crédit Suisse*,[162] the Cour de cassation considered a similar clause and came to the same conclusion, refusing to enforce the borrower's promise not to sue other than in the identified court. The lender had concluded two framework contracts for loans. The agreements included a jurisdiction clause which provided that the court of Zurich had exclusive jurisdiction, but that the bank was entitled to take action before any competent court. The borrower brought proceedings in France arguing that its negative obligation not to sue anywhere other than Zurich should not be enforced. The Cour de cassation agreed, holding that the clause was unenforceable because it did not set out an objective basis for the alternative jurisdictions which the bank could choose and that it was contrary, therefore, to the goal of certainty inherent in Art 23 of the Lugano Convention.[163]

In this case, the borrower was not an individual (see point (2) above). Furthermore, the court did not expressly refer to *potestatif* doctrine (point (1) above); the argument was based on a lack of certainty. However, it was unclear exactly how the clause was interpreted, in particular, whether the Cour de cassation interpreted the clause as seeking to confer jurisdiction (in favour of the bank) on any court, as opposed to any court with competent jurisdiction.

The final of the trio of cases is *Société eBizcuss.com v Apple*.[164] The jurisdiction agreement in this case provided:

> ... parties shall submit to the jurisdiction of the courts of the Republic of Ireland. Apple reserves the right to institute proceedings against Reseller in the courts having jurisdiction in the place where the Reseller has its seat [Ireland] or in any jurisdiction where a harm to Apple is occurring.

Proceedings had been commenced in France allegedly in breach of this agreement. However, in this case the Cour de cassation appeared to take a different view on the validity of the clause. The ratio of the decision is difficult to discern. An argument based on "potestatif character" was raised, but the Cour de cassation seemed to decide the case on a different basis. It held that:

> having noted that the jurisdiction clause required the eBizcuss company to bring its action before the Irish courts whereas it reserved the possibility for the other party, as an option, to seise another jurisdiction, the Court of Appeal correctly decided that this clause, which allowed the identification of the courts potentially to be seised to deal with a dispute arising between the parties in the course of performance or interpretation of the contracts, answered the imperative of foreseeability which jurisdiction clauses must satisfy. The ground of appeal is unfounded on this point.[165]

[162]French Supreme Court, First Civil Chamber, 25 March 2015, Case 13-27264 [2015] I L Pr 39.

[163]Which was in the same terms as Art 23 of the Brussels Regulation.

[164]French Supreme Court, First Civil Chamber, 7 October 2015 Case 14-16898.

[165]Translation [2016] I L Pr 13, [6].

On the facts the Cour de cassation concluded that the clause did not apply because it did not cover anti-competitive practices by Apple. However, the Cour de cassation's discussion of the clause seems to suggest that this clause was sufficiently certain to fall within Art 23 because it allowed the defendant to identify the courts in which Apple was entitled to sue, i.e. any jurisdiction where harm to Apple was occurring.

The *Rothschild* decision has been widely discussed[166] and followed in some other jurisdictions.[167] The Loan Markets Authority issued a memo in January 2013 warning of the risks now associated with the use of one-way jurisdiction clauses in lending documentation and advising its members of alternative approaches which might be taken.[168] This trio of decisions of the French Cour de cassation raised doubts about the validity of asymmetric agreements under Art 25 BIR recast in two different respects. The first is based on the *caractère potestatif* doctrine of French contract law. The second is a more general argument that such agreements breach requirements of certainty and foreseeability inherent in Art 25 itself.[169]

The reliance in *Rothschild* on the *caractère potestatif* doctrine in French law[170] raises two issues: first the role for national contract law in the application of Art 25 and, second, the application of the doctrine itself. Both of these points may need re-evaluation in the light of recent developments.

One of the criticisms of the *Rothschild* decision has been that any reliance on domestic contract law[171] was misplaced because the validity of a jurisdiction clause for the purposes of Art 23 BIR was a matter for Art 23 itself. For example, in *Roche Products Ltd v Provimi*[172] the judge, commenting on the role for national law in relation to the then equivalent provision in the Lugano Convention, said:

> There is some confusion here, in my view. Article 17 of the Lugano Convention is concerned with what English lawyers would probably call the 'formal' and 'material' validity of a

---

[166]See e.g. Fentiman (2013), p. 24: "*Rothschild* flies in the face of market practice and has caused consternation amongst practitioners. For many reasons the decision is as perplexing as it is controversial". Popplewell J in *Hestia* (in deciding whether or not the courts of Mauritius would be likely to follow *Rothschild*) commented at [34]: "The decision is controversial and has been subjected to criticism by commentators, both domestically and in the context of art. 23 which requires an autonomous interpretation. It is arguably inconsistent with previous decisions of the Cour de cassation, although consistent with decisions of the lower courts". Cf. Briggs (2014), para 4.190, suggesting that a clause which allowed one party to sue wherever he wishes, may overreach the limits of Art 25.

[167]See the summary in Financial Markets Law Committee (2016), [1.3] referring to decisions of the Bulgarian Supreme Court, French courts and Polish courts. A summary of relevant European legislation is set out in an Annex to the Report. See, for further comparative analysis, Draguiev (2014); Keyes and Marshall (2015), fn 4.

[168]See Beale and Clayson (2013), p. 464.

[169]Fentiman (2013), p. 25.

[170]It is unclear why the court referred to French law and not the law of Luxembourg, although the same doctrine is to be found in both: see Petch (2016), p. 320.

[171]Cf. Fentiman (2013), p. 25 suggesting that the French court did not apply French law directly so the decision contributes nothing to the familiar controversy about the relevance of national law in determining the validity of Art 23 agreements.

[172][2003] All ER (Comm) 683, [59].

> jurisdiction clause. It is clear that Article 17 defines the necessary and sufficient requirements for formal and material validity of jurisdiction clauses. Those requirements replace any requirements imposed by the various national laws.[173]

However, regardless of the position under the Brussels Convention and Art 23 BIR which was at issue in *Rothschild*, the position is more complex under Art 25 of the Recast regulation. As has been described in Sect. 2.3.2 above, Art 25 of the BIR recast provides that the courts designated in a jurisdiction agreement shall have jurisdiction "unless the agreement is null and void as to its substantive validity under the law of the [chosen] Member State."[174] This new proviso clearly reopens the door to reliance on national contract law in relation to questions of validity. However, the width of the proviso is yet to be established. Some commentators have argued that it should be narrowly construed and applies only to grounds which invalidate an existing agreement (such as fraud, duress or mistake), and not to all the requirements for a legally binding agreement, e.g. consideration, illegality etc.[175] Even if that narrow construction is right, it is not clear on what side of the line the *caractère potestatif* doctrine would fall.

Furthermore, there is also uncertainty about how the choice of law provision in Art 25 should work for asymmetric agreements. In an exclusive jurisdiction agreement, French contract law would be applicable if the chosen court would apply French contract law which would be most likely if the French courts were themselves the chosen courts.[176] In the case of an exclusive jurisdiction agreement in favour of England, a court even in France would almost certainly apply English contract law because that is the law which would be applied by the English court.[177]

[173]See also Briggs, noting that the CJEU had "gone out of its way to insist that the jurisdictional validity and jurisdictional effect of an agreement on jurisdiction, which falls within the domain of Art 23 is to be assessed not by reference to any national law, . . . but only by asking whether the consent of the party who is to be held to the agreement can be demonstrated with clarity and precision": (2008), p. 378.

[174]Recital (20) further provides "Where a question arises as to whether a choice of court agreement in favour of a court or the courts of a Member State is null and void as to its substantive validity, that question should be decided in accordance with the law of the Member State of the court or courts designated in the agreement, including the conflict of law rules of that Member State".

[175]Magnus and Mankowski (2016), Art 25 [33] conclude that the reference to national law in Art 25 relates only to grounds which invalidate an existing agreement, and not all the requirements for a legally binding agreement e.g. consideration etc. (see e.g. [81c].) See also Dickinson and Lein (2015), para 9.69: the reference to national law is, in principle, very limited: it only includes the grounds for material invalidity based on defects of consent (fraud, misrepresentation, duress or mistake), lack of authority or lack of capacity. It does not cover issues of contractual enforceability exogenous to the consent or capacity of the parties, such as illegality or public policy.

[176]Recital (20) provides that the question of validity should be decided in accordance with the law of the Member State of the court or courts designated in the agreement, including the conflict of law rules of that Member State.

[177]Agreements on choice of law are excluded from the scope of the Rome I Regulation (Art 1(2)(e)). At common law, although a choice of court agreement is a severable agreement, there is a presumption that it is governed by the same law as that which applies to the underlying agreement: *Mauritius Commercial Bank v Hestia* [2013] EWHC 1328 (Comm). If there is an exclusive jurisdiction agreement the underlying agreement is likely to be governed by English law: see, at

However, a further complication arises in the case of an asymmetric agreement as to which is the relevant "chosen court". This point was discussed in *Commerzbank v Liquimar*.[178] The judge rejected the argument that in order for Art 25 to operate there had to be a single court identified:

> This argument seems to overlook that in these asymmetric jurisdiction clauses the parties have designated the English court as having exclusive jurisdiction when the defendants sue. There is nothing in Article 25 that a valid jurisdiction agreement has to exclude any courts, in particular non EU Courts. Article 17, penultimate paragraph, of the Brussels Convention recognised asymmetric jurisdiction clauses. To my mind it would need a strong indication that Brussels 1 Recast somehow renders what is a regular feature of financial documentation in the EU ineffective.[179]

This would mean that the relevant chosen court, at least when the bank is suing, would be England in an asymmetric agreement where the lender has agreed to the exclusive jurisdiction of the English court. This would suggest that French contract law is only potentially likely to be relevant under Art 25 where France is the chosen court.

Further, and in any event, even if it is now possible, and indeed necessary, to look at national contract law under the new proviso to Art 25, there is a further development which might affect the *Rothschild* decision, namely the extensive changes made to French contract law by the new French Civil Code. Article 1170 of the version of the French Civil Code in force at the time of the cases referred to above provided: "A potestative condition is one which makes the execution of the agreement depend upon an event that one or the other of the contracting parties has the power to bring about or to prevent." Article 1174 of the same Code further provided: "Any obligation is null when it has been contracted subject to a potestative condition on the part of the party who binds himself."

The part of the French Civil Code dealing with contract law has been completely restructured and amended. The revised section came into force on 1 October 2016, the previous version having remained largely untouched since 1804. One of the aims was to get rid of out-of-date language, such as *potestatif*, and the express provisions set out above no longer appear. There are also changes of substance. Freedom of contract is now explicitly recognised as the first rule in a new article 1102. One of the other widely discussed changes is the removal of the notion of "cause", which used to be one of the four conditions set out in article 1008. The notion of objective cause (that is, that the contract must have an abstract goal, usually counter-performance

common law, *The Kominos S* [1991] 1 Lloyd's Rep; the Giuliano & Lagarde Report to the Rome Convention [1980] OJ C282/1 at 15–17 and Recital (12) to the RIR.

[178][2017] EWHC 161 (Comm), [80] per Cranston J.

[179]See also Magnus and Mankowski (2016), Art 25 [81h]. Dickinson and Lein (2015), para 9.65, also refer to this issue but conclude that the solution depends on the court before which the material validity of the clause is contested and, in the case of asymmetric agreements, that the validity should always be tested according to the designated court's law.

expected from the other party) was used by French courts as a ground to annul contracts which lacked any real reciprocity.[180]

It is too early to tell what effect these changes will have. Although there is no longer an express *caractère potestatif* doctrine, the courts may well be able to reach similar decisions on the basis of other provisions.[181] However, there is a strong argument that given these changes, and in particular, the greater emphasis apparently given to freedom to contract, the doubts as to the validity of asymmetric agreements raised by the Cour de cassation's reliance on the *caractère potestatif* doctrine should no longer apply.

The other objection relied on by the Cour de cassation is that asymmetric agreements are too uncertain and accordingly do not comply with the underlying requirements of Art 25. This does not seem to be an argument based specifically on French contract law. Nor does it depend on the one-sided nature of the agreement.

As has been described above, all agreements must be construed to discover what obligations they contain. Looking at asymmetric clauses purely from the point of view of this question of construction, the agreement by both parties to submit to the jurisdiction of the chosen court cannot be uncertain or unforeseeable. Nor can the promise by the lender not to sue in any other jurisdiction in itself be argued to be uncertain.

The issue seems to be with the other element of the clause, that is, the provision making it clear that, in relation to the bank, the agreement is not exclusive so that the bank can still sue in other jurisdictions. One of the problems with interpreting the French decisions is that it is not always clear what construction the court placed on the clause. For example, at first instance in *Rothschild* it seems that the court had found a general agreement on the part of the borrower to be sued in any court which the bank may choose.[182] However, as has already been described, English courts have not construed asymmetric clauses in this way. Rather they have tended to construe a clause submitting to the jurisdiction of "any competent court" more narrowly. English courts have construed such agreements as simply confirming that, from the point of view of the bank, the obligation is not exclusive, so that the bank can continue to sue in any other court in *which it could otherwise have sued* in accordance with the rules. If so, the underlying jurisdiction rules allocating jurisdiction to particular courts would be effectively incorporated.[183] If that is right, the borrower is in the same position as any other defendant who can be sued in any court

[180]Rowan (2017).

[181]For example, new clause 1169 which provides "An onerous contract is a nullity where, at the moment of its formation, what is agreed in return for the benefit of the person undertaking an obligation is illusory or derisory". Significant imbalance is also addressed in a consumer context: see Pillet (2016), p. 250.

[182]If that is right, the decision in *Apple* is distinguishable because it referred to courts where harm was suffered.

[183]For example, in China there is a general requirement that a chosen court must have a real connection with the dispute. A competent court would have to be one which includes conformity with rules on real connection: see Liang (2015), p. 345.

which has jurisdiction according to the Regulation rules. In one respect, indeed, the borrower is better off because the bank has agreed to submit to the chosen court's jurisdiction which might not otherwise have been available.

3.2.2 Asymmetric Agreements Under Article 31(2) BIR Recast

In cases where there are parallel proceedings in another Member State a different question arises. The BIR recast contains rules in Arts 29 and 30 which, in cases of either parallel or related proceedings, give precedence to the court first seised. As has been described at Sect. 2.3.2 above, the CJEU famously held in *Erich Gasser*[184] that the previous version of these rules applied even if there was a jurisdiction agreement in favour of the second seised court. This position has been reversed by Art 31 (2) BIR recast which provides: "where a court of a Member State on which an agreement referred to in Article 25 confers exclusive jurisdiction is seised, any court of another Member State shall stay the proceedings until such time as the court seised on the basis of the agreement declares that it has no jurisdiction under the agreement". The question whether an asymmetric clause triggers Art 31(2) was considered in *Commerzbank v Liquimar*.[185]

The bank had brought proceedings in England for the repayment of loans and on an associated guarantee. Both the loan agreement and guarantee contained a law and jurisdiction agreement in the following terms:

> 16.2 For the exclusive benefit of the Lender, the Guarantor irrevocably agrees that the courts of England are to have jurisdiction to settle any disputes which may arise out of or in connection with this Guarantee and Indemnity and that any proceedings may be brought in those courts.
>
> 16.3 Nothing contained in this Clause shall limit the right of the Lender to commence any proceedings against the Guarantor in any other court of competent jurisdiction nor shall the commencement of any proceedings against the Guarantor in one or more jurisdiction preclude the commencement of any proceedings in any other jurisdiction, whether concurrently or not.

Proceedings had already been commenced in Greece by the defendant against the bank concerning the same and/or related issues.[186] The Greek court was first seised, but the bank relied on Art 31(2) BIR recast, arguing that the Greek courts would have to stay in favour of the English court. The judge began by adopting[187] the standard construction of asymmetric agreements set out in *Mauritius Commercial Bank v Hestia* and in Sect. 3.1 above, that is, that the borrower was limited to English jurisdiction, but the bank was able to proceed in that jurisdiction or in other courts

[184] *Erich Gasser GmbH v MISAT Srl* Case C-116/02.

[185] [2017] EWHC 161 (Comm).

[186] There were essentially four proceedings, comprising two pairs of parallel proceedings in Greece and in England.

[187] At [40]–[41].

which have competent jurisdiction. Moreover, if the borrower sued in England, the bank would not be able to challenge the court's jurisdiction since it had agreed to it.[188] He noted that asymmetric jurisdiction agreements are a long-established and practical feature of international financial documentation. However, the question in this case was a novel one, namely, the correct interpretation of Art 31(2) BIR recast, which has effect where there is "a jurisdiction agreement which confers exclusive jurisdiction." On this question, the judge held, first, that this must be a question of autonomous interpretation under the Regulation, not a matter of English law.[189] He concluded: "the natural meaning of the words in Article 31(2) ...to my mind includes asymmetric jurisdiction clauses. ... *Considered as a whole*, they are agreements conferring exclusive jurisdiction on the courts of an EU Member State, namely, England. That this applies in respect of a claim by the defendant alone does not detract from this effect". [190]

The rationale for the new rule in Art 32(1) BIR recast is party autonomy. Recital (22) explains that the new rule was introduced "in order to enhance the effectiveness of choice-of-court agreements and to avoid abusive litigation tactics". In an asymmetric agreement, the borrower has promised not to sue anywhere other than the chosen jurisdiction. The question of whether the other party did or did not agree to do the same does not arise when the bank is seeking to enforce the agreement and should be irrelevant. Thus, the point is not so much that "considered as a whole" they are agreements conferring exclusive jurisdiction, as the judge put it in *Commerzbank*. Rather, each obligation can be considered on its own; the clause includes a promise by the borrower not to sue in any other jurisdiction and that promise is capable of being protected by Art 31(2). Each different obligation necessarily falls to be considered separately and the fact that the bank is not under a similar obligation is neither here nor there.[191]

3.3 Enforcement of Asymmetric Agreements Under the Hague Convention

Like the BIR recast, the Hague Convention contains rules which seek to enforce both the positive and negative aspects of jurisdiction agreements. Article 5(1) provides that the court or courts of a Contracting State designated in an exclusive choice of court agreement shall have jurisdiction, unless the agreement is null and void under the law of that State. Article 6 confirms the negative effect of an exclusive

[188] In this situation, the bank may not be able to sue elsewhere: *Lornamead Acquisitions Ltd v Kaupthing Bank* [2011] EWHC 2611, [112].

[189] At [52].

[190] At [64] (emphasis added).

[191] Compare Keyes and Marshall (2015), p. 352, concluding that an agreement will not be exclusive under the recast if it does not exclude the jurisdiction of all but the single chosen jurisdiction.

jurisdiction agreement providing that a court of a Contracting State other than that of the chosen court shall suspend or dismiss proceedings to which an exclusive choice of court agreement applies.

However, the Hague Convention applies only to "exclusive choice of court agreements" as defined in Art 3(a) as:

> an agreement concluded between two or more parties that . . . designates, for the purpose of deciding disputes which have arisen or may arise in connection with a particular legal relationship, the courts of one Contracting State or one or more specific courts of one Contracting State to the exclusion of the jurisdiction of any other courts.

It is commonly assumed that asymmetric agreements do not fall within the Hague Convention. The Explanatory Report to the Hague Convention by Professors Hartley and Dogauchi noted that asymmetric jurisdiction clauses are often used in international loan agreements. However, they continued, the Diplomatic Session had agreed that they "are not exclusive choice of court agreements for the purposes of the Convention".[192]

The Report noted that such clauses may be subject to the rules of the Convention if the States in question have made declarations under Art 22 which allows for reciprocal declarations on non-exclusive agreements.

However, the position is not entirely clear. An earlier report at the time of drafting of the Convention suggested that to make it clear that asymmetric jurisdiction clauses were excluded from the definition of what is now Art 3(a), it might be desirable to add the words "such an agreement must be exclusive irrespective of the party bringing the proceedings". That was not done.[193] In *Commerzbank*, Cranston J noted,[194] *obiter*, that "there are good arguments in my view that the words of the definition in article 3(a) of the Hague Convention cover asymmetric jurisdiction clauses". However, there was no reason for him to reach a concluded view. Presumably, his argument would have been analogous to that he adopted in relation to Art 31(2) BIR recast discussed above, that is, that "taken as a whole" an asymmetric agreement can be described as an "exclusive jurisdiction agreement". However, another way of putting it is that the effect of a clause can only be judged by considering the effect of a particular obligation on a particular party. There is nothing inherent in the structure or rationale of the Convention to mean that, if the claim is made against a borrower who has agreed to be sued in a particular jurisdiction and only that jurisdiction, the rules should not engage.

[192]Hartley and Dogauchi (2013), [106]. See also Keyes and Marshall (2015), p. 366, noting that Switzerland proposed that unilateral agreements should be brought within the scope of the Hague Convention, but that this proposal was rejected.

[193]See *Commerzbank v Liquimar Tankers Management Inc* [2017] EWHC 16, [39].

[194][2017] EWHC 161 (Comm), [74].

3.4 *Damages for Breach of an Asymmetric Jurisdiction Agreement*

Once an agreement, properly construed, includes a promise not to sue, if the borrower in breach of the promise does sue elsewhere there is no reason why a claim for damages should not be available. There seems to be no reason why this reasoning should not apply to a borrower in an asymmetric agreement who has similarly made such a promise. This was the view of the judge in *Barclays Bank PLC v Ente Nazionale de Previdenza dei Medici degli Odontoiatra.*[195] The judge noted that, as is frequently agreed for good practical reasons in financing transactions, the clause in question stipulated that exclusivity in favour of one court did not prevent the financing institution from bringing an action in the courts of any other jurisdiction. The judge continued by noting that there had been a short debate in the skeleton arguments as to whether such a clause can be regarded as "exclusive". While the judge would have accepted the submission that it was exclusive, he noted that:

> [T]he issue for decision in the present case is a more limited one. Regardless of how the clause is characterised in terms of exclusivity, the issue is whether ENPAM is right to say that it is not in breach of it by pursuing proceedings in the Milan courts. In the *Continental Bank*[196] case the court concluded that the clause at issue there evinced a clear intention that the defendant (though not the bank) was obliged to submit disputes in connection with the loan facility at issue to the English courts. I consider that the same construction should be placed upon the jurisdiction clause in the PCA. I do not accept ENPAM's submission that the supposed "non-exclusivity" of the clause means that the bringing of proceedings relating to the PCA by ENPAM in the Milan court is not a breach of the jurisdiction agreement. In my view, it clearly is a breach.

For the same reasons, a breach of a promise not to sue by a borrower might also provide the basis for a claim in tort against the borrower's advisers for inducing breach of contract (discussed in Sect. 2.5.2 above).

---

[195] [2015] EWHC 2857 (Comm), [127]–[128]. The clause at issue provided: ". . . each of the parties irrevocably:

(a) agrees for [C's] benefit that the courts of England shall have jurisdiction to settle any suit, action or other proceedings relating to this Agreement ("Proceedings") and irrevocably submits to the jurisdiction of such courts (provided that this shall not prevent us from bringing an action in the courts of any other jurisdiction); and

(b) waives any objection which it may have at any time to the laying of venue of any Proceedings brought in any such court and agrees not to claim that such Proceedings have been brought in an inconvenient forum or that such court does not have jurisdiction over it."

[196] *Continental Bank v Aeakos* [1994] 1 WLR 588.

3.5 Anti-suit Injunctions and Asymmetric Jurisdiction Agreements

There seems to be no reason why, at common law, an asymmetric agreement could not be relied on, in appropriate cases, as a basis for an anti-suit injunction. For the same reasons as apply in the damages cases, once it is seen that an asymmetric agreement contains a promise by the borrower not to sue in any other jurisdiction, that promise can be enforced in the normal way, including the possibility of an anti-suit injunction. It should not matter that the bank has not made a similar promise. This was exactly the case in *Bank of New York Mellon v GV Films*.[197] The documentation in a trust document in respect of a bond issue included an asymmetric agreement in favour of the bank in favour of the English courts. The defendant sued in India and the bank sought an anti-suit injunction. Field J[198] held that the wording of the clause, together with the express liberty conferred on the bank trustee, but not the defendant, to bring proceedings in any other court of competent jurisdiction, clearly showed that the intention of the parties was that the courts of England had exclusive jurisdiction so far as proceedings brought by the defendant were concerned. In the absence of strong reasons why not, the defendant's promise not to sue could be enforced by an anti-suit injunction.

Special rules may apply to consumers and other vulnerable parties such as employees both under the BIR recast and under other Consumer Protection legislation;[199] but the rules in relation to jurisdiction agreements themselves do not differ at common law because one of the parties is in a stronger position.

4 Reform

4.1 The Impact of Brexit on Jurisdiction in the UK

It is not possible to consider in any detail the implications of Brexit on the jurisdiction rules outlined above. At the time of writing, many aspects of the relationship of the UK to the EU remain to be determined. However, if, as seems inevitable, EU legislation ceases to become directly binding on the UK, important European private international law legislation, including the BIR recast, would cease to have effect,[200]

[197] [2009] EWHC 2338 (Comm).

[198] Following the reasoning in *Continental Bank v Aeakos* [1994] 1 WLR 588 discussed above in Sect. 3.1.

[199] For example, under the Consumer Rights Act 2015 or the Unfair Contract Terms Act 1977, and special rules apply under the BIR recast in relation to consumers, employees and insured parties. See also Draguiev (2014), p. 40 ("there is a degree of probability that unilateral clauses may be invalidated on grounds of consumer protection") and Fentiman (2015), para 2.108.

[200] The UK will also cease to be a party to the Lugano II Convention (2007) and the Hague Convention. For further discussion see: Dickinson (2016); Rogerson (2017); Harris (2016a, b);

at least on a properly reciprocal basis. However, the UK Government's March 2017 White Paper, "The UK's exit from and new partnership with the European Union"[201] set out the Government's plan to convert the *acquis*—the body of existing EU law—into British law, with the objective of providing "maximum certainty as we leave the EU. The same rules and laws will apply on the day after exit as on the day before. It will then be for democratically elected representatives in the UK to decide on any changes to that law, after full scrutiny and proper debate."[202] Explicitly, the UK Government aim is that, as the European Communities Act 1972 is repealed, directly-applicable EU laws will be converted into UK law and that the Withdrawal legislation will "preserve the laws we have made in the UK to implement our EU obligations". By section 3 of the European Union (Withdrawal) Act 2018

"(1) Direct EU legislation so far as operative immediately before exit day, forms part of domestic law on and after exit day."

Because the BIR recast is a reciprocal regime, it is not possible simply to implement equivalent provisions in a post Brexit Bill.[203] The effect of the rules without the reciprocity from Member States is severely diminished, both in respect to jurisdiction (parallel proceedings and jurisdiction agreements) and enforcement of judgments. Also, in some instances the interpretation of the Regulation depends on autonomous EU concepts to ensure uniformity across the EU to support the single market. It is also unclear what effect should be given to judgments of the CJEU both past and future on the interpretation of the Regulation.

If there is no negotiated replacement for the BIR recast as regards post-Brexit legal relations between the UK and EU27, this would have significant consequences for the enforcement of jurisdiction agreements.

In summary, the consequences would be as follows.

First, enforcement of jurisdiction agreements by British courts would be under the residual national rules discussed above.

Second, the position of English (or Scottish) jurisdiction agreements in other Member State courts would no longer be regulated by the BIR recast: rather it would become a matter for the relevant national law.

The enforcement of judgments would always be under the common law rules or relevant statutory scheme.

In relation to anti-suit injunctions, as discussed in Sect. 2.5.4 above, the principle of mutual trust and confidence between the courts of Member States means that British courts cannot issue an anti-suit injunction against the courts of another

---

Carruthers (2017); and Final Report of the House of Lords European Union Justice Sub-Committee "Implications of Brexit for the justice system" 14 March 2017; The EU and the Legal Sector, The Law Society of England and Wales 2015; Brexit Paper 4: Civil Jurisdiction and the Enforcement of Judgments; The General Council of the Bar.

[201]Department for Exiting the European Union and The Rt Hon David Davis MP (CM 9417) (2 February 2017).

[202]March 2017 White Paper, Foreword from the Prime Minister, p. 5.

[203]In contrast to the position in relation to the RIR which is not reciprocal and where it would be possible to implement equivalent rules into national domestic law.

Member State, even to enforce an arbitration agreement or jurisdiction agreement in favour of the English courts.[204] Once the UK has left the EU, it seems that such a remedy will become available again to enforce jurisdiction agreements.

Any issues concerning damages claims in a European context may also fall away.[205]

4.2 Possible Replacement Regimes

Once the UK has left the EU, it could rejoin the Hague Conference as a Contracting State. It could then accede to and ratify the Hague Convention on Choice of Court Agreements. This does not require the consent of the EU.

The UK (once it has left the EU) could apply to accede to and ratify the Lugano Convention. All the other contracting states would have to agree—the EU (possibly as separate Member States), Switzerland, Iceland and Norway. However, the Lugano Convention is an older and less attractive convention than the BIR recast in some ways. The rules on parallel proceedings within the Contracting States take no account of jurisdiction agreements. The rules also take no account of parallel proceedings in third States.

Alternatively, the UK could negotiate to continue to be within the BIR recast regime akin to Denmark's position.[206] This would ensure reciprocity on jurisdiction and enforcement of judgments, but may come at some political cost, depending on the EU's position.

In a Paper published on 22 August 2017, the Department for Exiting the EU published its plans for negotiations in this area.[207] The paper refers to the need for common rules to respect parties' agreements as to which court will have jurisdiction in order to "support business confidence to trade and to minimise the potential for delaying tactics in the event of a dispute".[208] The intention is said to be to seek a close and comprehensive framework of cooperation with the EU on a reciprocal basis which would mirror closely the current EU system;[209] to continue to participate in those Hague Conventions to which the UK is already a party, including the Hague

[204] *Turner v Grovit* Case C-159/02 and, in the context of arbitration, *Allianz SpA v West Tankers Inc* Case C-185/07.

[205] *Pace*, comments in Ahmed and Beaumont (2017).

[206] See Parliamentary Committee reports, the House of Lords European Union Committee, 17th Report of Session 2016/17, "Brexit: justice for families, individuals and businesses?" (HL Paper 134 (20 March 2017)), and the House of Commons Justice Committee, 9th Report of Session 2016/17, "Implications of Brexit for the Justice System" (HC 750 (22 March 2017)), each of which urges the UK Government to seek to negotiate a solution which keeps as close as possible to the existing private international law rules when negotiating their post-Brexit application.

[207] HM Government (2017).

[208] HM Government (2017), [15].

[209] HM Government (2017), [25].

Convention on Choice of Court Agreements; and to seek to participate in the Lugano Convention.[210]

References

Ahmed M, Beaumont P (2017) Exclusive choice of court agreements: some issues on the Hague Convention on Choice of Court Agreements and its relationship with the Brussels I recast especially anti-suit injunctions, concurrent proceedings and the implications of Brexit. J Private Int Law 13:386–410

Baatz Y, Sandiforth A (2010) Forum non conveniens further constrained. J Bus Law 6:522–528

Beale N, Clayson C (2013) One-way jurisdiction clauses: a one-way ticket to anywhere? J Int Bus Law 463

Briggs A (2008) Agreements on jurisdiction and choice of law. Oxford University Press, Oxford

Briggs A (2012) The subtle variety of jurisdiction agreements. Lloyd's Marit Commercial Law Q 364–381

Briggs A (2014) Private international law in English Courts. Oxford University Press, Oxford

Carruthers JM (2017) Brexit – the implications for civil and commercial jurisdiction and judgment enforcement. Scots Law Times (21):103–108

Collins L (2012) Dicey, Morris and Collins on the conflict of laws, 15th edn. Sweet & Maxwell, London

Crawford EB, Carruthers JM (2015) International private law: a Scots perspective, 4th edn. W Green, Edinburgh

Dickinson A (2016) Back to the future: the UK's EU exit and the conflict of laws. J Private Int Law 12:195–210

Dickinson A, Lein E (2015) The Brussels I Regulation Recast. Oxford University Press, Oxford

Draguiev D (2014) Unilateral jurisdiction clauses: the case for invalidity, severability or enforceability. J Int Arbitration 31:19–46

Fentiman R (2013) Unilateral jurisdiction agreements in Europe. Camb Law J 72:24–27

Fentiman R (2015) International Commercial Litigation, 2nd edn. Oxford University Press, Oxford

Financial Markets Law Committee (2016) Report on issues of legal uncertainty arising in the context of asymmetric jurisdiction clauses

Garvey S (2016) Hybrid jurisdiction clause: time for a rethink? Br J Int Bus Financ Law 1:6

Harris J (2016a) How will Brexit impact on cross-border litigation? Solicitors' J 160

Harris J (2016b) Brexit & cross-border dispute resolution. New Law J 166

Hartley T, Dogauchi M (2013) Explanatory report on convention of 30 June 2005 on choice of court agreements. Hague Conference on Private International Law, The Hague

Joseph D (2015) Jurisdiction and arbitration agreements and their enforcement, 3rd edn. Sweet & Maxwell, London

Keyes M, Marshall B (2015) Jurisdiction agreements: exclusive, optional and asymmetric. J Private Int Law 11:345–378

Liang W (2015) Unilateral jurisdiction clauses under Chinese law. J Int Bank Law Regul 30:341

Magnus U, Mankowski P (eds) (2016) European commentaries on private international law, Brussels Ibis Regulation. Otto Schmidt, Köln

Maher G, Rodger B (2010) Civil Jurisdiction in the Scottish Courts. W Green, Edinburgh

Petch T (2016) The treatment of asymmetric jurisdiction clauses in financial contracts in France and England. UCL J Law Jurisprudence 5:313–334

[210]HM Government (2017), [22].

Pillet G (2016) The reform of French contract law and the general rules on obligations: the civil code faces the challenges of the market. Int Bus Law J 235
Rogerson P (2013) Collier's conflict of laws, 4th edn. Cambridge University Press, Cambridge
Rogerson P (2017) Litigation post-Brexit. N Law J 166
Rowan S (2017) The new French Law of contract. Int Comp Law Q 66:805–831

Government Papers

HM Government (2017) Providing a cross-border civil judicial cooperation framework. A Future Partnership Paper, 22 August 2017

Louise Merrett is a Reader in International Commercial Law at the University of Cambridge and a fellow of Trinity College.

Janeen Carruthers is Professor of Private Law at the University of Glasgow.

United States: The Interpretation and Effect of Permissive Forum Selection Clauses

Hannah L. Buxbaum

1 Introduction

A forum selection clause[1] is a form of contractual waiver. By this device, a contract party waives its rights to raise jurisdictional or venue objections if a lawsuit is initiated against it in the chosen court. (If the forum selection is *exclusive*, then that party also promises not to initiate litigation anywhere other than in the chosen forum.) The use of such a clause in a particular case may therefore raise a set of questions under contract law. Is the waiver valid? Was it procured by fraud, duress, or other unconscionable means? What is its scope? And so on.

Unlike most contractual waivers, however, a forum selection clause affects not only the private rights and obligations of the parties, but something of more public concern: the jurisdiction of a court to resolve a dispute. The enforcement of such a clause therefore raises an additional set of questions under procedural law. For instance, if the parties designate a court in a forum that is otherwise unconnected to the dispute, must (or should) that court hear a case initiated there? If one of the parties initiates litigation in a non-designated forum that is connected to the dispute, must (or should) that court decline to hear the case?

This report analyzes the approach to these questions in the United States. Section 2 provides a brief background on the general attitude toward forum selection clauses. Section 3 surveys current state law on their use, in consumer as well as commercial contracts. Section 4 addresses the interpretation of forum selection

[1]Outside the United States, forum selection clauses are generally referred to as "choice of court agreements". In order to maintain consistency with the judicial opinions here analyzed, this chapter uses the U.S. terminology.

H. L. Buxbaum (✉)
Indiana University Maurer School of Law, Bloomington, IN, USA
e-mail: hbuxbaum@indiana.edu

M. Keyes (ed.), *Optional Choice of Court Agreements in Private International Law*, Ius Comparatum – Global Studies in Comparative Law 37,
https://doi.org/10.1007/978-3-030-23914-5_20

clauses as either permissive or exclusive. Section 5 analyzes the effect of permissive clauses in state and federal courts. Finally, Sect. 6 turns to choice of law problems, particularly as they arise in the course of litigation in federal courts.

2 Background

Historically, forum selection clauses were viewed as contrary to public policy and therefore invalid.[2] The most frequently invoked justification for this rule, relevant only in connection with exclusive clauses, was that parties should not be able to deprive a court of jurisdiction it would otherwise have over a dispute.[3] However, other explanations for the traditional approach—relevant in connection with permissive as well as exclusive clauses—appear in the case law as well. Some courts rejected forum selection clauses out of suspicion that the parties' intent in selecting a particular forum was to circumvent otherwise applicable substantive policies. Others worried that permitting parties to choose their forum would "bring the administration of justice into disrepute" by highlighting considerations such as the relative intelligence or impartiality of particular judges.[4] Overall, the sense was that "[t]he jurisdiction of our courts is established by law, and is not to be diminished, any more than it is to be increased, by the convention of the parties."[5]

Over time, and given increasing recognition of the need for certainty and predictability in interstate and international commerce, adherence to the traditional view diminished. This shift manifested itself in the case law[6] and elsewhere. For example, in 1968, the National Conference of Commissioners on Uniform State Laws adopted a Model Choice of Forum Act[7] based on the Hague Conference's 1964 Convention on the Choice of Court. Although the model law gave courts considerably more

---

[2]See generally Lenhoff (1961), pp. 430–431; Gruson (1982), pp. 138–139 (describing the traditional approach).

[3]See Home Ins. Co. v. Morse, 20 Wall. 445, 451 (1874); see also Lenhoff (1961), p. 431 (describing the "almost proverbial" status of the rule that parties cannot "oust" a court of jurisdiction).

[4]See Nute v. Hamilton Mut. Ins. Co., 6 Gray 174, 184 (1856).

[5]Meacham v. Jamestown, F. & C.R. Co., 211 N.Y. 346, 352 (1914) (Cardozo, J., concurring). See also Clermont (2015), p. 648 (under the traditional approach, "it was for the sovereign to decide what the sovereign's courts could or could not do; it was not for the parties to make private agreements as to the availability of public remedies").

[6]See, e.g., Krenger v. Pa. R.R., 174 F.2d 556, 561 (2d Cir. 1949) (Hand, J., concurring) (rejecting the notion of an "absolute taboo" against forum selection clauses, and stating that they are "invalid only when unreasonable" under the circumstances); Wm. H. Muller & Co. v. Swedish Am. Line Ltd., 224 F.2d 806, 808 (2d. Cir. 1955) (summarizing the new rule as follows: "[T]he parties by agreement cannot oust a court of jurisdiction otherwise obtaining; notwithstanding the agreement, the court has jurisdiction. But if in the proper exercise of its jurisdiction . . . the court finds that the agreement is not unreasonable in the setting of the particular case, it may properly decline jurisdiction and relegate a litigant to the forum to which he assented.").

[7]See Reese (1969).

discretion than the Convention did in enforcing forum selection clauses, its starting point was that the use of such clauses was desirable.[8] And the Restatement (Second) of Conflict of Laws, adopted in 1971, included a section stating that a forum selection clause will be given effect "unless it is unfair or unreasonable."[9]

The real turning point in U.S. doctrine was the Supreme Court's 1972 decision in *The Bremen v. Zapata Off-Shore Co.*[10] The case involved a forum selection clause included in a contract for towage negotiated by the U.S. owner of a drilling rig and a German towing company. The agreement designated the London Court of Justice as the exclusive forum for litigation; however, when its rig was damaged, the U.S. company brought suit in the United States District Court in Tampa, Florida. The defendant moved to dismiss or stay the action on the basis of the forum selection clause. Holding that such agreements were unenforceable, the court denied this motion, and its decision was upheld upon appeal. The U.S. Supreme Court then vacated and remanded, holding that the forum selection clause was entitled to a presumption of enforcement.

To make the discussion that follows as clear as possible, I want to separate strands of the Court's holding that have been frequently intertwined in subsequent cases and commentary.

- First, the holding rejected the notion that contractual provisions affecting matters of jurisdiction and venue were *invalid* as against public policy.[11] (The Court did suggest that the validity of a particular forum selection clause could be challenged on the basis of defects in contract formation, such as "fraud or overreaching," or lack of "free negotiation" by the parties.[12])
- Second, the holding introduced a rule of presumptive *enforceability* of exclusive (mandatory) forum selection clauses—meaning that, as a general matter, where the parties had agreed that any litigation would take place exclusively in the designated court, any other court should refuse to hear the case.[13]
- Third, the holding discussed two bases on which a court other than the designated court could refuse to enforce an otherwise valid and exclusive forum selection clause: (a) if enforcement would be "unreasonable" under the circumstances (by which the Court meant that the nominated forum would be so seriously inconvenient that the plaintiff would "for all practical purposes be deprived of his day in court"), or (b) if enforcement would violate a strong public policy of the forum in which suit was brought.[14]

[8]Reese (1969), p. 292.

[9]Restatement (Second) of Conflict of Laws § 80 (1971).

[10]The Bremen v. Zapata Offshore Co., 407 U.S. 1 (1972).

[11]The Bremen v. Zapata Offshore Co., 407 U.S. 1 (1972) at 10.

[12]The Bremen v. Zapata Offshore Co., 407 U.S. 1 (1972) at 12, 15.

[13]The Bremen v. Zapata Offshore Co., 407 U.S. 1 (1972) at 15.

[14]The Bremen v. Zapata Offshore Co., 407 U.S. 1 (1972) at 16–18.

The *Bremen* decision might have had limited effect for two reasons. To begin with, it involved an international contract. In justifying its adoption of a rule of presumptive enforceability, the Court referred repeatedly to the needs of international commerce; thus, the rule might have been limited to the international context. Moreover, the case involved the exercise of admiralty jurisdiction, and the decision was therefore binding neither on federal courts exercising different forms of jurisdiction nor on state courts.[15] Nevertheless, the *Bremen* rule quickly sprang these limits. Federal courts exercising jurisdiction in non-admiralty cases adopted the *Bremen* approach, applying it even in cases involving domestic contracts. State courts too began to apply the *Bremen* analysis, again in domestic as well as international cases.[16] In short, the decision has framed the modern U.S. approach to forum selection clauses.

The portions of the *Bremen* rule addressing the presumptive enforceability of forum selection clauses apply only to exclusive forum selection clauses, and so this report treats them only in passing. The first part of the Court's holding, though, relating to the general validity of private agreements as to forum choice, applies equally to permissive clauses. The following section addresses the treatment of such agreements under current law.

3 The Validity of Permissive Forum Selection Clauses Under U.S. Law

3.1 In General

In the vast majority of U.S. states, forum selection clauses, both permissive and exclusive, are viewed with approval. A few states have enacted statutes governing the treatment of such agreements,[17] based on the Model Choice of Forum Act mentioned above.[18] In most states, however, the validity and enforceability of forum selection clauses are governed by common law. Often that law explicitly adopts the *Bremen* rule; sometimes, it integrates the reasoning of that case into rules that achieve the same result. In New York, for example, courts have adopted a four-step test that analyzes (1) whether the forum selection clause was reasonably

[15]Indeed, the Court more or less suggested that the rule it articulated was applicable only in the admiralty context. The Bremen v. Zapata Offshore Co., 407 U.S. 1 (1972) at 10.

[16]In a two-part article published in the early 1990s, Walter Heiser provides an overview of the effect of the *Bremen* decision on analysis in both state courts and federal courts in the years following that case. See Heiser (1993a), pp. 369–371; Heiser (1993b), p. 565.

[17]See, e.g., Neb. Rev. Stat. §§ 25-414, -415; N.H. Rev. Stat. Ann. § 508-A; N.D. Cent. Code § 28-04.1.

[18]See note 7 and accompanying text. The Model Choice of Forum Act, approved in 1968 by the National Conference of Commissioners on Uniform State Laws, was loosely modeled on the 1964 Hague Convention on the Choice of Court. The Model Act was ultimately withdrawn in 1975.

communicated to the resisting party, (2) whether it should be classified as exclusive or permissive, (3) whether it covers the parties and the claims in question, and (4) whether the presumption in favor of enforcement has been rebutted by a showing that it is unreasonable under the circumstances or invalid for reasons such as fraud or overreaching.[19] Some states have also adopted specific legislation to permit (or attract) litigation involving high-value contracts. These statutes are discussed below.[20]

A handful of states maintain the traditional hostility to forum selection clauses. In one state, this position is reflected in the case law.[21] In three, legislation has been enacted that invalidates forum selection clauses.[22] Idaho's statute, for example, provides that "every stipulation or condition in a contract, by which any party thereto is restricted from enforcing his rights under the contract in Idaho tribunals ... is void as it is against the public policy of Idaho."[23] In some cases, however, courts have construed these statutes quite narrowly, reflecting recent movement toward the more liberal enforcement of forum selection clauses.[24] It is important to emphasize that—as the Idaho statute quoted above indicates—the focus of these general policies is on *exclusive* forum selection clauses that purport to deprive local courts of jurisdiction they would otherwise enjoy.

3.2 *In Particular Business Settings*

In addition, many states have enacted legislation invalidating the use of forum selection clauses in certain types of contract where the risk of bargaining inequality is particularly significant.[25] For instance, a number of states, including New Jersey,

---

[19]See, e.g., Phillips v. Audio Active Ltd., 494 F.3d 378, 383–384 (2d Cir. 2007); see also APR Energy Ltd. v. Greenhill & Co., LLC, 220 F. Supp. 3d 427, 430–431 (S.D.N.Y. 2016); Moose Toys Pty, Ltd., v. Creative Kids Far East Inc., 195 F. Supp. 3d 599, 602–603 (S.D.N.Y. 2016).

[20]See note 79 and accompanying text.

[21]See Davenport Mach. & Foundry Co. v. Adolph Coors Co., 314 N.W.2d 432, 437 (Iowa 1982) ("[C]lauses purporting to deprive Iowa courts of jurisdiction they would otherwise have are not legally binding in Iowa.").

[22]Mont. Code Ann. § 28-2-708 (Montana); Idaho Code § 29-110 (Idaho); N.C. Gen. Stat. § 22B-3 (North Carolina).

[23]Idaho Code § 29-110. See also Cerami-Kote, Inc. v. Energywave Corp., 773 P.2d 1143, 1147 (Idaho 1989) (applying this provision).

[24]See, e.g., Frontline Processing Corp. v. Merrick Bank Corp., 2013 WL 12130638, at *4 (D. Mont. 2013) (enforcing a forum selection clause despite Montana's legislation); see also Shelter Mutual Insurance Co. v. Rimkus Consulting Group, 148 So. 3d 871, 881 (La. 2014) (holding that a rule of Louisiana procedure stating that venue objections could not be waived prior to litigation did not prohibit the use of forum selection clauses).

[25]See generally Symeonides (2018), p. 1129 (noting the use of such legislation to address "consumer contracts, employment contracts, agency contracts, franchise contracts, and construction contracts").

Illinois, Minnesota, Wisconsin, and Washington, have adopted statutes designed to provide franchisees with a variety of substantive protections. Some include specific anti-waiver provisions relating to choice of court. Illinois's Franchise Disclosure Act, for instance, explicitly makes void "[a]ny provision in a franchise agreement that designates jurisdiction or venue in a [judicial] forum outside of this State."[26] Others include general anti-waiver language prohibiting any contractual provision that would operate as a waiver of the rights enjoyed by the franchisee under the law.[27] Provisions of the latter type require courts to analyze whether and to what extent a forum selection clause might operate as a waiver of any of the franchisee's rights.

Laws treating certain kinds of contracts are common. For example, New York's alcohol control law voids any contractual provision that operates as a waiver of any of the rights provided in the law.[28] A Virginia district court found the forum selection clause included in a distribution agreement to be unenforceable because it restricted the distributor's right to move for transfer, a right guaranteed by a local statute.[29] The Hawaii Motor Vehicle Industry Licensing Act generally prohibits any agreement that "requires that the dealer bring an action against the manufacturer or distributor in a venue outside of Hawaii."[30] And in Texas, forum selection clauses included in certain construction contracts are void.[31]

In the Reporter's view, these sorts of policies must be differentiated from a general policy of hostility toward forum selection clauses. Here, the target of regulation is not the power of private parties to affect matters of jurisdiction and venue. Rather, it is certain contractual relationships between parties of unequal bargaining power.[32] The effect of such policies on choice of court is incidental to the overall goal of protecting local residents from particular forms of unfair business practice.[33]

---

[26] 815 Ill. Comp. Stat. Ann. 705/4.

[27] E.g., Minn. Stat. Ann. § 80C.21.

[28] N.Y. A.B.C.L. § 55-c(11).

[29] Coors Brewing Co. v. Oak Beverage, Inc., 549 F. Supp. 2d 764, 771 (E.D. Va. 2008).

[30] Haw. Rev. Stat. Ann. § 437-52(1).

[31] Tex. Bus. & Com. Code Ann. 272.001.

[32] See generally Yackee (2004), pp. 48–49 (discussing the effect of protective legislation of this kind on the freedom of parties to choose a forum in advance). This distinction becomes important in the choice of law context; see Sect. 6.

[33] See Verdugo v. Alliantgroup, L.P., 237 Cal. App. 4th 141, 150 (Cal. Ct. App. 2015) (stating that both California's Franchise Investment Law and its Consumer Legal Remedies Act "share the common purpose of protecting California residents from unfair or deceptive business practices, and include a provision invalidating any waiver of the protections those laws provide," and at 154, stating that California's securities law "articulate[s] a strong public policy aimed at protecting the public from fraud and deception in securities transactions" and that a "cornerstone" of that law is an anti-waiver provision).

3.3 In Contracts of Adhesion

Like any clause in a contract, a forum selection clause can be challenged as invalid on the basis of formal defects (for instance, the absence of a required writing) or defects in the consent of one of the parties (for instance, that it was procured by duress, fraud, mistake, or the like). Formal validity is rarely an issue in practice, and allegations of duress and other similar practices are rare. However, parties frequently challenge the validity of forum selection clauses contained in adhesion contracts on the basis of unconscionability, arguing that it would be unconscionable to hold them to a clause that had not been freely negotiated.[34] *Bremen* itself recognized this potential limitation, focusing on the "freely negotiated" character of the clause at issue in that case.[35] And subsequent Supreme Court decisions did the same. In a 1985 case, for example, the Court echoed the position that where forum selection clauses "have been obtained through 'freely negotiated' agreements," their enforcement does not violate Constitutional norms.[36]

In 1991, however, in *Carnival Cruise Lines v. Shute*,[37] the Supreme Court undertook to "refine the analysis of *The Bremen* to account for the realities of form [maritime] passage contracts."[38] The case involved an exclusive forum selection clause included among the terms printed on a ticket for passage on a cruise ship. A federal court of appeals had concluded that the forum selection clause was "not freely bargained for," and on that basis declined to enforce it, permitting the plaintiffs to sue in a court other than the one nominated.[39] The Supreme Court reversed. The Court analyzed the forum selection clause the same way it would any clause in a contract offered on a "take it or leave it" basis: it scrutinized it for "reasonableness."[40] It concluded that both parties to the contract received benefit from an exclusive forum selection clause: the cruise line in the form of a limitation on the fora in which it could be sued by its passengers, and the passengers themselves "in the form of reduced fares" passing on the resulting cost savings.[41] Thus, the Court concluded, the clause was "reasonable" (i.e., not unconscionable). Although the clause was clearly not "freely negotiated," and although the parties had unequal bargaining power, the clause was therefore entitled to the *Bremen* presumption.

---

[34]See, e.g., Tucker v. Cochran, 341 P.3d 673, 687 (Okla. 2014) (party argues "that the forum-selection clause was never negotiated, bargained for, or discussed by the parties, and . . . there was no place for his initials to show agreement with the [clause]").

[35]407 U.S. at 12, 16.

[36]Burger King Corp. v. Rudzewicz, 471 U.S. 462, 472 n. 14 (1985).

[37]499 U.S. 585 (1991).

[38]499 U.S. 585 (1991) at 593.

[39]Shute v. Carnival Cruise Lines, 897 F.2d 377, 389 (9th Cir. 1988).

[40]499 U.S. at 593. The question here is not the reasonableness of the chosen forum, but rather the reasonableness of the "bargain" reflected in the contract provision.

[41]499 U.S. at 593 at 593–594.

Like *Bremen*, *Carnival Cruise* was an admiralty case, and therefore binding on lower federal courts and state courts only in that setting. Like *Bremen*, however, the decision has had much broader impact, and is now followed in all types of contract litigation. It is true that some courts have pulled back somewhat on the breadth of its holding in a number of ways. For instance, some lower courts have refused to enforce forum selection clauses included in consumer contracts on the basis of insufficient notice. (In *Carnival Cruise*, the plaintiffs conceded that they had notice of the forum selection clause.[42]) This is clearly a minority position, however. Most courts conclude that parties receive adequate notice of forum selection clauses if the relevant clauses are in capital letters, bold type, or otherwise set apart from other provisions in the contract—even if the parties did not in fact read the contract.[43] Similarly, some courts, reviewing forum selection clauses contained in agreements between parties of disparate economic and bargaining power, have held them to be invalid for overreaching.[44] This too is clearly a minority position. Overall, the general rule that such agreements are presumptively valid in the consumer as well as the commercial context is by now well established.[45]

3.4 In Asymmetrical Agreements

Under U.S. law, as long as each party's obligation is supported by consideration, mutuality of obligation is not required for a contract to be enforceable. Thus, as a general matter, the fact that a forum selection clause binds only one party does not render it unenforceable. And, indeed, courts are willing to enforce clauses that waive objections to jurisdiction and venue by only one of the contract parties.[46] The same is true of clauses that make the choice of court permissive for one party and exclusive for the other.

---

[42]In other words, in the Court's view, the plaintiffs had the opportunity after receiving the tickets in the mail to reject the contract if they objected to the forum selection clause. The dissenting opinion objected to this inference, questioning the effectiveness of notice contained in "the fine print on the back of the ticket." 499 U.S. at 593 at 597 (Stevens, J., dissenting).

[43]See, e.g., Campbell v. Marriott Ownership Resorts Inc., 2016 WL 817876, at ∗4 (Cal. Ct. App. 2016).

[44]See, e.g., Kubis & Perszyk v. Sun Microsystems, 680 A.2d 618, 627 (N.J. 1996) (holding "that forum-selection clauses in franchise agreements are presumptively invalid, and should not be enforced unless the franchisor can satisfy the burden of proving that such a clause was not imposed on the franchisee unfairly on the basis of its superior bargaining position").

[45]See Heiser (1993a), pp. 375–376 (concluding that the vast majority of states enforce valid and reasonable forum selection clauses); Mullenix (2015), p. 751 ("[T]he doctrinal bar to prevailing on an unconscionability objection to a forum-selection . . . clause is so great as to render that challenge practically moot.").

[46]See, e.g., Gen. Elec. Capital Corp. v. John Carlo, Inc., 2010 WL 3937313, at ∗2 (E.D. Mich. 2010) (giving effect to such a clause); Superior Nut & Candy Co., Inc., v. TDG Brands, Inc., 2017 WL 319149, at ∗2 (N.D. Ill. 2017) (asymmetrical clauses enforceable under Arizona law).

3.5 Conclusion

Overall, throughout the United States, there is a strong policy in favor of enforcing forum selection clauses. As many courts put it, "a party opposing enforcement of a forum-selection clause 'bears a heavy burden of proof.'"[47]

4 Distinguishing Exclusive from Permissive Agreements

Forum selection clauses can raise a number of questions of interpretation. These include whether the parties intended to cover only contractual claims arising out of their agreements or all claims, including statutory claims, relating to their relationship; whether they intended to select federal as well as state courts in a named location; and whether they intended the choice of court to be exclusive or merely permissive. This section focuses on the last of these questions.[48]

The general rule in the United States is that a forum selection clause will be construed as permissive unless it contains "language of exclusion."[49] In most cases, the presence or absence of such language is clear. A typical permissive forum selection clause simply indicates the parties' submission to jurisdiction and/or venue in an identified forum.[50] Conversely, a typical exclusive agreement not only identifies a forum but uses the word "exclusive" or "sole" in order clearly to foreclose litigation elsewhere.[51]

---

[47]See, e.g., Mount Carmel Ministries v. Seaway Bank & Tr. Co., 2015 WL 13375901, at *1 (S.D. Miss. 2015).

[48]For a recent empirical study of this and other questions of interpretation, see Coyle (2019).

[49]See, e.g., Converting/Biophile Labs., Inc. v. Ludlow Composites Corp., 722 N.W.2d 633, 641 (Wisc. App. 2006) ("Absent specific language of exclusion, an agreement conferring jurisdiction in one forum will not be interpreted as excluding jurisdiction elsewhere."); Golf Scoring Sys. Unlimited, Inc. v. Remedio, 877 So. 2d 827, 829 (Fla. Dist. Ct. App. 2004) ("Generally, a forum selection clause will be considered permissive where it lacks words of exclusivity."); Mark Grp. Int'l, Inc. v. Still, 566 S.E.2d 160, 162 (N.C. App. 2002) ("[T]he general rule is when a jurisdiction is specified in a provision of contract, the provision generally will not be enforced as a mandatory selection clause without some further language that indicates the parties' intent to make jurisdiction exclusive.").

[50]See, e.g., Michaluk v. Credorax (USA), Inc., 164 So. 3d 719, 721 (Fla. Dist. Ct. App. 2015) ("[E] ach party hereby submits to the jurisdiction of the Courts of Malta as regards any claim, dispute or matter arising out of or in connection with this Agreement, its implementation and effect."); Mark Grp. Int'l, Inc. v. Still, 566 S.E.2d 160, 161 (N.C. App. 2002) ("[T]he undersigned hereby submits itself to the jurisdiction of the 13th Judicial District Court of Hillsborough County Florida U.S.A. in order to resolve any such dispute.").

[51]See, e.g., Halpern Eye Assocs., P.A. v. E.A. Crowell & Assocs., Inc., 2007 WL 3231617, at *1 (Del. Com. Pl. Sept. 18, 2007) ("Each party hereto consents to the exclusive jurisdiction of the courts in the State of North Carolina.").

When a clause falls between these two poles, interpretation is more complicated. There is no uniform approach to determining what constitutes sufficiently exclusionary language.[52] Courts in most states have adopted what appears to operate as a presumption *against* exclusivity, perhaps as a vestige of the old prohibition against "ouster."[53] In one case illustrating this approach, the court stated that "the normal construction of the jurisdiction rules includes a presumption that, where jurisdiction exists, it cannot be ousted or waived absent a clear indication of such a purpose," thus supporting a requirement of "specific language of exclusion."[54] Courts in this camp require language that clearly excludes the jurisdiction of any other court: thus, for instance, clauses stating that the "place of jurisdiction shall be Dresden"[55] and "contract shall be governed by the law of the State of Florida, with proper venue in Palm Beach County"[56] were viewed as merely permissive, for lack of words such as "exclusive," "sole," or "only."

Other courts, though, are less restrictive, and interpret phrases like "shall be" as sufficient to create exclusivity.[57] Some are also willing to infer exclusivity even in the absence of such terms when they gather the parties' intent from the overall clause. In one illustrative case, for example, the court found a forum selection clause in which the parties consented to "Broward County, Florida, as the proper venue for all actions" to be exclusive because the definite article "the" operated as a venue limitation.[58]

5 The Effect of Permissive Forum Selection Clauses

Disputes arising from cross-border contracts, whether interstate or international, are typically subject (or at least arguably subject) to the jurisdiction of more than one forum. By selecting one of those fora in advance as the exclusive forum for eventual

[52]See Heiser (2010), p. 1015.

[53]See Lord (2002-2018), § 15:15 (relating the presumption in favor of permissive clauses to "the traditional reluctance of some courts to surrender their jurisdiction too readily").

[54]John Boutari & Son, Wines and Spirits, S.A. v. Attiki Imp. & Dist. Inc., 22 F.3d 51 (2d. Cir. 1994) (quoting City of New York v. Pullman, Inc., 477 F. Supp. 438, 443 (S.D.N.Y. 1979)).

[55]Hull 753 Corp. v. Elbe Flugzeugwerke GmbH, 58 F. Supp. 2d 925, 927 (N.D. Ill. 1999).

[56]Regal Kitchens, Inc. v. O'Connor & Taylor Condo. Const., Inc., 894 So. 2d 288, 290 (Fla. Dist. Ct. App. 2005).

[57]See, e.g., Sterling Forest Assocs., Ltd. v. Barnett-Range Corp., 840 F.2d 249, 251–252 (4th Cir. 1988) (holding that the language "shall be" created a mandatory forum selection clause); General Electric Co. v. G. Siempelkamp & Co., 29 F.3d 1095, 1099 (6th Cir. 1994) (holding that the language "all" and "shall" was mandatory). See also Born and Rutledge (2011), pp. 462–463 (collecting cases).

[58]Golf Scoring Systems Unlimited, Inc. v. Remedio, 877 So. 2d 827, 828 (Fla. Dist. Ct. App. 2004); accord Intershop Communications v. Sup. Ct., 104 Cal. App. 4th 191, 197 (Ct. App. First Dist. Calif. 2002).

litigation, parties are able to minimize the possibility of inefficient parallel proceedings as well as the costs of litigating jurisdictional matters. However, it is not uncommon for parties to deviate from such agreements. Most of the U.S. case law and commentary on forum selection clauses focuses on that situation, analyzing the effect of *exclusive* agreements when a party to such an agreement has contravened it by initiating litigation elsewhere. In other words, they focus on the function of forum selection clauses in derogating from the jurisdiction of a court. Permissive agreements do not serve this function, since they "constitute nothing more than a consent to jurisdiction and venue in the named forum"[59] without limiting either party's right to sue elsewhere.

However, all forum selection clauses, including permissive clauses, may serve a prorogation function as well, in that the parties may nominate a forum that is not otherwise connected with the dispute.[60] In such cases, the question arises whether the consent of the parties also has the effect of *conferring* jurisdiction on a court that would not otherwise have it. Section 5.1 below considers that function.

Section 5.2 turns to the effect of permissive forum selection clauses on venue. In the U.S. system, courts have the discretion to decline jurisdiction on the basis that litigation in another forum would be more convenient. Dismissal or transfer on this basis may be sought by the defendant or initiated by the court itself. The factors to be considered include not only the convenience of the parties, but a number of other private- and public-interest factors as well. Another effect of a permissive forum selection clause, then, is to waive the defendant's objection to the laying of venue in the nominated court, on the grounds that another court would have been more convenient. Here, the question is how much weight the court will give the parties' forum selection clause in considering whether to decline exercise of its jurisdiction.

5.1 The Effect of a Permissive Forum Selection Clause on Personal Jurisdiction

The outer limits of judicial jurisdiction over non-resident defendants derive from the right to due process guaranteed by the United States Constitution.[61] Both state and federal courts have repeatedly confirmed that the requirement of personal jurisdiction "recognizes and protects an individual liberty interest," and can therefore be waived by a defendant.[62] As a result, consent has long been recognized as a valid

[59]Garcia Granados Quinones v. Swiss Bank Corp. (Overseas), S.A., 509 So. 2d 273, 274–275 (Sup. Ct. Fla. 1987).

[60]This is common where the parties seek a neutral forum, or a forum with particular expertise in the subject matter of the contract.

[61]The Fifth Amendment applies to federal courts, the Fourteenth to state courts.

[62]Insurance Corp. v. Compagnie des Bauxites de Guinee, 456 U.S. 694, 702 (1982). See also Leroy v. Great Western United Corp., 443 U.S. 173, 180 (1979); Burger King, 471 U.S. at 472 n.14.

basis for the exercise of personal jurisdiction over a non-resident defendant.[63] The traditional rule, however, was that consent could be given only at the time of litigation.[64] On this basis, courts historically refused to enforce advance waivers by contract. Over time, this limitation eroded, and courts came to accept such waivers, in the form of forum selection clauses, as well.[65] As discussed above, this is true even with respect to adhesion contracts, although it is difficult to describe those as the knowing and intentional waiver of constitutional rights.[66]

Consistent with this view of the jurisdictional requirement as a purely individual right, courts generally conclude that asserting jurisdiction on the basis of consent is within constitutional limits even when the forum is otherwise unconnected with the dispute.[67] In a few states, courts have held that the designated forum "must bear a reasonable relationship to the transaction,"[68] but these decisions appear to be anomalous.[69]

The analysis of a forum selection clause's effect on personal jurisdiction has a statutory dimension as well. Over the course of the twentieth century, as the Supreme Court's due process jurisprudence expanded the circumstances under which it was viewed as constitutionally acceptable to assert jurisdiction over non-resident defendants, each state enacted a "long-arm statute" authorizing its courts to exercise jurisdiction within those expanded limits. Some of these statutes simply refer to the Constitutional limits, and give state courts blanket authorization to exercise jurisdiction on any basis not incompatible with them.[70] Others, however, enumerate particular categories of cases in which jurisdiction may be authorized over non-residents. In states that use this form of long-arm, a state court may assert

---

[63]Until the middle of the twentieth century, the jurisdiction of state courts was defined in a strictly territorial fashion to encompass only state domiciliaries and other persons served with process while within the state. See Pennoyer v. Neff, 95 U.S. 714, 720 (1877). However, even during that period, defendants not falling into either of those categories could consent to jurisdiction.

[64]"A man may not barter away . . . substantial rights," and thus cannot "bind himself in advance by an agreement, which may be specially enforced, thus to forfeit his rights at all times and on all occasions whenever the case may be presented." Home Ins. Co. v. Morse, 87 U.S. 445, 451 (1874).

[65]National Equipment Rental, Ltd. v. Szukhent, 375 U.S. 311, 315–316 (1964) ("[I]t is settled . . . that parties to a contract may agree in advance to submit to the jurisdiction of a given court . . . .").

[66]See Overmyer Co. v. Frick Co., 405 U.S. 174, 185 (1972) (a pre-*Carnival Cruise* case drawing this distinction, and suggesting that a waiver must be "voluntary, knowing, and intelligently made"); see also Sachs (2014), p. 4.

[67]See, e.g., RSR Corp. v. Sigmund, 309 S.W.3d 686, 704 (Ct. App. Tex. 2010) ("To the extent a party has consented to jurisdiction in a particular forum, the trial court's exercise of personal jurisdiction over it does not violate due process even in the absence of contacts with Texas.").

[68]See, e.g., KC Ravens LLC v. Nima Scrap, LLC, 369 P.3d 341 (Ct. App. Kansas 2016).

[69]See Born and Rutledge (2011), p. 115.

[70]See, e.g., Ann. Cal. Code Civ. Proc. § 410.10 ("A court of this state may exercise jurisdiction on any basis not inconsistent with the Constitution of this state or of the United States.").

personal jurisdiction over a non-resident defendant only on one of the enumerated bases.[71]

If a long-arm statute does not explicitly list consent as one of the approved bases of jurisdiction, then, the question arises whether the court is authorized to exercise jurisdiction *solely* on that basis if the litigation is otherwise unconnected with the forum. This question presents itself in federal courts as well, because they normally borrow the long-arm statute of the state in which they sit.[72] In almost all states using the enumerated-acts type of long-arm statute, courts in practice seem to enforce forum selection clauses despite the apparent lack of statutory authorization.[73] This is consistent with the general position that long-arm statutes are intended to expand, not restrict, the right to serve process upon non-residents.[74] Thus, consent—a basis on which it was always acceptable to assert jurisdiction over non-residents—should continue to suffice.[75] In some states, however, the position is that jurisdiction can be exercised only when specific statutory authority is present. If that is true, then a party to a forum selection clause may argue that despite its waiver of objections, the court lacks jurisdiction over it. In other words, if the statute of the chosen state does not include "contractual agreement" as one of the bases, then a forum selection clause should not be enforced unless there is some other statutory basis for the assertion of personal jurisdiction. This is the position in Florida.[76]

---

[71]See Casad et al. (2014), p. 441 ("[I]t remains a hornbook truism that personal jurisdiction proceeds in two steps, requiring state authorization in addition to satisfaction of due process requirements.").

[72]Fed. R. Civ. P. 4(k)(1).

[73]See, e.g., GP&W Inc. v. Daibes Oil, LLC, 497 S.W.3d 866, 869–870 (Mo. Ct. App. 2016) ("Although it is generally necessary to satisfy the Missouri long-arm statute to obtain *in personam* jurisdiction over a nonresident defendant . . . jurisdiction over the person may also be obtained by consent or by waiver; for example, parties to a contract may agree in advance to submit to personal jurisdiction in a given court by means of a forum selection clause."). See also Casad et al. (2014), pp. 446–447 ("[C]ourts in many states that have [enumerated-act] statutes have ruled that the statute is intended, despite its literal words, to authorize reach in all situations to the limits of due process.").

[74]Some statutes say so explicitly: see, e.g., Delaware 10 Del. C. § 3104 (i): "Nothing herein contained limits or affects the rights to serve process in any other manner now or hereafter provided by law. This section is an extension of and not a limitation upon the rights otherwise existing of service of legal process upon nonresidents." But see Heiser (1993a), p. 379 ("a state may choose to limit its jurisdiction over nonresident defendants to occasions that meet a list of specified factors, many of which are less expansive than what due process would permit. . .").

[75]Additional support for this position is found in Burnham v. Superior Court of California, 495 U.S. 604 (1990), which suggests that the exercise of jurisdiction on any of the traditional bases must be per se constitutional: at 619.

[76]See C.R. McRae v. J.D./M.D., Inc., 511 So. 2d 540, 543 (Fla. 1987) ("The legislature has set forth in our long arm statute the policy of this state concerning when Florida courts can exercise in personam jurisdiction over non-resident defendants. Conspicuously absent from the long arm statute is any provision for submission to in personam jurisdiction merely by contractual agreement." See also Maschino v. Val-Pak Direct Marketing Systems, Inc., 902 So. 2d 196, 197 (Dist. Ct. App. Fla. 2005) ("In Florida, the mere execution of a forum selection clause is insufficient to confer long-arm jurisdiction over out-of-state defendants. There must be an independent basis for

A number of states have enacted specific legislation under which they explicitly agree to accept jurisdiction on the basis of a forum selection clause. A few of these are based on the Model Choice of Forum Act, one section of which applies in situations where the court would lack jurisdiction but for the consent of the parties.[77] Others are designed to attract high-value disputes to the state in question. These statutes require that the contract in question also include a choice of law in favor of local law, and that the transaction involve a significant amount of money.[78] In these states, one assumes, consent in other types of contract disputes would *not* be sufficient to confer jurisdiction on the nominated court.

5.2 *The Effect of a Permissive Forum Selection Clause on Venue*

Even if the court in which the plaintiff initiates litigation enjoys jurisdiction over the claim and the parties, the defendant may argue that venue is either *improper* or *inconvenient*, and that the suit belongs in another court. The existence of a forum selection clause may affect the resulting procedural analysis.

5.2.1 In State Court

Removal

If a plaintiff initiates in state court a claim that also falls within the original jurisdiction of a federal district court located in that state, the defendant has a right to remove the case to the federal court.[79] When the defendant has agreed to a forum selection clause identifying the state court as a suitable venue, the question arises whether that agreement constitutes a waiver of the removal right. In answering this question, courts have adopted a requirement that such a waiver be "clear and unequivocal." That standard is met by explicitly waiving the right to remove, or by designating a particular state court as the exclusive forum for eventual

conferring long-arm jurisdiction."); Jetbroadband WV, LLC v. Mastec North America, Inc., 13 So.3d 159, 161 (Fla. App. 3 Dist. 2009) (confirming that Florida courts have personal jurisdiction only over cases that fall within the parameters of Florida's long-arm statute). This situation led to the enactment of a new provision explicitly authorizing jurisdiction on the basis of consent in certain types of contracts. See Steffan v. Carnival Corp., 2017 WL 4182203 (S.D. Fla. 2017).

[77] See Sect. 2 above.

[78] Cal. Civ. Proc. Code § 410.40 (California); Del. Code tit. 6, § 2708(b) (Delaware); Fla. Stat. Ann. tit. XXXIX §§ 685.101–102 (Florida); 735 Ill. Comp. Stat. Ann. 105/5-5, 5-10 (Illinois); N.Y. Gen. Oblig. Law §§ 5-1401–1402 (New York); Tex. Civ. Prac. & Rem. Code § 15.020 (Texas).

[79] 28 U.S.C.A. § 1441.

litigation.[80] A permissive forum selection clause does not meet this standard and therefore does not affect a defendant's right to remove.[81]

Forum Non Conveniens

There is no procedural mechanism by which a state court can transfer a case to a more convenient forum in another state (or another country).[82] However, a defendant can move to dismiss a case on the basis of inconvenience, under the doctrine of *forum non conveniens*.[83] Almost all states adhere to this common law doctrine, and some have incorporated it in procedural legislation. Although there is some variation among these states, in essence they follow the same approach that was announced as a rule of federal common law in *Gulf Oil Corp. v. Gilbert*.[84] In order to obtain dismissal on the basis of *forum non conveniens*, two conditions must be met. First, an adequate alternative forum must be available.[85] Second, because there is ordinarily a strong presumption in favor of the plaintiff's choice of forum,[86] the balance of private and public interests at stake in the case must weigh clearly in favor of dismissal.[87] The private interests of the litigants to be considered include ease of access to evidence, the availability of witnesses, and all the other elements that go into "mak[ing] trial of a case easy, expeditious, and inexpensive."[88] The public-interest factors include the state of the court's docket, the burden on jurors in a community that is not related to the dispute, and the familiarity of the court with the law to be applied.[89]

As discussed above, some states have adopted legislation that directs their courts to exercise jurisdiction over certain high-value contracts that contain forum selection clauses designating those courts. That kind of legislation is usually accompanied by companion clauses foreclosing the possibility of dismissal on the basis of inconvenience.[90] Otherwise, a court may always consider dismissal on that ground. This is

---

[80]See, e.g., Valspar Corp. v. Sherman, 211 F. Supp. 3d 1209, 1213 (D. Minn. 2016). This can raise the question of interpretation whether the designation of a particular location as the forum is intended to encompass federal as well as state courts there. See Coyle (2019), pp. 2–3.

[81]See, e.g., Carmen Group, Inc. v. Xavier Univ., 41 F. Supp. 3d 8, 13 (D. D.C. 2014).

[82]There is a mechanism for transferring a case from one state court to a more convenient forum within the same state, which this Report does not address.

[83]Many states also recognize the authority of courts to raise this basis for dismissal *sua sponte*.

[84]330 U.S. 501 (1947). See generally Heiser (1993a), pp. 394–395 (discussing the application of the doctrine in state courts). The operation of this doctrine in federal courts is discussed in Sect. 5.2.2.

[85]At a minimum, this means an alternative forum with jurisdiction over the defendant and the claim.

[86]Piper Aircraft v. Reyno, 454 U.S. 235, 255 (1981).

[87]Gulf Oil Corp., 330 U.S. at 508.

[88]Gulf Oil Corp., 330 U.S. at 508.

[89]Gulf Oil Corp., 330 U.S. at 508.

[90]See, e.g., N.Y. C.P.L.R. 327(b) (McKinney 2012) (stating that New York courts will not dismiss an action arising out of a contract to which section 5-1402 applies on the basis of inconvenient

true even when an exclusive forum selection clause is involved. While a forum selection clause may operate as a waiver of a party's own objection to the convenience of the designated forum, it does not affect the other relevant considerations. And permissive forum selection clauses, which by definition do not constrain the plaintiff's choice of forum, may be even less relevant to the analysis. The question, then, is how much weight a permissive forum selection clause should be given in *forum non conveniens* analysis.

Where Litigation Is Initiated in the Designated Forum

In this circumstance, the plaintiff has chosen to initiate litigation in the contractually designated forum, and the defendant moves to dismiss the claim in favor of some other forum. In practice, such a motion is highly unlikely to succeed. There is considerable variation, though, in the route that state courts take to this conclusion.

Some courts have held that a permissive forum selection clause "becomes mandatory" once suit is filed in the designated forum, and thus is entitled to "enforcement" under the *Bremen* standard.[91] On that view, assuming that the clause was valid as a matter of contract law, a party seeking to resist litigation there would need to establish that the designated forum was "unreasonable" under that standard. Most courts simply apply the traditional *forum non conveniens* analysis, but place a significant burden on the defendant who seeks to dismiss from a forum to which it previously agreed. This is generally achieved on the theory that the defendant has waived its right to object to that forum on the basis of its own inconvenience, which is traditionally one of the most significant factors in the analysis. Finally, some courts seem to conduct the usual analysis with no special adjustment for the forum selection clause at all. Even these, however, tend to decline to dismiss.[92]

Although it appears to be highly unusual, a court that has been designated in a valid and exclusive forum selection clause (and thus, *a fortiori*, in a permissive clause) may also invoke *forum non conveniens* on its own motion. In one recent case, a California court considered a breach of contract claim brought by a Taiwanese plaintiff against a Japanese defendant.[93] The contract included an exclusive forum selection clause in favor of California. The defendant moved to dismiss the claim on the basis of *forum non conveniens*. The court denied that motion, instead applying

---

forum). See also note 93 referring to Quanta Computer Inc. v. Japan Communications Inc., 230 Cal. Rptr.3d 334 (Cal. Ct. App. 2018) (noting that in California the rule foreclosing dismissal on the basis of inconvenience in such cases was no longer in effect).

[91]See, e.g., Paradise Enterprises Ltd. v. Sapir, 811 A.2d 516, 528 (Sup. Ct. N.J. 2002) ("Once plaintiff filed suit [in the designated forum], defendant was bound by that choice, whether the agreement's language be considered mandatory or permissive"); see also ICICI Bank Ltd. v. Essar Global Fund Ltd., 565 B.R. 241, 253 (S.D.N.Y. 2017); Mount Carmel Ministries v. Seaway Bank & Trust Co., 2015 WL 13375901 at *3 (S.D. Miss. 2015) (accord).

[92]But see Patel v. Patel, 2007 WL 3293379 (Ct. App. Ohio 2007) (applying the traditional *forum non conveniens* analysis and dismissing a claim brought in the designated forum).

[93]Quanta Computer Inc. v. Japan Communications Inc., 230 Cal.Rptr.3d 334 (Cal. Ct. App. 2018).

the *Bremen* rule and concluding that the defendant had failed to establish that enforcing the clause would be unfair or unreasonable.[94] However, it then went on to consider *forum non conveniens* on its own motion. Reasoning that the dispute had no connection with California, and that California had no interest in retaining the action, the court concluded that it would be unreasonable "to require California courts to accept the burden of litigation" and dismissed the claim.[95]

Where Litigation Is Initiated in a Non-designated Forum

Here the equities look different. The plaintiff initiates litigation somewhere other than the designated forum, and the defendant moves to dismiss in favor of the nominated forum.[96] Under U.S. law, great deference is given to a plaintiff's choice of forum,[97] and accordingly in this type of case the general rule is that dismissal will not be granted unless the traditional *forum non conveniens* analysis weighs in favor of declining jurisdiction. On that theory, some courts give no special weight to a permissive forum selection clause when considering these motions.[98] Other courts, however, recognize a few ways in which the existence of a permissive forum selection clause might affect the analysis. First, it may lead the court to give less deference to the plaintiff's choice of forum.[99] Second, it establishes the designated forum as an "adequate alternative forum," in the sense that the plaintiff has consented to jurisdiction there, thus satisfying the first prong of the *forum non conveniens* test.[100] And third, it shows that the plaintiff has waived its right to object to the convenience of that alternative forum.[101] In these courts, permissive forum selection clauses are in fact accorded substantial, although not determinative, weight.

---

[94] Quanta Computer Inc. v. Japan Communications Inc., 230 Cal.Rptr.3d 334 (Cal. Ct. App. 2018) at 340.

[95] Quanta Computer Inc. v. Japan Communications Inc., 230 Cal.Rptr.3d 334 (Cal. Ct. App. 2018) at 342.

[96] It is theoretically possible but practically unlikely for a defendant to move to dismiss in favor of an adequate alternative forum in a third location.

[97] See notes 86–87 and accompanying text.

[98] See, e.g., Animal Film, LLC v. D.E.J. Productions, Inc., 193 Cal. App. 4th 466, 471 (Ct. App. Calif. 2011) ("The existence of a permissive forum selection clause is one factor considered along with the other forum non conveniens factors in applying the traditional analysis.").

[99] See, e.g., Networld Communications Corp. v. Croatia Airlines, D.D., 2014 WL 4724625, at *5 (D.N.J. 2014).

[100] See, e.g., Waste Management of Louisiana., L.L.C. v. Jefferson Parish, 48 F. Supp. 3d 894, 913 (E.D. La. 2014) (a federal court decision recognizing that effect).

[101] See, e.g., Cohn v. Truebeginnings, LLC., 2009 WL 793925, at *3 (Ct. App. 2d Dist. Calif. 2009) (noting that "the parties expressly contemplated Texas as the appropriate forum pursuant to the permissive forum selection clause" and dismissing in favor of the designated forum).

5.2.2 In Federal Court

Venue in U.S. federal courts is regulated primarily by a general provision[102] that "govern[s] the venue of all civil actions brought in [federal] district courts," except as otherwise provided by law.[103] It sets forth the circumstances under which a plaintiff may initiate litigation in a particular district—including, for example, if a substantial part of the events giving rise to the claim occurred there.[104] A number of additional rules establish the procedures by which a defendant can challenge venue. Two of them apply when venue is *improper*—that is, when a case is filed in the "wrong" court.[105] Under Federal Rule of Civil Procedure 12(b)(3), a defendant can move to dismiss a case on this basis; and under 28 U.S.C. § 1406(a), the district court in which a case is wrongly filed can either dismiss it or transfer it to another district or division in which it could have been brought. Two additional rules apply when venue is proper but *inconvenient*: the doctrine of *forum non conveniens*, under which a case will be dismissed in favor of an alternative forum in a state or foreign court, and 28 U.S.C. § 1404(a), under which a case will be transferred to a more convenient court within the federal system.[106]

In a case decided in 2013, *Atlantic Marine Construction Co. v. U.S. District Court*,[107] the Supreme Court addressed the interplay between these rules and a forum selection clause. In that case, the plaintiff had initiated litigation in a forum other than that designated in an exclusive forum selection clause. Seeking to enforce that agreement, the defendant moved to dismiss the suit for improper venue under Rule 12(b)(3) and § 1406(a). The Court rejected this motion. It reasoned that the exclusive basis for concluding whether venue is proper or improper are the federal venue statutes; in other words, as long as the requirements of those statutes are met, venue is proper, whether or not the parties have agreed in advance to litigate in another court.[108] As a consequence, the Court held, the only appropriate pathway to use in effectuating a forum selection clause is an inconvenience-based argument:

[102] 28 U.S.C.A. § 1391(a).

[103] A number of federal statutes creating causes of action in particular substantive areas, including insurance regulation and securities regulation, contain specific venue provisions that displace § 1391 in those contexts.

[104] 28 U.S.C.A. § 1391(b).

[105] In other words, when the case does not fall within one of the categories laid out in the federal venue statutes.

[106] § 1404(a) provides that "[f]or the convenience of parties and witnesses, in the interest of justice, a district court may transfer any civil action to any district or division where it might have been brought or to any district or division to which all parties have consented."

[107] 134 S. Ct. 568 (2013).

[108] 134 S. Ct. 568 (2013) at 577 ("§ 1391 makes clear that venue in 'all civil actions' must be determined in accordance with the criteria outlined in that section. That language cannot reasonably be read to allow judicial consideration of other, extra statutory limitations on the forum in which a case may be brought.").

transfer to another federal court under § 1404(a), or, in the case of an agreement designating a state or a foreign court, dismissal under *forum non conveniens*.

The Court went on to analyze the effect of an *exclusive* forum selection clause on these forms of inconvenience-based analysis. The defendant in *Atlantic Marine* sought transfer to another court within the U.S. federal system, and so the Court discussed the weight that should be accorded a forum selection clause in § 1404 (a) analysis. It reasoned that the enforcement of valid forum selection clauses protects party expectations and "furthers vital interests of the justice system."[109] As a result, "[o]nly under extraordinary circumstances unrelated to the convenience of the parties should a § 1404(a) motion [in favor of the nominated court] be denied."[110] The Court identified three particular implications of a forum selection clause for venue analysis. First, when a plaintiff has agreed to bring suit only in a particular forum, its choice of any other forum should, contrary to the ordinary rule, be given no weight.[111] Second, in evaluating the possibility of transfer, the court should ignore arguments about the parties' private interests, considering only public-interest factors (which, as the Court points out, are rarely enough to defeat a transfer motion).[112] Third, when a party files suit in a non-nominated forum in disregard of a forum selection clause, a subsequent transfer to the nominated forum will not carry with it the original venue's choice of law rules.[113] As commentators have recognized, this decision altered the traditional § 1404(a) analysis quite significantly, giving nearly dispositive weight to exclusive forum selection clauses.[114]

Although *Atlantic Marine* involved a transfer between federal courts, the opinion also addressed the weight to be given a forum selection clause in a motion to dismiss on the basis of *forum non conveniens*, in cases involving the designation of a foreign (or state-court) forum. Like the state cases discussed above, the federal cases have not been uniform in the weight they give a forum selection clause when applying *forum non conveniens*. And some have proceeded on the assumption that the analysis under *forum non conveniens* should be more rigorous than under § 1404, since the former leads to outright dismissal of the claim rather than to transfer.[115] In *Atlantic Marine*, however, the Supreme Court echoed some previous cases in stating

---

[109]134 S. Ct. 568 (2013) at 581 (citing Stewart Organization, Inc. v. Ricoh Corp., 487 U.S. 22, 31 (1988)).

[110]134 S. Ct. 568 (2013) at 581.

[111]134 S. Ct. 568 (2013) at 581.

[112]134 S. Ct. 568 (2013) at 582.

[113]134 S. Ct. 568 (2013) at 582. This is an exception from the general rule that after a § 1404 transfer, the transferee court must apply the state law that would have been applied in the transferor court. See Van Dusen v. Barrack, 376 U.S. 612, 639 (1964); Ferens v. John Deere Co., 494 U.S. 516 (1990) (establishing this rule for transfer motions made by defendants and plaintiffs, respectively).

[114]See, e.g., Mullenix (2015), p. 728.

[115]See Norwood v. Kirkpatrick, 349 U.S. 29, 32 (1955) (noting this distinction); In re Volkswagen of America, Inc., 545 F.3d 304, 313 (5th Cir. 2008) (accord).

that § 1404(a) was a "codification" of the common law doctrine.[116] It went on to state that "the same standards should apply to motions to dismiss for *forum non conveniens* in cases involving valid forum-selection clauses pointing to state or foreign forums."[117]

There has already been a significant amount of litigation under *Atlantic Marine* considering whether its holding extends to permissive forum selection clauses. It is clear that the first and third of the specific implications the Court identified are relevant only when an exclusive forum selection clause is involved. And, indeed, on that basis, many lower courts have simply declined to extend the holding of *Atlantic Marine* to cases involving permissive forum selection clauses, proceeding instead with "traditional" transfer analysis.[118] Some courts, however, have adopted the "logic" of *Atlantic Marine*'s reasoning with respect to the second implication—both in cases initiated in the designated forum and in those initiated elsewhere. In one representative case, the defendant moved to transfer the case out of the forum designated in a permissive forum selection clause. The court stated that because the defendant had expressly waived its right to challenge the convenience of that forum, the private factors "automatically [fell] in favor of keeping the case" in the designated court, and that transfer would be appropriate only "if the public factors fall strongly in favor of a transfer."[119]

6 Choice of Law

As the foregoing discussion demonstrates, there are many points relating to the validity, enforceability, and interpretation of forum selection clauses on which applicable laws may differ. In both interstate and international disputes, choice of law is therefore an important threshold determination. There are a variety of laws

---

[116]Atlantic Marine, 134 S. Ct. at 580 (stating that "because both § 1404(a) and the *forum non conveniens* doctrine from which it derives entail the same balancing-of-interests standard, courts should evaluate a forum-selection clause pointing to a nonfederal forum in the same way that they evaluate a forum-selection clause pointing to a federal forum").

[117]Atlantic Marine, 134 S. Ct. at 583 n.8. For an analysis of this approach, see generally Effron (2015).

[118]See, e.g., Foundation Fitness Products, LLC v. Free Motion Fitness, 121 F. Supp. 3d 1038, 1043 (D. Oregon 2015); RELCO Locomotives, Inc. v. AllRail, Inc., 4 F. Supp. 3d 1073, 1085 (S.D. Iowa 2014).

[119]United American Healthcare Corp. v. Backs, 997 F. Supp. 2d 741, 750 (E.D. Mich. 2014). See also Perficient, Inc. v. Priore, 2016 WL 866090, at *4 (E.D. Miss. 2016) ("the forum selection clause, even though permissive, is determinative in the analysis of the first [forum non conveniens] factor—the convenience of the parties—and weighs against transfer"); AAMCO Transmissions, Inc. v. Romano, 42 F. Supp. 3d 700, 713 (E.D. Pa. 2014) ("the Supreme Court has explained [in *Atlantic Marine*] that the existence of a forum selection clause of any kind significantly undercuts any argument that the preselected forum is inconvenient for the parties or their witnesses.").

that might potentially be chosen to determine such matters: (a) the law of the forum; (b) the law chosen to govern the contract—either by the parties, in the case of contracts that also contain a choice of law clause, or through application of the forum's choice of law rule, in the case of contracts that do not; and (c) in a case in which the forum is *not* the nominated forum, the law of the nominated forum.

6.1 Practice in State Courts

In the United States choice of law is normally a matter of state rather than federal law, and state conflicts regimes differ. Nevertheless, there is one principle relevant to this analysis on which all states agree: a court will always apply forum law to matters of procedure. As discussed in the previous section, the effect of a permissive forum selection clause is on matters of procedure, including jurisdiction and venue. Accordingly, that effect is determined by forum law. A state court will apply its own long-arm statute when considering a forum selection clause's effect on its jurisdiction, for instance, and its own procedural rules when considering its effect on venue. Likewise, where a local statute sets forth the circumstances under which a forum selection clause shall be given effect, a court in that state will simply apply that law.[120]

Before considering the effect of a forum selection clause, however, a court must consider two antecedent questions: whether the agreement is valid, and whether it should be characterized as permissive or exclusive. These issues implicate substantive contract law, and therefore do require initial choice of law analysis.

6.1.1 Choosing the Law That Governs the Validity and Enforceability of Forum Selection Clauses

When a lawsuit is filed in a state other than that whose law governs the contract, it is possible for a conflict of laws problem to arise. For example, the forum state might have adopted a *Bremen*-like rule favoring the presumptive enforceability of a forum selection clause, while the state whose law governs the contract might have enacted legislation invalidating such agreements in order to protect parties with weaker bargaining power. While such conflicts are most problematic with respect to exclusive forum selection clauses, they can affect permissive ones as well. Consider a permissive forum selection clause that is valid under forum law but invalid, as against public policy, in the state whose law governs the contract. In that case, if the litigation is otherwise unconnected to the forum, applying the law that governs the contract to the question of validity would invalidate the forum selection clause,

[120]See generally Symeonides (2018), pp. 1124–1126 (discussing the application of such statutes in state courts).

and thereby eliminate the basis for jurisdiction over the defendant in the forum. Applying the law of the forum to the question of validity, by contrast, would yield the opposite result. Choice of law problems can also arise in considering the effect of a forum selection clause on a motion to dismiss on the basis of inconvenience. For instance, in a state that would consider a permissive forum selection clause as a salient factor in *forum non conveniens* analysis, applying foreign law to invalidate the agreement would change the subsequent procedural analysis.

Challenges to the validity of a forum selection clause come in a variety of forms. Some are clearly contractual challenges: for example, challenges based on fraud or duress, or the absence of a required writing. Others, though, relate more directly to the effect of a forum selection clause: for instance, challenges based on a policy of general hostility to private agreements affecting jurisdiction or venue. These are frequently characterized as procedural, and resolved pursuant to forum law. As one court put it, "as a general rule, whether the forum selection clause is valid and enforceable is a procedural issue that must be determined in accordance with the law of the forum state. . . . [T]he general rule prevails despite a choice of law provision in the contract."[121] In between, in the Reporter's view, are challenges based on anti-waiver provisions attached to specific substantive protections of contract parties.[122] However, under current practice, challenges based on such provisions are generally also treated as procedural and addressed under the law of the forum.[123] Overall, recent reviews of the case law conclude that the vast majority of U.S. courts apply *lex fori* to questions of validity.[124]

6.1.2 Choosing the Law That Governs the Interpretation of Forum Selection Clauses

Even in addressing questions of interpretation, which are quite clearly a purely contractual matter, state courts are divided. Some simply skip over choice of law analysis entirely, and begin with generally accepted principles of contract interpretation (such as "this court initially determines whether the 'language of the contract is clear and unambiguous; if it is, the contract will be enforced as written'"[125]). In interpreting forum selection clauses when the contract in question also includes a

[121] Golden Palm Hospitality, Inc. v. Stearns Bank Nat'l Ass'n, 874 So. 2d 1231, 1234–1235 (Fla. App. 2004).

[122] See notes 32–33 and accompanying text.

[123] For a critique of this practice, see Symeonides (2018), pp. 1158–1160.

[124] See Clermont (2015), p. 653; Symeonides (2018), p. 1136. For an example of an exception to this rule, see Hearst v. Calfund, LLC, 2016 WL 7661386 (Super. Ct. Conn. 2016) (applying the law selected by the parties to determine the enforceability of a forum selection clause).

[125] Am. First Fed. Credit Union v. Soro, 359 P.3d 105, 106 (Nevada 2015).

choice of law, many courts apply the chosen law to questions of interpretation.[126] Others do not, however, particularly but not exclusively in the context of international conflicts.[127] In these cases, the courts simply apply forum law in ascertaining the scope of a forum selection clause.

In interpreting forum selection clauses when the contract in question does *not* include a choice of law, courts are even more likely simply to apply forum law to questions of interpretation. Relatively few will go through the process of applying the forum's choice of law rules in an effort to identify the law governing the contract. Some courts justify this approach by concluding that the choice of court was implicitly also a choice of the forum's law.[128] Other courts may simply be avoiding complicated conflicts analysis.[129]

This tendency to apply forum law in interpreting the scope of forum selection clauses may lead to inappropriate outcomes. This is true particularly in international cases, where the U.S. approach to one critical issue—applying a presumption in favor of permissive rather than exclusive forum selection clauses in interpreting ambiguous clauses—is so different from that of other legal systems.[130]

6.2 *Practice in Federal Courts*

The subject-matter jurisdiction of U.S. federal courts is not limited to claims arising under federal law.[131] When there is diversity of citizenship between the parties to a lawsuit, the federal courts also have the authority to adjudicate claims based entirely on state law—including contract law. As a result, federal courts frequently hear disputes arising out of interstate and international contracts. Under the Rules of Decision Act,[132] as interpreted in *Erie v. Tompkins*,[133] federal courts sitting in diversity must apply the substantive law of the state in which they sit (including

[126]See, e.g., EnQuip Technologies Group v. Tycon Technoglass, 986 N.E.2d 469 (Ct. App. Ohio 2012) (applying the law chosen to govern the contract to determine whether the choice of court was mandatory or permissive).

[127]See, e.g., Turnkey Projects Resources v. Gawad, 198 So. 3d 1029, 1030–1031 (Ct. App. Fla. 2016) (applying forum law to determine whether a forum selection clause covered non-signatories).

[128]See Clermont (2015), p. 661.

[129]See Clermont (2015), p. 661.

[130]The Hague Choice of Court Convention, for instance, which is now in force in EU member states and elsewhere, adopts the opposite presumption. Hague Convention on Choice of Court Agreements (concluded 30 June 2005), Article 3(b).

[131]See generally U.S. Const. Art. III(2) (setting forth the scope of the federal judicial power).

[132]28 U.S.C. § 1652 provides that "The laws of the several states, except where the Constitution or treaties of the United States or Act of Congress otherwise require or provide, shall be regarded as rules of decision in civil actions in the courts of the United States, in cases where they apply."

[133]Erie R.R. Co. v. Tompkins, 304 U.S. 64 (1938).

that state's choice of law rules[134]). However, they apply federal, not state, procedural law. This regime generates complicated questions regarding the proper characterization of the issues that forum selection clauses raise.[135]

6.2.1 Choosing the Law That Governs the Validity and Enforceability of Forum Selection Clauses

In the Context of a Motion to Transfer Venue

As discussed above, federal courts frequently confront forum selection clauses in the context of a motion to transfer venue to another federal court. Here, a pair of Supreme Court decisions provides a definitive solution to the choice of law problem. In the first, *Stewart Organization, Inc. v. Ricoh Corp.*,[136] the plaintiff had initiated litigation in a district court in Alabama, in contravention of an exclusive forum selection clause. The defendant moved to transfer the case to the designated forum. The district court denied that motion on the grounds that the effect of the forum selection clause was "controlled by Alabama law," which disfavored such agreements as a matter of public policy.[137] When the case reached the Supreme Court, it held that the effect of a forum selection clause on the motion to transfer venue was a matter of federal procedural law, governed entirely by § 1404(a).[138] As a result, the federal courts were obligated to apply that law, to the exclusion of any otherwise applicable state law. This is essentially a holding that federal law, in the form of § 1404(a), has preempted any inconsistent state law regarding the enforceability of a forum selection clause.[139] (In that case, the Court indicated in a footnote that the federal rule would be applied to the exclusion of state law in cases predicated on federal-question jurisdiction as well.[140]) The Supreme Court recently confirmed this approach in the *Atlantic Marine* decision discussed above, effectively federalizing the law governing the enforceability of forum selection clauses in the context of transfer motions.[141] The case law reflects this approach: federal courts interpret §

[134]Klaxon Co. v. Stentor Elec. Mfg. Co., 313 U.S. 487, 495–497 (1941).

[135]See generally Farmland Indus., Inc. v. Frazier-Parrott Commodities, Inc., 806 F.2d 848, 852 (8th Cir. 1986) (noting this complexity). For more thorough background of this issue, see Heiser (1993b), pp. 556–563.

[136]487 U.S. 22 (1988).

[137]487 U.S. 22 (1988) at 24.

[138]487 U.S. 22 (1988) at 29.

[139]487 U.S. 22 (1988) at 31 ("This is thus not a case in which state and federal rules 'can exist side by side…'" (quoting Walker v. Armco Steel Corp., 446 U.S. 740, 752 (1978)).

[140]487 U.S. 22 (1988) at 26 n.3.

[141]See Mullenix (2015), p. 735.

1404(a) to supersede any inconsistent state law disfavoring forum selection clauses.[142]

In Other Cases

Outside the context of a motion to transfer venue, it is less clear what law a federal court should apply in determining the enforceability of a forum selection clause. Practice on this point is divided. Most federal courts sitting in diversity have concluded that the validity of a forum selection clause is clearly procedural, and should be controlled by the *Bremen* rule as a matter of federal common law.[143] By this approach, a federal court simply applies the rule of presumptive validity directly. Other courts have reached the opposite conclusion, characterizing questions of validity as a matter of substantive contract law.[144] This analysis should logically begin by applying local *choice of law* rules. Some courts follow that approach, which generally leads them to determine validity pursuant to the law chosen by the parties.[145] However, here, much like state courts, federal courts often skip over the choice of law analysis. They simply apply the substantive law of the forum in considering the validity of a forum selection clause.

6.2.2 Choosing the Law That Governs the Interpretation of Forum Selection Clauses

Although § 1404(a) may have preempted inconsistent state law regarding the effect of a forum selection clause, it did not displace state law on matters of substantive contract law. As noted above, forum selection clauses may present a number of questions under that law, including their construction as exclusive or permissive.

---

[142]See, e.g., Guest Associates, Inc. v. Cyclone Aviation Prods, Ltd., 30 F. Supp. 3d 1278, 1283 (N.D. Ala. 2014) ("[F]ederal law, not state law, applies to the enforceability of forum-selection clauses on a motion to transfer under § 1404(a).").

[143]See, e.g., Herr Indus., Inc. v. CTI Systems, SA, 112 F. Supp. 3d 1174, 1178 (D. Kansas 2015) ("The overwhelming majority of circuit courts consider the enforceability of forum selection clauses under federal law in diversity cases, based on the conclusion that venue presents a question of procedure for purposes of the *Erie* doctrine."); Jones v. Weibrecht, 901 F.2d 17, 19 (2d Cir. 1990) ("Questions of venue and the enforcement of forum selection clauses are essentially procedural, rather than substantive, in nature."). For an exploration of this approach, see Sachs (2014), pp. 17–26.

[144]For an early articulation of this approach, see Stewart Org., Inc. v. Ricoh Corp., 487 U.S. at 36 (Scalia, J., dissenting) ("§ 1404(a) was enacted against the background that issues of contract, including a contract's validity, are nearly always governed by state law." His opinion concludes that "no federal statute or Rule of Procedure governs the validity of a forum-selection clause.": 487 U.S. at 38.).

[145]See, e.g., Abbott Labs. v. Takeda Pharm., 476 F.3d 421, 423 (7th Cir. 2007); TH Agric. & Nutrition, LLC v. Ace European Group Ltd., 416 F. Supp. 2d 1054, 1075 (D. Kan. 2006).

Many federal courts sitting in diversity, following *Erie*, apply state law to those questions.[146] That approach is not uniform, however. Some federal courts simply apply federal precedent in interpreting forum selection clauses, without clearly identifying the source of applicable law.[147] Others apply what they describe as "federal common law"[148] to questions regarding interpretation of the contract, generally on the theory that "because enforcement of a forum clause necessarily entails interpretation of the clause before it can be enforced, federal law applies to interpretation of forum selection clauses [in diversity cases]."[149] (The federal law on this point, according to these courts, is that a choice of court must "clearly require" exclusivity in order to be characterized as mandatory.[150]) Others reason that although the "overriding framework governing the effect of forum selection clauses in federal courts ... is drawn from federal law," questions of interpretation—including whether a clause is exclusive or permissive—must be answered by applying "the body of law selected in an otherwise valid choice-of-law clause."[151] Although less commonly, some courts will, in the absence of a choice-of-law clause, apply the conflicts rules of the state in which they sit in order to select the substantive law governing the contract.[152] Still others simply duck the question by concluding that there are no "material discrepancies" between federal common law and the relevant state law in matters of contract interpretation.[153]

7 Conclusion

It is easy to articulate a general rule regarding the treatment of forum selection clauses in U.S. courts: almost always, in consumer as well as commercial contracts, they will be given effect. It is far more difficult to navigate the array of substantive,

---

[146]See Clermont (2015), p. 667.

[147]For citations to such cases, along with a lengthy critique of that practice, see Sabal Limited LP v. Deutsche Bank AG, 209 F. Supp. 3d 907, 918–919 (Dist. Ct. W.D. Tex. 2016).

[148]See Wong v. PartyGaming Ltd., 589 F.3d 821 (6th Cir. 2009).

[149]Manetti-Farrow, Inc. v. Gucci America, Inc., 858 F.2d 509, 513 (9th Cir. 1988). See also Foundation Fitness Products, LLC v. Free Motion Fitness, 121 F. Supp. 3d 1038, 1044 (D. Oregon 2015) ("To interpret the forum-selection clauses [as either mandatory or permissive], this Court, sitting in diversity, must apply federal law, despite the [contracts'] choice-of-law provisions selecting Utah law.").

[150]Foundation Fitness Products, 121 F. Supp. 3d at 1044.

[151]Martinez v. Bloomberg LP, 740 F.3d 211, 217–218 (2d. Cir. 2014); see also Yavuz v. 61 MM, Ltd., 465 F.3d 418, 430 (10th Cir. 2006); Phillips v. Audio Active Ltd., 494 F.3d at 385.

[152]See, e.g., Weber v. PACT XPP Technologies, AG, 811 F.3d 758, 770–773 (5th Cir. 2016) (applying the choice-of-law rules of Texas to determine that German law governed the contract, and then holding that under German law the forum selection clause in question was exclusive rather than permissive).

[153]See, e.g., Logic Energy Solutions, LLC v. Boulter, 2014 WL 12588521, at *3 (W.D. Oklahoma 2014).

procedural, and conflicts rules whose interplay yields that result. For any lawyer (and particularly for foreign lawyers) seeking to appreciate the complexity of procedural law within the U.S. federal system, there is no better subject of study.

References

Born GB, Rutledge PR (2011) International Civil Litigation in United States Courts. Wolters Kluwer, New York

Casad RC, Richman WM, Cox SE (2014) Jurisdiction in civil actions. LexisNexis, New York

Clermont KM (2015) Governing law on forum-selection agreements. Hastings Law J 66:643–674

Coyle JF (2019) Interpreting forum selection clauses. Iowa Law Rev 104:1791–1855

Effron R (2015) *Atlantic Marine* and the future of forum non conveniens. Hastings Law J 66:693–718

Gruson M (1982) Forum selection clauses in International and Interstate Commercial Agreements. Univ Illinois Law Rev 1982:133–206

Heiser WW (1993a) Forum selection clauses in state courts: limitations on enforcement after *Stewart* and *Carnival Cruise*. Fla Law Rev 45:361–401

Heiser WW (1993b) Forum selection clauses in federal courts: limitations on enforcement after *Stewart* and *Carnival Cruise*. Fla Law Rev 45:553–608

Heiser WW (2010) The Hague Convention on Choice of Court Agreements: the impact on forum non conveniens, transfer of venue, removal, and recognition of judgments in United States Courts. Univ Pa J Int Law 31:1013–1050

Lenhoff A (1961) The parties' choice of a forum: "Prorogation Agreements". Rutgers Law Rev 15:414–490

Lord RA (2002–2018) Williston on contracts. West Group, New York

Mullenix LS (2015) Gaming the system: protecting consumers from unconscionable contractual forum-selection and arbitration clauses. Hastings Law J 66:719–760

Reese WLM (1969) The model choice of Forum Act. Am J Comp Law 17:292–296

Sachs SE (2014) The Forum Selection Defense. Duke J Constitutional Law Public Policy 10:1–44

Symeonides SC (2018) What law governs forum selection clauses? La Law Rev 78:1119–1161

Yackee JW (2004) Choice of law considerations in the validity & enforcement of International Forum Selection Agreements: whose law applies? UCLA J Int Law Foreign Aff 9:43–96

Hannah L. Buxbaum is Vice President for International Affairs at Indiana University and the John E. Schiller Chair at the Indiana University Maurer School of Law. She holds a B.A. from Cornell University, a J.D. from Cornell Law School, and an LL.M. from the University of Heidelberg.

MIX
Papier aus verantwortungsvollen Quellen
Paper from responsible sources
FSC® C105338

If you have any concerns about our products,
you can contact us on
ProductSafety@springernature.com

In case Publisher is established outside the EU,
the EU authorized representative is:
Springer Nature Customer Service Center GmbH
Europaplatz 3, 69115 Heidelberg, Germany

Printed by Libri Plureos GmbH
in Hamburg, Germany